Interactivity in E–Learning:

Case Studies and Frameworks

Haomin Wang
Dakota State University, USA

Managing Director:	Lindsay Johnston
Senior Editorial Director:	Heather Probst
Book Production Manager:	Sean Woznicki
Development Manager:	Joel Gamon
Development Editor:	Hannah Abelbeck
Acquisitions Editor:	Erika Gallagher
Typesetters:	Jamie Snavely
Print Coordinator:	Jamie Snavely
Cover Design:	Nick Newcomer, Greg Snader

Published in the United States of America by
Information Science Reference (an imprint of IGI Global)
701 E. Chocolate Avenue
Hershey PA 17033
Tel: 717-533-8845
Fax: 717-533-8661
E-mail: cust@igi-global.com
Web site: http://www.igi-global.com

Library of Congress Cataloging-in-Publication Data

Interactivity in e-learning : case studies and frameworks / Haomin Wang, editor.
       p. cm.
  Includes bibliographical references and index.
  Summary: "This book provides a comprehensive examination of interactivity, combining key perspectives from communication and media studies, distributed cognition, system affordances, user control, and social interaction, intended for researchers working in the fields of communication and media, educational media, e-learning, and instructional technology"--Provided by publisher.
  ISBN 978-1-61350-441-3 (hardcover) -- ISBN 978-1-61350-442-0 (ebook) -- ISBN 978-1-61350-443-7 (print & perpetual access) 1. Educational technology. 2. Interactive multimedia. I. Wang, Haomin
  LB1028.3.I56634 2012
  371.33--dc23
                          2011035073

British Cataloguing in Publication Data
A Cataloguing in Publication record for this book is available from the British Library.

All work contributed to this book is new, previously-unpublished material. The views expressed in this book are those of the authors, but not necessarily of the publisher.

Table of Contents

Detailed Table of Contents

Section 1
Instructional Design to Promote Interactivity in E-Learning

Learning is becoming increasingly interactive as e-learning continues its growth. Technology advancement not only opens up more affordances for interactivity but also changes the ways people interact with the media and with one another through the media. This chapter attempts to identify key factors that contribute to effective interactivity in the e-learning environment and put the key factors in related perspectives for a holistic view of the interrelations. The key factors include media attributes, instructional values of visuals, audio, and video, digital text and e-reading, accessibility, distributed cognition, system adaptation, virtual space, and collaborative learning. From the interrelated perspective, an integrated approach is proposed for exploring and advancing research and practice in designing and promoting interactivity in the e-learning environment.

This chapter is concerned with interactivity of information representations in e-learning environments (ELEs)—where interactivity refers to the quality or condition of interaction with representations in an ELE. An ELE is any interactive computer-based software that mediates and supports learners' engagement with information. This chapter draws upon literature from the areas of human-information interaction, distributed cognition, and learning sciences with the goal of developing and exploring the features of a preliminary framework for thinking about interactivity in the context of ELEs. In this chapter we provide some background and motivation for such a framework, and identify and elaborate upon 10 structural elements of interaction that affect the interactivity of information representations: actual affordances and constraints, articulation mode, control, event granularity, focus, action flow, reaction flow, propagation, transition, and perceived affordances and constraints. Each of these has an effect on the learning and cognitive processes of learners, and the overall interactivity of an ELE is an emergent property of a combination of these elements. Collectively, these elements can serve as a framework to help thinking about design and analysis of interactivity in ELEs.

Chapter 3

Ann Leslie Claesson, Capella University, USA
Felicity Pearson, Capella University, USA
Jesse Rosel, Capella University, USA

This chapter examines the planning, process, and application of Riverbend City – an example of rich media developed by Capella University to enhance student interactivity in e-learning environments. Riverbend City is multidisciplinary scenario-based simulation project focusing on the disaster response of public service agencies in a fictional city. The ultimate goal of the project was, and continues to be, to empower learners to envision their ability to combine collaboration and leadership when working with multiple disciplines in a real-life situation. The primary focus of this chapter is how to provide a real-world scenario where skills and new knowledge can be applied in a safe practice situation, how rich media can be used to supplement existing course content, or be used as a means of initial content delivery. The focus for utilizing rich media in the Riverbend City project was to: (1) enhance learning; (2) challenge learners to have a multidisciplinary perspective; and (3) increase engagement with real-world scenarios. This chapter explores how rich media can be used in these three types of applications using the Riverbend City Simulation project for Capella's School of Public Service Leadership as a case study example. Riverbend City is a scenario-based simulation that provides a multidisciplinary, rich media experience to learners in an online, asynchronous university setting. The simulation provides real-world scenarios where student skills and knowledge can be applied and tested on specific subjects. The ultimate goal of the project is to empower learners to envision their ability to combine collaboration and leadership when working with multiple disciplines in a real-world situation.

Chapter 4

Deb Gearhart, Troy University, USA

The purpose of this chapter is to describe authentic learning, review the literature pertaining to authentic learning, discuss the benefits for online learning, and provide a model for the use of authentic learning in online course design. Students comment they are motivated by solving real-world problems and often express a preference for doing rather than listening. At the same time, most educators consider learning by doing the most effective way to teach (Lombardi, 2007). The chapter will be beneficial to instructors and instructional designers alike.

Chapter 5

Robert Z. Zheng, University of Utah, USA

This chapter focused the influence of cognitive styles on learners' performance in e-Learning. The author examined the existing practice of style matching where instructional conditions were matched with learners' cognitive styles and found that style matching did not necessarily provide learning gains for learners with different cognitive styles. Instead, he proposed ability building as an effective approach to improve learners' learning. Following the same line, the author further examined the relationship between cognitive styles and instructional situations where situated learning was implemented. The results revealed that instructional situations can significantly influence learners' learning in complex learning, and that cognitive style was not, as viewed by many people, a linear relationship between style and performance. Instead, it displayed multi-dimensional relationships with variables related to e-Learning. The author thus suggested that cognitive style should be examined in a broader manner where variables related to e-Learning be considered simultaneously.

This chapter presents a design framework of scaffolding that can be applied in designing adaptive e-learning systems. The framework is primarily grounded in socio-cultural theory and built on a critical analysis of literature on scaffolding. It addresses three key processes in scaffolding (i.e., diagnosis, supporting, and fading) and four conditions for designing scaffolding (i.e., who, what, how, and when). From the historical perspective, this chapter also provides a literature review of adaptive systems. The characteristics of adaptive systems from different paradigms are specifically examined through the lens of scaffolding. To illustrate the application of the scaffolding framework in system adaptation, four web-based e-learning systems are described to demonstrate how various scaffolding strategies are implemented through the design of the systems. In conclusion, issues related to designing scaffolds for adaptive e-learning systems are discussed, and research gaps are identified for future investigation.

Teachers teach to the level of their ability: novices can teach students to be novices: experts can teach students to be experts. Using the Buddhist Eightfold Path as a model, this chapter explores the expert/novice paradigm as a framework for helping novice become expert in the e-learning environment, particularly as offered through instructional design that can both scaffold novice instructors to teach to a higher level of learning, and also support experts to help students reach higher goals. Three facets of the teaching/learning dialogue are explored: expertise in a domain of knowledge (teacher), expertise in acquiring deep knowledge in a new domain through learning (learner), and expertise in the instructor/learner learning interface (instructional designer). Expert and novice teaching and learning and their relationship through instructional designers are discussed.

Section 2
Interactivity and Educational Games

Digital games and simulations are playing an important role in younger generations' lives. Their adoption to e-learning environments, however, is rather slow because educators are reluctant to change the way they teach. This chapter starts with a brief discussion of game and simulation terminology, including serious games, game-based learning, and game genres. It continues with a review of the current status of educational games and simulations being used in higher education institutions. Important case studies are provided to present examples to the higher education faculty. Finally, a discussion of teaching strategies, instructional design processes, and assessment issues for effective digital game incorporation in e-learning is included.

Game-based learning is a dynamic and powerful way to engage students to develop evidence-based reasoning, analytical and critical thinking skills, problem-solving skills, systems thinking, and connect with peers, all of which are 21st century skills. Games can lead students to become participatory learners and producers instead of passive recipients. This chapter considers the following three approaches to using games with students: (1) an instructor makes a game for a specific learner outcome, (2) students make a game, and (3) an instructor uses a commercial or online game. The chapter emphasizes the second and third methods. Specific examples of how games are being used with students illustrate ways to teach with games.

Motivation drives our learning behaviors. Our abilities to intentionally control our motivation to learn, however, remain largely limited because motivation is a subliminal and synthetic mental state derived from the interactivity between our prior experiences and the learning environment. In a digital game-based learning system (DGBLS), learners are always bombarded by a colossal amount of cognitive, social, and affective stimuli that afford and affect the interactivity, which can easily trigger learners' motivational responses and leads to the consequences of not being able to manage their motivation. As a result the intended learning processes can be interrupted. Although learners cannot control their motivation in this case, they can manage their interactivity with the DGBLS to select and process stimuli that are relevant to the learning task. Therefore, this chapter intends to propose a process framework to empower learners to autonomously manage their interactivity with the DGBLS in order to stay focused on the learning tasks. Specifically, this framework will draw literatures on learners' motivational processing and cognitive processing pertaining to learning in the DGBLS.

Chapter 11

Jillianne Code, University of Victoria, Canada
Jody Clarke-Midura, Harvard University, USA
Nick Zap, Simon Fraser University, Canada
Chris Dede, Harvard University, USA

Validating interactions in serious games and virtual worlds used in educational settings is critical for ensuring their effectiveness for learning. The effectiveness of any educational technology depends upon teachers' and learners' perception of the functional utility of that medium for teaching, learning, and assessment. The purpose of this chapter is to offer a framework for the design and validation of interactions in serious games and virtual worlds as they are linked to learning outcomes. In order to illustrate this framework, we present a case study of the Virtual Performance Assessment (VPA) project at Harvard University (http://vpa.gse.harvard.edu). Through our framework and case study, this chapter will provide educators, designers, and researchers with a model for how to effectively design immersive virtual and game-based learning environments for the purpose of assessing student inquiry learning.

Section 3
Interpersonal Interactivity through Media

Chapter 12

Ruth Xiaoqing Guo, Buffalo State College - State University of New York, USA

This case study examined a constructivist approach to creating an interactive learning environment on ANGEL for graduate students in a course designed to help students construct knowledge to develop professional websites. However, the class time was insufficient to meet the student learning needs and course objectives. The social interaction on ANGEL provided flexible time and space for participants to discuss the issues important to them. Findings revealed that practical action research combined with social interaction shed light on important issues of professional development through reflection on practice. The constructivist approach provided an interaction of two important sets of learning conditions: Internal and external levels for student cognitive development in authoring skills. Data were analyzed using a grounded theory approach. This study also identified issues for further research: The importance of curriculum design to meet students' needs, the effect of digital divide, and how student attitude impacts learning.

Chapter 13

This chapter explores the importance of collaborative and authentic learning in online distance learning environments. It focuses upon the interactive activities between the instructor, learners, online environment, and larger community, which are all engaged towards developing a community of learners in which meaningful connections enhance learner motivation and acquisition of learning objectives. Built-in opportunities are integral to the process for socialization-type learning activities and instructor's awareness, and alignment of those activities to the readiness of individual learners and collective learning community (i.e., zone of proximal development). Practical instructional ideas and activities for building an online learning community are presented.

Chapter 14

This chapter examines the support of social interaction in a cooperative, situated online learning environment, and the cultural barriers that hinder such intention and interactivity. The findings of a literature review suggest that the greatest challenge to intentional Community of Practice (CoP) is a sense of interdependence among CoP members, the authenticity of the practice or purpose, and a trajectory for the CoP's future. This case study attends to these issues with a cohort of practicing teachers. It explores an initiative to nurture CoP with cooperative projects and with the support of an online community portal. The case challenges CoP thoeory from an intentional or instructional standpoint, and informs design and technology in support of CoP.

Chapter 15

This chapter reports on one academic library's experiences with expanding instructional services by adding synchronous library instruction to better serve its online students and faculty located across the globe. Web conferencing software allows librarians to provide interactive, high-touch library instruction for online students equivalent to the experience of students in traditional face-to-face courses. While providing this real-time instruction on library resources and research skills, librarians are embedding themselves in online programs, becoming more readily accessible to online and distance students. By meeting the changing needs of academic library users wherever they are, librarians are reaffirming their integral role and relevance as partners in the educational endeavor.

Preface

As the Internet, rich media, social networking, portable devices, and other networked resources are increasingly used for e-learning, learning is expected to become increasingly interactive and flexible. Technology advancement not only opens up more affordances for interactivity but also changes the ways people interact with the media and with one another through media. Virtual space is continuing to expand with mobile computing and rich media development. People's perception and manipulation of time and space is evolving too. More media and modes of communication are becoming available for both synchronous and asynchronous interactivity. People's interactivity with media and with one another through media will become increasingly permeative and ubiquitous.

Interactivity can take place between human communicants mediated through an information carrier. Interactivity can also take place between a human and an information carrier without the direct involvement of another human. The former is qualitatively different from the latter primarily in terms of input and response spontaneity. In this book, interactivity is defined as mediated interaction that involves reciprocal message exchange between human communicants or between a human and an information carrier which can be any media, computer application, networked resource, and telecommunication device that carries information and can interact with a human.

Interactivity can be analyzed in terms of media attributes and affordances, distributed cognition, learner control, system adaptability, usability, spontaneity, and synchronicity. Much effort has been expended on classifying and topologizing interactivity from the perspective of media studies and information science. Empirical research work can also be found on interactivity in business website design to attract customers. Despite the efforts to categorize and classify interactivity, the concept of interactivity remains diverse and elusive. There is a lack of consolidated endeavor to put the studies of interactivity in related perspectives, to let findings from one field shed light on another, and to connect theoretical and empirical research to the practice of e-learning.

The current book addresses the issues mentioned above. The first objective of the book is to clarify the concept of interactivity, delineate its scope, and come forth with a definition and description that can be more readily applied to further research and practice in e-learning. The second objective is to propose a pragmatic framework for studying and promoting interactivity in e-learning. The third objective is to present the reader with a holistic view of interactivity, with different perspectives complementing and supplementing each other, providing a basis for conceptually and pragmatically informed design of interactive e-learning environment and boosting further research on interactivity in e-learning.

The book is intended for a broad range of audiences, including undergraduate and graduate students, instructors, professionals, and researchers working in the fields of communication and media, educational media, e-learning, and instructional technology. The book can also be a comprehensive library reference for the general audience.

ORGANIZATION OF THE BOOK

The book is organized into three sections: instructional design to promote interactivity, educational games, and interpersonal interactivity through media.

Section 1 includes a collection of articles that explore important areas of interactivity design in the e-learning environment and introduce innovative attempts to promote interactivity in e-learning. In Chapter 1, Haomin Wang of Dakota State University takes an integrated approach by looking at key factors that contribute to effective interactivity in interrelated perspectives for a holistic view of interactivity, with a particular interest in connecting media attributes and system affordances with distributed cognition, cognitive process, and collaborative learning. The focus is on studying how information exchange can be shaped by media and how media can be utilized and learning sources designed to support learning in interactive manners. It is hoped that this initial framework could be expanded and improved to become a conceptually helpful and pragmatically usable guide for interactivity design in e-learning.

Varied approaches have been taken and frameworks proposed for examining interactivity. In Chapter 2, Kamran Sedig and Paul Parsons from the University of Western Ontario identify and elaborate upon 10 structural elements of interaction that affect the interactivity of information representations. Each of these has an effect on the learning and cognitive processes of learners, and the overall interactivity of an e-learning environment is an emergent property of a combination of these elements. Collectively, these elements can serve as a framework to help thinking about design and analysis of interactivity in e-learning.

Media are becoming increasingly enriched with dynamic and interactive content. Immersed in virtual reality, rich media can be a powerful tool to simulate real-life like context and facilitate authentic learning. Chapter 3, by a group of scholars from the Capella University, presents a case that shows how the use of rich media and virtual reality can enable the presentation of a real-world scenario where skills and new knowledge can be applied in a safe-to-access practice situation.

Student engagement is a key attribute of interactive learning and can be greatly enhanced by providing authentic learning environment. In Chapter 4, Deb Gearhart of Troy University offers an overview of authentic learning that includes a literature review and discussion of the benefits for online learning. The chapter also provides a model for the use of authentic learning in online course design.

Learning style matching has long been believed a good way to meet learner needs and preferences. Chapter 5, by Robert Zheng from the University of Utah, presents an interesting finding: style matching did not necessarily provide learning gains for learners with different cognitive styles. Rather, cognitive skill development could be more constructive in helping students learn. This finding is expected to encourage instructional designers and instructors to reconsider the long-held belief about learning style matching and give more attention to cognitive skill development.

Another important dimension of student engagement is maintaining an appropriate level of challenge through a learning process. If a learning process is too easy, students tend to lose interest and motivation. On the other hand, when a learning process becomes too difficult, students may get frustrated, and their cognitive performance tends to be affected. Authored by Ge, Law, and Huang from University of Oklahoma & the University of North Texas Health Science Center, Chapter 6 is an endeavor to tackle a major challenge in maintaining an appropriate level of challenge: scaffolding, or more specifically promoting, dynamic and just-in-time help for learners in an interactive manner.

Using the Buddhist Eightfold Path as a model, Chapter 7, by Julie Shaw of the Empire State College of SUNY, explores the expert-novice paradigm as a framework for helping novice become expert in the e-learning environment, particularly through instructional design that can both scaffold novice instructors to teach to a higher level of learning, and also support experts to help students reach higher goals.

Section 2 explores an emerging field that holds great promises for promoting learner engagement and interactivity in e-learning: educational gaming. Chapter 8, by Betül Özkan Czerkawski from University of Arizona, provides a brief introduction to the basic concepts and terminology of gaming and then gives a review of the current status of educational games and simulations used in higher education institutions. Three case studies are provided to present examples. The chapter concludes with a discussion of teaching strategies, instructional design methods, and assessment issues for effective digital game incorporation in e-learning.

Following up on the instructional application aspect of educational games, In Chapter 9, Michelle Aubrecht of Ohio State University presents three approaches to using games for teaching and learning: (1) an instructor makes a game for a specific learner outcome, (2) students make a game, and (3) an instructor uses a commercial or online game. The chapter emphasizes the second and third methods. Specific examples of how games are used with students are provided to illustrate ways to teach with games.

In a digital game-based learning system (DGBLS), learners are often immersed in a large amount of stimuli that can distract or disrupt the intended learning processes. Chapter 10, by Wenhao Huang from University of Illinois at Urbana-Champaign and Dazhi Yang from Boise State University, proposes a process framework to empower learners to autonomously manage their interactivity with the DGBLS in order to stay focused on the learning tasks. The framework draws literatures on learners' motivational processing and cognitive processing pertaining to learning in a DGBLS.

As proposed by some other authors in this volume, interactivity should be assessed and evaluated in terms of its effectiveness in promoting intended learning objectives. Authored by Jillianne R. Code from University of Victoria, Jody Clarke-Midura (Harvard University), Nick Zap (Simon Fraser University), and Chris Dede (Harvard University), Chapter 11 presents a framework for the design and validation of interactivity in serious games and virtual worlds as they are linked to learning outcomes. Illustrated through a case study, the chapter aims to provide educators, designers, and researchers with a model for how to effectively design immersive virtual and game-based learning environments for the purpose of assessing student inquiry learning.

Section 3 involves another fast-growing field in education, particularly in e-learning: social networking. Among the various modes and tools of social networking are online forums, web conferencing, blogs, wikis, and virtual community. Chapter 12, by Ruth Guo from Buffalo State College, SUNY, is a case study that presents a constructivist approach to creating an interactive learning environment for graduate students in a course designed to help students construct knowledge and skills for developing professional web sites. To make up for the lack of time for practice and tutoring, online forums are used for participants to discuss the issues important to them. The study shows that practical action research combined with social interaction can shed light on important issues of professional development through reflection on practice.

A virtual community is an essential condition for interpersonal interactivity in the e-learning environment. In Chapter 13, Terri Edwards Bubb, Denise McDonald, and Caroline M. Crawford of University of Houston at Clear Lake explore learner virtual community development in which meaningful connections enhance learner motivation and acquisition of learning objectives. The chapter focuses on the interactive activities between the instructor, learners, online environment, and larger community. Practical instructional ideas and activities for building an online learning community are presented.

Function authenticity is often a key factor that affects the productivity of a learner community. In Chapter 14, Aaron Wiatt Powell suggests that the greatest challenge to intentional Community of Practice (CoP) is a sense of interdependence among CoP members, the authenticity of the practice or purpose, and a trajectory for the CoP's future. The chapter presents a case study with an initiative to nurture CoP with cooperative projects and with the support of an online community portal involving a cohort of practicing teachers. The chapter examines the support of social interaction in a cooperative, situated online learning environment, and the cultural barriers that hinder such intention and interactivity.

For virtual community interactivity, synchronous communication is becoming increasingly available. Chapter 15, by Sheila Bonnand and Mary Anne Hansen of Montana State University, is a report on extending library's instructional services by adding synchronous communication to better serve its online students and faculty located across the globe. The web conferencing tool enables the librarians to provide interactive, high-touch library instruction for online students, making librarians more readily accessible to online and distance students.

Haomin Wang
Dakota State University, USA

Section 1
Instructional Design to Promote Interactivity in E–Learning

Chapter 1
Interactivity Design in E-Learning:
An Integrated Approach

Haomin Wang
Dakota State University, USA

ABSTRACT

Learning is becoming increasingly interactive as e-learning continues its growth. Technology advancement not only opens up more affordances for interactivity but also changes the ways people interact with the media and with one another through the media. This chapter attempts to identify key factors that contribute to effective interactivity in the e-learning environment and put the key factors in related perspectives for a holistic view of the interrelations. The key factors include media attributes, instructional values of visuals, audio, and video, digital text and e-reading, accessibility, distributed cognition, system adaptation, virtual space, and collaborative learning. From the interrelated perspective, an integrated approach is proposed for exploring and advancing research and practice in designing and promoting interactivity in the e-learning environment.

INTRODUCTION

A great amount of literature can be found on typologizing interactivity. However, the concept of interactivity remains diverse and elusive due to divergent approaches from different perspec-

tives. In mass communication and information science, interactivity is often examined from a technological perspective with a focus on media attributes (Johnson, Bruner, & Kumar, 2006), or from a functional perspective with a focus on system affordances (Sims, 1997; Sundar, 2004), or user control (Jensen, 1998, 2008). In the psychological field from a learner-centered perspective,

DOI: 10.4018/978-1-61350-441-3.ch001

interactivity is generally seen as a process-related construct (Stromer-Gallery, 2004), rather than a characteristic of a medium (Rafaeli, 1988; Rafaeli & Sudweeks, 1998). The learner-centered approach is interested in internal cognition processes and instructional strategies to facilitate cognition (Hannafin, 1989; Jonassen, 1985, 1988). Stromer-Galley (2004) distinguishes between the media-centered and learner-centered perspectives by describing the former as product-oriented and the latter as process-oriented interactivity. The latter may involve person-to-person information exchange through media, or interpersonal interactivity (Massey & Levy, 1999).

While the media may have the potential to engage the learner, this potential is released only when the learner interacts with the media or through the media with other learners (Kennedy, 2004). From this perspective, interactivity is seen as a media's potential capability to let the user influence or modify the content and form of the mediated communication or as a measure of control over the communication process by both the sender and receiver (Jensen, 1998, 2008; Neuman, 1991; Steuer, 1995). Rogers and Scaife (1998) suggested that interactivity refers to perceptual and cognitive processes that occur when external representations are used, adapted, or constructed by the user in a given learning activity. In this view, the potential of interactivity is contingent upon the perception, cognition, and reaction of the human communicant. Interactivity is seen not as a function of the affordances of the learning system alone, or merely a function of the cognitive activities of the learner; it is seen as a dynamic process that involves both (Bucy, 2004b; Newhagen, 2004; Domagk, Schwartz, & Plass, 2010). As Stromer-Galley (2004) put it, product and process can interact reciprocally.

This chapter defines interactivity as information exchange between person and media, and information exchange between persons through media. Face-to-face interpersonal interaction without the use of media is excluded from this concept of interactivity. The process of interactivity involves the following phenomena:

- The sender of a message selects a medium or a combination of media to represent the message.
- The message is encoded and delivered to the receiver.
- The receiver decodes the message and responds to the sender.
- When the receiver responds to the sender, the receiver becomes the sender and the previous sender becomes the new receiver. This reciprocity can continue.

In the process above, both the sender and receiver can be persons or one is a person and the other is a media agent or learning system. The line between person-to-person interactivity and person-media interactivity can often be shifting and easily crossed in today's hypermedia and mobile computing environments. For instance, while most of the interactivity on a web page may be person-media, a chat or mail to link in a web page provides immediate access for a user to start a live conversation with or send an e-mail to a support person.

As mobile computing and networked resources continue expanding, e-learning is expected to become increasingly interactive and flexible. Technology advancement not only opens up more affordances for interactivity but also changes the ways people interact with the media and with one another through media. This chapter attempts to take a new approach to the study and design of interactivity by integrating the study of media attributes and technology affordance with distributed cognition and social interactions. Broadly speaking, e-learning includes any learning activities that employ electronic technology such as computer, digital media, and network resources to enable learning. In this chapter, e-learning primarily refers to learning enabled through the Internet and World Wide Web. However, e-learning can be found in face-to-face settings as well. For instance, an instructor can use clickers or Microsoft Interactive Classroom (Microsoft, 2010) to conduct quick polling and students can use mobile computing devices or networked computers to respond. Such interpersonal interactivity mediated by technology in a face-to-face setting is a rather different phenomenon (Stromer-Galley, 2004). It is occasionally mentioned in this chapter, but is not a focus of the chapter.

EVALUATION OF INTERACTIVITY AND INTERACTIVITY DESIGN

Before approaching the design of interactivity, it is helpful to discuss how interactivity should be assessed and evaluated. Focusing on quantifying interactivity does not help much to clarify its role in the learning process (Domagk et al, 2010). Observable behaviors such as user mouse click and button push are not necessarily an indication of learning. In terms of user action opportunities, more is not necessarily better for promoting learning. Even when research defines interactivity in a particular setting as high or low, users can have different feelings, experiences, or perceptions of interactivity of different levels of intensity (Rafaeli & Ariel, 2007). Bucy (2004a) finds that a moderate level of intensity is usually optimal for user satisfaction.

Defining interactivity in terms of amount of user control over the media interface is not as constructive to instructional design and practice either. Learner control over the user interface is not necessarily a reflection of cognitive engagement. Just as interactivity potential can attract, it can distract too. Liu and Shrum (2002) found that higher intensity of interactivity and elaboration on a web site generally requires more cognitive resources and makes it more difficult for the learner to control navigation and process related information. Plowman (1996) noted that giving the learner choices can disrupt the sequence of

events, affecting the final closure of the narrative. To keep the learner on an intended learning path, certain degree of system control and guidance is needed, and a simple user interface may encourage better cognitive concentration than a complex one. Likewise, for a communication task that involves mostly text or verbal information exchange without much visual data sharing, a text chat or audio conference may work better than a video conference with more interactive affordances.

For instructional benefits, what is more important is not the amount, but the type and quality, of interactivity. As Bucy (2004a) observes, interactivity research should not be satisfied with merely identifying when a communicative setting is interactive or not, but should ultimately address itself to the consequences of interactivity. Designers should be less concerned with the physical evidence of interactivity than with the cognitive activities that the lesson is designed to engender (Hannafin, 1989). The value and merit of interactive learning design should be determined by the degree to which instructional content and learning activities encourage beneficial cognitive processes and strategies in students (Kennedy, 2004). This author shares the point made by some researchers (Bucy, 2004a & 2004b; Liu & Shrum, 2002) that it is questionable to assume that two-way communication is uniformly desirable and predominantly associated with positive outcomes.

The primary goal of communication is to get a message across to the intended receiver. Therefore, interactivity should be evaluated in terms of effectiveness and efficiency for the message to be encoded, delivered, and decoded, and for response and feedback to be returned. How can the effectiveness and efficiency of interactivity be assessed then? In order for an interactivity process to be successfully carried out, appropriate media should be selected for the representation of the message. The message should be properly encoded in the selected media and successfully delivered to the receiver. Effective message encoding involves not only media selection but also content selection and presentation. Content relevance can be more important than media selection for successful comprehension by the receiver. The receiver should be able to receive and processes the message as it is originally intended, and respond to the sender in a manner available to the receiver. As carrier of the message exchange, media can have significant impact on the effectiveness and efficiency of interactivity. Media selection is therefore a primary constituent in the framework of interactivity design.

MEDIA MATTER

Our societies have been shaped by the nature of the media as well as by the content of the communication (McLuhan, 1967). Cognitive researchers observe that different media have different symbolic attributes (Mayer, 2001, Moreno & Mayer, 1999, Salomon, 1979) or information "bias" which can play a crucial role in revealing and communicating unique aspects of reality (Carpenter, 1960, Meringoff, 1980; Gardner, 1993). Information bias can be so unique that information coded within one medium may not be fully recoded in another without losing some of its features and content. A simple demonstration would be to challenge anyone who doubts this proposition to convey the content of a musical performance in verbal expression. The proposition can be demonstrated in other daily experiences as well. For example, the perceptions we have when watching an interactive weather map are usually different from what we perceive when reading the forecast in text. Such differences in perception are believed to be due to the different mental processes and skills involved in the information encoding and decoding (Salomon, 1974). From an instructional perspective, these information attributes or biases can suggest important guidelines in developing course materials and designing learning activities (Olson & Bruner, 1974; Clark & Salomon, 1986), particularly in media selection and content

development. Chris Dede (1996) contends that how a medium shapes its users and its message is a crucial issue in understanding the transformation of traditional distance education into e-learning.

Digital media allows information to be organized and structured in unprecedented ways that facilitate information access and search. The global network allows messages to be delivered to a large audience that cannot be easily gathered to meet in a face-to-face setting. Digital media can also be easily stored to hold message or data for on-demand access and retrieval. When feedback immediacy is not required or desired, communicants can take time to reflect and revise their messages. Saved records of communication can archive learning activities and can be used to review learning progress.

Media capabilities have greatly evolved since the birth of the Internet and World Wide Web. A broad range of digital interactive media have emerged: world-wide shareable resources, hypermedia, e-reading, search engine, distributed cognition, virtual space, augmented reality, social networking, and scalable audience. A new term "rich media" has been coined to highlight the dynamic and interactive characteristics of the new media. Related to rich media is virtual space, which might be considered a new genre of media, or perhaps more accurately a new realm of communication environment. Enhanced with distributed cognition and augmented reality, virtual space can effectively simulate actual physical space and provide a situational context the user can navigate through and interact with (see Figure 1). Coupled with mobile computing, virtual space can be augmented by networked resources and computer-generated 3D visuals and can be dynamically and interactively shifted in response to user actions and movement. Two good examples of such integration are GPS and Second Life which combines virtual reality, virtual space, and virtual community all in one.

In a virtual space, human communicants can make their presence known to other members of

Figure 1. Augmented reality: An integration of rich media, distributed cognition and virtual space

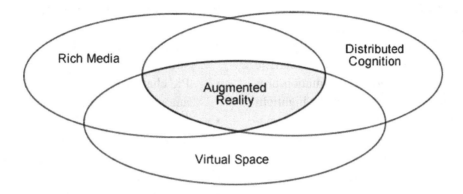

the virtual community, share digital materials and workspaces, and work on the same set of materials either synchronously or asynchronously. Virtual communities can function in online discussion forum, chat room, and web conferencing. The primary advantage of virtual meeting is time and space flexibility; participants do not have to travel and can join the meeting from anywhere with an Internet connection. However, web conferencing can do more. Some of the affordances offered by web conferencing would be difficult or inconvenient to deploy in a face-to-face setting, such as virtual breakout rooms, closed captioning, instant polling, and application sharing which allows a group of people simultaneous access to a shared application or document from their respective computers. In an application sharing, the host computer can give editing permission to any of the participants so that each participant can control the shared application and make contributions. All the changes and updates are sent back to the host computer and reflected on every participant's computer screen in real time. In recent years, the growth of social media has provided even more options for social interactivity. Built on the ideological and technological foundations of Web 2.0, popular social networking services include Facebook, MySpace, Twitter, and Wikipedia. An innovative case of using Facebook for

online mentoring is described in one of the chapters in this volume.

INSTRUCTIONAL VALUES OF VISUALS

The fundamental nature of visuals is that they are iconic. The primary value of visuals is their capacity to convey information that cannot be as effectively represented in other modalities (Gombrich, 1974). Functionally, visuals can be categorized into four groups: realistic representation, analogous or metaphoric representation, organizational representation, and perceptual enhancement. In some cases, distinction between categories can be blurred. For instance, perceptual enhancement and organizational representation may be blended in content layout design. Colors, lines, shapes, and allocations can be effective methods for both perceptual enhancement and organizational layout.

Realistic paintings and photographs are commonly used to re-present context, environment, and scenes from real life. Realism enhances content authenticity and facilitates content mapping. Most of us have experienced viewing a photo that was taken years ago on a vacation and recalling many details of the trips. Such recollections usually do not occur as easily with verbal stimuli. Using realistic visuals in e-learning can present life-like contexts to support situated learning.

Realistic visuals generally need to include enough details to make the representation look real. However, extraneous details in realistic representation can slow down information processing and add to cognitive load. To highlight important points and minimize possible distractions, it is often necessary to be selective in graphic encoding. Selective encoding can make the most relevant parts stand out, remove coverings, eliminate interfering details, and highlight or even exaggerate characteristics. Application examples can be found in X-ray photos, drawings of inner structural parts, and comic cartoons. However, caution needs to be taken when using selective encoding as over-simplified representation can make recognition difficult. Horn (1999) notes that recognizing a graphic representation depends on the context, frequency of usage, and scope of usage. This observation is particularly relevant when we use analogous and metaphorical graphic representations.

Sometimes, direct resemblance may not be applicable or conducive to visual perception and cognition, particularly in situations where easy recognition is needed. Using an analogous or metaphorical representation can usually speed up recognition and response, by removing less relevant details and highlighting the prominent characteristics of an object or phenomenon. Application examples include traffic and road signs, icons in computer-user interface, and logos. Appropriate use of icons and symbols in e-learning environment can enhance user interface and facilitate function recognition and perceptual response. However, instructional designers should avoid using icons or symbols that are not commonly recognizable.

Analogous representation is also found in the form of charts and diagrams to focus on spatial resemblance and to illustrate procedural and quantitative relationships. Here, the distinction between analogous and organizational representations can be blurred. Application examples include:

- Diagram to describe organizational structure.
- Pie chart to show proportional differences among comparable groups.
- Line chart to show changes or developmental trend along a timeline.
- Bar chart to show quantitative differences.
- Flowchart to illustrate procedures.
- 3D chart to show multi-dimensional relationships.

Sometimes, a diagram or chart alone may not be self-explanatory enough and some short text description or explanation can be helpful to highlight or point out key points to be conveyed by a diagram or chart. Most educators today are able to use common applications such as Microsoft Office to generate data-based diagrams and charts and deploy them in e-learning environments. More advanced visual data display is emerging. Combining highly advanced computational methods with sophisticated graphic display, Visual Data Analysis (VDA) can be effective for analyzing patterns and trends. VDA enables data to be interpreted holistically by exposing contextually meaningful attributes of the data to show interrelations, structures, directions of change, and other complex phenomena, such as climate modeling, environmental change, and earthquake prediction. Over 170 sample projects using VDA can be found in the Visual Complexity site at http://www.visualcomplexity.com/vc/. IBM also has many illustrative examples in its project titled Many Eyes at http://www-958.ibm.com/software/data/cognos/manyeyes/. VDA holds great potential for e-learning; it can help create intuitive and engaging learning aids and foster explorative and inquisitive learning, and can be easily deployed in the online environment.

Many VDA applications involve 3D visuals. Recent technology development has brought new functions and affordances for 3D video production and application. Technically, 3D video creates the perception of a differential between two slightly offset images when viewed by each of the two eyes. By presenting each eye with a slightly offset mage, the display can create an illusion of depth. When depth is perceivable, concepts that involve spatial comprehension would be easier to convey, and situated learning becomes more feasible. Here are some possible instructional applications for e-learning: (a) Virtually walking through famous architectural structures and feeling like one is right there, (b) Showing the nuances of the amazing anatomy in 3D detail, (c) Exploring topography to bring geography lessons to life, and (d) Presenting different cultural activities and settings to promote cross-cultural understanding. 3D projection and 3D television are already available on the market and educational applications have been experimented in some schools. Online 3D videos are also coming forth. Although the technology has arrived, the content is much slower to come. Questions remain as to what kind of content makes more sense for 3D production. Compatibility and technical standards are other issues to address. Vendors may have their own proprietary drivers, players, and protocols. Platform incompatibility could be barriers to adoption by educational institutions.

INSTRUCTIONAL VALUES OF AUDIO AND VIDEO

Aural input is an important part of our life. The auditory attribute of sound makes audio an unsubstitutable medium for music and language training, and for providing content for the visually impaired or those who cannot read text for other reasons. The appeal and effectiveness of speech come largely from the non-verbal expressiveness available in speech, but hardly replicable in writing. Non-verbal expressions include variations in vocal pitch, intonation, tone, rhythm, and stress.

Such variations can express attitude, feeling, mood, and points of interest in ways that are difficult to convey or even describe in writing. As hearing a voice talk can bring about a more personal feeling than a text message, an instructor can record greeting or weekly messages and post them as podcasts in the e-learning environments to help overcome the sense of alienation or isolation often felt by distance students.

Because listening in our native language is as automatic as breathing, we can combine audio messages with text or visuals to enhance learner-content interactivity without causing cognitive overload. On the other hand, because listening is usually not a conscious effort, it is hard for most people to remain concentrated on a listening task for an extended period of time. In e-learning, a long recorded speech would be better broken into several segments for easier delivery and processing, allowing learners to take short breaks between segments, and making it easier for students to select particular parts of the speech to listen to or replay.

Another constraint in listening to a speech is linearity. Because of the linear nature of speech, many information processing strategies applicable in reading are inapplicable in listening. For example, scanning and skimming are effective ways to get main ideas in reading, but not in listening, since the complete text is not available for perusal. Consequently, prediction in listening plays a more important role than in reading. The ability to predict in listening is partly based the listener's prior knowledge of the subject matter, and partly on the listener's familiarity with idiomatic expressions and special terms in the speech. To help the learner better comprehend a speech, a text introduction with necessary background information can be useful to facilitate prediction and comprehension. For extended messages, providing pre-listening questions can guide the learners and help them focus on major points. If there are many special terms in the speech that may be unfamiliar to the students, it can be a good idea to define or explain these items in the pre-listening activities. Finally, because sound is ephemeral, follow-up access and information retrieval may need to be provided by making the recording available for replay or providing scripts as redundant copy of the content. All these auxiliary or supplementary materials can be provided either through hyperlinks before and after each audio module or as e-mail attachment sent to students before or after a listening session.

Audio content is often an integral part of a video. Video production used to be a highly professional business. With the advancement of the camcorder and digital video technology, video making has now become something that many of us can do, and so is the distribution of digital video. A clear evidence is the increasing popularity of YouTube. Because video can integrate sound, action, and scene into one storyboard, it can be a great tool for recording and presenting field trips, lab experiments, debate sessions and project presentations. Compared with static images, the distinctive power of video is to show continuously changing scenes or evolving events. Video is therefore a good tool to demonstrate highly procedural and context-based events. Because the viewer of a video can be physically separate from the actual scene, we can use video to capture and represent scenes from remote or restricted areas, or scenes of hazardous or risky events, or contexts that would be impossible for students to access in person.

Seeing action in motion gives the viewer a more realistic experience of what is presented. The capabilities to show a scene as it appeared in real life makes video a powerful medium to bring about attitudinal and emotional impact. In the movie *Nuremberg*, the prosecutor of the International Military Tribunal started by presenting numbers of Jewish people who were murdered during World War II, but did not seem to be able to speak strongly with those figures. However, when the prosecutor presented a video that captured the scenes of the horrible war crimes, the emotional impact on the audience was far more shocking than those numbers and verbal descriptions.

Capturing and presenting scenes from remote or restricted areas is not the only power of video. Other techniques unique of video include montage, fast or slow motion, and zooming to re-create scenes that we do not normally see in our daily life or with our naked eye. Video can compress time by taking snapshots, in intervals, of a long process, such as the formation of a hurricane or the growth of a plant. With the capabilities of compressing and expanding durations, video can be very effective in demonstrating motor skills, even more effective than by having learners observe the actual performance in real life, because video can skip trivial parts and slow down to focus on important details for the learners.

Another type of video that many instructors find helpful is the capturing of screen actions that take place on the user interface of a computer application. Video of this type is most useful for illustrating procedural operations of a desktop application that involves visual details, such as digital graphic creation, application troubleshooting, program debugging, and manipulation of a graphic user interface. Many screen action capturing tools have editing functions that support zooming in, adding annotation and voice narration, callouts, and applying effects such as cursor and object highlighting. Popular tools include Adobe Captivate and Techsmith's Camtasia.

Video conferencing allows instructors to conduct live class sessions online where participants can interact with one another through networked computers with live audio and video support, text chat, and application sharing. New video technology even allows users to capture and present scenes from multiple sites on the same screen simultaneously, creating a virtual community with multimedia communication channels in web conferencing. Video conferencing is further discussed in the section Virtual Space and Collaborative Learning later in the chapter.

DIGITAL TEXT AND E-READING

Visuals can be more effective than text in representing and conveying certain type of information, but text is still the primary carrier of information in today's message exchange in e-learning environments. The digital revolution and mobile computing have brought about drastic changes in text writing and reading. In a study of 15,000 pieces of writing samples that cover in-class assignments, formal essays, journal entries, emails, blog posts, and chat sessions from 189 students, over a time span of five years from 2001 to 2006, Andrea Lunsford of Stanford University (2006) has found that young people today write far more than any generation before them, primarily because so much communication and socializing takes place online and involves text. Their writings are often short and brief with "haiku-like concision", though they can also write long and complex pieces of prose, often while working collaboratively with others.

Digital text storage and rendering have created new options and preferences for text composition, presentation, distribution, and processing. Digital text can be displayed and read on a variety of devices, including desktop computer screen, notebook, iPad, e-paper, smart phone, and other portable devices. Varied e-reading devices have greatly promoted flexibility and efficiency in text writing and reading. The power of e-reading has changed and will continue changing not only the way we read but also the way we write, and publishers publish. Writers try to make their writings more "e-friendly", more easily found and efficiently distributed through the Internet and other e-communication channels, and more effectively and efficiently processed by e-readers. When a variety of devices and e-readers are available for digital text, compatibility, portability, and interoperability become important issues to address in the production and consumption of e-text. In May 2011, the first World E-Reading Congress 2011 was held in London with representatives from leading publishers, software companies, and academic institutions around the world to discuss future business models and opportunities for e-reading.

In addition to easy storage and distribution, e-text has some other affordances that are not found in traditional text or quite different from what is available in traditional text. E-books can have built-in dictionaries and pronunciation guides. Multimedia can be more easily integrated into e-reading environment. E-books can now "talk to readers, quiz them on their grasp of the material, play videos to illustrate a point or connect them with a community of fellow readers" (Pham & Sarno, 2010). Bookmarks can be inserted as hyperlinks. Table of content can be easily created and updated through appropriate use of hierarchical levels of headings. Search by keyword or phrases or metadata can be done in most e-reading environment in a matter of seconds. Annotation can be added as a hide-on-side available at a click, and all the annotations to an e-text can be easily exported as a separate collection, archived or imported into other environments.

The developmental trends and emerging phenomena mentioned above are expected to have significant impact on the practice and prospect of e-learning. Reading and writing are becoming more of a communal event rather than an individual activity in the networked environment. The capability of search with varied scope, within a small virtual community or across the global village, enables the reader to find a right reading in a far more effective and efficient way. Integrated with social media and networking, e-text can be annotated by thousands or millions of readers and these annotations can be shared through blog, discussion forum, e-mail, listserv, twitter, web posting, notes directly attached to or embedded in the e-text. Editing on a text document can be tracked and can be shared with co-editors or target audience. Writing in a wiki environment allows a group of people to work on the same document, contributing and co-editing, and progressive versions of the document can be archived for future reference and tracking. All these affordances provided by e-text have opened up unprecedented possibilities for new forms of information architecture, data query, content search, collaborative learning, and meta cognition development.

While e-writing and e-reading offer great flexibility and convenience, there are constraints to be aware of for designers and writers. E-text is still not as legible as paper text due to the limitations of digital devices, such as surface glare, insufficient screen contrast, refresh rate, and screen size. Legibility is much improved and eye fatigue is less of an issue with e-paper. E-paper has seen some significant advancement in recent years. E-paper is now far more portable and much larger than most screens. However, content on e-paper currently available can only be updated periodically and cannot dynamically and interactively connect to network resources in real time. Most e-text is still posted as web page content.

In a study by Morkes and Nielsen (1997), 79% of the readers surveyed tended to scan web page content instead of reading word-by-word or even line by line, largely due to inadequate screen legibility. Short text is preferred over long text because it is easier to scan. Users also liked simple sentence structures and informal style. Similar findings are reported by McGovern, Norton, and O'Dowd (2001). Web authors have found ways to accommodate. Sub headings and topic sentences can make scanning easier. Text legibility and readability can be improved by sufficient contrast between background color and foreground text, by using colors to distinguish parts of content, such as important phrases and keywords, and appropriate use of font variations.

A prominent feature of e-text is the use of hypermedia. Hyperlink structure allows learners to traverse the content by selecting what is most relevant from among varied paths and multiple perspectives (Spiro, Feltovich, Jacobson, & Coulson, 1991). With a flexible and multidimensional organization of content nodes, hyperlink structure can be an effective way to promote cognitive flexibility in ill-structured domain by providing a "landscape crisscrossing" view of the content domain. As a facilitator of knowledge construction, hypermedia allows the learner to access a large knowledge base and seek out information that meets their particular needs, in terms of both their prior knowledge and their preferred learning style. Hypermedia is also a great tool for students to collect and organize their learning materials, share and critique information, reflect upon learning experiences, and revise and rebuild their knowledge base. In using hypermedia to present ideas, students will need to apply critical thinking and creative design by imposing some kind of knowledge structure on what they want to present, which can be intellectually challenging and engaging to learners (Jonassen, 2003), and can also entice meta cognition development.

The non-linear nature of hyperlink structure comes with problems too. Two commonly reported issues are user disorientation in navigation and cognitive overload (Yang & Moore, 1996). Dee-Lucas and Larkin (1992) point out that although accessing extra information while reading a text can compensate for initial deficiencies in vocabulary or background knowledge, continuous comprehension can be disrupted if the reader is frequently led away by external resource links. How to provide supplementary resources and customize learning paths without undue disruptions of continuous comprehension is a major challenge for hypermedia instructional designers. There is no one-fit-all solution here. Decisions will have to be based on learning contexts and learner needs.

ACCESSIBILITY AND USABILITY

The growing variety of rich media and flexibility of e-reading have come along with a subsequently important issue of accessibility, which must be taken into consideration in media selection, content development and delivery. Interactivity cannot take place if a message fails to reach the receiver.

For the general users, accessibility often means access speed: How fast the content can be retrieved and played on the user's end. Access speed is particularly a factor to consider for multimedia content and synchronous web conferencing. A web page that includes rich media usually takes more time to load than a page of mostly text content. A slow or unstable network connection can make web conferencing unusable.

For text content, accessibility includes legibility and readability. Text legibility can be affected by font size, type, and style, space between lines and between characters, and contrast between foreground and background. Readability can be affected by line length, paragraphing, grouping, listing, paging, headings, indexing, and table of content. Accessibility also includes compatibility: whether the content delivered can be displayed as intended on the user's platform. Customizing text display in a web page is now fairly easy in most web page editors. However, caution should be taken in customizing text display; some display may show up very nicely in one type of browser, but not in other browsers. As mobile computing and portable devices continue evolving, compatibility and portability will become more prominent. A generally recommended method to improve compatible text display is to use Cascading Style Sheet.

Apart from the broad sense of accessibility for the general public, accessibility can specifically refer to making content accessible to people with disabilities, particularly those with vision and hearing impairments who rely on assistive technology to access and process digital information. For educational institutions that receive federal funding in the United States, accessibility is a legal obligation, as mandated by Section 508 of the Rehabilitation Act. The criteria for web content accessibility are based on the guidelines developed by the Web Accessibility Initiative of the World Wide Web Consortium (www.w3.org/ WAI). A complete list with detailed description of the standards given by Section 508 is available from the web site of the Access Board (www.

access-board.gov), a federal agency devoted to accessibility for people with disabilities.

Accessibility requirements fall predominantly on graphic, audio and video content. Images, forms, and tables should have labels for vision-impaired users who access content with the help of screen reading software. All videos should be captioned for deaf and hard-of-hearing viewers. Videos should carry an audio component that describes images and visual cues for blind and low-vision users. For real-time online lectures, live captioning service should be provided for users with hearing or vision impairments. Applications should offer key combinations (on keyboard) for functions that are appropriate for users with mobility restrictions or vision impairments, and no key combination should require the use of more than one hand.

It could take a considerable amount of efforts and resources to meet some of these requirements. However, new technologies have emerged with functions and tools to greatly facilitate the accommodation of accessibility. Web development tools have some basic accessibility support built in and make it very easy to add labels and text descriptions for images, forms, and tables. Voice recognition software can now be versatile enough to provide transcription services. Dragon NaturallySpeaking (Nuance, 2011) is a popular speech recognition software application that can transcribe voice messages to text. Google Voice (Google, 2011) allows voice phone calls to be transcribed as text messages. Text messages are much easier to archive and search than voice mails.

Total accessibility is difficult to attain because users may have different types of disabilities, different language needs, and various hardware and software configurations. Nevertheless, a certain level of accessibility is usually possible. To determine which level of accessibility is feasible for a particular context, we recommend the reader consult the Web Content Accessibility Guidelines (WCAG) 2.0 by the World Wide Web Consortium (www.w3.org).

Accessibility can be closely related to the need of synchronicity. Synchronous communication typically has a higher demand on accessibility. Video conferencing has far more data to transfer and consequently has a higher demand for bandwidth. In real-time audio conferencing, a breakdown in network connection for only a few seconds can make a message hard to follow. Therefore, alternative backup channel of communication is highly desirable in case the primary channel of communication breaks down. Real-time captioning service needs to be provided for a live web conferencing when the audience includes hearing-impaired participants.

Accessibility is closely related to usability which is about whether a user can easily find the desired information in a given environment and accomplish the target task effectively and efficiently without undue frustration. In the e-learning environment, usability is often based on learner's perception of content, which can be influenced by several factors: (a) type of objects, (b) color of page components, (c) size of page components, (d) location of page components, and (e) division of page layout. In content layout design, Gestalt principles of perception have general referential values. The central point of Gestalt principles is that perception is more often determined by the structural relationships among the parts of a pattern, than by the individual elements of which the pattern is composed (Koffka, 1935; Bruce, Green, & Georgeson, 1996). Key principles include figure and ground, similarity, proximity, continuity, closure, area, and symmetry. Detailed discussion of the Gestalt principles is beyond the scope of this chapter.

DISTRIBUTED COGNITION

Media can not only provide a formal representation of a message but also embody human cognition. Distributed cognition theory holds that media and tools reflect the externalization and formalization of human cognition. Without some formalization of knowledge, knowledge accumulation across generations and knowledge exchange between people would be impossible. Without the accumulated wisdom embodied in the tools and environment, we would all have to find solutions from scratch. Such externalization helps extend human cognitive capacities and improve cognitive efficiency. Media and tools help learners to transcend their perceptual and cognitive limitations such as memory, information processing, and problem-solving (Pea, 1985). In the media objects and tools we use today, such accumulated knowledge and wisdom can be seen as functional properties and action opportunities, or affordances in Gibson's terms (1977). In active perceiving, organisms attend more to the functional properties and affordances implied by these properties than sensations and physical properties per se (Brock, Otto, Hoffman, 2004). In a broad sense, human language embodies the cognition mankind has accumulated through the centuries. The accumulated cognition is reflected in vocabulary, syntax, and composition, including text organization and rhetoric. With the growth of digital technology and networked resources, instructional functions and learning opportunities are more and more built into our living and working environments. As we build richer, more all-encompassing computational environments, it becomes more important than ever to understand the ways human cognitions and their cultural environments are tightly coupled enabling intelligent action (Hollan, Hutchings, & Kirsh, 2000).

At a user interface level, distributed cognition can be found in icons, signs, symbols, and content layout. Icons and menu items in a digital user interface can be so closely coupled to the actual operation of the intended object that we tend to feel we are acting on the real objects themselves rather than some symbols. This experience can be found in clicking an iconic button to save or delete or print, or dragging and dropping a file from one folder to another. Appropriate use of icons and symbols in e-learning environments can facilitate user recognition of and response to affordances and enhance usability.

In digital user interfaces, cues such as alert, prompts, and progress indicator are commonly used to facilitate perception and cognition. Computer applications and learning environments that have rich distributed cognition include databases, semantic networks, spreadsheets, modeling tools, information search engines, visualization tools, multimedia publishing tools, online communication environments, and expert systems (Jonassen, 2000). Distributed cognition can also be found in information architecture techniques such as categorization, grouping, indexing, list, menu, table of content, and navigation scheme.

Since the birth of the Internet and World Wide Web, digital distributed cognition is no longer confined to the desktop but reaches into a complex networked world of information, resources and mediated interactivity. A prominent application example of distributed cognition is Augmented Reality (AR). AR typically presents a live direct or indirect view of a physical real-world environment merged with and augmented by computer-generated imagery. It can enhance what we see, hear, and perceive and blur the line between what's real and what's virtual, thus creating a mixed reality. Application examples of AR can be found in 3D modeling, super-imposed imagery on sport events on TV, GPS, and smart phones.

AR can be combined with Virtual Reality (VR) to create applications such as flight simulator and tele-surgery. Employing 3-D graphics to simulate real world situations, VR allows the user to work with the simulations by moving around, zooming in and out, and interacting with objects in ways similar to what happens in real world, but with more convenience and flexibility. AR and VR have application values for many professional fields, including aviation, architectural and interior design, business modeling, city planning, medicine, performing arts, and law enforcement. Whether in e-learning environments or a face-to-face set-

ting, AR and VR can greatly expand and extend the range of realistic contexts that learners can experience and interact with.

Cognitive functions and processes can be distributed not only in objects and learning environment, but also across time and people. Processes may be distributed through time in such a way that the results or products of earlier events can transform the nature of later actions and events (Hollan, et al., 2000). Browsers can keep records of browsing history. Accrued history of menu choices of other uses of a system are indicated by highlighting more commonly used menu items. New browsers have intelligent auto completion or auto fill feature that can suggest or recommend entries as the user enters the first few letters into the browser's search box. Google Docs and Wikis can document who read or edited various sections of documents as well as the length of time they took. Such progressive monitoring allows the instructor to observe student performance in an interactive process so that the instructor can give guidance in a timely manner. Participants can look back on the revision history to see how their work has evolved, and how individual contributions have helped to shape a collective project. Collaborative team work and peer support are much easier by sharing documents and projects in progress.

The primary goal of incorporating distributed cognition in interactivity design is for cognitive efficiency and effectiveness. Cognitive efficiency is about minimizing unnecessary cognitive efforts spent to process and comprehend a message, whereas cognitive effectiveness is about maximizing the probability that the message gets through to the receiver as is intended by the message sender. While our cognition-enriched environment provides us with intellectual tools that enable us to accomplish things that we could not do otherwise, the existing environment may also constrain or blind us to habitual ways of thinking, leading us to assume that certain things are impossible when in fact they are possible when viewed differently (Hollan, et al., 2000). Interactivity design should help us to see enabling affordances and possible constrains so as to improve cognitive effectiveness and efficiency.

SYSTEM ADAPTATION AND CONSTRUCTIVE LEARNING

If cognitive growth is a primary goal of interactivity in e-learning, cognitive engagement is an essential condition that can be promoted by an adaptive learning system. Based on well-informed anticipation of learner needs, an adaptive learning system can provide options in learning paths to meet different learner needs, monitor and assess learner performances, give feedback when desired, and adjust instructional content to meet the evolving needs. Such an adaptive program aims to keep the learner cognitively engaged and moving forward in what Vygotsky (1978) called the zone of proximal development (ZPD). To engage the learner in a continuous dialogue with the instructional content, instructional systems must provide opportunities for learners to make active responses to the instructional content, and must be adaptive and responsive to learner actions and needs in the learning process. Adaptive instructional systems should also be capable of guiding learners in developing cognitive skills.

Developing truly adaptive instructional materials can be extremely challenging, requiring extensive analysis of information processing needs for a given learning task, well-informed anticipation of learner variations, well-planned instructional approach, systematic record keeping, and sophisticated programming that can dynamically assess learner performance and provide appropriate feedback and scaffolding. Adaptive instructional systems should also be capable of guiding learners in developing cognitive skills. In scaffolding, the instructional agent, whether an adaptive learning system or a human facilitator, will monitor the learning progress and determine when the learner needs help and what kind of help

is needed (Newman, Griffin, & Cole, 1989). In this apprenticeship approach, the instruction starts with an amount of help that has been found generally appropriate for the majority of learners. Based on the initial assessment of learner performance, the instruction adjusts the level of help until the learner appears to falter, and then increases help to the point where the learner can perform the task again with expected competence. Once the learner's performance becomes stabilized, the instruction reduces the help again to see if the learner can accomplish the task with less help. Scaffolding can be provided through navigation guidance, asking the learner questions, encouraging learner queries, and sustaining an appropriate level of task challenge to engage the learner. Ge, Law, and Huang (2011) in this volume describe some highly applicable examples of system adaptations to provide scaffolding.

Constrained by the theoretical limitations of our understanding of human cognition and technical limitations of intelligent programming, fully adaptive instructional content is still more of research and development efforts than of instructional applications. There are areas of human mental activities that are beyond the domain of logical information processing, but more under the influence by emotional traits and personality variations. Despite the difficulty in developing truly adaptive programs, certain level of adaptive capabilities can still be incorporated into e-learning environment, particularly in hypermedia navigation and customizable learning paths.

Adaptive hypermedia emerged in the early 1990s (Cristea, 2003; Park & Lee, 2004). Like non-hypermedia adaptive programs, an adaptive hypermedia system is based on a user model and a domain knowledge base, and is able to dynamically adjust the content and navigation paths to meet the needs and preferences of the user (Brusilovsky, 2000; De Bra, 2000). The user model is derived from the system's knowledge of learner's learning history and the learner's current knowledge in the target area (Eklund & Sinclair, 2000). It is possible to initialize the user model through a questionnaire or by observing the navigation behavior of the user (De Bra, Brusilovsky, & Houben, 1999). The primary advantage of hypermedia is flexible linkage that allows learning materials to be arranged in ways to encourage learners to find possible interconnections among concepts and ideas, and help learners to navigate through learning paths that are most relevant and engaging to their personal experiences. Through active exploration and cognitive navigation, learners are encouraged to build connections between their past experience and new knowledge.

In today's e-learning environment, the control of knowledge construction is more in the hands of the learner than that of the instructor. In constructive learning, the learner builds new knowledge and develops skills based on her or his existing knowledge and skills. A constructive learning environment is designed to relate learning to learners' personal experiences, making the learning authentic, situated in contexts meaningful to the learners. Authentic learning is characterized by content relevance and task salience. Authentic learning does not have to take place in real-life locations. Authentic learning activities can be carried out in virtual environments, through simulated scenarios, access to remote resources with expert consultation, collaborative online investigation, virtual space sharing, and team project. Mobile computing, rich media, augmented reality, 3D video, and live web conferencing can work together to bring about an e-learning context that can be even more authentic than a traditional face-to-face classroom setting since the former can let the learners experience what is generally not accessible without the facilitation of the technology. Gearhart (2011) in this volume has further discussions on authentic learning in the e-learning environment.

A critical feature of authentic and constructive learning is learner engagement. In this regard, educational gaming has many strategies that instructional designers and content developers

can use. Many important instructional principles can be readily found in educational gaming: a meaningful context, specific objectives, directions for activities, hands-on engagement, criteria for performance assessment, progress indicators, immediate feedback, and summative evaluation. In a game environment, what you learn is directly related to the context. Learning is not only relevant but is applied and practiced within that context. Interactivity in a game requires a constant cycle of hypothesis formulation, testing, and revision. Good games also maintain a certain level of challenge; games that are too easily solved will not be engaging (Eck, 2006). Johnson, Levine, Smith & Stone (2010) predict that game-based learning will be prevalent in schools in two to three years. However, limited research efforts have been made on the instructional applications of games in e-learning environment. In this volume, Czerkawski (2011) presents an overview of educational gaming in its current status; Aubrecht (2011) explores how games can teach and how teachers can use them; Huang and Yang (2011) propose a process framework to empower learners to autonomously manage their interactivity in a digital game-based learning system in order to stay focused on the learning tasks.

Complete integration of such dynamic monitoring of learner progress and adjustment of learning activities into an adaptive instructional program can be a major challenge and may not be practical in most cases. This is where a human instructional agent, whether an instructor or a tutor, or a peer learner can help. To make up for the lack of comprehensive and dynamic monitoring and programmed on-demand help, the instructor or a tutor could be virtually available to provide timely help when it is needed. In the e-learning environment, this means that the communication channels between instructor and students should remain open and students are free to contact the instructor whenever they need help. This also requires the instructor or tutor to stay informed of students' progress and provide help in a timely manner when help is needed. In addition to instructor's support, peer support and collaborative learning can be invaluable, oftentimes even more approachable and accommodating than instructor's help. Interpersonal communication and interactivity should therefore be generally encouraged and facilitated in e-learning.

VIRTUAL SPACE AND COLLABORATIVE LEARNING

Virtual Reality, 3D modeling, 3D video, and Augmented Reality have opened up new affordances for human perceptions of and interactivity with the physical environment in virtual space. In addition, virtual space has brought along a broad range of channels for interpersonal interactivity. Interpersonal communication and collaborative learning are valuable for distance learners not only because it helps learners to overcome the sense of alienation and learn from one another in the virtual environment, but also because it trains the students in effective team work which is becoming increasingly important in today's work place. Collaborative learning has its theoretical ground in Bandura's (1969, 1970) peer modeling and Vygotsky's (1978) emphasis on social construction of knowledge. Vygotsky believed that learners are capable of performing at higher intellectual levels when working with peers than when working alone. The competence they develop through collaborative learning will be transferable to their individual work. Compared with lecture-style teaching, collaborative learning environment provides relatively realistic, cognitively motivating, and socially enriched learning contexts. While collaborating with peers, learners often encounter fresh ideas, experience diverse interpretations, and see varied learning strategies that may not be congruent with one's prior knowledge and experiences. The reciprocal give-and-take will benefit not only tutees but also

tutors; people usually have a more solid grasp of what they know by tutoring others.

For today's students, social networking has become almost part of their lives. An e-learning environment without any use of social networking would be rather alienating for the e-generation. A great variety of media tools and mobile devices are available now to facilitate social networking and collaborative learning. Listserv is still very much in use today by many professional organizations. Newer social media include Facebook, Flickr, Google Docs, MySpace, Twitter, Wiki, and YouTube. In social networking, one person's comment on another person's blog may entice a third person to add comment, and this type of follow-up and threading can go on continuously. Google Docs and Wikis allow a group of people to work on a shared set of documents and can keep a revision history so that participants can track progress and see how individual contributions have helped to shape a collective project. Progressive monitoring allows the instructor to observe student performance in a dynamic and interactive process and can give formative guidance in a timely manner.

Several factors are to be taken into consideration in designing collaborative activities in e-learning, including task nature, group composition and size, synchronicity, and media preference. Some learning tasks require more collaborative learning than others, particularly those that require task analysis, concept clarification, process adjustment, solution negotiation, and peer evaluation. A learning task that encourages productive collaboration would be one in which participants have shared interests, but not shared views (Ragoonaden & Bordeleau, 2000). In other words, participants need to have a common core ground for the task in question, but the task should not have a clear-cut "correct" answer so that diverse views and multiple perspectives are encouraged, and discussion and negotiation become a natural requirement (Carroll, 1991).

Group composition and size can be important factors affecting the quantity and quality of interactivity. A very homogenous group tends to converge on most of the issues discussed and is less likely to benefit from sharing experiences and exchanging views. On the other hand, a heterogeneous group with rather incompatible academic backgrounds may have difficulty finding a "common language" of communication. For group interactivity and collaboration to be constructive and productive, group members need to have varied individual experiences as well as common core knowledge and background that constitute a shared reference base called "grounding" (Baker, Hansen, Joiner, & Traum, 1999). Group size can be important for synchronous interactive sessions. In a text chat session that involves several active participants, messages can keep popping up about divergent topics, making it difficult to follow a coherent thread. In a web conferencing, several people may try to speak simultaneously because they could not tell whether and when other people are about to speak. In a large group, dominant speakers are more likely to occur and less vocal participants would have less chance to talk or tend to remain quiet. Media selection may influence participants' willingness to interact too. Participants who are shy of microphone or camera may prefer text chat or asynchronous communication options over synchronous audio and video conferencing.

Interpersonal interactivity in e-learning environment can be synchronous or asynchronous, or a combination of both. The two modes differ primarily in the presence or absence of feedback immediacy. Synchronous communication can be carried out in text chat, audio and video conferencing. Asynchronous communication tools include e-mail, discussion board, text messaging, blog, twitter, and wiki. Synchronous communication has a higher technical demand than asynchronous communication. For audio and video conferencing, broadband Internet connection is usually necessary to ensure a continuous smooth flow of data. Sporadic delay or loss of data in audio communication can make a speech hard to comprehend. In text chat, participants need to be able to type with generally acceptable speed and accuracy. If one person cannot type as fast as the others, this person may feel inhibited from participation.

The primary benefit of synchronous communication is feedback immediacy and better perceived presence of participation. Synchronous communication usually works better for brainstorming, idea initialization, socializing and building interpersonal relationship, especially when people can hear and see one another. Jonassen (2000) observes that while in synchronous communication, participants are more focused on establishing identity, whereas in asynchronous conferences, participants tend to reflect more on issues being discussed. In a survey on student perceptions of asynchronous communication in e-learning, Wang (2001) has found that 50 out of 103 respondents indicated that conversing via discussion board allows individuals to be known for their thoughts rather than looks. Without hearing or seeing each other in real-time, participants tend to focus on ideas rather than on appearance. Additionally, introverted or shy students generally feel less inhibited and are more willing to express their views on discussion boards where there is no face-to-face presence or time pressures for instant responses. In fact, many introverted students often make more insightful observations than their more vocal peers when they do speak up.

Asynchronous communication is often more learner-centered since it gives the learner more control over the learning process and more time to reflect and revise. The learner-centered nature of asynchronous communication allows learning to be more inductive, explorative and problem-solving orientated in the virtual learning environment (Berge, 1999). In contrast, group-based synchronous approach is more often presenter-centered, instructor-led, and lecture-oriented, largely to replicate traditional "teaching by telling" across distance (Dede, 1996). The latter approach is generally considered more appropriate for tasks that are instructor-guided, deductive, introductory, and informing.

In a real-time chat, a conversation often takes on its own life as mini topics pop up. Unless controlled by an experienced coordinator or group leader, a live chat can follow spontaneous paths away from the planned track. In asynchronous communication, such digression is less likely to occur, since responses are more often targeted. Keeping a discussion on track is easier in asynchronous discussion than in real time conversation. Another possible constraint for synchronous sessions is that adult learners often have family and job-related commitments and scheduling synchronous sessions could be difficulty.

When immediate feedback is not needed, asynchronous communication is often more effective for learning tasks that require focused discussion, reflective thinking, and negotiation for team solutions. Messages posted in a discussion board are relatively permanent and typically organized in a way that allows the reader to see the path of the discussion. Participants can always review and follow up on previous postings, posting additional messages to clarify, and elaborating or modifying previous statements. Because it is easy to see who has and has not contributed in an online discussion forum, students tend to feel more obliged to participate and contribute. With more evenly distributed opportunities for participants to post and respond, dominant speakers are less likely to occur.

In practice, it is often possible to integrate synchronous and asynchronous communication or switch between the two modes. For instance, a synchronous brain-storming chat session can be followed by an asynchronous discussion to elaborate and expand on the initial ideas. In some web sites, there is a chat link that provides immediate access for a user to start a live conversation with a support person. Many colleges and universities now provide video conferencing services to support e-learning. Instructor and students can easily set up a time through e-mail to meet in the virtual room in real time. Instructors can also host virtual office hours during which students can pop in to ask questions or just to chat. As mobile computing and video conferencing technology continue growing, such integration can be expected to become increasingly popular.

AN INTEGRATED APPROACH

Based on the discussions made so far, an integrated approach is proposed with several key constituents that are expected to contribute to effective interactivity in e-learning. The framework centers around message exchange and consists of the following key components:

- Content
- Media modality
- Cognitive activity
- Distributed cognition
- Accessibility, readability, and usability
- User interface and system adaptation
- Collaborative needs
- Technology and time availability

The diagram in Figure 2 attempts to put the key components in interrelated perspectives, though the interrelations could be far more involving and interwoven than what the connecting lines can indicate. For instance, the selection of media is related not only to accessibility and content representation, but also to collaboration needs, technology availability and time constraints.

Content Representation and Media

Content is the essence of message exchange. Message is embodied in media. Message exchange cannot take place without media. Different media have different symbolic attributes. Information encoded in one modality may not be represented with comparable effectiveness in other modali-

Figure 2. Key components of interactivity design

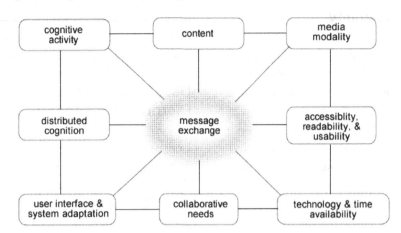

ties. Visuals can be more effective than in text in realistic representation, iconic recognition, and organizational illustrations for representing procedural and quantitative relationships. Colors, lines, shapes, and allocations can be effective methods to direct user attention and facilitate perception.

Content Representation and Distributed Cognition

Content representation can embody distributed cognition. When distributed cognition is seen in content representation, it is often coupled with user interface design and affordances. A diagram designed to illustrate a quantitative or spatial relationship reflects the author's understanding of the relationship and can be cognitively far more effective and efficient for the viewer to comprehend than a description in words. A spreadsheet can provide aggregated functions that can let the user sort content items, or get sums and averages easily. A visual data analysis may enable the viewer to see trends or interrelations that would be hard to see without the visuals.

Media and Cognitive Activity

Content represented in different media generally require different encoding and decoding skills. Memory load and cognitive processes involved in a listening task are very different from those in a reading task. Chunking or breaking content into more manageable modules may help to reduce cognitive load and improve cognitive effectiveness. Iconic representation may facilitate easy recognition and quick response.

Cognitive Activity and Content Relevance

Content should be meaningful to the learner. A good topic would be one that stimulates the learner's interest, one that the learner has some knowledge about, but still would like to learn more about. Content relevance can help the learner to identify with the content, activate the learner's prior knowledge, and facilitate cognitive involvement. Content relevance can be augmented by allowing selection of content topics, provision of multiple perspectives, adaptable learning paths, and alternative media modality. Adaptive hypermedia systems can be an effective means to support content relevance.

Media, Accessibility, and Technology Availability

The selection of media modality is not only related to content, but also to accessibility, collaboration needs, technology and time availability. Media selection and content development must be pursued with accessibility in mind. If content is not accessible to the user, interactivity is crippled. For many users, accessibility means access speed, particularly for multimedia content and web conferencing. Apart from access speed, accessibility also involves compatibility and interoperability. As learners' platforms and software availabilities may vary, designers and instructors need to make sure that the media selected and content delivered can be properly decoded and processed by all the users on their platforms. Documents generated from the latest version of a particular software application may be incompatible with the older version of the software on some users' computers. Web pages that display nicely in one type of browser may not show up properly in other types. Free web services are available for checking browser compatibility, such as http://browsershots.org/.

Readability and Usability

Related to accessibility and usability is text legibility and readability. As e-reading continues growing, writers are trying to make their writings more "e-friendly", more easily distributed through the Internet and other e-communication channels, and more effectively and efficiently accessed and processed by e-readers. A special feature of the e-learning environment is the integration of hypermedia and rich media with dynamic and interactive multimedia enhancement. Hyperlink structure allows readers to traverse the content by selecting what is most relevant among variable paths, supportive resources, and multiple perspectives. The navigation flexibility of hypermedia comes with two potential issues: user disorienta-

tion and cognitive overload. Designing adaptive hypermedia and providing adequate resources without undue disruption or disorientation is a major challenge for instructional designers.

User Interface and Distributed Cognition

Logistically, interactivity usually starts at the perceptual level when learner attention is activated. From a user interface perspective, user attention can be directed or constrained by distinctive colors, graphics, dynamic elements, and page layout including locations, sizes and shapes of objects. Good user interface design provides adequate affordances and guides learner navigation through learning paths. User interface design can be approached in light of distributed cognition. In e-text design, readability can be facilitated or constrained through text organization that includes headings, paragraphing, text layout, color distinctions, and font variations. At the conceptual level, learner attention can be affected by personal interest, content relevance, prior knowledge, topic novelty, and task commitment. By utilizing distributed cognition embodied in various artifacts and learning resources, instructional designers and instructors can design learning activities in ways that improve cognitive effectiveness and efficiency.

System Adaptation and Scaffolding

Once the learner is engaged into interactivity with the instructional source, cognitive scaffolding is a key to sustaining interactivity. Based on well-informed anticipation of learner needs, an adaptive learning system can provide options in learning paths, assess learner performances, monitor learning progress, give feedback when desired, and adjust instructional content to meet the evolving needs. Scaffolding can be provided through navigation guidance, by asking questions, encouraging learner queries, and sustaining an appropriate level of task challenge to engage the learner. A critical task in interactivity design is to determine where and when scaffolding is most likely to be needed and how it should be provided.

Collaboration

No matter how intelligent an adaptive learning system can be, cognitive scaffolding provided by a learning system cannot be as flexible and dynamic as a human facilitator. Help from a human facilitator may be needed from time to time. An instructor or a tutor or peer learner can often help not only cognitively, but affectively and socially. Collaborative learning can provide relatively realistic, cognitively engaging, and socially motivational contexts. The benefits of collaborative learning are often reciprocal; tutors often learn new things by helping tutees. Consideration for collaborative learning needs to be made in conjunction with accessibility, technology and time availability, particularly for synchronous sessions, which generally have higher demand for technology reliability and can be difficult to schedule for adult learners with family and job commitments.

The structure of the diagram in Figure 2 has a limited space and does not allow the insertion of additional text to indicate interrelations between the components, which could be far more involving and interwoven than what the connecting lines can suggest. The following list summarizes some of the relationships.

- Different media have different information attributes. Content representation can be facilitated and constrained by media selection.
- Different media require different perceptual and cognitive skills to encode and decode.
- Media can facilitate or constrain accessibility, readability, and usability. Media selection should be made in consideration of accessibility, readability, and usability.

- Likewise, the use of a particular technology can have impact on accessibility, readability, and usability. Technology adoption should therefore be evaluated and deployed in consideration of accessibility and usability.
- Technology and time availability can determine the range of options for collaborative learning activities, particularly regarding synchronous versus asynchronous communication, shared virtual space, and support of rich media.
- Content relevance can facilitate cognitive process and knowledge assimilation.
- Distributed cognition is embodied in media and content.
- Distributed cognition can reduce cognitive load and improve cognitive effectiveness and efficiency.
- At a more sophisticated level, distributed cognition can be found in adaptive learning systems and learning management system, such as user modeling, dynamic scaffolding, learning analytics, and educational gaming.
- Certain level of learner control is needed for learner engagement. Learner control can be enabled through user interface design, flexible course navigation, multiple perspectives, adjustable learning pace, and customizable learning paths, all of which can be implemented in adaptive learning systems.
- Learner control and system adaptation are inextricably coupled. Good user interface design provides adequate affordances and facilitates learner control. User interface design can be approached in the light of distributed cognition.
- No learning system can be as adaptive as a human facilitator. Human facilitators can often provide more flexible tutoring and adjustable scaffolding. Interpersonal interactivity is needed from time to time to ac-

commodate learners' affective, cognitive, and social needs.

CONCLUSION

This chapter defines interactivity as information exchange between person and media and interpersonal information exchange through media. A primary goal of this chapter is to identify key factors that can contribute to effective and efficient interactivity and to relate the study of interactivity to instructional practice in the e-learning environment. The key factors include content, media modality, cognitive process, accessibility, technology and time availability, distributed cognition, system adaptation, and collaboration. The focus is on studying how information exchange can be shaped by media and how media can be utilized and learning sources designed to support learning in interactive manners. An integrated approach is proposed that puts the key factors in related perspectives for a holistic view of interactivity, with a particular interest in connecting media attributes and system affordances with distributed cognition, cognitive process, and collaborative learning. It is hoped that this initial framework could be expanded and improved to become a conceptually helpful and pragmatically usable guide for interactivity design in e-learning. Although there is no guarantee that learners will carry out instructional events in the ways designers intend them to be, good interactivity design can improve the chance of interactivity potential to be realized as planned.

Due to space limit, many of the topics presented in this chapter can only receive an exploratory coverage. As technology continues advancing at an unprecedented pace, some of the observations in this text may be dated by the time this volume is published. It will be intriguing to see what new affordances and more sophisticated distributed cognition will become available to boost interac-

tivity in the e-learning environment, particularly with augmented reality, visual data analysis, 3D video, e-reading, and mobile computing supported by rich media.

Human cognition is expected to be increasingly embodied in media and distributed through virtual space. Reading will be more portable, communal, inter-connectable and integrated with rich media enhancement. Digital software and hardware will become increasingly intelligent and smart. Data warehousing can be used to build extensive user models to support more versatile adaptive courseware. Authentic learning will become more and more feasible and desirable in the e-learning environment as our living and working environment become increasingly enhanced with augmented reality and virtual space. In some cases, authentic learning may be better enabled in e-environment than in a traditional face-to-face setting.

While human-media interactivity is expected to become increasingly permeative, direct interpersonal communication is still indispensible, though probably more and more mediated. As virtual space continues to expand with mobile computing and rich media support, our perception of space and time will change too. More modes and tools will be available for both synchronous and asynchronous communication. As switching between the two modes can become so easy and seamless, the distinction between the two can become blurred. Just as our cognition-enriched environment can enable us to accomplish things that we could not do otherwise, the existing environment can also constrain or blind us to habitual ways of thinking, leading us to assume that certain things are impossible when in fact they are possible when viewed from different and fresh perspectives. Interactivity design should help us to see enabling affordances and possible constrains so as to improve the effectiveness and efficiency of learning.

REFERENCES

Baker, M., Hansen, T., Joiner, R., & Traum, D. (1999). The role of grounding in collaborative learning tasks. In Dillenbourg, P. (Ed.), *Collaborative learning: Cognitive and computational approaches* (pp. 31–63). Amsterdam, The Netherlands: Pergamon.

Bandura, A. (1969). *Principles of behavior modification*. New York, NY: Holt, Rinehart and Winston.

Bandura, A. (1970). Modeling theory: Some traditions, trends, and disputes. In Sahakian, W. S. (Ed.), *Psychology of learning: Systems, models, and theories*. Chicago, IL: Markham.

Berge, Z. (1999). Interaction in post-secondary web-based learning. *Educational Technology, 39*, 5–11.

Bloom, B. S. (1956). *Taxonomy of educational objectives, handbook I: The cognitive domain.* New York, NY: David McKay Co Inc.

Brock, S. A., Otto, R. G., & Hoffman, B. (2004). Media as lived environments: The ecological psychology of educational technology. In Jonassen, D. (Ed.), *Handbook of research on educational communications and technology* (pp. 215–241). Mahwah, NJ: Lawrence Erlbaum.

Bruce, V., Green, P. R., & Georgeson, M. A. (1996). *Visual perception: Physiology, psychology, and ecology.* Hillsdale, NJ: Erlbaum.

Brusilovsky, P. (2000). Adaptive hypermedia: From intelligent tutoring systems to web-based education. In G. Gauthier, C., Frasson, & K. ValLehn (Eds.), *Intelligent tutoring systems. Lecture notes in computer science* (vol. 1839, pp. 1-7). Berlin, Germany: Springer Verlag.

Bucy, E. P. (2004a). Interactivity in society: Locating an elusive concept. *The Information Society, 20*, 373–383. doi:10.1080/01972240490508063

Bucy, E. P. (2004b). The interactivity paradox: Closer to the news but confused. In Bucy, E. P., & Newhagen, J. E. (Eds.), *Media access: Social and psychological dimensions of new technology use* (pp. 47–72). Mahwah, NJ: Lawrence Erlbaum Associates.

Carpenter, E. (1960). The new languages. In Carpenter, E., & McLuhan, M. (Eds.), *Explorations in communication*. Boston, MA: Beacon Press.

Carroll, J. M. (1991). The Kittie House Manifesto. In Carroll, J. M. (Ed.), *Designing interaction: Psychology of the human-computer interface* (pp. 1–16). Cambridge, UK: Cambridge University Press.

Clark, R., & Salomon, G. (1986). Media in teaching. In Wittrock, M. C. (Ed.), *Handbook of research on teaching* (3rd ed., pp. 464–478). New York, NY: Macmillan Publishing Company.

Cox, J. (2004). E-books: Challenges and opportunities. *D-Lib Magazine, 10*(10). Retrieved April 26, 2011, from http://www.dlib.org/dlib/october04/cox/10cox.html

Cristea, A. (2003). Adaptive patterns in authoring of educational adaptive hypermedia. *Journal of Educational Technology & Society, 6*(4), 1–5.

De Bra, P. (2000). Pros and cons of adaptive hypermedia in web-based education. *Journal of CyberPsychology and Behavior, 3*(1), 71–77. doi:10.1089/109493100316247

De Bra, P., Brusilovsky, P., & Houben, G. (1999). Adaptive hypermedia: From systems to framework. *ACM Computing Surveys, 31*(4). Retrieved April 26, 2011, from http://www.cs.brown.edu/memex/ACM_HypertextTestbed/papers/25.html

Dede, C. (1996). Emerging technologies and distributed learning. *American Journal of Distance Education, 10*(2), 4–36. doi:10.1080/08923649609526919

Dee-Lucas, D., & Larkin, J. H. (1992). *Text representation with traditional text and hypertext.* Pittsburgh, PA: Carnegie Mellon University.

Domagk, S., Schwartz, R. N., & Plass, J. L. (2010). Interactivity in multimedia learning: An integrated model. *Computers in Human Behavior, 28*, 1024–1033. doi:10.1016/j.chb.2010.03.003

Eck, R. V. (2006). Digital game-based learning: It's not just the digital natives who are restless…. *EDUCAUSE Review, 41*(2), 16–30.

Eklund, J., & Sinclair, K. (2000). An empirical appraisal of adaptive interfaces for instructional systems. *Educational Technology and Society Journal, 3*(4), 165–177.

Gardner, H. (1993). *Multiple intelligence.* New York, NY: Basic Books.

Gibson, J. J. (1977). The theory of affordances. In Shaw, R., & Bransford, J. (Eds.), *Perceiving, acting, and knowing: Toward an ecological psychology* (pp. 67–82). Hillsdale, NJ: Lawrence Erlbaum.

Gombrich, E. H. (1974). The visual image. In Olson, D. (Ed.), *Media and symbols: The forms of expression, communication and education.* Chicago, IL: University of Chicago Press.

Google. (2011). *Google Voice.* Retrieved from http://www.google.com/googlevoice/about.html.

Hannafin, M. J. (1989). Interaction strategies and emerging instructional technologies: Psychological perspectives. *Canadian Journal of Educational Communication, 18*(3), 167–179.

Hollan, J., Hutchins, E., & Kirsh, D. (2000). Distributed cognition: Toward a new foundation for human-computer interaction research. *ACM Transactions on Computer-Human Interaction, 7*(2), 174–196. doi:10.1145/353485.353487

Horn, R. E. (1999). *Visual language: Global communication for the 21st century.* Bainbridge Island, WA: MacroVU, Inc.

Jensen, J. F. (1998). Interactivity: Tracking a new concept in media and communication studies. *Nordicom Review, 1*, 185–205.

Jensen, J. F. (2008). The concept of interactivity – Revisited. *Proceeding of the 1st International Conference on Designing Interactive User Experiences for TV and Video.* Retrieved May 19, 2011, from http://portal.acm.org/citation.cfm?id=1453831

Johnson, G. J., Bruner, G. C., & Kumar, A. (2006). Interactivity and its facets revisited. *Journal of Advertising, 35*(4), 35–52. doi:10.2753/JOA0091-3367350403

Johnson, L., Levine, A., Smith, R., & Stone, S. (2010). *The 2010 horizon report.* Retrieved from http://wp.nmc.org/horizon-k12-2010/chapters/game-based-learning/#0

Jonassen, D. H. (1985). Interactive lesson designs: A taxonomy. *Educational Technology, 25*(6), 7–17.

Jonassen, D. H. (1988). Integrating learning strategies into courseware to facilitate deeper processing. In Jonassen, D. H. (Ed.), *Instructional designs for microcomputer courseware* (pp. 151–181). Hillsdale, NJ: Lawrence Erlbaum.

Jonassen, D. H. (2000). *Computers as mindtools for schools.* Upper Saddle River, NJ: Prentice-Hall.

Jonassen, D. H. (2003). *Learning to solve problems with technology: A constructivist perspective.* Upper Saddle River, NJ: Merrill/Prentice Hall.

Kennedy, G. E. (2004). Promoting cognition in multimedia interactivity research. *Journal of Interactive Learning Research, 15*(1), 43–61.

Koffka, K. (1935). *Principles of Gestalt psychology.* London, UK: Lund Humphries.

Liu, Y., & Shrum, L. J. (2002). What is interactivity and is it always such a good thing? Implications of definition, person, and situation for the influence of interactivity on advertising effectiveness. *Journal of Advertising*, *31*(4), 53–64.

Lunsford, A. (2006). *The Stanford study of writing*. Retrieved February 28, 2011, from http://ssw.stanford.edu/

Massey, B. L., & Levy, M. R. (1999). Interactivity, online journalism, and English-language Web newspapers in Asia. *Journalism & Mass Communication Quarterly*, *76*(1), 138–151.

Mayer, R. E. (2001). *Multimedia learning*. New York, NY: Cambridge University Press.

Mayer, R. E. (2003). Elements of science of e-learning. *Journal of Educational Computing Research*, *29*, 297–313. doi:10.2190/YJLG-09F9-XKAX-753D

McGovern, G. Norton, R., & O'Dowd, C. (2001). *Web content style guide: The essential reference for online writers, editors, and managers*. Upper Saddle River, NJ: FT Press.

McLuhan, M. (1967). *The medium is the massage*. Corte Madera, CA: Gingko Press.

Meringoff, L. K. (1980). Influence of the medium of children's story apprehension. *Journal of Educational Psychology*, *72*, 240–249. doi:10.1037/0022-0663.72.2.240

Microsoft. (2010). *Microsoft Interactive Classroom*. Retrieved May 20, 2011, from http://support.microsoft.com/kb/2395492.

Moreno, R., & Mayer, R. E. (1999). Cognitive principles of multimedia learning: The role of modality and contiguity. *Journal of Educational Psychology*, *91*, 358–368. doi:10.1037/0022-0663.91.2.358

Morkes, J., & Nielsen, J. (1997). *Concise, scannable, and objective: How to write for the Web*. Retrieved March 2, 2011, from http://www.useit.com/papers/webwriting/writing.html

Neuman, W. R. (1991). *The future of the mass audience*. New York, NY: Cambridge University Press.

Newhagen, J. E. (2004). Interactivity, dynamic symbol processing, and the emergence of content in human communication. *The Information Society*, *20*, 395–400. doi:10.1080/01972240490508108

Newman, D., Griffin, P., & Cole, M. (1989). *The construction zone: Working for cognitive change in school*. New York, NY: Cambridge University Press.

Nuance. (2011). *Dragon NaturallySpeaking*. http://www.nuance.com/dragon/index.htm.

Olson, D., & Bruner, J. (1974). *Media and symbols: The forms of expression, communication and education* (Olson, D., Ed.). Chicago, IL: University of Chicago Press.

Park, O., & Lee, J. (2004). Adaptive instructional systems. In Jonassen, D. (Ed.), *Handbook of research on educational communications and technology* (pp. 651–684). Mahwah, NJ: Lawrence Erlbaum.

Pea, R. D. (1985). Beyond amplification: Using the computer to reorganize mental functioning. *Educational Psychology*, *20*, 167–182. doi:10.1207/s15326985ep2004_2

Pham, A., & Sarno, D. (2010, July 18). The future of reading: Electronic reading devices are transforming the concept of a book. *Los Angeles Times*.

Plowman, L. (1996). Narrative, interactivity and the secret world of multimedia. *The English & Media Magazine*, *35*, 44–48.

Rafaeli, S. (1988). Interactivity: From new media to communication. In Hawkins, R., Wiemann, J., & Pingree, S. (Eds.), *Advancing communication science: Merging mass and interpersonal processes* (pp. 110–134). Newbury Park, CA: Sage.

Rafaeli, S., & Ariel, Y. (2007). Assessing interactivity in computer-mediated research. In Joinson, A. N., McKenna, K. Y. A., Postmes, T., & Rieps, U. D. (Eds.), *The Oxford handbook of internet psychology* (pp. 71–88). Oxford University Press.

Rafaeli, S., & Sudweeks, F. (1998). Interactivity on the Nets. In Sudweeks, F., McLaughlin, M., & Rafaeli, S. (Eds.), *Network and netplay: Virtual groups on the Internet* (pp. 173–189). Menlo Park, CA: AAAI Press/MIS Press.

Ragoonaden, K., & Bordeleau, P. (2000). Collaborative learning via the Internet. *Educational Technology & Society, 3*(3). Retrieved April 26, 2011, from http://www.ifets.info/journals/3_3/d11.html.

Rogers, Y., & Scaife, M. (1998). How can interactive multimedia facilitate learning? In Lee, J. (Ed.), *Intelligence and multimodality in multimedia interfaces: Research and applications*. Menlo Park, CA: AAAI. Press.

Salomon, G. (1974). What is learned and how it is taught: The interaction between media, message, task and learner. In Olson, D. (Ed.), *Media and symbols: The forms of expression, communication and education*. Chicago, IL: University of Chicago Press.

Salomon, G. (1979). *Interaction of media, cognition and learning*. San Francisco, CA: Jossey-Bass.

Sims, R. (1997). Interactivity: A forgotten art? *Computers in Human Behavior, 13*(2), 157–180. doi:10.1016/S0747-5632(97)00004-6

Spiro, R., Feltovich, P., Jacobson, M., & Coulson, R. (1991). Cognitive flexibility, constructivism, and hypertext: Random access instruction for advanced knowledge acquisition in ill-structured domains. *Educational Technology*, (May): 24–33.

Steuer, J. (1995). Defining virtual reality: Dimensions determining telepresence. In Biocca, F., & Levy, M. R. (Eds.), *Communication in the age of virtual reality* (pp. 33–56). Hillsdale, NJ: Lawrence Erlbaum Associates.

Sundar, S. S. (2004). Theorizing interactivity's effects. *The Information Society, 20*, 385–389. doi:10.1080/01972240490508072

Vygotsky, L. (1978). *Mind in society*. Cambridge, MA: Harvard University Press.

Wang, H. (2001). Effective use of WebBoard for distance learning. In T. Okamoto, R. Hartley, Kinshuk, & J. P. Klus (Eds.). *IEEE International Conference on Advanced Learning Technologies*. Las Alamitos, CA: IEEE Computer Society.

Yang, C. S., & Moore, D. M. (1996). Designing hypermedia systems for instruction. *Educational Technology Systems, 24*, 3–30.

ADDITIONAL READING

Allesi, S. M., & Trollip, S. (2001). *Multimedia for learning: Methods and development* (3rd ed.). Needham, MA: Allyn & Bacon.

Clark, R. (1983). Reconsidering research on learning from media. *Review of Educational Research, 53*, 445–460.

Dede, C. (2002). Interactive media in an interview with Chris Dede. *Syllabus, 15*(11), 12–14.

Dede, C. J., & Palumbo, D. (1991). Implications of hypermedia for cognition and communication. *International Association for Impact Assessment Bulletin, 9*, 15–28.

Gardner, H. (1985). *The mind's new science: A history of the cognitive revolution.* New York: Basic Books.

Gibson, D., Aldrich, C., & Prensky, M. (2006). *Games and simulations in online learning: Research and development frameworks.* Hershey, PA: IGI Global. doi:10.4018/978-1-59904-304-3

Gibson, J. J. (1979). *Ecological approach to visual perception.* Hillsdale, NJ: Lawrence Erlbaum Associates.

Jonassen, D. H. (1999). Designing constructive learning environments. In Reigeluth, C. M. (Ed.), *Instructional-design theories and models: A new paradigm of instructional theory* (*Vol. II*, pp. 217–239). Mahwah, NJ: Lawrence Erlbaum.

Kosma, R. B. (1994). Will media influence learning? Reframing the debate. *Educational Technology Research and Development, 42,* 7–19. doi:10.1007/BF02299087

Leggett, H. (2009). *Best science visualization videos of 2009.* Retrieved February 25, 2011 from http://www.wired.com/wiredscience/2009/08/visualizations/all/1

Lombardi, M. M. (2007). *Authentic learning for the 21st century: An overview.* Retrieved February 19, 2011 from net.educause.edu/ir/library/pdf/ELI3009.pdf

McGovern, G., & Norton, R. (2001). *Content critical: Gaining competitive advantage through high-quality web content.* Upper Saddle River, New Jersey: FT Press.

McLellan, H. (2004). Virtual realities. In Jonassen, D. (Ed.), *Handbook of research on educational communications and technology* (pp. 461–497). Mahwah, NJ: Lawrence Erlbaum.

Moreno, R., & Mayer, R. E. (2002). Learning science in virtual reality environments: Role of method and media. *Journal of Educational Psychology, 94,* 598–610. doi:10.1037/0022-0663.94.3.598

Nielsen, J. (1998). *2D is better than 3D.* Retrieved April 2, 2011 from http://www.useit.com/alertbox/981115.html.

Nielsen, J. (2000). *Designing web usability.* Indianapolis, IN: New Riders.

Olson, D. (1974) (Ed.). *Media and symbols: The forms of expression, communication and education* (73rd annual yearbook of the National Society for the Study of Education). Chicago: University of Chicago Press.

Park, O., & Lee, J. (2004). Adaptive instructional systems. In Jonassen, D. (Ed.), *Handbook of research on educational communications and technology* (pp. 651–684). Mahwah, NJ: Lawrence Erlbaum.

Pea, R. D. (1993). Practices of distributed intelligence and designs for education. In Salomon, G. (Ed.), *Distributed cognitions: Psychological and educational considerations* (pp. 47–87). Cambridge, UK: Cambridge University Press.

Pea, R. D., & Gomez, L. (1992). Distributed multimedia learning environments. *Interactive Learning Environments, 2*(2), 73–109. doi:10.1080/1049482920020201

Prensky, M. (2005). "Engage me or enrage me": What today's learners demand. *EDUCAUSE Review, 40*(5), 60–65.

Prensky, M. (2007). *Digital game-based learning.* St. Paul, MN: Paragon House.

Romiszowski, A. J. (1993). Developing interactive multimedia courseware and networks: Some current issues. In Latchem, C., Williamson, J., & Henderson-Lancett, L. (Eds.), *Interactive multimedia: Practice and promise* (pp. 79–96). London: Kogan Page.

Romiszowski, A. J., & Mason, R. (2004). Computer-mediated communication. In Jonassen, D. (Ed.), *Handbook of research on educational communications and technology* (pp. 397–431). Mahwah, NJ: Lawrence Erlbaum.

Russell, T. L. (1999). *The no significant different difference phenomenon*. Chapel Hill, NC: Office of Instructional Telecommunications, North Carolina State University.

Salomon, G. (1993) (Ed.). *Distributed cognitions: Psychological and educational considerations*. Cambridge, UK: Cambridge University Press.

Schimmel, B. J. (1988). Providing meaningful feedback in courseware. In Jonassen, D. H. (Ed.), *Instructional designs for microcomputer courseware* (pp. 183–196). Hillsdale, NJ: Lawrence Erlbaum.

Schwier, R. A., & Misanchuk, E. R. (1993). *Interactive multimedia instruction*. Englewood Cliffs, NJ: Educational Technology Publications.

Sims, R. (2000). An interactive conundrum: Constructs of interactivity and learning theory. *Australian Journal of Educational Technology*, *16*(1), 45–57.

Stromer-Galley, J. (2004). Interactivity as process and interactivity as product. *The Information Society*, *20*(5), 391–394. doi:10.1080/01972240490508081

Suchman, L. A. (1987). *Planned and situated actions*. New York: Cambridge University Press.

Sundar, S. S. (2007). Social psychology of interactivity in human-website interaction. In Joinson, A. N., McKenna, K. Y. A., Postmes, T., & Reips, U.-D. (Eds.), *The Oxford handbook of internet psychology* (pp. 89–104). Oxford, UK: Oxford University Press.

KEY TERMS AND DEFINITIONS

Accessibility: The degree to which a digital content or service can be accessed through the Internet or in an electronic environment.

Augmented Reality: A direct or indirect live view of a physical real-world environment is merged with (augmented by) computer-generated imagery

Distributed Cognition: Externalization and formalization of human cognition embedded in media and objects that can facilitate cognition.

E-Learning: Broadly speaking, e-learning includes any learning activities that employ electronic technology such as computer, digital media, and network resources to enable learning. In this chapter, e-learning primarily refers to learning enabled through the Internet and World Wide Web.

E-Reading: Digital text to be read on an electronic device such as computer screen or e-paper

Interactivity: Mediated interaction between human communicants or between human communicant and media agent

Modality: Perceptual form or mode in which information is encoded and represented. Graphic, audio, text, and video are different modalities

Rich Media: A broad range of digital interactive media. Rich media typically exhibit dynamic motion that can occur over time or in direct response to user action. Rich media can be downloadable or may be embedded in a web page.

System Adaptation: Capabilities of a learning source that can adapt its form and content in response to learner actions and needs

Virtual Space: Space perceived via an electronic device that may simulate a physical context or creates an electronic environment where participants can perceive the presence of each other, exchange messages, and share digital work.

Chapter 2
Interactivity of Information Representations in e-Learning Environments

Kamran Sedig
The University of Western Ontario, Canada

Paul Parsons
The University of Western Ontario, Canada

ABSTRACT

This chapter is concerned with interactivity of information representations in e-learning environments (ELEs)—where interactivity refers to the quality or condition of interaction with representations in an ELE. An ELE is any interactive computer-based software that mediates and supports learners' engagement with information. This chapter draws upon literature from the areas of human-information interaction, distributed cognition, and learning sciences with the goal of developing and exploring the features of a preliminary framework for thinking about interactivity in the context of ELEs. In this chapter we provide some background and motivation for such a framework, and identify and elaborate upon 10 structural elements of interaction that affect the interactivity of information representations: actual affordances and constraints, articulation mode, control, event granularity, focus, action flow, reaction flow, propagation, transition, and perceived affordances and constraints. Each of these has an effect on the learning and cognitive processes of learners, and the overall interactivity of an ELE is an emergent property of a combination of these elements. Collectively, these elements can serve as a framework to help thinking about design and analysis of interactivity in ELEs.

DOI: 10.4018/978-1-61350-441-3.ch002

INTRODUCTION

Interactive e-learning environments have the potential to facilitate learning; their effectiveness, however, has not lived up to original optimistic expectations (Kulik & Kulik, 1991; Jonassen & Reeves, 1996; Alessi & Trollip, 2001). In this chapter we use the term e-learning environment (ELE) to refer to any interactive computer-based software that mediates and supports learners' engagement with information. Examples of ELEs include interactive mathematical software, interactive physics simulations, interactive biology animations, and interactive geovisualizations. These ELEs facilitate learning through activities such as reasoning about the growth of fractal patterns, analyzing the workings of a cell, exploring weather patterns and ocean currents, investigating the structure of chemical bonds, and so on. The main characteristic of ELEs is that they display and allow interaction with information in order to facilitate learning. As such, the framework proposed in this chapter treats ELEs as technology-independent; that is, they may be implemented with desktop computers, tabletop computers, tablets, and so on, all of which may or may not be networked to other sources of information such as the internet.

When ELEs are designed well they can support information processing functions of their learners to carry out cognitive activities (Brey, 2005). In the past, many ELEs have played a secondary role in cognition and learning; that is, they served simply as aids or amplifiers of cognitive abilities (Dror, 2007). This is especially the case when ELEs are thought of as vehicles for passively maintaining and displaying information, rather than as technologies that engage learners in reflective, critical thinking (Jonassen & Reeves, 1996; Jonassen, Peck, & Wilson, 1998). When designed with their interactive features at the forefront of consideration, ELEs not only can amplify learners' cognitive abilities, but also can become partners in cognition (Salomon & Perkins, 2005; Dror, 2007; Bruner, 2005). In this manner, ELEs have

the potential to reorganize learners' thoughts and to facilitate deeper understanding of information (Pea, 1985). ELEs, by distributing the information-processing load of the visual information, can allow learners to think in partnership with the represented information (Sedig & Sumner, 2006). The theory of distributed cognition states that the internal mental processes of the learner, combined with external representations of information, form a system with which the learner's cognition is distributed across. Thus learning cannot be analyzed from the perspective of an individual in isolation, since it requires an interplay between the mind of an individual and things in the external world. In other words, learning is an emergent property of interactions among internal and external representations of information (Karasavvidis, 2002). This is true of a learner solving a problem using an abacus, a slide rule, or a computer. In order to perform high-level learning activities, such as reasoning and decision making, one often combines and processes information from both internal and external representations, in an integrative and dynamic manner (Zhang, 2000). In the case of ELEs, representations such as text, maps, and images comprise the interface, and the learner's cognition is distributed across their mental representations and the representations of the ELE. Thus the careful design of appropriate representations is of critical importance for supporting learners' thought processes.

It is often the case that researchers discuss only high-level details of ELEs, such as pedagogy and learning theory (Alessi & Trollip, 2001). However, if the low-level details of ELEs, such as interaction and interactivity, are not recognized and taken into consideration systematically, they may not achieve their intended goals, and can even have negative effects on learners (Dascal & Dror, 2005). A number of studies have shown that these low-level details affect the quality of learning (e.g., Golightly, 1996; Sedig, Klawe, & Westrom, 2001; Liang, Parsons, Wu, & Sedig, 2010). For example, Sedig et al. (2001) showed that by not using appropriate representations and interactions, an ELE inadvertently constrained learners' understanding of concepts. In another study, Liang et al. (2010) have demonstrated that the design of interactivity can affect how deeply learners engage with information, and, in turn, can have effects on learning performance.

The effective design of ELEs is complex and challenging, and requires careful consideration of the elements of the interface of ELEs. The interface of ELEs is comprised of two main components: representation and interaction (Sedig, 2004; Yi, Kang, Stasko, and Jacko, 2007). The representation component displays the external encodings of information from a certain domain. The interaction component allows learners to act upon these representations and receive responses from the system. As an example, in the domain of biology, information about a cell may be represented with a dot, an image, a table, a plot, and so on. A learner could act upon the table to rearrange its rows, or could act upon the image to animate it. The interfaces of all ELEs—ELEs from any domain—are comprised of these two main components. The New Oxford American Dictionary defines *interface* as "a point where two systems, subjects, organizations, etc., meet and interact" (Interface, 2005). As such, the interface of an ELE is the place where the mind of a learner meets and interacts with information, making it the epistemic locus of any ELE. The interface allows for the learner and information to hold a conversation together—a dialogue. The effectiveness of this dialogue depends on the quality of the learner's interaction with the represented information. This quality determines the interactivity of information representations. This is different from a representation being interactive—being 'interactive' suggests that learners can act upon the representation and receive responses. Adding '-ity' to the end of the term 'interactive' changes the adjective to suggest the quality and condition of the interactiveness of the representation. Accordingly, we define interactivity as the

quality, feel, or properties of interaction. Although interaction and interactivity are closely related, they are conceptually distinct, and each needs to be examined carefully. The relationship between interaction and interactivity is that interactivity depends upon the operationalization of an interaction. For example, a learner can interact with a representation so as to rearrange its elements. This interaction can be operationalized either by acting directly upon the representation, such as by clicking and dragging, or by acting indirectly, such as by clicking a button or entering a command to tell the ELE to move the elements to other locations. In either case the interaction is the same, but its feel and properties are different, and each may require differing amounts of cognitive effort and engagement with the information. Accordingly, it is necessary to consider not only interactions in the design of ELEs, but also the elements of interaction that affect interactivity of the representations.

There are several existent problems in designing and evaluating interactivity. First, often times, the research community does not make a clear distinction between interaction and interactivity. Second, the research community is not clear about how to distinguish between the interactivity of ELEs and other non-educational software. That is, the underlying frameworks, principles, and metrics have not been investigated sufficiently. Third, the notion of interactivity in the context of ELEs has not been clearly characterized. As a result, it is not easy to systematically design and assess interactivity of ELEs. This chapter attempts to address some of these problems.

Part of the challenge when it comes to designing ELEs is a lack of suitable conceptual frameworks that can guide their design and evaluation. Such frameworks serve to describe and characterize the main components of a design space (Sedig & Liang, 2008). Frameworks serve to organize and give structure to a space of ideas by classifying and characterizing its constituent elements and by providing a common language for referring to elements within the space. Therefore, frameworks bring order and coherence to a set of fragmented elements and provide opportunities for their systematic analysis and comparison. They can help evaluators and designers clarify their thinking and provide a shared vocabulary to inform, express, and substantiate their design decisions. The problem of lack of frameworks is compounded by the fact that the terms interaction and interactivity have not been clearly characterized and are often used synonymously in a loose manner. Designers and evaluators are usually not clear, nor specific, about what types of interactions are available in ELEs, how these interactions support the epistemic activities of the learners, how their design can influence the cognitive processes of the learners, and how to analyze the interactivity of the representations and the tools. As a result, an ELE can be "interactive," yet its interactive features may not fit the cognitive and epistemic needs of learners. This non-specificity of interactive features of representations is partly due to the fact that there is lack of a coherent language when describing and characterizing the interactive features and properties of these representations. Without suitable frameworks to guide the design process, designers tend to develop tools in a haphazard fashion, relying mostly on personal anecdotes and intuition. Therefore, the unavailability of systematic frameworks can lead to designs that may not be able to achieve their intended epistemological and/or functional goals. Studies have shown that haphazard design with respect to interactivity can have negative effects on learning (e.g., Sedig et al., 2001; Liang & Sedig, 2010).

There are two broad categories of frameworks: prescriptive and descriptive. Descriptive frameworks characterize the elements of a design space so as to provide a common language that can assist thinking about the landscape of a design area. Prescriptive frameworks prescribe design rules and guidelines that can provide best-practice examples of existing designs. Generally, the development of prescriptive frameworks requires the existence of descriptive frameworks. As there is a lack of descriptive frameworks that deal with interactivity, this chapter is an attempt at exploring and developing a preliminary descriptive framework that deals with interactivity of representations in ELEs. As such, this chapter does *not* provide any prescriptive guidelines for design. This chapter discusses a number of structural elements of interaction that affect the interactivity of information representations of ELEs. Collectively, these elements can serve as a framework to help thinking about design and analysis of interaction in ELEs.

The rest of the chapter is divided into three main sections: (1) a discussion of human-information interaction and its relationship with learning and; (2) the proposed framework—the elements of interaction that affect the interactivity of any ELE, and how these affect learning and human-information interaction; and, (3) a summary of the chapter and some proposed future directions.

HUMAN-INFORMATION INTERACTION

From a cognitive perspective learning involves a set of internal mental processes such as reasoning, recalling, comparing, attending, and evaluating (Ormrod, 1995). These processes regulate how the mind interacts with external information and processes it internally (Eysenck & Keane, 1990; Thagard, 1996).

Cognitive artifacts, such as ELEs, mediate our access to information by maintaining, displaying, or operating upon information to serve a representational function (Norman, 1991). Many researchers have suggested that external cognitive artifacts can greatly influence thinking and learning processes (Norman, 1993; Salomon, 1993; Zhang & Norman, 1994; Hutchins, 1995; Zhang, 1997). While performing any type of learning activity with ELEs, learners are using, working with, or thinking with information that is given some representational form. While performing such activities, there is a coupling between the mind of a learner and the artifact (i.e., the represented information). When a cognitive artifact is static and does not provide mechanisms for interaction, this coupling is weak. In such a case, especially if the information being represented is complex, learners are forced to exert a great deal of mental effort in order to reason and think about the information. ELEs, however, are inherently interactive. Interaction strengthens this coupling, as it allows a learner to perform actions on the represented information and to receive responses to those actions. In this manner it allows for a dialogue to take place between the learner and the represented information, such that the learner can adapt the information to fit his/her epistemic and cognitive needs. Human-information interaction design focuses on this dialogue, and is concerned with information, how it is represented, the interaction of a learner and the represented information, and the effects of interaction on learning and other cognitive activities. Figure 1 provides a conceptual model of the structure of human-information interaction.

Figure 1. A model of human-information interaction in ELEs

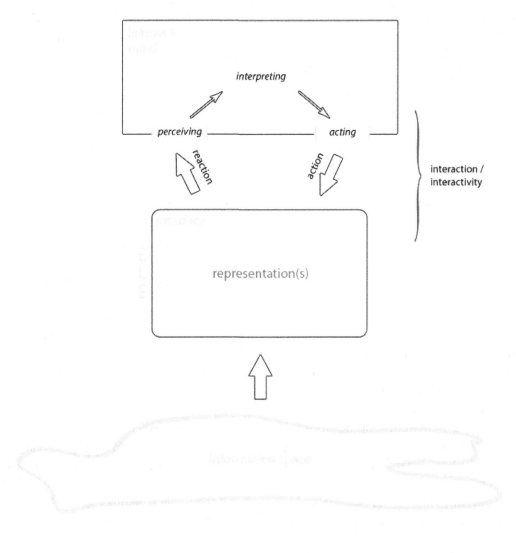

Information space, representation, and interaction and interactivity are briefly discussed next.

Information Space

When performing learning activities with ELEs, learners explore and investigate information that originates from some source. For instance, the human body is a source from which information can be derived and investigated, as are a planet and an atom; bodies of information about mathematics, philosophy, or economics, are also sources of information. In this chapter we refer to any source of information as an information space—that is, some place or area of containment of information. In digital environments, such as ELEs, information has no natural form; consequently, all information must be represented and given a tangible and perceptible form. This is done at the interface of an ELE in the form of representations. When learners are exploring an information space through the mediation of representations, they are trying to make sense of and learn about the elements, properties, relations, and processes that exist as part of any information space. The goal of human-information interaction design is to effectively facilitate the exploration of information spaces through the medium of interactive information representations that are situated at the interface of ELEs.

Representation

Since a great deal of learning occurs through interaction with the external world, representations provide many general benefits for the exploration of information spaces (Norman, 1993). For instance, by making use of external representations, cognitive effort can be offloaded onto the representations, reducing the amount of effort required to perform mental activities (Larkin & Simon, 1987). Accordingly, representations can alleviate memory load by maintaining and displaying information and by performing operations and calculations. This can free-up cognitive resources and allow learners to focus on higher-level cognitive processes (Lajoie, 2005). As such, representations can facilitate complex mental activities that are necessary for learning such as planning, sense-making, reasoning, and decision making. Representations embody aspects of an information space to make them tangible and accessible to learners. One of the reasons why representations are so powerful is due to the primal unity of the external and internal symbols in human cognition (Cole & Derry, 2005). That is, learners have access to an information space only through representations; consequently, learners think with and through representations. Representations are not simply forms that are perceived, but rather they are the means by which reality is perceived (ibid.). Therefore, representations can guide, constrain, and determine cognitive behavior (Zhang, 1997; 2000).

Interaction and Interactivity

Interaction and interactivity are at the heart of ELEs (Sedig & Liang, 2006). Without provisions for interaction, information representations are limited in their communicative and epistemic utility. This can be especially true when representing large information spaces, where much of their structure remains hidden and latent. That is, due to the size and/or complexity of the information space, only a subset of the information is represented and made perceptually accessible. By providing mechanisms for acting upon representations, such that the form and content of a representation can be changed and manipulated to fit the needs of learners, virtually any representation becomes more powerful (Dix & Ellis, 1998). As such, interaction essentially acts as an 'epistemic extension' of static representations (Sedig & Liang, 2006). It is generally accepted that adding interaction to representations increases their utility (Dix & Ellis, 1998; Sedig & Sumner, 2006; Spence, 2007). Nevertheless, no systematic framework exists to explicate the design of interactions that support reasoning, problem solving, and other learning activities (Sedig, 2004; Thomas & Cook, 2005; Pike, Stasko, Chang, & O'Connell, 2009). Much of the research that has been done in regards to interactive representations has focused on the representation aspect at the expense of their interactive aspects (Yi et al., 2007). As more ELEs are being developed for educational use, a more systematic and comprehensive understanding of interaction and its effects on learning must be developed. Books like this one are an important step towards this end, as interaction and interactivity are multifaceted and require consideration of many more aspects than are mentioned in this chapter. For instance, Ge, Law, & Huang (this volume) propose a design framework for scaffolding in ELEs, an important consideration for any interactive ELE. Additionally, as ELEs can be used in many different ways to promote learning, their context of use is also important. One area of increased attention in recent years is digital games and serious games for learning. Other chapters in this volume (e.g., Huang & Yang; Code, Clark-Midura, Zape, & Dede) make important contributions to these areas. As more attention is placed on the many aspects of interaction and interactivity, there can be a synthesis of ideas that motivate effective interaction design of ELEs.

In this chapter we define interaction in terms of two components: action and reaction. That is, a learner performs an action upon a representation, and the representation provides some reaction for the learner to interpret. As a learner performs an action, the resulting reaction can be a change in a representational form and/or a change in how the information space is represented (e.g., more or less of the information space may become represented). Just as there can be different ways of representing information, there can also be varied ways by which learners can interact with these representations (Sedig & Sumner, 2006). Some ways are more conducive to reflective thinking and learning purposes, while others can have unwanted

learning outcomes (Svendsen, 1991; Sedig et al., 2001). When learners think with information, they often need to process it—that is, decode, deconstruct, and understand its layers of meaning—in order to make sense of it and/or to apply it (Sedig, 2009). Earlier research has developed a framework that categorizes and characterizes a set of interaction techniques by which learners can explore and investigate representations in ELEs. Sedig and Sumner (2006) have characterized a number of techniques for interacting with visual mathematical representations according to their common features. As an example of this characterization, interaction techniques such as magic lenses, pop-up dialogs, panning, and zooming all share the same goal; namely, interacting with a representation so as to focus on or drill into an aspect of it to get more detail. That is, they all belong to one abstract pattern of interaction. Accordingly, these techniques can be aggregated and given a common label—probing. By characterizing these techniques, educators and designers of ELEs can think more systematically about higher-level goals of learners and about how to assist them in achieving these goals with proper interaction design. Even though the framework was designed for mathematical visualizations, its interactions are applicable in most ELEs. Table 1 provides a list of these interactions and a brief description of each.

This previously devised framework, however, looks only at interaction with representations, and does not address their interactivity—that is, the quality, feel, or properties of the interaction. In this chapter we are interested in strengthening the epistemic coupling between a learner and an ELE, and in examining and characterizing the structural elements and features of interaction that affect this coupling. These elements are what determine the interactivity of the different representational components of an ELE and the ELE as a whole, and are the focus of this chapter.

Table 1. A preliminary framework of interactions

Interaction	Description
Animating	Generating movement within a representation
Annotating	Augmenting a representation with additional information
Chunking	Grouping similar or related elements together
Composing	Putting together separate visual elements to form a new representation
Cutting	Removing unwanted or unnecessary portions of a representation
Filtering	Showing, hiding, or transforming a subset of information based on certain criteria
Fragmenting	Breaking a representation into its component parts
Probing	Focusing on or drilling into an aspect of a representation for further analysis
Rearranging	Changing the spatial arrangement of representations
Repicturing	Displaying a representation in an alternative manner
Scoping	Adjusting the field of view of a representation to see its compositional development
Searching	Seeking the existence of certain features or elements of a representation

ELEMENTS OF INTERACTION AFFECTING INTERACTIVITY

Here we present and discuss a number of structural elements of interaction that affect the interactivity of information representations of ELEs. The interactivity of the ELE itself is an emergent property, which results from the interactivity of the information representations at the interface level as a whole. The interaction elements presented here provide a descriptive framework to help designers think about their design choices in a systematic manner. As this chapter is a preliminary framework, it does not claim to be exhaustive, and there may be other elements or issues that are not discussed here. As interaction is concerned with both action and reaction, some of these elements are concerned with the action component and some with the reaction component. Here we identify 10 such elements: 6 that are concerned with action, 3 that are concerned with reaction, and 1 (perceived affordances / constraints) that is concerned with the overall conceptual model that an ELE communicates. The elements concerned with action are: actual affordances / constraints, articulation mode, control, event granularity, focus, and action flow. The elements concerned

with reaction are: reaction flow, propagation, and transition. Figure 2 provides a diagram depicting these structural elements of interaction. Some of these elements have overlapping features, but each is conceptually distinct enough to deserve its own consideration. Some have been previously investigated and studied as separate elements—i.e., not in the context of a coherent framework. Some are new and/or require more empirical verification. The following sections discuss each of these elements affecting interactivity.

Actual Affordances / Constraints

Affordances are concerned with interaction possibilities of representations, and constraints are concerned with restrictions in the possible interactions. There are two types of affordances and constraints: actual and perceived. Actual affordances and constraints refer to what actions are possible and what limitations are provided by an ELE. Perceived affordances and constraints refer to what actions and limitations a learner perceives to be in existence. Thus actual affordances and constraints are concerned with the action component of interaction, whereas perceived affordances and constraints are concerned more

Figure 2. The structural elements of interaction affecting interactivity

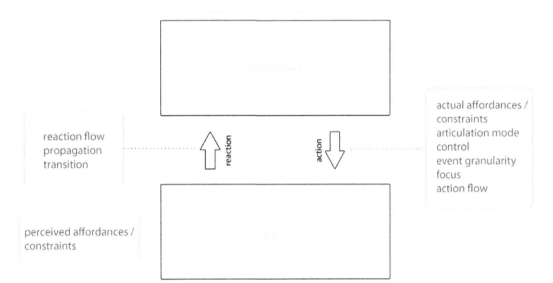

with the overall conceptual model that an ELE communicates. In general, effectively designed interactive representations should communicate their affordances and constraints such that learners easily perceive the actual affordances and constraints offered by the ELE.

The element of affordance affects learners' perceptive and attentive processes by facilitating awareness of possible actions. Interaction possibilities can be advertised by such means as color change in visual elements or cursor change resulting from mouse-over actions. For example, an ELE, *Polyvise* (Morey & Sedig, 2004), allows learners to investigate four-dimensional geometric solids. Figure 3 shows two screenshots of the ELE. As seen in the figure, the ELE affords the learner to turn a polytope representation in two directions along a circle (see Figure 3). However, as one of its constraints, the polytope representation cannot be dragged on the screen. As affordances provide suggestions for action, constraints set limits for action. Thus what a learner is allowed to do or constrained from doing with representations can serve to focus, canalize, and direct their cognitive processes—that is, to attract attention towards

certain salient representational elements and properties, to guide thinking and reasoning during interaction, and to narrow and direct the course of goal formulation while exploring representations. As such, affordances and constraints serve to balance one another. Some researchers (e.g., Trudel & Payne, 1995) have suggested that exploratory learning can be significantly improved when learners' interactions and explorations are constrained and restricted. Different types of affordances and constraints and their effects on quality of learning need to be explored and studied more systematically if ELEs are to be designed to meet their epistemological and pedagogical functions.

Articulation Mode

Articulation mode is concerned with the manner in which a learner actualizes an intention. There are three types of articulation mode: conversing, manipulating, and navigating. These modes are based on the root metaphors derived from how people use different parts of their body to act upon the physical world—i.e., mouth/talking, hands/ handling, and feet/walking (Sedig & Sumner,

Figure 3. A polytope representation's actual affordance and constraint

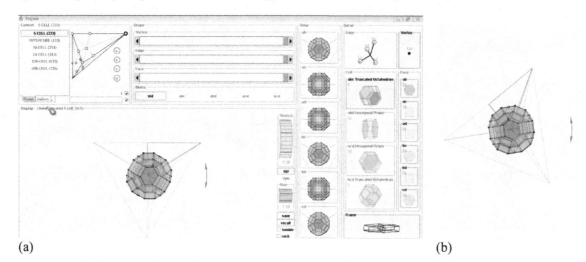

(a) (b)

Figure 4. Both indirect and direct focus in an ELE

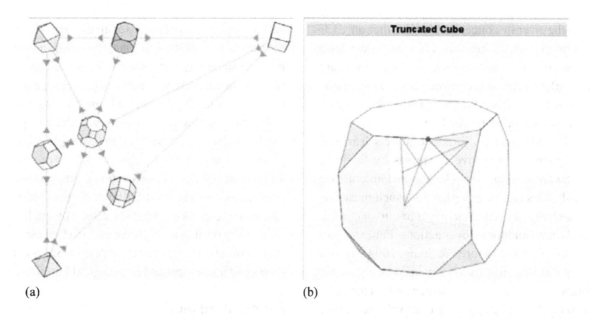

(a) (b)

2006; Sherman & Craig, 2003). Just as people use these to explore and make sense of objects in the physical world, learners can act upon representations in a similar fashion to make sense of and reason about them.

While performing an action by conversing, a representation is thought of as an entity that understands language. As such, a learner is ex-

pressing an action through symbolic language. For instance, a learner can issue an action command to a representation to give it instructions, query it, and so on. Conversational action is often more effective when learners need to express repetitive and recursive activities, which may not be as easy to express using the other modes of articulation (Sedig & Sumner, 2006). While performing an action by manipulating, a representation is thought of as an object that can be handled. Learners express an action by pointing and touching, handling, or grasping a representation. During this mode of articulation, representations can be thought of as virtual manipulatives (Moyer, Bolyard, & Spikell, 2001). Learners generally manipulate objects by performing actions such as dragging, dropping, rotating, morphing, and so on. While performing an action by navigating, a representation is thought of as a space, area, or map. Learners express an action by moving on, over, or through a representation. Navigation can be used to help learners develop an internal spatial cognitive map of a representation (Golledge, 1999; Spence, 1999; Sedig, Rowhani, Morey, & Liang, 2003). Navigating can also help learners gain knowledge about details of specific locations on an interface and about the structure of and relations among elements in an information space.

The above three modes of articulation can be explained by using Figure 5 as an example. With this ELE, a learner is exploring the information space of our planet. If the learner wishes to investigate the surface structure of the planet,

she can articulate her action through conversing, manipulating, or navigating. For example, the learner could type a command to the ELE such as 'rotate 120 degrees'. She could also click and drag on the representation so as to manipulate it (e.g., Figure 5a). Or she could also navigate through or around the representation so as to develop a cognitive map of its features (e.g., Figure 5b). Each of these articulation modes can have different effects on the cognitive processes of learners, and may affect learning in different ways.

Control

Control is concerned with a learner's ability to set or change some parameters of action. The degree of control can be anywhere from zero control (i.e., action parameters are fixed and predetermined) to complete control (i.e., action parameters are completely under the learner's control). For example an ELE may allow learners to have some control over modifying the parameters of an action, such as animating. In such a situation, learners may be able to set the speed at which representational frames are animated. Control can also be with regard

Figure 5. Different types of interaction flow

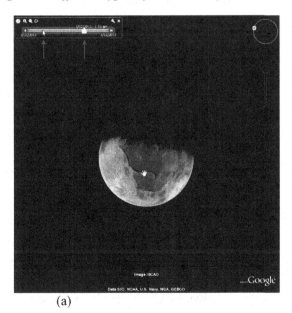

(a)

(b)

to other elements of interactivity. For instance, while acting upon a representation, a learner may be given control over the mode of articulation by which he wants to express the action (see *articulation mode*); an ELE may allow a learner to choose whether to act directly upon a representation or through an intermediary (see *focus*); an ELE may allow a learner to choose between acting in a continuous manner or in a discrete manner (see *flow*); and so on. Some researchers suggest that having control is desirable (e.g., Benyon, Turner, & Turner, 2005), however the degree of control given to a learner and which parameters should be made available for control are not clear and require further investigation.

Event Granularity

Event granularity is concerned with how many events need to take place in order to achieve an intended action. Events refer to the micro-level occurrences such as mouse clicks or drags, keyboard strokes, and menu-item selections. Actions such as probing, rearranging, and composing, for example, may require many sequential events to accomplish or may be performed with only one event. While a low degree of event granularity may lead to greater ease of use and therefore be desirable for productivity tools, such may not be the case with ELEs where the goal is to engage learners in mindful and reflective thinking. For instance, given a representation of a geometric shape to rotate on the screen, two potential ways in which the action can be implemented are as follows: (1) the learner must right-click on the shape to rotate it in a clockwise direction and left-click it to rotate it in a counterclockwise direction; or (2) the learner must click on a button to specify what type of rotation is desired, then specify the angle of rotation, and finally commit the action. As can be noted from this simple example, the first implementation requires one event to achieve the action and the second requires at least 3 events. More research needs to be done to understand the effects of event granularity on learning. A number of questions regarding event granularity for different actions can be posed and investigated. For instance, does fragmenting a representation into its component parts by a single button click versus requiring many events to complete the same action result in more elaborative thinking about the underlying information space? If so, is this always the case? Is there an ideal number of events? And so on.

Focus

Focus is concerned with the locus of attention of the learner while acting upon a representation. Focus can be either direct or indirect. If the focus of action is direct, a learner acts upon a representation directly. On the other hand, if the focus of action is indirect, a learner acts upon intermediary representations to affect the representation of interest. An example of direct focus would be a learner clicking on a 3D representation of a molecule so as to rotate it to investigate its structure. An example of indirect focus would be a learner acting upon a representation of an arc of rotation to adjust rotational parameters of the molecule. In the early days of computing, interaction was primarily symbolic or command-based, which employs indirect focus to affect representations. As direct focus (e.g., "direct manipulation", see Shneiderman, 1983) gained more popularity, it became the prevalent technique used both in productivity tools as well as in ELEs. The main goal of directness of action was to minimize learners' cognitive load by allowing them to engage with the representations directly (Hutchins, Hollan, & Norman, 1986). Although direct focus can make interaction easier by reducing cognitive load, it is not necessarily conducive to reflective and effortful engagement with information—an important aspect of learning. For instance, Svendsen (1991) found that subjects who used a command-based interface (i.e., indirect focus of action) engaged in more reflective thought that lead to better learning.

Golightly (1996) had subjects solve the 8-puzzle game and found that moving the puzzle pieces by clicking on adjacent buttons (i.e., indirect focus) resulted in learners paying more attention to each move than they would with the direct focus option. The results were interpreted to suggest that direct focus would involve less planning.

It is not always clear which type of focus is the best option. Sedig, Rowhani, and Liang (2005) conducted a study in which learners were investigating an information space of 3D geometric solids. Learners were given two representations with which they could interact: a diagrammatic map of the transitional relationships among a set of solids (Figure 4a), and a geometric solid (Figure 4b). Learners could interact directly with either the solid or the map. As they directly acted upon one, they would indirectly act upon the other—that is, the two representations were dynamically linked such that changes in one would cause changes in the other. What the researchers found is that the subjects used each type of focus for different purposes. For instance, learners would focus action upon the map to reason about transitions, and would focus action upon the solid to reason about its structure. Since the reaction was reciprocal, the learners could benefit from the fact that they indirectly acted upon the other representation as well. In this study, the results suggest that having access to both direct and indirect focus of action can help learners develop a deeper understanding of an information space. Further research is needed to investigate how focus affects how learners act upon representations and the degree to which it influences their cognitive processes. Additionally, it is still unclear how the chain of indirection can affect learning of content.

Flow

Flow is concerned with the duration of interaction with a representation. The flow element is part of both the action as well as the reaction part of interaction. As such, flow can be thought of as two distinct but related components: action flow and reaction flow. In the context of this framework, these are considered as separate elements; however, since they share an underlying conceptual similarity they are discussed under one section for ease of description. Because both action and reaction occur within time, flow can happen in two ways: continuous and discrete. Continuous flow refers to action and/or reaction occurring over a span of time in an uninterrupted, fluid manner. Discrete flow refers to action and/or reaction occurring at an instance in time. Some researchers (e.g., Spence, 2007) refer only to continuous action, or to continuous action coupled with continuous reaction, which is then referred to as continuous interaction. That is, no distinction is made between the continuity or discreteness of the action and that of the reaction. Such an approach may be fine for productivity tools, but for the purpose of facilitating learning these issues should be examined in greater detail.

As flow can happen in two ways there are four possibilities for interaction flow: continuous action followed by continuous reaction; continuous action followed by discrete reaction; discrete action followed by continuous reaction; and discrete action followed by discrete reaction. Figure 5 shows a tool that can be used as an ELE, *Google Earth (earth.google.com)*, which provides a simple and easily accessible example of each form of interaction flow. Learners can interact with C-C flow by clicking on the earth (hand cursor in Figure 5a) and dragging (i.e., continuous action) such that it rotates simultaneously in response to the action (i.e., continuous reaction). Learners can also double-click on a point of the earth (i.e., discrete action) and the ELE will fluidly zoom-in on the area (i.e., continuous reaction). A learner can also click on a slider (shown with arrows in Figure 5a) to change the time of day (i.e., discrete action) and receive a response in an immediate fashion (i.e., discrete reaction). In the maps view (Figure 5b) the learner can click and drag on the slider (i.e., continuous action) and the map will react instantaneously once the mouse is released (i.e., discrete reaction).

To investigate the effects of each type of flow on learning, Liang et al. (2010) conducted a study using an ELE that supports learning about 3D mathematical shapes. Based upon the four types of flow, four versions of the ELE were created in which learners had different combinations of flow. In the C-C version both action upon and reaction from representations of geometric shapes were continuous. For example, learners could rotate a given shape by positioning the mouse-cursor on it and dragging it towards the direction of their preference (i.e., continuous action). The shape responded by being updated in a fluid and continuous manner (i.e., continuous reaction). The D-D version operationalizes both action and reaction discretely, and so on. The results of the study showed that although the C-C version was most liked and considered the most intuitive to use, the D-D version resulted in the learners obtaining the most improvement in post-test scores. Additionally, the D-C version resulted in the second-highest improvement. The results of this study seem to challenge the recent popularity of having continuous flow in educational tools. This study showed that getting learners to act in a discrete manner promoted more effortful and reflective thinking by encouraging learners to be more economical in their use of actions. This study, if nothing, suggests that learning can be affected by how the flow of interaction is designed. Even though the conclusions from this study are inconclusive, they do suggest that further research is needed to investigate the effects of this interaction element on learning in different contexts.

Propagation

Propagation is concerned with how action on a representation affects other representations in terms of their properties and relationships. For instance, a learner may perform an action on a representation, and the ELE may respond by propagating

an effect to other areas of the interface such that there is a change in the representational forms. When an interface consists of multiple representations, the set of representations is either connected or disconnected. Propagation is concerned with connected sets of representations, which can be of four types: sink, star, network, and directed pair. Figure 6 shows these types of propagations represented as directed graphs. With sink propagation, actions performed on different representations all propagate to one specific representation. With star propagation, an action performed on a specific representation propagates to all other representations. Network propagation exists when an action on any representation is propagated to all other representations in the interface. With directed pair propagation, an action performed on a specific representation is propagated to another specific representation. Finally, Figure 6 also shows a disconnected set configuration, which occurs when representations are independent of each other. As each of these may affect cognitive processes differently, further investigation of their effects on learning is required.

Transition

Transition is concerned with visual changes that occur as a result of an action. Many actions that are performed upon representations result in a visual change in a representation—i.e., a transition in its structure and form. There are two ways in which a transition can be communicated: stacked or distributed. With stacked transition, any change in a representation's state is stacked on top of the original representation in a single location, such that the new representation replaces the one temporally previous to it. While stacked transition constrains the visual change to one location, distributed transition can communicate changes to the representation over a region of space. That is, distributed transition shows the effect of changes in the original representation by displaying the transitional stages of the original representation

Figure 6. Different types of propagation (from L to R): sink, star, network, directed pair, disconnected set

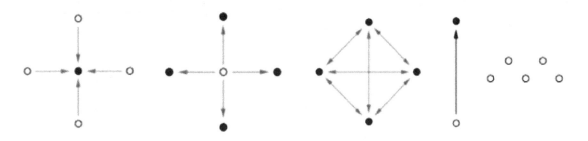

Figure 7. An example of stacked transition

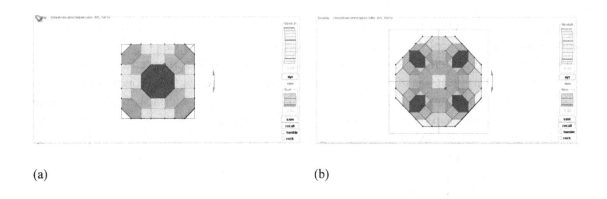

(a)   (b)

at different locations on the screen. Spatial distribution of transitional states makes use of the human visual system's ability to compare multiple different representations that can be perceived in our visual field (Tufte, 1997). Figure 7 shows an example of stacked transition, where Figure 7a is the original representation and Figure 7b is the resulting representation displayed at the same spot as the original one. Figure 8 shows an example of distributed transition, where Figure 8a is the original representation and Figure 8b shows how the changes in the representation are displayed as a series of small multiples.

Each type of transition has its own inherent strengths and weaknesses. For instance, stacked transition avoids forcing the learner to make constant back-and-forth movements of the eye

that spatially distributed transition does (Tufte, 1997). However, distributed transition forces learners to compare different states from memory, as they cannot see multiple states of the representation simultaneously, a limitation that stacked transitions do not have. As these have different perceptual and cognitive effects, they can influence learning in different ways. As such, they require more systematic investigation and explication in this framework.

SUMMARY AND FUTURE RESEARCH DIRECTIONS

This chapter is concerned with the interactivity of information representations in e-learning

Figure 8. An example of distributed transition

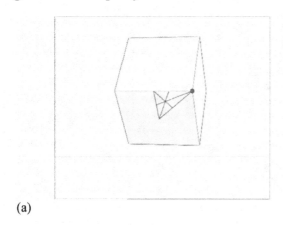

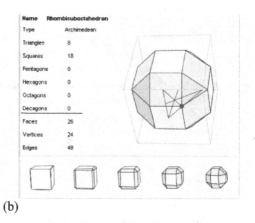

(a)   (b)

environments (ELEs), where an ELE refers to any computer-based software that mediates and supports learners' engagement with information. When ELEs are designed well they can facilitate reflective and effortful processing of information that is conducive to learning. Currently there are several existent problems when designing and evaluating the interactivity of information representations in ELEs. First, it is often the case that researchers do not make any clear distinction between interaction and interactivity. Additionally, these terms are often used interchangeably and in a loose manner. This chapter has made a clear distinction between interaction and interactivity and has defined their meanings. Interaction involves two components, action and reaction. Thus the term 'interactive' suggests that learners can act upon a representation and receive responses to their actions. Adding '-ity' to the end of the term 'interactive' changes the adjective to suggest the quality and condition of the interaction. That is, interactivity refers to the feel, quality, or properties of interaction. Second, there is no clear guidance on how to distinguish between the interactivity of ELEs and other non-educational software. That is, the underlying frameworks, principles, and metrics have not been investigated sufficiently. Third, the notion of the interactivity of information representations has not been clearly character-

ized. As a result, it is not easy to systematically design and assess the interactivity of information representations in ELEs.

This chapter has proposed a preliminary framework that addresses these concerns. This chapter is concerned with interface of ELEs, the space in which a learner's mind interacts with information representations to construct knowledge. Many researchers have suggested that external cognitive artifacts, such as ELEs, can greatly influence thinking and learning processes. While performing any type of activity with an ELE, learners are using, working with, or thinking with information that is given some representational form, such that there is a coupling between the mind of a learner and the information representations. This coupling is epistemic in nature, as it pertains to the acquisition of knowledge. When a cognitive artifact is static and does not provide mechanisms for interaction, this coupling is weak. In such a case, especially if the information being represented is complex, learners are forced to exert a great deal of mental effort in order to reason and think about the information. Interaction strengthens this coupling, as it allows a learner to perform actions on representations and to receive responses to those actions. In this manner it allows for a dialogue to take place between learners and the ELE that is maintaining and representing information, such

Table 2. Structural elements of interaction affecting interactivity of information representations

		Element	Description
Interaction	Action	Actual affordances / constraints	What actions are possible and what limitations are provided
		Articulation mode	The mode in which an intention is actualized (types: conversing, manipulating, navigating)
		Control	Degree to which a learner can set or change parameters of action
		Event granularity	How many events need to take place in order to achieve an intended action
		Focus	Locus of learner's attention while acting upon a representation (types: direct, indirect)
		Action flow	Temporal duration of action upon a representation in time (types: continuous, discrete)
	Reaction	Reaction flow	Temporal duration of reaction from a representation (types: continuous, discrete)
		Propagation	How action on a representation affects other representations in terms of their properties and relationships
		Transition	Visual changes that occur as a result of an action (types: stacked, distributed)
		Perceived affordances / constraints	What actions and limitations a learners perceives to be in existence

that the learner can adapt the information to fit their epistemic and cognitive needs. In this chapter we are interested in strengthening the epistemic coupling between a learner and information, and in examining and characterizing the structural elements of interaction that affect this coupling. The proposed framework identifies and elaborates upon 10 structural elements of interaction. These are listed with a brief description of each in Table 2. These elements collectively affect the interactivity of the information representations in ELEs. As many of these structural elements were offered only brief treatment in this chapter, future research will develop these further. As these are developed further, empirical studies can be conducted to assess their effects on learning and cognitive processes. These elements can eventually be incorporated into a larger framework that deals with other aspects of design and evaluation, such as representations and actions. Such a framework could be used as a comprehensive guide for design and analysis of interactive information representations.

REFERENCES

Adams, W. K. (2009). Student engagement and learning with PhET interactive simulations. *Proceedings of Multimedia in Physics Teaching and Learning*.

Alessi, S. M., & Trollip, S. R. (2001). *Multimedia for learning: Methods and development* (3rd ed.). Needham Heights, MA: Allyn and Bacon.

Benyon, D., Turner, P., & Turner, S. (2005). *Designing interactive systems*. Essex, England: Pearson Education.

Brey, P. (2005). The epistemology and ontology of human-computer interaction. *Minds and Machines*, *15*, 383–398. doi:10.1007/s11023-005-9003-1

Bruner, J. (2005). Foreward. In Sternberg, R., & Preiss, D. D. (Eds.), *Intelligence and technology: The impact of tools on the nature and development of human abilities* (pp. ix–xi). Mahwah, NJ: Lawrence Erlbaum.

Code, J. R., Clarke-Midura, J., Zap, N., & Dede, C. (in press). *Virtual performance assessment in serious games and immersive virtual reality environments.*

Cole, M., & Derry, J. (2005). We have met technology and it is us. In Sternberg, R., & Preiss, D. (Eds.), *Intelligence and technology: The impact of tools on the nature and development of human abilities* (pp. 210–227). Mahwah, NJ: Lawrence Erlbaum.

Dascal, M., & Dror, I. E. (2005). The impact of cognitive technologies: Towards a pragmatic approach. *Pragmatics & Cognition, 13*(3), 451–457. doi:10.1075/pc.13.3.03das

Dix, A., & Ellis, G. (1998). *Starting simple – Adding value to static visualization through simple interaction.* Paper presented at the Working Conference on Advanced Visual Interfaces (AVI '98), L'Aquila, Italy.

Dror, I. E. (2007). Gold mines and land mines in cognitive technology. In Dror, I. E. (Ed.), *Cognitive technologies and the pragmatics of cognition* (pp. 1–8). Philadelphia, PA: John Benjamins.

Eysenck, M. W., & Keane, M. T. (1990). *Cognitive psychology* (2nd ed.). Hillsdale, NJ: Lawrence Erlbaum.

Ge, X., Law, V., & Huang, K. (in press). *Diagnosis, supporting, and fading: A scaffolding design framework for adaptive e-learning systems.*

Golightly, D. (1996). Harnessing the interface for domain learning. In M. J. Tauber (Ed.), *Proceedings of the CHI '96 Conference Companion on Human Factors in Computing Systems: Common Ground* (pp. 37-38). Vancouver, BC.

Golledge, R. G. (1999). Human wayfinding and cognitive maps. In Golledge, R. G. (Ed.), *Wayfinding behavior: Cognitive mapping and other spatial processes* (pp. 5–45). Baltimore, MD: The Johns Hopkins University Press.

Huang, W.-H. D., & Yang, D. (in press). *Empowering digital learners: A self-managing learning process framework for digital game-based learning systems (DGBLS).*

Hutchins, E. (1995). *Cognition in the wild.* Cambridge, MA: MIT Press.

Hutchins, E., Hollan, J. D., & Norman, D. A. (1986). Direct manipulation interfaces. In Norman, D. A., & Draper, S. W. (Eds.), *User centered system design: New perspectives in human-computer interaction.* Hillsdale, NJ: Lawrence Erlbaum.

(2005). Interface. In McKean, E. (Ed.), *New Oxford American dictionary* (2nd ed.). Oxford, UK: Oxford University Press.

Jonassen, D. H., Peck, K. L., & Wilson, B. G. (1998). *Learning with technology: A constructivist perspective.* Columbus, OH: Prentice-Hall.

Jonassen, D. H., & Reeves, T. C. (1996). Learning with technology: Using computers as cognitive tools. In Jonassen, D. H. (Ed.), *Handbook of research for educational communications and technology* (pp. 693–719). New York, NY: Macmillan.

Karasavvidis, I. (2002). Distributed cognition and educational practice. *Journal of Interactive Learning Research, 13*(1/2), 11–29.

Kulik, C.-L. C., & Kulik, J. A. (1991). Effectiveness of computer-based instruction: an updated analysis. *Computers in Human Behavior, 7*(1/2), 75–94. doi:10.1016/0747-5632(91)90030-5

Lajoie, S. P. (2005). Cognitive tools for the mind: The promises of technology—Cognitive amplifiers or bionic prosthetics? In Sternberg, R., & Preiss, D. (Eds.), *Intelligence and technology: The impact of tools on the nature and development of human abilities* (pp. 87–101). Mahwah, NJ: Lawrence Erlbaum.

Larkin, J., & Simon, H. (1987). Why a diagram is (sometimes) worth ten thousand words. *Cognitive Science, 11,* 65–99. doi:10.1111/j.1551-6708.1987.tb00863.x

Liang, H.-N., Parsons, P. C., Wu, H.-C., & Sedig, K. (2010). An exploratory study of interactivity in visualization tools: 'Flow' of interaction. *Journal of Interactive Learning Research, 21*(1), 5–45.

Liang, H.-N., & Sedig, K. (2010). Role of interaction in enhancing the epistemic utility of 3D mathematical visualizations. *International Journal of Computers for Mathematical Learning, 15*(3), 191–224. doi:10.1007/s10758-010-9165-7

Morey, J., & Sedig, K. (2004). Using indexed-sequential geometric glyphs to explore visual patterns. In. *Proceedings of Interactive Visualisation and Interaction Technologies, ICCS, 2004,* 996–1003.

Moyer, P., Bolyard, J., & Spikell, M. (2001). Virtual manipulatives in the K-12 classroom. In A. Rogerson (Ed.), *Proceedings of the International Conference on New Ideas in Mathematics Education* (pp. 184–187). Palm Cove, Australia: Autograph.

Norman, D. A. (1991). Cognitive artifacts. In Carroll, J. M. (Ed.), *Designing interaction: Psychology at the human-computer interface.* Cambridge, UK: Cambridge University Press.

Norman, D. A. (1993). *Things that make us smart: Defending human attributes in the age of the machine.* New York, NY: Addison-Wesley.

Ormrod, J. E. (1995). *Human learning.* Englewood Cliffs, NJ: Prentice-Hall.

Pea, R. D. (1985). Beyond amplification: Using the computer to reorganize mental functioning. *Educational Psychology, 20*(4), 167–182. doi:10.1207/s15326985ep2004_2

Peterson, D. (1996). *Forms of representation.* Exeter, UK: Intellect Books.

Pike, W. A., Stasko, J., Chang, R., & O'Connell, T. A. (2009). The science of interaction. *Journal of Information Visualization, 8*(4), 263–274. doi:10.1057/ivs.2009.22

Salomon, G. (Ed., 1993). *Distributed cognitions: Psychological and educational considerations.* Cambridge, UK: Cambridge University Press.

Salomon, G., & Perkins, D. (2005). Do technologies make us smarter? Intellectual amplification with, of, and through technology. In Sternberg, R., & Preiss, D. D. (Eds.), *Intelligence and technology: The impact of tools on the nature and development of human abilities* (pp. 71–86). Mahwah, NJ: Lawrence Erlbaum.

Sedig, K. (2004). Need for a prescriptive taxonomy of interaction for mathematical cognitive tools. In. *Proceedings of Interactive Visualisation and Interaction Technologies, ICCS, 2004,* 1030–1037.

Sedig, K. (2009). Interactive mathematical visualizations: Frameworks, tools, and studies. In Zudilova-Seinstra, E., Adriaansen, T., & van Liere, R. (Eds.), *Trends in interactive visualization: State-of-the-art survey* (pp. 343–363). London, UK: Springer-Verlag. doi:10.1007/978-1-84800-269-2_16

Sedig, K., Klawe, M., & Westrom, M. (2001). Role of interface manipulation style and scaffolding on cognition and concept learning in learnware. *ACM Transactions on Computer-Human Interaction, 1*(8), 34–59. doi:10.1145/371127.371159

Sedig, K., & Liang, H.-N. (2006). Interactivity of visual mathematical representations: Factors affecting learning and cognitive processes. *Journal of Interactive Learning Research, 17*(2), 179–212.

Sedig, K., & Liang, H.-N. (2008). Learner-information interaction: A macro-level framework characterizing visual cognitive tools. *Journal of Interactive Learning Research, 19*(1), 147–173.

Sedig, K., Rowhani, S., & Liang, H.-N. (2005). Designing interfaces that support formation of cognitive maps of transitional processes: An empirical study. *Interacting with Computers: The Interdisciplinary Journal of Human-Computer Interaction, 17*(4), 419–452.

Sedig, K., Rowhani, S., Morey, J., & Liang, H. (2003). Application of information visualization techniques to the design of a mathematical mindtool: A usability study. *Journal Information Visualization, 2*(3), 142–160. doi:10.1057/palgrave.ivs.9500047

Sedig, K., & Sumner, M. (2006). Characterizing interaction with visual mathematical representations. *International Journal of Computers for Mathematical Learning, 11*(1), 1–55. doi:10.1007/s10758-006-0001-z

Sherman, W. R., & Craig, A. B. (2003). *Understanding virtual reality: Interface, application, and design*. San Francisco, CA: Morgan Kaufmann.

Shneiderman, B. (1983). Direct manipulation: a step beyond programming languages. *IEEE Computer, 16*(8), 57–69.

Spence, R. (1999). A framework for navigation. *International Journal of Human-Computer Studies, 51*(5), 919–945. doi:10.1006/ijhc.1999.0265

Spence, R. (2007). *Information visualization: Design for interaction* (2nd ed.). Essex, UK: Pearson.

Svendsen, G. B. (1991). The influence of interface style on problem solving. *International Journal of Man-Machine Studies, 35*(3), 379–397. doi:10.1016/S0020-7373(05)80134-8

Thagard, P. (1996). *Mind. Introduction to cognitive science*. Cambridge, MA: MIT Press.

Thomas, J. J., & Cook, K. A. (2005). *Illuminating the path: The research and development agenda for visual analytics. National Visualization and Analytics Center*. Richland, WA: IEEE Press.

Trudel, C., & Payne, S. J. (1995). Reflection and goal management in exploratory learning. *International Journal of Human-Computer Studies, 42*, 307–339. doi:10.1006/ijhc.1995.1015

Tufte, E. R. (1997). *Visual explanations: Images and quantities, evidence and narrative*. Cheshire, CT: Graphics Press.

Yi, J. S., Kang, Y. A., Stasko, J., & Jacko, J. (2007). Toward a deeper understanding of the role of interaction in information visualization. *IEEE Transactions on Visualization and Computer Graphics, 13*, 1224–1231. doi:10.1109/TVCG.2007.70515

Zhang, J. (1997). The nature of external representations in problem solving. *Cognitive Science, 21*(2), 179–217. doi:10.1207/s15516709cog2102_3

Zhang, J. (2000). External representations in complex information processing tasks. In Kent, A. (Ed.), *Encyclopedia of library and information science* (*Vol. 68*, pp. 164–180). New York, NY: Marcel Dekker.

Zhang, J., & Norman, D. (1994). Representations in distributed cognitive tasks. *Cognitive Science, 18*, 87–122. doi:10.1207/s15516709cog1801_3

ADDITIONAL READING

Ainsworth, S., & Peevers, G. J. (2003). The interaction between informational and computational properties of external representations on problem solving and learning. In R. Alterman, & D. Kirsh (Eds.), *Proceedings of the 25th Annual Conference of the Cognitive Science Society* (pp. 67-72). Boston, MA: Cognitive Science.

Albers, M. J. (2008). Human-information interaction. In *Proceedings of the 26th annual ACM international conference on design of communication* (pp. 117-124). New York: ACM.

Carroll, J. M. (Ed., 1991). *Designing interaction: Psychology at the human-computer interface.* Cambridge, MA: Cambridge University Press.

Clark, A., & Chalmers, D. (1998). The extended mind. *Analysis, 58*(1), 7–19. doi:10.1111/1467-8284.00096

Hollan, J., Hutchins, E., & Kirsh, D. (2000). Distributed cognition: Toward a new foundation for human-computer interaction research. *ACM Transactions on Computer-Human Interaction, 7*(2), 174–196. [TOCHI]doi:10.1145/353485.353487

Jones, W., Pirolli, P., Card, S. K., Fidel, R., Gershon, N., & Morville, P. (2006). "It's about the information stupid!": why we need a separate field of human-information interaction. In *CHI '06 extended abstracts on human factors in computing systems* (pp. 65–68). New York: ACM. doi:10.1145/1125451.1125469

Kastens, K. A., Liben, L. S., & Agrawal, S. (2008). Epistemic actions in science education. In C. Freksa, N. S. Newcombe, P. Gärdenfors, & S. Wölfl (Eds.), *Spatial cognition VI-Learning, reasoning, and talking about space: International Conference Spatial Cognition (LNAI 5248)* (pp. 202-215). Berlin: Springer-Verlag.

Kirsh, D. (1997). Interactivity and multimedia interfaces. *Instructional Science, 25*(2), 79–96. doi:10.1023/A:1002915430871

Kirsh, D. (2006). Distributed cognition: A methodological note. *Pragmatics & Cognition, 14*(2), 249–262. doi:10.1075/pc.14.2.06kir

Kirsh, D. (2009). Interaction, external representations and sense making. In *Proceedings of the 31st Annual Conference of the Cognitive Science Society* (pp. 1103-1108). Austin, TX: Cognitive Science Society.

Kirsh, D., & Maglio, P. (1994). On distinguishing epistemic from pragmatic action. *Cognitive Science, 18*, 513–549. doi:10.1207/s15516709cog1804_1

Lovett, M. C., & Shah, P. (Eds., 2007). *Thinking with Data.* Mahwah, NJ: Lawrence Erlbaum.

Maglio, P. P., Matlock, T., Raphaely, D., Chernicky, B., & Kirsh, D. (1999). Interactive skill in Scrabble. In M. Hahn & S. C. Stoness (Eds.), *Proceedings of Twenty-first Annual Conference of the Cognitive Science Society* (pp. 326-330). Mahwah, NJ: Lawrence Erlbaum.

Morey, J., & Sedig, K. (2004a). Adjusting degree of visual complexity: An interactive approach for exploring four-dimensional polytopes. *The Visual Computer: International Journal of Computer Graphics, 20*, 1-21. Berlin: Springer-Verlag.

Morey, J., & Sedig, K. (2004b). Archimedean Kaleidoscope: A cognitive tool to support thinking and reasoning about geometric solids. In Sarfraz, M. (Ed.), *Geometric modeling: techniques, applications, systems and tools* (pp. 376–393). Norwell, MA: Kluwer Academic Publisher.

Nickerson, R. S. (2005). Technology and cognition amplification. In Sternberg, R. J., & Preiss, D. D. (Eds.), *Intelligence and Technology: The impact of tools on the nature and development of human abilities* (pp. 3–28). Mahwah, NJ: Lawrence Erlbaum.

Parsons, P., & Sedig, K. (In Press). The role of interactive representations in cognitive tools for learning. In Abramovich, S. (Ed.), *Computers and education.* Hauppauge, NY: Nova.

Preece, J., Rogers, Y., & Sharp, H. (2002). *Interaction design: Beyond human computer interaction.* NY: John Wiley and Sons.

Rogers, Y., & Scaife, M. (1997). How can interactive multimedia facilitate learning? In *Proceedings of the First International Workshop on Intelligence and Multimodalities in Multimedia* (pp. 123-142), Palo Alto, CA: The Live Oak Press.

Rowhani, S., & Sedig, K. (2005). E-books plus: Role of interactive visuals in exploration of mathematical information and e-learning. *Journal of Computers in Mathematics and Science Teaching, 24*(3), 273–298.

Rowhani, S., & Sedig, K. (2009). Classifying interactive features of scientific cognitive tools. In G. Siemens & C. Fulford (Eds.), *Proceedings of World Conference on Educational Multimedia, Hypermedia and Telecommunications 2009* (pp. 1015-1020). Chesapeake, VA: AACE.

Scaife, M., & Rogers, Y. (1996). External cognition: how do graphical representations work? *International Journal of Human-Computer Studies, 45*, 185–213. doi:10.1006/ijhc.1996.0048

Sedig, K. (2008). From play to thoughtful learning: A design strategy to engage children with mathematical representations. *Journal of Computers in Mathematics and Science Teaching, 27*(1), 65–101.

Zhang, J. (1991). The interaction of internal and external representations in a problem solving task. In *Proceedings of the Thirteenth Annual Conference of Cognitive Science Society*. Hillsdale, NJ: Lawrence Erlbaum.

KEY TERMS AND DEFINITIONS

Distributed Cognition: A theory that proposes that cognition is not confined to the individual, but rather is a coordination between the individual and their environment. ELEs are part of a learner's cognitive system, and the interactivity of an ELE affects learning and cognitive processes.

E-Learning Environment (ELE): Interactive computer-based software that mediates and supports learners' engagement with information. The interface of an ELE is its epistemic locus.

Human-information interaction: The discipline concerned with information, how it is represented, the ways with which it can be interacted, and the effects of interaction on learning and other cognitive activities.

Information Space: The source of information that a learner is investigating. Aspects of an information space are made tangible by representations. Through interaction with representations, a learner explores different features of an information space.

Interaction: Actions performed by a learner on representations and the subsequent reactions. Interaction allows a learner to have a discourse with information, creating a strong coupling between the learner's mind and the information.

Interactivity: The quality, feel, or properties of interaction. This chapter identifies 10 structural elements of interaction that affect interactivity: actual affordances and constraints, articulation mode, control, event granularity, focus, action flow, reaction flow, propagation, transition, and perceived affordances and constraints.

Interface: The meeting place between a learner's mind and an information space. An interface has two main components: representation and interaction.

Representation: A visual form that embodies some aspects of an information space. It is only through representations that learners have access to information.

Chapter 3
Simulation to Enhance Interactivity in E-Learning:
The Capella Story

Ann Leslie Claesson
Capella University, USA

Felicity Pearson
Capella University, USA

Jesse Rosel
Capella University, USA

ABSTRACT

This chapter examines the planning, process, and application of Riverbend City – an example of rich media developed by Capella University to enhance student interactivity in e-learning environments. Riverbend City is multidisciplinary scenario-based simulation project focusing on the disaster response of public service agencies in a fictional city. The ultimate goal of the project was, and continues to be, to empower learners to envision their ability to combine collaboration and leadership when working with multiple disciplines in a real-life situation.

The primary focus of this chapter is how to provide a real-world scenario where skills and new knowledge can be applied in a safe practice situation, how rich media can be used to supplement existing course content, or be used as a means of initial content delivery. The focus for utilizing rich media in the Riverbend City project was to: (1) enhance learning; (2) challenge learners to have a multidisciplinary perspective; and (3) increase engagement with real-world scenarios.

This chapter explores how rich media can be used in these three types of applications using the Riverbend City Simulation project for Capella's School of Public Service Leadership as a case study example. Riverbend City is a scenario-based simulation that provides a multidisciplinary, rich media experience

DOI: 10.4018/978-1-61350-441-3.ch003

to learners in an online, asynchronous university setting. The simulation provides real-world scenarios where student skills and knowledge can be applied and tested on specific subjects. The ultimate goal of the project is to empower learners to envision their ability to combine collaboration and leadership when working with multiple disciplines in a real-world situation.

INTRODUCTION

Welcome to Riverbend City, where a chemical spill has interrupted the day of medical personnel, school children, city officials, and about 200 other "residents" of this simulated metropolis. Based loosely on Minneapolis, Riverbend City has been developed at Capella University to enrich School of Public Service Leadership courses. (Riverbend City introduction, Rockler-Gladen, N. personal communication, February, 2011, Media Course Developer).

The Riverbend City Simulation Project at Capella University provided a vehicle by which rich, interactive media was used as the best solution for a multidisciplinary approach where learners would greatly benefit from real world scenarios. The fact that Capella is an online university added to the challenge. This chapter will present an overview of the use of rich media as a means to enhance learner engagement with a focus on the experience of the Riverbend City Simulation project from Capella University

Concerns that have been voiced by faculty and accrediting agencies related to "How does one translate knowledge and skills into practice in an e-learning environment?" "How do we really know if they 'get it'?" In today's virtual and technology-rich social networks and environments, the public has grown accustomed to the inclusion of media (particularly rich media) as a part of daily life and interaction. Since these technological resources are so applicable to the content and curriculum of online courses, to not include such tools would be questionable not only to today's learners, but also to faculty and regulatory agencies.

We had originally targeted 19 courses to include Riverbend City simulation missions. The 19 courses quickly expanded to 29 and current plans are to soon include Riverbend City in more than 60 courses. Our original intent was to develop the core storyline, assets and locations up front, and then customize the simulation as necessary for each individual course later on. It was a surprise to the project team to discover early on that this approach would not work. The challenge with this approach is that each course would be developed separately over 2010 and 2011.

Through the use of rich media, it is possible to critique a student's application of knowledge as well as provide an environment where students can engage with real world problems in a manner that is exciting, stimulating, and congruent with learner needs and expectations.

BACKGROUND

The Role of Rich Media and Simulation in E-Learning

Changes in technology, societal expectations, globalization and ability to pursue academic goals through an expansion of funding (Kantrowitz, M., 2010, February 4; Lauerman, 2011, February 14) have changed the way we approach course development and design. Students and accrediting agencies (AACN, 2008; Boller & Jones, 2008) expect more than lecture, testing and discussions in both traditional face-to-face and online environments. Academic learning can take a variety of forms such as active learning, cooperative / collaborative learning, and technology, but one key method of knowledge and skill delivery that is effective in today's academic environment and continues to meet learner expectations is that of problem-based learning. (McKeachie & Svinicki, 2006, p. 221). Problem-based learning is funded on the assumption that learners are individuals who are motivated to solve problems and that as problem solvers they will continue to seek, learn, and explore whatever is needed to acquire knowledge and answers. (McKeachie & Svinicki, 2006, p. 222)

Social networking, computers, and increased globalization through the Internet have influenced student expectations and perceptions of how to acquire information, how to use it, and what to do with it once acquired. Virtual gaming and virtual worlds and networks have become a part of life for many. How does this impact the way we design and develop academic courses and offerings? How can educators draw on student expectations to provide relevant and innovative course material and ways to present knowledge and test skills?

One way is through the use of media in e-leaning and online classrooms. Current advances in technology have provided course developers and designers with a variety of ways to enhance academic course content through the use of rich media, particularly simulation.

What is rich media and how can it be used to enhance learning in the online classroom? Media, rich media and simulation are all forms of communications which can be used to enhance academic learning and enhance learner experience, particularly in an online and e-learning environment. Table 1 provides an overview of definition of these concepts that will be discussed in this chapter.

Rich media can be downloaded and viewed offline thorough media players and devises such as Real Networks' RealPlayer, Microsoft Media Player, or Apple's QuickTime, or it can be embedded in wcb pages. Rich media is characterized by its dynamic motion over time or by direct interaction with a user such as streaming video, a prerecorded webcast and synchronized slide show with

Table 1. Distinguishing characteristics of media and media-based applications

Term	Definition	Source
Media	"main means of communication" such as newspapers, radio, and television or as a specific means of mass communication (OED, 2010). Media can also be a form of communication which relies upon graphic representation of a real or imaged event, situation or item. This type of media is used in academia as animations, illustrations, or videos and is primarily used to deliver content and information to be used in a specific course or educational offering.	OED, 2010a
Rich media in web-based advertising or networking	An Internet advertising term for a Web page ad that uses advanced technology such as streaming video, downloadable programs (applets) that immediately interact with the user. Rich media can also be advertisements that change when a user's mouse passes over them.	TechTarget, 2005, April 5
Rich Media	"Information that consists of any combination of graphics, audio, video and animation, which is more storage and bandwidth intensive than ordinary text." "it exhibits dynamic motion. This motion may occur over time or in direct response to user interaction."	PCmag,1981- 2011 University of Washington,2010, September 8
Simulation	The technique of imitating the behavior of a situation or process through the application of a suitably analogous situation or apparatus, particularly for the purpose of study or personnel training. Simulation in e-learning and academic are generally considered to be scenarios that engage learners in real-world settings with experience representing learning goals.	OED, 2010b

user control or an animated, interactive file embedded in a web page (University of Washington, 2010, September 8).

Rich Media as Simulation

One form of rich media that is gaining popularity in e-learning and web-based educational offering is simulation. Adams & Valiga (2009) noted that "simulations can be acted out in a classroom, played on a board, or run on a computer, and they can be incorporated into almost any course. Research suggests that well-chosen simulations can enhance student learning and motivation (DeNeve & Heppner, 1997; McCarthy & Anderson, 2000; Hertel & Millis, 2002; as cited in Adams & Valiga, 2009). Simulations may take different formats such as role playing, board and computer games, and virtual worlds (Educause Learning Initiative, 2006; Frederick, 1981; New Media Consortium and Educause Learning Initiative, 2007; Rymaszewski, Au, Wallace, Winters, Ondrejka, Batstone-Cunningham & Rosedale, 2006; Van Eck, 2006; Adams & Valiga, 2009). Some colleges and universities use virtual worlds for role playing and scenario building where learners can engage in interactivities that enhance course assessment and application of new knowledge and skills (Adams & Valiga, 2009, p. 231.)

Nehring (2010) noted that the application of simulation "in its many forms, has been a beneficial adjunct to teaching nursing since the beginning of formalized nursing education" (p. 6) with its purpose being to replicate some aspects of the clinical situation to be more easily understood when encountered in real clinical practice (Morton, 1995, p. 76; as cited in Nehring, 2010, p. 6)

The effectiveness of simulations as with other forms of learning and rich media require a certain degree of instructional support or structure (Nehring, 2010, p. 226). One of the most important factors concerning rich media and simulations is that learners are active participants in the learning process rather than passive observers as with

many forms of traditional education such as lecture and test taking (Nehring, 2010, p. 226). Studies by Leeper and Malone (1985) on motivational elements found in computer games noted that primary motivators were challenge, self-competence, curiosity, personal control, and fantasy.

The application of simulation, particularly high-fidelity simulation, has been seen for decades in nursing education and curriculum. The sixth essential in the Revised Essentials of Baccalaureate Nursing Education (AACN, 2008), stated that "Interpersonal communication and collaboration for improving patient health outcomes" – specifically addressing the use of simulation. NCSBN, 2006; Nehring, 2010).

A combination of Patricia Benner's (1984) Novice to Practice Model for nursing skill acquisition and simulation have been noted by a number of nursing experts and clinicians such as Ferguson and colleagues' (2004) nursing staff model, Long' (2005) high-fidelity patient simulation for resuscitation skill learning, and Waldner and Olson's (2007) combination of Benner's first three stages with Kolb's (1984) experiential learning as a framework for using high-fidelity simulation in nursing curriculum (Nehring, 2010).

The use of simulation in clinical settings has been also recommended by the Health Resources and Services Administration (HRSA, 2002) and implied that faculty develop skills on the use and application of simulation (Nehring, 2010, p. 6). Boller & Jones (2008) identified the need for the revision of existing nursing curricula to include the use of simulation with appropriate infrastructure needs developed and supported. Bristol, 2006; Oregon Nursing Leadership Council, 2005; Waneka, 2008 noted that this perspective has been supported by state nursing workforce reports 15 states as a way to enhance nursing student experience, increase numbers of nursing students and provide a cost-effective utilization of scarce faculty resources.

Alternate forms of simulation in e-learning include the concept of the simulation as a freestanding virtual world or course-hosting device (Adams & Valiga, 2009, p. 231). Some universities and colleges house courses or parts of them on virtual worlds or simulation web sites such as Second Life (Rymaszewski, Au & Wallace, et al., 2006; Educause Learning Initiative, June 2008) or the open source software Croquet (Saulnier, D. (2008, January 23).

With these environments, learners create their own avatars and participate in real and virtual meetings, avatars communicate with each other though text media or VoIP (Voice over Internet protocol) allowing learners to speak with each other (Educause Learning Initiative, June 2008; as cited in Adams & Valiga, 2009, p. 231). In conclusion, rich media, especially simulation can be a valuable tool for e-learning educators to enhance course content and provide safe virtual real-world scenarios where learners can interact and practice newly discovered skills and knowledge. The remainder of this chapter will focus on the Riverbend City Simulation project at Capella University as an example of how simulation can be effectively applied in an online e-learning academic setting.

ISSUES, CONTROVERSIES AND PROBLEMS

The Capella Story: The Beginning

One cold winter day in December, a casual conversation between two colleagues at Capella University in Minneapolis, Minnesota turned from technology and infrastructure to how to enrich the current eLearning environment with rich media and simulation. This initial conversation between Jesse Rosel, MS, Manager of Interactive Media; Next Generation Learning Department and Ann Leslie Claesson, PhD, PDP, FACHE, core faculty member in the School of Public Service Leadership at Capella University began the dialogue of how to bring new forms or rich media into the

online classroom. Initial ideas involved the use of course-specific gaming, simulation with extension decision-tree branching, and even virtual worlds (Claesson, A. personal communication, February 2011). As the excitement built it was quickly decided that the first step must be to narrow down the possibilities to one type of rich media: simulation.

Early conversations focused on basic simulations, educational games and the newly announced nursing program. Conversations quickly evolved into a multidisciplinary approach that would span several programs and dozens of courses. In collaboration with the Portfolio Strategies team and the School of Public Service Leadership, we identified a scenario-based, multimedia simulation as the best possible solution to meet the learning objectives of the program (Rosel, J. personal communication, February 2011).

Capella University is an accredited online university that offers degree programs for working adults in a variety of professional disciplines. Among Capella's many offerings are advanced degrees in public service fields such as nursing, public health, public administration, and public safety. Capella takes a cross-disciplinary approach to instruction in these fields, since it is critical that professionals in these disciplines learn how to work effectively with each other.

It was critical that the School of Public Service Leadership provide learners with an experience where they could develop and demonstrate their ability to collaborate in multidisciplinary and interagency situations (Council on Education for Public Health, n.d; National Center for Healthcare Leadership, 2010-2011,a,b) Professional organizations and accrediting entities had stressed the importance of teaching these skills, and the school's challenge was how to do so in an asynchronous online setting (National Council of State Boards of Nursing, 2005; Waneka, 2008)

After brainstorming with faculty and business leadership, several iterations of project proposals, and the development of an Interactive Media Simulation team, it was determined that a scenario-based, multimedia simulation was the best solution. The simulation would allow learners to observe, analyze, and discuss situations that had been specifically created for their program and course. This scenario-based learning model provides a greater level of engagement than other models as well as encouraging critical thinking and creative problem solving (Davis, 2009; Bristol, 2006; Hertel & Millis, 2002).

In order to highlight multidisciplinary collaboration, it was decided that the simulation would present a consistent storyline based on an emergency incident—a train derailment and chemical spill set in a fictional location named Riverbend City. This storyline would allow the team to integrate and present the perspectives of leadership within each of the public service disciplines. The ultimate goal of the project was, and continues to be, to empower learners to envision their ability to combine collaboration and leadership when working with multiple disciplines in a real-life situation.

The core engine, which includes proprietary code and assets (UI, characters, and locations), had been completed by April, 2010 and the first course to launch with Riverbend City "missions" went live in July 2010. Since then, more than 30 courses and over 70 missions have been completed. As a result of having reached organizational criteria, plans have been made to expand the project.

Riverbend City was integrated into the courses through missions, which consisted of several related scenes in the simulation specific to the course competencies. Missions were self-contained and are a more detailed expansion of a set of specific scenes linked together to provide learners with objectives to be accomplished both in the simulation and in course activities such as discussion or assignments.

Many U.S.-based academic institutions rely upon primarily Flash-based media integrated into online classrooms bringing such features as animations, illustrations, and interactive exercises into the e-Learning environment. It was decided that we should begin with a basic simulation type of media using our current media software and design capabilities; hence the Riverbend City simulation was born. Initially it was hoped that this could expand into a type of virtual world with avatars, interaction between students across programs and courses with and aspect of gaming thrown in for excitement. The reality of this project required that we start small and work up to a larger scale depending on how our offering was accepted. Our "simulation" was to be set in a virtual city (that was static), be designed large enough to include room for expansion later on, and use illustrations rather than video to deliver content. A key factor, scalability, was included early to ensure adaptability to potential new programs as the simulation gained acceptance and demand grew.

Key Players

In June 2009, the newly formed School of Public Service Leadership approached Capella's Interactive Media team to explore multimedia solutions that support the learning objectives for their programs. These programs included health administration, non-profit administration, nursing, public administration, public health and public safety. Within six months, our proposal had been accepted and the project kicked off in December 2009.

Key players were chosen and the groundwork for the project began in the summer of 2009 shifting to project status based in the Interactive Media Department; Next Generation Learning Department. It was imperative that the initial development team involve:

- management

Figure 1. Riverbend City initial opening decision mission

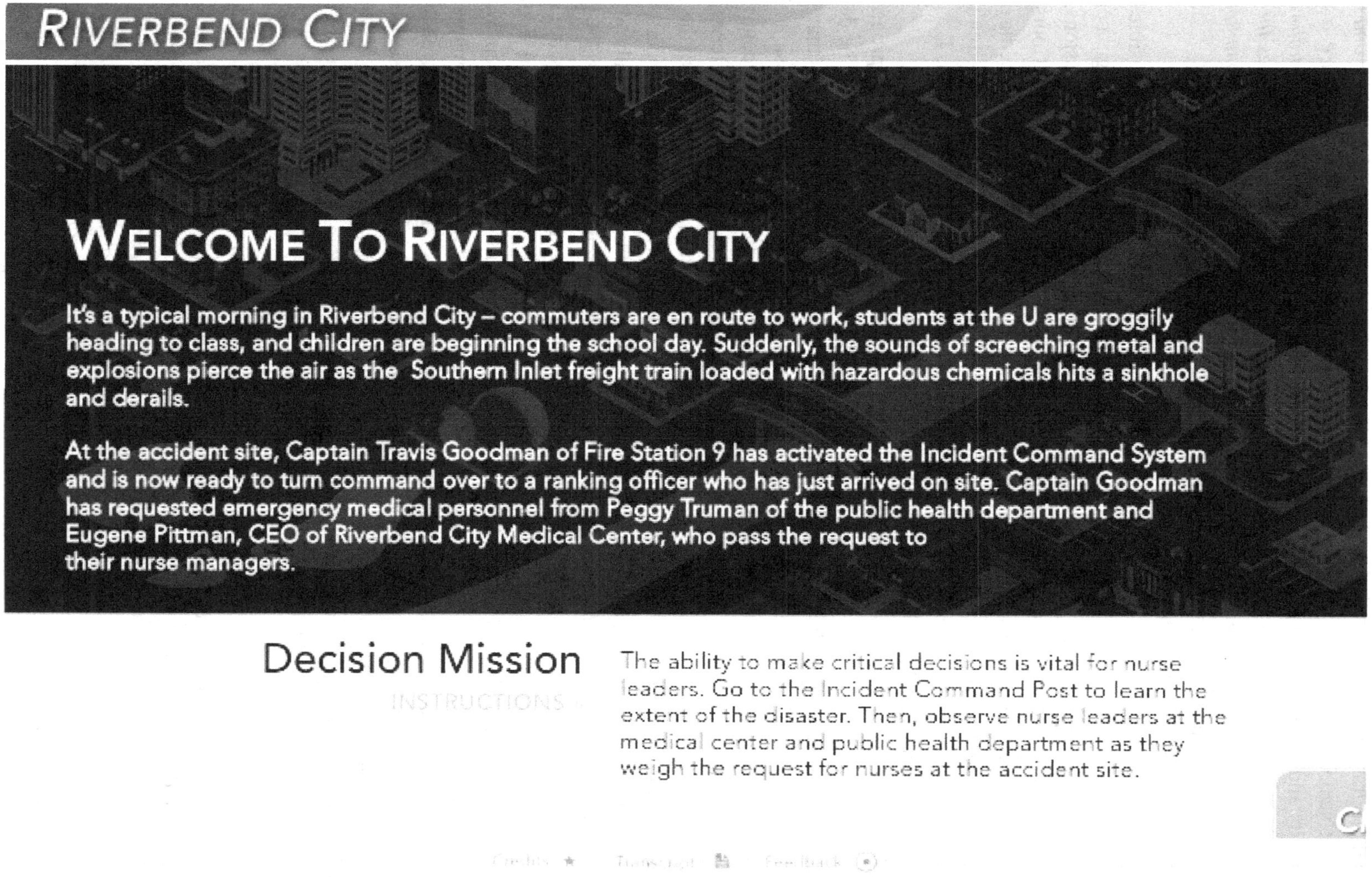

RIVERBEND CITY

WELCOME TO RIVERBEND CITY

It's a typical morning in Riverbend City – commuters are en route to work, students at the U are groggily heading to class, and children are beginning the school day. Suddenly, the sounds of screeching metal and explosions pierce the air as the Southern Inlet freight train loaded with hazardous chemicals hits a sinkhole and derails.

At the accident site, Captain Travis Goodman of Fire Station 9 has activated the Incident Command System and is now ready to turn command over to a ranking officer who has just arrived on site. Captain Goodman has requested emergency medical personnel from Peggy Truman of the public health department and Eugene Pittman, CEO of Riverbend City Medical Center, who pass the request to their nurse managers.

Decision Mission
INSTRUCTIONS

The ability to make critical decisions is vital for nurse leaders. Go to the Incident Command Post to learn the extent of the disaster. Then, observe nurse leaders at the medical center and public health department as they weigh the request for nurses at the accident site.

- course development, interactive design and programming from the media perspective (Next Generation Learning)
- faculty and organizational input (School of Public Service Leadership) on course application, learner interface
- interaction with curriculum and one school (Public Service Leadership) in Capella University.

The key players in the Riverbend City Simulation Project Interactive Media Team were: Jesse Rosel, MS, Manager of Interactive Course Media; Felicity Pearson, Media Course Developer; LaVonne Carlson, Interactive Designer, Matthew Johnson, Programmer; and Ann Leslie Claesson, PhD, PSP, FACHE, Core Faculty and Instructional Designer.

Jesse Rosel's role, in addition to the initial concept, concerned the management and coordination of the project as well as acquisition of resources, staff and university support.

I manage the Interactive Media team at Capella. Our team is responsible for designing and delivering the educational multimedia for Capella's online courses. We collaborate with course developers (aka: instructional designers) and subject matter experts (faculty) to determine how multimedia can support the learning objectives of each course. Multimedia solutions may include illustrations, animations, videos, interactive activities and simulations. The team is composed of designers, developers, writers and project managers (Rosel, J., personal communication, February 2011).

It was Felicity Pearson's role as Media Course Developer, to design and direct scripting for the simulation and subsequent "missions" that guided learners in each course.

My role is to find a narrative approach to the competencies that the Riverbend City simulations are intended to address. My contribution of the story line to the custom interactive and learning activities helps learners experience a realistic scenario that has been specifically tailored to the competencies and learner outcomes for a given course (Pearson, F., personal communication, February 2011).

LaVonne Carlson was responsible for the illustrations and interactive design portion of the simulations and individual missions. "As an interactive designer on the Capella Course Media team, I help plan and create multimedia elements that align to course competencies and enhance the courseroom experience "(Carlson, L., personal communication, February 2011).

Matthew Johnson's unique programming abilities enabled the simulation to be developed on a scalable, flexible "engine" that allowed designers to efficiently create missions and add new interactivity tools. "My role contributes to a unique learning experience by offering sophisticated I interactive tools tailored to the creative imaginations of our course developers. Custom interactive and learning activities allow us to set Capella apart from other programs "(Johnson, M., personal communication, February 2011).

Ann Leslie Claesson's role in addition to the initial brainstorming and concept with Jesse Rosel, involved faculty involvement, subject matter expertise and development of the initial storyline with Lead Media Course Developer, Felicity Pearson, and coordination of input from the School of Public Service Leadership.

If we can capture the interest of our learners and allow them to demonstrate what they know through the Riverbend City simulation perhaps when they encounter a similar situation in the real world they will be better equipped to deal with it in a rationale and effective manner." (Claesson, A. L., personal communication, February 2011).

Phase I: Brainstorming and Initial Idea Development

Curriculum and Media Matching

It was critical that the School of Public Service Leadership provide learners with an experience where they could develop and demonstrate their ability to collaborate in multidisciplinary and interagency situations. Professional organizations and accrediting entities had stressed the importance of teaching these skills, and the school's challenge was how to do so in an asynchronous online setting (Adams & Valiga, 2009; McCarthy & Anderson, 2000; McKeachie & Svinicki, 2006; NCHL, 2010-2011, a, b; CePH, n.d; AACN, 2008).

After brainstorming with faculty and business leadership, and several iterations of project proposals, the team determined that a scenario-based, multimedia simulation was the best solution. The simulation would allow learners to observe, analyze, and discuss situations that had been specifically created for their program and course. Scenario-based learning provides a greater level of engagement than other models as well as encouraging critical thinking and creative problem solving.

In order to highlight multidisciplinary collaboration, it was decided that the simulation would present a consistent storyline based on an emergency incident—a train derailment and chemical spill set in a fictional location named Riverbend City. This storyline would allow the team to integrate and present the perspectives of leadership within each of the public service disciplines. The ultimate goal of the project was, and continues to be, to empower learners to envision their ability to combine collaboration and leadership when working with multiple disciplines in a real-life situation. The central storyline was designed around a disaster scenario involving a train derailment and chemical spill in a metropolitan city divided by a river (RiverBend City).

Case Study 1—Riverbend City: Getting Started

As the Lead Media Course Developer, the job of scripting the initial storyline and coordinating subsequent min-stories (missions) per course fell to Felicity Pearson.

As a course developer for Capella, my focus has always been on aligning the competencies with the course room activities. So, from my perspective, the direction was always toward alignment – what is the purpose of the mission? What competency does it allow the learner to practice? (Pearson, F., personal communication, February 2011).

The initial storyline development was exciting, stimulating and at times overwhelming as it was difficult to conceptualize something specific enough to address competencies for courses from multiple programs including nursing, emergency management, and public administration. Alignment of course objectives and competencies was paramount for new and existing courses, particularly those who were accredited by external accrediting bodies such as the nursing and public health (Pearson, F., personal communication, February 2011; Claesson, A. L. personal communication, February 2011; AACN, 2008).

Early missions centered around the hospital and the impact of the chemical spill disaster on health care. The story revolved around hospital administrators and medical personnel reacting to the crisis. This included a response to what happened at the school yard – children injured, and one died. Another important early theme was the development of three ethnic neighborhoods to reflect cultural issues in the city and in response to the disaster. The Shoals neighborhood was primarily Hmong, Longley is Somali, and Ruby Lake was Latino. A mission in the Shoals community evolved around a Hmong child who was brought into the ER exposed to fumes. He

Figure 2. Riverbend City introduction

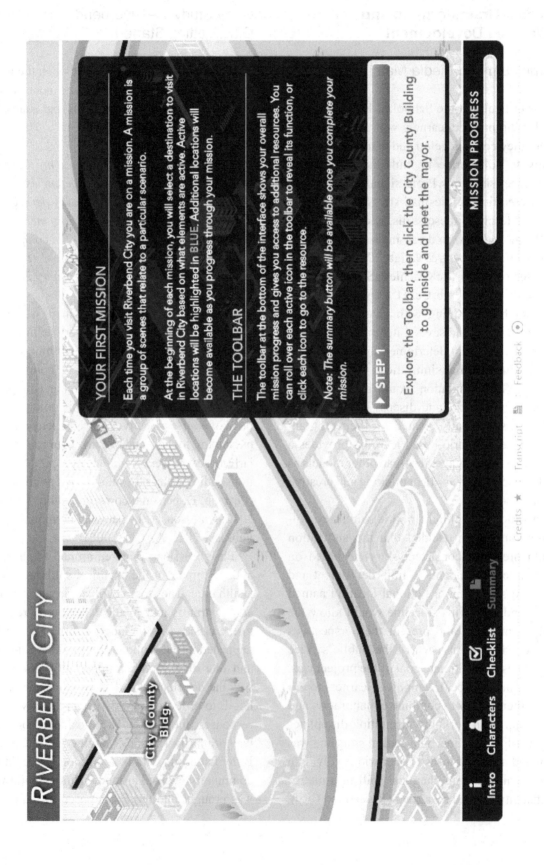

Figure 3. Case study 2: Riverbend City principles of cultural competence

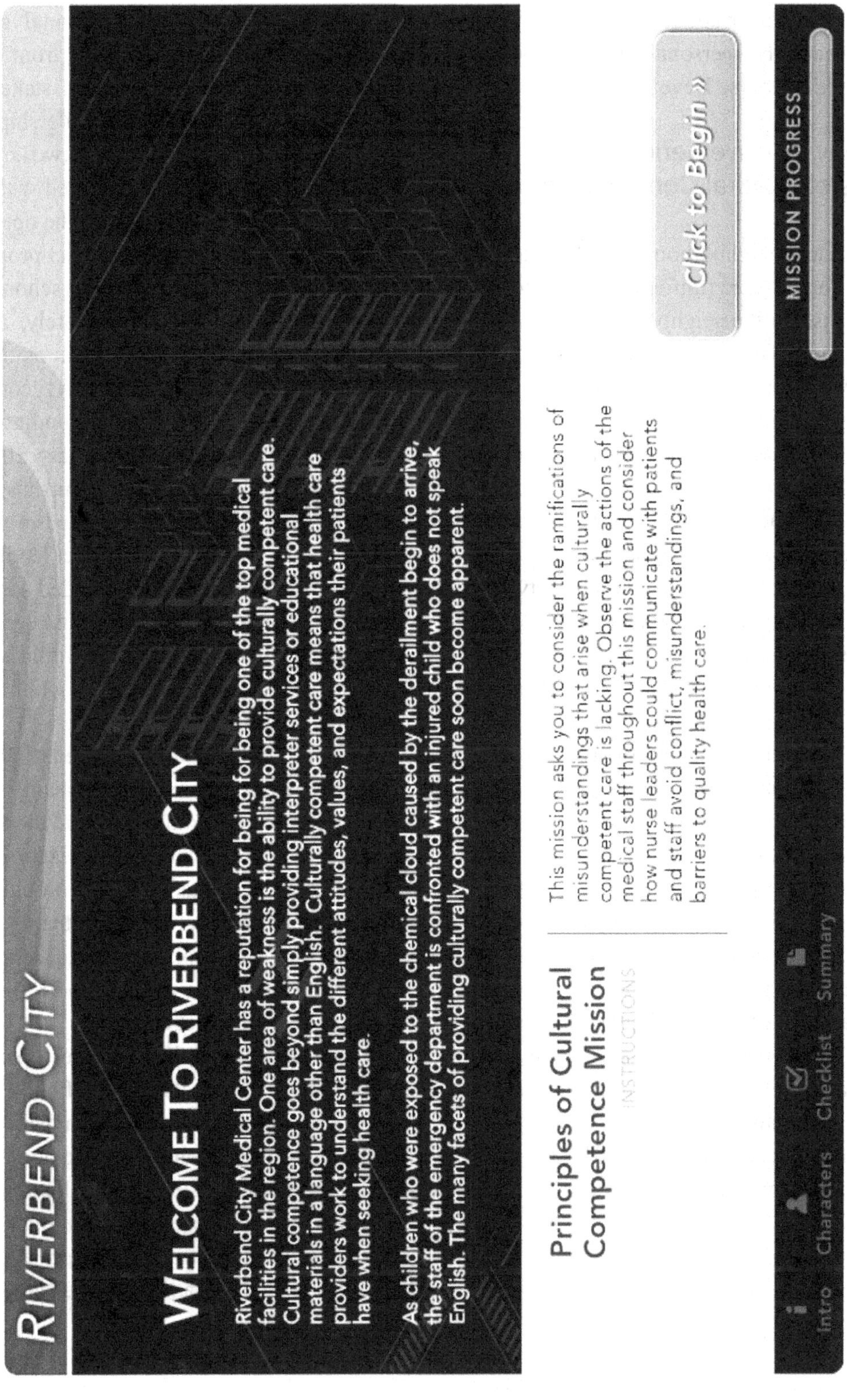

had "welts" on his back that were the result of coining, a traditional Hmong healing practice. A nurse thought he'd been abused and called CPS, prompting a discussion about cultural sensitivity (Rockler-Glader, B., personal communication, February Media Course Developer).

Case Study 2—Riverbend City Principles of Cultural Competence

In the Longley neighborhood, public service courses explored a lead (unfounded) that home-grown terrorists in the neighborhood caused the train derailment. The Ruby Lake, the neighborhood which has been developed the most, provided multiple explorations into the evacuation of the neighborhood after the spill, and then the experience neighborhood people had at the shelter. Later developments expanded into exploration of the effects of the chemical spill on a nearby Indian reservation, a nearby rural community, and the bordering country of Canexico. In late 2010 we started moving away from the chemical spill story and into more spinoff stories focusing on events about a year after the spill.

While the initial concept revolved around strategies for implementing complex multimedia scenarios in the nursing program, it soon expanded to include all of the programs in the School of Public Service Leadership! "Everyone wanted to be included and were determined that they to be left behind" (Claesson, A.L., personal communication, February 2011). In short, the original concept was to create a multimedia simulation that would allow learners to engage with real-world scenarios related to their discipline with a less linear, more game-like simulation (Rosel, J., personal communication, February 2011; Johnson, M., personal communication, February 2011).

Organizational Considerations: Phases and Plans

Capella University's organizational structure required that we obtain "buy-in" from multiple groups and internal and external stakeholders. The School of Public Service Leadership and the Portfolio Strategies team were the two key groups that had input. Next, they partnered with the Interactive Media team to identify the opportunity and propose a solution. The project proposal required support from the sponsoring school (Public Service Leadership) and, ultimately, approval from the Portfolio Strategies team as they held the decision-making responsibility concerning which initiatives would receive funding (Rosel, J., personal communication, February 2011). The School of Public Service Leadership has a Health Advisory Board which participated in the early brainstorming phase of the project lending their expertise and advice. They provided some great ideas/advice and confirmed that a disaster scenario was a good way to go; hence it would allow for the most "multidisciplinary" interaction between characters and agencies.

Once the project was approved, the Interactive Media team partnered with faculty to begin development of the simulation, and the Portfolio Strategies team and University leadership continued to be key stakeholders throughout the project. The key management team included executive sponsorship, program leadership, and stakeholder engagement and support from Day 1 and throughout project duration.

It should be noted that this interdepartmental collaboration of the School of Public Service Leadership, the Interactive Media team, and the Portfolio Strategies team proved to be a very successful partnership. Departmental and specialty expertise was provided without overstepping boundaries and bogging down the project. Project duties were divided among these stakeholders:

subject matter expertise for course-specific curriculum was provided by the School of Public Service Leadership, business and budget expertise was provided by the Portfolio Strategies team and instructional design, script writing and multimedia expertise was supplied by the Interactive Media team (Rosel, J., personal communication, February 2011; Claesson, A.L., personal communication, February 2011).

Since this was the first project of this scope and complexity at Capella for the Interactive Media team there was no existing groundwork or infrastructure to build upon. To acquire knowledge and expertise of media projects of this magnitude it was decided to hire a consultant from Filament Games to advise us in how to get started based on their experience in developing educational games. The consultant held a workshop for the project team to begin organizing ideas into an initial set of requirements. Using templates that Filament games uses to design educational games, the consultant walked us through their processes as an example for how to approach a project like the Riverbend City Simulation.

Once project work officially began after the consulting sessions with Filament Games, the initial approach was to develop all aspects of the storyline, including characters and locations, up front. However, as the simulation project began to grow it quickly became evident that we needed to shift our approach due to the need for input from subject matter experts (Rosel, J., personal communication, February 2011). We revised our approach to focusing on the developing the details of the storyline as we developed each individual course. This was "similar to writing chapters of a book over time instead of writing the entire book in one setting" (Rosel, J., personal communication, February 2011). The main point was that we needed to collaborate with each subject matter expert assigned to a course to ensure that we were meeting the objectives of each course and delivering content and a simulated real-world experience that was appropriate to the course and program

(Rosel, J. personal communication, February 2011; Claesson, A.L., personal communication, February 2011).

Assumptions

Part of the evolution of creative projects such as Riverbend City are the assumptions and expectations that each member of the team beings with them.

Assumptions that Were True

Initial assumptions from a technology and programming perspective were that the simulation would be browser based and delivered via Flash technology since "Flash is an efficient way to deliver complex, interactive multimedia without additional software requirements" (Johnson, M., personal communication, February 2011). Primary assumptions for technology and programming pertained to implementing the ideas of others and presumed expertise of technical limitations and complexity. This assumption turned out to be true as the team was limited by the available software and resources to build a simulation beyond what we were capable of at this point in time.

Management and stakeholder assumptions were more from a pedagogical perspective where the assumption that the storyline of the simulation would focus on a multidisciplinary experience. It was absolutely essential that there was effective collaboration between script writers (Media Course Developers) and subject matter experts (Faculty) in order to meet the learning objectives of the Public Service Leadership programs (Rosel, J., personal communication, February 2011).

Assumptions that Were False

There was the assumption that learners would be able to move freely throughout Riverbend City, that they could interact with one another and that there would be a decision-tree type of interactive mechanism where learners could affect the outcome of a mission (Claesson, A.L. personal communication, February 2011). External assumptions by internal and external stakeholders included a simulation comparable to a video game with avatars and gaming characteristics, and that new missions and even storylines could be developed rapidly and incorporated into any and all courses in a program or school (Claesson, A.L. personal communication, February 2011). In the end, Riverbend City turned out to not be an open-ended, virtual environment where learners could use avatars to interact with their fellow learners; hence this assumption turned out to be false.

Case Study 3—Riverbend City: Vulnerable Populations

Phase II: Development and Logistics

Curricular Considerations and Learner Interactivity

One of the first steps in the development Riverbend City simulation was to define the basic storyline. It needed to be interesting enough to appeal to learners, be able to be incorporated into multiple programs, and "fit" within the current curricular structure used by Capella University. "Capella's approach to course development is to create a course in which all activities can be clearly linked to the defined course competencies" (Pearson, F., personal communication, February 2011). All of the activities assigned to a course need to be specific enough to accurately address the learner outcomes and provide a method for assessment of knowledge and skill acquisition at the curricular level.

While it seemed easy initially, this proved to be rather challenging as the excitement of developing the baseline story gained momentum. Riverbend City, in its current form, is based upon a central storyline of a disaster scenario in a large metropolitan city. There is a train derailment due to a

sinkhole developing under the train track. This led to a chemical spill and subsequent environmental and health hazards that spread across the city.

Individual "missions" were used to create scenes within the simulation specific to courses and learning objectives. There could be two or more missions per course tied directly to course discussions or assignments. These missions could be used to delineate knowledge acquisition, provide data and scenario-based interaction or show how information could be applied in a simulated real-world experience with positive or negative results. It was the learner's responsibility to view the simulation, obtain required data and information needed to complete the assessment activity, and then analyze the scenario based on the requirements of the assessment (e.g., discussion, assignment, etc.).

In addition to the fundamental storyline, learner engagement and interactivity with the simulation was needed beyond the scenarios to link simulation to the curricular requirements. Interactive elements were needed that required learners to prioritize steps or walk a character through a decision to enhance the learner's experience of the mission beyond that of merely observation. "By asking them to make choices in the context of the scenario and then defend those choices in discussions with their peers and instructors, we bring them into the multidisciplinary setting that we've developed" (Pearson, F., personal communication, February 2011).

Capella learners and faculty in School of Public Service Leadership programs are the key beneficiaries of the project. To date, simulation missions are integrated in 36 courses with more courses planned for development in 2011. As mentioned above, learners with disabilities are also able to benefit from the simulation. The key benefit, or more specifically the critical learning objective, is an experience that will: (1) enhance learning; (2) challenge learners to have a multidisciplinary perspective; and (3) increase engagement with real-world scenarios.

Figure 4. Case Study 3. Riverbend City – Vulnerable Populations Learner Interactivity

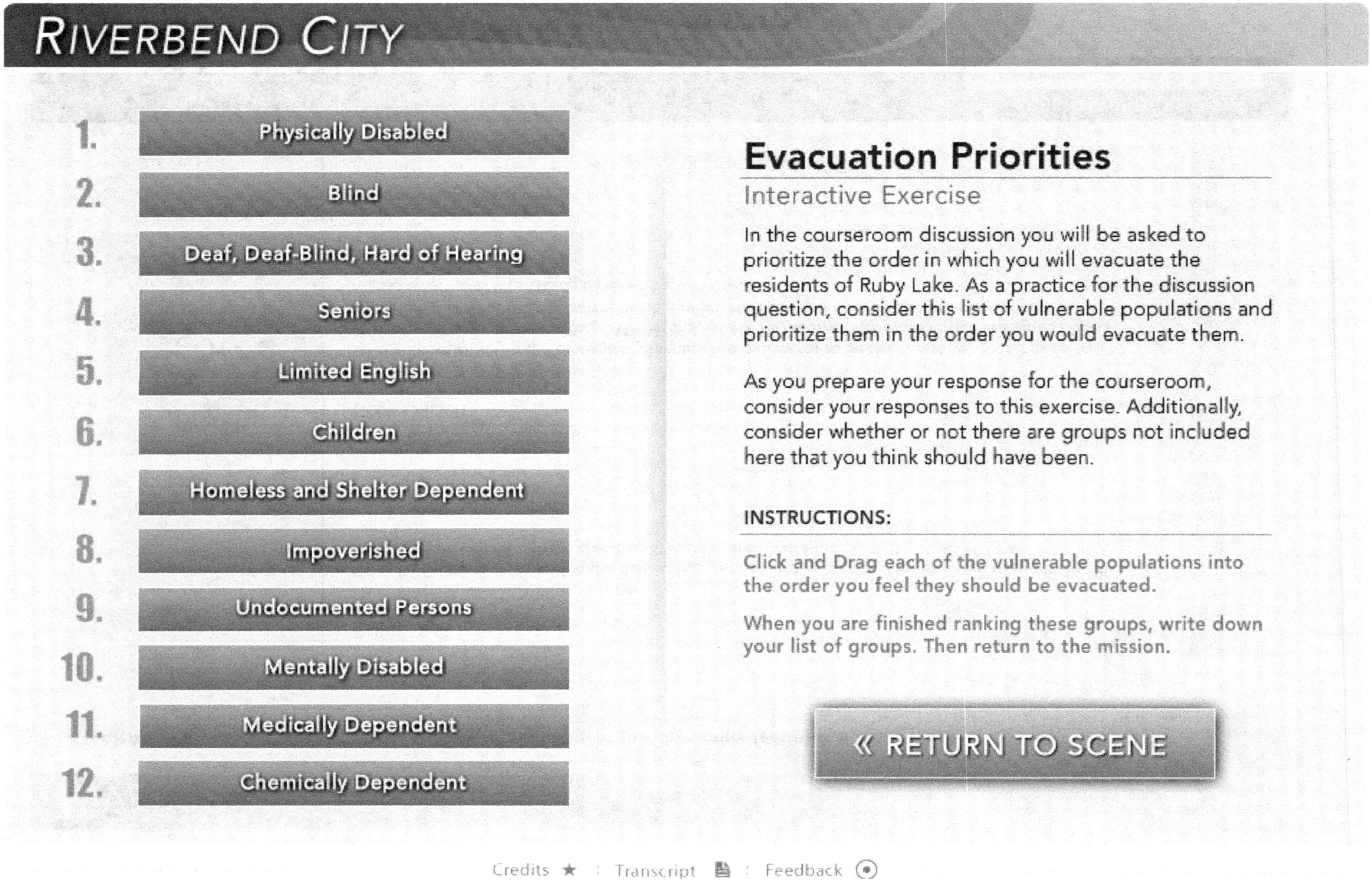

RIVERBEND CITY

Evacuation Priorities

Interactive Exercise

In the courseroom discussion you will be asked to prioritize the order in which you will evacuate the residents of Ruby Lake. As a practice for the discussion question, consider this list of vulnerable populations and prioritize them in the order you would evacuate them.

As you prepare your response for the courseroom, consider your responses to this exercise. Additionally, consider whether or not there are groups not included here that you think should have been.

INSTRUCTIONS:

Click and Drag each of the vulnerable populations into the order you feel they should be evacuated.

When you are finished ranking these groups, write down your list of groups. Then return to the mission.

« RETURN TO SCENE

1. Physically Disabled
2. Blind
3. Deaf, Deaf-Blind, Hard of Hearing
4. Seniors
5. Limited English
6. Children
7. Homeless and Shelter Dependent
8. Impoverished
9. Undocumented Persons
10. Mentally Disabled
11. Medically Dependent
12. Chemically Dependent

Credits ★ : Transcript 📖 : Feedback ◉

Figure 5. RiverBend City downloadable items in mission

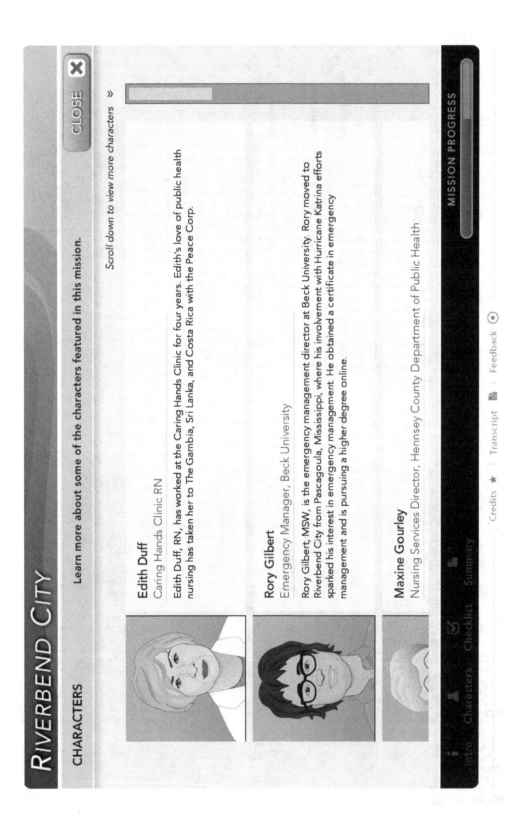

Graphics, Audio and Video

Initial considerations for the look and sound of the Riverbend City Simulation were based on a number of factors:

- Professional & realistic look and feel (i.e. realistic looking characters)
- Scalability (we knew this would be an ongoing project and not just a one-time initiative, so being able to efficiently create new missions was essential. This is why we decided to go with static illustrations instead of 3D and/or character animations).
- Narration that added to the realism of the experience (this is why we went with voice actors).
- Current skill sets already on the team

Several different styles of graphics and interactivity were presented and once the "look" had been agreed upon the graphics, audio, scripting and character development began. Character development involved descriptions in terms of age, gender, ethnicity, and physical appearance. Casting the audio portion, particularly matching the voices to the graphic character proved to be more difficult and complex than we'd first imagined. "We are using voice talent who are primarily geared toward commercial or industrial work. Finding people who can create compelling characters with their voices is a key element to creating engaging scenarios" (Pearson, F., personal communication, February 2011).

It became clearer that the character development was becoming the focus of each mission, the decision was made that by using voice talent and more detailed portraits we could enhance our capabilities of capturing the essence of each character as opposed to just written text and generic people icons (Carlson, L., personal communication, February 2011).

As the scope of the project increased it became clear that the level of detail that could be feasibly

produced needed to be defined. This led to a concentration on creating illustrated assets that could easily be repurposed. For instance, locations were drawn in an isometric view so that objects could be easily reused no matter where they were located in the scene. In addition, instead of creating detailed illustrations for each dialog scene, we created portraits to represent the people in a conversation (Carlson, L., personal communication, February 2011). This prevented the need to create a unique illustration for every new conversation.

It was also important for us to take in account the skill-set of our team. Early on, we did discuss creating a 3D city, but decided against it because this was not something we had a lot of experience in, so it might strain the timeline, and at that point it was clear that we might not know the exact needs of a course until a month before the deadline (Carlson, L., personal communication, February 2011).

To take advantage of existing resources, media course developers have been encouraged to reuse existing characters for multiple purposes whenever possible. For example, school superintendent Bruce Greenburg typically appears in school related missions, but was "borrowed" from the End of Life mission, where he deals with his father's terminal illness. Media course developers are also encouraged to reuse existing locations.

Time constraints did restrict the final product in some ways, but overall the team and stakeholders were pleased with the final project and its user ability. The team had to stagger feature enhancements instead of rolling them all out at once. For example, a branching interactive option wasn't something we added until the third full development cycle.

Recently, Capella conducted an anonymous, online survey with 30 learners who have encountered the Riverbend City simulation in their courses. The results have been overwhelmingly

Figure 6. RiverBend City characters

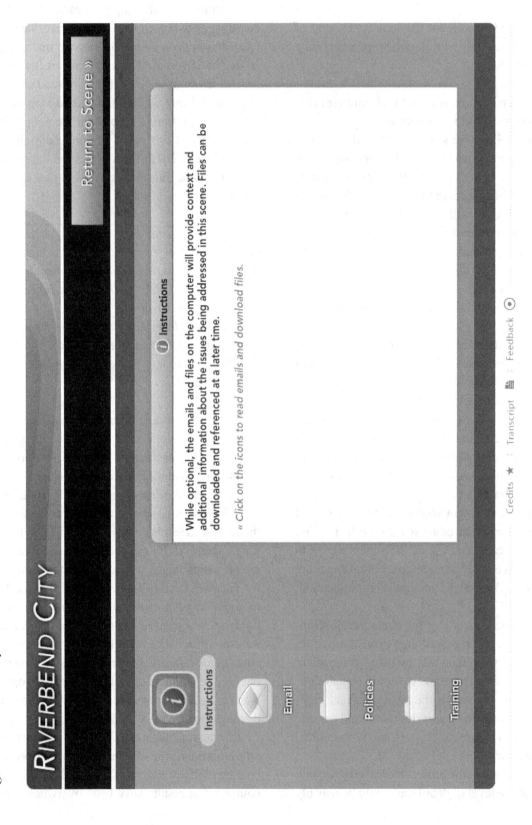

positive and confirm that the simulation has successfully met the learning objectives. Table 2 is a summary of the results.

Open-ended questions concerning learner perception of Riverbend City simulation experience included: "Hands-on learning puts a visual to an actual emergency management situation," "I liked the realistic issues discussed," and "It provided an artificial real life experience. I could easily relate to the issues being explored more so than merely reading about it."

The missions were built so that simple animation could be added to scenes with more detailed illustrations in the dialog scenes as needed (Carlson, L., personal communication, February 2011). Advantages of the final product provided flexibility and a streamlined production. Illustration assets could be pieced together to create new scenes, and this greatly speeded up the production process allowing new locations and characters to be easily created as needed (Carlson, L., personal communication, February 2011).

Programming, User Interface and Functionality

Riverbend City was designed as large infrastructure and user interface that could be expanded due to the demand of future projects and requirements. The basic structure of Riverbend City was designed and developed on a "core engine" or framework that included the backend code and the design assets that would serve as the building block for all future missions. The backend code drove the functionality and interactivity of the simulation while the design assets were the locations, buildings and user interface elements. "The most I interesting part for me is how I was able to build a general framework that will make many of our media projects easier to develop. The framework applies far beyond the Riverbend City project" (Johnson, M., personal communication, February 2011).

The technology used to deliver the simulation experience is Flash and an internally developed Flash markup language nicknamed ActionML. We chose Flash because it is a ubiquitous plug-in in modern Web browsers. Flash does not require additional downloads for the end-user and it efficiently delivers interactivity over the Web. These are must-have requirements for Capella since 100 percent of courses are offered online.

The internally developed markup language, a full-featured ActionScript framework utilizing XML, allows designers to create interactivity for the simulation without relying on a developer to write the code. This technology enhances efficiency and reduces cost of producing simulation

Table 2. Riverbend City simulation survey results

Question	Agree or strongly agree	Average score
The Riverbend City scenario simulation will enhance my learning experience in future courses.	24/30 (80%)	4.0 out of 5
The Riverbend City simulation helped me understand the importance of multi-disciplinary collaboration.	26/30 (87%)	4.1 out of 5
The Riverbend City scenario simulation provided realistic issues for me to analyze.	29/30 (97%)	4.2 out of 5
The voice actors added value to the experience of the Riverbend City simulation.	25/28 (89%)	4.1 out of 5
I find these types of scenario simulations to be more engaging than reading articles, case studies, etc.	24/29 (83%)	4.0 out of 5
Likert Scale Questions (1 = strongly disagree, 3 = neither agree or disagree, 5 = strongly agree)		

missions for Capella courses. Flash was the main skill set supported by Capella's Course Media team. Choosing Flash as the technology meant that we could leverage the existing talent and expertise on the team.

Initially, it was decided that each mission would begin with a map of the entire city where learners could explore different geographic locations that would highlight when their cursor moved across them if they were a part of the mission for that course. Soon it became apparent that this could be redundant and that most courses only needed to focus on 1-3 locations: hence the idea of the larger city map was shelved. "The removal of this initial city map was a change to the User Interface that we eventually decided to make" (Carlson, L., personal communication, February 2011).

The Lead Designer created a collection of illustration assets, audio snippets, and functionality that could be "pieced" together to create unique missions which enabled her to re-use and polish existing characters and missions as needed. Once the first mission was created we tested its functionality and appeal through user usability tests or a pilot test of the mission from a learner perspective. "We spent a lot of time building animated transitions between scenes, but in usability tests, it was shown that most people found these distracting and felt that it slowed their progress through a mission" (Carlson, L., personal communication, February 2011). It was the access to information rather than visual effects that held the appeal for the users.

Case Study 4. Riverbend City – National Response Framework (NIMS) Mission

Implementation

Implementation of the RiverBend City simulation began with its infusion into courses in three different programs (nursing, public health and public administration) and three different academic levels (bachelor's, master's and doctoral). As the start dates for these courses came closer and RiverBend simulation went "live" it was met with praise and wonder by the faculty and learners alike. Finally there was a new way to acquire knowledge and apply skills based on a simulated real-world scenario where multi-disciplinary interaction was *de rigeur*. No longer were programs and learners relegated to traditional academic silo effect where learners only interacted with like members of their profession, Now, they were required to participate in interdisciplinary interactive exercises simulating the real-world encounters among disciplines that learners would encounter upon graduation or immersion onto their chosen field or profession (Claesson, A.L., personal communication, February 2011).

Courses at Capella are designed to clearly indicate how a given activity within a course aligns to the instructional goals of that particular course. The writers on the Riverbend City project (who are instructional designers) work with faculty subject matter experts to identify learning outcomes that could be illustrated through the simulation. During brainstorming sessions, the writers and subject matter experts would identify the various stakeholders in a given scenario and create situations that demonstrate opportunities for or challenges to collaboration.

Capella's courses are delivered through the Blackboard learning management system (LMS). Instruction is provided through assigned study activities, discussion opportunities, and graded assessments. The Riverbend City simulation is integrated into the course in the form of discrete missions. Missions are a collection of self-contained, competency-based scenes; a learner might encounter several missions in selected Public Service Leadership courses.

A learner accesses the Flash-based mission via a link in the study section of their course, launching a new browser window. The introductory screen

Figure 7. National response framework learner interactivity I

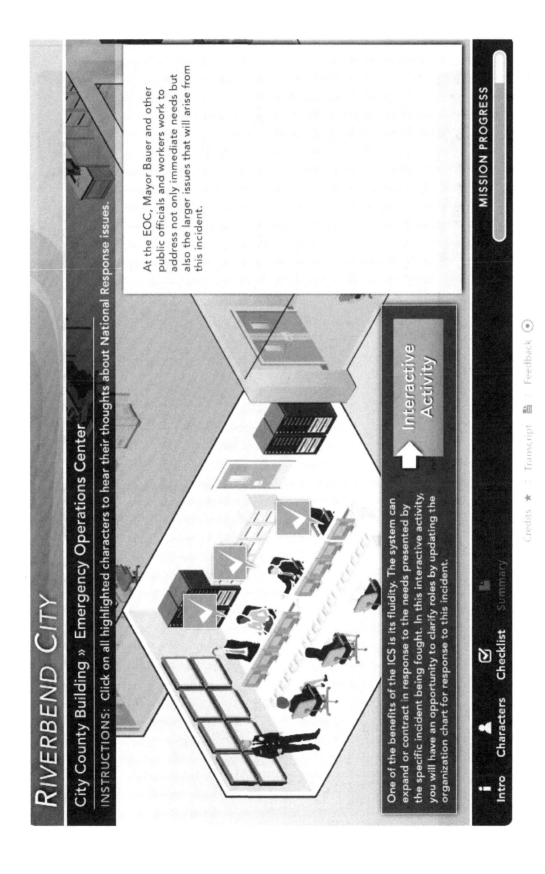

Figure 8. National response framework learner interactivity II

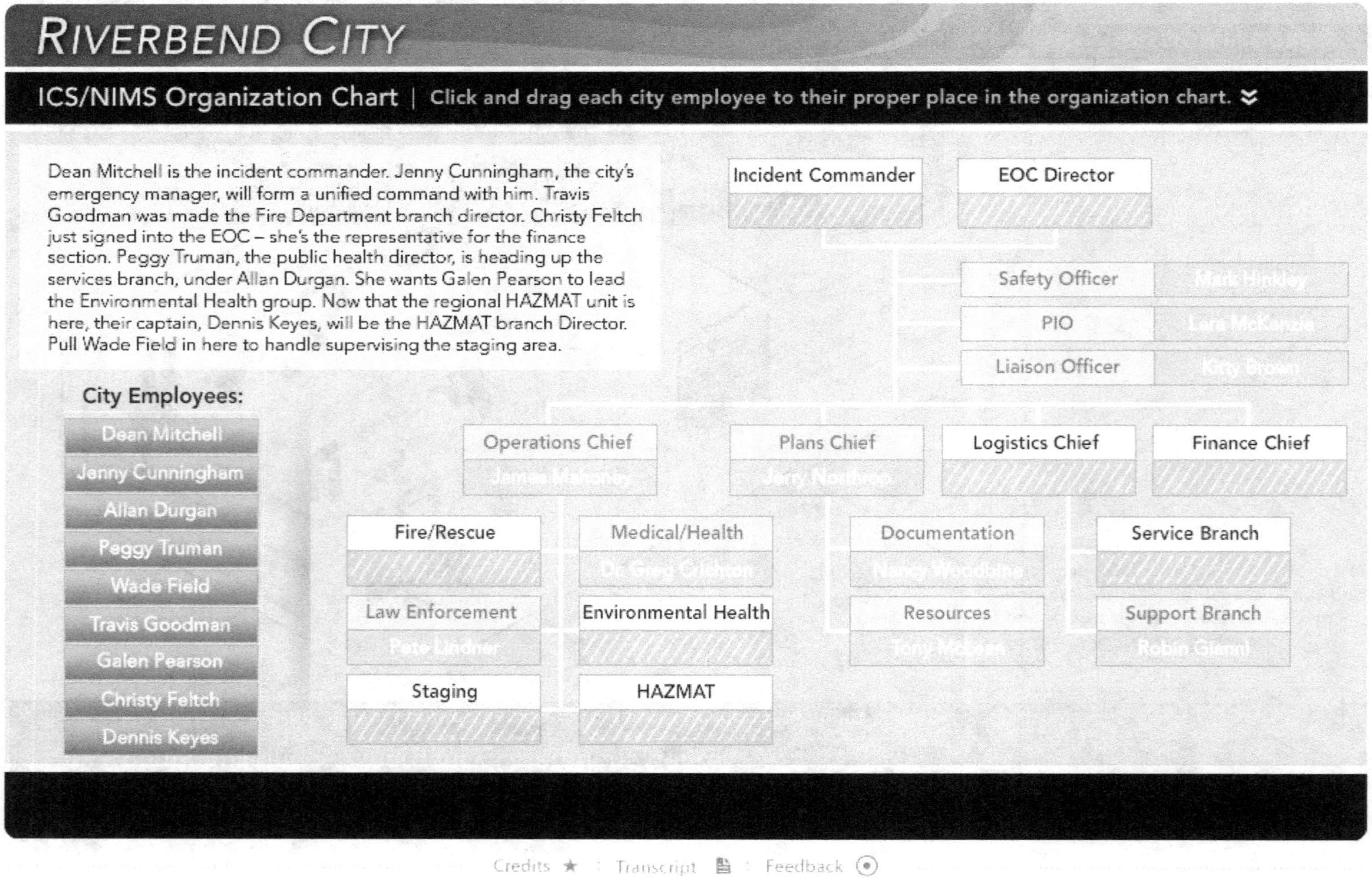

RIVERBEND CITY

ICS/NIMS Organization Chart | Click and drag each city employee to their proper place in the organization chart. »

Dean Mitchell is the incident commander. Jenny Cunningham, the city's emergency manager, will form a unified command with him. Travis Goodman was made the Fire Department branch director. Christy Feltch just signed into the EOC – she's the representative for the finance section. Peggy Truman, the public health director, is heading up the services branch, under Allan Durgan. She wants Galen Pearson to lead the Environmental Health group. Now that the regional HAZMAT unit is here, their captain, Dennis Keyes, will be the HAZMAT branch Director. Pull Wade Field in here to handle supervising the staging area.

City Employees:

Dean Mitchell
Jenny Cunningham
Allan Durgan
Peggy Truman
Wade Field
Travis Goodman
Galen Pearson
Christy Feltch
Dennis Keyes

Incident Commander   EOC Director

Safety Officer
PIO
Liaison Officer

Mark Hinkley
Lara McKenzie
Kitty Brown

Operations Chief   Plans Chief   Logistics Chief   Finance Chief

Fire/Rescue   Medical/Health   Documentation   Service Branch

Law Enforcement   Environmental Health   Resources   Support Branch

Staging   HAZMAT

James Moriarty
D. Gary Oldman
City Newhouse
Nancy Woodrine
Tony Nelsen
Robin Glienni
Pete Ulricher

Credits ★   Transcript 📖   Feedback ⊙

of the Riverbend City mission explains the focus of a particular mission and provides instruction to the learner about what she or he should do while moving through the mission. The learner then navigates through each scene, listening to conversations between characters and downloading relevant documents. The learner may also be required to complete a knowledge check, such as a mini-branching scenario or a drag-and-drop quiz. In the online course room, the learner writes a response to a discussion question or assignment that specifically addresses the topics and issues explored in the mission.

Some challenges noted during the implementation phase included keeping the plotlines straight especially, because the scenes were designed to be modular components that can be reused in future missions. There was a push to "always be thinking ahead when we write the story lines" (Pearson, F., personal communication, February 2011), especially after two new media course developers joined the project.

We faced these challenges: from the technology and programming perspective the greatest challenges was "figuring out what we wanted to build... [and] detail" (Johnson, M., personal communication, February 2011), and from the Interactive Media perspective on the implementation and launch of the first course mission" not knowing the exact needs of the courses before we started development" (Carlson, L., personal communication, February 2011). A high point in the implementation phase occurred when the team, while working separately on their respective components in order to meet the deadline, was able to see all pieces come together to form the first mission and see the results of the preliminary user testing (Carlson, 2011; Claesson, A.L., personal communication, February 2011).

Phase III: Evaluation, Solutions, and Plans for the Future

Evaluation and Progress

When we began the Riverbend City Simulation project, we found that it was too difficult to anticipate all of the aspects of the storyline that needed to be included in a multidisciplinary simulation without input from each and every subject matter expert. It quickly became apparent that it was essential to collaborate with the faculty who were teaching the course to ensure that the simulation missions were tailored to truly meet the learning objectives for the course.

Once we concluded the need to shift our focus, the approach changed to create more modular and customized missions for courses. In other words, we maintained the overarching storyline, but the elements of the story had to unfold for each individual course as we developed them.

Primary areas noted when evaluating this initial design and implements experience can be categorized into two main areas: (1) interactive media, design and curriculum; and (2) management. While the self-evaluation did identify a number of "pain points" we are able to utilize this information to improve and expand our initiative into a sub-department within Interactive Course Media, Next Generation Learning dedicated to simulations and rich media add-ins to enhance our course offerings. Listed below you will find some of the major areas of concern divided into Interactive Media, Design and Curriculum, and Management. Primary recommendations for future projects and those who might be contemplating such an endeavor are to hire a project manager at the beginning of the initiative, and take the time to understand the specific needs of the courses where the media (simulation) will be used when developing the "core" and initial storyline. Table 3 defines key areas of "pain" from the initial team evaluation of the Riverbend City Simulation project.

In a recent retrospective evaluation of the Riverbend City simulation project from its beginning, individual team members identified a variety of techniques for measuring success. Felicity Pearson (2011) stated" When the subject matter experts and chairs tell us that we have, in fact, captured the complexity of their profession, I know I've done my job. Getting the details right is a challenge, but it is so rewarding in the end" (Pearson, F., personal communication, February 2011). "I measure my success by the opinion of the course and interactive designers. If they are happy I am happy. I leave measuring overall success to others (Johnson, M., personal communication, February 2011).

From an interactive design perspective the Lead Designer stated that she relied upon "usability testing and surveys" to determine success or failure of a specific mission or interactive (Carlson, L., personal communication, February 2011). Regarding the evolution of the development process, the team noted that it seemed to move from a case study built around a single incident to a profile of a town where many case studies or narratives could stem from, a more streamlined approach (Carlson, L., personal communication, February 2011; Johnson, M., personal communication, February 2011).

Another surprise or "Ah Hah!" moment was the recognition of the increasing complexity of managing a growing storyline, list of locations and characters. For example, there were more than 200 characters created for the simulation. The project team included three writers, and they had begun to add steps in the process for formal collaboration to ensure there were no inconsistencies in the scripts. The team is currently using spreadsheets to manage the list of characters, locations, scenes and missions. However, an important next step is to explore more sophisticated software to efficiently manage these assets.

What Makes it Unique?

The Riverbend City Simulation project is unique in that it is a large scale–and scalable–simulation that creates a multidisciplinary learning experience for dozens of asynchronous, online courses across

Table 3. Post mortem evaluation of initial RiverBend City simulation experience

Pain Point
Interactive Media, Design and Curriculum
Trying to build the "core" and the main storyline without understanding the specific needs of the courses * Spending time on requirements up front * Not taking an iterative approach until later in the project
Not enough time for mockups and review
Non-English speaking parts of the scripts for audio recording the narration; challenges in finding people and cost
Management
Trying to schedule the work based on a waterfall approach vs. an iterative approach
Managing the demand (overwhelming positive reaction from people)
Articulating what Riverbend City was in the early courses without much to show them and managing expectations
Communicating workload for adding new locations Estimating in general for the illustration assets is more time-consuming
Not having a project/program manager fully dedicated to project
Challenge of estimating early on: revisit for any new core simulations. Note that baseline costs for first simulation will provide historical foundation for future estimates

several programs. Because missions are custom built for each course, the narrative can evolve to include new disciplines or new methodology or technology within the professions (such as the use of GIS technology in public administration and public safety) without abandoning the assets that have already been developed.

The Riverbend City Simulation differs from other public service simulations in that it can be customized to meet the competencies of an individual course and its modular design and catalogue of assets allow it to be quickly and easily integrated into new programs with no change in the existing development process.

To our knowledge, while there are other simulations which target specific fields, such as emergency management or HAZMAT response, our focus on the collaborative process and multiple professional disciplines is unique. Furthermore, the course-specific development process represents a level of customization that is unique.

From a technical standpoint, the simulation is unique in that ADA 508 accessibility best practices are integrated throughout the end-user experience. On-screen text is used in conjunction with audio, navigation is keyboard accessible, and an HTML version of the transcript is included for compatibility with screen-reader software.

Most importantly, faculty and departmental chairs in the School of Public Service Leadership are the strongest proponents for integrating the simulation into their programs. Faculty leadership views of how the Riverbend City simulation as a unique, standout project includes:

"Riverbend City allows our learners to assess problems and implement solutions similar to what many will face in their careers. What sets it apart is the multidisciplinary nature of the simulation, with the challenges, organizations and individual characters designed by a talented creative team of interactive design specialists and faculty subject matter experts across the broad field of public service" (Kochanowski, Y.J., Interim Fac-

ulty Chair; Public Administration and Nonprofit Management and Leadership Programs; cited in Campus Technology Award Nomination, 2011).

We plan to utilize our Riverbend City simulation in our courses to teach and model the very best practices of interagency collaboration. The beauty of the simulation missions is that they have applicability to nursing, public administration, healthcare, public health, emergency management, homeland security and law enforcement. Today's complex challenges require leaders who have a skill set honed on just such a platform (Tiffin, C. M., Dean; School of Public Service Leadership; cited in Campus Technology Award Nomination, 2011).

"At [a recent] cultural awareness presentation for the American Association of Critical-Care Nurses (AACN), I shared the positive impact of Riverbend City on our nursing programs. I explained that it affords our students the opportunity for decision making, critical thinking, and multicultural exploration...all in an accurate representation of a nursing environmental I was asked if it was for sale" (Bemker, M., Faculty Chair; Nursing Programs; cited in Campus Technology Award Nomination, 2011).

Management Pearls

What can be learned from the Capella Simulation Experience that could benefit others when adding rich media such as simulation into eLearning environments? Jesse and Karen Dodd, Project Manager for the Simulation Project, noted a number of challenges along the way as well as strategies for improvement.

Challenges

What were the greatest challenges with this project from a management perspective? One of the greatest challenges noted (Rosel, 2011) was taking on an initiative of this size and scope which had never been done before at Capella, perhaps anywhere in an organization of this size.

Managing a creative project that is breaking new ground without an established process can be difficult. Allowing room for creativity and innovation while maintaining scope and meeting aggressive deadlines is a balancing act, to say the least. But the key is finding that balance (Rosel, J., personal communication, February 2011).

During the initial development and brainstorming and beginning storyline development phases we noted a number of areas that we could go such as developing multiple different storylines as opposed to a single one with multiple missions branching off of it, but this would have slowed down the momentum not to mention administrative support, by not meeting deadlines. On the other hand, it was possible that we would have missed out on some truly innovative ideas if we had solely focused on meeting deadlines and limiting the scope of the project. "In the end, all decisions came down to whether or not this would enhance learning and the learner experience while not blowing away budget and timelines "(Rosel, J., personal communication, February 2011).

Performance Improvement from a Management Perspective

Using hindsight, what could have been done differently in the beginning? The initial cost estimations fell below the actual costs and expenditure; hence it would have been beneficial to have started with more conservative estimates and a better idea of what to expect (Rosel, J., personal communication, February 2011). What advice can we provide from a management and course media perspective to somebody starting a similar project? Due to the iterative nature of this process the best advice for others pursuing similar project would be to plan

for and incorporate continuous improvement steps. As each development cycle ends, the simulation team needs to meet to discuss lessons learned and process enhancement that should be made.

It is essential that any team pursuing a similar project be prepared to constantly reevaluate their process as the project matures. The process improvements we have made since the project began have contributed significantly to improved efficiency in the brainstorming process, script development, asset creation, and mission production. To date, these improvements have translated into a 33 percent reduction in simulation team resource hours per course (Rosel, J., personal communication, February 2011).

From a project management perspective, Karen Dodd (personal communication, February 2011) noted that it was imperative for anybody considering a creative project of this scope to let go of any preconceptions about how the project will work.

Classic waterfall project management or iterative project management aren't flexible and responsive enough to accommodate fluid work efforts. Creative projects are non-linear, fast-paced, and open-ended. The core development of function and engine is similar to software development, the interface design and framework is similar to web page design and development, and the subject matter development is a hybrid of script writing, competency-based design, and media. It all needs to fit together into the final media product for a course, running on the core framework and engine (Dodd, K., personal communication, February 2011).

Dodd recommended the following Project Management techniques that do work for designing and implementing effective creative projects such as rich media and simulation into eLearning environments (Table 4).

Table 4. Dodd's project management techniques that do work

Scheduling Tools	Use a scheduling tool to forecast resource needs and load level resources during each phase
Scope Due Dates	Scope management-negotiating function and date trade-offs
Stakeholders	Stakeholder communication including weekly in person updates along with written status – essential in early stages to maintain sponsor confidence, faculty engagement;
Communication	Team communication in multiple approaches, including weekly team meetings, ad hoc meetings for unplanned events; 1:1 check-ins with team members
Cost Management	Cost and expenditure management (corporate time keeping, vendor invoices)
Co-locate the team	"Drop by communication" and convenience enhances problem resolution in a timely manner.

Lessons Learned

Evaluation of any project includes a careful critique of what worked well and what did not work well. Key aspects that worked well in the initial development of the Capella Simulation Project included: (1) scene collaboration across courses; (2) character reuse greater this launch; (3) improvements made to network folder system the organization of the aid search and standards; (4) "Mission Synopses Reviews" by Media Course Developers were helpful to determine potential re-use, size of missions, possible swap of due date slots if course is "larger" or more "complex"; (5) great job of recruiting and organizing multi-lingual talent (aids in maximum use of individual talent); and (6) script review meetings rock!

Areas that were noted for improvement included: (1) clarification of how new interactive are different from a programming and interactive media perspective; (2) scheduling and communication challenges with collaboration related to alignment of due dates and whether a component can be re-used in whole or in part; (3) need backup for staff and talent off-time and vacations (? cross-training among disciplines); (4) coordination of talent and characters for audio talent consolidating scheduling; (5) Finding reuse for courses; and (6) keeping list of existing missions updated to reflect growing inventory of missions, especially as we offer Riverbend to new stakeholders.

CONCLUSION: FUTURE DIRECTIONS AND RECOMMENDATIONS

Future plans include considerations for expansion into other schools/departments in Capella University to complement existing course content and test student knowledge and skills with application in this scenario-based, real-world, rich media setting. The Riverbend City Simulation project has been quite successful with requests to expand into different areas and programs. We will continue to add enhancements and create more Riverbend City missions to meet the needs of our learners and programs. "The more learner engagement we can build into the missions, the better the learning experience will be" (Pearson, F., personal communication, February 2011).

It is our anticipation that this experience might provide some valuable tools for others who may consider the addition of rich media such as simulation into eLearning-based courses. Recommendations from the Capella Simulation Riverbend City Project Team for potential similar projects would include building on existing knowledge and toolsets to allow for more options for interactive and content, think about the organization and documentation up front, obtaining engaged committed sponsorship at both the business and school levels, and balancing multiple deadlines with a manageable and achievable set of interim deliverables.

Due to the fact that this process has been extremely iterative, the best advice for institutions pursuing similar projects would be to plan for and incorporate continuous improvement steps. After each development cycle, the Riverbend City team meets to discuss lessons learned and process enhancements that should be made. In a project this large in scope, the process is bound to evolve. It is essential that any team pursuing a similar project be prepared to constantly reevaluate their process as the project matures. The process improvements we have made since the project began have contributed significantly to improved efficiency in the brainstorming process, script development, asset creation, and mission production. To date, these improvements have translated into a 33-percent reduction in simulation team resource hours per course from the initial offering.

One final piece of advice from Karen Dodd (personal communications, February 2011) regarding the potential of creating a similar project is:

One of the earlier challenges was describing Riverbend City when there was no prototype or example to show. Recommend starting out with a small subset of content and building that so the team has sense of accomplishment, stakeholders see something real, users get to use it early and provide feedback, and team can learn early on. Then expand offerings from there (Dodd, K., personal communication, February 2011).

REFERENCES

Adams, M. H., & Valiga, T. M. (2009). *Achieving excellence in nursing education.* New York, NY: National League for Nursing.

American Association of Colleges of Nursing. (2008). *The essentials of baccalaureate nursing education.* Washington, DC: Author.

Benner, P. (1984). *From novice to expert.* Menlo Park, CA: Addison-Wesley.

Boller, J., & Jones, D. (2008). *Nursing education for California: White paper and redesign and strategic action plan recommendations.* Berkeley, CA: California Institute for Nursing and Health Care.

Bristol, T. J. (2006). *Evidence-based e-learning for nursing educators.* Iowa City, IA: Center for Health Workforce Planning, Bureau of Health Care access, Iowa Department of Public Health.

Council on Education for Public Health (CePH). (n.d.). *Accreditation criteria.* Council on Education for Public Health. Retrieved March 14, 2011, from http://www.ceph.org/pg_accreditation_criteria.htm

Crawford, C. (2005). *Chris Crawford on interactive storytelling.* Berkeley, CA: New Riders.

Davis, B. G. (2009). *Tools for teaching* (2nd ed.). San Francisco, CA: Jossey-Bass.

DeNeve, K. M., & Heppner, M. J. (1997). Role play simulations: The assessment of an active learning technique and comparisons to traditional lectures. *Innovative Higher Education, 21*(3), 231–246. doi:10.1007/BF01243718

Educause Learning initiative. (2006, June). *7 things you should know about virtual worlds.* Retrieved from http://connect.educause.edu/Library/ELI/7ThingsYouShouldKnowAbout/39392

Educause Learning initiative. (2008, June). *7 things you should know about Second Life.* Retrieved from http://connect.educause.edu/Library/ELI/7ThingsYouShouldKnowAbout/46892

Ferguson, S., Beeman, L., Eichorn, M., Jaramillo, Y., & Wright, M. (2004). High-fidelity simulation across cultural settings and educational levels. In Loyd, G. E., Lakem, C. L., & Greenberg, R. B. (Eds.), *Practical health care simulations* (pp. 184–203). Philadelphia, PA: Elsevier.

Frederick, P. (1981). The dreaded discussion: Ten ways to start. *Improving College and University Teaching, 29*(3), 109–114.

French, J., Blair-Stevens, C., McVey, D., & Merritt, R. (Eds.). (2010). *Social marketing and public health theory and practice.* Oxford, UK: Oxford University Press.

Health Resources and Services Administration. (2002). *National advisory council on nurse education and practice: Second report to the Secretary of Health and Human Services and Congress.* Rockville, MD: Author.

Hertel, J. P., & Millis, B. J. (2002). *Using simulations to promote learning in higher education.* Sterling, VA: Stylus.

Kantrowitz, M. (2010, February 4). *Higher education funding in President Obama's FY 2011 budget.* Council on Law in Higher Education. Retrieved March 14, 2011, from http://www.clhe.org/marketplaceofideas/financial-aid/higher-education-funding-in-president-obamas-fy-2011-budget/

Lauerman, J. (2011, February 14). Higher education funding cut by $89 billion over 10 years in Obama budget. *Bloomberg.* Retrieved March 14, 2011, from http://www.bloomberg.com/news/2011-02-14/higher-education-funding-cut-by-89-billion-over-10-years-in-obama-budget.html

Long, R. E. (2005). Using simulation to teach resuscitation: An important patient safety tool. *Critical Care Nursing Clinics of North America, 17*, 1–8. doi:10.1016/j.ccell.2004.09.001

MacKay, C. (2000). The trial of Napoleon, a case study for using mock trials. *Teaching History: A Journal of Methods, 25*(2).

McCarthy, J. P., & Anderson, L. (2000). Active learning techniques versus traditional teaching styles: Two experiments from history and political science. *Innovative Higher Education, 24*(4).

McKeachie, W. J., & Svinicki, M. (2006). *McKeachie's teaching tips: Strategies, research and theory for college and university teachers.* Boston, MA: Houghton Mifflin, Co.

National Center for Healthcare Leadership (NCHL). (2010-2011a). *Graduate health management education demonstration project.* National Center for Healthcare Leadership. Retrieved March 14, 2011, from http://nchl.org/static.asp?path=2851,3223

National Center for Healthcare Leadership (NCHL). (2010-2011b). *NCHL measures of success.* National Center for Healthcare Leadership. Retrieved March 14, 2011, from http://nchl.org/Documents/NavLink/NCHL_Board_Measures_of_Success_7.09_uid8202009959251.pdf

National Council of State Boards of Nursing (NCSBN). (2005). *Meeting the ongoing challenge of continued competence.* Chicago, IL: Author.

Nehring, W. M. (2010). History of simulation in nursing. In Nehring, W. M., & Lashley, F. R. (Eds.), *High-fidelity patient simulation in nursing education.* Sudbury, MA: Jones and Bartlett Publishers.

Nehring, W. M., & Lashley, F. R. (2010). *High-fidelity patient simulation in nursing education.* Sudbury, MA: Jones and Bartlett Publishers.

Oregon Nursing Leadership Council. (2005). *Oregon nursing leadership council strategic plan: Solutions to Oregon's nursing shortage, 2005-2008.* Portland, OR: Author.

Oxford English Dictionary Online. (2010a, November). *Media.* Retrieved 27 February 2011, from http://oed.com/view/Entry/115635?rskey=IM0rW9&result=2#

Oxford English Dictionary Online. (2010b, November). *Simulation.* Retrieved February 27, 2011, from http://oed.com/view/Entry/180009?redirectedFrom=simulation#

Rosel, J. (2011). *Campus technology award nomination*. Capella University. Unpublished manuscript.

Rymaszewski, M., Au, W. J., & Wallace, M. Winters, C., Ondrejka, C., Batstone-Cunningham, B., & Rosedale, P. (2006). *Second Life: The official guide*. Indianapolis, IN: Wiley.

Saulnier, D. (2008, January 23). *Immersive education and virtual worlds: Croquet and MPK20/ Wonderland/Darkstar*. Retrieved February 25, 2011, from http://saulnier.typepad.com/learning_technology/2008/01/immersive-educa.html

TechTarget. (2005, April 5). *Rich media*. Retrieved February 25, 2011, from http://whatis.techtarget.com/definition/0,sid9_gci212901,00.html

Van Eck, R. (2006). Digital-based learning: It's not just the natives who are restless. *Educator Review*, *41*(2), 17–30.

Waldner, M. H., & Olson, J. K. (2007). Taking the patient to the classroom: Applying theoretical frameworks to simulation in nursing education. *International Journal of Nursing Education Scholarship*, *4*(1), 18. doi:10.2202/1548-923X.1317

Waneka, R. (2008). *California Board of Registered Nursing 2006-2007 annual school report: Pre-licensure nursing programs data summary*. San Francisco, CA: Center for Health Professions.

ADDITIONAL READING

Caladine, R. (2008). *Enhancing E-Learning with Media-Rich Content and Interactions*. IGI Global. *ISBN*, *13*, 978–1599047324.

Miller, C. H. (2008). *Digital Storytelling, Second Edition: A creator's guide to interactive entertainment*. Focal Press. ISBN-13: 978-0240809595

Spierling, U., & Szilas, N. (Eds.). Interactive Storytelling: First Joint International Conference on Interactive Digital Storytelling, ICIDS 2008 Erfurt, Germany, November 26-29, 2008, ... Applications, incl. Internet/Web, and HCI). Springer Publishing. ISBN-13: 978-354089424

University of Washington. (2010, September 8). What is rich media and how can I learn more about its accessibility? The National Center on Accessible Information Technology in Education. Retrieved February 25, 2011 from: http://www.washington.edu/accessit/articles?1146

KEY TERMS AND DEFINITIONS

Media Course Developer: A course development specialist who works specifically with media applications to curriculum. In the Riverbend City Simulation, media course developers work with Subject Matter Experts to write the mission scripting and design interactive challenges for learners to meet the mission and course objectives.

Mission: A mission in the Riverbend City Simulation consists of several related scenes specific to the course competencies. Missions are self-contained and are a more detailed expansion of a set of specific scenes linked together to provide learners with objectives to be accomplished both in the simulation and in course activities such as discussion or assignments.

Rich Media: Information consisting of a combination of graphics, audio, video and animation, which is more storage and bandwidth intensive than ordinary text. It also displays dynamic motion which may occur over time or in direct response to user interaction.

RiverBend City: A multidisciplinary scenario-based simulation project focusing on the disaster response of public service agencies in a fictional city developed at Capella University in Minneapolis, Minnesota.

Simulation: The technique of imitating the behavior of a situation or process through the application of a suitably analogous situation or apparatus, particularly for the purpose of study or personnel training. Simulation in e-learning and academic are generally considered to be scenarios that engage learners in real-world settings with experience representing learning goals.

Subject Matter Expert: A faculty member whose expertise in a specific area is used to design and develop curriculum. Subject matter experts (SME) work directly with course developers and in the case of the Riverbend City Simulation, SMEs work with Media Course Developers to identify areas in new and existing courses where the simulation would be applicable to enhance learner experience and assess attainment of learning objectives.

Chapter 4
Authentic Learning in Online Courses:
A Course Design Model

Deb Gearhart
Troy University, USA

ABSTRACT

The purpose of this chapter is to describe authentic learning, review the literature pertaining to authentic learning, discuss the benefits for online learning, and provide a model for the use of authentic learning in online course design. Students comment they are motivated by solving real-world problems and often express a preference for doing rather than listening. At the same time, most educators consider learning by doing the most effective way to teach (Lombardi, 2007). The chapter will be beneficial to instructors and instructional designers alike.

INTRODUCTION

It is clear that in today's environment employers are expecting university graduates to be able to walk right into the workforce with the skills needed to do their jobs; they want employees who are innovative and communicate in their chosen profession. Traditional approaches to higher education do not necessarily provide graduates with those skills. Many faculty members have looked to authentic learning approaches to content to help prepare students for the workforce in their chosen profession. But, what exactly is authentic learning? First, let's look at the tool that has advanced the use of authentic learning, particularly for online learning.

The Internet has fundamentally changed the instructional process in higher education. The

DOI: 10.4018/978-1-61350-441-3.ch004

Internet has provided educators with a powerful tool to create effective and immersive learning environments and provides efficient and collaborative forms of communication for students with their instructors and with each other (Herrington & Oliver, 2006). Most common of the learning environments are online courses.

Online learning's use of the Internet to focus on real-life problems and projects allows students to explore and discuss these problems in ways that are relevant to them. Embedded in this concept is the idea that authentic instructional approaches include a focus on real-life questions and issues, active pedagogy, collaboration, and connectedness. Authentic learning, based in constructivism, engages students in constructing new ideas or concepts that build on previous experiences and knowledge. Authentic approaches to teaching and learning recognize the importance of collaboration (Mathur & Murray, 2006). There are many strengths of the Internet for authentic learning. It supports lifelong learning; it shifts the instructional paradigm from a teaching environment to a learning environment; it provides communication tools that support dialog within and between diverse communities of learners; it fosters the collaboration needed for scaffolding, support, and shared meaning-making; it supports "deep learning" though meaningful dialog; it provides easy access to broad, deep sources of information and supports meaningful interaction with this information; and it provides a flexibility and convenience for learners that are not feasible in the traditional face-to-face classroom (Mathur & Murray, 2006).

Interactivity in Authentic Learning for Online Learning

The emphasis of the book is on interactivity in online courses. Interactivity refers to the interaction between the learner and the instructional source. Interactivity in online courses deals mainly with print and digital media. It is more predesigned and programmed, needing to prompt and engage learners (Wang & Gearhart, 2006). This chapter progresses first with defining authentic learning and describes how it is used in successful online course design.

Defining Authentic Learning

Authentic learning is a pedagogical approach that allows students to explore, discuss, and meaningfully construct concepts and relationships in contexts that involve real-world problems and projects relevant to the learner. Students are presented with problem-solving activities that incorporate authentic, real-life questions and issues in a format that encourages collaborative effort, dialogue with informed expert sources, and generalization to broader ideas and application (Donovan, Bransford, & Pellegrino, 1999; Christensen, 1995).

According to Cornelius-White and Harbaugh (2010) many students find much of their education to be irrelevant, especially students who struggle academically. Particularly, adult students find it hard to connect the value from traditional teaching of facts to real world situations. Adult learners are drawn to online learning for its flexibility and convenience and adult learners want to find relevance of their learning to their real world situations. Transfer of learning is one of the biggest challenges teachers face in teaching from an authentic curricula. This is particularly compounded when taking authentic curricula from the traditional classroom to the online course.

Authentic learning and inquiry-based teaching are interrelated methods of knowledge construction and skill development consistent with learner-centered facilitation, engagement, and achievement. Characteristics of authentic learning include high perceived relevance and direct redressing of simulated and real-world problems. Authentic learning methods can support distance students desire to include their experiences in their learning, recognizing the rarity with which learners generalize academic learning reached through traditional methods to real-world applications. Authentic learning helps students engage their intrinsic motivation and environmental demands with a supportive context in which to learn. Authentic learning represents a guided integration of the cognitive with the emotional, behavioral, and social elements of learning as most real-life situations call for (Cornelius-White and Harbaugh, 2010).

The following characteristics of authentic learning summarize the concept of authentic learning:

- **Provides an authentic context that reflects the way the knowledge will be used in real life.** A course with a more authentic context is presenting a realistic problem preserving the complexity of the real-world setting.
- **Provides authentic activities.** The tasks that students perform are arguably the crucial aspect of course design and ideally these tasks should have real world relevance. Learning is centered on authentic tasks that are of interest to the learners and the students are engaged in exploration and inquiry.
- **Provides access to expert performances and modeling of processes.** To expose students to expert performance is to give them a model of how a real practitioner behaves in a real situation.
- **Provides multiple roles and perspectives.** In a more authentic learning environment, it is important to enable and encourage students to explore different perspectives. Learning, most often, is interdisciplinary.
- **Provides for collaborative construction of knowledge.** The opportunity for users to collaborate is an important design element, particularly for students who may be learn-

ing at a distance. Collaborative groupings enable students to reflect and engage in meaningful discussion on issues presented.
- **Provides for reflection.** Reflection is both process and product. Reflection is not only solitary, but also collaborative and can be collected in journals, portfolios blogs, discussions, etc.
- **Provides articulation.** Authentic tasks require articulation of ideas in one form or another. Students become engaged in complex tasks and higher-order thinking skills, such as analyzing, synthesizing, designing, manipulating, and evaluating information.
- **Provides for coaching and scaffolding.** Authentic learning environments need to provide collaborative learning where instructors and mentors can assist with scaffolding and coaching to support learning.
- **Provides authentic assessment.** To provide authentic assessment the learning environment needs to ensure the assessment is seamlessly integrated with the activity (Herrington & Herrington, 2006; Donovan et al., 1999; Newman & Associates, 1996; Newman et al., 1995; Nolan & Francis, 1992).

Keeping in mind that interactivity in an online course is a key component to a well designed online course; this chapter develops into a model for authentic online course design where interactivity through authentic content and assessment provides the basis for learning. The following figures displays a model that sets the stage for authentic course design, starting with the change of role for the instructor, developing content using authentic learning theory and conducting authentic instruction with authentic learning objects, followed through with authentic assessment and finally conduct quality assurance for continuous course improvement.

ROLE OF THE INSTRUCTOR

In the process of redefining and developing the role of the instructor in authentic learning, student learning is enhanced when the instructor provides coaching and scaffolding support as a central and important pedagogical element as an alternative to didactic forms of teaching (Herrington & Oliver, 2006). Providing this scaffolding and support is part of the roles of instructors and instructional designers alike in online courses and should consist of the skills and strategies needed for the students to complete the tasks. Scaffolding includes the following levels: providing support; functioning as a tool, much like the text and other tools in an online course; extending the range of the student with the authentic approaches used in the online course; allowing the student to accomplish a task not otherwise possible; and is used selectively to aid the student where needed, aiding the student's acquisition of the content.

Teaching in an online environment involves far more than simply transferring teaching skills from the classroom. The successful instructor will need to learn strategies for developing skills for humanizing the online environment and new ways to guide students to discuss, critique, and reflect together as they engage in the construction of meaning. Instructors also need skills to blend communication technologies to foster a sense of community. Most importantly, instructors need strategies to deal with student frustrations caused by technology failures and other technology and software related problems (Herrington & Oliver, 2006).

Providing for interactivity in an online course is another skill that faculty and instructional designers need to emphasize in authentic online course

Figure 1. Model for an authentic online course design ©Gearhart, 2011

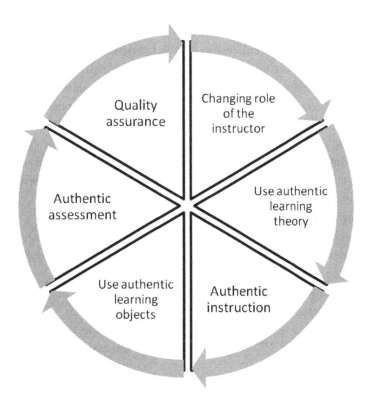

Authentic Learning Theories

design. As mentioned in the previous paragraph the need to humanize the online environment is not done in the traditional forms of communication. Interactivity is completed through digital media and print. According to Wang and Gearhart (2006) there are many factors that affect interactivity: content factors, legibility, readability, relevance and modality options; task challenge; programmed feedback; learner control over learning paths and learner input opportunities.

Although authentic learning is appropriate for online learning there are few examples of successful authentic online courses, typically because institutions are slow in adopting innovative approaches to conventional teaching. Authentic learning offers a powerful approach that draws upon a wealth of research in constructivist and situated approaches to learning (Herrington & Oliver, 2006). One way to help instructors learn about and adapt authentic learning applications is to have them trained in an authentic online course.

There are successful authentic learning approaches in the classroom that can easily be adapted to online learning. Examples in social science with the project designed by Borthwick, et. al. (2007) using models such as apprenticeship, situated reality, and enminding; the comparative study of Correia, et. al. (2010) using service-learning and student engagement; and the PALs project by Hancock, et. al (2010) all support the use of authentic learning theory in online course design and the use of authentic assignments and assessment, demonstrated in the following sections of the authentic online course design model.

With understanding the instructor's changing role in developing authentic online courses, the second stage of the model involves the theoretical base for authentic learning. The following section of the chapter describes authentic learning theories that can be used as the basis of an interactive authentic online course.

In order to set the stage for describing the learning theories which are incorporated in authentic learning it is important to understand the learning process. The learning process can be described as a continuum:

- Acquiring and storing of facts, skills, and methods for reproduction of what is learned;
- Relating parts of subject matter to each other and making sense of that relationship; and
- Understanding and interpreting reality in a different way – comprehending the world by reinterpreting knowledge (Parry & Reynoldson, 2006).

Theories of learning can be viewed in two lenses; one distinguishes surface learning (learning is given knowledge; learning is reproduction for assessment; learning is applying knowledge to problems) from deep learning (learning as making sense by abstracting meaning from the learning experience; and learning enables the student to see the world differently). Deep learning involves both relating external personal experiences and personal development integrating into the total experience (Parry & Reynoldson, 2006).

Constructivism is the first theory discussed and the most commonly used learning theory for online education. The principles of constructivist learning include:

- To make learning outcomes transferable, learners need both content and context learning;
- Learners are active constructors of knowledge;
- Learning is in a constant state of growth and evolution;
- Learners bring their own needs and experiences to learning situations;

- Learners acquire skills and knowledge within realistic contexts; and
- Assessment is realistic and holistic (Parry & Reynoldson, 2006).

The next form of authentic learning theory discussed is work-based learning. A key, identifying feature of work-based learning is that it is an accredited, assessed and an integral component of degree programs. The institution, the student and the workplace typically design individual, work-based learning programs collaboratively developing discipline-specific and globally transferable skills (Hunt, 2006). Models of work-based learning used in higher education include: recognition of prior work experience, independent work-based modules, and internships or practicum. Some of the goals of authentic work-based learning include:

- The creation of supportive environments
- Policy development
- Community action
- Development of personal and professional skills (Hunt, 2006).

Work-based learning fits authentic learning pedagogy because it links the theoretical knowledge of universities with the real-life application of the knowledge in the work environment.

Authentic learning often incorporates elements of action learning, learning by doing. Real tasks are used as the vehicle for learning. The learning is immediately relevant and useful to the work setting. Learning in the workplace provides authentic contexts and activities as well as opportunities to learn from best practice. The application of theoretical knowledge to real, workplace problems creates opportunities for students to recreate and scaffold knowledge flexibility, in accordance with the task at hand. This also provides for the authentic assessment of learning within tasks. Embedded in authentic learning pedagogy, work-based learning recognizes the importance of interaction and socialization among learners. Instructors and

students work on projects in partnership which enhance the concepts of classrooms without borders, opportunities for networking, and freedom to work in unstructured ways.

The fourth form of authentic learning theory which can be used in authentic online courses is experience-based learning, where learning is based on experiences and stories about experiences. People learn from their own (first-person) experiences as well as from others' (third-person) experiences; both types of experiences can be incorporated into online learning environments. Using an online authentic assignment requiring collaboration through small online groups incorporates several key features: learning will be goal-based, ensure shared responsibility, and have students acting as coaches and scaffolds for each other within their groups and between the groups (Koenders, 2006).

Among the many facets of authentic learning is problem-based learning. Learning is authentic when students are faced with solving *real* world problems based in the theory and practice of the content. As technology continues to open up possibilities for innovative and effective teaching and learning opportunities, students and instructors are no longer satisfied to accept familiar classroom based pedagogies that rely on content delivery and little else (Herrington & Herrington, 2006).

Problem-solving, to be worthwhile, has to be challenging, and requires the instructor's support which can be very involved and intense. Problem-solving is often time consuming and hard to manage. These issues, challenging content, time for development and managing the instruction and grading of problems need to be kept in mind when designing problem-solving into online courses. Problem-solving is a complex intellectual process involving the coordination of a range of demanding and interrelated skills including:

- Understanding and representing the problem (including identifying what kinds of information are relevant to its solution);

- Gathering and organizing relevant information;
- Constructing and managing a plan of action, or a strategy;
- Reasoning, hypothesis-testing and decision-making;
- Using various problem-solving tools (Whitebread, 1997, pg. 17).

A student based authentic learning theory is Situated learning - a form of authentic learning which helps students improve confidence in their own ability, a greater awareness of quality, more self-reflection and a greater responsibility for their own learning. Situated learning emphasizes the idea that much of what is learned is specific to the situation in which it is learned (Anderson, et. al., 1996). Situated learning often deals with the physical or social situation the student is in at the time of the learning (Cobb & Bowers, 2011), such as being enrolled in an online course. Using situated learning in an online course can be developed through the concept that the physical and social situation for the students is the community established in the online course. Some ways to incorporate situated learning include: access to experts in the content; use of multiple roles and perspectives; use of collaboration, reflection, articulation; coaching and scaffolding; and authentic assessment (Koenders, 2006).

The final authentic learning theory to be discussed is Technology-based learning which is designed to expose students to concepts and issues in a complex and evolving content domain; designed in a tasked-based format rather than a sequence of content related to evaluation (Agostinho, 2006). Technologies that enhance authentic learning include personal computers, digital video and still cameras, projectors, graphic tablets and SMART boards, audio recorders and players, handheld computers, phones, and other hand-held devices. The use of technology enhances authentic learning by having learning move from being instructor-directed to being learner-centered (Cornelius-White and Harbaugh, 2010). In simple terms, the computer offers access to information in a flexible format, which can be manipulated and explored. It also offers scenarios where events are altered as a result of a learner's actions (McFarlane, 1997).

When designing an authentic online course, the goal is purposeful deep learning of the content. Using the different authentic learning theories described above should be geared to deep learning. In deep learning, students relate the content to previous knowledge and experience, a crux of authentic learning. However, deep learning goes on where students look for patterns and underlying principles; they check for evidence and relate it to their conclusions, examining the logic of the content critically to develop understanding while learning (Weigel, 2002). Ultimately students become actively interested in the course content, easily developed in authentic online learning.

Once an authentic learning theory has been determined as the basis for the authentic online course the next step is to review authentic learning objects to be used in the course content.

Learning Objects in Authentic Learning

Learning objects are renewable learning resources which are easily used in authentic learning. Students need to be provided with scaffolds and supports that enable them to complete activities they cannot yet do. In authentic learning environments where students are frequently required to undertake tasks outside their comfort zone and capability, scaffold and supports are very important. Examples of reusable learning objects include:

- Information and reference material;
- Websites and links;
- Journal and newspaper articles;
- Books;
- Online tutorials and self-paced instructional materials;

- Quizzes and self-tests;
- Training manuals;
- Previous student work samples and projects;
- Workplace documents (Oliver, 2006).

The list above is not all inclusive; resources used in authentic learning settings are diverse and varied. Authentic learning objects should be selected based on the content to be taught and the desired outcome of the learning, which leads to next step of the model, the development of authentic assessment. But again, the object of well designed authentic learning objects is to develop deep learning of the content through the authentic learning theory selected for the design of the content for online delivery, using authentic and learning objects to achieve a transformational learning experience providing deep learning.

AUTHENTIC ASSESSMENT

According to Tileston (2005), all assessment begins with effective planning on the part of the instructor and the students. Assessment is built on declarative and procedural information. Declarative information is factual and procedural information deals with processes. In assessing both forms of information the instructor provides opportunities to use declarative information followed by assessing by procedural methods. Traditional assessment is generally curriculum driven, where in authentic approaches, assessment drives the curriculum. Authentic learning focuses on process as well as content, on how one is learning and not just what is being learned. Authentic assessment is an important means through which the practical experience of authentic learning can be theorized and integrated into an online course. The authentic experiences encourage reflective and critical thinking about real problems in real settings. Assessment is normally based on port-

folios and journals, and includes a high degree of self-direction (Hunt, 2006).

Alternative assessment, a form of authentic assessment, refers to methods that both evaluate broad learning processes and outcomes and facilitate learning (which can incorporate traditional assessments). Alternative assessments allow connections between the cognitive and affective, share power and control, and usually call for learners to create rather than select meaning and products, thereby incorporating more in the learning process. Authentic assessment is a means of directly assessing student performance on the meaningful tasks at hand. Alternative assessments also include the use of formative assessments, rubrics, and self- and peer evaluations (Cornelius-White & Harbaugh, 2010).

The next step in developing authentic assessment is to provide the students the criteria for success; which is often done through rubrics. The following table describes the characteristics, processes, models and strategies for developing authentic online assessments.

Authentic assessment strategies need to provide sufficient time to complete the authentic assignment as developing authentic projects is time consuming. Authentic assessments need to develop from the competency level at the start of the course. Competencies that require cognitive skill building are best suited for authentic assessment. Authentic assessment strategies must be fair to students – ethnic, language, economic, and gender-based groups. Table 2 presents a checklist which can be used to determine the authenticity of an online assessment strategy.

The final step in the design model for an authentic online course is the quality assurance process. All quality course design, in class or online, is cyclical providing for continuous improvement through a variety of means including such as, student course evaluation and currency of content.

Table 1. Characteristics, processes, models and strategies for developing authentic online assessments

Authentic assessments have four common characteristics:	Process for planning and executing assessment activities:
1. They are designed to be truly representative of performance in the field. **2.** The criteria used in assessments seek to evaluate the essentials of performance against well-articulated performance standards. **3.** A major goal of authentic assessment is to help students develop the capacity to evaluate their own work against public standards, to revise, modify, and redirect their energies, taking initiative to assess their own progress. **4.** Students are often expected to present their work publicly and orally.	• Diagnose students competency through pre-assessment • Define learning goals collaboratively with students • Determine expected outcomes • Determine task for authentic learning • Determine standard for excellence • Determine schedule for formative assessment • Select strategies for authentic assessment • Collaboratively develop rubrics for assessments with students
Learner centered models for authentic assessments include:	**Authentic online assessment strategies:**
• Heterogeneous and inter-age groupings • The creation of a learning community • Collaboration: small groups and interaction with the instructors • Emphasis on critical thinking skills and in-depth study • Active learning: students work extensively on problem solving and projects • The authentic assessments use multiple perspectives	• Electronic portfolios • Electronic journal entries • Online discussions • Online self-testing • Rubrics
Obstacles to authentically assessing in an online classroom:	
• Perceptions of authentic assessment as too labor intensive • Perceptions of authentic assessment as too expensive and time consuming • Questions of public faith in the objectivity and reliability of judgment-based scores	

Sources: Wiggins in Darling-Hammond, et. al., 1995, pgs. 11-12; Mathur & Murray, 2006.

Table 2. Checklist to determine the authenticity of an online assessment strategy

√	Strategy
	Is the assessment strategy fair to students of all ethnic, language, color, and gender based groups?
	Does the assessment strategy link content with students authentic needs?
	Does the assessment strategy adequately demonstrate the student's ability to solve real life problems/situations?
	Does the assessment strategy provide sufficient time to complete the authentic task?
	Is the assessment strategy guided by student competency at entry point of the curriculum?
	Is the assessment strategy flexible and adaptable in that it can be modified if the context of learning changes?
	Does the assessment include a combination of strategies?
	Does the assessment strategy raise questions that have more than one correct solution?
	Is there provision for multiple raters?
	Does the assessment strategy provide a built-in mechanism for adequate and timely feedback?
	Are the assessment strategies described in a way that is understandable to the student and other raters?
	Is the authentic assessment strategy co-created by the instructor and the student?
	Does the authentic assessment strategy serve as a motivator for learning?

Source: Mathur & Murray, 2006, page 256

Quality Authentic Learning

Quality assurance is becoming a necessity, particularly for online learning, and in many places is legislatively mandated. Institutions must look to benchmark teaching and learning standards and within the institution to come to agreement on which benchmarks and standards quality will be based on. This section of the chapter will look at quality standards for teaching and learning and will apply them to authentic learning.

Commonly accepted benchmarked quality indicators for teaching and learning include:

- Learning and teaching plans
- Course development processes
- Scholarly teaching
- An interactive teaching environment
- Effective academic review processes
- Appropriateness of courses
- Student progress ratio
- First- to second- term/semester/year retention trends
- Appropriate course assessment
- Student satisfaction
- Employability of graduates (Oliver, et. al. 2006)

These quality indicators are not all inclusive, but representative of common quality indicators. Institutions decide within their own structures what the appropriate benchmarks will be related to their mission. However, developing a quality assurance process within an institution and particularly for authentic online learning can face many challenges. Challenges to developing a quality assurance process include: establishing quantifiable and meaningful metrics for all elements so that they can be assessed and recorded in an objective and reliable fashion; discovering strategies for assessing those elements which are hard to quantify rather than discarding them because they are difficult to assess; coming to a common agreement and common understanding

on minimum standards that might be applied across teaching and learning in the whole university; having staff and institutions take ownership of the process and the standards and seeing them as agents for quality assurance and continuous improvement and not simply instruments for monitoring and checking; and establishing the degree to which the use of such a system actually contributes to the improvement of teaching and learning in the institution (Oliver, et. al. 2006).

Within the author's institution the quality assurance process developed for online courses was based on the Quality Matters rubric. The process is a peer review process to enhance the quality of the online courses and is not considered punitive or used in faculty evaluation. The process is a peer review process reviewing both the design of the online course and the currency, breadth, and depth of the content.

CONCLUSION

What then does this model and subsequent authentic online course delivery lead to? In most cases online learning is geared to adult learners and their lifestyle. Authenticity is personal attitude that aims to take responsibility for choices that involve freedom and obligation; freedom as causal and logical. Choices are made by faculty to develop an online course that incorporates authentic learning. Students want authentic assessment in their courses to provide them the opportunity to use their experiences and knowledge. In turn, authenticity helps students develop the necessary skills for the workforce. This leads to making an authentic career choice involving career exploration and development through researching information regarding developing a career plan that is true to one's self and occupations and the world of work as it relates to one's major and participating in an experimental learning program (Leahy, 2009). This should be the institution's, faculty members', and student's goal.

The goal of this chapter was to review the literature of authentic learning to provide a background on the learning theory and to provide a model for developing an authentic online course, which centered on rich, immersive, and engaging tasks; considered participatory using real-world applications, situations or problems.

REFERENCES

Agostinho, S. (2006). Using characters in online simulate environments to guide authentic tasks. In Herrington, A., & Herrington, J. (Eds.), *Authentic learning environments in higher education.* Hershey, PA: Information Science Publishing. doi:10.4018/978-1-59140-594-8.ch007

Anderson, J. R., Reder, L. M., & Simon, H. A. (1996). Situated learning and education. *Educational Researcher, 25*(4), 5–11.

Borthwick, F., Bennett, S., LeFoe, G., & Huber, E. (2007). Applying authentic learning to social science: A learning design for an inter-disciplinary sociology subject. *Journal of Learning Design Designing for Effective Learning, 2*(1).

Christensen, M. (1995). *Critical issues: Providing hands-on, minds-on, and authentic learning experience in science.* Retrieved September 27, 2010, from http://www.ncrel.org/sdrs/areas/issues/content/cntareas/science/sc500.htm

Cobb, P., & Bowers, J. (1999). Cognitive and situated learning perspectives in theory and practice. *Educational Researcher, 28*(2), 4–15.

Cornelius-White, J. H., & Harbaugh, A. P. (2010). *Learner-centered instruction: Building relationships for student success.* Thousand Oaks, CA: SAGE Publications, Inc.

Correia, A., Yusop, F. D., Wilson, J. R., & Schwier, R. A. (2010). *A comparative case study of approaches authentic learning in instructional design at two universities.* Paper presented at the American Educational Research Association 2010 Annual Meeting, Denver, CO, April 30-May 4, 2010.

Darling-Hammond, L., Ancess, J., & Falk, B. (1995). *Authentic assessment in action.* New York, NY: Teachers College Press, Teachers College, Columbia University.

Donovan, M. S., Bransford, J. D., & Pellegrino, J. W. (1999). *How people learn: Bridging research and practice.* Washington, DC: National Academy Press.

Hancock, T., Smith, S., Timpte, C., & Wunder, J. (2010). PALs: Fostering student engagement and interactive learning. *Journal of Higher Education Outreach and Engagement, 14*, 4.

Herrington, A., & Herrington, J. (2006). What is an authentic learning environment? In Herrington, A., & Herrington, J. (Eds.), *Authentic learning environments in higher education.* Hershey, PA: Information Science Publishing. doi:10.4018/978-1-59140-594-8.ch001

Herrington, J., & Oliver, R. (2006). Professional development for the online teacher: An authentic approach. In Herrington, A., & Herrington, J. (Eds.), *Authentic learning environments in higher education.* Hershey, PA: Information Science Publishing. doi:10.4018/978-1-59140-594-8.ch020

Hunt, L. (2006). Authentic learning at work. In Herrington, A., & Herrington, J. (Eds.), *Authentic learning environments in higher education.* Hershey, PA: Information Science Publishing. doi:10.4018/978-1-59140-594-8.ch019

Koenders, A. (2006). An authentic online learning environment in university introductory biology. In Herrington, A., & Herrington, J. (Eds.), *Authentic learning environments in higher education.* Hershey, PA: Information Science Publishing. doi:10.4018/978-1-59140-594-8.ch004

Leahy, R. (2009). *Authentic educating.* Lanham, MD: University Press of America, Inc.

Lombardi, M. M. (2007). Authentic learning for the 21st century: An overview. *ELI Paper, 1,* 2007.

Mathur, S., & Murray, T. (2006). Authentic assessment online: A practical and theoretical challenge in higher education. In Williams, D. D., Howell, S. L., & Hricko, M. (Eds.), *Online assessment, measurement, and evaluation: Emerging practices.* Hershey, PA: Information Science Publishing. doi:10.4018/978-1-59140-747-8.ch014

McFarlane, A. (1997). Where are we and how did we get there? In McFarlane, A. (Ed.), *Information technology and authentic learning.* New York, NY: Routledge. doi:10.4324/9780203440674

Newman, F. (1996). *Authentic achievement: Restructuring schools for intellectual quality.* San Francisco, CA: Jossey-Bass Publisher.

Newman, F., Secada, W., & Wehlage, G. (1995). *A guide to authentic instruction and assessment: Vision, standards and scoring.* Alexandria, VA: Association for Supervision and Curriculum Development.

Nolan, J., & Francis, P. (1992). Changing perspectives in curriculum and instruction. In Glickman, C. (Ed.), *Supervision in transition.* Alexandria, VA: Association for Supervision and Curriculum Development.

Oliver, R. (2006). Reusable resources and authentic learning environments. In Herrington, A., & Herrington, J. (Eds.), *Authentic learning environments in higher education.* Hershey, PA: Information Science Publishing. doi:10.4018/978-1-59140-594-8.ch018

Oliver, R., Herrrington, A., Stoney, S., & Millar, J. (2006). Authentic teaching and learning standards that assure quality higher education. In Herrington, A., & Herrington, J. (Eds.), *Authentic learning environments in higher education.* Hershey, PA: Information Science Publishing. doi:10.4018/978-1-59140-594-8.ch021

Parry, G., & Reynoldson, C. (2006). Creating an authentic learning environment in economics for MBA students. In Herrington, A., & Herrington, J. (Eds.), *Authentic learning environments in higher education.* Hershey, PA: Information Science Publishing. doi:10.4018/978-1-59140-594-8.ch006

Tileston, D. W. (2005). *10 best teaching practices* (2nd ed.). Thousand Oaks, CA: Corwin Press, a SAGE Publications company.

Weigel, V. B. (2002). *Deep learning for a digital age: Technology's untapped potential to enrich higher education.* San Francisco, CA: Jossey-Bass Publisher.

Whitebread, D. (1997). Developing children's problem-solving: the educational uses of adventure games. In McFarlane, A. (Ed.), *Information technology and authentic learning.* New York, NY: Routledge.

ADDITIONAL READING

C-Shaper. (n.d.). *Website.* Retrieved from www.c-shaper.com

MERLOT. (n.d.). *Website.* Retrieved from www.merlot.org

National Educational Association guide to online teaching. (n.d.). *Website.* Retrieved from www.nea.org/technology/image/onlineteachguide.pdf

NCLOR. (n.d.). *Website.* Retrieved from www.explorethelor.org

North American Council for Online Learning. (n.d.). *Website*. Retrieved from www.nacol.org

Oliver, R., Herrington, A., Herrington, J., & Reeves, T. C. (2007). Representing authentic learning designs supporting the development of online communities of learners. *Journal of Learning Design.*, *2*, 2.

Online, N. A. S. A. (n.d.). *Website*. Retrieved from www.knowitall.org/nasa/simulations/science.html

Pan, N., Lau, H., & Lai, W. (2010). Sharing e-Learning innovation across disciplines: an encounter between engineering and teacher education. *Electronic Journal of e-Learning. 8:*1. Pgs. 31-40. Retrieved from www.ejel.org.

Repository. (n.d.). *Website*. Retrieved from www. softchalkconnect.com

Simulations: National Library of Virtual Manipulatives. (n.d.). *Website*. Retrieved from http://nlvm.usu.edu

WebQuests. (n.d.). *Website*. Retrieved from www. WebQuests.org

Wisc-Online. (n.d.). *Website*. Retrieved from www.wisc-online.org

Chapter 5
The Influence of Cognitive Styles on Learners' Performance in e-Learning

Robert Z. Zheng
University of Utah, USA

ABSTRACT

This chapter focused the influence of cognitive styles on learners' performance in e-Learning. The author examined the existing practice of style matching where instructional conditions were matched with learners' cognitive styles and found that style matching did not necessarily provide learning gains for learners with different cognitive styles. Instead, he proposed ability building as an effective approach to improve learners' learning. Following the same line, the author further examined the relationship between cognitive styles and instructional situations where situated learning was implemented. The results revealed that instructional situations can significantly influence learners' learning in complex learning and that cognitive style was not, as viewed by many people, a linear relationship between style and performance. Instead, it displayed multi-dimensional relationships with variables related to e-Learning. The author thus suggested that cognitive style should be examined in a broader manner where variables related to e-Learning be considered simultaneously.

INTRODUCTION

With the increasing presence of the Internet in education, research on e-Learning has drawn attention from educators, researchers and other professional practitioners. According to Sedig (2011), e-Learning refers to using digital technologies including the Internet and other computer-based technologies to mediate and support learners' engagement with information (Also see Moore, Dickson-Deane, & Galyen,

DOI: 10.4018/978-1-61350-441-3.ch005

2011). Evidence has shown that e-Learning in general and web-based learning in particular, has great potentials for future education due to its unique affordances in learning (Gonzalez, Jover, & Cobo, 2010). For example, Skylar (2009) studied the differences between synchronous and asynchronous instructional delivery venues and the learning benefits associated with them. The author concluded that the asynchronous delivery venue entails learning flexibility that facilitates self-paced learning whereas the synchronous delivery venue galvanizes learners' interactivity in the web and promotes collaborative learning. Taking from a different perspective, Martin (2008) investigated the instructional function of the linear and non-linear web-based learning. According to Martin, differences in information presentation, that is, linear vs. non-linear, may affect learners' information processing in terms of knowledge association as well as learner control during learning. While previous research has demonstrated relative benefits of the Internet in learning, researchers (e.g., Buckingham, 2004; Lloyd, 2002; Greenfield & Yan, 2006) argue that research on e-Learning should go beyond media effects to examine the underlying cognitive function that affects learners' learning. Lloyd (2002) proposed that the existing research on e-Learning should integrate media effects into a broader understanding of the cognitive functioning of e-Learning and its influence on individuals' performance.

One effort to understand the relationship between cognition and e-Learning is to examine the influence of individual differences such as cognitive styles in e-Learning. Research suggests that cognitive styles can significantly influence the way people process information, thus affect their performance in learning (Liu & Reed, 1994; MacNeil, 1980; Zheng, 2010). For example, Shany and Nachmias (2000) examined the relationship between learners' thinking styles and their performance in a web-based learning environment. They found a significant difference between global and local thinking learners in terms of their per-

formance and online communication behaviors. Similar findings were obtained by Liu, Magjuka, and Lee (2008) who noted that cognitive styles can leverage learners' orientation in learning, particularly in team work, decision making, and so forth. Evidently, cognitive styles bear a strong correlation with learners' online behaviors in e-Learning including online networking, social communication, and web-based information processing. Nonetheless, the extant literature on the relationship between individual differences and e-Learning is primarily characterized by qualitative studies focusing on case analysis (Crown, 1999; Holt & Oliver, 2002) and descriptive research (Koc, 2005; Santo, 2006). Although the above methods have their merits in many ways, a lack of quantitative effort could limit the generalization of the findings which would further affect the scalability, sustainability and maintenance of new knowledge in the cognate area. Moreover, lacking quantitative effort in the above area has begun to hamper the practices of e-Learning. Therefore, the current chapter is set forth to explore the influence of cognitive styles on learners' performance in e-Learning by considering learners' differing orientations and adaptation of e-Learning environments when engaged in web-based learning.

BACKGROUND

Despite the differences including delivery, location, structure, etc. among the learning environments, it is widely recognized that success in any kind of learning environments is attributed to such critical factors as learner characteristics and individual differences (Jonassen & Grabowski, 1993). Jonassen and Grabowski maintained that individual differences such as attitude, aptitude, cognitive styles, learning styles, motivation, and prior knowledge play an important role in learning. Within a rich literature of individual differences, cognitive styles are one of those that have been heavily studied. In the last half century, researchers have studied the learner's cognitive styles and their relations with learning. These studies encompass a wide range of topics: from brain hemisphere function (Samples, 1975; Springer & Deutch, 1985), to temperament (Gregorc, 1982), to impulsive/reflective cognitive tempo (Kagan, 1966), and to field dependent and field independent theory (Witkin & Goodenough, 1977), just to name a few. In an early study Kirby (1979) provided a comprehensive summary of 19 cognitive styles and concluded that all learners learn differently. According to Chinien and Boutin (1992), cognitive styles refer to "the information processing habits representing the learners' typical mode of perceiving, thinking, problem solving, and remembering" (p. 303). They claimed that cognitive styles constitute important dimensions of individual differences among learners and have important implications for teaching and learning.

One of the most studied areas pertinent to cognitive styles is field dependence (FD) and field independence (FI) (Angeli & Valanides, 2004; Liu & Reed, 1994; Noble, 2006). Previous research indicates that FD and FI (hereinafter called FDI) can significantly influence learners' behavior and their consequent learning outcomes during the learning process. The following section thus discusses the characteristics of FDI and its relationship with learning.

Field Dependence and Field Independence

The word "field" can be a set of thoughts, ideas, or feelings. People with field dependent (FD) or field independent (FI) cognitive style are different in their interpersonal behavior, social skills, and information processing. In the early 1970s Witkin and his colleagues developed what is now known as *Group Embedded Figures Test* (GEFT) in order to measure the cognitive traits associated with people's perceptual ability in separating the figures from their surroundings (Witkin, Oltman, Raskin, & Karp, 1971). Although FDI is primar-

ily concerned with learner's visual perceptiveness, it is highly correlated with other individual abilities such as reasoning, learning preferences and information processes (Angeli & Valanides, 2004; Liu & Reed, 1994; Zheng, Flygare, Dahl, & Hoffman, 2009b).

According to Witkin and Goodenough's (1977), FD people tend to make use of external social referents whereas FI people function with greater autonomy under such conditions. FD people are more attentive to social cues than are FI people. As a result, FD people show more interest in others, prefer to be physically close to people, are emotionally more open, and gravitate toward social situations. In contrast, FI people are characterized by an impersonal orientation, less interested in others, show physical and psychological distancing from people, and prefer non-social situations (Ikegulu & Ikegulu, 1999; Liu & Reed, 1994; Witkin, Moore, Goodenough, & Cox, 1977). Research on FDI has indicated that differences in cognitive styles reflect individuals' differing orientations in learning, thus bear direct impact upon their achievement performance. Some researchers found that FI people tend to outperform FD people in various learning settings (Griffin & Franklin, 1996; Ikegulu & Ikegulu, 1999; Liu & Reed, 1994; Richards, Fajen, Sullivan, & Gillespie, 1997). Others contended that the extent to which the influence of FDI on individual learners' performance should be considered broadly to encompass such factors as instructional conditions, motivation, and so forth (Zheng et al, 2009b; Zheng, Flygare, & Dahl, 2009a).

FDI and Instructional Conditions

Evidence has shown that learning succeeds when instructional conditions optimally match with learners' cognitive styles (Ford, 1995; Ford & Chen, 2001; Liu & Reed, 1994). It is widely acknowledged that the learner's cognitive style should be matched with the relevant instructional condition so that the learner will learn best under the optimal circumstances. For example, Danili and Reid (2004) studied 105 Greek pupils aged 15 to 16 in a chemistry course. A learning gain was detected for FI learners when self-initiated instructional strategy was used. For FD learners, grouping appeared to be the most effective strategy in learning. Richards et al. (1997) conducted two experiments, one in listening and one in reading, in connection to learners' FDI cognitive styles. The results indicated that FI subjects' note taking skill in both reading and listening improved when a tacit structure strategy was matched to their cognitive styles. Similar progress was found for FD subjects when a different instructional strategy was selected to match their cognitive styles. The above studies and others (e.g., Ford & Chen, 2001; Liu & Reed, 1994) suggest that humans have unique ways of processing information; our brain becomes actively engaged when the external condition, i.e., instructional environment, is optimally matched with our way of thinking. This is evidenced in the research of FDI studies where FD and FI learners are found to be sensitive to the instructional conditions they are involved in.

Zheng et al. (2009b) examined the differences between FD and FI learners in terms of instructional conditions and found that FD learners differ from their counterparts when selecting instructional conditions for their learning. For example,

FD learners prefer structural support with salient cues whereas FI learners like abundant content resources and reference materials to sort through. In addition, FD learners require clear directions and guidance and rely on timely and detailed feedback in instruction. In contrast, FI learners prefer minimal guidance and directions. They like inquire-based discovery learning, are comfortable with independent, contract-based self-instruction (e.g., independent study), and welcome inductive methods in instruction and learning. Table 1 summarizes the preferred instructional conditions as well as challenges for FD and FI learners.

FDI and e-Learning

Our previous discussion focused on the relationship between FDI and learning in general. The following section will zero in on the characteristics of FDI and e-Learning. That is, given the unique affordances of web technology, what are the connections between FDI and e-Learning?

Research on e-Learning and FDI is scarce. A search of ERIC database with key word search of "e-Learning" and "FDI" generated fewer than ten studies, of which only two were relevant. The scarcity of research in this area calls for an immediate attention to the relationship between FDI and e-Learning. Despite of the scarcity of research

Table 1. *Instructional conditions that capitalize on the preferences of and challenges to FD-I learners. (Adopted with the permission from Zheng et al., 2009b).*

Instructional Conditions Capitalized on the Preferences of FD Learners and Challenges to FI Learners	Instructional Conditions Capitalized on the Preferences of FI Learners and Challenges to FD Learners
• Providing structural support with salient cues • Including an advance organizer • Including an outline or graphic organizer of the content • Giving clear directions and guidance in instruction • Giving prototype examples • Facilitating a synergetic, social learning environment • Providing timely and detailed feedback • Embedding questions throughout learning • Providing multiple cues including visual, oral, and auditory, etc. • Providing detailed steps for deductive or inductive instruction	• Providing abundant content resources and reference material to sort through • Employing inquiry and discovery methods • Including minimal guidance and direction • Providing independent, contract-based self-instruction • Facilitating an independent learning environment • Encouraging learners to self-initiate questions • Employing inductive methods for instruction and learning • Employing outlines, pattern notes, concept maps as instructional strategies for teaching and learning • Using theoretical elaboration sequences

in FDI and e-Learning, new understanding has been generated to share light on the idiosyncratic nature of e-Learning and its influence on FDI learning behavior.

Cognitive Control and e-Learning

Researchers (Jonassen & Grabowski, 1993; Messick, 1984; Rittschof, 2010) found FDI to be synonymous to cognitive control because it (a) indicates a unipolar, value directional construct and (b) reflects specific intervening variables or mechanisms affecting the information processing operations and effectiveness. Thus, on the continuum of FDI, FI learners tend to more organized and in control of their learning process whereas FD learners rely heavily on the external support. Since e-Learning is characterized by a non-linear, unstructured learning environment, anonymity, anytime-anywhere access, synchronous and asynchronous learning modes in e-Learning can be a challenge to FD learners but would be a benefit to FI learners because the non-linear, unstructured e-Learning environment provides the flexibility FI learners need to control their learning process.

Cognitive Dependence and e-Learning

Like the affordances in e-Learning that give FI learners the ability to control their learning processes, the same affordances offered by e-Learning subjugate FD learners to seeking cognitive dependence in e-Learning. In a study by Zheng et al. (2009b), the authors found that FD learners actively joined FI learners in an online learning environment to form a discussion group. They found a high level of cognitive dependence of FD learners on FI learners when the discussions in an online threaded forum became spontaneously cross-referential, unstructured, and unorganized.

In short, there are notable differences between FD and FI learners in terms of seeking cognitive help and asserting cognitive control in e-Learning

environment. Due to the flexibility and ubiquity of e-Learning environment, the desire to control or depend on external learning mechanism can be conveniently fulfilled. As such, both FDI factor and e-Learning environment should be carefully studied to understand the dynamic relationship between the two.

FDI and Instructional Situations

Differing from instructional conditions which are concerned with the presence of social and visual cues, feedback, as well as resources in learning, instructional situation reflects the epistemological thinking in learning by focusing on knowledge generation and transfer (Herbst, 2006). The term instructional situation is broadly defined in both research and practice ranging from general education to corporate training, from instructional design to field instruction, and from daily practices to epistemological considerations. Due to the space limitation, our discussion in instructional situations will limit primarily on the epistemological aspect by focusing on knowledge generation and transfer in learning. Although areas like general education are important in the study of instructional situations, we argue that understanding the epistemology of instructional situations would significantly contribute to the improvement of educational practices in general, and instructional design and professional training in particular. This is because views of how knowledge is/should be generated significantly influence the way (1) people teach in schools and (2) the instructional situations is designed and developed. For example, using cognitive as opposed to situative approach can bear direct influence on learners' performance. Our discussion therefore focuses on the epistemological aspects of instructional situations by introducing cognitive and situative perspectives on knowledge generation and transfer.

Cognitive vs. Situated Perspectives on Knowledge Generation and Transfer

There has been a debate on the nature of the instructional situation and its associated functions with respect to knowledge generation and transfer (Anderson, Reder, & Simon, 1996; Greeno, 1997). Cognitive and situated perspectives differ in four areas pertaining to knowledge generation and transfer: (a) contextualization of learning, (b) conditions of learning, (c) knowledge transfer, and (d) abstract representation of instruction (Anderson et al., 1996; Greeno, 1997). First, the cognitive group viewed knowledge generation to be a process that can be manipulated independent of the social context. They conceptualized the learning context as something manipulatable by the instructor where instructional variables are manipulated to understand the relationship between the context and learning. As a result, the instructional situation is designed in such a way that learning becomes detached from its social context. The cognitive theorists argue that social context may not be necessary in situations like developing learners' general mathematical reasoning abilities (Anderson et al., 1996). Lave and Wenger (1991) argued that "learning is an integral part of generative social practice in the lived-in world" (p. 35). Situative learning theorists insisted that any type of learning is situationally grounded (Greeno, 1997; Lave & Wenger, 1991). They further pointed out that all learning activities, individual and collective, entail social context and therefore reflect social practice of human being. The difference between cognitive and situative perspectives with regard to contextualization of learning thus lies in their differing views on the context in which learning occurs, with former assuming learning context as a manipulatable variable for cognitive information process and the latter defining learning to be a social context where knowledge is distributed among learners (Hutchins, 2000). This difference, as Cobb and Bowers (1999) pointed out, reflects "the differing treatments of meaning, the alternative ways in which instructional goals are cast, and conflicting views of the relationship between theory and classroom practices" (p. 4).

Second, the cognitive perspective presumed that complex cognitive skills can be learned more successfully if their independent subskills are learned first in situations involving individual practices (Hicks & Young, 1972). Consequently, the instructional situation is characterized by a hierarchical learning process where learning is subordinated to a set of steps called cognitive skills acquisition. This approach was challenged by the situative learning theorists who argued that developing students' abilities to participate in valued social practices and their identities as learners is more important in any learning situation than merely learning a collection of subskills (Greeno, 1997). Choi and Hannafin (1995) defined the conditions of situated learning as everyday cognition which entails authentic and collaborative environments. They pointed out that in the formal learning environment skills and knowledge are operationalized very differently from how experts and practitioners use them in real life. Students may be able to pass tests and exams but be unable to apply the same knowledge in everyday circumstances. Situated learning model, in contrast, creates a learning environment in which the inextricability of thinking and the contexts is recognized through the revelation of the inherent significance of real-life contexts in learning.

Third, significant differences exist between cognitive and situative perspectives on knowledge transfer. Cognitive perspective viewed knowledge transfer as a two-step process which involves the mapping of knowledge between base and target domains (Holyoak & Thagard, 1989). The mapping process may involve far and near transfers with positive or negative results (Besnard & Cacitti, 2005; Mariano, Doolittle, & Hicks, 2009). Evidently, the cognitive perspective on knowledge transfer carried an assumption that knowledge transfer is a static concept, in that it can be measured in separate stages defined by a single point in time. This view is best shown in the instructional situations where learners are scaffolded to perform knowledge transfer tasks that render their knowledge inertia. That is, learners still fail to successfully transfer the knowledge they learned in school to the real world even though they receive substantial practices on knowledge transfer. Contrary to cognitive perspective, situative perspective argued that knowledge transfer is a dynamic process in which a person participates in "interactions with other people and with material and representational systems" (Greeno, 1997, p. 11). The view that knowledge transfer is a dynamic social interaction has been shared by researchers and social psychologists across the disciplines (Cobb & Bowers, 1999; Engle, 2006; Pea, 1987). For example, Bowers (1996) studied third-grade students' math learning and noticed the influence of social participation on knowledge transfer. Similar findings were obtained by Harris (2009) who used situated learning model to facilitate subject matter experts' (SME) tacit knowledge transfer.

In sum, cognitive and situative perspectives differ significantly on the issues of learning context, learning conditions and knowledge transfer. The above differences have already mirrored different practices in education in terms of (a) the types of instructional situations that should be implemented in teaching and learning, (b) the way the knowledge is generated and transferred in both formal and informal learning environments, and (c) the learning experience learners derive from instructional situations that reflect different epistemological perspectives. Despite of the significant improvement in understanding the differing epistemological perspectives pertaining to instructional situations, the extant literature fails to account for the individual differences, especially cognitive styles that would affect the learners' experience and performance. It is thus

appropriate to include a discussion on the issue of cognitive styles and instructional situations.

Cognitive Styles and Instructional Situations

As it was discussed above, research on situated learning has demonstrated positive results with regard to knowledge generation and transfer (Bowers, 1996; Harris, 2009). Nonetheless, this body of literature has failed to account for one important aspect in learning, especially in situated learning; that is, the extent to which learners' performance in situated learning is influenced by their differences in cognitive styles. As it was mentioned elsewhere in this chapter, cognitive styles can significantly leverage learners' way of information processing, their orientations as well as performance in learning. It should be noted that situative perspective recognizes "individual uniqueness" in learning (Harley, 1993). Commenting on the learning context and individual learning Harley pointed out that "Situation is defined as the awareness by which the individual determines his/her moment-by-moment reality … individual as an actor in the social world defines the reality he encounters" (p. 46). Apparently, the individual uniqueness defined in situated learning refers to a situation in which individuals try to make sense of the situated learning he/she is engaged in. In other words, situated learning becomes a world that transposes into an individual world of biographical situation (Harley, 1993). Nonetheless, research in situated learning still fails to account how learning is influenced by the individual differences in learning. Recently, researchers have called attention to the role of individual differences in situated learning (Huang & Andrews, 2010; Zheng, 2010). Zheng (2010) notes that the advantages of instructional situations as shown in situated learning research can be mediated by factors like individual differences, especially the differences in cognitive styles. He thus points out that it is essential that research on situated learning puts in perspective the differences of cognitive styles among learners "to understand how such differences may affect learners' performance in learning" (p. 468).

MAIN FOCUS OF THE CHAPTER

Issues, Controversies, Problems

One of the important innovations in education in the late 1990s is e-Learning which utilized the Internet and other digital technologies to provide education to individuals who have been otherwise denied the education opportunity due to distance, schedule conflict, job, and so forth. While there are some arguments about the quality of e-Learning as opposed to face-to-face classroom learning (Harasim, 2001), the impact of e-Learning on the existing educational system is palpable. Duncan (2008) pointed out that e-Learning has challenged the traditional curriculum, the pedagogy, and educational policies related to student assessment and faculty evaluation. Snelbeck, Miller, and Zheng (2008) accorded, "The proliferation of Internet use in general and online learning in particular has dramatically changed the landscape in K-16 education" (p. 2). Because of the critical role e-Learning has played in education, researchers begin to explore issues that affect the successful implementation of online teaching and learning. One variable that has drawn researchers' attention is the relationship between cognitive styles and learners' performance in e-Learning. Some researchers suggested that instruction should focus on the match of cognitive styles with instructional conditions (Ford & Chen, 2001); others found such approach to be less instructionally sound since there was no evidence showing the relationship between cognitive styles and learners' performance (Vincent-Morin & Lafont, 2005). The equivocal results shown above thus led to the first question this chapter would like to address:

Research Question 1: *Does learning become more effective when instructional conditions are matched with learners' cognitive styles in an e-Learning environment?*

Next, we examine FDI learners' behavior and their consequent learning performance when they are placed in different instructional situations (i.e., traditional vs. situative learning). Since the instructional situation reflects the epistemological perspective in learning, understanding the influence of cognitive styles on learners' performance in different instructional situations would contribute to the theoretical advancement as well as practices of the field. Thus, the second question that this chapter aims to answer is:

Research Question 2: *To what extent do cognitive styles affect learners' performance in situated learning or traditional learning environment?*

THE STUDY

Two main studies were carried out to address the two research questions. The first main study consisted of two sub-studies to explore the style matching and ability building in e-Learning. The second main study investigated the relationship between FDI and instructional situations in e-Learning.

Does Learning Become More Effective When Instructional Conditions Are Matched With Learners' Cognitive Styles in An e-Learning Environment?

The first study explored the issues of style matching and ability building in e-Learning. The following section presents the sub-studies that were conducted in two separate semesters.

Study 1

Study 1 was conducted using a hybrid online learning mode where learners learned the content in classroom and were asked to participate in online discussions via WebCT as part of their course work. The study purported to determine whether matching instructional conditions with learners' cognitive styles would produce better learning results in online learning. Forty-two undergraduates were recruited from an educational department. Participants were assigned readings related to their content area and required to post their comments online. There were two types of postings. The first posting asked the learners to post messages individually online after reading the articles. The second required the learners to challenge others' postings based on the individual postings already posted online. The first posting was called self posting (SP) and the second was called challenging others (CO). Using a quasi-experimental design, participants were divided into group and non-group with group learners receiving group support while posting comments online, and the non-group learners receiving no group support while engaging in online posting. Participants were first given a cognitive style test called Group Embedded Figure Test (GEFT) (Witkin et al., 1971) and were divided into FD and FI learners using a median split method with the median score being 13 and the range from 3 to 18.

It was hypothesized that FD learners would do well in well-structured task like SP as well as in ill-structure task like CO when they learned collaboratively since FD learners prefer social environment and that collaborative learning would promote their critical thinking skills, especially in tasks that require higher level thinking such as *challenging others*. It was also hypothesized that FI learners would perform better in SP tasks since FI learners prefer working individually with less social support. To test above hypotheses, we assigned FD learners to group instructional condition and FI learners to non-group instructional condition based on the literature that FD learners would like to be taught in a learning environment rich with social cues whereas FI learners prefer independent studies with minimal guidance and directions (Witkin & Goodenough, 1977). The study lasted about fourteen weeks. The postings were rated by two independent raters based on the rubrics developed by the author. The reliabilities for SP and CO task ratings were .91 and .84 respectively.

Results showed that FD learners had a higher mean average than their counterparts in SP tasks although the data revealed no significant difference between the groups. However, FD learners failed to perform well in ill-structured (CO) tasks. It was found that there was a big confusion among FD learners who did not know how to identify key issues and how to challenge others in ill-structured learning even though the style matching strategy was used to support their learning (For the details of the results, please refer to Zheng et al., 2009a).

The above findings challenged the previous assumption about style matching which stated that effective learning would occur when there was a match between instructional strategies and learners' cognitive styles (Ford & Chen, 2001; Liu & Reed, 1994). The results indicate that learners' performance was not determined by the style matching since we matched FD learners with instructional conditions (grouping) in both SP and CO tasks, but they performed well only in SP tasks. If we looked closely at the SP and CO tasks, SP was well-structured which required less higher level thinking skills whereas CO was ill-structured which required considerable degree of higher level thinking skills. It can thus be concluded that learners' performance was not so much dependent on style matching as on individual learner's cognitive ability. This is supported by the view that style matching only removes negative influences and keeps learning effective at minimum and that learning becomes more efficient and effective when there is an improvement in learners' cognitive abilities (Macpherson & Stanovich,

2007; Riding, 2000). Given the results of study 1, we hypothesized that learning would be more effective if the effort was gravitated toward ability building rather than style matching. Therefore, a second study was conducted which investigated learners' ability building through a scaffolding approach in online learning.

Study 2

Study 2 followed the similar research design as study 1 except that instead of matching instructional conditions (group vs. non-group) with FD and FI learners, the technique of cognitive scaffolding (i.e., teacher modeling, guided practice, and practice application. See Cazden, 1988) was used to improve FD learners' ability in critical and analytical thinking. The scaffolding was provided online by the instructor who assessed the student's performance in online postings followed by an appropriate scaffolding strategy based on the student's performance.

Seventy-nine participants were recruited from multiple sections of an undergraduate educational technology course from the same university as in study 1. Five did not complete the study and were therefore excluded from final analyses. Thus, the number of participants included in the final analysis was 74 undergraduate students. Participants first took the GEFT test. Based on the results of GEFT, participants were identified as FD or FI learners using a median split method. As with study 1, study 2 took a quasi-experimental design in which FD learners were assigned to the experimental group (with scaffolding) and FI learners to control group (without scaffolding) based on the assumptions that FD learners required extensive social cues and external support in complex learning whereas FI learners preferred to working independently and thus required little external guidance (Liu & Reed, 1994; Witkin et al., 1971, 2002b). That FI learners received no scaffolding support in CO tasks was also based on the fact

that FI learners had performed well in complex learning under the preferred condition in study 1.

As was discussed previously, ill-structured online learning demands cognitive resilience and the ability to deploy various cognitive strategies in an evolving and emerging learning environment (DeSchryver & Spiro, 2008). Therefore, helping learners develop critical thinking skills and the ability to become cognitively resilient to adjust to the evolving content is essential. Evidence has shown that scaffolding is effective in developing learners' critical thinking skills and their abilities to deploy cognitive strategies in ill-structured complex learning (Berthold, Nuckles, & Renkl, 2007; Milliken, 2007). It was thus hypothesized that FD learners would improve their performance in CO tasks resulting from an enhancement in cognitive ability in critical thinking due to cognitive scaffolding. The findings of study 2 confirmed our prediction that scaffolding as a cognitive tool improves FD learners' cognitive abilities which in turn increase their performance in ill-structured (CO task) learning. Although there was a learning gain with scaffolding for FD learners in SP tasks, no significant difference was found between the groups. FD learners demonstrated a trend of improvement in CO tasks over the course of study and outperformed their counterparts in complex learning (For the detail of the results, please refer to Zheng et al., 2009a).

The above findings indicate that merely matching instructional conditions with learners' cognitive styles is not sufficient to attain quality learning for students in online environment. The author argues that ability cultivation rather than style matching empowers FD and FI learners to succeed in learning including online learning. This is particularly true for FD learners as they developed their cognitive abilities in analyzing and synthesizing what has been presented and flexibly deploying appropriate cognitive strategies to deal with the complexity of the tasks (i.e., challenging other people's comments) in online learning.

To What Extent Cognitive Styles Affect Learners' Performance in Situated Learning?

The second question this chapter aims to address is the relationship between cognitive styles and instructional situations, particularly pertaining to situated vs. traditional learning. We predicted that there would be differences between FD and FI learners in situated and traditional learning in terms of knowledge acquisition. We also tried to find out what other variables that may influence the relationship between cognitive styles and instructional situations in learning.

The study was designed to compare the instructional effects between traditional learning and situated learning with a focus on individual differences (i.e., FD vs. FI) in a hybrid online learning environment. The instructional situations consisted of two learning environments: situated learning and traditional lectures. In situated learning, students were assigned an authentic task by working with a local company to design and develop instructional materials for professional training. Students formed a group of 3 to 4 to work on the instructional design project. The group was asked to select one instructional design model covered in the class to design and develop their project. Students in situated learning group critiqued each other's projects, gave feedback and made revisions accordingly. Most collaborative activities such as critiques, feedback, revisions were carried out in WebCT. Students in the traditional learning group received the same amount of information except the project was developed based on a hypothetical scenario provided by the instructor. The entire learning process was dominated by lectures in which the instructor explained and delineated the components of the instructional design models and the implementation process. Students submitted their assignments to WebCT and received critiques and feedback from the instructor online.

Seventy-nine participants were recruited from graduate classes in a large research I university in the western United States. Using a block design model, the classes were randomly assigned to experimental and control groups. The study lasted about 16 weeks. At the beginning of the study, all participants took a cognitive test called Group Embedded Figure Test (GEFT) (Witkin et al., 1971). Learners with higher GEFT scores were defined as field independent (FI) learners and those with lower GEFT scores were considered field dependent (FD) learners. At the end of the 16-week period both situated and traditional learning groups took an achievement test that measured their declarative knowledge in instructional design. A rubric was developed for the final assessment of the projects for both situated and traditional learning groups. The rubric included nine items covering three major areas of performance: identifying problems, integrating an instructional design model to solve the problems and presenting solutions by developing an instructional training unit. To find out the role of cognitive styles in situated learning and determine if other variables may interact with cognitive styles to influence learners' performance, we conducted a survey study for the situated learning group asking how the presence of situated learning characteristics would affect their performance in learning.

The results of the study confirmed our prediction that there was a significant difference between FD and FI learners in situated learning as measured by their projects. However, no significant difference was found between FD and FI learners in traditional learning. Overall, both FD and FI learners did better in situated learning than in traditional learning in terms of declarative knowledge acquisition as measured by achievement tests. This suggests that instructional situation did influence learners' performance when it came to learning like declarative knowledge acquisition. Meanwhile, the findings suggest that when engaging in tasks like projects which require analytical thinking and decision making, situated learning appeared to benefit learners more than did traditional learning. Next, the findings from our survey study revealed, at a deeper level, the relationships among the variables in situated learning. The results indicated that the influence of cognitive styles on learners' learning was not simply a linear relationship but with significant complexity showing a web-like relationship among the variables involved in e-Learning (Figure 1).

Figure 1 indicates that authentic context, articulation, authentic activity, authentic assessment, multiple perspectives are directly correlated with performance, and that FDI has multi-dimensional relationships with articulation, authentic activity, and multiple perspectives which suggest a mediation effect that needs further empirical verification. It also shows that scaffold and collaboration correlate well with authentic activity and authentic context. Evidently, the existing research paradigm on cognitive style and performance can be limited in explaining the complex-

ity of the relationship between FDI and e-Learning. The above findings suggest that situated learning can improve learners' learning by providing authentic and meaningful context which facilitates knowledge acquisition and transfer (Cobb & Bowers, 1999; Greeno, 1997). They also suggest that situated learning can be affected by learners' cognitive styles such as FDI in learning.

In conclusion, our studies have shown that cognitive styles can significantly influence learners' behavior and performance in e-Learning. The results of our studies challenged the existing practices in terms of style and instructional conditions matching. Our findings indicate that ability building is more important than merely matching instructional conditions with learners' cognitive styles in e-Learning. We also found that instructional situations (e.g., situated learning) can significantly influence learners' performance, particularly those with different cognitive styles. More importantly, we identified the critical role of FDI in situated learning. Despite of the advancement

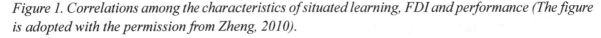

Figure 1. Correlations among the characteristics of situated learning, FDI and performance (The figure is adopted with the permission from Zheng, 2010).

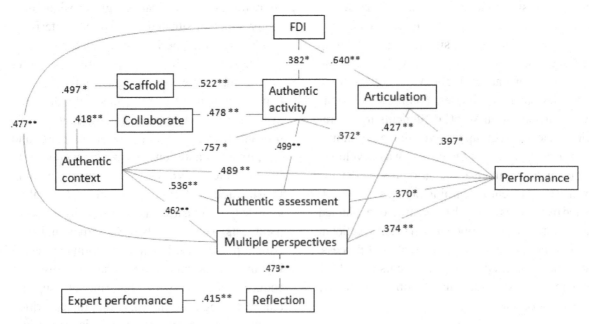

in the research of cognitive styles and e-Learning as evidenced by our findings along with those of others, significant challenges still remain in terms of how to effectively design and develop an e-Learning environment that promotes learners' cognitive abilities and higher level thinking skills while engaging in meaningful and robust online learning.

SOLUTIONS AND RECOMMENDATIONS

To meet the above challenges, research in cognitive style and e-learning needs to consider broadly variables in e-learning by taking a systematic approach. It is suggested that a comprehensive research agenda that looks at the relationship among the factors and variables involved in e-learning is necessary. Oftentimes, a narrowly defined research agenda can bias the researcher into a few isolated topics which result in the negligence of more important issues. Therefore, we propose a comprehensive research agenda based on the correlation model as identified above (Figure 1) and suggest that future research should consider the relations among variables related to e-learning. As such, we offer our recommendations for future research on cognitive styles and e-learning:

- Research on cognitive styles and e-Learning should encompass both direct and latent variables that impact the learner's behavior and performance in e-Learning
- More robust research methods such as path analysis and structural equation modeling (SEM) should be taken to explicate the relationship of the variables under study.
- More advanced interventions should be developed that will reflect the findings of research resulting from the adoption of above suggested methodologies.
- Related to No. 2 and 3 above, rigorous research methods and intervention should be

employed to generate findings that will accurately describe and explain the phenomenon related to e-Learning. Thus, the results can be replicated in various situations and generalized to a larger population.

FUTURE RESEARCH DIRECTIONS

This chapter examined the variables associated with e-Learning by putting in perspective the influence of cognitive styles on learners' performance. As it was mentioned elsewhere in this chapter, the current research paradigm in cognitive styles and performance often takes a narrow approach by limiting their studies to a few key variables while neglecting the roles of other variables that play critical roles in e-Learning. Future research should consider investigating the relationship and the roles of variables in learning by employing robust research methodology such as SEM and path analysis. Future research should ground its work in developing theoretical framework that would explicate the complexity of the phenomenon in e-Learning. This can be accomplished by first identifying fundamental factors/constructs through exploratory and confirmatory factor analyses, followed by more sophisticated research methodologies that verify the explanatory power of the factors/constructs identified. Till then, we will have a better grasp of the underlying variables/constructs that influence the behavior and performance of learners in e-Learning.

CONCLUSION

The goal of this chapter is to identify the influence of cognitive styles in e-Learning. The author examined the roles of cognitive styles in e-Learning by focusing on two important issues that relate to the current practices in e-Learning; that is, the matching of instructional conditions with cognitive styles and the role of cognitive style in instructional situations. Our first study which consisted of two sub-studies revealed that merely matching instructional conditions with learners' cognitive styles does not necessarily help learners learn more effectively. Rather, building learners' cognitive abilities using such techniques as scaffolding can significantly enhance learners' performance in e-Learning. Our next study explored the relationship between cognitive styles and instructional situations. We found that instructional situations can influence the performance of learners who differ in their cognitive styles. This is particularly true in situations where learners learned with traditional approach or with situated learning. Our findings indicated that situated learning can significantly improve learners' ability in critical thinking and decision making when engaging in complex task like project-based learning. Another important finding derived from the second study was that the influence of FDI on learners' performance is not unilateral or one-way impact. Rather, FDI has multi-dimensional relationships with other variables including authentic activity, performance and learners' perspectives in learning. This challenges the existing research paradigm that often focuses on the linear relationship between cognitive styles and performance. In that regard, the current chapter has filled the gap in research by identifying the role of FDI in e-Learning which calls for a more comprehensive approach in the research on cognitive styles and e-Learning.

As with any other empirical studies, the findings of the studies described in this chapter require further verification and empirical research so the results can be generalized to a larger population. In addition, the existing findings can be further enhanced by taking a systematic approach that examines the relationship among the variables in e-Learning, identifies the critical factors that undergird the learners' behavior and performance in e-Learning, and develops a theoretical framework that explicates the complexity of e-Learning.

The findings reported in this chapter have significant ramifications for the design and de-

velopment of e-Learning. By identifying the role of FDI and the limitation of matching practice, the design of e-Learning can benefit from focusing more on building learners' cognitive ability rather than matching their cognitive styles with instructional conditions. Moreover, researchers, educators, and other professional trainers can utilize the findings of the studies to improve their design and development of e-Learning where cognitive styles are looked upon as a dynamic variable that correlates with the variables in e-Learning and where learners become engaged in meaningful and robust online learning that would consequently lead to effective knowledge acquisition and transfer.

REFERENCES

Anderson, J., Reder, L., & Simon, H. (1996). Situated learning and education. *Educational Researcher*, *25*(4), 5–11.

Angeli, C., & Valanides, N. (2004). Examining the effects of text-only and text-and-visual instructional materials on the achievement of field-dependent and field-independent learners during problem solving with modeling software. *Educational Technology Research and Development*, *52*, 23–36. doi:10.1007/BF02504715

Bernardi, R. (2003). Students performance in accounting: Differential effect of field dependence–independence as a learning style. *Psychological Reports*, *93*, 135–142.

Berthold, K., Nuckles, M., & Renkl, A. (2007). Do learning protocols support learning strategies and outcomes? The role of cognitive and metacognitive prompts. *Learning and Instruction*, *17*(5), 564–577. doi:10.1016/j.learninstruc.2007.09.007

Besnard, D., & Cacitti, L. (2005). Interface changes causing accidents. An empirical study of negative transfer. *International Journal of Human-Computer Studies*, *62*, 105–125. doi:10.1016/j.ijhcs.2004.08.002

Bowers, J. (1996). Conducting developmental research in a technology-enhanced classroom (Doctoral dissertation, Vanderbilt University, 1996). *Dissertation Abstracts International, 57,* 3433A.

Buckingham, D. (2004). New media, new childhoods? Children's changing cultural environment in the age of digital technology. In Kehily, M. J. (Ed.), *An introduction to childhood studies* (pp. 108–122). Maidenhead, UK: Open University Press.

Cazden, C. B. (1988). *Classroom discourse: The language of teaching and learning.* Portsmouth, NH: Heinemann.

Chinien, C. A., & Boutin, F. (1992). Cognitive style FD/I: An important learning characteristic for educational technologies. *Journal of Educational Technology Systems*, *21*(4), 303–311.

Choi, J., & Hannafin, M. J. (1995). Situated cognition and learning environments: Roles, structures, and implications for design. *Educational Technology Research and Development*, *43*(2), 53–69. doi:10.1007/BF02300472

Cobb, P., & Bowers, J. (1999). Cognitive and situative learning perspectives in theory and practice. *Educational Researcher*, *28*(2), 4–15.

Crown, S. W. (1999). Web-based learning: Enhancing the teaching of engineering graphics. *Interactive Multimedia Electronic Journal of Computer Enhanced Learning, 1*(2). Retrieved on November 17, 2010, from http://imej.wfu.edu/articles/1999/2/02/index.asp

Danili, E., & Reid, N. (2004). Some strategies to improve performance in school chemistry, based on two cognitive factors. *Research in Science & Technological Education*, *22*(2), 203–226. doi:10.1080/0263514042000290903

DeSchryver, M., & Spiro, R. (2008). New forms of deep learning on the Web: Meeting the challenge of cognitive load in conditions of unfettered exploration in online multimedia environments. In R. Zheng (Ed.), *Cognitive effects of multimedia learning* (pp. 134-152). Hershey, PA: IGI Global Publishing.

Duncan, J. (2008). Learning and study strategies for online teaching. In Kidd, T., & Song, H. (Eds.), *Handbook of research on instructional systems and technology* (pp. 532–546). Hershey, PA: Information Science Reference/IGI Global Publishing. doi:10.4018/978-1-59904-865-9.ch037

Engle, R. A. (2006). Framing interactions to foster generative learning: A situative explanation of transfer in a community of learners classroom. *Journal of the Learning Sciences*, *15*(4), 451–498. doi:10.1207/s15327809jls1504_2

Ford, N. (1995). Levels and types of mediation in instructional systems: An individual differences approach. *International Journal of Human-Computer Studies*, *43*, 241–259. doi:10.1006/ijhc.1995.1043

Ford, N., & Chen, S. (2001). Matching/mismatching revisited: An empirical study of learning and teaching styles. *British Journal of Educational Technology*, *32*(1), 5–22. doi:10.1111/1467-8535.00173

Gonzalez, J. A., Jover, L., & Cobo, E. (2010). A web-based learning tool improves student performance in statistics: A randomized masked trial. *Computers & Education*, *55*(2), 704–713. doi:10.1016/j.compedu.2010.03.003

Greenfield, P., & Yan, Z. (2006). Children, adolescents, and the Internet: A new field of inquiry in developmental psychology. *Developmental Psychology, 42*, 391–394. doi:10.1037/0012-1649.42.3.391

Greeno, J. (1997). On claims that answer the wrong questions. *Educational Researcher, 26*(1), 5–17.

Gregorc, A. (1982). *An adult's guide to style.* Columbia, CT: Gregorc Associates.

Griffin, R., & Franklin, G. (1996). Can college academic performance be predicted using a measure of cognitive style? *Journal of Educational Technology Systems, 24*(4), 375–379.

Harasim, L. (2001). Shift happens: Online education as a new paradigm in learning. *The Internet and Higher Education, 3*, 41–61. doi:10.1016/S1096-7516(00)00032-4

Harley, S. (1993). Situated learning and classroom instruction. *Educational Technology, 33*(3), 46–51.

Harris, R. (2009). Improving tacit knowledge transfer within SMEs through e-collaboration. *Journal of European Industrial Training, 33*(3), 215–231. doi:10.1108/03090590910950587

Herbst, P. G. (2006). Teaching geometry with problems: Negotiating instructional situations and mathematical tasks. *Journal for Research in Mathematics Education, 37*(4), 313–347.

Hicks, R. E., & Young, R. K. (1972). Part-whole list transfer in free recall: A reappraisal. *Journal of Experimental Psychology, 96*(2), 328–333. doi:10.1037/h0033643

Holt, R. D., & Oliver, M. (2002). Evaluating web-based modules during and MSc programme in dental public health: A case study. *British Dental Journal, 193*(5), 283–286. doi:10.1038/sj.bdj.4801546

Holyoak, K. J., & Thagard, P. (1989). Analogical mapping by constraint satisfaction. *Cognitive Science, 13*, 295–355. doi:10.1207/s15516709cog1303_1

Huang, J. S., & Andrews, S. (2010). Situated development and use of language learner strategies: Voices from EFL students. *Language Learning Journal, 38*(1), 19–35. doi:10.1080/09571730902717430

Hutchins, E. (2000). *Distributed cognition.* Retrieved October 5, 2009, from http://eclectic.ss.uci.edu/~drwhite/Anthro179a/DistributedCognition.pdf

Ikegulu, P. R., & Ikegulu, T. N. (1999). *The effectiveness of window presentation strategy and cognitive style of field dependence status on learning from mediated instructions.* Ruston, LA: Center for Statistical Consulting. (ERIC Document Reproduction Service No. ED428758)

Jonassen, D. H., & Grabowski, B. L. (1993). *Handbook of individual differences, learning, and instruction.* Hillsdale, NJ: Lawrence Erlbaum.

Kagan, J. (1966). Reflection-impulsivity: The generality and dynamics of conceptual tempo. *Journal of Abnormal Psychology, 71*, 17–24. doi:10.1037/h0022886

Kirby, P. (1979). *Cognitive style, learning style and transfer skill acquisition.* Columbus, OH: The National Center for Research in Vocational Education, The Ohio State University.

Koc, M. (2005). Individual learner differences in web-based learning environments: From cognitive, affective and social-cultural perspectives. *Turkish Online Journal of Distance Education, 6*(4), 12–22.

Lave, J., & Wenger, E. (1991). *Situated learning: Legitimate peripheral participation.* Cambridge, UK: Cambridge University Press.

Liu, M., & Reed, W. M. (1994). The relationship between the learning strategies and learning styles in a hypermedia environment. *Computers in Human Behavior, 10*(4), 419–434. doi:10.1016/0747-5632(94)90038-8

Liu, X. J., Magjuka, R. J., & Lee, S. H. (2008). The effects of cognitive thinking styles, trust, conflict management on online students' learning and virtual team performance. *British Journal of Educational Technology, 39*(5), 829–846. doi:10.1111/j.1467-8535.2007.00775.x

Lloyd, B. T. (2002). A conceptual framework for examining adolescent identity, media influence, and social development. *Review of General Psychology, 6*, 73–91. doi:10.1037/1089-2680.6.1.73

MacNeil, R. (1980). The relationship of cognitive style and instructional style to the learning performance of undergraduate students. *The Journal of Educational Research, 73*(6), 354–359.

Macpherson, R., & Stanovich, K. E. (2007). Cognitive ability, thinking dispositions, and instructional set as predictors of critical thinking. *Learning and Individual Differences, 17*(2), 115–127. doi:10.1016/j.lindif.2007.05.003

Mariano, G. J., Doolittle, P., & Hicks, D. (2009). Fostering transfer in multimedia instructional materials. In Zheng, R. (Ed.), *Cognitive effects of multimedia learning* (pp. 237–258). Hershey, PA: Information Science Reference/IGI Global.

Martin, F. (2008). Effects of practice in a linear and non-linear web-based learning environment. *Journal of Educational Technology & Society, 11*(4), 81–93.

Messick, S. (1984). The nature of cognitive styles: Problems and promise in educational practice. *Educational Psychologist, 19*, 59–74. doi:10.1080/00461528409529283

Milliken, J. (2007). Scaffolding cognitive processes in a marketing curriculum. *Higher Education in Europe, 32*(2-3), 185–191. doi:10.1080/03797720701840740

Moallem, M. (2008). Accommodating individual differences in the design of online learning environments: A comparative study. *Journal of Research on Technology in Education, 40*(2), 217–245.

Moore, J. L., Dickson-Deane, C., & Galyen, K. (2011). e-Learning, online learning, and distance learning environments: Are they the same? *The Internet and Higher Education, 14*(2), 129–135. doi:10.1016/j.iheduc.2010.10.001

Noble, K. (2006). *Effect of the NePPHRO program on the learning of students of physiology who exhibit variation in cognitive style.* Unpublished PhD Thesis, Temple University, Pennsylvania, PA.

Pea, R. D. (1987). Socializing the knowledge transfer problem. *International Journal of Educational Research, 11*(6), 639–664. doi:10.1016/0883-0355(87)90007-3

Richards, J. P., Fajen, B. R., Sullivan, J. F., & Gillespie, G. (1997). Signaling, notetaking, and field independence-dependence in text comprehension and recall. *Journal of Educational Psychology, 89*(3), 508–517. doi:10.1037/0022-0663.89.3.508

Riding, R. (2000). *Cognitive style analysis – Research administration.* Birmingham, UK: Learning and Training Technology.

Rittschof, K. A. (2010). Field dependence–independence as visuospatial and executive functioning in working memory: Implications for instructional systems design and research. *Educational Technology Research and Development, 58*, 99–114. doi:10.1007/s11423-008-9093-6

Samples, R. E. (1975). Are you teaching online one side of the brain? *Learning, 3*(6), 25–28.

Santo, S. A. (2006). Relationships between learning styles and online learning. *Performance Improvement Quarterly, 19*(3), 73–88. doi:10.1111/j.1937-8327.2006.tb00378.x

Sedig, K. (2011). Interactivity of information representation in e-learning environments. In Wang, H. (Ed.), *Interactivity in e-learning: Case studies and frameworks*. Hershey, PA: Information Science Reference/IGI Global Publishing.

Shany, N., & Nachmias, R. (2000). *The relationship between performances in a virtual course and thinking styles, gender, and ICT experience*. Retrieved November 15, 2010, from http://muse.tau.ac.il/publications/64.pdf

Skylar, A. (2009). A comparison of asynchronous online text-based lectures and synchronous interactive web conferencing lectures. *Issues in Teacher Education, 18*(2), 69–84.

Snelbecker, G., Miller, S., & Zheng, R. (2008). Functional relevance and online instructional design. In Zheng, R., & Ferris, S. P. (Eds.), *Understanding online instructional modeling: Theories and practices* (pp. 1–17). Hershey, PA: Information Science Reference/IGI Global Publishing.

Springer, S., & Deutch, G. (1985). *Right brain, left brain*. San Francisco, CA: W. H. Freeman.

Vincent-Morin, M., & Lafont, L. (2005). Learning-method choices and personal characteristics in solving a physical education problem. *Journal of Teaching in Physical Education, 24*, 226–242.

Witkin, H. A., & Goodenough, D. R. (1977). Field dependence and interpersonal behavior. *Psychological Bulletin, 84*, 661–689. doi:10.1037/0033-2909.84.4.661

Witkin, H. A., Moore, C. A., Goodenough, D. R., & Cox, P. W. (1977). Field dependent and field independent cognitive styles and their educational implications. *Review of Educational Research, 47*(1), 1–64.

Witkin, H. A., Oltman, P. K., Raskin, E., & Karp, S. A. (1971). *Group embedded figures test manual*. Menlo Park, CA: Mind Garden.

Zheng, R. (2010). Effects of situated learning on students' knowledge acquisition: An individual differences perspective. *Journal of Educational Computing Research, 43*(4), 463–483. doi:10.2190/EC.43.4.c

Zheng, R., Flygare, J., & Dahl, L. (2009a). Style matching or ability building? An empirical study on FDI learners' learning in well-structured and ill-structured asynchronous online learning environments. *Journal of Educational Computing Research, 41*(2), 195–226. doi:10.2190/EC.41.2.d

Zheng, R., Flygare, J., Dahl, L., & Hoffman, R. (2009b). The impact of individual differences on social communication pattern in online learning. In Mourlas, C., Tsianos, N., & Germanakos, P. (Eds.), *Cognitive and emotional processes in web-based education: Integrating human factors and personalization* (pp. 321–342). Hershey, PA: Information Science Reference/IGI Global Publishing. doi:10.4018/978-1-60566-392-0.ch015

Zheng, R., Yang, W., Garcia, D., & McCadden, B. P. (2008). Effects of multimedia on schema induced analogical reasoning in science learning. *Journal of Computer Assisted Learning, 24*, 474–482. doi:10.1111/j.1365-2729.2008.00282.x

ADDITIONAL READING

Adey, P., & Shayer, M. (1993). An exploration of long-term far-transfer effects following an extended intervention program in the high school science curriculum. *Cognition and Instruction, 11*(1), 1–29. doi:10.1207/s1532690xci1101_1

Atkinson, S. (2004). A comparison of pupil learning and achievement in computer aided learning and traditionally taught situations with special reference to cognitive style and gender issues. *Educational Psychology, 24*(5), 659–679. doi:10.1080/0144341042000262962

Brown, A., & Campione, J. (1990). Communities of learning or a context by any other name. In Kuhn, D. (Ed.), *Contributions to human development* (*Vol. 21*, pp. 108–126). New York: Oxford University Press.

Browne-Ferrigno, T., & Muth, R. (2006). Leadership mentoring and situated learning: Catalysts for principalship readiness and lifelong mentoring. *Mentoring & Tutoring, 14*(3), 275–295. doi:10.1080/13611260600635530

Danili, E., & Reid, N. (2004). Some strategies to improve performance in school chemistry, based on two cognitive factors. *Research in Science & Technological Education, 22*(2), 203–226. doi:10.1080/0263514042000290903

Ford, N. (1995). Levels and types of mediation in instructional systems: an individual differences approach. *International Journal of Human-Computer Studies, 43*, 241–259. doi:10.1006/ijhc.1995.1043

Graff, M. G. (2003). Learning from web-based instructional systems and cognitive style. *British Journal of Educational Technology, 34*(4), 407–418. doi:10.1111/1467-8535.00338

Hambrick, D. Z., Pink, J. E., & Meinz, E. J. (2008). The roles of ability, personality, and interests in acquiring current events knowledge: a longitudinal study. *Intelligence, 36*(3), 261–278. doi:10.1016/j.intell.2007.06.004

Harnad, S. (2005). Distributed processes, distributed cognizers and collaborative cognition. *Pragmatics & Cognition, 13*(3), 501–514. doi:10.1075/pc.13.3.06har

Hill, J. R., & Hannafin, M. J. (1997). Cognitive strategies and learning from the World Wide Web. *Educational Technology Research and Development, 45*(4), 37–64. doi:10.1007/BF02299682

Lajoie, S. P. (2008). Metacognition, self regulation, and self-regulated learning: A rose by any other name? *Educational Psychology Review, 20*(4), 469–475. doi:10.1007/s10648-008-9088-1

Lave, J., & Wenger, D. (1991). *Situated learning: Legitimate peripheral participation.* Cambridge: University of Cambridge Press.

Lever-Duffy, J., McDonald, J. B., & Mizell, A. P. (2003). *Teaching and learning with technology.* Boston, MA: Allyn & Bacon/Pearson.

Lim, J., Reiser, R. A., & Olina, Z. (2009). The Effects of part-task and whole-task instructional approaches on acquisition and transfer of a complex cognitive skill. *Educational Technology Research and Development, 57*(1), 61–77. doi:10.1007/s11423-007-9085-y

O'Leary, M., Calsyn, D., & Fauria, T. (1980). The Group Embedded Figures Test: A measure of cognitive style or cognitive impairment. *Journal of Personality Assessment, 44*(5), 532–537. doi:10.1207/s15327752jpa4405_14

Resnick, L. (1987). Learning in school and out. *Educational Researcher, 16*(9), 13–20.

Wolfson, L., & Willinsky, J. (1998). Situated learning in high school information technology management. *Journal of Research on Computing in Education, 31*(1), 96–109.

Workman, M. (2009). Cognitive styles and design interactions in web-based education. In Mourlas, C., Tsianos, N., & Germanakos, P. (Eds.), *Cognitive and emotional processes in web-based education: integrating human factors and personalization* (pp. 58–71). Hershey, PA: Information Science Reference/IGI Global Publishing. doi:10.4018/978-1-60566-392-0.ch004

Zheng, R., Miller, S., Snelbecker, G., & Cohen, I. (2006). Use of multimedia for problem-solving tasks. *Journal of Technology, Instruction. Cognition and Learning, 3*(1-2), 135–143.

Zheng, R., & Zhou, B. (2006). Recency effect on problem solving in interactive multimedia learning. *Journal of Educational Technology & Society, 9*(2), 107–118.

KEY TERMS AND DEFINITIONS

Cognitive Styles: One's way of thinking, perceiving, and remembering information. In an early study Kirby (1979) provided a comprehensive summary of 19 cognitive styles and concluded that all learners learn differently. According to Chinien and Boutin (1992), cognitive styles refer to "the information processing habits representing the learners' typical mode of perceiving, thinking, problem solving, and remembering" (p. 303). They claimed that cognitive styles constitute important dimensions of individual differences among learners and have important implications for teaching and learning. Differing from learning styles which describe the conditions (i.e., auditory, visual, haptic, etc.) under which we best learn, cognitive styles are about how we perceive and think (Lever-Duffy, McDonald, & Mizell, 2003). The construct of cognitive style has been considered as a consistent, stable variable in learning.

Cognitive Ability: one's cognitive capability in processing information. The cognitive ability may refer to aptitude, intelligence, and skill. Riding (2000) made a distinction between cognitive style and cognitive ability by showing that performance on tasks would improve as the ability increased, whereas the effect of style on performance would either be positive or negative depending on the nature of the task. Atkinson (2004) added that cognitive styles are characterized by a bipolar nature that would either positively or negatively influence learner performance whereas cognitive abilities reflect a continuum of individual's psychological functions relating to information processing. Thus, the pedagogical benefits for style matching would be at most to alleviate the negative influence and maintain positive influence on learner performance. However, such approach may not necessarily result in an increase in cognitive ability. In other words, removing negative influence only keeps learning effective at a minimal level. Learning becomes more efficient and effective when the improvement is made in learners' cognitive abilities (Hambrick, Pink, & Meinz, 2008; Macpherson & Stanovich, 2007).

E-Learning: Using electronic venues to deliver the content. It essentially employs computer network to transfer skills and knowledge. E-Learning applications and processes include Web-based learning, computer-based learning, virtual classroom opportunities and digital collaboration. Content is delivered via the Internet, intranet/extranet, audio or video tape, satellite TV, and CD-ROM. It can be self-paced or instructor-led and includes media in the form of text, image, animation, streaming video and audio. E-Learning can be either full online version or hybrid that uses both online and face-to-face environments to deliver the content.

Field Dependence and Field Independence: The word "field" can be a set of thoughts, ideas, or feelings. People with field-dependent (FD) or field-independent (FI) cognitive style are different in their interpersonal behavior, social skills, and information processing. According to Witkin and Goodenough's (1977), FD people tend to make use of external social referents whereas FI people function with greater autonomy under such conditions. FD people are more attentive to social cues than are FI people. As a result, FD people show more interest in others, prefer to be physically close to people, are emotionally more open, and gravitate toward social situations. In contrast, FI people are characterized by an impersonal orientation, less interested in others, show physical and psychological distancing from people, and prefer non-social situations.

Instructional Conditions: Concerned with the presence of cues and scaffolds in learning environments. Instructional conditions include such variables as structural support, feedback, directions and guidance in learning, available resources, and so forth. It also refers to the conditions under which the learning occurs such as collaborative vs. individual learning, self-paced vs. instructor directed learning, and with visual, social cues vs. without visual, social cues, etc.

Instructional Situations: Differing from instructional conditions which are concerned with the presence of cues and scaffolds in learning, instructional situation reflects the epistemological thinking in learning by focusing on knowledge generation and transfer (Herbst, 2006). The term instructional situation is broadly defined in both research and practice ranging from general education to corporate training, from instructional design to field instruction, and from daily practices to epistemological considerations. In this chapter, the instructional situations refer to epistemological differences regarding the design of instructional situations. Specifically, they refer to the differing views between situated learning and cognitive learning in terms of learning conditions, knowledge acquisition and transfer.

Situated Learning: First proposed by Jean Lave and Etienne Wenger as a model of learning in a community of practice. The situated learning advocates maintained that learning should take place in the same context in which it is applied. Thus, situated learning emphasizes authentic context, authentic activities and authentic assessment while learning takes place. Lave and Wenger (1991) argue that learning should not be viewed as simply the transmission of abstract and decontextualised knowledge from one individual to another, but a social process whereby knowledge is co-constructed; they suggest that such learning is situated in a specific context and embedded within a particular social and physical environment.

Style Matching: An educational practice where educators match instructional conditions with learners' cognitive styles. Research suggests that relevant instructional strategies should be employed to match learners' cognitive styles due to the differences between learners in information processing, social interaction, and demands for support (Ford, 1995; Ford & Chen, 2001; Liu & Reed, 1994). For example, Danili and Reid (2004) studied 105 Greek pupils aged 15 to 16 in a chemistry course. They found a learning gain for FI learners when self-initiated instructional strategy was used and for FD learners, grouping appeared to be the most effective strategy in learning. Ford and Chen (2001) studied the instructional consequences of matching and mismatching instructional strategies with students' cognitive styles in a computer-based learning environment and concluded that learning became effective when a style matching was implemented.

Chapter 6
Diagnosis, Supporting, and Fading:
A Scaffolding Design Framework for Adaptive E-Learning Systems

Xun Ge
University of Oklahoma, USA

Victor Law
University of Oklahoma, USA

Kun Huang
University of North Texas Health Science Center, USA

ABSTRACT

This chapter presents a design framework of scaffolding that can be applied in designing adaptive e-learning systems. The framework is primarily grounded in socio-cultural theory and built on a critical analysis of literature on scaffolding. It addresses three key processes in scaffolding (i.e., diagnosis, supporting, and fading) and four conditions for designing scaffolding (i.e., who, what, how, and when). From the historical perspective, this chapter also provides a literature review of adaptive systems. The characteristics of adaptive systems from different paradigms are specifically examined through the lens of scaffolding. To illustrate the application of the scaffolding framework in system adaptation, four web-based e-learning systems are described to demonstrate how various scaffolding strategies are implemented through the design of the systems. In conclusion, issues related to designing scaffolds for adaptive e-learning systems are discussed, and research gaps are identified for future investigation.

DOI: 10.4018/978-1-61350-441-3.ch006

INTRODUCTION

With the rapid advancement of information and communication technology, the word "interactivity" has been taken for granted as a key characteristic of and an essential requirement for e-learning. Yet, interactivity has been defined or interpreted differently in different contexts and from different perspectives, ranging from the human-computer perspective to the communication and media view. The former perspective views interactivity as the capability to allow a human being to act on the computer screen, such as a mouse click (e.g., Betrancourt, 2005), and the latter views interactivity as personal communications (verbal & non-verbal) over different media (FtF or CMC) (Burgoon et al., 2002). Tung and Deng (2006) argued that interactivity is a means of developing sociable technology that enhances social presence in an e-learning environment. In the e-learning environment we contend that interactivity is a dynamic process that allows exchanges not only between human and computer, but also among people through computer systems, involving control or ability to act.

An important aspect of interactivity is system adaptation. System adaptation, in its broad sense, refers to "an artificial organism that alters its behavior according to the environment" (Shute & Zapata-Rivera, 2008, p. 278). In the context of e-learning, system adaptation refers to the capability of a technology system to monitor individuals' learning processes and consequently provide optimal dynamic adaptations according to the needs and characteristics of individual learners (Leutner, 2004; Shute & Zapata-Rivera, 2008). In this chapter, we are particularly interested in examining system adaptation that facilitates learners' deep cognitive and metacognitive processes.

The concept scaffolding originated from Vygotsky's (1978) socio-cultural theory. When a child is being assisted by an adult or a more capable peer in a social context, he or she is capable of carrying out a task that would have been otherwise too difficult to accomplish alone. The assistance that a learner receives in this situation is described as scaffolding. This kind of support, or scaffolding, is "temporary and adjustable" (Palincsar, 1986, p. 75), which means that scaffolding will be gradually withdrawn as learners gain competence in performing a task. Conventionally, scaffolds are described in the form of instructional strategies or procedures (e.g., Palincsar, 1986; Palincsar & A. Brown, 1984; Scardamalia & Bereiter, 1985; Scardamalia, Bereiter, & Steinbach, 1984); however, the use of scaffolding began to find its way in the context of computer-supported learning environments in the 80s. For example, Salomon, Globerson, and Guterman (1989) proposed using computers as Reading and Writing Partners to scaffold learners' metacognitive activities and assist learners to complete their reading and writing tasks. Scardamalia and her colleagues (1989) embedded procedural prompts in a computer-supported collaborative learning environment as a form of scaffolding to guide learners through their writing tasks.

In the context of computer-supported learning environments, Lajoie (2005) defined scaffolding as "a temporary framework to support learners when assistance is needed and is removed when no longer needed" (p. 542). In such environments, adaptive instruction can be considered a method of scaffolding because instructional approaches, strategies and techniques are geared to accommodate individuals' needs and abilities within their zone of proximal development (ZPD) (Vygotsky, 1978). As learners develop their skills over time and no longer depend on the assistance, scaffolding can be withdrawn gradually (Corno & Snow, 1986).

PURPOSE

In the past three decades, there is a myriad of research and practice on developing scaffolds for computer-supported learning environments

(Lajoie, 2000a; Lajoie & Derry, 1993), yet there is an absence of synthesis of literature on scaffolding strategies in e-learning, particularly a lack of conceptual framework to guide the integration of scaffolding methods with e-learning systems to provide adaptive assistance or instructional support. In addition, the relationship between scaffolding and system adaption has not been closely and distinctively examined in literature. Therefore, the goals of this chapter are to clarify the relationships between scaffolding and adaptation, identify major components of scaffolding, and synthesize scaffolding strategies for designing adaptive e-learning systems.

This chapter provides a comprehensive literature review on both scaffolding and adaptive systems from a historical perspective. Following the literature review, this chapter discusses various processes of scaffolding and examines how adaptation can be designed to provide scaffolding of different processes, from diagnosing difficult areas, identifying learners' needs, providing support with tools, to implementing fading strategies. Next, scaffolding strategies are classified and discussed in e-learning contexts. Towards the end, examples are presented to illustrate how various scaffolding strategies are implemented and how adaptations are achieved. In conclusion, research gaps are identified, implications for future research are discussed, and practical guidelines are provided for designing e-learning systems with effective adaptation and scaffolding mechanisms.

THEORETICAL BACKGROUND

Scaffolding

To design scaffolding mechanisms and adaptive systems, it is important to first examine the definition of scaffolding. The term *scaffolding* is rooted in Wood, Bruner and Ross' (1976) work, which defines scaffolding as "the process that enables a child or novice to solve a problem,

carry out a task or achieve a goal which would be beyond his unassisted efforts" (p.90). Wood et al.'s (1976) concept of scaffolding was similar to Vygotsky's concept of ZPD, which is defined as "the distance between the actual developmental level as determined by independent problem solving and the level of potential development as determined through problem solving under adult guidance or in collaboration with more capable peers" (Vygotsky, 1978, p. 86). The notion of ZPD is important for understanding scaffolding (Pea, 2004). First, there is a need for scaffolding because a novice cannot solve a problem independently. Second, a more capable other is going to provide the needed support to help the novice solve the problem. The more capable other can be a teacher, a parent, a peer in the same class who has more knowledge, or even a partner in a computer system (Ge & Land, 2004; Salomon, 1993a, 1993b). Third, scaffolding is both temporal and adjustable (Palincsar, 1986). One of the central characteristics of scaffolding is gradual fading or withdrawal of support as a learner gains competence in his or her problem-solving skills. Lastly, scaffolding is a continual process that constantly adjusts to meet individuals' needs because individuals' ZPD is subject to change over time. Our definition of scaffolding highlights three key processes in scaffolding: dynamic diagnosis, calibrated support, and fading (Puntambekar & Hubscher, 2005), which is discussed specifically below.

Dynamic Diagnosis

Dynamic diagnosis refers to the continuous assessment of students' learning processes and outcomes. In order to provide appropriate scaffolding, novices' prior knowledge has to be assessed in order to determine whether assistance is needed. Further, formative assessment must be carried out constantly to determine whether assistance needs to be adjusted or if it is no longer needed. Given the flexibility of human scaffolding, research in the past twenty years has focused on understanding how human beings provide scaffolding and how technology can be designed to provide similar kind of scaffolding. Drawing research on artificial intelligence, Intelligence Tutoring Systems (ITSs) are capable of diagnosing students' learning by comparing their problem solutions to an expert's solution. Although computer tutors have the capability of tracing learners' behaviors or input, it is difficult to perform diagnoses when tasks become more ill-defined and ill-structured (Lajoie, 2000a). It is particularly a challenge to map all the possible solution paths to ill-structured problems. As a result, dynamic diagnosis is often neglected in many tutoring systems that are designed to support complicated tasks. The responsibility of diagnosis is often offloaded from the tutor to the tutee.

Calibrated Support

Similarly, as a result of examining human scaffolding, researchers have studied how computer tutors can be designed to provide human-like scaffolding. Examples of such computer systems include the *Reading Partner* and the *Writing Partner* (Salomon, et al., 1989; Zellermayer, Salomon, Globerson, & Givon, 1991) and *Computer-Supported Intentional Learning Environments* (CSILE) (Scardamalia & Bereiter, 1994). In these computer-supported learning environments, the calibration of support is provided through computer tools that guide learners' cognitive and metacognitive processes. Prompts, hints, or cues are some mechanisms to guide learners through problem-solving (e.g., Ge & Land, 2003; Scardamalia & Bereiter, 1994), self-regulation (e.g., Manlove, Lazonder, & de Jong, 2006), and inquiry processes (e.g., van Joolingen, de Jong, Lazonder, Savelsbergh, & Manlove, 2005).

Technology systems not only facilitate or guide students' individual learning, but also enable students to work with peers and learn from each other (e.g., Ching & Kafai, 2008; Lai & Law, 2006). For instance, van Joolingen and his colleagues (2005) designed *Co-lab*, a system

supporting scientific discovery learning, including hypothesis generation, experimental design, data interpretation, self-regulation, and model building. The *Co-lab* system has features such as online chat rooms and forums to facilitate collaboration. Obviously, a scaffolding system can be designed to facilitate both individual and group learning processes.

Fading

Fading is an essential but often overlooked component in the scaffolding literature. Pea (2004) and Puntambekar and Hubschur (2005) suggested that scaffolding should be naturally faded or removed when learners acquire desired skills or concepts. Two main issues are related to fading. First, evaluation mechanisms are needed to assess whether learners are ready or not to perform a task without support. This issue points to the need for dynamic diagnosis. The second issue is related to the design of fading mechanisms. In e-learning systems, we often use a popular approach called *passive fading*, which refers to situations where learners voluntarily stop using the support provided to them. More often, however, scaffolding is faded by design, as found in many studies in which scaffolding is provided for a fixed period of time and then is removed. Lai and Law's (2006) study represents one such case. In their study, twenty-two Canadian students who were more experienced in an online learning environment spent time working with a group of twenty-two students from Hong Kong who had no prior experience with this kind of environment. After one and a half months, the Canadian students "left" the environment, i.e., the peer scaffolding was withdrawn from the Hong Kong students. In this case, Lai and Law (2006) observed how the Hong Kong students were able to collaborate among themselves when the Canadian students' support faded.

System Adaptation

After a critical analysis of the literature on scaffolding, we now turn to the discussion of technology systems that can be adapted to support learning. Understanding how adaptive systems develop through different paradigms and the characteristics of each paradigm can inform us the design of effective adaptive systems to scaffold diagnosis, supporting, and fading processes.

Adapting instruction to individual learners has been practiced throughout the human history (Corno & Snow, 1986). With increased understanding about how people learn, the challenge of high student-teacher ratio in today's education, and the advancement of technologies, researchers have developed and studied various adaptive systems for the purpose of tailoring instructions to individual differences. In the context of e-learning, system adaptation refers to the capability of a computer-based system to monitor important learner characteristics and accordingly provide adaptations in response to the needs and characteristics of individual learners for the purpose of supporting their learning (Leutner, 2004; Shute & Zapata-Rivera, 2008).

CAI Paradigm

Computer-Assisted Instruction (CAI) is the early form of adaptive instructional systems, which provides fixed and static adaptations to support self-paced learning. From the behaviorist perspective, the CAI paradigm holds that learning is a behavioral change resulting from stimulus and response (Ertmer & Newby, 1993). The role of instruction is to identify a specific set of observable learning goals and objectives and carefully arrange a sequence of instructional activities that eventually lead to the achievement of the originally identified learning objectives. Therefore, testing learners' knowledge both prior to learning and at the end of an instructional unit is a key feature in designing CAI systems because it helps an instructor to determine if a learner is ready to proceed to the next unit, if remedial instruction is needed, and if the prescribed objectives have been achieved. Rooted in Skinner's (1974) works of *Programmed Instruction*, the *PLATO Learning Management System* was one of the examples representing the CAI paradigm (Hart, 1981). Learners took pretest before a new learning event, and the system prescribed appropriate learning activities based on the results of the pretest. At the end of an instructional unit, learners were tested to determine their mastery of the content covered by the unit. If they did not pass the test, students could repeat the instruction. When a satisfactory score was obtained, students would then be allowed to move on to the next unit.

During the 70s, research on individual differences indicated that a learner's knowledge level should not be the only area of focus in the design of instructional systems (Cronbach & Snow, 1977). Instead, the effectiveness of instruction depends on a variety of learner characteristics (Carrier & Jonassen, 1988), including (a) aptitude (intelligence and academic achievement), (b) prior knowledge, (c) cognitive styles, and (d) personality variables (motivation, locus of control, etc.). Studies on instructional systems that adapt to various learner characteristics are still ongoing. For example, E. Brown, Cristea, Stewart, and Brailsford (2005) proposed a taxonomy of learning styles to guide the authoring of adaptive instructional systems. Fillippidis and Tsoukalas (2009) introduced an instructional system that taught spreadsheet functions by presenting different types of images that were adapted to individual students' learning styles. While pre-task measures of learner characteristics and the subsequent prescriptions of learning activities enabled certain levels of system adaptation, the adaptation was mostly fixed and static, insensitive to the learning processes (Lee & Park, 2007).

ITS Paradigm

Dissatisfied with the fixed and static nature of adaptation, researchers started to build new adaptive systems in the early 70s in the hope of tracing learners' on-task performance and providing timely diagnosis and prescription. Intelligent tutoring systems (ITSs) were built on the works on artificial intelligence (AI) and rooted in the cognitivist paradigm, which views learning as acquisition, organization, and storage of information in human mind. Being referred to as modelers by Derry and Lajoie (1993), the ITS researchers believed that underlying problem-solving expertise is a set of production rules (i.e., condition-action), which can be modeled with computer systems (Anderson, 2000). There are three important components in an ITS: (a) an expert model which represents the expert knowledge to be taught, (b) a tutor model that represents the instructional strategies, and (c) a student model which monitors students' status of knowledge (Lee & Park, 2007). For example, in *LISP*, an ITS that teaches an AI programming language, the expert model consists of about 500 production rules that represent the expert knowledge of LISP programming. As a student interacts with the tutor, the student model of the system monitors the student's application and acquisition of the production rules. Once the system detects the student's mistake, the tutor model will provide the student with the remedial instruction (Anderson, 2000).

ITSs have been widely used and generally successful in well-structured domains, including geometry, programming, physics, and algebra (Anderson, 2000). However, when encountering complex problem-solving domains, researchers are challenged as they attempt to map all the possible solution paths, generate all the possible production rules, and identify all the possible learner errors (Lajoie & Derry, 1993). Meanwhile, researchers argue that computer systems should not be the only responsible party for diagnosing learners' performance; rather learners themselves should play an active role in reflecting upon and monitoring their own performance (Lajoie & Derry, 1993). The latter argument reflects a departure from the cognitivist paradigm toward the constructivist paradigm, which views learning as individuals actively constructing knowledge. Hence, just as Lajoie (2000b) argued, the question for instructional systems should not be "to model or not to model" (p.2), but rather *who* or *what* should be responsible for modeling in students' learning process. The movement toward the constructivist paradigm and the advent of hypermedia and the World Wide Web has led to the development of adaptive hypermedia systems (AHS). AHS is not only adaptive (e.g., adapt the content of a page to particular learner characteristics), but more importantly it is adaptable (e.g., offering learner control and guidance on which page to visit next) (Brusilovsky, 2001). Further, while past instructional systems have been criticized for the lack of pedagogy (Lee & Park, 2007), AHSs have begun to incorporate pedagogical approaches in the design. Since then, the metaphoric wall between modelers and non-modelers have collapsed (Lajoie, 2000a), and various pedagogies have been implemented and explored (Lee & Park, 2007).

CSCL Paradigm

Starting from the 90s, with its distributed nature the World Wide Web has gradually evolved from providing adaptive instruction to individual learners to facilitating collaborative learning among multiple learners (Koschmann, 1996). The beginning of computer-supported collaborative learning (CSCL) marked a new era in adaptive instructional systems when peer learners and computer systems shared the responsibility of adaptation together. Koschmann (1996) argued that previous computer-supported learning mainly addressed the psychological aspects of learning, but CSCL, rooted in the socially oriented constructivist perspective, brought social learning to the foreground. Web-based collaborative systems provide platforms to support collaborative learning. In *Knowledge Forum* (Scardamalia & Bereiter, 2006), an example of CSCL system, various tools are designed to support learners' social discourse. For example, the note tool allows students to write ideas or ask questions which can then be reviewed by other students. As students write notes, they can tag with labels such as "My theory", "I need to understand", and "This theory cannot explain", to guide their collaborative theory-building process and facilitate knowledge construction. The *Web-based Inquiry Science Environment* (WISE) (Linn, Clark, & Slotta, 2003) is another CSCL system that provides tools and scaffolding structures (e.g., inquiry map) to facilitate collaborative inquiry learning. In the CSCL paradigm, cognition is regarded as distributed among multiple individuals, tools, and artifacts (Hutchins, 1995; Salomon, 1993a). Correspondingly, adaptive systems are no longer conceptualized as the only tutor in learning. As Pea (1993) indicated, the computer systems in the CSCL paradigm provided two dimensions of distributed cognition: the material dimension (i.e., information, tools, and artifacts provided by the computer system itself) and the social dimension (i.e., the affordances of computer systems to facilitate collaboration with social others). On the other hand, learners in the CSCL paradigm are, for the most part, still the "consumers" of adaptive systems. Because web publishing still required sophisticated computer programming skills, web-based adaptive systems were largely contributed and controlled by a small group of content providers (e.g., the *Knowledge Forum*) (Greenhow, Robelia, & Hughes, 2009). The paradigm provided only modest opportunities for learners to create and share their knowledge.

Web 2.0 Paradigm

The recent rise of the Web 2.0 technologies has greatly reduced the technical thresholds of creating and sharing web-based information. Web 2.0 is a term coined in 2004, which indicates the Web's break away from predominantly read-only to read-and-write (McManus, 2005). The web 2.0 technology features applications and tools such as social networks, media sharing, social bookmarking, collaborative knowledge creation, content aggregation and organization; all of which allow users to create, share, collaborate, and interact with minimal technical barriers (Greenhow, et al., 2009). Web 2.0 has found its way to education. For example, Harvard University launched the H2O project that provides an educational platform for the free creation and exchange of ideas within and beyond the traditional university community. Such technologies have transformed learners who are mostly passive recipients or consumers of knowledge in the Web 1.0 era to knowledge creators and disseminators in the Web 2.0 era (Cormode & Krishnamurthy, 2008). From the perspective of distributed cognition, the distribution of knowledge among learners and learner-created artifacts are magnified in the Web 2.0 era. As Bonk (2009) theorized, e-learning in the Web 2.0 age can be conceptualized as pipes (i.e., platforms or infrastructures that allow users to access and search information), pages (i.e., user created content and resources), and a participatory learning culture. The Web, as of today, can be considered as a vast adaptive system that is undergirded by numerous tools and users from all over the world. It is evident that learner communities and the Web 2.0 technologies have coupled together to share the responsibility of providing adaptive instruction to one another. Technologies provide unprecedented infrastructure, offer opportunities for individuals to generate, create, and share endless open educational resources (OER) that are growing and dynamically updating every minute, and cultivate a participatory learning culture (Bonk, 2009). In such a new era, pedagogical guidance is needed more than ever to facilitate the collaboration among learners and the interactions between learners and e-learning systems.

We have witnessed the paradigm shifts in the design of adaptive systems influenced by different learning theories and philosophical perspectives. As noted by Mayer (1997), the learning theories have evolved from behaviorist emphasis of strengthening learning with reinforcement, cognitivist emphasis of information processing and knowledge construction, to social constructivist emphasis of collaborative knowledge building. Parallel to the paradigm shifts in learning theories, adaptive systems have evolved from CAI paradigm, ITS paradigm, CSCL paradigm, to the recent Web 2.0 paradigm. The design of adaptive systems has evolved from emphasizing pre- and post-task measures and feedback mechanisms, to continuously monitoring and supporting learners' acquisition of production rules, to allowing the learner to take control of learning with system guidance, to facilitating system-supported collaborative learning, and to sharing information and building knowledge among communities of learners. Similar to the literature on scaffolding, the major concerns of the literature on system adaptation are (a) diagnosing through testing and measuring learners' knowledge, (b) providing learner support through practice and feedback, expert modeling, and monitoring learners' progress, and (c) fading after determining that a learner is ready to proceed to the next instructional unit. We believe that the features of adaptive systems from different paradigms can inform the design of scaffolding mechanisms for e-learning systems to better facilitate learners' knowledge building through diagnosing, supporting, and fading.

A DESIGN FRAMEWORK FOR SCAFFOLDING

Our literature review reveals three important processes in scaffolding, including *diagnosis*, *supporting*, and *fading*. Furthermore, some researchers pointed to several key issues in scaffolding, including *who*, *what*, *how*, and *when* (WWHW) (Azevedo & Jacobson, 2008; Lajoie, 2005). *Who* refers to the entity that provides scaffold, *what*

refers to knowledge, skills or learning processes, *how* refers to scaffolding mechanisms, and *when* refers to the timing of scaffolding. The design of scaffolding is a complex undertaking because it involves not only the three key scaffolding processes but also the consideration of WWHW. For example, in Co-Lab (van Joolingen, et al., 2005) scaffolding is mainly provided by a computer tutor, but peers are also involved during the collaborative inquiry process. Various scaffolding tools are presented to students throughout the inquiry process. For instance, discussion forums are used to facilitate clarification, explanation and justification during peer interactions, model editors are used to depict students' understanding of problems, and a planning tool is used to display and keep track of students' inquiry processes. Fading occurs when students choose not to use the scaffolds any more. As summarized in Table 1, we will further explicate the WWHW issues in the context of the three main scaffolding processes: diagnosis, support, and fading.

Diagnosis Process

Azevedo and Jacobson (2008) suggest that one of the key issues in scaffolding research is the mode of scaffold, that is, who provides the scaffold. In the context of diagnosis, the first question is whether diagnosis should be carried out by *human tutors*, *peers*, *computer tutors*, or even *students themselves*. The advantage of human tutor diagnosis is that human tutors not only use artifacts and tools (e.g., tests and surveys) to assess students' understanding, but also rely on non-verbal cues to aid the diagnosis, which are absent in an e-learning environment. Peers are able to diagnose their peers' learning process, but they may not be motivated to help their peers, or they do not know what to look for (Ching & Kafai, 2008). Therefore, it is important to guide the students, such as providing question prompts to them so that they understand what to look for during the peer learning process. Diagnosis can also be performed by individual

Table 1. A design framework for scaffolding

	Diagnosis	**Support**	**Fading**
Who	• Human tutors • Peers • Computer tutors	• Human tutors • Peers • Computer tutors	• Human tutors • Peers • Computer tutors
What	• Prior knowledge • Learning processes • Learning outcomes	• Knowledge construction • Articulation of investigation • Explanation and justification • Self-monitoring, self-reflecting, and revising projects	• Single scaffold • Multiple scaffolds
How	• Multiple-choice tests • Short-answer questions • Open-ended essay questions • Causal mapping • Projects • Behavioral measures such as tallying number of posting in a discussion forum	• Process display • Question prompts • Process modeling • Social discourse through forum discussions • Access to online resources	• Sequence of fading • Pace of fading
When	• At the beginning of learning process • At the end of learning process • Throughout the learning process	• Just-in-time • Pre-designed • All the time	• When students no longer need the scaffold • Pre-designed • Students' choice • Peers' choice

students. For instance, students could be asked to evaluate their own knowledge construction (de Wever, van Keer, Schellens, & Valcke, 2009), problem-solving process, and self-reflection process (Kauffman, Ge, Xie, & Chen, 2008). Tools can be provided to assist students in planning, monitoring, and evaluation processes. Empirical evidences revealed that computer tools that support students' self-regulation could enhance their learning outcomes (Manlove, et al., 2006).

When a computer tutor, such as an ITS, provides diagnosis, it traces students' problem-solving processes, which are compared with the *correct* problem states in an expert model to provide accurate assessment of students' problem-solving performance. As discussed earlier, an ITS works well for well-structured problems, in which problem states are finite and solutions are deterministic. However, in an ill-structured problem-solving situation, a computer tutor has to rely on additional means to obtain accurate assessment of students' performance. In an e-learning environment, a large amount of information, including students'

activities, communications, artifacts and tool usage data, can be traced and utilized to assess students' needs and monitor their progress. For example, *gStudy* – a tool to support collaboration and self-regulation – is capable of collecting a variety of student data, such as the time students spent in the system, timestamp records of mouse clicks, students' actions such as scrolling and text entry (Hadwin, Oshige, Gress, & Winne, 2010). *Signals* – a computer system monitoring students' learning progress – identifies at-risk students and alerts instructors in order to provide additional help to at-risk students (Arnold, 2010). Besides collecting and analyzing individual students' data, *Social Networks Adapting Pedagogical Practice* (SNAPP) utilizes social network analysis and data mining techniques to provide instructors and students with visual display of students' interactions in a Learning Management System (Dawson, 2010; Macfadyen & Dawson, 2010). Instructors and students will be able to see not only who contribute to a discussion forum, but also how students interact; for example, how often they communicate with each other, who is left off from the discussion, who is communicating with whom, and so on. With the use of learning analytics, instructors will be able to identify in advance who might face learning difficulties so that they can help those students effectively.

The second issue of diagnosis involves *what to diagnose*. Before students enter a learning environment, their prior knowledge should be assessed. Assessment of students' prior knowledge provides a baseline for determining students' ZPD, based on which instructors can provide appropriate support to bridge learners' knowledge gap, which can be concepts, rules and principles, problem solving, critical thinking, or transfer skills. Another issue regarding diagnosis is *how to diagnose*. Some traditional methods such as multiple-choice tests and opened-ended essay questions can be used to assess students' knowledge level. Multiple-choice tests have the advantage of providing quick feedback; yet they may not be appropriate to assess higher-order thinking skill such as ill-structured problem-solving and creativity. Opened-ended questions or project-based assessments are some appropriate diagnostic tools for higher-order thinking, but they require human resources and additional time for grading, which means that timeliness of feedback can be affected compared with multiple-choice tests. Recently, some researchers have developed tools to assess the mental models of problem solvers. An example of such tools is *Highly Integrated Model Assessment Technology and Tools* (HIMATT), an application that measures students' problem-solving ability by assessing student-created causal maps (Pirnay-Dummer, Ifenthaler, & Spector, 2010).

The final issue regarding diagnosis is *when to diagnose*. In order to determine whether someone needs scaffolding, we need to carry out an assessment at the very beginning of a learning process. In addition, diagnosis is also needed at the end of the learning process in order to determine whether scaffolding needs to be removed or not. Lajoie (2005) suggested that diagnosis be performed throughout the learning process so that decisions can be made on what to scaffold, when to scaffold, and when to fade.

Support Process

After diagnosis, calibrated support should be provided to students. One of the key issues in designing support is to decide *who provides the support*: a human tutor, a peer, or a computer tutor. Azevedo, Cromley and Seibert (2004) compared the effects of a human tutor with those of a computer-based system that provided question prompts to scaffold students' self-regulation. Although the study found that the human tutor was more effective than the self-regulation question prompts provided by the computer system, Ge, Planas, and Er (2010) argued that in an e-learning system where either a human tutor or the immediate feedback from a human tutor was unavailable, the system played an important role by providing helpful learning support. An e-learning system can provide support by asking questions to guide students in problem-solving processes and encouraging them to reflect on their problem-solving experience, evaluate their solutions, and modify the solutions if needed. Support can also be provided by peers, which has been found effective in complex problem solving (Ge, Chen, & Davis, 2005; Kauffman, et al., 2008).

The next issue is *what to support*. Land and Zembal-Saul (2003) suggested three scaffolding strategies for scientific inquiry and problem-based learning in a technology-supported learning environment. First, students should be directed to various aspects of investigation. Second, students' explanations and justifications can be elicited by using question prompts or other tools. Finally, student's monitoring, reflection, and revision processes should be supported throughout their scientific inquiry.

When it comes to *how to support*, there is a variety of strategies to support student learning. Lin and her colleagues (Lin, Hmelo, Kinzer, & Secules, 1999) suggested four ways to scaffold students in a technology-supported environment: process display, question prompts, process modeling, and social discourse. *Process display* visually demonstrates students' learning and thinking processes, which makes students aware of what they have learned. For example, Manlove and her colleagues (2006) developed tools to display all the sub-goals of an inquiry task in order to support students' planning in an inquiry-based learning environment.

Question prompts guide students' thinking and problem solving processes. Ge and Land (2004) categorized three kinds of question prompts: procedural prompts, elaboration prompts, and reflection prompts. Procedural prompts guide learners through the processes of completing a specific problem-solving task; elaboration prompts help learners to articulate thoughts and elicit explanation; reflection prompts encourage learners to reflect upon their learning experiences. Empirical evidences support that question prompts are effective in supporting complex learning, such as ill-structured problem solving (e.g. Ge & Land, 2003; Kauffman, et al., 2008; Molenaar, van Boxtel, & Sleegers, 2010).

Process modeling, based on the concept of cognitive apprenticeship (J. Brown, Collins, & Duguid, 1989; Collins, J. Brown, & Newman, 1989), is designed to demonstrate experts' reasoning and problem-solving processes to novices. The concept of expert modeling is to make expert's thinking explicit so that novices can develop problem-solving skills by learning from the expert model. Pedersen and Liu (2002) used videos to demonstrate expert problem-solving processes, and found that expert modeling improved the quality of students' rationale in developing solutions.

Social discourse encourages learners to articulate their thoughts and seek feedback from peers. Research shows that putting peers together does not guarantee learning success (e.g., Ge & Land, 2003); structure and tools are necessary to support peer collaboration and support. *CSILE* (Scardamalia & Bereiter, 1994), *Belvedere* (Suthers, 1998),

and *Co-Lab* (van Joolingen, et al., 2005) are some of the collaborative learning systems that support social discourse via chats and other technology-supported shared problem-solving spaces.

Another popular approach to developing learners' expertise in ill-structured problem solving is to provide them with access to cases (Jonassen & Hernandez-Serrano, 2002). Williams (2005) suggested that case-based learning encouraged self-reflection and fostered science inquiry. Based on the theory of case-based reasoning (Kolodner & Guzdial, 2000), studies found that case-based learning had a positive impact on learning outcomes (e.g. Choi & Lee, 2009; Ertmer & Stepich, 1999; Hernandez-Serrano & Jonassen, 2003).

Finally, the last question to ask about the support process is *when to provide the support*. Many e-learning systems provide support at predetermined times, for instance, at the beginning of a learning process. However, van Merriënboer, Clark and de Croock (2002) suggested that we should provide just-in-time information to students. In other words, information should be given when students need it so that they would not feel overwhelmed. Diagnosis must be performed constantly if we need to provide just-in-time support. In addition, by providing support in the form of a help menu, a button, or a link, learners will be able to access support any time they need the information.

Fading Process

After it is ascertained that learners acquire the desired knowledge and skills, scaffolding should be faded. Fading is another area that is largely ignored in the research of scaffolding (Puntambekar & Hubscher, 2005). Most of the studies on scaffolding focused on investigating different types of support processes without investigating the fading of scaffolding (e.g., Azevedo, et al., 2004; Oh & Jonassen, 2007). In a few studies, fading was discussed, but it was never tested (e.g. Cho & Jonassen, 2002; Sharma & Hannafin,

2004). Recently, some studies began to examine the effects of fading, and the results from these limited studies indicated that fading had mixed effect on learning processes and outcomes (e.g., Bulu & Pedersen, 2010; Kester & Kirschner, 2009; McNeill, Lizotte, Krajcik, & Marx, 2006). Some of the key issues for fading are *who decides fading*, *what to fade out*, and *when to fade out*. Naturally, the *decision of fading* should be based on the results of diagnosis, performed by either a human tutor, a peer, or a computer tutor.

With regard to the question *what to fade out*, Lin and her colleagues (1999) suggested that we incorporate a system of scaffolds in a learning environment, which would allow testing and examining different scaffolds one at a time. When multiple scaffolding methods are used, instructors not only need to decide on which scaffolds to fade, but also on the sequence of fading. Bulu and Pedersen's (2010) study provided a great example of sequencing fading in a problem-solving context. The participants in the study were required to work on four problem-solving activities, with three types of support – examples, question prompts, and sentence starters. The researchers faded out examples in the second activity, followed by the fading of question prompts in the third activity, and finally faded sentence starters in the last activity. It was found that the students demonstrated better problem-solving performance in the third and last activities when additional scaffolds were faded. Bulu and Pedersen's (2010) findings suggested that, when implemented effectively, fading of scaffolding could promote the transfer of problem-solving.

The final question regarding the design of fading in an e-learning system is the *timing of fading*. Ideally, fading should be administered at the time when learners no longer need scaffolding. However, in several studies, fading was administered at a fixed time. Molenaar and colleagues (2010) used examples of self-regulation and question prompts to scaffold elementary school students' metacognitive skills. The experiment

was conducted in six one-hour lessons, and the scaffolds were removed starting from the third hour. The authors tried to test the lasting effect of scaffolding, but it was unclear why they assumed that the first two hours of scaffolding would be sufficient for the students to acquire metacognitive skills. In some e-learning systems where support was provided through hyperlinks or tools (e.g., Manlove, et al., 2006; Manlove, Lazonder, & de Jong, 2009), the timing of using or removing scaffolds was determined by learners. In other words, when learners no longer felt the need for support, they could choose not to click on the hyperlinks nor use the tools.

DESIGNING ADAPTIVE E-LEARNING SYSTEMS: EXAMPLES

In this section, we illustrate how the design framework for scaffolding has guided us to design four adaptive e-learning systems to support ill-structured problem-solving: *the Virtual Clinic*, the *Virtual Drug Lab*, *the Problem-Solving Support System* (*PSSS*), and *the Concept Challenge*. We discuss particularly how different aspects of scaffolding (diagnosis, support, and fading) are operationalized as design features of the adaptive e-learning systems. The *Virtual Clinic* employs three case scenarios and a set of scaffolding mechanisms in a simulated clinical environment to guide nursing students in ethical decision-making processes (Huang, Ge, & Bowers, 2006). The *Virtual Drug Lab* is designed to scaffold nursing students' conceptual understanding on pharmacokenetics through tutorials and cases (Law, Ataman, & Ge, 2010). The *PSSS* is a cognitive support system offering a suite of cases and scaffolding mechanisms to guide pharmacy students through complex and ill-structured problem-solving (Ge & Er, 2005). The *Concept Challenge* provides a design shell with embedded scaffolding tools that allow a community of teachers to design instruction with the purpose of correcting students' misconceptions in science.

Design for Diagnosis Process

In the four examples of e-learning systems, diagnoses are performed at different times of learning processes. In the *Virtual Drug Lab*, the first diagnosis is performed right after students launch the system. The interface presents two options to students – they can either choose to review prerequisite pharmacology topics that are necessary to solve problems in subsequent cases or skip the review section and jump directly to case studies. At this point, students take the responsibility of assessing their own prior knowledge to determine whether or not they need the review. If students believe that they are competent in a given topic and do not need to review it, they can click on a Skip button to proceed directly to patient cases. Otherwise, they can choose to go through tutorials to review relevant information. At the end of the tutorial, the system performs a second diagnosis to assess students' understanding using true-or-false questions, which is shown in Figure 1. When students select an answer by clicking on T (true) or F (false) button, they will receive instant feedback. Based on the system diagnosis and feedback, students can determine how much

they know about a topic and whether or not they are ready to start working on the cases.

In the *Virtual Clinic*, system performs diagnosis throughout students' ethical decision-making processes. As students encounter an ethical dilemma and ponder upon the situations, the system presents a list of six ethical principles and asks students to consider which principles are applicable to the current patient case (Figure 2). As students make a selection by clicking on an appropriate button, they would receive immediate feedback to their response and the rationales underlying the decision. Similarly, students are also asked to choose a nursing code of ethics that would best address the ethical dilemma in the patient case, and the system provides instant feedback upon receiving students' responses. Additionally, in the final decision-making stage, different options are presented through red radio buttons. For each choice students make, corresponding feedback is provided on the subsequent screen.

In the *Concept Challenge*, students' misconceptions are diagnosed as they answer the pre-designed multiple-choice questions (Figure 3). The distracters of the questions represent common misconceptions held by students on a given topic. Depending on students' responses, the system would direct them to different pages with

Figure 1. The system diagnosis in the Virtual Drug Lab is designed to assess students' prerequisite knowledge.

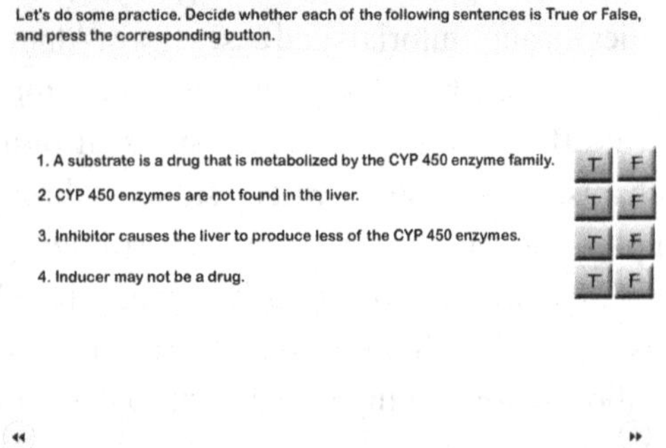

Figure 2. In the Virtual Clinic, as students select an ethical principle that is in conflict in a patient case, they will receive instant feedback.

Let's do some practice. Decide whether each of the following sentences is True or False, and press the corresponding button.

1. A substrate is a drug that is metabolized by the CYP 450 enzyme family. T F
2. CYP 450 enzymes are not found in the liver. T F
3. Inhibitor causes the liver to produce less of the CYP 450 enzymes. T F
4. Inducer may not be a drug. T F

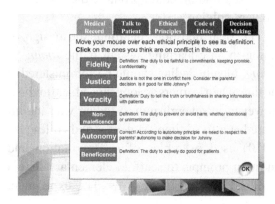

Figure 3. The Concept Challenge system presents multiple-choice questions to diagnose students' misconceptions.

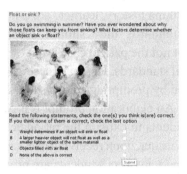

different learning activities designed to refute their misconceptions. The *Concept Challenge* is a design shell. While it is the system that performs the diagnosis, it is actually teachers or instructional designers who design and author the multiple-choice questions at the back end. The system allows authoring teachers or designers to make changes to the diagnosing questions whenever necessary, e.g., when a new misconception on a topic is discovered.

In the *PSSS*, diagnosis is conducted by both instructors and students. Before a group of students start working on a problem in the *PSSS*, their instructor can determine students' level of problem-solving expertise and use built-in features to set the appropriate level of support for the students. After students individually work on a case and

submit their answers, they can performance self-diagnosis by viewing and comparing their answers with both peers' and expert's solutions (Figure 4). In addition, students are prompted to articulate their reflections on the differences between their responses and the expert's responses. The comparison and reflection activities enable students to assess and evaluate their own problem-solving performance. Although the *PSSS* system does not directly diagnose students' performance and provide canned feedback, the system provides a platform for collaboration and cognitive apprenticeship, with tools and scaffolding mechanisms to support diagnosis and feedback. The *PSSS* offloads the task of diagnosis to individual learners and peers (Koschmann, 1996; Lajoie & Derry, 1993), which demands a higher level of metacognitive skills from learners.

Design for Support Process

In the literature of scaffolding, typical ways to provide support include process display, question prompting, process modeling, social discourse, and access to a case library (Lin, et al., 1999). The different supporting mechanisms are demonstrated in the four example systems.

Figure 4. In the PSSS, students can compare their case responses to those of their peers.

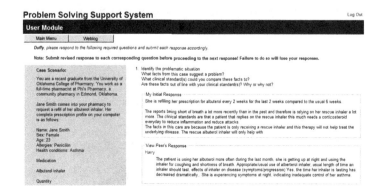

Process Display

Process display visually demonstrates expert problem-solving processes (Lin, et al., 1999). It provides guidance on *what to consider* when facing a task (Hannifin, Land, & Oliver, 1999). In the *Virtual Clinic*, the process display appears in the form of a set of tabs at the top of the screen, showing the ethical decision-making process (Figure 3): checking medical records, interacting with patients, identifying ethical principles, applying code of ethics, and making ethical decisions. The process display makes explicit to learners what would have been implicit in problem-solving processes (Lin, et al., 1999).

Question Prompts

Ge and Land (2004) specified three types of question prompts, which serve different cognitive functions in scaffolding ill-structured problem-solving processes: procedural prompts, elaboration prompts, and reflection prompts. Procedural prompts guide students through ill-structured problem-solving processes and direct students to important aspects in solving a problem; elaboration prompts require students to elaborate their thoughts and reasoning; reflection prompts ask students to reflect on their learning experiences.

In the *PSSS*, one of the cases involves an asthma patient who is requesting to refill at a pharmacy. After examining the patient's prescription profile and her asthma history, learners are asked which clinical standards they should consider and whether or not the patient case is out of line with the clinical standards. Here, a procedural prompt is executed by prompting students to the clinical standards. An elaboration prompt is provided by asking students to explain the rationale for their answers. Further, upon receiving peer review and seeing expert answers, students are prompted to reflect on the gaps between their reasoning and the expert's reasoning, thus reflection prompts are provided. Ge, Planas, and Er (2010) found that students who received question prompts embedded in the *PSSS* achieved better problem-solving outcomes than those who did not receive the prompts. The *Virtual Clinic* and the *Virtual Drug Lab* provide similar types of question prompts via an agent (e.g., an expert nurse) (Figure 5).

It is worth noting that the PSSS has some distinct question prompt features. First, question prompts are offered at several levels depending on the learners' levels of expertise. The top level provides questions that prompt students to consider only major aspects of problem-solving. This particular level is appropriate for those students who have high levels of problem-solving expertise

Figure 5. In the Virtual Clinic, an experienced nurse asks a question to prompt the learner to think about the ethical dilemma in a patient case.

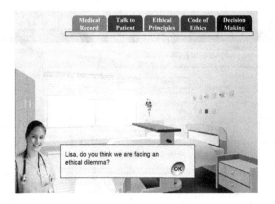

Figure 6. In the PSSS, different levels of questions are used to prompt learners' elaboration of thoughts.

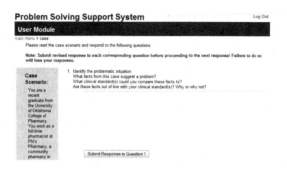

and need minimal guidance. For those students with less expertise, more specific question prompts are provided for each problem-solving aspect. As shown in Figure 6, under the main question prompt "Identify the problematic situation," three sub-questions are presented to provide more specific support for student thinking. The design of different levels of question prompts helps to adjust the level of scaffolding based on students' ZPD.

Similarly, the *Concept Challenge* has embedded question prompts to promote students' conceptual change in science. Question prompts are one of the scaffolding strategies that have been used for science investigation (Land & Zembal-Saul, 2003). When students answer a multiple-choice question incorrectly, the system would prompt them to further elaborate their ideas based on their selected answers, which not only allows the instructor to diagnose students' misconceptions, but also provides an opportunity for students to articulate their thinking and become more aware of what they know (Land & Zembal-Saul, 2003; Scardamalia, et al., 1989). For each pre-identified misconception, instructors can use the *Concept Challenge* system to set up a sequence of examples or experiments to help students to refute their misconceptions. Throughout the process, students are prompted to interpret and explain the results of experiments, evaluate their findings, and revise their conceptual understanding. At the end, students can see a progression of their ideas and are

prompted to reflect on the changes to their initial ideas.

Process Modeling

In all the four e-learning systems, *process modeling* is designed to make the expert thinking visible to the students. In the *Virtual Drug Lab*, an expert nurse draws students' attention to the important aspects of a case and offers an expert perspective during the process of problem-solving. In the *Virtual Clinic* and the *PSSS* systems, after students submit their solutions on a case study, they are presented with the expert's perspective and solutions to the problem. The systems provide students with expert modeling that enables students to examine the expert's reasoning and problem-solving processes. Ge, Planas, and Er (2010) found that the expert modeling in the *PSSS* had positive impact on pharmacy students' reasoning and problem-solving processes.

Social Discourse

Opportunities for *social discourse* are available in the *PSSS* and the *Virtual Clinic*. In the *PSSS*, a peer review mechanism is designed for students to review their peers' responses to a case study and receive peers' feedback to their own responses. In addition, based on the peer feedback, students can revise their initial case responses. In the *Virtual Clinic*, after students complete three ethical cases, students are directed to visit an online nursing ethics forum, in which students can join in a professional community of nurses to interact with practicing nurses, discuss real-life ethical issues, and share and exchange their perspectives.

Case Library

While both the *Virtual Clinic* and the *Virtual Drug Lab* have three predefined cases, the *PSSS* and the *Concept Challenge* provide mechanisms to build a library of searchable cases - in the *PSSS* the cases are patient scenarios, and in the *Concept Challenge*, the cases are scenarios that are tied to particular science misconceptions. Both systems have an instructor interface, where instructors can log on and follow on-screen instruction to create cases. Further, student responses recorded in the systems also provide input and feedback mechanisms, which help instructors to revise or add cases.

Design for Fading Process

Fading is available in the three examples of the e-learning systems. In the *Virtual Clinic*, support is gradually decreased through three cases. In the first patient case, learners have full support: process display (e.g., tabs appearing at the top of the screen), question prompting (e.g., questions asked by an expert nurse), and process modeling (e.g., expert advice and solutions). Upon completing the first case, the expert nurse summarizes the main decision-making process as a way to help the student reflect on her learning experience. In the second case, the expert nurse no longer accompanies the student in the patient room, and the student is no longer provided with question prompts. The only scaffold available is the process display appearing at the top of the screen to help the student tackle the second ethical dilemma. After the student nurse makes the decision for the second case, she leaves the patient room and comes into the hallway, where the expert nurse

greets her and shares with her how she would approach the second case as an expert nurse. In the third case, the student is still on her own in making a decision about a new ethical dilemma. Although the process display is still available, the student does not have to click through all the tabs in a fixed order to make a decision. The fading illustrated in the *Virtual Clinic* is based on the assumption that learners' problem-solving competence would improve over time with all the scaffoldings. The fading is static and pre-designed instead of dynamically adjusting according to students' subtle changes in their learning process.

The *PSSS* and the *Virtual Drug Lab* offload the control of fading to the instructor or learners themselves. As discussed earlier, in the case of the *PSSS*, the instructor has the option to set different levels of question prompting for solving the problem in the patient cases. Therefore, as students become more proficient in problem-solving, the instructor can set the question prompts at a lower scaffolding level. In the *Virtual Drug Lab*, the system provides options that allow students to determine when fading or reinforcement is needed; for instance, students have free access to any of the three cases and can go back to review any topic at any time.

DISCUSSION AND CONCLUSION

This chapter offers a comprehensive analysis and synthesis of the literature on scaffolding research conducted in the past years. It is an attempt to make the linkage between two bodies of literature: scaffolding and system adaptations. Although the two bodies of literature have co-existed and have been developing simultaneously over the years, there has been little effort to relate them theoretically and pedagogically. This chapter allows us to re-examine adaptive systems using the lens of scaffolding, and therefore we consider it a contribution to the existing literature concerning scaffolding and system adaptation. Furthermore, this chapter presents a design framework for scaffolding based on a critical literature review. Grounded in socio-cultural learning theories, this design framework has both theoretical and practical values for guiding instructional designers and educators to conceptualize and design adaptive e-learning systems with effective scaffolding mechanisms. It is hoped that the four examples illustrated in this chapter are insightful to the understanding on how the scaffolding framework is applied in designing adaptive e-learning systems.

Through literature review, we also identify some issues that indicate gaps or challenges in the research of scaffolding. For instance, as important as the role of diagnosis in scaffolding, it seems to be an area that has been understudied in recent scaffolding research. In the ITS paradigm, dynamic diagnosis is performed quite consistently by computers which monitor learners' performance. However, most of the recent studies on scaffolding focus on supporting different processes of learning tasks such as ill-structured problem-solving (Ge & Land, 2003), science inquiry (Quintana et al., 2004), and metacognitive processes of online inquiry (Quintana, Zhang, & Krajcik, 2005), yet they fail to examine the role of diagnosis in scaffolding. One of the possible reasons for the lack of diagnosis is probably due to the fact that the responsibility for diagnosis is often offloaded to learners in many cases.

The problem with offloading diagnosis to learners is that often students do not have the ability to diagnose their own learning needs due to a lack of domain knowledge, metacognitive skills, or a felt need for scaffolding. In the studies conducted by Manlove, de Jong and Lazonder (2006, 2009), it was found that high school students did not use embedded monitoring and evaluating tools as much as desired, even though the tools were available at all time. It is often the case when students are not required to use the tools or scaffolds provided, they may choose not to use them at all because they do not see the needs. Ge and colleagues (2010) found that

some pharmacy students were unable to identify the gaps between their reasoning and the expert's reasoning in solving the same problem when they were asked to make the comparison; rather, they felt that their solutions were fairly close to the expert's solutions with only minor differences; for example, they only saw that the expert was more thorough and elaborative in their reasoning. These findings suggest that not all students are capable of diagnosing their learning insufficiency, and it would be an issue if a learning system relies completely on learners' diagnosis and voluntary use of scaffolds. How much autonomy do we want to give to students? How can we balance system control and learner control in diagnosis and supporting? How can we develop students' metacognitive ability so that they will be able to accurately assess their learning difficulties and needs? These are some of the challenges to be addressed by future research.

Another issue warranting future research includes comparing the effects of various scaffolding methods. In the past, the research on scaffolding mostly focuses on testing the effect of one scaffolding method at a time. However, many recent adaptive systems involve more than one scaffold or tool in order to maximize the effect of scaffolding in an e-learning environment. While some researchers (Lin, et al., 1999) advocate a system approach by combining different scaffolding techniques and methods to provide more powerful scaffolding, it makes it difficult for researchers to examine individual effect of each scaffolding method or tool. In fact, all the four learning systems illustrated in this chapter provide a suite of scaffolding mechanisms. Therefore, robust scientific experiments should be conducted to examine the interactive effects of multiple scaffolding methods and tools. In addition, there is a need to compare the effects of different scaffoldings. Some studies are moving in that direction. For example, Ge and Land (2003) examined the effect of question prompts and peers scaffolds on ill-structured problem-solving, and Azevedo and his colleagues (Azevedo, et al., 2004; Azevedo, Cromley, Winters, Moos, & Greene, 2005) used both static question prompts and human tutors to scaffold students' understanding of complex systems. However, little research has investigated the effects of hard scaffolding (i.e., system scaffolding) as compared with soft scaffolding (i.e., human scaffolding) and the interaction effect between hard and soft scaffolding. Further, little research has investigated the appropriateness of a given scaffold for a particular situation or learner type.

As discussed earlier, fading – a key component of scaffolding (Pea, 2004; Puntambekar & Hubscher, 2005), is an area that has been overlooked in the past research on scaffolding. Although we begin to see some studies focusing on the fading effect of scaffolding (e.g., Bulu & Pedersen, 2010; McNeill, et al., 2006), research in this area is still scant. Further research is needed to understand the conditions and methods of fading, sequence of fading, as well as issues influencing the effectiveness of fading.

In conclusion, we hope that this chapter will serve as a catalyst for instructional designers and e-learning system developers to work together in creating and researching effective pedagogical scaffolds for e-learning. As Lee and Park (2007) observed, it is time to move pedagogy to the foreground of e-learning design. We encourage instructional designers to use the scaffolding design framework advanced in this chapter as a blueprint to develop adaptive e-learning systems to support students' learning, especially complex learning tasks such as ill-structured problem-solving. The three main processes – diagnosis, support, and fading – are integral parts of scaffolding since effective support and fading are contingent upon accurate diagnosis and constant assessment. Therefore, the three processes should be continuously coordinated, and the design of e-learning systems should be aligned with the three scaffolding processes.

From the literature review, we found that it is possible to offload the responsibility of scaffolding to human (instructors or learners) through well-designed, technology-mediated scaffolding strategies. Opportunities such as social discourse and process modeling provide means to realize potential dynamic scaffolding/system adaptation. The advent of Web 2.0 and associated tools have greatly increased such opportunities to provide scaffolding *through* e-learning systems. Moreover, e-learning system designers and developers should take advantage of the new technological tools to effectively involve instructors and learners as active contributors and knowledge creators who are an integral part in adaptive e-learning systems.

REFERENCES

Anderson, J. R. (2000). *Cognitive psychology and its implications* (5th ed.). New York, NY: Worth Publishers.

Arnold, K. E. (2010). Signals: Applying academic analytics. *EDUCASE Quarterly Magazine, 33*(1).

Azevedo, R., Cromley, J. G., & Seibert, D. (2004). Does adaptive scaffolding facilitate students' ability to regulate their learning with hypermedia? *Contemporary Educational Psychology, 29*(3), 344–370. doi:10.1016/j.cedpsych.2003.09.002

Azevedo, R., Cromley, J. G., Winters, F. I., Moos, D. C., & Greene, J. A. (2005). Adaptive human scaffolding facilitates adolescents' self-regulated learning with hypermedia. *Instructional Science, 33*(5), 381–412. doi:10.1007/s11251-005-1273-8

Azevedo, R., & Jacobson, M. (2008). Advances in scaffolding learning with hypertext and hypermedia: A summary and critical analysis. *Educational Technology Research and Development, 56*(1), 93–100. doi:10.1007/s11423-007-9064-3

Betrancourt, M. (2005). The animation and interactivity principles in multimedia learning. In Mayer, R. E. (Ed.), *The Cambridge handbook of multimedia learning* (pp. 287–296). New York, NY: Cambridge University Press.

Bonk, C. (2009). *The world is open: How Web technology is revolutionizing education*. San Francisco, CA: Jossey-Bass.

Brown, E., Cristea, A., Stewart, C., & Brailsford, T. (2005). Patterns in authoring of adaptive educational hypermedia: A taxonomy of learning styles. *Journal of Educational Technology & Society*, *8*(3), 77–90.

Brown, J. S., Collins, A., & Duguid, P. (1989). Situated cognition and the culture of learning. *Educational Researcher*, *18*(1), 32–42.

Brusilovsky, P. (2001). Adaptive hypermedia. *User Modeling and User-Adapted Interaction, 11*, 87–110. doi:10.1023/A:1011143116306

Bulu, S., & Pedersen, S. (2010). Scaffolding middle school students' content knowledge and ill-structured problem solving in a problem-based hypermedia learning environment. *Educational Technology Research and Development*, *58*(5), 507–529. doi:10.1007/s11423-010-9150-9

Burgoon, J. K., Bonito, J. A., Ramirez, A., Dunbar, N. E., Kam, K., & Fischer, J. (2002). Testing the interactivity principle: Effects of mediation, propinquity, and verbal and nonverbal modalities in interpersonal interaction. *The Journal of Communication*, *52*(3), 657–677. doi:10.1111/j.1460-2466.2002.tb02567.x

Carrier, C., & Jonassen, D. (1988). Adapting courseware to accommodate individual differences. In Jonassen, D. (Ed.), *Instructional designs for microcomputer courseware* (pp. 61–96). Mahwah, NJ: Lawrence Erlbaum Associates.

Ching, C. C., & Kafai, Y. B. (2008). Peer pedagogy: Student collaboration and reflection in a learning-through-design project. *Teachers College Record*, *110*(12), 2601–2632.

Cho, K.-L., & Jonassen, D. (2002). The effects of argumentation scaffolds on argumentation and problem solving. *Educational Technology Research and Development*, *50*(3), 5–22. doi:10.1007/BF02505022

Choi, I., & Lee, K. (2009). Designing and implementing a case-based learning environment for enhancing ill-structured problem solving: Classroom management problems for prospective teachers. *Educational Technology Research and Development*, *57*(1), 99–129. doi:10.1007/s11423-008-9089-2

Collins, A., Brown, J. S., & Newman, S. E. (1989). Cognitive apprenticeship: Teaching the crafts of reading, writing, and mathematics. In Resnick, L. B. (Ed.), *Knowing, learning, and instruction: Essays in honor of Robert Glaser* (pp. 453–494). Hillsdale, NJ: Lawrence Erlbaum Associates.

Cormode, G., & Krishnamurthy, B. (2008). Key differences between Web 1.0 and Web 2.0. *First Monday*, *13*(6). Retrieved from http://www.uic.edu/htbin/cgiwrap/bin/ojs/index.php/fm/article/view/2125/1972.

Corno, L., & Snow, R. (1986). Adapting teaching to individual differences among learners. In Wittrock, M. C. (Ed.), *Handbook of research on teaching* (*Vol. 3*, pp. 605–629). New York, NY: MacMillan.

Cronbach, L., & Snow, R. (1977). *Aptitudes and instructional methods: A handbook for research on interactions*. New York, NY: Irvington.

Dawson, S. (2010). Seeing the learning community: An exploration of the development of a resource for monitoring online student networking. *British Journal of Educational Technology*, *41*(5), 736–752. doi:10.1111/j.1467-8535.2009.00970.x de Wever, B., van Keer, H., Schellens, T., & Valcke, M. (2009). Structuring asynchronous discussion groups: The impact of role assignment and self-assessment on students' levels of knowledge construction through social negotiation. *Journal of Computer Assisted Learning, 25*(2), 177–188. doi:10.1111/j.1365-2729.2008.00292.x

Derry, S., & Lajoie, S. (1993). A middle camp for (un)intelligent instructional computing: An introduction. In Lajoie, S., & Derry, S. (Eds.), *Computers as cognitive tools* (pp. 1–11). Hillsdale, NJ: Lawrence Erlbaum Associates.

Ertmer, P. A., & Newby, T. J. (1993). Behaviorism, cognitivism, constructivism: Comparing critical features from an instructional design perspective. *Performance Improvement Quarterly, 6*(4), 50–72. doi:10.1111/j.1937-8327.1993.tb00605.x

Ertmer, P. A., & Stepich, D. A. (1999). *Case-based instruction in post-secondary education: Developing students' problem-solving expertise.* Paper presented at the Annual Conference of the Midwestern Educational Research Association (MWERA).

Filippidis, S. K., & Tsoukalas, I. A. (2009). On the use of adaptive instructional images based on the sequential-global dimension of the Felder-Silverman learning style theory. *Interactive Learning Environments, 17*(2), 135–150. doi:10.1080/10494820701869524

Ge, X., Chen, C.-H., & Davis, K. A. (2005). Scaffolding novice instructional designers' problem-solving processes using question prompts in a web-based learning environment. *Journal of Educational Computing Research, 33*(2), 219–248. doi:10.2190/5F6J-HHVF-2U2B-8T3G

Ge, X., & Er, N. (2005). An online support system to scaffold real-world problem solving. *Interactive Learning Environments, 13*(3), 139–157. doi:10.1080/10494820500382893

Ge, X., & Land, S. (2003). Scaffolding students' problem-solving processes in an ill-structured task using question prompts and peer interactions. *Educational Technology Research and Development, 51*(1), 21–38. doi:10.1007/BF02504515

Ge, X., & Land, S. M. (2004). A conceptual framework for scaffolding ill-structured problem-solving processes using question prompts and peer interactions. *Educational Technology Research and Development, 52*(2), 5–22. doi:10.1007/BF02504836

Ge, X., Planas, L., & Er, N. (2010). A cognitive support system to scaffold students' problem-based learning in a web-based learning environment. *Interdisciplinary Journal of Problem-Based Learning, 4*(1), 30–56.

Greenhow, C., Robelia, B., & Hughes, J. (2009). Learning, teaching, and scholarship in a digital age. *Educational Researcher, 38*(4), 246–259. doi:10.3102/0013189X09336671

Hadwin, A. F., Oshige, M., Gress, C. L. Z., & Winne, P. H. (2010). Innovative ways for using gStudy to orchestrate and research social aspects of self-regulated learning. *Computers in Human Behavior, 26*(5), 794–805. doi:10.1016/j.chb.2007.06.007

Hannifin, M. J., Land, S. M., & Oliver, K. (1999). Open learning environments: Foundations, methods, and models. In Reigeluth, C. M. (Ed.), *Instructional-design theories and models: A new paradigm of instructional theory* (*Vol. II*, pp. 115–140). Mahwah, NJ: Lawrence Erlbaum Associates.

Hart, R. (1981). Language study and the PLATO IV System. *Studies in Language Learning, 3*, 1–24.

Hernandez-Serrano, J., & Jonassen, D. H. (2003). The effects of case libraries on problem solving. *Journal of Computer Assisted Learning, 19*(1), 103–114. doi:10.1046/j.0266-4909.2002.00010.x

Huang, K., Ge, X., & Bowers, B. (2006). *Virtual Clinic: Simulated ethical decision making in nursing education*. Paper presented at the Annual Meeting of the Association for Educational Communications and Technology.

Hutchins, E. (1995). *Cognitions in the wild*. Cambridge, MA: MIT Press.

Jonassen, D., & Hernandez-Serrano, J. (2002). Case-based reasoning and instructional design: Using stories to support problem solving. *Educational Technology Research and Development, 50*(2), 65–77. doi:10.1007/BF02504994

Kauffman, D., Ge, X., Xie, K., & Chen, C.-H. (2008). Prompting in web-based environments: Supporting self-monitoring and problem solving skills in college students. *Journal of Educational Computing Research, 38*(2), 115–137. doi:10.2190/EC.38.2.a

Kester, L., & Kirschner, A. (2009). Effects of fading support on hypertext navigation and performance in student-centered e-learning environments. *Interactive Learning Environments, 17*(2), 165–179. doi:10.1080/10494820802054992

Kolodner, J. L., & Guzdial, M. (2000). Theory and practice of case-based learning aids. In Jonassen, D. H., & Land, S. M. (Eds.), *Theoretical foundations of learning environments* (pp. 215–242). Mahwah, NJ: Lawrence Erlbaum.

Koschmann, T. (1996). Paradigm shifts and instructional technology: An introduction. In Koschmann, T. (Ed.), *CSCL: Theory and practice of an emerging paradigm* (pp. 1–23). Mahwah, NJ: Lawrence Erlbaum.

Lai, M., & Law, N. (2006). Peer scaffolding of knowledge building through collaborative groups with differential learning experiences. *Journal of Educational Computing Research, 35*(2), 123–144. doi:10.2190/GW42-575W-Q301-1765

Lajoie, S. (2000a). *Computers as cognitive tools: No more walls (Vol. II)*. Mahwah, NJ: Lawrence Erlbaum Associates.

Lajoie, S. (2000b). Introduction: Breaking camp to find new summits. In Lajoie, S. (Ed.), *Computers as cognitive tools: No more walls*. Mahwah, NJ: Lawrence Erlbaum Associates.

Lajoie, S. (2005). Extending the scaffolding metaphor. *Instructional Science, 33*(5), 541–557. doi:10.1007/s11251-005-1279-2

Lajoie, S., & Derry, S. J. (1993). *Computer as cognitive tools*. Hillsdale, NJ: Lawerence Erlbaum Associates.

Land, S., & Zembal-Saul, C. (2003). Scaffolding reflection and articulation of scientific explanations in a data-rich, project-based learning environment: An investigation of progress portfolio. *Educational Technology Research and Development, 51*(4), 65–84. doi:10.1007/BF02504544

Law, V., Ataman, I., & Ge, X. (2010). *Virtual Drug Lab - Pharmacokinetics in an open-ended learning environment*. Paper presented at the The Annual Conference of Association for Educational Communications and Technology.

Lee, J., & Park, O.-C. (2007). Adaptive instructional systems. In Spector, J. M., Merrill, M. D., van Merriënboer, J., & Driscoll, M. P. (Eds.), *Handbook of research for educational communications and technology* (3rd ed., pp. 469–484). New York, NY: Routledge.

Leutner, D. (2004). Instructional-design principles for adaptivity in open learning environments. In Seel, N. M., & Dijkstra, S. (Eds.), *Curriculum, plans, and processes in instructional design: International perspectives* (pp. 289–308). Mahwah, NJ: Erlbaum.

Lin, X., Hmelo, C., Kinzer, C., & Secules, T. (1999). Designing technology to support reflection. *Educational Technology Research and Development, 47*(3), 43–62. doi:10.1007/BF02299633

Linn, M., Clark, D., & Slotta, J. (2003). WISE design for knowledge integration. *Science Education, 87*(4), 517–538. doi:10.1002/sce.10086

Macfadyen, L. P., & Dawson, S. (2010). Mining LMS data to develop an "early warning system" for educators: A proof of concept. *Computers & Education, 54*(2), 588–599. doi:10.1016/j.compedu.2009.09.008

Manlove, S., Lazonder, A. W., & de Jong, T. (2006). Regulative support for collaborative scientific inquiry learning. *Journal of Computer Assisted Learning, 22*(2), 87–98. doi:10.1111/j.1365-2729.2006.00162.x

Manlove, S., Lazonder, A. W., & de Jong, T. (2009). Trends and issues of regulative support use during inquiry learning: Patterns from three studies. *Computers in Human Behavior, 25*(4), 795–803. doi:10.1016/j.chb.2008.07.010

Mayer, R. (1997). Learners as information processors: Legacies and limitations of educational psychology's second metaphor. *Educational Psychologist, 32*(3/4), 151–161.

McManus, R. (2005). Web 2.0 is not about version numbers or betas. *Read/WriteWeb*. Retrieved July 18, 2011, from http://www.readwriteweb.com/archives/web_20_is_not_a.php

McNeill, K. L., Lizotte, D. J., Krajcik, J., & Marx, R. W. (2006). Supporting students' construction of scientific explanations by fading scaffolds in instructional materials. *Journal of the Learning Sciences, 15*(2), 153–191. doi:10.1207/s15327809jls1502_1

Molenaar, I., van Boxtel, C. A. M., & Sleegers, P. J. C. (2010). The effects of scaffolding metacognitive activities in small groups. *Computers in Human Behavior, 26*(6), 1727–1738. doi:10.1016/j.chb.2010.06.022

Oh, S., & Jonassen, D. H. (2007). Scaffolding online argumentation during problem solving. *Journal of Computer Assisted Learning, 23*(2), 95–110. doi:10.1111/j.1365-2729.2006.00206.x

Palincsar, A. S. (1986). The role of dialogue in providing scaffolded instruction. *Educational Psychologist, 21*(1 & 2), 73–98.

Palincsar, A. S., & Brown, A. L. (1984). Reciprocal teaching of comprehension-fostering and comprehension-monitoring activities. *Cognition and Instruction, 1*(2), 117–175. doi:10.1207/s1532690xci0102_1

Pea, R. (1993). Practices of distributed intelligence and designs for education. In Salomon, G. (Ed.), *Distributed cognitions* (pp. 47–87). New York, NY: Cambridge University Press.

Pea, R. (2004). The social and technological dimensions of scaffolding and related theoretical concepts for learning, education, and human activity. *Journal of the Learning Sciences, 13*(3), 423–451. doi:10.1207/s15327809jls1303_6

Pea, R. D. (2004). The social and technological dimensions of scaffolding and related theoretical concepts for learning, education, and human activity. *Journal of the Learning Sciences, 13*(3), 423–451. doi:10.1207/s15327809jls1303_6

Pedersen, S., & Liu, M. (2002). The effects of modeling expert cognitive strategies during problem-based learning. *Journal of Educational Computing Research, 26*(4), 353–380. doi:10.1092/8946-J9N7-E79U-M7CR

Pirnay-Dummer, P., Ifenthaler, D., & Spector, J. M. (2010). Highly integrated model assessment technology and tools. *Educational Technology Research and Development, 58*(1), 3–18. doi:10.1007/s11423-009-9119-8

Puntambekar, S., & Hubscher, R. (2005). Tools for scaffolding students in a complex learning environment: What have we gained and what have we missed? *Educational Psychologist, 40*(1), 1–12. doi:10.1207/s15326985ep4001_1

Quintana, C., Reiser, B. J., Davis, E. A., Krajcik, J., Fretz, E., & Duncan, R. G. (2004). A scaffolding design framework for software to support science inquiry. *Journal of the Learning Sciences, 13*(3), 337–386. doi:10.1207/s15327809jls1303_4

Quintana, C., Zhang, M., & Krajcik, J. (2005). A framework for supporting metacognitive aspects of online inquiry through software-based scaffolding. *Educational Psychologist, 40*(4), 235–244. doi:10.1207/s15326985ep4004_5

Salomon, G. (1993a). No distribution without individuals' cognition: A dynamic interaction view. In Salomon, G. (Ed.), *Distributed cognitions: Psychological and educational considerations* (pp. 111–138). Cape Town, South Africa: Cambridge University Press.

Salomon, G. (1993b). On the nature of pedagogic computer tools: The case of the writing partner. In Lajoie, S. P., & Derry, S. J. (Eds.), *Computers as cognitive tools* (pp. 179–196). Hillsdale, NJ: Lawrence Erlbaum Associates.

Salomon, G., Globerson, T., & Guterman, E. (1989). The computer as a zone of proximal development: Internalizing reading-related metacognitions from a Reading Partner. *Journal of Educational Psychology, 81*, 620–627. doi:10.1037/0022-0663.81.4.620

Scardamalia, M., & Bereiter, C. (1985). Development of dialectical processes in composition. In Olson, D. R., Torrance, N., & Hildyard, A. (Eds.), *Literacy, language, and learning: The nature and consequences of reading and writing* (pp. 307–329). Cambridge, UK: Cambridge University Press.

Scardamalia, M., & Bereiter, C. (1994). Computer support for knowledge-building communities. *Journal of the Learning Sciences, 3*(3), 265–283. doi:10.1207/s15327809jls0303_3

Scardamalia, M., & Bereiter, C. (2006). Knowledge building: Theory, pedagogy, and technology. In Sawyer, K. (Ed.), *Cambridge handbook of the learning sciences* (pp. 97–118). New York, NY: Cambridge University Press.

Scardamalia, M., Bereiter, C., McLean, R., Swallow, J., & Woodruff, E. (1989). Computer-supported intentional learning environments. *Journal of Educational Computing Research, 5*(1), 51–68.

Scardamalia, M., Bereiter, C., & Steinbach, R. (1984). Teachability of reflective processes in written composition. *Cognitive Science, 8*(2), 173–190. doi:10.1207/s15516709cog0802_4

Sharma, P., & Hannafin, M. (2004). Scaffolding critical thinking in an online course: An exploratory study. *Journal of Educational Computing Research, 31*(2), 181–208. doi:10.2190/TMC3-RXPE-75MY-31YG

Shute, V. J., & Zapata-Rivera, D. (2008). Adaptive technologies. In Spector, J. M., Merrill, M. D., van Merriënboer, J., & Driscoll, M. P. (Eds.), *Handbook of research for educational communications and technology* (pp. 277–294). New York, NY: Routledge.

Skinner, B. F. (1974). The technology of teaching. In Bart, W. M., & Wong, M. R. (Eds.), *Psychology of school learning: Views of the learner* (*Vol. 2*, pp. 38–54). New York, NY: MSS Information Corporation.

Suthers, D. (1998). *Representations for scaffolding collaborative inquiry on ill-structured problems.* Paper presented at the AERA Annual Meeting.

Tung, F.-W., & Deng, Y.-S. (2006). Designing social presence in e-learning environments: Testing the effect of interactivity on children. *Interactive Learning Environments, 14*(3), 251–264. doi:10.1080/10494820600924750

van Joolingen, W. R., de Jong, T., Lazonder, A. W., Savelsbergh, E. R., & Manlove, S. (2005). Co-Lab: Research and development of an online learning environment for collaborative scientific discovery learning. *Computers in Human Behavior, 21*(4), 671–688. doi:10.1016/j.chb.2004.10.039

van Merriënboer, J. J. G., Clark, R., & de Croock, M. (2002). Blueprints for complex learning: The 4C/ID-model. *Educational Technology Research and Development, 50*(2), 39–61. doi:10.1007/BF02504993

Vygotsky, L. S. (1978). *Mind in society: The development of higher psychological processes.* Cambridge, MA: Harvard University Press.

Williams, B. (2005). Case based learning – A review of the literature: Is there scope for this educational paradigm in prehospital education? *Emergency Medicine Journal, 22*(8), 577–581. doi:10.1136/emj.2004.022707

Wood, D., Bruner, J. S., & Ross, G. (1976). The role of tutoring in problem solving. *Journal of Child Psychology and Psychiatry, and Allied Disciplines, 17*(2), 89–100. doi:10.1111/j.1469-7610.1976.tb00381.x

Zellermayer, M., Salomon, G., Globerson, T., & Givon, H. (1991). Enhancing writing-related metacognitions through a computerized writing partner. *American Educational Research Journal, 28*(2), 373–391.

ADDITIONAL READING

Azevedo, R., & Jacobson, M. (2008). Advances in scaffolding learning with hypertext and hypermedia: A summary and critical analysis. *Educational Technology Research and Development, 56*(1), 93–100. doi:10.1007/s11423-007-9064-3

Bonk, C. (2009). *The world is open: How Web technology is revolutionizing education.* San Francisco, CA: Jossey-Bass.

Brown, J. S., Collins, A., & Duguid, P. (1989). Situated cognition and the culture of learning. *Educational Researcher, 18*(1), 32–42.

Collins, A., Brown, J. S., & Newman, S. E. (1989). Cognitive apprenticeship: Teaching the crafts of reading, writing, and mathematics. In Resnick, L. B. (Ed.), *Knowing, learning, and instruction: Essays in honor of Robert Glaser* (pp. 453–494). Hillsdale, NJ: Lawrence Erlbaum Associates.

Corno, L., & Snow, R. (1986). Adapting teaching to individual differences among learners. In Wittrock, M. C. (Ed.), *Handbook of research on teaching* (*Vol. 3*, pp. 605–629). New York, NY: MacMillan.

Ge, X., & Land, S. (2003). Scaffolding students' problem-solving processes in an ill-structured task using question prompts and peer interactions. *Educational Technology Research and Development, 51*(1), 21–38. doi:10.1007/BF02504515

Ge, X., & Land, S. M. (2004). A conceptual framework for scaffolding III-structured problem-solving processes using question prompts and peer interactions. *Educational Technology Research and Development, 52*(2), 5–22. doi:10.1007/BF02504836

Kester, L., & Kirschner, A. (2009). Effects of fading support on hypertext navigation and performance in student-centered e-learning environments. *Interactive Learning Environments, 17*(2), 165–179. doi:10.1080/10494820802054992

Koschmann, T. (1996). *CSCL: Theory and practice of an emerging paradigm.* Mahwah, NJ: Lawrence Erlbaum.

Lajoie, S. (2000). *Computers as cognitive tools: No more walls* (*Vol. II*). Mahwah, NJ: Lawrence Erlbaum Associates.

Lajoie, S. (2005). Extending the scaffolding metaphor. *Instructional Science, 33*(5), 541–557. doi:10.1007/s11251-005-1279-2

Lajoie, S., & Derry, S. J. (1993). *Computer as cognitive tools.* Hillsdale, NJ: Lawerence Erlbaum Associates.

Land, S., & Zembal-Saul, C. (2003). Scaffolding reflection and articulation of scientific explanations in a data-rich, project-based learning environment: An investigation of progress portfolio. *Educational Technology Research and Development, 51*(4), 65–84. doi:10.1007/BF02504544

Lee, J., & Park, O.-C. (2007). Adaptive instructional systems. In Spector, J. M., Merrill, M. D., van Merriënboer, J., & Driscoll, M. P. (Eds.), *Handbook of research for educational communications and technology* (3rd ed., pp. 469–484). New York, NY: Routledge.

Lin, X., Hmelo, C., Kinzer, C., & Secules, T. (1999). Designing technology to support reflection. *Educational Technology Research and Development, 47*(3), 43–62. doi:10.1007/BF02299633

Linn, M., Clark, D., & Slotta, J. (2003). WISE design for knowledge integration. *Science Education, 87*(4), 517–538. doi:10.1002/sce.10086

Palincsar, A. S. (1986). The role of dialogue in providing scaffolded instruction. *Educational Psychologist, 21*(1 & 2), 73–98.

Palincsar, A. S., & Brown, A. L. (1984). Reciprocal teaching of comprehension-fostering and comprehension-monitoring activities. *Cognition and Instruction, 1*(2), 117–175. doi:10.1207/s1532690xci0102_1

Pea, R. D. (2004). The social and technological dimensions of scaffolding and related theoretical concepts for learning, education, and human activity. *Journal of the Learning Sciences, 13*(3), 423–451. doi:10.1207/s15327809jls1303_6

Puntambekar, S., & Hubscher, R. (2005). Tools for scaffolding students in a complex learning environment: What have we gained and what have we missed? *Educational Psychologist, 40*(1), 1–12. doi:10.1207/s15326985ep4001_1

Quintana, C., Reiser, B. J., Davis, E. A., Krajcik, J., Fretz, E., & Duncan, R. G. (2004). A scaffolding design framework for software to support science inquiry. *Journal of the Learning Sciences, 13*(3), 337–386. doi:10.1207/s15327809jls1303_4

Quintana, C., Zhang, M., & Krajcik, J. (2005). A framework for supporting metacognitive aspects of online inquiry through software-based scaffolding. *Educational Psychologist, 40*(4), 235–244. doi:10.1207/s15326985ep4004_5

Salomon, G. (1993). No distribution without individuals' cognition: A dynamic interaction view. In Salomon, G. (Ed.), *Distributed cognitions: Psychological and educational considerations* (pp. 111–138). Cape Town: Cambridge University Press.

Salomon, G., Globerson, T., & Guterman, E. (1989). The computer as a zone of proximal development: Internalizing reading-related metacognitions from a Reading Partner. *Journal of Educational Psychology, 81*(4), 620–627. doi:10.1037/0022-0663.81.4.620

Scardamalia, M., & Bereiter, C. (1985). Development of dialectical processes in composition. In Olson, D. R., Torrance, N., & Hildyard, A. (Eds.), *Literacy, language, and learning: The nature and consequences of reading and writing* (pp. 307–329). Cambridge: Cambridge University Press.

Shute, V. J., & Zapata-Rivera, D. (2008). Adaptive technologies. In Spector, J. M., Merrill, M. D., van Merriënboer, J., & Driscoll, M. P. (Eds.), *Handbook of research for educational communications and technology* (pp. 277–294). New York, NY: Routledge.

Vygotsky, L. S. (1978). *Mind in society: The development of higher psychological processes.* Cambridge, MA: Harvard University Press.

Wood, D., Bruner, J. S., & Ross, G. (1976). The role of tutoring in problem solving. *Journal of Child Psychology and Psychiatry, and Allied Disciplines,* *17*(2), 89–100. doi:10.1111/j.1469-7610.1976.tb00381.x

KEY TERMS AND DEFINITIONS

Adaptive Systems: Any computer-based instructional interventions aiming at accommodating individual learner characteristics and needs.

Diagnosis: As one of the three major processes of scaffolding, diagnosis refers to the continual assessment of students' learning processes and outcomes.

Fading: The removal of support when a learner is gaining competence and confidence in desired concepts and skills.

Scaffolding: A temporary framework to support learners when assistance is needed; it is removed when it is no longer needed. It is adjustable based on individuals' change of zone of proximal development.

Support: As one of the three major processes of scaffolding, support represents the needed assistance that enables a learner accomplish a task, solve a problem, or acquire a skill.

System Adaption: The capability of a computer-based system to monitor and adapt to the characteristics and needs of learners for the purpose of supporting their learning.

Chapter 7
A Noble Eightfold Path:
Novice to Expert in E-Learning and the Efficacy of Instructional Design

Julia Penn Shaw
State University of New York - Empire State College, USA

ABSTRACT

Teachers teach to the level of their ability: novices can teach students to be novices: experts can teach students to be experts. Using the Buddhist Eightfold Path as a model, this chapter explores the expert/ novice paradigm as a framework for e-learning, particularly as offered through instructional design that can both scaffold novice instructors to teach to a higher level of learning, and also support experts to help students reach higher goals. Three facets of the teaching/learning dialogue are explored: expertise in a domain of knowledge (teacher), expertise in acquiring deep knowledge in a new domain through learning (learner), and expertise in the instructor/learner learning interface (instructional designer). Expert and novice teaching and learning and their relationship through instructional designers will be discussed.

EXPERTS AND NOVICES IN E-LEARNING

You probably already know much of what is presented in this chapter about advantages of instructional design in e-learning environments.

DOI: 10.4018/978-1-61350-441-3.ch007

What might be different is to view it from the expert/novice perspective. The expert/novice paradigm is one more conceptual tool in the tool-bag of the teacher, the instructional designer, and/or the learner. For example, would learners respond differently to the challenges of learning within a domain if they consciously identify themselves as seeking to become experts? Are there effective ways to measure the characteristics identified with expertise, such as 'flow', 'discipline', etc? What are the particular hurdles of a domain expert in teaching a novice? How can the backbone of essential knowledge within a domain be built such that details fall into place effectively and with greatest retention and potential usefulness? The expert/novice paradigm opens up interesting questions and may lead to additional rich and productive dialogue between teachers, learners, and instructional designers.

Significant work has established the value of researching differences between novices and experts in various domains (Gills, 1999; Ortega, 1987; Greening, 1998; Wiedenbeck, 1985). Initially, differentiated levels of skill were used to create computerized knowledge engines or knowledge systems that replicated processes used by experts guiding novices toward higher levels of achievement in the military, particularly airline pilots (Endsley, Farley, Jones, McKiff & Hansman, 1998; Morrow, Miller, Ridulfo, Kokayeff, Chang, Fischer & Stein-Morrow, 2004) and in industry, particularly computer programmers (Perkins & Martin, 1986). As the continuum of novice to expert became better known, its relationships to other types of learning, knowledge-acquisition, and skill-building for both children and adults became a source of interest, connecting novice/ expert frameworks to business applications (business management, Reuber & Fischer, 1992); social constructivist education (Meyer, 2004; Duckworth, 2006); and adult learning process (Rich & Almozlino, 1999; Meyer, 2004; Shaw, 2005).

The focus of this chapter is on using the expert/ novice paradigm to improve reused (not 'one off') undergraduate e-learning environments through instructional design. Because of its digital base, e-learning can support knowledge-engines and algorithmic skill training. Skills which require over-practice to build expertise are especially promising e-learning applications. Expertise is shown through demonstration and application of identified sequences that are measureable against quantifiable standards. Educational domains having known skill paths (e.g., science, music, and project management) attract application of the expert/novice paradigm into e-learning (Burns, Parlett & Redfield, 2009; Keefe & Jenkins, 1997).

'Expert' and 'novice' are ends of a continuum from novice to advanced beginner, to competent, to proficient, and to expert (Dreyfus & Dreyfus, 1985), but most instructors and learners have skill-levels between these two poles. Three types of expertise are distinguished here – domain expertise, learning expertise, and instructional design expertise – as related to three roles: teacher, learner and instructional designer. This is an oversimplification, but perhaps a useful one to isolate areas that can effectively use the expert/ novice paradigm to provide authentic learning for students at all levels. Table 1 outlines these relationships.

Although the continuum is a high level look at the map of the learning exchange, exposing only some of the covered territory, it highlights major features of learning. Ideal teachers and learners are experts, but because this is rare, especially in an undergraduate class setting that we

Table 1. Relationships among levels of expertise (expert/novice), areas of expertise (domain/interface/ learning) and roles (teach/instructional designer/learner)

	Expert	Novice
Teaching	Domain Experts	Domain Novice
Interface	Expert Instructional Designer	Novice Instructional Designer
Learning	Expert Learner	Novice Learner

are describing, expertise in instructional design is sought to bridge the gap. In an established online program, effective instructional design augments the learning environment in ways that encourage expertise in both teaching and learning.

Both experts and novices enrolled in an online course must invest time to learn the language, skills, and conceptual tools of the domain. Research shows that both see the surface features of the domain ((Wiedenbeck, 1985; Perkins & Martin, 1986; Blanton, Moorman, Hayes & Warner, 1997) and there is no significant difference in their memory capacities: Experts do not have better memories than novices, just better ability to organize meaningful information in a familiar domain (Wiedenbeck, 1985). Domain experts and novices do not differ in innate abilities, but in their relationship to domain knowledge. Chess players show superior memory for regular chess positions, but that superior memory does not generalize to other environments (Djakow, Petrowski & Rudik, 1927). IQ was not shown to distinguish the best chess players (Doll & Mayr, 1987), or successful and creative artists and scientists (Taylor, 1975). Superior training seemed to be a critical factor in the differences across levels of expertise, and competency in narrow areas of expertise did not transfer well to other domains (Ericsson & Lehman, 1996).

Differences between experts and novices start with the time invested to achieve excellence. The rule for ten thousand hours of practice (Ericsson, 1996) is invoked by Daniel Levitin in *This is your brain on music: The science of a human obsession* (2006):

... ten thousand hours of practice is required to achieve the level of mastery associated with being a world-class expert — in anything. In study after study, of composers, basketball players, fiction writers, ice skaters, concert pianists, chess players, master criminals, and what have you, this number comes up again and again. Ten thousand hours is the equivalent to roughly three hours per day, or twenty hours per week, of practice over ten years. Of course, this doesn't address why some people don't seem to get anywhere when they practice, and why some people get more out of their practice sessions than others. But no one has yet found a case in which true world-class expertise was accomplished in less time. It seems that it takes the brain this long to assimilate all that it needs to know to achieve true mastery. (p. 197).

EXPERTS AND NOVICES, TEACHERS AND LEARNERS

"Teacher" is the name given to subject matter/domain expertise in this chapter. Looking at the online experience from the teacher's perspective, what different types of knowledge are required to be an expert teacher for the subject domain? Is the teacher a novice or an expert in the field of study? Is the teacher a novice or expert in pedagogy for the level of the learner? Is the teacher able to bridge between her/his own level of skill and that of the learners being instructed?

"Learner" is the term here for expertise in scaffolding oneself to construct new knowledge. What different types of knowledge are required to be an expert learner? Is the learner a novice or expert in this subject area? Is the learner a novice or expert skilled in bridging between current knowledge and new learning? Has the learner been traumatized by former learning, increasing scaffolding required to follow the path towards expertise?

In a course, both teacher and learners want to do their best within their time and commitment constraints: teachers want motivating learners and learners want motivating teachers, both having expectations that may be hard to meet. Unguided, the blind do sometimes lead the blind, and novice teachers may lead novice learners to attend to superficial aspects of a subject. The structure of an online template can help novice instructors guide learners toward practice, patterns and analogies leading to knowledge of basic principles, a reduction in field dependence on surface features of the terrain of the new domain (Zheng, in press). All new learners need ample opportunities to practice syntax and semantics in a new domain so basics can become automatic (Rich & Almozlino, 1999), but expert learners strive to gain the automaticity that elevates them to the next level of expertise. Novice learners may resist practice if they have never before gained conscious expertise in a subject area, not realizing the importance of learning the domain 'language'. "Expertise and experience are not identical, but... experience is a necessary component of expertise" (Rich & Almozlino, 1999).

Surprise is a necessary part of deep learning (Kagan, 2004), as initial primitive relationships are restructured with experience. Novice learners are surprised by their surprise, not expecting it and not welcoming it when it happens, treating learning as 'an accumulation of more bits of information" (Meyer, 2004), but expert learners expect deviations from the rules, seeking them out through extensive practice. Using a reading example, young learners of English as a first language are surprised to learn that some words do not follow the rules of phonics, but learners of a second language expect, and may even seek, experiences that expose such anomalies. Both expert and novice learners need small learning chunks, but expert learners know they do, and independently combine identifiable units. All learners create spontaneous constructions and analogies, but those created by novice learners are more likely to be disjointed, distracting, and frail because they are focused on surface rather than fundamental aspects of the subject (Perkins & Martin, 1990). As a course progresses, expert teachers are sensitive to inappropriate applications of principles by students knowing that errors can create misunderstanding of basic principles if not caught early – but augment understanding of basic principles if noticed early and used to create a cognitive dissonance in the learner between a pseudo-principle and a basic principle (Piaget,

1967; Shaw, 2005). Ge, Law & Huang (in press) scaffold learners using a 'diagnosis, support and fade' model to overcome these learning hurdles.

Accustomed to using analogies to learn (Brown, 1997), expert learners create opportunities to generate and test hypotheses, self-correcting their errors. Many expert learners intentionally create novel hypotheses that lead them off the beaten path of the course template, just to learn about the limits of their new domain (Brown, 1997). An expert in one domain adapts to being an expert learner in similar domains where principles are constructed in a similar manner and where the same rich neural networks can be accessed (Zull, 2002). Experts in one domain entering a new domain look for its foundational principles, expecting instructors to clarify them, to provide ample opportunities to exercise those principles in rich and diverse contexts, to ask provocative questions, and to relate surface structure to deep structure (Schoenfield & Hermann, 1982). For example, expert readers in one language expect to be taught an alphabet, words, and larger units of thought for the language that they are learning.

Insightful judgment of information is needed to successfully move toward the goal (Ortega, 1987) and experts need less information to successfully achieve a goal, selecting the best options from those available. They spot red herrings and dodge artificial barriers, identifying missing elements and filling in gaps. They create short-term goals and long-term strategies based on the reality of the domain (Schoenfield & Hermann, 1982).

Novice learners value social support based on 'let's do this together,' looking for instructor support and course formatting that scaffolds each new step (Blanton, Moorman, Hayes & Warner, 1997). Expert learners prefer collegial support, acting as co-constructors of knowledge, frequently offering improvements to the course material. While creating and testing models for success they create their own analogies and craft practice routines which they verify themselves. Many get a reputation for asking instructors challenging questions, even as they make the best use of guidance. The more expert learners are about their own learning process, the more effectively they communicate about what they need in instruction to learn well. Such learners are often called self-regulated learners (Moore, 1993). As a learning process continues, expert learners and teachers create an interactive system (Moore, 1993) that elicits continual attention, reflection, practice, and critique. Obtaining expertise, however, is not linear, but rather the result of many, many transformations, contextual shifts and bypasses. In language learning for example, we learn to use language effectively by stages, some of which are identifiable (i.e., letters, words, chunks of meaning, expression of thoughts and experiences), and some of which are not (i.e., motivations to read and write, what language invokes internally, what language is evoked from external events).

Using the metaphor of the "forest and the trees", novices see separate trees of different shapes, sizes and distributions, whereas experts see unique aspects of specific trees, how they interact with each other, and what constitutes a forest from the perspective of many systems (ecological, biological, chemical, geological, etc.). The growth of knowledge fits with the epigenetic principle (Werner and Kaplan, 1960) that the development of knowledge leads to an increased integration and flexibility of concepts within the domain and in relationship to other domains; and also to increased differentiation of details and specific knowledge of parts and wholes in different contexts.

EXPERTS AND NOVICES, INSTRUCTIONAL DESIGNERS

'Instructional Designer' is the name here for expertise in bridging between the learner and domain knowledge. The roles of the teacher and course designer can be fused – but since sometimes the domain expert is not an interface expert, interface

expertise is identified here with the role of the instructional designer. Are there aspects of cognitive, social and cultural presence that are critical to learner success (Shaw & Chen, in press)? What significant visual experiences must be included to make the online experience salient? From the instructional designer's perspective, what are the fundamental principles of the e-learning domain? How can they best be reinforced? What is the general complexity level of thought of the learners? Specifically, what can be done from an instructional design perspective to build on the expertise of the teacher to reach the expertise of the learner, the question most directly addressed here?

Effective learning can be systematically assessed, evaluated, reinforced and critiqued in online environments (Harasim, 2000). For example, based on prior research on expertise, we know that it takes time to develop a new domain language, a conceptual base, and the skills to use them (Brown, 1997). An online environment offers a stage for knowledge-based learning with branches to different levels of skill-practice based on input from the learner. Flexible guidelines can support teachers with different levels of domain expertise to reach learners with different levels of learning expertise. Systematic procedures can support varied paths for novices and experts in a domain based on diverse learning patterns. For example, students who demonstrate their knowledge of a scientific principle through correct application of a formula to a problem move on to a more complex application. If they do not, they are redirected to exercises that reinforce the smaller learning chunks they still need to learn.

Effective instructional design can scaffold at least three levels of the learning environment: scaffold domain experts to bridge between their high level of knowledge and the levels of knowledge that learners can receive; scaffold domain novices to convey deeper knowledge to learners; and scaffold novice learners to construct knowledge with increasing skill (Vygotsky, 1978). Learners value connecting their previous cognitive and motivational insights with deep foundational knowledge. Zull (2002) among others notes that rich, deep, neuronal connections must be tapped. Somehow the online course must construct motivational experiences, reduce pitfalls in understanding, and present successful paths to new understanding and useful meta-cognitive critiques. Learners use online opportunities to connect relational principles of the new domain with their rich neural networks in other areas (i.e., connecting baseball or cooking to physics). With effective counter-examples, learners discriminate effectively between true principles and pseudo-principles.

Instructional design enhances the expertise of both teachers and learners. Examples, exercises, problem sets, discussions, journals, games and reflections provided by an instructional designer to an online course augment expert teaching. Instructional designers use pedagogical frameworks such as the Zone of Proximal Development to scaffold understanding of critical points (Vygotsky, 1978; Fischer, Zheng & Stewart, 2002; Duckworth, 2009). Together, teachers and instructional designers provide clear labels for the conventions of the domain, reinforce precise vocabulary, and enable learners to relate their prior learning to current experience (Meyer, 2004). E-learning can provide 'teaching moments' at points in learning when many students become confused about surface features and deep structure of a subject (Schoenfield & Hermann, 1982). The challenging points in learning are easier to spot on online learning, because the student responses are captured in the course template. An instructional designer can then search for materials in the public domain that reinforce the deep structure. Such materials are frequently available, because students in other institutions experience similar problems, and many excellent teachers are willing to share their time-tested approaches.

Online templates may provide permanency of classroom experiences for future view as books provide permanency to spoken words. As online learning experiences become more common,

analysis of classroom experiences may have some of the appeal to educators that literature has to narratologists. Teaching can be studied in ways that are not now available, and one can envision courses in the future that focus almost solely on online exchanges as the source of pedagogical knowledge.

AN EIGHTFOLD PATH FROM NOVICE TO EXPERT

Creating a path from novice to expert is not a new concept. In ancient Greece, neophyte philosophers learned from more elder mentors; in the Middle Ages, apprentices became masters as determined by trade guilds; in Native American cultures Shamans follow rituals to gain access to spiritual depths.

In *Writing down the Bones: Freeing the writer within* (2005), author Natalie Goldberg described an experience with her Zen master, as he guided her spiritual path using sitting meditation as a practice. He said, "Why do you come to sit meditation? Why don't you make writing your practice? If you go deep enough in writing, it will take you everyplace (p. 3)." In this, Natalie links her path for writing expertise to a search for higher consciousness. The Zen master suggested that a path of disciplined practice may be as effective in writing as it is in meditation. Although seeking a path to Enlightenment is on a scale vastly greater than the goal of gaining expertise in a subject domain, as Goldberg's quote suggests one can reinforce the other through mindful daily practice

It is from such an integrative approach, that the Buddhist Noble Eightfold Path to Enlightenment is linked here to the path from novice to expertise in e-learning. In Buddhism, it is through the practice of Wisdom (through Right View and Right Intention), of Ethical Conduct (through Right Speech, Right Action, and Right Livelihood) and of Mental Development (through Right Effort, Right Mindfulness, and Right Concentration), that a higher level of existence can be reached (Bodhi, 2000). Although the goals are different, the structure of an eightfold path proves workable to guide instructional design in e-learning.

- The title, The Noble Eightfold Path, conveys a holistic recognition that a path has a 'right' direction with the implication that even first steps build toward success, and non-constructive habits need to be changed.
- Organizing the aspects of the learning path into eight 'chunks' is good teaching practice, with each chunk being clear and distinct, connecting with each of the others, and together providing necessary and sufficient coverage of the learning required for the path.
- The eight aspects are not presented as linear or sequential, but as simultaneous perspectives upon the whole of the learning experience. All are necessary.

The 'Eightfold Path from Novice to Expert' presented here is derived from research about novice to expert learning in the context of years of experience with e-learning environments. It is intended to provide a high-level map for the very complex, engaging, and time-intensive experience of conceiving of, developing, teaching and monitoring e-learning environments. Some of the take-away points are presented as 'either/or' options in the statements below. In Table 2, the "aspect of attention" provides simple mnemonics to guide the instructional designer to attend to differences between novice and expert responses. These polar responses (e.g., junky or chunky organization) can be used as simple assessments for the effectiveness of activities. That is, a design element to increase 'motivation' can be assessed to see if it helps learners become more 'mindful', or if the learner continues to be 'muddled' in identifiable ways. Each of these aspects is explained briefly along with some instructional design elements that augment it, with the intention to be suggestive rather than inclusive.

1. Motivation: Muddled or Mindful

Dr. Ellen Winner, Professor of Psychology at Boston University, provided an insight, at the 2010 Association for Psychological Science Annual Convention, into motivation towards expertise: a strong indicator that a young musician will continue to practice was the answer to this simple question: "How long do you think you will play the violin?" Students who said they expected to play it life-long were the ones most likely to continue successful practice (Winner, 2010) Practicing a minimum of 10,000 hours of practice fits with this lifelong commitment. A commitment of about twenty hours of practice a week suggests that

Table 2. The eightfold path from novice to expert

Aspect of Attention	Novice Response	Expert Response
1. Motivation	Muddled	Mindful
2. Process	(prematurely) Closed	Exposed
3. Organization	Junky	Chunky
4. Presentation	(stiltedly) Formal	Flowing
5. Approach	Distressed	Disciplined
6. Goals	Fixed	Flexible
7. Focus	Buckshot	Bulls-eye
8. Direction	Flooded	Futuristic

the work is part of one's life, connected to one's identity and social network, and to one's current or projected livelihood. Mentoring at critical points may make the difference between continuing and stopping the effort. Examples abound of families of child experts, such as swimmers, ice skaters and pianists, who modify their activities and budgets to accommodate the expectations and stresses of their child's practice and performance; and the commitment to excellence may be not only to the self and family, but also to one's country. Adults who seek expertise have even more challenges, frequently balancing adult work and family expectations with hours spent in practice.

Relevant research in psychology augments novice/expert studies. Here are some highlights of studies that inform mindfulness in motivation:

- Identification with successful models for learning leads to the development of good habits, prevents wasteful digressions, builds professional networks, keeps motivation strong, and provides answers to questions as they arise (Dewey, 1916; Montessori, 1949, 1994; McCarthy, in press).
- Self-regulation is something that successful learners bring to their online studies. Even as early as preschool, self-regulation is a predictor for a child's subsequent success in school because the child is able to forego immediate pleasures for a longer term goals (Bandura, 1986).
- Envisioning is a capacity that can be developed, particularly from adolescence (Shaw, 2002). The ability to envision goals keeps small challenges within the perspective of larger efforts.

Instructional Design
Support for Motivation

Although one online course will not lead to expertise, it can set clear expectations and sup-

port habits essential for future success, possibly catching (and grounding) student dreams for future achievements through journaling and self-narratives. It can address muddledness about identity with a domain by providing models and mentors, examples of expert work, motivating biographies, and possibly opportunities for student/ faculty work. It can address the cost of pursuing expertise in a domain by providing information to help determine that cost. More effectively it can address questions about whether one has ability in a domain, what changes need to be made in habits to be more successful, and what steps can be taken to move forward.

Online mentors can encourage identification with professional standards, and provide avenues for personal identification, including easy access to local branches of national professional organizations. E-portfolios enable self-examination in ways that bare grades do not; service learning encourages deep connection to community with immediate feedback about the importance of doing work well. Increasingly, open communication and blogs can connect novices directly to experts in the field, to peek in on their dialogue with each other or join in discussions of interest. Through blogs, professional listservs and other electronic communication vehicles, online environments provide avenues for building paths for future learning beyond the course. Learners can smoothly be introduced to experts with whom they may choose to continue a relationship, through journals and conferences. We know that modeling from experts provides a level of learning that no other experience provides (McCarthy, in press). As Thomas Kuhn pointed out, knowledge about the 'human stories' behind the formal presentation of expertise enables learners to better envision themselves, as human beings, in the shoes of the admired expert (Kuhn, 1996). Teachers and students quickly learn the level of commitment that each has for the course with some institutions, such as premiere colleges, setting higher standards for learners than others.

2. Process: (Prematurely) Closed or Exposed

Teaching for coverage to pass examinations leads to a superficial view of a domain, if not paired with opportunities to explore more deeply (Schoenfield & Hermann, 1982). An overview is not a handicap, because a surface picture is required to get a map of the territory, but it is not a place to stop. Teachers, expert instructional designers, and expert learners will tend to focus on goals exposing fundamentals in a domain. Novice teachers, novice instructional designers and novice learners will tend to have goals for premature closure, settling for a first successful answer, rather than exploring situations where that first answer fails. Expert learners relate new knowledge to prior experience and seek natural breaking points in knowledge where closure is appropriate. Novice learners may seek to end their exploration when they learn rules and procedures – an initial point of closure.

Even those who have achieved identified expertise must be ready for change. Economic growth in our society is based on "creative destruction' (Cowan, 2004), so expertise may change fast, faster in some domains (computer applications) than in others (swimming). For example, physics may have a high cycle of creative destruction, but the mathematical tools used in physics may have higher stability. Even Einstein's expertise became displaced within his lifetime. Music performance may have a lower cycle of creativity and higher stability in tools. Because many breakthroughs come from outside an established domain of expertise, experts may not anticipate where the next foundational change comes from, but they are less likely to be surprised by it than novices, because they are aware of cycles of paradigm shift (Kuhn, 1996). Such shifts are common to all areas and eras, leading to the emergence of new areas of expertise and the demise of others.

Instructional Design Support for Process

Sound habits build expertise, but how can students assure that their habits are effective? Expert teachers are likely to have experienced a few key exercises that led to their own success, understanding the value of foundational exercises and rigorous training. A process that provides corrective feedback of increasing granularity may lead a pianist to work on one piece for five years, and perfect it over a lifetime (Gladwell, 2008). Courses can provide exemplary models from various experts as templates for coursework so that students experience different styles of practice and expression. In some domains verification of success comes directly: a computer program or mathematical equation either works as expected or it does not; a musical piece either sounds as expected or does not; a medical procedure or mediation brings the result or not; a golf ball hits the green or does not. Online courses can provide time-lapse simulations for processes such as geology that enable a view of future based on current actions. Tools for conceptual mapping enable a learner to explore interacting facets of a domain, exposing both emic (internal) and etic (external) connections. An intense group review of a challenging case study opens learners up to options they would not otherwise consider, and even in TV shows such as *House* and *CSI* experts challenge each other, explore false paths, and integrate disparate elements. If paired with appropriate challenges and anomalies about the domain, conceptual maps and hyperlinks may provide learners with just-in-time insights (Novak, 1990), and lead learners to further inquiry.

3. Organization: Junky or Chunky

Experts create meaningful chunks at larger and larger levels of relevant abstraction are more flexible in chunking so that the level of abstraction is right for a problem, and are better at immediate switching from one level to the other, as needed (Miller, 1956; Gobet, Lane, Crocker, Cheng, Jones, Oliver & Pine, 2001). Experts in meaningful situations can remember larger chunks than novices, leading to superior solutions. Using reading as an example, an experienced reader can remember words of very long lengths, but will remember nonsense words of about the same length as novices (Ortega, 1987). Because of the effective 'chunking' of letters into meaningful words, readers execute the actions leading to the goal of reading. Novice readers cannot yet envision the same goal of reading words that an experienced reader can (e.g., reading the words in a sentence), because they are still analyzing letter chunks.

Through extensive practice, experimentation, and application in foundational and peripheral contexts, experts build small subroutines, assembling them flexibly to meet larger goals. The smaller procedures may be musical units for a performer, computer subroutines for a programmer, chess play sequences for a chess master, visual scans for an airplane pilot, dives for a swimmer, mathematical equations for a mathematician, etc. These subroutines serve as successful solutions to small problems, as elegant parts of larger units, and as lubrication for streamlined paths to sophisticated goals. When a part of the 'language' of the expert, they enable focus on the larger issues in the domain. With this knowledge, experts have confidence that they can function swiftly and surely. The chunking capacity enables the expert to know what to test when something goes wrong, and to switch quickly from one intuitively sound hypothesis to another. Experts have both divergent and convergent skills in their domain and can move from one strategy to another as needed.

Instructional Design Support for Organization

Practice, practice, practice. Knowledge about chunking comes from experience. First the basic elements must be over-taught: letters (and then words) for a language; computer instructions (and then algorithms) for a computer language; moves (and then strategies) for a game: strokes (and then styles) for a sport. Understanding the nuances and skillfully manipulating the variations in perspectives to create effective 'chunking' can be demonstrated online, but direct experience through exercises provides the opportunities to learn the 'rules' of the domain, create short 'flows' which can then be creatively assembled, and to relate short-term skill-building to long-term strategies. This knowledge must be in the body as well as in the mind. My personal experience leads me to believe that instructional design can be of particular use in over-practice of basic concepts and skills, with very concrete feedback about strengths and weaknesses of skill development. Games, competitions, applications, exercises, experiences all contribute, and no longer have to be developed in-house since so many are available through the web. Over-practice is, to me, the most obvious area for instructional design to support the path to expertise.

With practice comes differentiation, knowledge about attributes of the basic chunks and how those attributes create larger structures (i.e., chess roles and chess moves). Chunks are organized by relationships across time and across space, and relationships through sequences, partitions, rankings and visual images emerge (Shaw, 2002). Online courses can use examples of past successes and failures (champion games, key competitions) to make critical distinctions, and offer specific challenges.

4. Presentation: (Stiltedly) Formal or Flowing

Novices see a domain as 'out there', seeing the tops of the trees; Experts understand individual trees, the forest from floor to canopy, and the root system that supports it. Expert learners desire for domain knowledge to become a part of themselves, changing not only their skills but also their identity.

Learning for an expert learner binds new knowledge to the self. Wiedenbeck (1985) identifies three stages of expertise: (1) *Cognitive* (textbook or declarative), where rules rule; (2) *Associative*, where functional procedures are used; (3) *Autonomous*, where high speed, flexibility, intuition, and flow preside. Expert teachers provide opportunities for learners to make personal connections with the domain knowledge because the teachers either consciously or intuitively understand the stages of learning of which Wiedenbeck speaks, having passed through them themselves.

Flow has an aesthetic quality. Teachers with flow can lead learners through complex paths of information, differentiating major from minor points by accent, pace, tone, informative comments, length of attention to that part of the story and more attention to the details that support it. The information leads the learner to the next step linking connections between the last element, the current one, and the next one; separating the 'backbone' (narrative) of the domain from the auxiliary points; and fleshing out the domain leading to knowledge of methods of investigation as well as the resulting foundational knowledge.

Expertise is characterized by fluidity in using syntactical, semantic, and functional knowledge to create meaningful gestalts (Wiedenbeck, 1985), providing unity among successive actions as 'flow' (Csikszentmihalyi & Csikszentmihalyi, 1988). There is a story in cognitive science about an alien who discovers a toaster. The alien can visually grasp all of the elements, can take the toaster apart and put it back together again, but without the concept of 'toast' the toaster remains strange. Perhaps the alien has already figured out that electricity becomes available by plugging the end of the cord into a hole in the wall, but may not be able to 'tell the story' about how the toaster is used, when, by whom, and why it would appear in a home on this planet. The alien has 'novice' experience with our culture. Experts, unlike novices, can piece together disparate elements into meaningful pictures and logical stories that would elude novices. That is part of the appeal of CSI television shows, theories about the origin of the universe, reconstruction of ancient civilizations through shards of pottery, and envisionment of ancient hominids through shards of bone. "Experts" create whole stories from bits and pieces of evidence that for novices appear merely to be fragments.

Instructional Design Support for Presentation

The concept of *Gestalt* was discovered as a psychological experience in the early 1900s, by Max Wertheimer in his seminal work on the Phi Phenomenon. His experiments demonstrated that the human eye automatically blends a series of discrete individual points of light into a continuous line of light when the presentation of the individual lights exceeds a certain speed. Later gestalt psychologists identified this phenomenon with the human propensity to link disparate pieces into wholes (King & Wertheimer, 1997; Kohler, 2007). The internal experience of unity, lift, and ease was given the name 'flow' by Csikszentmihalyi and Csikszentmihalyi (1988). Instructional designers can encourage students to experience flow by creating a compelling narrative that links the essential 'backbone' information together, augmenting it with captivating auxiliary information. An expert teacher can make a story from even the driest subject, using new domain language with syntactic, semantic, visual and aural coherence and building the narrative from simpler to more complex elements as the course moves on. The bold highlighting of key points with enticing sidebars keeps students on track while enriching their learning: clear distinction between essential and non-essential information (figure/ground differentiation) helps students 'stay with the flow'. Visuals, precise discussions, video examples, and simulations support the mainline messages.

5. Approach: Distressed or Disciplined

Expertise breeds confidence, and confidence breeds openness (Foa, Keane, Freidsman, & Cohen, 2004). Stress results in premature closure, tunnel vision, and fear (Foa et. al., 2004). When we think of teaching, we think about experts transferring their love of learning, and the insights gained through life-dedication to acquiring the skills, attitudes, life-frames, and mental compass associated with their domain. Expertise is about immersion in a domain but also about immersion in a life. Novice teachers may be stressed about lacking sufficient depth of knowledge in the domain and attempt to keep learners from asking the difficult questions, deviating from the assigned path, and exploring deeply. Stress imposed by the instructor on students in an online course is a sign of an attempt to gain order through command (distress) rather than through knowledge (discipline). Expert learners are most apt to resist the conformity that the novice teacher requests. A course template can assist a nervous novice teacher by providing alternatives at points where expert students have been shown to become confused and ask the most questions.

Depth and breadth of knowledge cannot be gained without immersion for many years in a discipline, with the watershed seeming to be about ten thousand hours of practice over a period of at least ten years (Chase & Simon, 1973). Even geniuses in a field need immersion to develop their nascent talents. Through practice experts gain discipline to master many points of challenge and opportunity, as well as plateaus and milestones – a discipline they demonstrate to their students. Discipline is a both a precursor to, and a result of, excellence. The Beatles had about ten years of prior practice before gaining their international reputation (Gladwell, 2008). Bill Gates was immersed on complex computer challenges by high school, preparing him for his 'early' entry into the digital business world (Gladwell, 2008). According to

critics, although Mozart wrote respectable piano pieces by the age of six, some musical analysts believe he did not create his monumental works until he passed his teens. Writers as diverse as George Bernard Shaw, Jane Austin, Isaac Asimov, Virginia Woolf, and William Shakespeare all started writing at an early age and were disciplined about writing daily throughout their lives. Isaac Newton, admired for his tireless discipline, ignored his assigned farm chores, dedicating his teenage years to exploring the stars, light, and motion of materials, and spending his twenties in daily independent research. In all cases, expertise was developed by a focus in a domain accompanied by continual active experimentation, exploration, and self-critique. Experts approach their domain with respect, determination, courage and stamina, and model that approach for others.

Instructional Design Support for Approach

One characteristic of an effective learning/teaching dialogue is that, on some level, it is fun. Perhaps it is not the kind of fun that leads to laughing out loud (although sometimes one cannot help oneself), but the kind of fun that keeps the learner engaged, where an effective back-and-forth exchange is almost impossible to stop, where effective questions emerge from the contexts created by the learning environment, and where exercises to build skill are not always drudgery. Effective instructional design can play a key role in augmenting the presentation of the material of a domain expert with engaging supportive materials.

Online games provide models for engaging approaches to a domain. Instructional design contains game design. To succeed in online games, competitors are compelled to over-practice, through 'play'. The sales of environments such as Wii and Leapster are a measure of the success of this approach. Where possible, such as foreign language learning, why not have games associated with online courses to develop required basic skills? Over-practice of esoteric vocabulary even applies in social science courses: When students learn to work with people in clinical settings, their vocabulary must be precise but also receptive. Through role-play students become accustomed to using particular language which they then apply in service learning situations.

Images, both visual or visionary, attract students. Images of desired results are influential, such as military training showing strong young men completing complicated maneuvers, a human development course showing a contented mother and child, or an accounting course showing a confident CPA with an appreciative client. An effective motivation attracts a learner to the domain: access to deep knowledge in science through disciplined investigative processes; successful athletic competition based on physical strength and skill, or academic inquiry into unanswered philosophical questions. A successful approach taps into prior motivation and elicits sustained alert attention, balancing between high stress and unfocused relaxation (Kagan, 2002).

6. Goals: Fixed or Flexible

The goals of experts and novices are different in the same environment. Experts are much clearer about their goals which are experientially-based. Experts know that their goals will change as they gain experience in the new domain (Ortega, 1987). Experts have knowledge of goal structure, the perception of the goal, and single-mindedness towards reaching the goal (Chi, et al, 1981). According to his autobiography, *Snowball*, Warren Buffett integrated a focus on building his wealth into almost every life activity, literally counting his pennies as a boy, (Schroeder, 2008). Charles Darwin also started investigating differences in species as a boy, taking meticulous notes at an early age. Expertise takes significant time to develop and no one becomes an expert without a notable single-mindedness of purpose, but taking advantage of opportunities to exercise that purpose

requires flexibility. Darwin, for example, would not have become the naturalist he was without spending nearly five years on the ship, Beagle, traveling to exotic places – an opportunity he primed. When the Black Plague swept England in 1665-1666 and scholars were sent home from Cambridge to prevent further outbreaks, Isaac Newton spent his 'miracle year' in a barn discovering the optic qualities of the spectrum, creating a calculus, and exploring a theory of universal gravitation (Gleick, 2004). Expertise is intrinsic to the person, but the environment can highlight or inhibit talents upon which expertise is built.

Instructional Design Support for Goals

Confidence in approaching problems flexibly comes with using a set of tools in diverse ways. Online courses can help students become flexible in using learned skills to meet myriad goals, once a set of basics is learned. Group activities work well for this, with class members taking on various projects and reporting back to relay success, to solicit help with challenging problems, and to get past stuck points. Tried and true case studies, such as those used in medical training and business management, demand creative approaches from students who can chew over possibilities, and then compare their proposed solutions with the opinions of experts or with stories of what was done in actual practice. Interviews and biographies of experts can help students understand how goals change for a given expert, and also how different experts achieve success having different goal paths. Darwin, for example, because of the inflammatory nature of his theory of evolution, had intended to have that part of his work published after his death. When he learned that Alfred Russel Wallace had arrived at similar conclusions, he had to prepare quickly so that their theories could be presented together at the Linnean Society of London in 1858. Tracking the path of an expert like Darwin shows the role played by goal flexibility.

What distinguishes Motivation and Goals? Emotional impetus drives excellence (motivation), and flexibility is required to achieve that excellence (goals). Motivations are complex, intertwined, and multiple, likely to reinforce each other and to continue as long as the drive for excellent remains – most likely a lifetime. Excellence is not static, but a moving target. The motivation to sustain excellence requires flexibility in goals.

Instructional design can encourage students to continue to be mindful of their own goals, and to consider pursuing more challenging goals as the course unfolds. Many courses have an initial Icebreaker Question that asks why a student is in the course, with encouragement at the course's end to see if those goals have been met. This is a very simple method to encourage positive direction, and effective reflective practice.

7. Focus: Buckshot or Bulls-Eye

Experts cull information necessary to achieve complex goals. An expert reader achieves comprehension with much less information than a novice (Blanton et al, 1997). For example, even if letters are left out of words, expert readers can fill in the missing letters based on the context of the words in sentences.

Because experts have expertise at all levels of knowledge within a domain – from the smallest to the largest chunks – they may immediately recognize or sense when something is not 'right' although it may take a while to identify what is missing or awry. They more easily identify whether a change, large or small, will make a difference in a solution. It is because of their depth of experience with both knowledge and contexts of the domain that experts have superior focus, and flexible ability to switch from very small to very large focus within an instant. They are sought as consultants to identify when a goal is at risk or a foundational element is threatened. Conversely, they can divergently assemble elements within the

domain to connect to contexts outside the domain or to solve newly-posed problems.

Additionally, experts in one domain recognize experts in other domains. They recognize and seek out expert teachers in a new domain, attracting associates who are experts in their fields. Experts more effectively evaluate the competency of others. They recognize who incorporates foundational elements in their thinking, who has built key subroutines for the domain, and who has flexibility to flow quickly and intuitively from big picture issues to detailed analysis. Experts recognize the power of focus in others as well as in themselves.

Instructional Design Support for Focus

In online environments, a course template, a course sequence, multimedia aids and social media can assist a teacher to address learner needs by presenting educational material in logical and approachable formats; by making concepts salient and deeply meaningful (capturing learner attention and relating the subject to pre-existing learner interests); by structuring sequences of learning steps appropriate to the range of learner capabilities, and by introducing domain concepts in multiple contexts where fundamental concepts can be explored and skills built. Flexibility and effectiveness of focus is a higher-level capacity of experts gained by their years of experience. Focus cannot be obtained without supporting skills and conceptual knowledge. Instructional design assists focus by providing successful practice, meaningful chunks, and challenging problems that are solved by connecting divergent and convergent thinking.

Guidelines for evaluation of assignments help novice teachers focus on the foundational aspects of learner work. Concept maps aid both the learners and novice teachers to see the relationships between and among domain concepts (Novak, 1990). Novice teachers will continue to be drawn to surface aspects of the domain, the trees, and benefit from well-crafted online templates that help both themselves and their learners focus on deep structure. They need support built into the online template for specification and elaboration of the foundations of the domain as modeled in clear examples (e.g., the alphabet and how letters become words).

8. Direction: Flooded or Futuristic

Experts demonstrate effective selection of detail to create solutions to complex problems, strategies to set direction, and integration of multiple interacting but isolated or conflicting points of view. Novices, as we know, are more apt to focus on extraneous (or even interfering) variables and miss important opportunities to move past the present. Experts are effective in self-critique and in predicting future events (Meyer, 2004; Ericsson, 1996). Because experts have flexibility in the domain at both the detail and big picture levels, they can predict logical paths toward future events (location of undiscovered stars, discovery of unearthed civilizations, new uses for nanotechnology, novel musical methods, etc.). Experts not only predict well, they seek opportunities to explore and apply what they know to new realms. Creativity on some level is a byproduct of excellence, and probably a source of the ability to create 'test cases' for practicing the skills thoroughly. Ericsson (2000) captures these attributes succinctly in this quote:

"The superior qualities of the experts' mental representations allow them to adapt rapidly to changing circumstances and anticipate future events in advance. The same acquired representations appear to be essential for experts' ability to monitor and evaluate their own performance (Ericsson, 1996; Glaser, 1996) so they can keep improving their own performance by designing their own training and assimilating new knowledge."

Many differences between novices and experts are based on the fact that "novices are more dependent on surface features of a problem" (Wiedenbeck, 1985; Perkins & Martin,

1986; Blanton et al, 1997), and experts relate to foundational and frequently non-apparent aspects of a problem. Only with scaffolding to the next meaningful level (but not too far beyond) will the learner get past the surface variations in the new domain. For example, the novice reader will find it challenging to understand that letters come in different sizes and shapes. The next meaningful level might be to realize that whatever the size and shape of the letters they combine to make words. The problem for the more-expert reader is to read the word, no longer concerned with the problem of isolating variations in the letters. The goal of the novice reader is different from the goal of the more-experienced reader.

Instructional Design Support for Direction

Some people have a talent for identifying a core problem and spending years developing an elegant solution. That is a step beyond expertise but built upon it. Scaffolding by former experts only goes so far, and then learners are left with their own skills to handle the problems of the future, Will new concepts lead to new chunking, and new chunking lead to new solutions?

Instructional design is especially important at learning points where surface features mislead students about deep structure. Differentiation between effective and ineffective solutions at these points will help direct a student toward successful solutions in the future. Open-ended exercises provide opportunities for learners to identify which existing resources can be transformed for solving new problems. Learners should get help discriminating between solved problems and those left for discovery. Learners learn best from high expectations: if learners are expected to create Human Subject Proposals for IRB (Institutional Review Board) approval, they are more likely to create a viable research project; if asked to write and submit a letter to the editor proposing a solution to a local problem, they may end up running for local office: if a teacher offers a chance to co-author a paper for a local conference, then many students become peers-in-training. The expectation of real work creates real work. The practice of 'being' a professional within the protected environment of an online course leads to the confidence to practice professionalism beyond the course. Learners recognize when they are given real problems to solve, and appreciate knowing why over-practice of fundamental routines is important.

FUTURE RESEARCH DIRECTIONS

Instructional support can mean the difference between a student becoming passionately engaged in a subject, or finding it dry and uninviting. From a domain expert's perspective, support via an effective online template can mean the difference between continuing to teach or moving on to more lucrative venues. Expert teachers and learners recognize and appreciate authentic learning experiences. Even if the online environment is foreign at first, it will soon become second nature, similar to contact lenses or calculators, if the course draws interest.

Unique to the online environment is the archiving of completed course templates which contain the responses of both learners and teachers. These stored past courses are a treasure for researchers who analyze patterns of teacher-learner communication so that future courses can be modified on successful patterns observed. Online learning provides views that are both diachronic (comparison of course events across time) and synchronic (comparison of course events in one term). Teachers and instructional designers can explore this stored warehouse of knowledge to determine which course templates, which teachers, and which learners are most successful – and why. Using diachronic and synchronic stored data from past and current courses to view the course in a long term framework, the instructional designer may be the first to identify course improvements

for future terms and to suggest meaningful areas for research. Appropriate research could augment expert learning. How can the novice/expert paradigm make e-learning more effective?

- What are the operational ramifications of the model of an Eightfold Path for Novices and Experts? How can it lead to better instructional design, and better assessment of instructional design?
- This chapter briefly discusses aspects of expertise that are common across domains, although we know that cognitive aspects of expertise differ across domains (expertise in wine tasting will not require the same skills as expertise as an airline pilot). At a deeper level of analysis, how do different types of expertise differ, and how do those differences impact choices made in instructional design support for a particular subject?
- Experts think differently about their domain than others do. Are there characteristics of expert teaching that cross domains or differences in expert thinking which can be identified with particular domains? How do these differences influence classroom dynamics?
- Would the conscious understanding of levels of expertise make a difference in the level of learning for the learner, or the level of teaching for the teacher? What if a learner could, without penalty, declare at the beginning of the course the level of expertise they wanted to ultimately achieve in this subject and different assignments were given to learners whose goals were different?
- Would an explanation of what it takes to build expertise help to motivate learners to practice the relevant skills? To what degree can expertise be built into a survey course for those learners who seek it?

- Identification with experts and modeling by experts are likely to make a significant difference in expert learning. What are the qualities of the domain expert and learners that lead to exceptional learning dialogue?
- Can effective 'chunks', as identified by domain experts, be effectively taught through gaming technology, using game levels to identify levels of 'expertise' in the domain?

CONCLUSION

There is a synergy between the venerated Noble Eightfold Path of Buddhism and the dynamic development of experts from novices. Both emphasize correct practice because it is only through vigilant exercise of principles that higher levels of excellence can be achieved. Although the expert/novice paradigm failed to revolutionize our knowledge of consciousness, it did succeed in transforming interactions on the scale of daily routine, influencing interactions through websites, automated phone tellers, and digital games. Instructional designers can model teaching excellence which leads to more effective use of teacher time, higher probability of student success, and increased consistency of instruction across multiples sections of an online course. Minimally, these impacts will help offset the shortage of domain experts as teachers, especially in domains where the pay difference between teaching and other uses of expertise is great. More fundamentally, however, even small design changes increase student and teacher motivation, save time and energy, increase overall satisfaction in e-learning experiences, and may lead learning to higher levels of excellence.

ACKNOWLEDGMENT

Special thanks to Fabio Chacon, Suzanne Hayes and Ken Charuk for reviewing this chapter prior to its submission. Their input was appreciated, and when possible, incorporated into this work.

REFERENCES

Ausubel, D. (1968). *Educational psychology*. New York, NY: Holt, Rinehart & Winston.

Bandura, A. (1985). *Social foundations for thought and action: A social cognitive theory*. New York, NY: Prentice Hall.

Blanton, W., Moorman, G., Hayes, B., & Warner, M. (1997). Effects of participation in the 5th dimension on far transfer. *Journal of Educational Computing Research*, *16*(4), 371–396. doi:10.2190/0YAW-FYAN-2T2B-0LP3

Blaton, W. E. (n.d.). *Teaching and the 5th dimension: Novice and expert*. Retrieved from http://129.171.53.1/blantonw/5dClhse/teaching/expert.html

Bliss, C. A., & Lawrence, B. (2009). From posts to patterns: A metric to characterize discussion board activity in online courses. *Journal of Asynchronous Learning Networks*, *13*(2), 15–32.

Bodhi, B. (1999). *The noble eightfold path: The way to the end of suffering*. Retrieved from http://www.accesstoinsight.org/lib/authors/bodhi/waytoend.html.

Brown, A. L. (1997). Transforming schools into communities of thinking and learning about serious matters. *The American Psychologist*, *52*(4), 399–413. doi:10.1037/0003-066X.52.4.399

Burns, H., Parlett, J., & Redfield, C. L. (2009). *Intelligent tutoring systems: Evolution in design*. New York, NY: Psychology Press.

Carter, K., & Sabers, D., Cushing, Pinnegar, S., & Berliner, D. C. (1987). Processing and using information about students: A study of expert, novice, and postulant teachers. *Teaching and Teacher Education*, *3*(2), 147–157. doi:10.1016/0742-051X(87)90015-1

Chase, W. G., & Simon, H. A. (1973). The mind's eye in chess. In Chase, W. G. (Ed.), *Visual information processing* (pp. 215–281). New York, NY: Academic Press.

Chi, M. T. H., Feltovich, P. J., & Glaser, R. (1980). Categorization and representation of physics problems by experts and novices. *Cognitive Science, 5*, 121–152. doi:10.1207/s15516709cog0502_2

Cowan, T. (2004). *Creative destruction: How globalization is changing the world's cultures.* Princeton, NJ: Princeton University Press.

Csikszentmihalyi, M., & Csikszentmihalyi, I. S. (Eds.). (1988). *Optimal experience: Psychological studies of flow in consciousness.* Cambridge, UK: Cambridge University Press.

Dewey, J. (1916). *Democracy and education: An introduction to the philosophy of education.* New York, NY: MacMillan.

Dreyfus, H., & Dreyfus, S. (1985). *Mind over machine: The power of human intuition and expertise in the era of the computer.* New York, NY: Free Press.

Duckworth, E. R. (2006). *The having of wonderful ideas and other essays on teaching and learning* (3rd ed.). New York, NY: Teachers College Press.

Endsley, M., Farley, T., Jones, W. M., Midkiff, A. H., & Hansman, R. J. (1998-09). *Situation awareness information requirements for commercial airline pilots.* International Center for Air Transportation. ICAT 98-0.1

Ericsson, K. A. (1996). The acquisition of expert performance: An introduction to some of the issues. In Ericsson, K. A. (Ed.), *The road to excellence: The acquisition of expert performance in the arts and sciences, sports, and games* (pp. 1–50). Mahwah, NJ: Erlbaum.

Ericsson, K. A. (2000). *Expert performance and deliberate practice: An updated excerpt Ericsson.* Retrieved from http://www.psy.fsu.edu/faculty/ericsson/ericsson.exp.perf.html

Fischer, K. W., Zheng, Y., & Stewart, J. (2002). Adult cognitive development: Dynamics in the developmental web. In Valsiner, J., & Connolly, K. (Eds.), *Handbook of developmental psychology* (pp. 491–516). Thousand Oaks, CA: Sage.

Foa, E. B., Keane, T. M., Friedsman, M. J., & Cohen, J. A. (2009). *Effective treatments for PTSD, 2nd ed: Practice guidelines from the International Society for Traumatic Stress Studies.* New York, NY: Guilford Press.

Ge, Z., Law, V., & Haung, K. (in press). Diagnosis: Supporting and fading: A scaffolding design framework for adaptive el-learning systems. In Song, H. (Ed.), *Interactivity in e-learning: Cases and frameworks.* Hershey, PA: IGI Publishers.

Gladwell, M. (2008). *Outliers: The story of success.* New York, NY: Little, Brown and Company.

Gleick, J. (2004). *Isaac Newton.* New York, NY: Vintage Books.

Gobbet, F., Lane, P. C. R., Croker, S., Cheng, P. C. H., Jones, G., Oliver, I., & Pine, J. M. (2001). Chunking mechanisms in human learning. *Trends in Cognitive Sciences, 5*, 236–243. doi:10.1016/S1364-6613(00)01662-4

Goldberg, N. (2005). *Writing down the bones: Freeing the writer within.* Boston, MA: Shambhala Press.

Harasim, L. (2000). Shift happens: Online education as a new paradigm in learning. *The Internet and Higher Education, 3*(1-2), 41–61. doi:10.1016/S1096-7516(00)00032-4

Henningsson, S. (2003). *Deep learning with e-learning?* Master's thesis. Department of Informatics. Lund University. Lund, Sweden.

Hmelo-Silver, C. E., Marathe, S., & Lui, L. (2007). Fish swim, rocks sit, and lungs breathe: Expert-novice understanding of complex systems. *Journal of the Learning Sciences, 16*(3), 307–331. doi:10.1080/10508400701413401

Jacoby, S., & Gonzales, P. (1991). The constitution of expert-novice in scientific discourse. *Issues in Applied Linguistics, 2*(2), 149–181.

Kagan, J. (2002). *Surprise, uncertainty and mental structures.* Cambridge, MA: Harvard University Press.

Keefe, J., & Jenkins, J. (1996). *Instruction and the learning environment.* West Larchmont, NY: Eye on Education.

King, D. B., & Wertheimer, M. (2007). *Max Wertheimer and gestalt theory.* New York, NY: Transaction Publishing.

Kohler, W. (1992). *Gestalt psychology: The definitive statement of the gestalt theory.* New York, NY: Liveright Publishing. (Original work published 1947)

Kuhn, T. (1996). *The structure of scientific revolutions* (3rd ed.). Chicago, IL: University of Chicago Press.

Levitin, D. (2007). *This is your brain on music: The science of a human obsession.* New York, NY: Plume/Penguin.

McCarthy, J. (in press). Connected: Online mentoring in *Facebook* for final year digital media students. In Song, H. (Ed.), *Interactivity in e-learning: Cases and frameworks.* Hershey, PA: IGI Publishers.

McPherson, S. L. (2000). Expert-novice differences in planning strategies during collegiate singles tennis competition. *Journal of Sport & Exercise Psychology, 22*(1), 39–62.

Meyer, H. (2004). Novice and expert teachers' conceptions of learners' prior knowledge. *Science Education, 88,* 970–983. doi:10.1002/sce.20006

Miller, G. A. (1956). The magical number seven, plus or minus two: Some limits on our capacity for processing information. *Psychological Review, 63,* 81–97. doi:10.1037/h0043158

Mishra, P., & Koehler, M. J. (2006). Technological pedagogical content knowledge: A framework for teacher knowledge. [New York, NY: Columbia University.]. *Teachers College Record, 108*(6), 1017–1054. doi:10.1111/j.1467-9620.2006.00684.x

Montessori, M. (1949). *The absorbent mind.* Madras, India: The Theosophical House.

Montessori, M. (1994). *From childhood to adolescence* (pp. 7–16). Oxford, England: ABC-Clio.

Moore, M. G. (1993). Three types of interactive learners. In K. Harry M., John, & D. Keegan (Eds.), *Distance education: New perspectives* (pp. 19-24). London, UK: Routledge.

Morrow, D., Miller, L. S., Ridolfo, H., Kokayeff, N., Chang, D., Fischer, U., & Stine-Morrow, E. (2004). Expertise and aging in a pilot decision-making task. *Human Factors and Ergonomics Society Annual Meeting Proceedings. Aging, 5,* 228–232.

Novak, J. D. (1990). The concept mapping: A useful tool for science education. *Journal of Research in Science Teaching, 27*(10), 937–950. doi:10.1002/tea.3660271003

Ortega, K. A. (1987). *Problem solving: Expert/ novice differences.* IBM Technical Report. TR54.422.

Paulus, T. (2009). Online, but off-topic: Negotiating common ground in small learning groups. *Instructional Science, 37*(3), 227–245. doi:10.1007/s11251-007-9042-5

Perkins, D. N., & Martin, F. (1986). Fragile knowledge and neglected strategies in novice programmers. In Soloway, E., & Iyengar, S. (Eds.), *Empirical studies of programmers.* Norwood, NJ: Ablex.

Piaget, J. (1967). *The child's conception of space.* New York, NY: Norton & Company.

Reuber, A. R., & Fischer, E. M. (1992). Does entrepreneurship experience matter? *Journal of Small Business and Entrepreneurship, 9*(4), 50–62.

Rich, Y., & Almozlino, M. (1999). Educational goal preferences among novice and veteran teachers of science and humanities. *Teaching and Teacher Education, 15*, 613–629. doi:10.1016/ S0742-051X(99)00010-4

Schoenfield, A. H., & Hermann, D. J. (1982). Problem perception and knowledge structure in expert and novice mathematical problem solvers. *Journal of Experimental Psychology. Learning, Memory, and Cognition, 8*(5), 484–494. doi:10.1037/0278-7393.8.5.484

Schroeder, A. (2008). *Snowball: Warren Buffet and the business of life*. New York, NY: Bantam Dell Publishers.

Shafto, P., & Coley, J. D. (2003). Development of categorization and reasoning in the natural world: Novices to experts, naïve similarity to ecological knowledge. *Journal of Experimental Psychology. Learning, Memory, and Cognition, 29*(4), 641–649. doi:10.1037/0278-7393.29.4.641

Shaw, J. P. (2002). *A model for reflective processing using narrative symbols: Time and space coordinates in adult reflection*. Unpublished doctoral dissertation, Harvard Graduate School of Education. Cambridge, Massachusetts.

Shaw, J. P. (2005). Building meaning: Experts and novices in on-line learning. In *Proceedings for EdMedia International Conference*, Montreal, Canada.

Shaw, J. P., & Chacon, F. (2010). Structure and change in elearning: An ecological perspective. In Song, H. (Ed.), *Distance learning technology, current instruction, and the future of education: Applications of today, practices of tomorrow* (pp. 316–338). Hershey, PA: IGI Global Publishers.

Shaw, J. P., & Chen, J. (in press). Transactional distance and teaching presence in e-learning environments. *International Journal for Innovation and Learning*.

Sloutsky, V. M., & Yarlas, A. S. (2000). Problem representation in experts and novices: Part 2. Underlying processing mechanisms. In L. R. Gleitman & A. K. Joshi (Eds.), *Proceedings of the 22nd Annual Conference of the Cognitive Science Society* (pp. 475-480). Mahwah, NJ: Erlbaum.

Vygotsky, L. S. (1978). *Mind in society: The development of higher psychological processes* (Cole, M., John-Steiner, V., Scribner, S., & Souberman, E., Trans.). Cambridge, MA: Harvard University Press.

Werner, H., & Kaplan, P. (1960/1984). *Symbol formation*. New York, NY: Psychology Press. (reprint).

Wiedenbeck, S. (1985). Novice/expert differences in programming skills. *International Journal of Man-Machine Studies, 23*, 383–390. doi:10.1016/ S0020-7373(85)80041-9

Winner, E. (2010). *Cognitive and brain consequences of learning in the arts*. Association for Psychological Science 22nd Annual Convention, Boston, Massachusetts.

Yarlas, A. S., & Sloutsky, V. M. (2000). Problem representation in experts and novices. Part 1. Differences in the content of representation. *Proceedings of the 22nd Annual Conference of the Cognitive Science Society*.

Zheng, R. Z. (in press). The influence of cognitive styles on learner's performance in e-learning. In Song, H. (Ed.), *Interactivity in e-learning: Cases and frameworks*. Hershey, PA: IGI Publishers.

Zull, (2002). *The art of changing the brain – Enriching teaching by exploring the biology of learning*. Sterling, VA: Stylus Publishing.

ADDITIONAL READING

Bates, T. (2005). *Technology, E-learning and Distance Education* (2nd ed.). London: Routledge-Falmer Studies in Distance Education.

Bliznak, M. (2007). *Virtualization technologies as an e-learning support in the academic environment. Annals of Proceedings*. DAAAM International Vienna.

Bloom, H. (2000). *How to read and why*. New York: Scribner.

Brown, J. S. (2000). *Growing up digital: How the web changes work, education, and the ways people learn. Change Magazine* (pp. 11–20). March/April.

DeVoogd, G., & Kritt, D. (1997). Computer-mediated instruction for young children: Teachers and software missing the zone. In Willis, J., Price, J. D., McNeil, S., Robin, B., & Willis, D. A. (Eds.), *Technology and teacher education annual, 1997*. Charlottesville, VA: Association for the Advancement of Computing in Education.

Erikson, E. H. (1959/1980). *Identity and the Life Cycle*. New York: Norton.

Gardner, H. (2008). *Five minds for the future*. Cambridge, Massachusetts: Harvard University Press.

Garrison, D. R., & Anderson, T. (2003). *E-Learning in the 21st Century: A Framework for Research and Practice*. London: Routledge/Falmer. doi:10.4324/9780203166093

Gibbs, G. (1992a). Improving the quality of student learning through course design. In R. Barnett (Ed.). *Learning to Effect*. Buckingham: SRHE/Open University Press. Part I Using research to improve student learning.

Gibbs, G. (1992b). *Improving the quality of studentlLearning*. Bristol: Technical and Educational Services.

Hall, S. S. (2010). *Wisdom: From philosophy to neuroscience*. New York: Alfred A. Knopf.

Kroger, J. (2004). *Identity in adolescence: The balance between self and other*. London: Routledge. doi:10.4324/9780203346860

Langer, E. (1997). *The power of mindful learning*. Cambridge, MA: Perseus Publishing.

Langer, S. (1951). *Philosophy in a new key*. Cambridge, MA: Harvard University Press. (Original work published 1942)

Manovich, L. (2001). *The language of New Media*. Cambridge, Mass: The MIT Press.

Marton, F., & Saljo, R. (1976). On qualitative differences in learning: Outcome and process. *The British Journal of Educational Psychology, 46*, 4–11. doi:10.1111/j.2044-8279.1976.tb02980.x

Merrill, M. D. (2000). "Knowledge objects and mental models." In D. A. Wiley (Ed.), *The Instructional Use of Learning Objects: Online Version*. Retrieved June 7, 2008, from the World Wide Web: http://reusability.org/read/chapters/merrill.doc

Moore, M. G. (1993). Theory of transactional distance. In Keegan, D. (Ed.), *Theoretical principles of distance education* (pp. 22–38). London, New York: Rutledge.

Piaget, J. (2003). *The psychology of intelligence*. London: Routledge. (Original work published 1947)

Pinch, T. J., & Bijker, W. E. (1987). The social construction of facts and artifacts: Or how the Sociology of Science and the Sociology of Technology might benefit each other. In Bijker, W. E., Pinch, T. J., & Hughes, T. P. (Eds.), *The social construction of technological systems* (pp. 17–50). Cambridge, MA: MIT Press. doi:10.1177/030631284014003004

Salomon, G. (1979a). *Interaction of media, cognition, and learning: An exploration of how symbolic forms cultivate mental skills and affect knowledge acquisition.* San Francisco: Jossey-Bass.

Salomon, G. (1979b). Media and symbol systems as related to cognition and learning. *Journal of Educational Psychology, 71*(2), 131–148. doi:10.1037/0022-0663.71.2.131

Sternberg, R. J. (2003). *Wisdom, intelligence, and creativity synthesized.* Cambridge, United Kingdom: Cambridge University Press. doi:10.1017/CBO9780511509612

Vygotsky, L. S. (1987). *Thought and language* (Kozulin, A., Trans.). Cambridge, MA: MIT Press. (Original work published 1934)

Wertsch, J. V., McNamee, G. D., McLane, J. B., & Budwig, N. A. (1980). The adult-child dyad as a problem-solving system. *Child Development, 51*, 1215–1221. doi:10.2307/1129563

Wexler, S., Grey, N., Adams-Miller, D., Nguyen, F., & van Barneveld, A. (2008), Learning Management Systems: The good, the bad, the ugly ... and the truth. Santa Rosa, CA: *The eLearning Guild Publications*.

Wiley, D. A. (Ed.). *The Instructional Use of Learning Objects: Online Version.* Retrieved Jan 30, 2008, from the World Wide Web: http://www.reusability.org/read/

KEY TERMS AND DEFINITIONS

Eightfold Path: The Noble Eightfold Path is one of the principal teachings of the Buddha and the fourth of Buddha's Four Noble Truths providing guidance to end personal suffering and achieve self-awakening. The concept is adapted here as an eightfold path for providing guidance to gain expertise.

E-Learning: E-learning is an abbreviation for electronic learning, designating intentional instruction of skills and knowledge through electronic media, particularly through the world wide web as facilitated by increasingly prevalent digital media. E-learning includes not only direct instruction, but also the institutions that support it. E-learning is distinguished from a broader concept of e-communication, which includes accidental or supplemental learning through general internet contact.

Expert: An expert has gained recognition from peers and the public for reliable and extensive knowledge and ability in an identifiable and valued domain, based on extensive experience, research, and acumen. An expert is granted status as an authority, and frequently has an occupation related to their expertise.

Expertise: Recognized extensive knowledge and skill in a valued domain.

Instructional Design: A term frequently associated with e-learning, instructional design is the adaptation of technology to enhance learning, usually in established learning environments, using effective teaching methods (appropriate pedagogy and andragogy) to adjust to learners of different skill levels. Ideally, instructional design includes an evaluation step to determine if the teaching assistance offered by the instructional design was successful.

Learning Dialogue: In this context, a learning dialogue refers to the engaged, interactive, communication between one (or more) who teaches and one (or more) who learns with the possibility of role-reversal at any point in the communication cycle. This is in contrast to more structured AI or programmed learning environments.

Novice: A person who is new to an identified domain. The domain frequently has paths to achievement which are sought after and which others have explored, such as sports, computer programming, religion or music.

Section 2
Interactivity and Educational Games

Chapter 8
Digital Games:
Are They the Future of E-Learning Environments?

Betül Özkan-Czerkawski
University of Arizona South, USA

ABSTRACT

Digital games and simulations are playing an important role in younger generations' lives. Their adoption to e-Learning environments, however, is rather slow because educators are reluctant to change the way they teach. This chapter starts with a brief discussion of game and simulation terminology, including serious games, game-based learning, and game genres. It continues with a review of the current status of educational games and simulations being used in higher education institutions. Important case studies are provided to present examples to the higher education faculty. Finally, a discussion of teaching strategies, instructional design processes, and assessment issues for effective digital game incorporation in e-Learning is included.

INTRODUCTION

Games are defined as "organized play" (Prensky, 2001, p.119), or "a competitive activity that is creative and enjoyable in its essence, which is bounded by certain rules and requires certain skills" (Akilli, 2006, p. 4). Gee (2007b) argued

about the importance of video games as "action-and-goal-directed preparations for, and simulations of, embodied experience" (p. 26). Currently, there are many different game platforms (computer games; console games such as Xbox, PlayStation, Nintendo or Wii; or games played on mobile devices); forms (single-player; multiplayer; massively multiplayer games) and game genres (first-shooter; strategy, turn-based, etc).

DOI: 10.4018/978-1-61350-441-3.ch008

In addition, there are numerous terms related to games and simulations, such as core games, casual games, video games, and many acronyms, such as alternative reality games (ARGs), massively-multiplayer online games (MMOG), etc.

If we ignore all the differences and varieties in the gaming literature, we can focus on some of the common traits shared by all games. One of these traits is *goal* or *purpose*. Goal is what gamers will achieve at the end of playing a game. This end goal keeps players attentive and active participants throughout the game play. The second trait is *rules*. This trait can also be defined as the game play and it refers to what players can do and how they can do to achieve a game's purpose. The third trait is *feedback*, where players get immediate information about their progress in a game. This may be expressed in points, levels or verbal feedback. The last trait that can be found in every game is *voluntary participation*. It refers to the players' willingness to participate or quit the game anytime they want. It also refers to willingness to accept the gameplay -goal, rules and feedback system (McGonigal, 2011).

What makes games so attractive to younger generations? Why has almost every child in the country played at least one game regularly before graduating high school? While it is very difficult to get younger generations' attention for traditional academic disciplines, why can they play hours of games without even a single complaint? How will these developments in the digital gaming world affect future of e-Learning practices? Will games and game-based learning replace traditional e-Learning courses or are game-based learning and e-Learning represent a natural partnership?

This chapter seeks answers to these questions. It is the author's hope that this information will benefit the e-Learning faculty and enable them to catch up with the latest developments in educational gaming, make learning a fun, engaging and interactive activity. To do this, a basis for discussion will be provided by reviewing the current status of educational games and simulations in higher education e-Learning environments. This discussion will also include interactive teaching strategies along with examples from various e-Learning or hybrid courses. It will then discuss learning outcome and content, teaching strategies, instructional design processes, and assessment issues which will lay the groundwork for a successful implementation plan. Finally, the chapter will discuss recommendations for educators who are planning to use games in their online courses.

This chapter will use three of the gaming terms: serious games, game-based learning and digital games. Michael and Chen (2006) define *serious games* as "games that do not have entertainment, enjoyment, or fun as their primary purpose" (p.21). In other words, serious games can be entertaining but this is not their main purpose. They are used in education, military, health care, religion, politics, and many other industries. *Game-based learning* is considered a branch of serious games that refers to the learning outcomes that are achieved through games. Johnson, Levine, Smith & Stone (2010) predict that game-based learning will be prevalent in schools in two to three years, because it "has tremendous potential to transform education, and includes open-ended, challenge-based, truly collaborative games" (para.11). Johnson et al. also emphasize that "games, which occur in both massively multiplayer online (MMO) and non-digital forms, can draw on skills for research, writing, collaboration, problem-solving, public speaking, leadership, digital literacy, and media-making" (para.11). The third term that is used in this chapter is *digital games*, which are games played on computers.

DIGITAL GAME GENRES

Gameplay or *game mechanics* refer to the interactive elements within a game. This includes player's interaction with the plot, game's rules and structures. Depending on the gameplay characteristics, games are categorized under game genres: action, adventure, strategy, role playing, and simulation. Although there isn't any agreement on these genres or there are overlaps between genres, it might be helpful to educators to know their major characteristics.

Action games embrace the most popular games in the market. The basic purpose here is to respond quickly to game challenges or combat. In this category, shooter games (first-person shooter, third-person shooter, massively played online first-shooter to name a few subcategories), fighting or combat games are the most common subgenres. America's Army, BioShock, Halo Series are popular action games. *Adventure games* are where players solve a problem interacting with the game mechanics. Compared to action games, players in adventure games do not perform combat or confront challenges but they respond to quests. Myst, Dragon's Lair, King's Quest are some of the examples of popular adventure games. *Strategy games* require players to carefully think and plan victory or overcome a game's challenges. World of Warcraft, Command and Conquer, Civilization series, Age of Empires are the well-known strategy games. In *role playing games*, the focus is on progressing through characters that have specialized skills to achieve a game's goals or progress through the storyline. Runescape, Lord of the Rings Online, Oblivion and Final Fantasy are some examples of role playing games. *Simulation games* simulate a fictional or real life situation, and they represent another common category in game genres. SimCity, Spore and the Caesar series are some of the best known simulation games.

Different people may develop different competency levels in each of these game genres. Some players will enjoy and play action games, while others prefer strategy games. According to Gee (2007b) this is because different game genres represent different literacy skills, and people need to be literate in different semiotic domains (an area where one or more modalities affect the way people act, think and value) represented in each game genre.

When selecting game genres, educators should pay attention to a learners' age, gender and their prior gaming experience, as well as available resources, time, technical requirements, and instructor's role in the gaming experience. Moreover, e-Learning faculty should consider their teaching preferences and chosen teaching strategies in addition to their students' learning styles.

PEDAGOGICAL CONSIDERATIONS FOR DIGITAL GAMES AND SIMULATIONS

Today, 67 percent of all heads of household in the Unites States play computer and video games. This percentage goes even higher, 97 percent of youth play computer and video games, when it comes to younger generations (Entertainment Software Association, 2010). What makes digital games so appealing? According to Gee (2007b), gaming is a "pleasantly surprising" experience and also "good learning principles built into game design –that is, if it facilitates learning in good ways- then games will sell and do better" (p.3-4). In the latter case, game designers use principles of cognitive science or learning sciences that include higher order thinking and problem solving to create more challenging, long-lasting and collaborative games. If we understand the relationship between good game design and learning, we can create similarly challenging, long-lasting learning experiences. Furthermore, Gee (2007b) argues that "learning is learning to play a game" (p. 7). If educators can understand how game play is closely related to the learning process, they will also understand how to design motivating and engaging learning environments.

Game-based learning can play a significant role in engaging students in e-Learning, by creating a more interactive, immersive and participatory environment. According to Kebritchi and Hirumu (2008) digital games are effective teaching tools because "they (1) use action instead of explanation,

(2) create personal motivation and satisfaction, (3) accommodate multiple learning styles and skills, (4) reinforce mastery skills and (5) provide interactive and decision-making contexts" (in Kebritchi, 2010, p.256). Moreover, digital games can contribute to alternative performance assessments that are more engaging. For instance, Orlando (2011) argues that "too often, teachers assign only a few large works during a class, and thus put off rewards for many weeks. Instead, (with the use of games) teachers can assign continual short pieces with a narrower focus and clearer goals to achievement" (para. 6-7). Orlando also suggests that teachers use a point-accumulating approach towards scoring, so students will move upward in the system. Therefore, rather than diminishing the advantages of games, educators should look for "integrating gaming principles in teaching to improve motivation and outcomes" (Orlando, 2011, para.8).

Although games and simulations are gaining more acceptance in today's higher education institutions, there is still controversy about their 'non-educational' and 'distractive' content. Part of this misconception derives from the fact that research is scarce about:

- Types of learning outcomes achieved through game play,
- Instructional design processes related to the incorporation of games and simulations,
- Assessment and evaluation procedures appropriate for these new technologies,
- Differences in learning (learning styles and expectations) when playing games and simulations.

Negative perceptions about games limit their prospects in today's schools but educational games can and should exist in both formal and informal educational settings. According to Klopfer, Osterweil and Salen (2009) designers shouldn't,

assume that teachers will figure out how best to use an educational game as a teaching tool. Therefore, teacher training and support materials should always be provided. These materials and the design of the game should take into account classroom constraints. When these constraints are too onerous, the game should target an out of school audience. Finally, the game should clearly state, at least for the teacher, which knowledge or understanding it's trying to impart, and be transparent about its assumptions. This helps teachers and players focus their inquiry on those aspects of the game that were designed to be probed (p.49).

For digital games to be successful in e-Learning environments, a few issues should be considered carefully. For instance, it should be clear how games align with the content that educators should cover; educators should feel comfortable using the chosen digital games and enough technical support and training should be provided to those instructors who will be using games in their classrooms. Even after these issues are overcome, the objections that may come from other educators, administrators, and parents may prevent individual educators to avoid using games altogether. Following sections and case studies will address some of these concerns and help educators to understand how digital games can innovate the learning.

Case Study 1: Portal Game for Undergraduate Freshman Students

In 2010, Wabash College in Indiana required all freshman students to play, understand and discuss the Portal game in order to graduate from college. Portal was planned to be part of a mandatory seminar called "Enduring Questions", where students explore "fundamental questions of humanity" through "classical and contemporary works." In this course, a small group of students (approximately 15 students) discuss what it means to be human, how humans understand themselves, each other and the world surrounding them. Student assessments are based on written and oral expression of ideas. Michael Abbott, a professor of theater initiated the idea by designing this seminar course. Dr. Abbott's inspiration for this gaming experience comes from Erwing Goffmann's seminal book, *The Presentation of Self in Everyday Life* published in 1959. In his book Goffmann "discusses social intercourse under the metaphor of actors performing on a stage. As with the theater, we have a place where we manage the performance and a place where we give that performance" (Johnson, 2009, para.1-2). Portal game does exactly the same by allowing students to express their ideas as an actor on stage. The Wabash College doesn't require Portal for every section of the undergraduate seminar course, due to the technical difficulties that may arise when a large group of students play a game in the campus. At this point, the project is still being pilot tested by Dr. Abbott and his colleagues at Wabash, and is being implemented only in select classes. Dr. Abbott considered *BioShock* and *Planescape Torment*, for this seminar as well but chose Portal, a puzzle shooter game because it is accessible, smart, cross-platform, relatively short nature. Although still in its pilot testing stages, Portal and Wabash College is an interesting case of requiring a game as a graduate requirement.

LEARNING OUTCOMES AND CONTENT

For games to be used as instructional tools or strategies in e-Learning environments, it is essential to match game purpose, goals, actions and feedback with the instructional outcomes. There is a lack of empirical data, on this aspect of educational gaming. It is clear that not even serious games that are designed for educational purposes in mind are effective or good for all educational outcomes just as one learning activity cannot be effective for all educational outcomes. When learning outcomes

are considered, many also argue about effectiveness of games in educational settings.

Gee (2007a) thinks that educational or serious games do not necessarily have positive or negative effects on learning. "Rather, they have different effects depending on the different uses we make them, the different contexts in which we place them, and the different social systems that are built around them" (p.133). In this regard, the effectiveness of games should be measured by considering curriculum, content areas that games support, related content areas, relationships between each content area, social interactions, and assessment strategies that provide the context and social environment of learning. This means that evaluating games or any other technology per se will not yield any valid or meaningful result in terms of their effectiveness unless researchers consider multitude of factors. In terms effectiveness of games, Hirumi, Appelman, Rieber, and Van Eck (2010) point out a deeper issue:

The problem is, like many rapidly growing industries, advances in video game technology are far outpacing research on its design and effectiveness. Relatively little is understood about how to apply what we know about teaching and learning to optimize game-based learning (p. 27).

Similarly, the content of commercial digital games is much broader than traditional academic disciplines such as math, science or social sciences. McFarlane, Sparrowhawk and Heald (2002) categorize learning outcomes supported by games in three groups: "learning as a result of tasks stimulated by the content of the games, knowledge developed through the content of the game, skills arising as a result of playing the game." (p. 11) Playing games may stimulate and highly motivate children. Teachers can channel this energy to creative work in arts, science and math or out of school activities that can feed back school learning and activities. In terms of content related learning, the relevance of game content to academic subjects is usually low, and even serious games or educational games have little potential to teach every content area to school children. According to McFarlane and et al. simulation games have more potential than any other game genre to be useful to supplement academic disciplines represented in schools. In addition, elementary schools might have a higher adaption rate, whereas middle school or high school curriculum might have little room to utilize games for teaching certain subject areas. Higher education and e-Learning environments provide the best learning environments to successfully adapt games. When it comes to skill learning, games can teach a wide range of skills, such as problem solving, decision making, reasoning, collaboration and social skills. In higher education, games can teach specific content areas or tasks in innovative ways or help gain broader skills that are required in the information age. Democracy 2, Civilization Series, Budget Hero and Portal are some of the examples of such games that can be used to teach certain content areas for undergraduate students.

Hirumi, Appelman, Rieber, and Van Eck (2010) indicate a major problem with the learning goals and outcomes. While goals and outcomes are sacred to instructional designers, in the game play they are not the most important elements, so game designers focus on engaging and motivating game play rather than the instructional outcomes. According to Van Eck (2010), "when developing instructional games, we cannot allow the goals and objectives to trump game play, nor can we sacrifice learning goals for the sake of playability" (p. 32). The best solution to this issue is integrating desired learning outcomes in game play, while not spoiling the 'fun' factor of digital games.

In the latest edition of Horizon Report (2011) it is argued that "gaming related specifically to course content helps student gain a fresh perspective on material and can potentially engage them in that content in more complex and nuanced ways" (p. 21). Some of the examples of such games are World without Oil, The Tower of Babel,

Free Culture Game and Oligarchy, all of which allow students to role play and resolve problems in novel ways.

TEACHING AND LEARNING ENVIRONMENTS

The ways games are used in educational settings directly determines their success in achieving desired learning outcomes. Digital games are not designed to replace teachers or entire teaching situations or tasks, so they are almost always part of a larger teaching plan. Instructors should also remember that teaching and learning are contextual activities, and they have to consider their learners, learning styles, social environment and relations, content, technology available, and other available resources and materials.

Using a game for instructional purposes requires serious instructional planning. According to Prensky (2007), games need to be targeted towards an audience; subject matter should be evaluated for its appropriateness and then an interactive teaching strategy should be employed to put the first two factors together. In terms of teaching strategies, digital games strongly favor interactive teaching strategies. Prensky proposes several interactive strategies that can be used with a game such as practice and feedback, learning by doing, learning from mistakes, goal-oriented learning, discovery learning and guided discovery, role playing, coaching, and intelligent tutoring.

Practice and feedback become important strategies when a skill needs to be practiced over time. Learning by mistakes is also a valuable approach. Digital games provide a safe environment for the players because they are not judged by their mistakes. Each time they fail, they get some kind of feedback from the system, so they are more motivated to do better in the game. In goal-oriented learning, the focus is achieving goals of the game as opposed to memorizing facts about the game. In this sense, it provides a more active and engaging role to the players. Discovery learning refers to the players' own exploration of the game mission. Players investigate game play and strategies on their own and this approach grants a more meaningful learning experience. Role playing is a crucial part of many digital games that they have their own genre. This strategy enables players to take responsibility for acting out in certain roles and this experience usually ends up with players' making decisions in their roles. For instance, in a study conducted by Adams (2009) Neverwinter Nights used in teaching reading skills while engaging students in read-aloud while interacting with the game. Intelligent tutoring is a much more structured gaming strategy and it is based on providing regular feedback to players so they can correct their misconceptions and go through a process of problem solving in a certain field. Intelligent tutoring systems use common misconceptions in learning and decision making. Based on players' moves, they present hints so players can tackle the problem in hand. Although the idea of intelligent tutoring is not new, their integration with the games is pretty recent. In a study conducted by Burton and Brown (1982) the intelligent tutor was designed to teach arithmetic and operator precedence. The students reported that they found the game more enjoyable than the original version of the game.

Case Study 2: EcoRacer to Teach Engineering Classes

In 2008, Dr. Idowu of Penn State University School of Science, Engineering and Technology started using E-Trax, a two-player car racing game. The purpose of this game was to teach electric power and energy and increase student engagement. From this initial trial, another game called EcoRacer emerged. EcoRacer is a single player game and it requires players to complete laps around a racing track by choosing one of the engines: gasoline; solar; wind; hydrogen. Each of these engines has different strengths and weaknesses, and they also

have various effects on the environment. The players try to get high scores by using more eco-friendly, more efficient engine options in the least amount of time. What is different in EcoRacer is that learning outcomes are carefully aligned with the purpose of the game. Engineering students learn the impact of different energy sources, availability of energy sources and energy-environment relations by playing this game. EcoRacer is one of the many projects that has been undergoing at Penn State's Educational Gaming Commons. In addition to the games, Educational Gaming Commons also designs projects with the virtual worlds and promotes meaningful learning, and teaching, and research practices at Penn State.

INSTRUCTIONAL DESIGN FOR GAME-BASED LEARNING

The purpose of instructional design is to optimize effectiveness of instruction and learning after a careful planning and design of learner needs, learning outcomes, content, learning materials and technology, and assessment strategies. If games will be used to increase student learning, it is essential that instructional designers understand elements of game design and use these elements to plan instruction. Along the same lines, Akilli (2006) believed that "instructional designers should strive to seamlessly integrate game elements into their designs and to create game-like environments, so that they can prepare students for the future and build powerful learning into their designs" (p.15). However, the guidelines for instructional designers seem insufficient. Becker (2006, in Gibson, Aldrich & Prensky) argues that "instructional design for games must come *out of* the games design itself and cannot be imposed upon it" (p. 43). By doing this, we create games like *Civilization* and *Black & White* which are very engaging, realistic and graphically rich rather than artificially created *Mathblaster* which has distracting background noise or graphics with a redundant game play (Becker, 2006, in Gibson, Aldrich & Prensky).

Another important factor that affects instructional design is flow and motivation theories. Csikszentmihalyi's *Flow Theory* has been used extensively as a method to understand and implement motivation, especially in the gaming research. In this theory, Csikszentmihalyi (1975) defines a specific state of happiness and creativity called flow. Individuals experience flow as a satisfying, gratifying and exhilarating feeling when they involve in activities that are challenging but at the same time, engaging and balanced. Csikszentmihalyi "found a depressing lack of flow in everyday life, but an overwhelming abundance of it in games and game-like activities" (McGonigal, 2011, p. 35). Today, many game designers and researchers believe that "the flow theory is a theoretical bridge between the concerns of instructional design and motivational design theory" (Chan & Ahern, 1999) because games promote play; play increases a state of flow, which helps increase motivation. At the end, motivation supports the learning process, and causes meaningful learning experiences. The study of flow theory contributed very positively to the game design. For instance, when players set their goals, engage in game activities that create a perfect state of flow, and receive positive feedback about their progress, quality game play is created for even more flow-inducing games. Not all game designers have adopted Csikszentmihalyi's theory to keep the player in the 'flow', but some games such as Civilization, Everquest, Age of Empires, and World of Warcraft have implemented this so successfully that players stay in the 'flow zone' for hours.

While instructional design plays a vital role in game-based learning, there are other problems in regards to instructional design process. According to Hirumi, Appelman, Rieber, and Van Eck (2010),

For the most part, instructional designers know little about game development and video game developers may know little about training, education and instructional design. As a result, instructional designers may not realize the potential of play, game, and story to create engaging and memorable learning experiences, and game developers may fail to apply basic pedagogical principles that are vital for facilitating learning (p.27).

It is clear that digital games present new learning environments that have their own strengths and weaknesses. Instructional designers must be equipped with the required design skills as well as the new literacies, to take the advantage of them. They also need to understand what is involved in designing successful environments.

ASSESSMENT ISSUES IN GAME-BASED LEARNING

Assessment activities in education ensure that learning outcomes are achieved and confirms that students have learned the desired outcomes. In other words, assessment provides proof of learning. Michael and Chen (2005) state that this proof of learning is important for the following reasons:

- Student advancement from one level of education to another,
- National and international comparison of students,
- Demonstration that the student has completed a particular training program (para. 9).

Over the decades, instructors used multiple-choice tests, quizzes, surveys, or essays to test student's understanding of the content. However, it is obvious that digital games cannot follow a similar method of student testing. One of the assessment methods used with the digital games is tutorial assessment. Most games have tutorials built into their structure and they assess a player's understanding of the game play, game rules, user control and interaction mechanisms. As players accomplish game challenges, they move towards more difficult tasks taking into account that they understood the previous challenges and game play. Another assessment method that is commonly used with digital games is scoring. Almost all games have a scoring chart that shows players how well they are progressing through game challenges. In massively played multi-player online games, the scoring could be against other players in the game. In addition to a scoring chart, progress bars or levels are also used in most digital games to indicate a player's advancement through the game challenges. As players move from one level to another, they are introduced to more challenging tasks, and sometimes they gain additional bonuses, strengths and capabilities. For instance, in World of Warcraft, players gain flying capabilities after they reach level 12. This helps them complete game missions in a shorter time but at the same time, missions become more difficult.

While traditional assessment methods may not work with digital games, serious game designers have been trying new methods. Michael and Chen (2005) list these alternatives as follows:

- **Completion Assessment:** Did the player complete the lesson or pass the test?
- **In-Process Assessment:** How did the players choose their actions? Did they change their mind? If so, at what point?
- **Teacher Evaluation:** Based on observations of the student, does the teacher think the student now knows/understands the material? (para. 22).

Completion assessment is a good way to gauge a student's progress. Not all games are designed to finish, but if certain scores, progress, levels or missions are achieved, students can be considered to have passed the test. The second method of game assessment, in-process assessment, can be done in two ways. Either, an instructor observes students' progress (which may not be possible in e-Learning settings) or students report their own

game reflections after they played the game. What did work for them? What was challenging? How did they cope out with the challenges? When did they solve the problems or accomplish the missions? All these points can be discussed in the virtual environment with the rest of the class. More and more serious games are adopting internal tracking features into their structure, so in the future it might be possible for instructors to observe a student's progress. At this point, current structures of most digital games do not offer much room for instructor observations. The last method of game evaluation, teacher-evaluation, includes a combination of completion and in-process assessments of the students.

In the context of current digital games, game designers rarely include any evaluation of learning. In order to do this, the game play needs to be revised by the game designers. Similarly, "what instructional designers need to understand is that evaluation must also include game play, which may require modification of strategies, sequence of learning, and the development of challenges and strategies that extend beyond the attainment of instructional objectives" (Hirumi, Appelman, Rieber, and Van Eck, 2010, p. 36).

Case Study 3: Tragedy of the Tuna to Teach Business Classes

Inspired by an article by Hardin published in 1968, Learning Lab at the Wharton University of Pennsylvania developed Tragedy of Tuna. This game is another good example of integrating educational games into e-learning environments while engaging students in collaborative decision-making and problem solving situations. Garret Hardin's paper was called "Tragedy of the Commons" and it claimed that all the open sources in the world will vanish eventually because all people use these sources but nobody takes responsibility for preserving them. Tragedy of Tuna uses a similar idea and places students in a situation where they are faced with such a challenge. In the game play, students are assigned to a country where a tuna fishing fleet is based. They make decisions about where to deploy their fleet, where to fish, and the size of the fleet. Each decision has different consequences and the team of players should fight to keep their fleet alive because in time, keeping the fish alive becomes more and more difficult. There are certain interactive components in the game. For instance, each team can communicate through a chat window and discuss their relations with the other teams, which will cause partnerships with the other teams. Teams can order more fishing boats with a cost and when the next turn becomes available they can use their boats. Selling or trading boats are also possible in the market. Last but not the least, teams can create public or private contracts and these contracts set rules about boat deployments and also set up rules if anyone breaks the contracts. Each team's achievement is calculated once they enter their decisions in the system. The tuna population is calculated based on the fishing results, money spent, and profits made.

HOW TO USE DIGITAL GAMES IN E-LEARNING

When a university faculty decides to integrate game-based learning to their online courses, the following suggestions may help them:

- **Start small.** As with any other new technology or teaching technique, instructors should employ games slowly into their teaching. As they observe their students' reactions, adjustments should be made.
- **Consider overall purpose of the course/ unit.** What is the game's overall goal? Does this match with the learning objectives? Does the game provide multiple levels of goals? Do students have any power to customize the game's goals? How does the game support social interactions? The

faculty member should ponder on these points before implementation.

- **Focus on learner experience.** Does the difficulty level of the game match with the students' abilities? Can students have any control over difficulty level? Is there a built-in feedback system? How will a faculty member help students when they need help? At the higher education level, formative evaluation instruments may be very helpful to get students' feedback on their gaming experience. Instructors could also set up quick online polls to get immediate student feedback.
- **Prepare for the technicalities.** How will students access the game? Is it easier to integrate it in the course/learning management system or provide a separate link? Is there a help line for technical problems? Does faculty lay out technical requirements early in the process?
- **Provide mentoring and modeling.** When students are assigned to play games in an online environment, it might be challenging to provide immediate feedback or mentoring. It might be helpful to introduce students to the game in a synchronous online meeting and provide a 'frequently asked questions'. Also, if the game is a commercial one, providing a list of online resources, community wiki or webpage information could positively support learning experiences.
- **Include reflective exercises or use reflection as an assessment.** One of the criticisms of digital games is that their fast-facing nature doesn't give students enough time to reflect on their learning experiences. Provide exercises (or reflective assessments) in the online course so students will think about their learning, game play, and social interactions.

WHAT IS THE FUTURE OF GAME-BASED LEARNING?

After a careful analysis of the literature it is clear that a few themes are emerging as trends in the game-based learning.

- **Growth in popularity of simulation games.** When it comes to serious games, more and more simulation games have been designed in the recent years such as war games, role-play simulation games, business and economics games. Simulation games provide students situated learning experiences where they can control real life situations in a simulated online environment. In such games, students have plenty of opportunities for creating strategies or tactics, role play, plan and social interactions.
- **Online learning on the rise.** Learning and teaching supported by various forms of electronic and web-based platforms has become a valid, valuable and convenient format of instruction in the 21st century. Using game-based learning in such environments makes a great fit.
- **Increased collaboration between game designer and educators.** Most of the games that are used in education today are created without a sound pedagogical basis. The issue for the future is: "who will create these digital games and will they be based on sound theories of learning and socially conscious educational practices?" (Shaffer, Squire, Halverson & Gee, 2005, p. 110). The rapid growth in the body of research in the past decade shows that game-based learning is a new area of exploration for many education researchers today, and this will cause the production of more sophisticated and serious games in the near future.
- **Accessibility of the technology.** Today almost all college students have access to a computer with high speed internet access. As online learning becomes mainstream, students' access to higher broadband, better memory and processing power and quality video cards is becoming more common. The developments in personal access to this technology will make it easier for game-based learning as an essential learning strategy.

ARE DIGITAL GAMES THE FUTURE OF E-LEARNING?

Digital games are changing the way today's students are learning. When students can practice and improve their leadership, digital literacy, collaboration, and problem solving skills in a fun and motivating way, it is impossible to ignore the potential of educational games and simulations. It is crucial for educators to start understanding how commercial games are developed, how they motivate students and lock them onto a computer for hours so educators will be more equipped with skills to develop serious and educational games. A few important questions need to be studied carefully nevertheless:

- What are the design practices of commercial game businesses? How can these experiences and practices help educators to design effective learning environments?
- How can we transfer learning gained through games to other cognitive domains?
- How are social skills fostered in game-based learning and how do these skills align with 21st century skills?
- What skills are required from online educators to design game-based learning environments?
- What kinds of interactive learning are happening in games and how this experience can be transferred to online format?

Digital games are at the beginning of their progress. While they represent a new form of learning, they are not a significant part of today's education practices. While searching for answers to above questions, perhaps "we must strive to push the boundaries of what games can be, in form and in function. As games move from being solely a technological tool to becoming a pervasive culture of play, we may yet unlock generations of curious, confident investigators and collaborators" Klopfer, Osterweil and Salen (2009, p. 43).

REFERENCES

Adams, M. G. (2009, July). Engaging 21st-century adolescents: Video games in the reading classroom. *English Journal, 98*(6), 56–59.

Akilli, G. K. (2006). Games and simulations: A new approach in Education? In Gibson, D., Aldrich, C., & Prensky, M. (Eds.), *Games and simulations in online learning* (pp. 1–20). Hershey, PA: IGI Global. doi:10.4018/978-1-59904-304-3. ch001

Burton, R., & Brown, J. S. (1982). An investigation of computer coaching for informal learning activities. In Sleeman, D., & Brown, J. S. (Eds.), *Intelligent tutoring systems*. Orlando, FL: Academic Press. doi:10.1016/S0020-7373(79)80003-6

Chan, T. S., & Ahern, T. C. (1999). Targeting motivation: Adapting flow theory to instructional design. *Journal of Educational Computing Research, 21*(2), 152–163.

Csikszentmihalyi, M. (1975). *Beyond boredom and anxiety*. San Francisco, CA: Jossey-Bass.

Entertainment Software Association. (2010). *Sales, demographics and usage data: Essential facts about the computer and video game industry*. Retrieved from http://www.theesa.com/facts/pdfs/ESA_Essential_Facts_2010.PDF

Gee, J. P. (2007a). *Good video games + good learning: Collected essays on video games, learning and literacy*. New York, NY: Peter Lang.

Gee, J. P. (2007b). *What video games have to teach us about learning and literacy*. New York, NY: Palgrave MacMillan.

Gibson, D., Aldrich, C., & Prensky, M. (2006). *Games and simulations in online learning: Research and development frameworks*. Hershey, PA: IGI Global. doi:10.4018/978-1-59904-304-3

Hirumi, A., Appelman, B., Rieber, L., & Van Eck, R. (2010). Preparing instructional designers for game-based learning: Part I. *TechTrends, 54*(3), 27–37. doi:10.1007/s11528-010-0400-9

Johnson, D. (2009). *Analysis and deconstruction of the institution. Gamasutra: The art and business of making games*. Retrieved from http://www.gamasutra.com/view/news/23960/Analysis_Portal_and_the_Deconstruction_of_the_Institution.php

Johnson, L., Levine, A., Smith, R., & Stone, S. (2010). *The 2010 Horizon report*. Austin, TX: The New Media Consortium. Retrieved from http://wp.nmc.org/horizon-k12-2010/chapters/game-based-learning/#0

Kebrichi, M. (2010). Factors effecting teachers' adoption of educational computer games: A case study. *British Journal of Educational Technology, 41*(2), 256–270. doi:10.1111/j.1467-8535.2008.00921.x

Klopfer, E., Osterweil, S., & Salen, K. (2009). Moving learning games forward: Obstacles, opportunities, openness. *The Education Arcade*. Retrieved from http://education.mit.edu/papers/MovingLearningGamesForward_EdArcade.pdf.

McFarlane, A., Sparrowhawk, A., & Heald, Y. (2002). *Report on the educational use of games*. Retrieved from http://www.teem.org.uk/publications/teem_gamesined_full.pdf

McGonigal, J. (2011). *Reality is broken: What games make us better and how they can change the world.* New York, NY: The Penguin Press.

Michael, D., & Chen, S. (2005). *Serious games: Games that educate, train, and inform.* Course Technology PTR.

Michael, D., & Chen, S. (2005). *Proof of learning: Assessment in serious games. Gamasutra: The art and business of making games.* Retrieved from http://www.gamasutra.com/view/feature/2433/proof_of_learning_assessment_in_.php

Orlando, J. (2011). What games teach us about learning? *Faculty Focus.* April, 2011. Retrieved from http://www.facultyfocus.com/articles/teaching-with-technology-articles/what-games-teach-us-about-learning/

Orts, E. W. (2011). *Tragedy of the tuna.* Retrieved from http://beacon.wharton.upenn.edu/learning/management/tragedy-of-the-tuna/

Prensky, M. (2007). *Digital game-based learning.* St. Paul, MN: Paragon House.

Report, H. (2011). *The New Media Consortium and Educause.* Retrieved from http://net.educause.edu/ir/library/pdf/HR2011.pdf

Shaffer, D. W., Squire, K. R., Halverson, R., & Gee, J. P. (2005, October). Video games and the future of learning. *Phi Delta Kappan,* 104–111. Retrieved from http://ddis.wceruw.org/docs/08%20ShafferSquireHalversonGee%20PDK.pdf.

Wikipedia. (n.d.). *Serious games.* Retrieved from http://en.wikipedia.org/wiki/Serious_game

KEY TERMS AND DEFINITIONS

Digital Game: An electronic and computerized game.

Game-Based learning: "Game based learning (GBL) is a branch of serious games that deals with applications that have defined learning outcomes" (Wikipedia, 2011, para.1)

Serious Game: "A serious game is a game designed for a primary purpose other than pure entertainment" (Wikipedia, 2011, para.1).

Teaching Strategies: Goals, methods, techniques and processes that facilitate teaching performance.

Chapter 9
Games in E-Learning:
How Games Teach and How Teachers Can Use Them

Michelle Aubrecht
Ohio State University, USA

ABSTRACT

Game-based learning is a dynamic and powerful way to engage students to develop evidence-based reasoning, analytical and critical thinking skills, problem-solving skills, systems thinking, and connect with peers, all of which are 21ˢᵗ century skills. Games can lead students to become participatory learners and producers instead of passive recipients. This chapter considers the following three approaches to using games with students: (1) an instructor makes a game for a specific learner outcome, (2) students make a game, and (3) an instructor uses a commercial or online game. The chapter emphasizes the second and third methods. Specific examples of how games are being used with students illustrate ways to teach with games.

INTRODUCTION

"Can games teach?" and "What do they teach?" are two questions that are at the forefront of pedagogy. In the name of accountability, educators are confronted with demands from legislators who mandate testing as the primary indicator

of success (Gee & Shaffer, 2010; Squire, 2011; Valli, Croninger, Chambliss, Graeber, & Buese, 2008). However, analysis of these accountability measures by the National Research Council (2011) report *Incentives and Test-Based Accountability in Public Education* has shown them to be ineffectual in increasing student achievement. Concurrently, there is a growing awareness about the importance of incorporating 21ˢᵗ century learning skills, many

DOI: 10.4018/978-1-61350-441-3.ch009

of which can be met with digital video games (smartbean, November 2009; Wellings, 2009) and new media literacies into the curriculum. This requires that both the role of the teacher and the way that schools are organized undergo examination and transformation. Gee & Shaffer (2010) call for a "radical" transformation of assessment in order "to succeed in introducing the new ways of learning that computers make possible" (p. 6). Technology, in general, can allow a teacher to move into the role of facilitator (Morrison, Lowther, & DeMeulle, 1999), partner (Prensky, 2010) and coach and advisor (Squire, 2011). Teachers can guide students in thoughtful and researched sharing of ideas, recognizing that they themselves do not have to know all of the answers. The role of the student can also be transformed from passive receiver of knowledge to active producer (Jenkins, 2006; Gee & Hayes, 2010; Prensky, 2010; Squire, 2011).

Because students grow up in a visual culture, it is imperative that they be able to understand and navigate within it. Video games, now well established as an entertainment medium, have the potential to change the way that students and teachers think about learning (McLellan, 1996; Jenkins, Clinton, Purushotma, Robison, & Weigel, 2006; Prensky, 2006; Annetta, 2008; Gee & Hayes, 2010). According to Thai, Lowenstein, Ching, and Rejeski (2009),

Educational digital games offer a promising and untapped opportunity to leverage children's enthusiasm and help transform teaching and learning in America. These games allow teachers to tap into their students' existing enthusiasm for digital games to engage, expand, and empower them as learners. (as cited in Wellings & Levine, 2009, p. 10)

Video games provide powerful and complex learning tools and environments through their inherent ability to combine such multimedia as video, sound, text (including narrative), vi-

sual information (images, tables, graphs), and simulations, including pulling information from databases in real time. MIT's Ubiquitous Games project features games in production that are intended for mobile devices and handhelds. Smallab Learning at Arizona State University uses wall- or ceiling-mounted projection equipment and sensors to make use of motion-capture technology to create multimodal, embodied learning games that are projected on the floor. Smallab is also developing a new product, the 3D Interactive Whiteboard, so that the games they are developing can be used with an interactive whiteboard. Tested in classrooms and museums, their library of embodied learning content spans several disciplines including Science, Technology, Engineering, Mathematics (STEM), Language, Special Education, Gaming, and the Arts.

Video games can be an alternative way to demonstrate learning without testing (Gee & Shaffer, 2010). Essentially, games are designed to test and challenge players. Players are actively engaged in problem solving, understanding complex relationships, building upon what they have learned in order to progress, and experiencing the consequences of their choices. David Shaffer (2006) explains the difference between testing and learning by doing as the "difference between … declarative knowledge and procedural knowledge, or being able to explain something and being able to actually do it" (pp. 91-92).

In this chapter, the author will discuss teaching methods, specific games that have been used to teach, and student projects as well as the educational benefits of students making and designing games. While many of the examples herein are from physical classroom environments, there are also many web-based games that are free and easily lend themselves to online learning environments. The author will distinguish the terms "simulation", "simulation game", and "game", and discuss the ways that "play" and "game" can be understood in an educational context.

BACKGROUND: WHY USE GAMES?

Video games in the classroom can provide students with opportunities to work together, including expanding the walls of the school to include other classrooms in other cities and countries through massively multi-player online role-playing games (MMORPG) and online tools. Students can collaborate through game spaces, social networks, forums, blogs, and wikis. In the hands of a skilled educator, video games are well suited to lessons that teach multiple perspectives in the same way that novels, documentaries, and current events have traditionally been used by teachers. Additionally, games provide a visual impact that is multiplied by interactivity, providing context for the content and allowing students to make decisions and choices.

Gee (2007) refers to contextual content found in games as "situated learning", in which students access information that they need when they need it, or "just in time," in order to progress in a game. Medina (n.d.), a developmental molecular biologist, explains that "the brain processes meaning before it processes details." Educators often give students details without context, expecting that students will process details to find meaning. If a student can contextualize and apply information, he or she is more likely to remember it (or build in knowledge of the process through which the goal was reached) and be encouraged to tackle more challenging tasks. Pokémon, a role-playing game that uses cards involving 250 characters and a complex rule system, is often played by elementary-age children. Gee uses the example of how some students who exhibit the ability to learn and master Pokémon's complex naming structure and game play seemingly lack the ability to learn specific academic domains and language (Gee, 2004). This is not due to the students' inability to learn domain-specific language, but rather to the student lacking motivation or any understanding of why it is important to learn material. Basically, students lack the connection to the context. Their

learning is not "situated." Game environments can situate terms within the context, helping the students to grasp the relevance and application of the terms and knowledge (Gee, 2004).

There is growing evidence that strongly suggests that non-traditional learners are more motivated when games are used in the classroom (Steinkuehler, 2010; Klopfer, Osterweil, & Hass, 2009) and that children with learning disabilities are better able to learn with games (Marino, 2011). Games seem to be finding their way into teaching environments, and for solid reasons. According to Van Eck (2006), "the core principle [of serious game is] that games can promote learning at higher taxonomic levels" (p. 22). Also, "games are good at involving students in a procedural experience" (Magerko, 2009, p. 1276). The 2011 Horizon Report projects that game-based learning will be widely adopted by higher education within two to three years. It states that "research and experience have already shown that games can be applied very effectively in many learning contexts, and that games can engage learners in ways other tools and approaches cannot" (Johnson, Smith, Willis, Levine, & Haywood, 2011, p. 22).

One study found that digital games can considerably improve students' knowledge of the subject matter as well as their enjoyment, engagement, and interest in learning. The findings were the same for both boys and girls (Papastergiou, 2009). Papastergiou's study supports other prior studies on the same topic while also showing increased student academic achievement and motivation (Klawe, 1999; Rosas, Nussbaum, Cumsille, Marianov, Correa et al., 2003; Ke & Grabowski, 2007).

There is a need for more studies that demonstrate how games help students learn (Becker, 2010; Ng, Plass, & Zeng, 2009; Wellings & Levine, 2009) and how learning is facilitated (Charsky, 2010). However, evidence about the benefits of game-based learning is hard to categorize, especially if we assume that scientifically designed studies are to be conclusive. Conclusively determining whether or not a game is successful or useful for educating children is like creating the optimal diet. Individual needs preclude a one-size-fits-all solution. There are too many variables to take into account, such as allergies, birth defects, environmental influences, and so on. Likewise, individuals have different learning styles and abilities, which may be affected by their health and living environments. Individuals have access to different opportunities to learn outside of school, and they may or may not have parents who encourage learning and provide a computer, books, discussion, and trips to libraries, parks, and museums. All of these factors make sound research studies hard to design and conclusive evidence for success elusive.

Squire (2011) superbly describes the momentous difficulty in conducting meaningful research in the Appendix of his book *Video Games and Learning: Teaching and Participatory Culture in the Digital Age*. Access to classrooms for research is just one difficulty. Creating controls that conclusively determine what factors influence student learning is virtually impossible. Squire (2011) concludes that the best research models are ones "that instantiate pedagogical ideas in interventions co-constructed with teachers" (p. 234). Furthermore, he pointedly states that instead of dwelling on which measurements to use, we should rethink assessment and evaluation procedures, taking into account that we live in a participatory culture. He charges us to,

Imagine students, teachers, and parents discussing what evidence constitutes successful participation in science. Imagine performance not being reduced to a single score on a normed test, but rather, a battery of assessments (including those from peers) indicating what the student has done, is good at, and needs to work on in areas from game design to verbal communication. (p. 418)

Gee and Shaffer (2010) also support this view. They argue that nearly everything relevant to typical assessment methods should be reconsidered.

We argue that three fundamental properties of assessment need to change in the 21st Century: *what* is assessed, *how* the assessment takes place, and the *purpose* of assessment in the first place. (p. 6)

They also explain that using digital media is an ideal way to collect and organize information, potentially using this "information to help learners and to judge the success of programs, processes, and practices for learning" (pp. 8-9)

How to use technology is a more pressing question than whether or not it should be used (Wellings & Levine, 2009). There are numerous benefits to using it, among which are building 21st century skills, engaging students in content creation, providing access to virtual communities and expertise, supporting STEM fields and differentiated instruction, and reducing the dropout rate (Wellings & Levine, 2009). Before students can benefit from playing educational games, support materials (Baek, 2008) and training for teachers are needed so that games can be integrated into the curriculum (Becker, 2010; Oblinger, 2006; Thai, et al., 2009). According to Oblinger, (2006) "integration requires an understanding of the medium and its alignment with the subject, the instructional strategy, the student's learning style, and intended outcomes" (p. 7). Through training and support, teachers can gain understanding, confidence, and the ability to use games with students (Becker, 2007).

Baek (2008) identified several barriers to using games in the classroom, including teacher concerns about the negative effects of gaming, student uneasiness, fixed class schedules, inflexible curriculums, and limited budgets. Rice (2007) also identified lack of adequate computer hardware, fixed class schedules, and a lack of alignment to state standards as barriers to integrating games into the curriculum. Other factors inhibiting the use of games include objections from those who are concerned about negative influences from games (Rice, 2007) or who consider games to be inappropriate for education (Charsky & Mims, 2008; Oblinger, 2006). Additionally, non-gamer students may feel concerned about their ability to figure out how to use games (Baek, 2008; Charsky & Mims, 2008).

There are many constraints that vary from school to school and teacher to teacher, including availability of computers, internet access and speed, working with IT, and, in most cases, obtaining approval for accessing online games. Teachers may not have time to play a game long enough to feel confident in using it with students, creating a lesson or unit based on it, or adapting a game lesson guide to meet specific curricular needs. Also, because games differ widely, figuring out how to assess student learning may present difficulties.

DEFINING GAMES AND PLAY

While many game scholars have discussed the difficulty of defining game and play, Salen and Zimmerman, in their book *Rules of Play*, plumb the depths of this conundrum. After exploring and discussing the merits of multiple definitions and the implications of those definitions, they settle on the following definitions:

Game: "A game is a system in which players engage in an artificial conflict, defined by rules, that results in a quantifiable outcome" (p. 80).

Play: "Play is free movement within a more rigid structure" (p. 304).

Play and games: "Games are a subset of play: Games constitute a formalized part of all activities considered to be play. And Play is an element of games: Play is one way to frame the complex phenomenon of games" (p. 311).

A succinct characterization of games is given by McGonigal (2011): "All games have four defining traits: a goal, rules, a feedback system,

and voluntary participation" (p. 21). McGonigal explains that voluntary participation means that the player accepts the goals, rules, and feedback of a game.

Play is a controversial subject in the context of school. Many would argue that fun, which is closely connected to play, is not necessary to a learning environment. However, play can lead us to think creatively, and it can also have educational results. Salen suggests that play has much to offer: learner engagement, it produces knowledge and understanding, it produces culture and encourages students to be producers as well as to help others, and it offers new ways of seeing that can be transformative. She explained that when play is connected back to learning, it can be leveraged. (Salen, 2011)

Agreeing with Salen and Zimmerman's definitions of "play" and "game", Bogost (2008) explains that play allows the creation of a "possibility space" that is "created by constraints of all kinds. Play activities are not rooted in one social practice, but in many social and material practices" (p. 120). Huzinga's book *Homo Ludens* (1950) is a seminal work about play and games. In it, Huzinga states that "play is non-serious," which is not to say "not serious" (p. 5). He further contends that "play lies outside morals" (p. 213). Huzinga (1950) coined the phrase "magic circle" to explain how a play space transports us to a consecrated spot that finds its place among temples, stages, courts of justice, tennis courts, and card tables "dedicated to the performance of an act apart," with special rules, actions, and goals that we may voluntarily perform (p. 10).

For the purposes of this chapter, "game" will be understood to be a subset of "play", which corresponds to the definitions given above by Salen and Zimmerman. It should also be understood that the author considers play as a part of the engagement and risk taking that allows creative experimentation and exploration that leads to understanding and knowledge growth.

PLAY AND CREATIVITY ARE NECESSARY TO LEARNING

Play is a topic that is receiving widespread discussion as people revisit the purpose and necessity of it in our lives. Physical activity is essential to our physical and mental well-being. Students who exercise right before a test score higher than those who do not (Medina, 2008). The neuroscience of play has shown that students need art, music, and recess to develop creativity that is necessary for the workplace (Brown & Vaughan, 2009). However, physical education and art programs are being cut from school curriculums so that there is more time to prepare for mandated testing. Brown and Vaughan cited Panksepp's research involving animals that indicated that "depriving young animals of play might delay or disrupt brain maturation," which is similar to how ADHD in humans affects self control. "Without play, Panksepp suggests, optimal learning, normal social functioning, self-control, and other executive functions might not mature properly" (as cited in Brown & Vaughan, 2009, p. 100). Brown and Vaughan also discuss the findings of Byers, who studies animal play.

Byers speculates that during play, the brain is making sense of itself through simulation and testing. Play activity is actually helping sculpt the brain. In play, most of the time we are able to try out things without threatening our physical or emotional well-being. We are safe precisely because we are just playing. (Brown & Vaughan, 2009, p. 34)

Brown and Vaughan (2009) conclude:

Play is nature's greatest tool for creating new neural networks and for reconciling cognitive difficulties. The abilities to make new patterns, find the unusual among the common, and spark curiosity and alert observation are all fostered by being in a state of play. (p. 127)

Playfulness is necessary to creativity, exploration of ideas, taking risks, trying new strategies, and creating new ways to organize data and ideas. Games employ these elements of playfulness. "Good games always involve play and schooling rarely does" (Klopfer, Osterweil, & Salen, 2009, p. 4). Games also support learning styles that fall outside of traditional learning methods. Gardner's (1999) multiple intelligences theory supports the idea that people learn in different ways. Prensky explains that in games students learn by doing, learn from mistakes, and experience "goal-oriented learning, discovery learning, task-based learning, question-based learning, situated learning, role playing, coaching, constructivist learning and multi-sensory learning" (as cited in Akilli, 2007, p. 157). To be competitive in the 21st century, students must be guided in developing all of their intelligences, including the emotional and physical aspects, thereby equipping them to solve problems, think critically and analytically, and use the ever-changing internet, communication systems, and software tools (Galarneau, 2007).

DEFINING GAME, SIMULATION, AND SIMULATION GAME

Educators have many different applications for the terms "simulation", "simulation game", and "game". In 1996, these terms were differentiated in *Instructional Media and Technologies for Learning*. Heinich (1996) explained that while "these are separate concepts, they do overlap and have been used interchangeably," causing confusion (p. 327). David Shaffer (2006) would say that all games are simulations because they are representational or models of reality. Becker (2010) clarifies that "all digital games are computer simulations, although the reverse is not true" (p. 29). Having clear distinctions can help sort out the options when selecting the appropriate interactive media for a given learning outcome. Below the author distinguishes the terms "game", "simulation", and "simulation game" to describe three variations of interactive digital media. The author will briefly look at early educational games and discuss virtual worlds and how those can be leveraged for learning environments.

Game

The definition of game herein is broad and encompasses simulation games as well as all non-digital games. (Refer back to the definitions from Salen and Zimmerman and McGonigal in the Defining Games and Play section above.) A video game may or may not attempt to simulate a time in history, include a narrative, or model something realistic. Games can be abstract, like tic tac toe, chess, or *Tetris*. In *The Video Game Explosion*, Wolfe (2008) identifies 43 game genres. Categorizing games can be confusing. It is worth noting that games are also aesthetic objects and cultural objects (Zimmerman, 2011). While the focus herein is on games that can be used for teaching, it is not meant to exclude games that do not fit neatly within the serious or educational game genre. Klopfer, et al. (2009) explains the purpose of an educational game: "learning games…target the acquisition of knowledge as its own end and foster habits of mind and understanding that are generally useful or useful within an academic context" (p. 21). With this definition in mind, many games that were not intended for education could be repurposed by a skilled teacher. Simply put, a game is educational if it is being used to teach.

Simulation

Simulation accurately describes a user-directed model that demonstrates a phenomenon, allowing for dynamic and interactive engagement with the subject matter. This is especially useful in the sciences. Watching a science demonstration is good, but doing it oneself is even better. Sometimes setting up experiments for large numbers of students is impractical; a digital simulation could be the best alternative. Simulations can also be extremely useful in online learning environments.

Meen's 1993 study claimed that if people learn by doing something, even through a simulation, they will retain 90 percent of what they have learned, compared to only 10 percent if they read and 50 percent if they watch someone performing the task (as cited in Klopfer, et al., 2009).

Many examples of digital simulations are available through the PhET project at the University of Colorado (http://phet.colorado.edu/). This project has created research-based, interactive simulations for physics, biology, chemistry, earth science, and math. The buoyancy simulation, for example, allows the user to explore how density, mass, volume, and the material of an object can affect its buoyancy. The user can adjust the sliders to change properties of the object. This is an example of a simple simulation. It prompts one to ask, "what happens if…?" As with a flight simulation, one is not actually flying, but it feels as if one were.

Simulation Game

A simulation game builds upon the idea of representation or modeling of real-world phenomena. The more complicated simulations also share some similarities to simulation games. In a simulation game, specific goals are added, thereby introducing the possibilities of success, failure, the option to try different things, and risk taking. Players have options to employ and develop multiple strategies, and in some cases they can work together with multiple players online, as in *World of Warcraft*, *Age of Empires*, and *Civilization*. In these examples, one can see how fluid the line is between "simulation" and "simulation game". Some of the simulation games could also share characteristics with the physics simulation example above. The major difference is that a simulation game does not have to be completely accurate, or it may reflect the designer's interpretation. For example, in *Civilization* there are historical biases or limitations of the game environment that prevent it from being 100% accurate.

Figure 1. PhET Buoyancy simulation. Players can move the blocks, bottle and adjust the fluid density or reset the simulation if they want to start over. (© 2011, PhET Interactive Simulations, University of Colorado. Used with permission.)

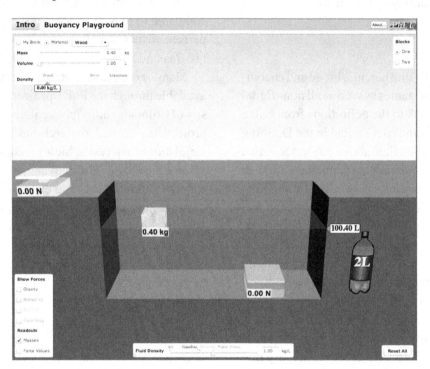

Furthermore, a simulation game is an interactive model that allows students to understand a system without being hindered by minutia. The game designer decides the most important information to communicate and how much detail to include. As Squire describes, "if the model gets too complex, then you can't observe the consequences, and it is not entertaining, nor educational. … We don't want a 1:1 map of the world. We want a model to illustrate ideas" (2011, p. 23). Simulation games also provide defined goals and rule systems. In understanding buoyancy, there is no inherent task that leads one to reach a particular goal. The goal of the simulation is to allow a student to explore and manipulate until understanding is reached. "A simulation game combines the attributes of a simulation (role playing, a model of reality) with the attributes of a game (striving toward a goal, specific rules)" (Heinich, et al., 1996, p. 332).

Some simulation games create environments in which players take on roles, such as "game designer" in *Gamestar Mechanic* and "urban planner" in *Urban Science*. Shaffer has been researching educational games in the epistemic game group. Epistemic games engage students by involving them in a community of practice.

Epistemic games are games that help players learn the ways of thinking–the epistemologies–of the digital age. …Creative professionals learn innovative thinking through training that is very different from traditional academic classrooms because innovative thinking means more than just knowing the right answers on a test. It also means having real-world skills, high standards and professional values, and a particular way of thinking about problems and justifying solutions. (Epistemic Games Website, 2011)

At the time of publication, epistemic games, such as *Digital Zoo*, *Urban Science*, and others featured on the website, are not available for use because they are still in the research stage.

Early Educational Games

Historically, Ito (2008) identifies three categories of video games that have been designed for children: educational, entertainment, and construction. Educational games used in schools are typically drill-and-practice exercises that are tied closely to curricular goals. Examples can be found in games such as *Reader Rabbit* and *Math Blasters* that focus on memorization. Trying to disguise drill and practice as fun tasks that are rewarded by game play doesn't really fool children; they are still answering traditional multiple-choice questions and math problems. Entertainment games are defined as those that are "exploratory, narrative-based games that privilege play" (Klopfer, et al. 2009, p. 17), such as *Where in the World is Carmen San Diego?* Finally, construction games are those that allow a player to make or operate something, such as *SimCity* and *Zoo Tycoon*. Some of the entertainment games are educational, teaching valuable skills sets, while some of the games designed to be educational were a porting of typical educational approaches to a digital medium, such as demonstrating learning through quizzing and drill and practice exercises. In an effort to make educational games more engaging, many educational game designers are using methods similar to those that the entertainment industry uses.

Virtual Worlds

Virtual worlds provide an online 3-D environment where participants can "walk" around as an avatar and communicate with other online participants in real time. *Whyville* and *Kidscom. com* are two educational spaces developed for children, both of which have games embedded within them. *Quest Atlantis* is a 3-D, multi-user, immersive environment that offers quests, blogging, and interviewing and social opportunities. While it has some game elements, it is more a virtual world than a game. Similarly, *River City* is a multi-user environment that was created for middle school students in which they explore a River City where several illnesses are affecting the town. Students work in teams to do research, and they compare their evidence and hypotheses after they have explored the virtual world.

DIGITAL GAME-BASED LEARNING AND STUDENTS

How Games Teach

The theoretical underpinnings of learning in game environments come from constructionist theory attributed to Dewey and Vygostky and built upon by play theorists such as Sutton-Smith. Squire (2011) suggests that the Montessori method of teaching "provides a model of what a game-based learning system should look like" (p. 49). In a Montessori school, students are encouraged and allowed to follow their interests and learn from the materials provided in an "ordered environment designed to pique their interests, instill a sense of order and pattern to the world, and push them toward developing deep understanding." It is freedom within boundaries (Squire, p. 51).

Games are structured environments that allow freedom within boundaries. Klopfer, et al. (2009) explain how play allows one to exercise freedom along five axes: freedom to fail (taking steps towards mastery), freedom to experiment, freedom to fashion identities (defining the self/ understanding the relationship to others and the world), freedom of effort (alternating between intense and relaxed), and freedom of interpretation (p. 4). These freedoms allow children to grow through failure and exploration. Oblinger (2006) states that "games embody many attributes associated with how people learn: games are social and experiential, they require players to recall prior learning and develop new understanding, and being successful depends on problem-solving" (p. 6).

For the player to remain engaged in game play, there must be a balance between challenge and the player's ability to succeed. This is referred to as "flow" (Csikszentmihalyi, 2000). Flow theory can apply to any activity wherein one becomes absorbed in something and time passes quickly. Game designers have used flow theory to explain the optimal game-play experience. Players can become immersed in a play experience for hours as they navigate through a series of challenges within a game. If a game is too easy, players become bored. If it's too difficult, players become anxious or frustrated. Chen (2007) cites Csikszentmihali's eight primary components of flow:

- a challenging activity requiring skill;
- a merging of action and awareness;
- clear goals;
- direct, immediate feedback;
- concentration on the task at hand;
- a sense of control;
- a loss of self-consciousness; and
- an altered sense of time. (p. 31-32)

Being in a state of "flow" is important not just to games but to any learning activity (Shernoff, Csikszentmihalyi, Schneider, & Shernoff, 2003).

Games that incorporate the components of flow are engaging and effective. The most effective games are those that incorporate the right degree of challenge, providing the information required to succeed as it is needed, offering more than one way to reach the goal, requiring critical and analytical thought and decision-making, and giving the player feedback and a feeling of satisfaction and pleasure in accomplishments within the game. Within a good game, learning is scaffolded. As the player advances in the game, she builds upon what she already knows. Advancing to the next level lets the player know that she has achieved a level of mastery. The next level provides new

challenges that build upon what the player has already learned. As the challenges increase, the player's skill will have increased as well. Gee (2010) argues that if an educational game is properly structured, winning the game indicates mastery. In such a case, there would be no need to test whether or not the student had learned the lessons of the game.

According to Salen (2008), "games, like other forms of media, are systems of meaning that are read, interpreted, and performed by players" (p. 10). Salen further explains that "the term system refers not just to the game itself, but to the entire tool-set available to the player within a gaming practice, including FAQs or strategy guides, cheats, forums, and other players in and out of multiplayer settings" (p. 13). Playing a game can encourage collaboration and shift the student's role from passive consumer to active producer (Squire, 2011; Gee & Hayes, 2010).

In playing a game and understanding how the game system works, patterns emerge. As Koster (2005) explains, humans are natural pattern seekers. There are patterns in nature, politics, ethics, and social behavior, all of which can be expressed dynamically in a game. As each person uses an acquired knowledge of systems and identifies her place within those systems, she creates a frame or multiple frames for viewing reality. According to Lakoff (2008), human beings can hold contradictory frames of understanding and belief. In a learning environment, a teacher can guide a student in exploring systems of understanding to identify the frames that she is constructing while also challenging her to examine them.

A teacher must identify the best games for teaching and understand how to use them. Not all games are well-suited to the educational environment and not all educational games serve the purpose of advancing 21st century skills. Many educational games mimic traditional educational methods, doing little to incorporate the innovative ways that video games can interactively engage students. Gee states that a good game is one where the way a game is designed to be played is perfectly married to the problem to be solved (2011). Consensus about what constitutes a quality educational video game is still being researched and has yet to be established. To this end, Squire (2010) stated that there is a need for designers of serious and educational games to establish common standards for creating good games.

Using This Medium as a Teaching Tool

While teachers must determine how games meet curricular needs, many online games and accompanying websites provide teaching materials and guides. Most games have built-in tutorials that guide a player in learning how to play the game. The biggest obstacle to using digital game-based learning is the time it takes to evaluate the game (Oblinger, 2006). There must be "careful analysis and a matching of the content, strengths, and weaknesses of the game to the content to be studied" (Van Eck, 2006, p. 22). Similarly, assigning game making depends upon the tools that students will use, their available time, and the curricular goals.

Once a teacher has determined the curricular goal, she can then decide what game genre would be best suited for her purpose. For example, Van Eck (2006) suggests that *Sim City* could be a great supplement to a civil engineering course because it requires a grasp of city planning and calls attention to several problems, both logistically and socially, that are inherent in creating sustainable city and regional planning.

Video games require different amounts of time to play. A teacher must decide how much instructional time can be devoted to playing a game and whether it will be played individually, in small groups, or as a class. If the course is online, students may be assigned to play an online game. In a classroom, some games lend themselves to a team's approach that might use a SMART board or projector during a single class period. The simulation about buoyancy mentioned above could be

used to illustrate a point or given as an assignment for individuals or teams to use in conjunction with a lecture, reading, or lab assignment. For some lessons, it may be appropriate to use a game that can be played over a few days or weeks. Many commercial games take 50-60 hours of time to play, so using them would require a teacher to plan carefully. Alternatively, nonprofit organizations and museums have created or gathered many useful titles on their websites, offering shorter and often free games. (Please see suggestions below.)

Evaluating student learning can be done in several ways; it depends upon the assessment tools that the teacher uses. A class discussion may be a viable way to evaluate and expand upon student learning. Students can be given worksheets, asked to write journals, or papers, give demonstrations, diagram aspects of game play demonstrating systems thinking, or use screens shots from the game to analyze how they made choices within the game that demonstrate problem solving or analytical thinking (McCall, 2011). In some cases, looking at the end or win state can indicate how the student thought and reasoned through the game challenges. Actually, all games provide player feedback. According to Gee and Shaffer (2010), "games are nothing *but* good assessment. The player is always being tested, given feedback, and challenged to get better" (p. 16). Some games provide a small amount of user and teacher feedback such as how far a student is in a game and their final score. At this point, "technology development has outpaced the assessment development" (Steinkuehler, 2011). Incorporating this into educational games is a growing field, but at present there are few examples of it. Embedded assessment allows a student to be assessed as part of the learning activity rather than with a test that occurs at a later time. "When diagnostic learning tasks continually assess the development of learners, we get a portrait of problem solving decisions in real time. We can provide feedback to customize learning, and we can probe the strengths and weaknesses of students' thinking" (Gee & Shaffer, 2010, p. 9).

Examples from Learning Environments

In a review of the literature, Van Eck (2006) identified three ways that games are being used with students:

- Educators build educational games themselves or with a game developer;
- Students design and build or modify games; and
- Educators integrate commercial off-the-shelf (COTS) and online games into the curriculum.

These different approaches frame the choices about how teachers can use games with students. Using video games with students requires planning and a degree of familiarity with video games, such as being able to select game genres to meet curriculum goals, knowing basic game terms, and taking time to play games that one selects for use with students.

This section will focus primarily on Van Eck's second and third methods, having students design and make games and using existing games, after briefly addressing the first method. The section will provide several examples of how students have designed games and learned from playing them, as well as examples of how existing games have been used with students. The first part highlights how a math teacher created a game for his students. The second part provides examples of students making games in several venues: a Global Kids community program, a graduate level Architecture class, and Quest to Learn, a middle school in New York City. This is followed by brief descriptions of "modding" (changing an existing game) and using game engines. The third part includes examples of how games can or are being used as teaching tools, including an elementary art classroom using

Gamestar Mechanic, iCivics games being used to learn about the U.S. government, simulation games in high school history classes, and how *World of Warcraft* was used after school in a high school to increase retention. Because these examples include a wide age range (fourth grade through graduate school), some may be more relevant than others for different readers. In these examples, the term "game" is used in a general way to designate video games and simulations games. It is worth mentioning that an educator who takes the time to build a game with a simple game engine may gain valuable knowledge about game design that could inform an assignment that requires students to make a game.

1. Educators Build Educational Games

There are varying degrees of complexity involved in making a video game to use with students. A common obstacle is lack of programming skills. Game engines vary along a continuum of complexity that may or may not require the user to know how to program. Many of the simulations found on the Phet website mentioned above were made by a single person. Making less complex games or simulations may be within the ability of many people, especially since software tools are becoming more and more available and easy to use.

How a Math Teacher Made a Game for Middle School Students

It usually requires a team of people to build a complex, well-researched game that addresses relevant curriculum goals and includes artwork, working game mechanics, and embedded assessment. However, sometimes a teacher familiar with content and student difficulties is in the best position to design a game.

Ko's Journey (from Imagination Education) is a video game that teaches math concepts to middle school students in a rich story environment that requires the player to learn mathematics concepts. Scott Laidlaw (2009) has been teaching mathematics for several years. As a teacher, he understood the potential of games to teach and capture students' imagination, especially in the case of underachieving students. Explaining his process, Laidlaw (2010) describes four steps:

- Pick a story;
- Make a goal;
- Have a turn-based structure; and
- Make a prototype and test it with students.

To make the game, Laidlaw had help from the school community. Parent volunteers painted hand-sewn deer hides to make the prototype. Students moved stone totems around the deer-hide playing area that was spread on the floor. Students played the prototype game before it was developed into a story-based web application.

In the game, the main character, Ko, has to use her mathematics skills to navigate the terrain by learning Cartesian coordinate mapping. She also learns a whole curriculum of core mathematics concepts, including linear equations, ratios, and fractions. These are concepts that most kids do not have any context for learning. In the game's environment, though, they are motivated to learn so they can progress and complete the journey. By the end, they have experienced real applications for mathematics skills.

2. Students Make Games

Building games inherently teaches good teamwork skills, technology literacy, brainstorming skills, and time management. ... Beyond the intrinsic lessons of building games, games are potentially a positive and engaging medium for representing models on various topics of study." (Magerko, 2009, pp. 1276-1277)

Playing a game teaches players how the game system works, providing choices and user feedback. Students use their analytical and problem-solving skills and evidence-based reasoning to figure out what they need to know to do a given task or reach a goal. Making a game requires these same skills, but on an even deeper level. It is comparable to the way that being able to teach a topic requires that one really knows the material. Making a game requires that one really understand strategies, relationships, and interactions between both the game system and its content. It also requires the designer to consider how the game will provide user feedback and assess progress.

Making a game can be a creative act for students. Much like writing a novel, making artwork, or designing a science experiment, they are all ways to "play" with ideas. Robinson (2006) cites two different ways of knowing—"rational and emotional"—which he attributes to the work of Daniel Goleman (p. 146). Balancing the rational and emotional selves gives people the freedom both to make significant connections and to create. Making a game combines many ways of knowing and understanding. It requires an understanding of design principles, the creation artwork, the combination of visual images to represent ideas, and demonstrations of relationships, connections, and influences. Games give users a way to control these variables, thereby making their own meaning.

Problem solving, which is necessary for many academic tasks, is a creative act (Robinson, 2006). As Robinson (2006) explains, this understanding is often ignored in academia. Exiling our "feelings [from academic content] is a structural feature of academicism. The division between intellect and emotion was a deliberate strategy in the intellectual revolutions of the Enlightenment and in the cultural reaction of Romanticism" (p. 140). The author asserts that in considering games, academics should reconsider this situation. While many discussions about using video games for teaching and learning focus on how games support STEM areas, integrating socioemotional intelligence and art as part of the educational experience are also necessary (Gee & Hayes, 2010). According to Gee and Hayes, "there is no real divide between technology and art." They argue that it is the arts that "drive us to see things in new ways leading to new solutions" (2010, p. 15).

Below are a few examples that illustrate how students making games supports learning. Students making games is an important aspect of students as producers. Making games allows them to play with systems (Zimmerman, 2011). He explained that designers see the world as "constructible" and that as world issues are increasingly interdisciplinary and complex, bringing innovation and creativity to bear in game-making is how students can learn systems thinking and thus be able to address and understand complex problems such as pandemics, global poverty, or financial collapse.

Global Kids: Making Games in a Non-academic Environment

Realizing the power of games to express and understand social situations, Global Kids, a nonprofit educational organization, uses game design as a way for young people to learn about global issues and create serious games through its Playing 4 Keeps program. *Consent!* is a game that was created by high school students to explore the life of an African American male who is sentenced to 50 years in prison and subjected to medical research. It was created in Teen Second Life, an online virtual environment. (See the project video here: http://www.youtube.com/watch?v=Jx9XJDYOC 9s&feature=player_embedded#at=24.)

Ayiti: The Cost of Life is a game about poverty in Haiti. Players must manage a rural family of five, keep them healthy, and educate them through the course of the game. (See a video about it here: http://www.youtube.com/watch?v=vfhW V7kQQdM&feature=player_embedded#at=19.) The students who designed *Ayiti* did such a good

job that it was developed into a fully conceived video game.

Another group of students researched human trafficking. Their project used Second Life to make a dramatic video or *Machinima*. The heroine of the video is "Talia," a girl who is taken from Mexico to the US on the pretense of becoming a model, when in reality she was forced into prostitution and treated as a prisoner. Although the video is not technically a game, it is an extension and repurposing of the game environment. (See the video here: http://www.olpglobalkids.org/library/)

Architecture Class: Graduate Students Make Games

Ann Pendleton-Jullian, a professor of architecture, uses game making to change the way her students think about their design projects. While at Cornell, she designed an undergraduate studio that "began with the playing of games, the analysis of game-play and then the design of the games themselves" (Pendleton-Jullian, 2010a, p. 154). She states that the studio experience of playing, analyzing, and designing games made her students more successful with their architectural projects. Pendelton-Jullian thinks that making a game requires students to "construct society and negotiate relationships" (2010b, presentation). This belief has stayed with her over the years, and she continues to use game making as a teaching method.

Working at Ohio State University (OSU), Pendleton-Jullian gave her graduate students a series of game-related activities. The first assignment was for students to work together in pairs to choose a game from a provided list and analyze their game play. Hristina Panovska, one of her students, explained that this deep level of analysis really helped her to think strategically. Following the initial assignment, she created *Duplo*, a physical game (see Figure 2).

Panovska was able to transfer her deeper sense of spatial relationships to her final project. She

Figure 2. Designed and built by Panovska, Duplo has a game board on top and a magnetized game board underneath with a mirror to reflect the underside. Some of the spaces connected both sides of the game board, represented by the see-through game spaces on the grid. (© 2008, Hristina Panovska. Used with permission.)

defined her project by setting up a "playing field" with three variables: a game board and game pieces #1 and #2. The land is analogous to a playing board used in games. The live objects are game pieces #1: humans, animals, insects, and trees. The constructed objects are game pieces #2. A tree grid dictates where the "architectural pieces" go (see Figure 3). She also considered the vertical spaces to be "playing fields" (see illustration of tiers below, Figure 4). Panovska explains:

The vertical striations (the tiers) is an exploration of the site vertically and setting up another "playing field"—the experiential field as one navigates the architecture as they occupy the space below, in between, and above the tree grid. This sets up a combination of variables of how you would "play" or "use" the site. (personal communication, February 28, 2011)

Pendleton-Jullian (2010b) used game making with students because she believes it fosters "elastic dispositions." She explains that students who will be successful in the future are those who are willing to change their focus and change their minds, thereby able to see things differently and collaborate as part of a diverse team.

Figure 3. The tee grid "playing field". (© 2008, Hristina Panovska. Used with permission.)

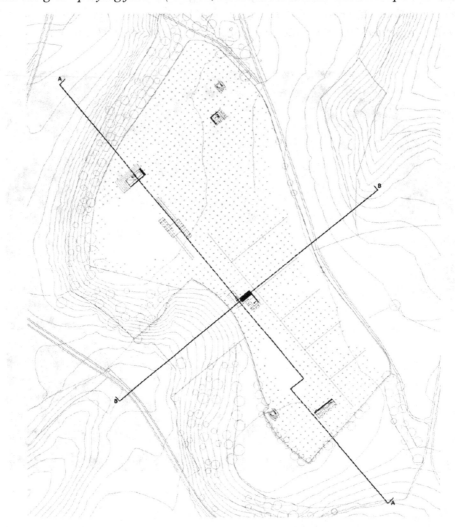

Figure 4. Vertical "playing fields" or tiers. (© 2008, Hristina Panovska. Used with permission.)

BIOMASS

CANOPY

GRID

PASTURE

Quest to Learn: A School Where Students Both Make and Play Games

Quest to Learn is a public school in New York City that is focused on systems thinking and game design while incorporating a standards-based curriculum. "The big idea of the school is we looked at how games work—literally how they're built and the way they support learning—and we thought could we design a school from the ground up that supported learning in the way games do," explained Salen, one of the Executive Directors at the school (Chaplin, 2010).

There are four primary ways that the school structures learning at Quest to Learn: learning is rigorous but engaging, games are used purposefully (meaning that the "learning itself is structured like a game"), digital media are well integrated, and digital literacy is supported (Salen, 2010). For example, structuring learning like a game means that students are given a problem that creates a need to know fractions and decimals.

Salen (2010) explained that there are three dimensions of competency that are measured or assessed: 21st century skills, state standards, and social, emotional, and physical dimensions that focus children's attention on what it means to be both human and a citizen. The teachers use models, simulations, and social networks; they encourage students to do and produce, making connections with their lives inside and outside of the school. Their goal is to make school relevant and engaging, resulting in deep learning. Salen (2010) defines 21st century skills as "complex problem-solving, models and simulation, working in cross-functional teams, participatory learning, intelligent resourcing or knowing how to find information and resources, credibility, and judgment" (presentation).

At Quest to Learn, data visualization tools are put into the hands of students. Each morning, a typical student logs on to *About Me*, a non-academic school site that focuses on wellness. Students can create an image or emoticon using drag and drop features to make a face that represents how they are feeling. This data can be charted so that students can make connections between how they are feeling and what they are doing, enabling them to identify patterns about themselves.

All of the units are structured as missions, with smaller, scaffolded quests that build knowledge. Students work in teams to discuss what they are learning and to collaborate in building theories. For example, social studies is combined with language. In order to understand how civilizations operate as systems, they look at its components: geography, technology, forms of government, and forms of religion in a given community. Then students considered how those elements work together to form systems. "Systems thinking," Salen said, "gives you a tool to manage complexity" (as cited in Chaplin, 2010, Section, para. 4).

Al Doyle (personal communication, May 25, 2010), a former teacher at Quest to Learn, described one student's experience. Doyle asked the student, "what have you learned by designing games?" The student responded, "it made all my other work seem easy." Doyle continued to explain that this was a student who had previously struggled with math, science, and history, feeling overwhelmed by the topics:

because he's doing these very complex games, and he's breaking things down into little pieces, and he's seeing relationships. It really made those other things manageable. (personal communication)

Modding

Modding is similar to what teachers have done for years, adapt existing content to fit their particular needs. Game environments are allowing players to do something similar. This emerging 21st century skill is an activity whereby an existing game can be changed or "modified" by the users, allowing them a great deal of control and self-expression (Wright, 2006). At one time, this was an achievement accomplished only by hackers. However, the desire to change one's game map, add levels, change the game play, and add content has resulted in many game companies providing modding tools and source code. *World of Warcraft, Civilization, Sims,* and *Little Big Planet* (a game designed to teach players to become level designers) are a few examples of games that support modding. Modding has created a thriving and growing community of producers and designers who communicate and share through websites, collaborative-learning communities, and forums. Communities that players have created "display a great deal of what has been called social and emotional intelligence," terms Gee and Hayes (2010) attribute to Goleman, mentioned above. (p. 39) Modding is a clear example of students as active producers. It gives students an opportunity to actively engage with content in a meaningful and creative way. Additionally, thinking through how to modify a game can be easier for some students than designing a whole game.

Using Game Engines

Making games is another example of how students can become producers. Game making is also a means of demonstrating learning. In addition, game making requires students to use many 21st century skills. Game engines are software systems that supply the game maker with readymade actions, sprites (images or animations), and environments. Using game engines can simplify the process and some can be used without knowing how to write code. When assigning game making, be aware that making games is an iterative process and has similarities to designing a scientific experiment. Before using game engines or software tools, students can make a prototype, using paper, pencils, scissors, tokens, or dice to create and test out initial designs.

Gamestar Mechanic is a game engine that requires no programing skills. Players learn game design by playing and fixing a series of games.

Another example of a game engine is Microsoft's *Kodu,* an easy 3-D game engine. *Scratch* is another game making and animation tool for beginning programmers. Students using these game engines can share their projects with others online. All three have companion teacher resources. Other game engines include *Sploder* and *Gamemaker*. More sophisticated game engines include *Unity 3D, Panda 3D, Torque,* and *Thinking Worlds*. Wikis, forums, and tutorials are available for those who want to learn to use game engines.

3. Use of an Existing Game or COTS Game

Games are a new medium. Teaching students how to use a game is similar to teaching them how to use a book. One must be as critical when teaching games as one would in any other medium. Games put forward social commentary, they are made for advertisement and propaganda, and they can be compared and contrasted. Students can question a designer's message by explaining how a game is persuading or putting forth a particular frame for how to understand a given topic. As described above, Global Kids uses making games as a way to discuss and research social problems and issues. Many subjects can be explored through games, including anthropological issues concerning identity, race, feminism, and the concept of "other." Students can question how games are both changing and being used in society. In addition, games can be used to make the world a better place, encouraging people to work together for common goals and even creating a collective intelligence through crowdsourcing.

Jane McGonigal is well-known for her Alternate Reality Games (ARG), such as *World without Oil*. ARGs are interactive narratives that involve multiple people, media, and game elements to create games that happen in the real world. At the time of this writing, her latest game is *Evoke*. According to McGonigal, "the goal of the social network game is to help empower young people all over the world, and especially young people in Africa, to come up with creative solutions to our most urgent social problems" (Alchemy, 2010). Playing *Evoke* teaches players what they need to know in order to start a business.

McGonigal is doing something really remarkable. After considering the skills that are developed playing games, she has found ways to direct that knowledge and enthusiasm for games into making the world a better place. Through playing ARGs, people can effect real-world change that makes their learning significant and meaningful. Playing an ARG can change you; and it can contribute to something real, like discovering a cure for cancer by figuring out how proteins fold by playing *Foldit*. *Foldit*, which was developed at the University of Washington (http://fold.it/portal/), is a multiplayer online game that engages non-scientists in solving hard prediction problems. *Foldit* players interact with protein structures using direct manipulation tools and user-friendly versions of algorithms from the Rosetta structure prediction methodology, while they compete and collaborate to optimize the computed energy. (Cooper, Khatib, Treuille, Barbero, Lee, Beenen, Leaver-Fay, Baker, Popović, & Foldit players, 2010)

The players of *Foldit* were cited as authors on a published paper. Interviews with players described adults who come home after work and want to play *Foldit* to relax with an engaging activity. In this case, playing a game can change the world. See *Foldit: Biology for gamers* by Nature Video (2010).

Using Gamestar Mechanic in an Elementary Art Classroom

Gamestar Mechanic is unique in that it is both a game and a game engine. Its purpose is to teach game design through playing and fixing games. It is designed for 4th through 9th graders, although it could be used with older students. Math, reading, writing, and story composition, including how music and artwork contribute to storytelling, can all be easily combined with the activities in *Gamestar Mechanic*. As students work through levels, they learn the principles of game design and how to use tools to make games. Art class is an ideal place to teach game design because it incorporates the concepts of balance, use of space, color, and how these elements can combine to tell a story or describe a social issue.

Figure 5. Gamestar Mechanic website. (© 2011, E-Line Media. Used with permission.)

The author and an elementary art teacher used *Gamestar Mechanic* with fourth-grade students. The teacher led a preliminary unit on comic books that was adapted so that it would support making games. Students made a three-panel comic with an avatar/main character, an obstacle to overcome, and a goal. This became the story for students to draw upon when they designed their first game. Students played *Gamestar Mechanic* for eight classes over a four-week period.

To introduce the topic, the author discussed games in general by using examples of games the students were familiar with, such as football, *Monopoly*, and chess. Virtual game space was related to physical game spaces: a football field, a monopoly board, and a chessboard. Similarly, the author also discussed how the game tokens represent the player in *Monopoly*, and how this compared to how an avatar virtually represents a player. As a class, we also identified the goals

of each game. Further discussion examined how obstacles in the game are part of the rules of the game. In *Gamestar Mechanic*, the rules and obstacles comprise the game mechanics, or what the player can and cannot do. Using game design terms, relating them to familiar games, and introducing some of these terms in the comic book lesson helped the students grasp the concepts.

After the first few days of playing *Gamestar Mechanic* in the computer lab, the author discussed principles of game design with the students as it related to the *Gamestar Mechanic* environment and the games they had already played. Using a projector connected to the internet, students were shown episodes and missions within the game in order to discuss how they related to game design: space, rules, game mechanics, enemy and avatar settings, stationary obstacles, moving enemies as obstacles, and creating a goal. This reinforced

Figure 6. In the workshop, players use the sprites they have earned on the left to make games. Clicking the settings allows players to create levels, write directions, make choices about the game environment and adjust settings. Using the toolbar on the right, players can select, delete, copy, and adjust setting on the sprites. (© 2011, E-Line Media. Used with permission.)

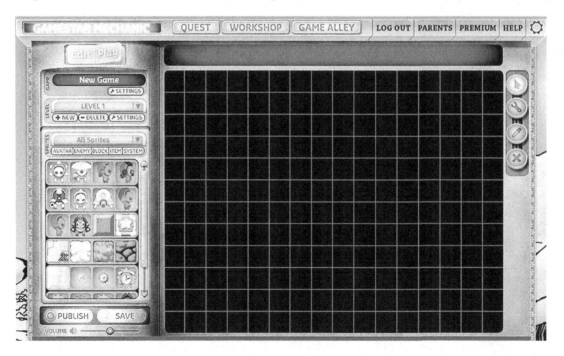

the game terminology that had been introduced in the initial lesson.

Students may make games at any point using the toolbox in the workshop area; sprites are earned by winning games. Students who complete Episode 5 may post their games in Game Alley, an area where *Gamestar Mechanic* games can be shared with other game makers. It provides a section called *my class* where all of the students' work can be gathered together. Each game provides an area for reviewers to make comments, and the author gave students individual feedback about their games, making suggestions for improvements, new levels, and things to consider trying.

During the last class, a few students were asked to present their games. As each game was presented, a classmate played the game while other students watched on the classroom projector. Students and instructors gave feedback on what they liked about the games and suggestions for improvements.

Using iCivics Games in the History Classroom

iCivics is a website that provides several fun, engaging, and easy-to-learn games about U.S. government. It was created in response to Sandra Day O'Connor's vision of providing educational games that could be used in school and at home to teach people about how the U.S. government functions. In the "for teachers" section of the site there are webquests (an inquiry-based, online tool where students explore and evaluate information from websites that are selected by the teacher), descriptions of how to use the games through curriculum units, lesson plans, worksheets, and a list of state standards that each game addresses. The games, which can be played during a single class period or saved and played over several days, have simple embedded assessments that provide teachers and students with a few statistics about how each game was played. In these games, achieving

particular goals and advancing to new levels does indicate levels of content mastery.

Do I Have a Right? is a game that explores the Bill of Rights within a constitutional law firm. It would probably take a few class periods for everyone to play through the whole game, but when students finish it they will have a firm grasp of several constitutional amendments and how lawyers apply them to determine what rights citizens have and which amendments are applicable to certain courtroom cases. Through the game play, "clients" come into a law firm and request legal counsel. The player decides if the problem is a legal issue and which lawyer (based upon their amendment expertise) can help the client. As the players win more cases, they can make their office more comfortable for clients and hire more lawyers, thereby increasing the number of amendments that the lawyers specialize in, which in turn helps the players win more cases.

Another game on the iCivics website is *Executive Command*, a game about what it is like to be the President of the United States. Players have a lot of choices about how to spend their time: diplomacy, speaking to congress about special interests, stopping or starting wars, and reading proposed bills related to energy policy, spending, education, and health.

These are just two of several games on the website. They are especially well-suited to middle school students, although they could also be used with older students. Students could be asked to make connections to current presidential policies, initiatives, and positions and then discuss or write about the connections.

Using Simulation Games to Teach High School History

Jeremiah McCall, a high school history teacher, uses simulation games such as *Rome: Total War* because they help students visualize and comprehend complex historical situations. McCall (2011) stresses that knowing how to play

Figure 7. Do I have a Right? In the upper left corner is the opening title screen. As players begin, there are messages that help the player quickly learn how the interface works. The background fades and messages appear to point out where the tools are and what to do (upper right). As the player progresses, clients come more often. As the lawyers win their cases, the player gains points so she can hire more lawyers (lower left). The interface on the lower right helps the players to decide which lawyers to hire next. Choices include lawyers with different amendment specialty. (© 2011, iCivics Inc. Used with permission.)

the game himself is essential so that he can give students a solid introduction to the game and help them when they are confused or stuck by offering strategies. He notes that more game-savvy students can help those who are unfamiliar with playing video games. Students who can step in as experts to guide others have a genuine opportunity to contribute to the class. In some cases, McCall provides some strategies upfront so that students can progress more quickly.

To use a game with students, McCall (2011) lists four activities that need to occur: "students need to learn to play, gain solid play experience, observe and analyze the game in action, and have time to reflect and debrief" (p. 72). McCall explains that he first teaches students how to play the game. He also provides observation sheets and prompts to guide student thinking and game play. Students demonstrate their work through blogs, journals, formal papers, charts or annotated screen shots to analyze content, and diagrams of systems identified in the game. For McCall (2010), playing games is about learning—whether or not it is fun is not his primary concern. He explained that writing a paper is not necessarily fun, but that's no reason to stop assigning them (presentation).

After asking about the accuracy of something in the game environment, students may be asked to "extrapolate from that system to consider real world past and present problems" (p. 98).

Using *World of Warcraft* after School to Encourage Retention

Steinkuehler (2010), who has done extensive research on multi-player online environments, is exploring how games can ameliorate the problem of struggling readers who are failing in schools. In working with students who play *World of Warcraft*, she found that students who were reading at the sixth or seventh grade level were able to read at the twelfth grade level or higher if they were allowed to choose their own texts about the game. Their self-correction rates were 33%, which is much higher than is typical. These students were so interested in the topic that they took the time to figure out what the texts meant.

Peggy Sheehy is an ITF/Media Specialist who created a special after school program using *World of Warcraft*. She worked with a guidance counselor to select a group of "fringe kids with no tribe," many of whom had learning disorders. After school, the students gathered for 2 hours to play *World of Warcraft* and, through the process, wrote character descriptions. Because of this process, the students' writing improved, as was confirmed by the school's English teacher. *World of Warcraft* served as a narrative space, making learning relevant. In other activities, the students negotiated naming their guild, wrote campaign speeches for themselves or others who they nominated for guild position; after the elections, they had an induction ceremony. The students were invested, as a group, in *World of Warcraft*, and their school behavior, grades, and school attendance rates improved. As part of *World of Warcraft*, Sheehy's students became part of something bigger than themselves, learned social skills, and became motivated to do their classwork (P. Sheehy, personal communication, 2010).

FUTURE RESEARCH

The author has identified three areas where more research is needed:

- Game researchers, scholars, and designers need to create standards and establish best practices for what constitutes a quality educational game.
- More studies that demonstrate how games support learning in the classroom are needed.
- More research about designing and incorporating assessment into a learning game is needed.

Once games that provide assessments for teachers become more available, research that establishes how to rethink and redesign the existing evaluation and grading processes will be needed.

The first would contribute to creating quality educational games. The second would yield needed data about using games with students in classrooms, and the third would enable teachers to rely upon assessment data from game play rather than test scores. It would also allow the teacher to evaluate a student's thinking process and student would receive in-game feedback.

In addition, more research is needed about how to overcome barriers to using games in the classroom and other learning environments. From reviewing the literature, this researcher believes that teacher training is essential. Research is needed to determine whether short training videos about specific games would enable teachers to quickly learn what a game is about without having to play the game for several hours or read through a long teacher's guide. That is not to say that a teacher who wants to use games shouldn't play games. Having an understanding about current games and how to play different kinds of games will help a teacher understand the student experience and, potentially, boost teacher confidence about using games. This combined with training could go a long way toward creating avenues for games to enter learning environments.

CONCLUSION

As Dewey explained in 1897, "the teacher is not in the school to impose certain ideas or to form certain habits in the child, but is there as a member of the community to select the influences which shall affect the child and to assist them in properly responding to these influences" (2008, p. 129). We now view what Dewey was describing as a paradigm shift from "sage on the stage" to "guide on the side". Over 100 years have passed since Dewey wrote *My Pedagogic Creed* and we are still entrenched in the factory model of education, ignoring much of what we know from research about learning and cognitive development. Digital games and their effectiveness in teaching 21st century learning skills may provide the impetus to embrace Dewey's idea about the nature of learning and the purpose of formal education: It is primarily a social institution. He believed that education should support both the psychological and sociological aspects of a child's development, building upon children's interests and abilities and connecting them to the community. He stated that "education ... is a process of living and not a preparation for future living" (p. 127). Game-based learning advocates students' use of games as a process of engaging in real-world activities, participating in communities of practice, and becoming producers (Jenkins, 2006; Gee & Hayes, 2010; Gee & Shaffer, 2010; Prensky, 2010; Shaffer, 2006; Squire, 2011).

As more games are created with assessment features for teachers, the burden on teachers to evaluate student learning with tests and quizzes can be lifted (Gee & Shaffer, 2010) and move us from the testing frenzy that has captivated the minds of legislators and engendered fear in the teaching community. Furthermore, how to use embedded assessment in games has to be under-stood and incorporated into teaching practices. Games and simulated game environments that create a community of practice for players could potentially transform the way that students think about what they are learning, fulfilling Dewey's vision of education as a "process of living" and making education more relevant for students.

REFERENCES

Akilli, G. K. (2007). Games and simulations: A new approach in education? In Gibson, D., Aldrich, C., & Prensky, M. (Eds.), *Games and simulations in online learning: Research and development frameworks* (pp. 1–20). London, UK: Information Science Publishing, Idea Group, Inc.

Alchemy. (January 2010). *About the EVOKE game*. Retrieved from http://blog.urgentevoke.net/2010/01/27/about-the-evoke-game/

Annetta, L. A. (2008). Video games in education: Why they should be used and how they are being used. *Theory into Practice, 47*, 229–239. doi:10.1080/00405840802153940

Baek, Y. K. (2008). What hinders teachers in using computer and video games in the classroom? Exploring factors inhibiting the uptake of computer and video games. *Cyberpsychology & Behavior, 11*(6), 665–671. doi:10.1089/cpb.2008.0127

Becker, K. (2007). Digital game-based learning once removed: Teaching teachers. *British Journal of Educational Technology, 38*(3), 478–488. doi:10.1111/j.1467-8535.2007.00711.x

Becker, K. (2010). Chapter 2: Distinctions between games and learning: A review of current literature on games in education. In R. Van Eck (Ed.), *Gaming and cognition: Theories and practice from the learning sciences* (pp. 22-54). Hershey, PA: Information Science Reference, IGI Global.

Bogost, I. (2008). The rhetoric of video games. In K. Salen (Ed.), *The ecology of games: Connecting youth, games, and learning* (pp. 117-139). The John D. and Catherine T. MacArthur Foundation Series on Digital Media and Learning. Cambridge, MA: The MIT Press.

Brown, S. L., & Vaughan, C. (2009). *Play: How it shapes the brain, opens the imagination, and invigorates the soul*. New York, NY: Avery.

Campbell, G. (Interviewer) & Medina, J. (Interviewee). (n.d.). *Personal interview*. Retrieved from http://hw.libsyn.com/p/5/c/6/5c614405b3bd577f/37-brainscience-Medina.mp3?sid=6341d3776c2c99f93b0aa9d671dd523b&l_sid=18369&l_eid=&l_mid=1550378

Chaplin, H. (June 28, 2010). Schools use video games to teach thinking skills. *National Public Radio*. [radio news station]. Retrieved from http://www.npr.org/templates/story/story.php?storyId=128081896.

Charsky, D. (2010). Chapter 9: Making a connection: Game genres, game characteristics, and teaching structures. In R. Van Eck (Ed.), *Gaming and cognition: Theories and practice from the learning sciences* (pp. 189-212) Hershey, PA: Information Science Reference, IGI Global.

Charsky, D., & Mims, C. (2008). Integrating commercial off-the-shelf video games into school curriculums. *TechTrends, 52*(5), 38–44. doi:10.1007/s11528-008-0195-0

Chen, J. (2007). Flow in games (and everything else). *Communications of the ACM, 50*(4), 31–34. doi:10.1145/1232743.1232769

Cooper, S., Khatib, F., Treuille, A., Barbero, J., Lee, J., & Beenen, M. … Foldit players. (2010) Predicting protein structures with a multiplayer online game. *Nature, 466*, 756-760. Retrieved from http://www.nature.com/nature/journal/v466/n7307/full/nature09304.html.

Csikszentmihalyi, M. (1990). *FLOW: The psychology of optimal experience*. New York, NY: Harper and Row.

Dewey, J. (2008). My pedagogic creed. In Pestritto, R. J., & Atto, W. J. (Eds.), *American progressivism: A reader* (pp. 125–134). New York, NY: Lexington Books.

Epistemic Games. (2011). *Website*. Retrieved February 20, 2011, from http://epistemicgames.org/eg/category/games/front/

Galarneau, L., & Zibit, M. (2007). Online games for 21st century skills. In Gibson, D., Aldrich, C., & Prensky, M. (Eds.), *Games and simulations in online learning: Research and development frameworks* (pp. 59–88). Hershey, PA: Information Science Publishing, Idea Group, Inc.

Gardner, H. (1999). *Intelligence reframed: Multiple intelligences for the 21st century*. New York, NY: Basic Books.

Gee, J. P. (2004). *Situated language and learning: A critique of traditional schooling*. New York, NY: Routledge.

Gee, J. P. (2007). *What video games have to teach us about learning and literacy*. New York, NY: Palgrave Macmillan.

Gee, J. P. (May 26, 2010). *Games and assessment discussion*. Games for Change Conference. New York.

Gee, J. P. (June 17, 2011). *The invective-filled tirade I would like to give if I wasn't so nice: A chat*. Games+Learning+Society Conference. Madison, Wisconsin.

Gee, J. P., & Hayes, E. R. (2010). *Women and gaming: The Sims and 21st century learning*. New York, NY: Palgrave Macmillan.

Gee, J. P., & Shaffer, D. W. (2010). Looking where the light is bad: Video games and the future of assessment. *Edge, 6*(1), 1–19.

Heinich, R., Molenda, M., Russell, J. D., & Smaldino, S. E. (1996). *Instructional media and technologies for learning, 5/E.* Englewood Cliffs, NJ: Prentice-Hall, Inc., Simon & Schuster Company.

Huzinga, J. (1950). *Homo Ludens: A study of the play-element in culture.* Boston, MA: Beacon Press.

Jenkins, H. (2006). *Convergence culture: Where old and new media collide.* New York, NY: New York University Press.

Jenkins, H., Clinton, K., Purushotma, R., Robison, A. J., & Weigel, M. (2006) *Confronting the challenges of participatory culture: Media education for the 21st century* [white paper]. MacArthur Foundation.

Johnson, L., Smith, R., Willis, H., Levine, A., & Haywood, K. (2011). *The 2011 horizon report.* Austin, TX: The New Media Consortium.

Ke, F., & Grabowski, B. (2007). Gameplaying for maths learning: Cooperative or not? *British Journal of Educational Technology, 38*(2), 249–259. doi:10.1111/j.1467-8535.2006.00593.x

Klawe, M. M. (1999). *Computer games, education and interfaces: The E-GEMS project,* (pp. 36-39). Retrieved from http://www.informatik.uni-trier.de/~ley/db/conf/graphicsinterface/graphicsinterface1999.html

Klopfer, E., Osterweil, S., Groff, J., & Haas, J. (2009a). *Using the technology of today, in the classroom of today: The instructional power of digital games, social networking, simulations and how teachers can leverage them* [white paper]. The Education Arcade, MIT.

Klopfer, E., Osterweil, S., & Salen, K. (2009b) *Moving learning games forward: Obstacles, opportunities, & openness* [white paper]. The Education Arcade, MIT.

Koster, R. (2005). *A theory of fun for game design.* Scottsdale, AZ: Paraglyph Press.

Laidlaw, S. (2009, October 3). *The top 10 most important concepts in middle-school math.* Retrieved from http://www.imagineeducation.org/matharticles/

Laidlaw, S. (2010, January 31). *History of imagine education and our story-based math.* Retrieved from http://www.imagineeducation.org/matharticles/

Lakoff, G. (2008). *The political mind: Why you can't understand 21st-century American politics with an 18th-century brain.* New York, NY: Viking, Penguin Books.

Magerko, B. (2009). The future of digital game-based learning. In Ferdig, R. E. (Ed.), *Handbook of research on effective electronic gaming in education* (*Vol. III*, pp. 1274–1288). Hershey, PA: Information Science Reference.

Marino, M. T., Basham, J. D., & Beecher, C. C. (2011). Using video games as an alternative science assessment for students with disabilities and at-risk learners. *Science Scope, 34*(5), 36–41.

McCall, J. (October 4, 2010). *Gaming the past: Simulation games in history class.* Goldberg Center and Digital Union Game-based Learning Conference. Columbus, Ohio.

McCall, J. (2011). *Gaming the past: Using video games to teach secondary history.* New York, NY: Routledge.

McGonigal, J. (1011). *Reality is broken: Why games make us better and how they can change the world.* New York, NY: Penguin Group.

McLellan, H. (1996). Being digital: Implications for education. *Educational Technology, 36*(6), 5–20.

Medina, J. (2008). *Brain rules: 12 principles for surviving and thriving at work, home, and school.* Seattle, WA: Pear Press.

Medina, J. (n.d.). *Interview by Ginger Campbell*. Retrieved from http://hw.libsyn.com/p/5/c/6/5c614405b3bd577f/37-brainscience-Medina.mp3?sid=6341d3776c2c99f93b0aa9d671dd523b&l_sid=18369&l_eid=&l_mid=1550378.

Mizuko, I. (2008) Education vs. entertainment: A cultural history of children's software. In K. Salen (Ed.), *The ecology of games: Connecting youth, games, and learning* (pp. 89–116). The John D. and Catherine T. MacArthur Foundation Series on Digital Media and Learning. Cambridge, MA: The MIT Press.

Morrison, G. R., Lowther, D. L., & DeMeulle, L. (1999). *Integrating computer technology into the classroom*. Upper Saddle River, NJ: Prentice Hall.

National Research Council. (2011). *Incentives and test-based accountability in public education. Committee on Incentives and Test-Based Accountability in Public Education*. Washington, DC: The National Academies Press.

Nature Video. (2010). *Foldit: Biology for gamers* [video].Retrieved from http://www.youtube.com/watch?v=axN0xdhznhY

Ng, F., Plass, L., & Zeng, H. (2009). Research on educational impact of games: A literature review [white paper]. Institute for Games for Learning.

Oblinger, D. G. (2006). Games and learning: Digital games have the potential to bring play to the learning experience. *EDUCAUSE Quarterly, 29*(3), 5–7.

Papastergiou, M. (2009). Digital game-based learning in high school computer science education: Impact on educational effectiveness and student motivation. *Computers & Education, 52*(1), 1–12. doi:10.1016/j.compedu.2008.06.004

Pendleton-Jullian, A. (2010). *Four (+1) Studios*. CreateSpace. Self-published. Retrieved from http://4plus1studios.com/

Pendleton-Jullian, A. (February 26, 2010). *Higher education and game-based learning: A faculty panel*. Digital Union Game-Based Learning Group Conference. Columbus, Ohio.

Prensky, M. (2006). *"Don't bother me Mom, I'm learning!": How computer and video games are preparing your kids for twenty-first century success and how you can help!*St. Paul, MN: Paragon House.

Prensky, M. (2010). *Teaching digital natives: Partnering for real learning*. Thousand Oaks, CA: Sage.

Rice, J. (2007). New media resistance: Barriers to implementation of computer video games in the classroom. *Journal of Educational Multimedia and Hypermedia, 16*(3), 249–261.

Robinson, K. (2006). *Out of our minds: Learning to be creative*. New York, NY: Wiley, John & Sons.

Rosas, R., Nussbaum, M., Cumsille, P., Marianov, V., Correa, M., & Flores, P. (2003). Beyond Nintendo: Design and assessment of educational video games for first and second grade students. *Computers & Education, 40*(1), 71–94. doi:10.1016/S0360-1315(02)00099-4

Salen, K. (Ed.). (2008). *The ecology of games: Connecting youth, games, and learning. The John D. and Catherine T. MacArthur Foundation Series on Digital Media and Learning*. Cambridge, MA: MIT Press.

Salen, K. (May 25, 2010). *Future of digital media talks*. Games for Change Conference. New York.

Salen, K. (June 16, 2011). *Keynote: "What is the work of play?"* Games+Learning+Society Conference. Madison, Wisconsin.

Salen, K., & Zimmerman, E. (2003). *Rules of play: Game design fundamentals*. Cambridge, MA: MIT Press.

Shaffer, D. W. (2006). *How computer games help children learn*. New York, NY: Palgrave Macmillan. doi:10.1057/9780230601994

Shernoff, D. J., Csikszentmihalyi, M., Schneider, B., & Shernoff, E. S. (2003). Student engagement in high school classrooms from the perspective of flow theory. *School Psychology Quarterly, 18*(2), 158–176. doi:10.1521/scpq.18.2.158.21860

Smartbean. (November, 2009). *What are 21ˢᵗ century skills?* Retrieved June 10, 2011, from http://www.thesmartbean.com/magazine/21st-century-skills-magazine/what-are-21st-century-skills/

Squire, K. D. (May 27, 2010). *Toward a theory of game-based assessment*. Games for Change Conference. New York.

Squire, K. D. (2011). *Video games and learning: Teaching and participatory culture in the digital age*. New York, NY: Teachers College Press.

Steinkuehler, C. (March 25, 2010). *Keynote: Massively multiplayer online games, learning and the new pop cosmopolitanism*. New Media Consortium Conference. Retrieved from, http://www.nmc.org/2010-nml-symposium/steinkuehler-keynote

Steinkuehler, C. (June 15, 2011). *Keynote: National Research Council report: Learning science through computer games and simulations*. Games+Learning+Society Conference. Madison, Wisconsin.

Thai, A. M., Lowenstein, D., Ching, D., & Rejeski, D. (2009). *Game changer: Investing in digital play to advance children's learning and health* [policy brief]. The Joan Ganz Cooney Center at Sesame Workshop. Retrieved from http://www.joanganzcooneycenter.org/Reports-abc.html

Valli, L., Croninger, R. G., Chambliss, M. J., Graeber, A. O., & Buese, D. (2008). *Test driven: High-stakes accountability in elementary schools*. New York, NY: Teachers College Press.

Van Eck, R. (2006). Digital game-based learning: It's not just the digital natives who are restless. *EDUCAUSE Review, 41*(2), 16–30.

Wellings, J., & Levine, M. H. (2009). *The digital promise: Transforming learning with innovative uses of technology. A white paper on literacy and learning in a new media age* [white paper]. The Joan Ganz Cooney Center at Sesame Workshop. Retrieved from http://www.joanganzcooneycenter.org/Reports-abc.html

Wolf, M. J. P. (Ed.). (2008). *The video game explosion: A history from Pong to Playstation and beyond*. Westport, CT: Greenwood Press.

Wright, W. (April 2006). Dream machines. *Wired*. Retrieved from http://www.wired.com/wired/archive/14.04/wright.html

Zimmerman, E. (June 15, 2011). *Keynote: Games are not good for you: a designer's perspective on learning and game*. Games+Learning+Society Conference. Madison, Wisconsin.

ADDITIONAL READING

Brown, S. L., & Vaughan, C. (2009). *Play: how it shapes the brain, opens the imagination, and invigorates the soul*. New York: Avery.

Ferdig, R. E. (Ed.). *Handbook of research on effective electronic gaming in education, Vols. I, II, III* (pp. 1274-1288). Hershey, NY: Information Science Reference, IGI Global.

Gee, J. P. (2007). *What video games have to teach us about learning and literacy*. New York: Palgrave Macmillan.

Gee, J. P., & Shaffer, D. W. (2010). Looking where the light is bad: Video games and the future of assessment. *Edge, 6*(1), 1–19.

Klopfer, E., Osterweil, S., Groff, J., & Haas, J. (2009). *Using the technology of today, in the classroom of today: The instructional power of digital games, social networking, simulations and how teachers can leverage them* [white paper]. The Education Arcade, MIT.

McCall, J. (2011). *Gaming the past: Using video games to teach secondary history*. New York: Routledge.

Medina, J. (2008). *Brain rules: 12 principles for surviving and thriving at work, home, and school*. Seattle, Washington: Pear Press.

Prensky, M. (2010). *Teaching digital natives: Partnering for real learning*. Thousand Oaks, CA: Sage.

Robinson, K. (2006). *Out of our minds: Learning to be creative*. New York: Wiley, John & Sons.

Salen, K. (Ed.). (2008). *The ecology of games: Connecting youth, games, and learning. The John D. and Catherine T. MacArthur Foundation Series on Digital Media and Learning*. Cambridge, Massachusetts: MIT Press.

Shaffer, D. W. (2006). *How computer games help children learn*. New York: Palgrave Macmillan. doi:10.1057/9780230601994

Squire, K. D. (2011). *Video games and learning: Teaching and participatory culture in the digital age*. New York: Teachers College Press.

Thai, A. M., Lowenstein, D., Ching, D., & Rejeski, D. (2009). *Game changer: Investing in digital play to advance children's learning and health* [policy brief]. The Joan Ganz Cooney Center at Sesame Workshop. Retrieved from http://www.joanganzcooneycenter.org/Reports-abc.html

Van Eck, R. (Ed.). *Gaming and cognition: Theories and practice from the learning sciences* (pp. 22-54). Hershey, PA: Information Science Reference, IGI Global.

Wellings, J., & Levine, M. H. (2009) *The digital promise: Transforming learning with innovative uses of technology. A white paper on literacy and learning in a new media age* [white paper]. The Joan Ganz Cooney Center at Sesame Workshop. Retrieved from http://www.joanganzcooneycenter.org/Reports-abc.html

KEY TERMS AND DEFINITIONS

21st Century Skills: These skills include: critical thinking and problem solving, communication (including media, technology, and information skills), collaboration, and creativity and innovation, including career and life skills. These skills blend with content knowledge, expertise, and literacies that are emerging as technology and internet tools become ubiquitous.

Embedded Assessment: Within a game environment, embedded assessment means that the assessment is integrated with the game play, giving the user feedback about her choices. This process can also be used to give feedback to an instructor. Achievements in the game can be used to indicate mastery, meaning that testing is unnecessary.

Game Based Learning: Learners play a game that has defined or intended learning outcomes.

Game Engines: Game development tools that allow the user to create a video game that includes a user interface and physics algorithms for simulating real-world motion and perspective. Game engines are available along a continuum from easy-to-use to difficult-to-use and simplicity to complexity.

Modding: Any alteration of content or addition of content to modify an existing game by adding a new level, changing the game play, etc.

Participatory Learning: Learners take an active rather than passive role, actively researching and producing as opposed to passively listening and taking notes.

Systems Thinking: the ability to understand how complex entities work, how the parts are related to the whole; the ability to understand how things are connected, such as how cars are part of the transportation system and affect other parts.

APPENDIX

Must Read Websites

- Education Arcade: http://www.educationarcade.org/
- Smallab Learning, http://smallablearning.com/home
- Ubiquitous Games: http://education.mit.edu/projects/ubiquitous-games

Sources for Finding Specific Games to use with Students

- Bakery Shop, economics for 2nd graders: http://www.thebakeryshop.org/
- Budget Hero: http://marketplace.publicradio.org/features/budget_hero/
- Gamestar Mechanic: http://gamestarmechanic.com/
- Immune Attack, Federation of American Scientists: http://www.fas.org/immuneattack/
- Ko's Journey, math for middle school students: http://www.kosjourney.com/
- World of Goo: http://www.worldofgoo.com/

Websites that Provide Multiple Games or Lists of Games

- K-12 learning: http://www.spreelearninggames.com/
- Education Arcade: http://www.educationarcade.org/
- Filament Games, educational game company: http://www.filamentgames.com/
- Gambit!: http://gambit.mit.edu/
- Games about the U.S. government system: http://www.icivics.org/
- Games and simulations related to Nobel Prize topics: http://nobelprize.org/educational/
- *Games for Change* website provides titles and descriptions; (these can be sorted for grade level): http://www.gamesforchange.org/play
- Games for instruction, persuasion, and activism: http://www.persuasivegames.com/ & http://www.socialimpactgames.com/.
- Games for younger children: http://pbskids.org/games/
- *games2train* provides games and templates: http://www.games2train.com/.
- Health Games: http://www.healthgamesresearch.org/database/results/content_type:game
- Jason Project, National Geographic: http://www.jason.org/public/whatis/start.aspx
- Ubiquitous Games: http://education.mit.edu/projects/ubiquitous-games

Chapter 10

Empowering Digital Learners:
A Self-Managing Learning Process Framework for Digital Game-Based Learning System (DGBLS)

Wenhao David Huang
University of Illinois at Urbana-Champaign, USA

Dazhi Yang
Boise State University, USA

ABSTRACT

Motivation drives our learning behaviors. Our abilities to intentionally control our motivation to learn, however, remain largely limited because motivation is a subliminal and synthetic mental state derived from the interactivity between our prior experiences and the learning environment. In a digital game-based learning system (DGBLS), learners are always bombarded by a colossal amount of cognitive, social, and affective stimuli that afford and affect the interactivity, which can easily trigger learners' motivational responses and leads to the consequences of not being able to manage their motivation. As a result the intended learning processes can be interrupted. Although learners cannot control their motivation in this case, they can manage their interactivity with the DGBLS to select and process stimuli that are relevant to the learning tasks. Therefore this chapter intends to propose a process framework to empower learners to autonomously manage their interactivity with the DGBLS in order to stay focused on the learning tasks. Specifically this framework will draw literatures on learners' motivational processing and cognitive processing pertaining to learning in the DGBLS.

DOI: 10.4018/978-1-61350-441-3.ch010

INTRODUCTION

The digestive process of humans is a complex process. Numerous chemical and physiological elements must be mixed properly in order to help us digest our food intake effectively. As a result, we might feel hungry, which is a common experience among us. The occurrence of such sensation and the digestive process, however, are out of our conscious control. We cannot tell our bodies when to feel hungry. Luckily we do know how to respond to such physiological signal. When we are hungry, we respond with eating. But there is more to the "eating" part of the digestive cycle. In order to stay healthy, we should monitor when we eat, what we eat, and how we eat. In other words, we should manage our eating behaviors in response to the feeling of hunger. If we eat whatever we want whenever we are hungry, after a while our digestive systems might not be able to handle the unregulated (and often abusive) processes. Just by looking at all those dieting and fitness publications on a magazine stand has illuminated the fact that we actually "can" manage our eating behaviors with many proven strategies.

Interestingly the relationship between motivation and learning behaviors is strikingly similar to the connection between feeling hungry and eating. Feeling motivated is analogous to the sensation of hunger; learning behaviors stimulated by motivation parallels with eating activities that intake and process information. This comparison implies two possibilities when viewing the relationship between motivation and learning. First is that excessive motivational stimuli can interrupt the intended learning process by overloading learners' cognitive processing capacity. Second, it is possible to manage learning processes via proven strategies.

Learning processes interrupted by excessive motivational stimuli are prone to occur in Digital Game-Based Learning Systems (DGBLS) where learners are immersed in and often overwhelmed by enhanced interactions, enriched multimedia presentations, and explicit extrinsic performance incentives (Huang, Huang, & Tschopp, 2010). DGBLS are known for providing abundant of stimuli to motivate learners. Current bodies of literature, however, are lacking in enabling learners in DGBLS to effectively manage their learning processes while playing in the game-based environment. To address this motivational-cognitive overloading issue, we assert that although we cannot consciously control our motivation as a psychological state derived from complex internal processing, we still can manage our learning behaviors in DGBLS with planned processes. These processes should be based on proven learning theories and instructional design models with specific focus on motivational and cognitive processing because motivation drives cognitive learning in DGBLS.

The following sections will first examine existing literatures relevant to DGBLS, motivational design, cognitive processing, and integrative approaches in understanding the relationship between motivation and cognition in digital game environments. Secondly we will propose a process framework to help digital learners manage their learning processes in DGBLS by synthesizing reviewed design models and theories. The final section will conclude our chapter by proposing a research agenda.

BACKGROUND

In this section we first review literatures on learning motivation and cognitive learning. We also discuss relevant instructional design models to put those theories in the context of designing actual learning processes. The second part discusses design models for DGBLS that have specific emphasis on motivational as well as cognitive processing. Finally a review of additional DGBLS design heuristics concludes this section.

Digital Game-Based Learning System (DGBLS)

A game, regardless of its delivery mechanism, is a context in which individual and teamed players compete to attain game objectives by following rules and principles. The playing process is intended to overcome challenges (Gredler, 1994; Suits, 1978). In DGBLS, playing becomes "serious" activities that require players to achieve the game and learning objectives (Apt, 1970). The game playing process therefore supports the learning process by allowing players with full control to acquire interactive and social learning experiences in complex learning environments (Avedon & Sutton-Smith, 1971; Johnson & Huang, 2008; Pannese & Carlesi, 2007).

While the learning process in online DGBLS might be promising to engage learners, the inherent complexity of interacting with DGBLS might pose problems for learners. Huang and Johnson (2008) identified ten digital game features that are often seen in computer-based instructional games, all requiring learners' significant cognitive investment while identifying essential learning cues. If managed improperly the learning process could be interrupted early, because learners' limited motivational processing as well as cognitive processing capacity could be overloaded (Ang, Zaphiris, & Mahmood, 2007; Keller, 2008).

Corporations and organizations are no strangers to applying DGBLSs for training because they understand that humans have enjoyed learning through playing for generations (Rieber & Noah, 2008). In recent years, many have embraced serious games (i.e., digital educational games) (Federation of American Scientists, 2006) as a major training venue. Companies such as Cold Stone Creamery, Cisco Systems, and Sun Microsystems have applied DGBLSs in their training programs (Edery & Mollick, 2009). The U.S. Navy has also adopted computer games in its Naval Service Training Command to accommodate the gaming generation recruits (Thornbloom, 2009). In 2007,

Microsoft launched a software platform to allow users to develop digital training games (Jana, 2007). IBM also entered the serious game market in 2009 by providing customizable digital game-based training solutions (IBM, 2009). In order to optimize DGBLSs' effect on training, owing to their inherently complex affective, cognitive, and social stimuli structures, their interactions with learners must be closely monitored to ensure that learners' processing capacities are efficiently responding to information stimuli in DGBLS (Huang & Aragon, 2009; Huang et al., 2010). DGBLS should properly motivate learners so that they do not intend to process too much information at the same time. It is rather challenging, however, to incorporate a just right level of motivational support for effective learning in DGBLS.

Learning Motivation

Motivation is an internal state that drives our actions, directs our attention, and sustains our behaviors (Ormrod, 1999). Goal-directed behaviors are often stimulated and maintained by such state (Berliner & Gage, 1998), which plays a critical role in learning (Weiner, 1985). Studies have identified motivation's positive impact on learning (ChanLin, 2009; Sankaran & Bui, 2001). Its complexity involving self-regulatory skills, learner control and meta-cognitive activities, however, prevents it from being fully integrated into learning processes (Armstrong, 1989; Lee, 1990; Zimmerman, 1989). Motivation also drives people's performance at work (Vroom, 1964). Herzberg (1966) categorizes motivation into the "motivator" and the "hygiene" factors while DeCharms (1968) proposes the extrinsic and intrinsic motivation. Extrinsic motivation (or the hygiene factor) is derived from factors that are external to the work itself (e.g., working conditions, pay). It is often associated with rewards or incentives. Intrinsic motivation (or the motivator factor), in contrast, drives behaviors via employees' internalized values or enjoyable feelings toward the work

(Deci, 1975; Etzioni, 1975). Challenging tasks, for instance, have been associated with enjoyable work experiences (Deci, 1975).

Similar division on motivation has also been applied in the context of learning. Learners are suggested to be motivated by intrinsic motives that are inherent with learning task itself or by extrinsic motives that associate learning behaviors with external rewards (Newby & Alter, 1986; Pintrich, 1988; Scheifele, 1991). In technology-mediated environments, one must increase the perceived importance of the task to extrinsically motivate users and in the meantime, enhancing the enjoyment of the task to make it intrinsically appealing (Davis, Bagozzi, & Warshaw, 1989; 1992). Nevertheless, learning motivation is complex to measure due to its multiple constructs inherent within the domain (Driscoll, 2000). The increasing complexity of today's DGBLSs further challenges the current understanding of motivational processing. For instance, since extrinsic motives are inherently embedded in a game system (e.g., scores), an integrative view to equally emphasize the effect of intrinsic and extrinsic motivation in DGBLS might be more appropriate than a compartmentalized approach (Huang et al., 2010).

From the viewpoint of instructional design, the ARCS model of motivational design (Keller, 1983, 1987a, b) suggests that learning motivation is dependent on four perceptual components: attention, relevance, confidence and satisfaction (Keller, 2008). *Attention* refers to the learner's response to perceived instructional stimuli provided by the instruction (Keller, 1983). *Relevance* helps learners associate their prior learning experience with the new information. *Confidence* stresses the importance of building learners' positive expectation towards their performance. *Satisfaction* is derived from the evaluation and reflection at the end of the learning process (Keller, 1987b). ARCS model is derived from various learning, instructional, and motivation theories (Driscoll, 2000; Small & Gluck, 1994). Although its applications are initially aimed at the "design" aspects of

learning environments to maximize the amount of *effort* invested by learners to achieve the learning goal (Song & Keller, 2001), motivational strategies derived from the model are promising to inform learners how to effective manage their motivation before, during, and after the learning tasks.

Cognitive Learning and Cognitive Load Theory (CLT)

Cognitive learning consists of processes of information selection, information acquisition, knowledge construction, and knowledge integration (Pintrich, 1988). Considering various information processing theories, cognitive learning involves components of sensory registers, working memory, and long-term memory. Information needs to be located, encoded, stored, decoded, and retrieved between the aforementioned memory structures, to enable the completion of learning tasks (Driscoll, 2000; Ormrod, 1999). Based on the assumption that learning is supported by schema construction and automation within the constraints of memory structures, Cognitive Learning Theory (CLT) proposes a comprehensive framework to bridge the gap between information structure design and human cognitive structures (Paas, Tuovinen, Tabbers, & van Gerven, 2003; van Merriënboer, Clark, & de Croock, 2002).

In CLT, cognitive load is a multidimensional construct that includes task-based mental load induced by learning tasks, learners' performance, and mental effort invested by students in their working memory to process information (Paas et al., 2003; Paas & van Merrienboer, 1994). Mental load is the learners' cognitive capacity and it represents the learning task's novelty and complexity in relation to learners' prior learning experiences and existing knowledge. Tasks with high complexity usually demand a high cognitive capacity from learners. Learners' performance refers to learners' achievement in terms of performance outcome and time spent on learning. It is often used to confirm the occurrence of learning.

Mental effort reflects the actual cognitive load, which indicates the cognitive load allocation by learners as the result of interacting with learning tasks (Kalyuga, 2007; Paas et al., 2003).

There are three types of cognitive load: intrinsic, extraneous, and germane cognitive load that compose the total cognitive load. For learning to occur, the total cognitive load can never exceed the learner's working memory capacity.

Intrinsic cognitive load is associated with the element interactivity – the degree to which information can be understood without other elements' involvement – inherent to the instructional material itself. Information with high element interactivity is difficult to understand thus inducing a high intrinsic cognitive load, since the instruction requires more working memory for information processing (Paas et al., 2003). For instance, the intrinsic cognitive load induced by an introductory calculus lesson is higher than learning simple additions. In contrast, we can manipulate the extraneous cognitive load and germane cognitive load through careful instructional design (Brünken, Plass, & Leutner, 2003).

Extraneous cognitive load is also known as ineffective cognitive load. It only involves the process of searching for information and can be influenced by information structures and presentations (Paas et al., 2003; Sweller, van Merriënboer, & Paas, 1998). Considered a necessary cognitive cost of processing information, yet not related to the understanding of the information or the construction of new schema or mental models, extraneous cognitive load must be reduced (Brüken et al., 2003). One instructional design approach found to be successful in reducing extraneous cognitive load is the use of well-structured instructional multimedia components that lower the cognitive load by utilizing multiple modalities to process information (Khalil, Paas, Johnson, & Payer, 2005; Mayer & Moreno, 2003).

In contrast to the desired low degree of the extraneous cognitive load, instructional materials should be designed to *increase* the germane cog-

nitive load. Germane cognitive load, also known as the *effective cognitive load*, is described as the mental effort students invest in order to facilitate the process of schema construction and automation (Paas et al., 2003). A higher germane cognitive load level can induce a deeper learning experience, which in turn, supports both near and far transfer of performance (van Merriënboer et al., 2002). The essential design principle for enhancing germane cognitive load is to deliver instruction in ways that compel students to constantly reexamine every new piece of information while accessing their long-term memory (de Crook, van Merriënboer, & Paas, 1998; Kalyuga, 2009).

The total of extraneous and germane cognitive load is assumed to be equal to the total cognitive load minus the intrinsic cognitive load. Since we cannot manipulate the intrinsic cognitive load via instructional interventions, the design of learning should strive to optimize the combination of extraneous and germane cognitive load. That is, all design efforts and learner actions should aim to reduce the extraneous while increasing the germane cognitive load (van Gerven, Paas, van Merriënboer, & Schmidt, 2006).

Review of Design Models for DGBLS

A considerable amount of effort has been devoted to the development of design models for DGBLS. The following section reviews recent studies with specific focus on the motivatioanl and cognitive design aspects of DGBLS.

Integrative Theory of Motivation, Volition, and Performance

In a recent rendition of motivational design, the integrative theory of motivation, volition, and performance (MVP), Keller (2008) argues that a complete motivational learning cycle consists of several stages: motivational and volitional processing, motivational and information processing interfacing, information and psychomotor processing, and finally, the outcome processing. Motivational processing helps learners set up initial performance goals that are critical for sustainable learning processes. First learners should have sufficient level of curiosity to explore the learning task (attention). Then, learners should understand the value of the learning task (relevance), and evaluate the possibility of attaining successful performance (confidence), to identify and confirm the performance goal. These processes, in turn, prepare learners for the follow-up actions of learning. The satisfaction component seen in the ARCS model, however, is only considered at the end of the learning cycle.

The next stage is the volitional processing that converts learners' learning intentions into executable learning actions. At this stage, learners should apply action control strategies to implement needed activities that move them towards the performance goal. At the effect of volitional processing learners enter the interface between motivation and information processing. This is where learners apply meta-cognitive strategies to actively manage their learning processes within the limited cognitive processing capacity. The next stage, information and psychomotor processing, learners should focus on how to utilize a variety of mental activities to process information that leads to the desired performance. Learners at this stage carry out learning activities that help them create and automate transferrable mental models. The processing capacity, however, is limited by learners' working memory.

Finally, the outcome processing stage allows learners to evaluate the discrepancy between the performance consequence and their invested efforts. Learners reflect upon all previous stages' experiences emotionally and cognitively, and develop a collective sense of satisfaction towards the learning process.

The implication of the theory of MVP is three-fold. First, motivation and cognition cannot be viewed separately in designing DGBLS (Huang, 2011). Second, since motivational processing is crucial at the early stage of the learning process, instructional designers must be cautious to neither overwhelm learners' processing capacity nor distract them with competing stimuli. Third, motivational processing directs the focus of cognitive processing, and learners' cognitive processing activities could play a substantial role in sustaining learners' motivation. Learners with little motivational stimuli are less likely to fully invest their cognitive processing effort. On the other hand, learners overloaded with cognitive stimuli, regardless of their initial attention, confidence, and relevance levels (motivational processing results), are very likely to be unmotivated by exhausting cognitive information processing tasks.

Four Components Instructional Design Model (4C/ID-model) for DGBLS Design

4C/ID-model is a non-linear, systematic, and performance transfer-oriented instructional design model (van Merriënboer et al., 2002). This model helps reduce extraneous cognitive load while increasing germane cognitive load in complex learning environments. The model includes four non-linear, interrelated design components: Learning Tasks, Supportive Information, Just-In-Time (JIT) information, and Part-task practice. All design actions center around the Learning Tasks component.

Learning Tasks are concrete, authentic, comprehensive experiences that promote schema construction for nonrecurring aspects and, to a certain degree, rule automation. For instance, learning to apply mathematical skills to figure out how much to tip after a meal in the restaurant is a holistic Learning Task. The scenario of tipping is one concrete activity in our daily life; learners' involvement in calculating the right amount of tip makes it a comprehensible process (i.e., receiving the full meal cost, applying the appropriate percentage of tip, calculating the tip amount); tipping based on different amount of meal cost is the nonrecurring aspect of the learning task since it might change from time to time; and finally the ultimate objective for learners to achieve is being able to calculate the right amount of tip quickly and effortlessly, which would require some level of automation. Learning Tasks must be complex and require the coordination and integration of all relevant skills. They should be categorized with simple-to-complex task classes. Learning Tasks within a particular class are equivalent in the sense that the tasks can be performed on the basis of the same body of knowledge (i.e., mental models and cognitive strategies). When given a higher task class, however, learners are expected to elaborate upon their existing knowledge base. Going back to the tip calculation example, a higher class of task could be adding more people to contribute to the pool of tip. This then would require learners to apply additional mathematical skills to solve the problem. Two types of supports are also provided with Learning Tasks, to inform learners about the problem in hand and guidance for generating effective solutions. Product-support provided solution models in terms of worked-out examples and case studies. Process-oriented support explains performance requirement and criterion reference for learners. In sum, the design of Learning Task should primarily aim at the induction process that enables learners to extract abstract problem-solving principles from concrete tasks.

Supportive Information component mainly supports the learning and performance of nonrecurring aspects of intended tasks. Theories and models are often included in supportive information since learners can apply them universally for problem-solving in the same task class. The design of learning environments focuses on constructing meaningful relationships between learners' prior experiences and the Learning Tasks. More importantly the design of learning environments should promote the elaboration process with cognitive feedback (Reigeluth, 1999) thus to enable learners to develop complex schemata. The design of Supportive Information component must facilitate the learner-driven abstraction processes by making relevant theories and models readily available. Although this type of information is abstract by nature, it offers explanations for learners to make sense of activities required by the given Learning Tasks.

Just-In-Time (JIT) Information component facilitates learners' development in generating automated responses, which differs from the Supportive Information by providing on-demand contextual information pertaining to Learning Tasks' rules and principles of problem-solving. JIT Information is also applied with practices and exercises (Part-task Practice), the next component of the 4C/ID- model, by providing demonstrations and instances to effectively explain the rules for all classes of Learning Tasks.

Part-task Practices (PtP), often are presented as small parts of the Learning Task, promote rule automation for selected recurrent aspects of the intended complex task. In the tip calculation example the PtP can be designed as various exercises on simple multiplications to help learners familiarize with basic multiplication rules. The design should aim to gradually develop learners' ability to automate the performance of recurrent skills via small task building blocks.

The 4C/ID-model operates under the following assumptions: (1) an upper level learning skill can be attained by assembling sets of simplified task procedure; and (2) performance transfer can be achieved after completing simplified Learning Tasks (van Merriënboer & Sweller, 2005). It further divides constituent skills into two categories: non-recurrent skills and recurrent skills. Non-recurrent skills vary from problem to problem. As a result they require learners' cognitive reasoning since every situation is different from their previous experiences. Cognitive strategies are applied to extract existing schema in order to facilitate the problem-solving process in a novel context. Recurrent skills, on the other hand, are less effortful for learners to process and perform. Problem-solving process, in the case of recurrent skills, is very close to what learners have experienced previously. The design of the learning environment should focus on the abstraction of effective problem-solving process for non-recurrent skills since the goal is to enable learners to redevelop their own schema under various scenarios. In other words, the abstraction helps learners transfer the desired performance from context to context.

By applying 4C/ID-Model to DGBLS design, Huang and Johnson (2008) proposed to align games' main features (e.g., challenge, rules, competition, fantasy) with a purposed combination of the four components. For instance, when designing games' challenges, the focus should be primarily on the Learning Task to connect learning objectives with game tasks, secondarily on the Supportive Information to properly inform learners, and tertiarily on both the Part-Task Practice and JIT Information. When designing for game competitions, on the other hand, the primary design focus should be on Supportive Information and JIT Information to provide immediate feedback to learners. Learning Task in this case, might only require tertiary level of design focus since competition is extraneous to learning objectives.

Other DGBLS Design Heuristics

In addition to the motivation- and cognition-oriented DGBLS models discussed earlier, in recent years a substantial amount of efforts have been invested in developing design frameworks that are conceptually sound, technically deployable, and practically feasible. Crawford (1982) proposed representation, interaction, conflict, and safety as four interconnected computer game components. The representation of the game system situates players in the context of playing via agents and tasks, which enables intended interactions. Conflict is the outcome of players' interactions against the game's underlying rules. The safety component enables players to learn from their mistakes with an experiential learning approach.

Similarly the Game Object Model (Amory, 2007) suggested that games should include game space (play, exploration, authenticity, tacit knowledge), visualization space (critical thinking, storylines, relevance), elements space (fun, emotive, graphics, sounds, technology), problem space (communication, literacy level, memory), and social space (communication tools and social network analysis). For example, the problem space bridges the game space and the social space while within each space are clusters of concrete and abstract "interfaces" to interact with game players. The applicability of Game Object Model in realistic design settings that are constrained by resources and pre-determined learning objectives, however, requires further investigations (Westera, Nadolski, Hummel, & Wopereis, 2008).

By integrating considerations on instructions, game design, motivation, and learning, Garris, Ahlers, and Driskell (2002) proposed the Input-Process-Outcome Game Model. The input consists of instructional content and game characteristics; the process includes a 3-stage cyclic game play (user judgment, user behavior, and system feedback); connected by a debriefing procedure, the outcome focuses on the attainment of learning outcomes. This model further argues for the need to establish empirical connections among game features, motivational support, and learning outcome attainment. With a focus on motivation, Dickey (2007) analyzed one type of DGBLS, modern massively multiple online role-playing games (MMORPGs) and concluded that such digital game-based environments could provide practical design models for creating learning environments to support the development of complex competencies. Character design and narrative environments in the MMORPGs could foster players' intrinsic motivation to continuously participate in the game playing. It is the role-playing process (character) immersed in a story-telling setting (narrative) that deeply engages players cognitively and affectively.

Emerging from concepts of learning theories, motivational design, and cognitive load, the Relevance Embedding Translation Adaptation Immersion & Naturalization (RETAIN) model focuses on the relevance of game content and activities due to their potential impact on learners' cognitive processing (Gunter, Kenny, & Vick, 2008). The main thesis of the model suggests that the content and activities should be situated in a fantasy world to support immersive learning experiences. Although the model was supported by a detailed design and evaluation rubrics, the empirical validation of this evaluation model was not further discussed.

Considering the heavy developmental cost associated with digital instructional games in higher education, Westera and colleagues (2008) proposed a design framework to reduce the design complexity of DGBLSs. They identified four design components (environments, learning activities, multi-user, and methodology) in the DGBLS where the environments should be challenging, learning activities should be complex and based on expert problem-solving processes, multi-user should encourage collaborative learning, and the methodology represents the rules of the game. The framework also presents a 3-tier design process consisted of conceptual, technical, and practical levels. This framework, nevertheless, did not address the connection between specific game features with intended motivational or learning outcomes. Furthermore, it used the decision-tree approach to reduce the design complexity, which might limit the versatility of the game-based learning environments to satisfy learners' diverse needs.

DGBLSs are often praised for their support in motivating and engaging learners across contexts (Garris et al, 2002; Gee, 2003; Prensky, 2001). Recent studies in DGBLSs have mostly focused on their support on intrinsic motivation. Van Eck (2006) argued that the design of games should stress Malone and Lepper's four motivational factors manifested by explicit game features (i.e.,

challenge, curiosity, rules, and fantasy) (1987) in order to promote positive attitudes toward learning games. Similarly Papastergiou (2009) incorporated intrinsic motivational factors to measure digital games' motivational appeal in teaching computer science with DGBLSs. Although it is encouraging to see these motivational game features that are available to support learning, some have implied that DGBLSs' instructional effectiveness could be compromised by motivational and engagement issues (Eow, Ali, Mahmudb, & Baki, 2009), because the motivational features might be possible to overload learners' cognitive and motivational processing capacities thus disrupting the intended learning process (Nelson & Erlandson, 2008).

In the integrated model of multimedia learning and motivation, Astleitner and Wiesner (2004) suggested that the design of multimedia learning environments must be cautious not to overload learners' motivational processing capacities with excessive stimuli. Otherwise learners' cognitive processing could be interrupted. Situated in serious games with an experimental design, Ritterfeld, Shen, Wang, Nocera, and Wong (2009) confirmed the critical role of multimedia learning processing in affecting learner motivation. Scheiter and Gerjets (2007), focusing on the self-control factor in hypermedia learning that is commonly seen DGBLSs, suggested that motivational stimuli in such environments might impose high demand on learners' processing capacities. For motivational factors to be effective in supporting intended learning processes, the learning environments must prevent learners from being distracted and overloaded by extraneous cognitive stimuli (Keller, 2008).

Deficiency in Current Research on DGBLS

In reviewing the aforementioned literatures on DGBLS, it is clear that much effort (conceptual and empirical) has been devoted in mainly two fronts. First, research is highly interested in how to reduce the design complexity of DGBLS while maintaining their viability to provide substantial motivational support and cognitive engagement. Despite the recognition that DGBLS design is more of a creative art and less of a scientific manipulation (Hirumi, Appelman, Reiber, & van Eck, 2010), this aspect of research effort strives to identify systematic and replicable design procedures to align DGBLS features with intended learning outcomes. The second front of research focuses on the interactions between DGBLS and learners. This aspect of studies often reported findings of evaluative studies where learners self-reported their experiences after participating in certain playing processes (Huang, 2011). Learners in this context often passively react to the DGBLS environments where their actions can be freely chosen within a rigid game playing structure bound by pre-determined game tasks and rules (Salen & Zimmerman, 2010). Considering a comprehensive instruction-to-learning cycle must include learning environments, learners, and interactions between learners and learning environments, current DGBLS research is deficient in informing how to empower learners in a highly distracting DGBLS where they are vulnerable facing excessive amount of motivational and cognitive stimuli. To preliminarily address this issue, the following section presents a process framework for learners in DGBLS to manage their learning processes.

Considering the frameworks of motivation and cognition discussed earlier, the proposed Self-Managing Learning Process Framework for learners in DGBLS maintains the perspective that both motivational processing and cognitive processing need to be proactively managed by learners. The goal of this framework is to help learners reach a reciprocal and dynamic equilibrium between the receiving of motivational stimuli and the investment of cognitive efforts. As a result, learners can attain intended learning outcomes without being overwhelmed.

THE SELF-MANAGING LEARNING PROCESS FRAMEWORK FOR DGBLS

Target Audience and Learner Competencies

Metacognitive skills need to be developed via experiences acquired by learners through time. Learners might be aware of certain metacognitive learning strategies but might not have first-hand experiences in applying them to different learning environments. This characteristic poses some concerns for learners to apply metacognitive learning strategies in the DGBLS because there are more distracting stimuli in DGBLS than other digital learning environments (e.g., static web pages). Therefore to make this framework feasible for learners in DGBLS to apply, we suggest that learners need to have prior experiences in both playing digital games and participating in interactive online learning.

As for learners' competencies, learners need to develop self-regulatory skills that can help them consciously regulate their motivational and cognitive engagement activities in DGBLSs. Self-regulatory activities can help address the major issue of learning in DGBLSs (Eow, Ali, Mahmudb, & Baki, 2009), which is motivational features of DGBLSs often overload learners' cognitive and motivational processing capacities and disrupt the intended learning process (Keller, 2008; Nelson & Erlandson, 2008). For motivational factors to be effective in supporting intended learning processes in DGBLSs, learners must prevent themselves from being distracted and overloaded by extraneous cognitive stimuli –one of the major issues of learning in DGBLSs (Eow et al., 2009; Ke, 2008). Combined the limited cognitive processing capacity with the overwhelming motivational features a DGBLS typically entails, the achievement of the ultimate learning goal of serious games leaves largely to the self-regulatory ability of the learners during the learning process. Since self-regulatory skills consist of both the affective and cognitive processes (McMahon & Luca, 2001), it seems that self-awareness, thoughts and emotions can either positively or negatively influence learning outcomes in DGBLSs. Fortunately, learner's thoughts and emotions can exert a positive influence on learning and performance (Kanfer & Ackerman, 1996) and a strong sense of confidence and self-efficacy result in better learning outcome and performance (Bandura, 1991). This positive influence of learner's thoughts and emotions is possible to obtain giving digital learners are better tuned to take more ownership over how and when learning takes place (McMahon & Luca, 2001).

Assumptions of the Framework

The proposed framework is based on the following assumptions:

- Motivation drives cognitive learning processes and implementations of relevant learning strategies. An excessive level of motivation, however, might deter learners to sustain their performance (Keller, 2009).
- Cognitive processing capacity is limited by working memory. Learners are also subject to invest mental efforts that can be explained by various types of cognitive load (extraneous and germane).
- Multiple game features are situated in DGBLS simultaneously. Studies have identified a list of features such as challenging, competitive, regulated by rules, role-playing, controllable, unrealistic, task-based, multimedia-rich, and guided by storylines (Huang & Johnson, 2008)
- The DGBLS seamlessly integrates learning into the gameplay. In other words, upon participating fully in the playing process, learners will be able to attain intended learning objectives in terms of knowledge

acquisition, skill development, and attitudinal change.

The Framework

The framework parallels with the progression of game playing. Pre-Game, Game Starts, During Game, Game Ends, and Post-Game are the five stages identified in the framework. The following sections describe how learners need to apply different metacognitive strategies in relation to a variety of game features at different stages of playing, in order to stay motivationally and cognitively capable in DGBLSs. See Figure 1 for the conceptual diagram.

Pre-Game Stage

Motivation Management

While in a learning management system learners are able to interact with a new online course with similar activity and behavioral patterns, a new DGBLS often requires learners to get used to a set of completely foreign interface, rules, tasks, and challenges within a relatively short amount of time. As an unfortunate result, learners can be demotivated by this initial learning curve and fail to engage with the playing and learning process further. Therefore the framework suggests that learners should devote their main efforts to the following tasks in this stage to maintain a sufficient level of motivation:

- **Developing interface control skills:** Interfacing skills such as controlling the game avatars and interacting with handheld controllers/computer keyboards need to be sufficiently developed here. In turn learners can feel confident in accomplishing the rest of game playing.
- **Understanding game goals and rules:** Game goals and rules inform learners the

Figure 1. Conceptual diagram of the framework

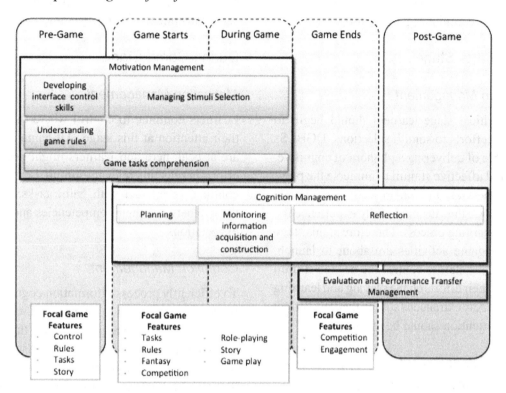

end and boundaries of their actions in the game. They also explain the underlying relationships between participating game elements. In DGBLS game rules are interwoven with intended learning goals so learners can follow them to attain intended learning objectives. Understanding goals and rules enables learners to acquire a sense of predictability and structure for the playing and learning processes.

- **Comprehending game tasks in the context of learning:** In DGBLS the game tasks integrate intended learning objectives and performance criteria into the gameplay. The pedagogical elements of game tasks, however, are often concealed under the playing activities. Learners at this stage need to mindfully connect the game tasks with the learning goal. This process, span-

ning from Pre-Game to During Game, enables learners to stay on the track of learning while being immersed in playing.

Focal Game Features

In order to efficiently manage motivation at the Pre-Game stage, learners need to purposefully seek out information and activities pertaining to game control, game goals, game rules, game tasks, and the underlying storyline. In most computer-based games, for example, learners can access the aforementioned information by spending time to go through the game control tutorial and game mission statements. Some learners, however, would dive into the playing process without acquiring these knowledge and skills first. As a consequence they would terminate the play prematurely due to a loss of motivation resulted from unsuccessful attempts for continuous participation.

Game Starts Stage

Motivation Management

At this critical stage learners should begin to shift their efforts to stimuli selections. DGBLSs are capable of delivering a plethora of cognitive, social, and affective stimuli to immerse the players. If learners take them all in, learners might feel overwhelmed thus unable to fully experience the intended learning process. Therefore at this stage where all game activities are about to launch, learners must start to control the needed stimuli and focus their efforts on the playing and learning processes. Any extraneous stimuli that can distract learners' attention should be avoided.

Cognition Management

Learners need to mindfully plan their actions in the DGBLS at this point upon digesting the information retrieved from Pre-Game. Learners should take the advantage of any resources external to the DGBLS to make the planning process tangible. For instance, learners can use a notepad to outline the plan of actions and use it as a reference of activities. Learners also need to consider the amount of time devoted to the playing and learning processes. Learners should not spend too little time on the game tasks since it might prohibit a deep learning process. Neither should learners spend too much time on the DGBLS as it could overtax the cognitive processing capacity. Learners should allocate a fixed amount of time per day (or feasible time intervals) for activities in the DGBLS.

Focal Game Features

For motivation management, learners can consider features such as fantasy, role-playing, story, and competition. They support the cognitive processing of primary stimuli such as game tasks,

rules, and game play that are critical for the task accomplishment.

During Game Stage

Motivation Management

Learners continue to control where they invest their attention at this stage. All game activities are at peak here and learners might need more efforts in selecting relevant stimuli. Learners also continue to interact with game tasks to gauge the gap between their competencies and the task expectations.

Cognition Management

To efficiently process information cognitively, it is crucial for learners to be aware of where they are and where they are going during the playing and learning processes. Learners also need to relate newly acquired knowledge and skills to their existing schemas. Therefore at the During-Game stage learners should focus on monitoring how they have processed the information in the working memory (acquisition) and the new information modifies their existing mental models (construction).

Focal Game Features

Learners ought to focus more on the competition and story aspects of the game playing to immerse themselves into the DGBLS environments affectively. Game tasks and rules remain essential for the cognitive aspect of the playing and learning processes.

Game Ends Stage

Cognition Management

Here is where learners need to connect everything together. Specifically at this stage learners should elaborate newly acquired knowledge and skills in the context of intended learning goals. Furthermore learners need to reflect upon the playing and learning processes in terms of their effectiveness in achieving the game and learning goals.

Evaluation and Performance Transfer Management

Learners should begin to make sense of the game playing and learning experiences at this point. Specifically they need to evaluate whether or not the investment of efforts during the playing and learning processes are worthy of the outcome they have perceived. The outcome could be derived from both the level of enjoyment and the level of learning induced by interacting with the DGBLS. If the effort investment significantly outweighs the perceived outcome, learners might decide not to continue the playing and learning processes in the future.

Focal Game Features

The competition aspect of the game playing might mean more than anything else at this point. Most learners would enjoy winning at the end. Learners now can redirect their attention to reasons of winning (or losing) and devise plans to improve their future participation. Furthermore, the ability of DGBLS to engage learners might enable learners to come back to the same environment for more similar playing and learning experiences.

Post-Game Stage

Cognition Management

The process of reflection continues. Learners are encouraged to discuss their reflections with peer players who have finished the game. Since the playing and learning processes in DGBLS are often iterative (i.e., players would repeat one game task multiple times to get higher scores), the final outcome of cognition management here is to help learners improve their learning processes next time around.

Evaluation and Performance Transfer Management

In addition to justify the relationship between invested efforts and perceived outcomes, learners also need to situate the newly acquired skills and knowledge in the performance settings so they can be applied to different problem-solving situations. Discussions with peer players and instructors could significantly facilitate this process.

Limitations of the Framework

The Self-Managing Learning Process Framework for DGBLS, at its current rendition, is not meant for the design of DGBLSs. To a certain extent the framework is advising DGBLS users to act against the design of the game. DGBLS designers, however, could benefit from the framework to understand the necessities of managing learners' motivational and cognitive processing during the playing and learning process. The framework is also incapable of explaining the dynamic relationship between game features and the actual learning outcomes, which remains a critical research agenda to pursue. Finally, augmenting auxiliaries to evaluate the viability and effectiveness of this framework could further enhance its scalability.

CONCLUSION AND FUTURE RESEARCH

This chapter intends to provide a unique and much needed perspective to decipher learners' interactions with the DGBLS that has not been purposefully addressed in prior research. In particular we set out to conceptualize how learners can consciously manage their motivation and cognitive learning in complex and distracting DGBLSs. Upon synthesizing current literature on learning motivation, cognitive load theory, and digital educational game design, the Self-Managing Learning Process Framework for DGBLS is proposed to enable and empower learners to control their learning via playing digital educational games. This framework is a vanguard to shift the control of DGBLS learning from designers to learners. Considering the rich literatures in learning motivation, cognitive learning, meta-learning strategies, we are optimistic about the future development of this fertile research agenda. In terms of refining the conceptual structure of the framework, future research must synthesize proven instructional design theories, learning theories, and game design models to hypothesize the relationship among game features, learner actions, and learning outcomes. Using the hypotheses as a blueprint, future research efforts can focus on devising both inductive and deductive studies to verify and validate the aforementioned relationships.

REFERENCES

Amory, A. (2007). Game object model version II: A theoretical framework for educational game development. *Educational Technology Research and Development*, 55, 55–77. doi:10.1007/s11423-006-9001-x

Ang, C. S., Zaphiris, P., & Mahmood, S. (2007). A model of cognitive loads in massively multiplayer online role playing games. *Interacting with Computers*, 19(2), 167–179. doi:10.1016/j.intcom.2006.08.006

Apt, C. C. (1970). *Serious games: The art and science of games that simulate life in industry, government and education.* New York, NY: Viking.

Armstrong, A. M. (1989). Persistence and the causal perception of failure: Modifying cognitive attributions. *Journal of Educational Psychology*, 70, 154–166.

Astleitner, H., & Wiesner, C. (2004). An integrated model of multimedia learning and motivation. *Journal of Educational Multimedia and Hypermedia*, 13, 3–21.

Avedon, E., & Sutton-Smith, B. (1971). *The study of games.* New York, NY: Wiley.

Bandura, A. (1991). Self-efficacy mechanism in physiological activation and health-promoting behavior. In Madden, J. IV, (Ed.), *Neurobiology of learning, emotion and affect* (pp. 229–270). New York, NY: Raven.

Berliner, D. C., & Gage, N. L. (1998). *Educational Psychology*. Boston, MA: Houghton Mifflin Company.

Brünken, R., Plass, J., & Leutner, D. (2003). Direct measurement of cognitive load in multimedia learning. *Educational Psychologist*, 38, 53–61. doi:10.1207/S15326985EP3801_7

ChanLin, L. (2009). Applying motivational analysis in a Web-based course. *Innovations in Education and Training International*, 46(1), 91–103. doi:10.1080/14703290802646123

Crawford, C. (1982). *The art of computer game design*. Retrieved from http://www.vancouver.wsu.edu/fac/peabody/game-book/Coverpage.html

Davis, F. D., Bagozzi, R. P., & Warshaw, P. R. (1989). User acceptance of computer technology: A comparison of two theoretical models. *Management Science*, 35(8), 983–1003. doi:10.1287/mnsc.35.8.982

Davis, F. D., Bagozzi, R. P., & Warshaw, P. R. (1992). Extrinsic and intrinsic motivation to use computers in the workplace. *Journal of Applied Social Psychology*, 22(14), 1111–1132. doi:10.1111/j.1559-1816.1992.tb00945.x

de Crook, M. B. M., van Merriënboer, J. J. G., & Paas, F. G. W. C. (1998). High versus low contextual interference in simulation-based training of troubleshooting skills: Effects on transfer performance and invested mental effort. *Computers in Human Behavior*, 14, 249–267. doi:10.1016/S0747-5632(98)00005-3

DeCharms, R. (1968). *Personal causation: The internal affective determinants of behavior*. New York, NY: Academic Press.

Deci, E. L. (1975). *Intrinsic motivation*. New York, NY: Plenum.

Dickey, M. D. (2007). Game design and learning: A conjectural analysis of how massively multiple online role-playing games (MMORPGs) foster intrinsic motivation. *Educational Technology Research and Development*, *55*(3), 253–273. doi:10.1007/s11423-006-9004-7

Driscoll, M. P. (2000). Introduction to theories of learning and instruction. In Driscoll, M. P. (Ed.), *Psychology of learning for instruction* (2nd ed., pp. 3–28). Boston, MA: Allyn and Bacon.

Edery, D., & Mollick, E. (2009). *Changing the game: How video games are transforming the future of business*. Upper Saddle River, NJ: FT Press.

Eow, Y. L., Ali, W. Z. B. W., Mahmud, R., & Baki, R. (2009). Form one students' engagement with computer games and its effect on their academic achievement in a Malaysian secondary school. *Computers & Education*, *53*, 1082–1091. doi:10.1016/j.compedu.2009.05.013

Etzioni, A. (1975). *Comparative analysis of complex organizations*. New York, NY: MacMillan Publishing Co.

Federation of American Scientists. (2006). *Harnessing the power of video games for learning*. Summit on Educational Games. Washington, DC: Federation of American Scientists.

Garris, R., Ahlers, R., & Driskell, J. E. (2002). Games, motivation, and learning: A research and practice model. *Simulation & Gaming*, *33*, 441–467. doi:10.1177/1046878102238607

Gee, J. (2003). *What video games have to teach us about learning and literacy*. New York, NY: Palgrave Macmillan.

Gredler, M. (1994). *Designing and evaluating games and simulations: A process approach*. Houston, TX: Gulf Publishing Company.

Gunter, G. A., Kenny, R. F., & Vick, E. H. (2008). Taking educational games seriously: Using the RETAIN model to design endogenous fantasy into standalone educational games. *Educational Technology Research and Development*, *56*, 511–537. doi:10.1007/s11423-007-9073-2

Herzberg, F. (1966). *Work and the nature of man*. Cleveland, OH: World.

Hirumi, A., Appelman, B., Reiber, L., & van Eck, R. (2010). Preparing instructional designers for game-based learning: Part 2. *TechTrends*, *54*, 19–27. doi:10.1007/s11528-010-0416-1

Huang, W., & Aragon, S. (2009). An integrated evaluation approach for e-learning systems in career and technical education. In Wang, V. C. X. (Ed.), *Handbook of research on e-learning applications for career and technical education: Technologies for vocational training*. Hershey, PA: IGI Global. doi:10.4018/978-1-60566-739-3.ch031

Huang, W., & Johnson, T. (2008). Instructional game design using cognitive load theory. In Ferdig, R. (Ed.), *Handbook of research on effective electronic gaming in education* (pp. 1143–1165). Hershey, PA: Information Science Reference. doi:10.4018/978-1-59904-808-6.ch066

Huang, W. H. (2011). Learners' motivational processing and mental effort investment in an online game-based learning environment: A preliminary analysis. *Computers in Human Behavior*, *27*, 694–704. http://dx.doi.org/10.1016/j.chb.2010.07.021. doi:10.1016/j.chb.2010.07.021

Huang, W. H., Huang, W. Y., & Tschopp, J. A. (2010). Sustaining iterative game playing processes in DGBL: The relationship between motivational processing and outcome processing. *Computers & Education*, *55*(2), 789–797. .doi:10.1016/j.compedu.2010.03.011

IBM. (2009). *"Serious game" provides training to tackle global business challenges*. Retrieved from http://www-03.ibm.com/press/us/en/press-release/26734.wss

Jana, R. (2007). *Microsoft's games get serious*. Retrieved from http://www.businessweek.com/innovate/content/dec2007/id20071220_808794.htm

Johnson, T. E., & Huang, W. D. (2008). Complex skills development for today's workforce. In Ifenthaler, D., Spector, J. M., & Pirnay-Dummer, P. (Eds.), *Understanding models for learning and instruction: Essays in honor of Norbert M. Seel* (pp. 305–325). New York City, NY: Springer. doi:10.1007/978-0-387-76898-4_15

Kalyuga, S. (2007). Enhancing instructional efficiency of interactive e-learning environments: A cognitive load perspective. *Educational Psychology Review, 19*, 387–399. doi:10.1007/s10648-007-9051-6

Kalyuga, S. (2009). Instructional design for the development of transferable knowledge and skills: A cognitive load perspective. *Computers in Human Behavior, 25*, 332–338. doi:10.1016/j.chb.2008.12.019

Kanfer, R., & Ackerman, P. (1996). A self-regulatory skills perspective to reducing cognitive interference. In Sarason, I. G., Pierce, G. R., & Sarason, B. R. (Eds.), *Cognitive interference: Theories, methods, and findings* (pp. 153–171). Mahwah, NJ: Lawrence Erlbaum Associates.

Keller, J. M. (1983). Motivational design of instruction. In Reigeluth, C. M. (Ed.), *Instructional design theories and models: An overview of their current status* (pp. 386–434). Hillsdale, NJ: Lawrence Erlbaum Associates.

Keller, J. M. (1987a). Strategies for stimulating the motivation to learn. *Performance and Instruction, 26*, 1–7. doi:10.1002/pfi.4160260802

Keller, J. M. (1987b). The systematic process of motivational design. *Performance and Instruction, 26*(9/10), 1–8. doi:10.1002/pfi.4160260902

Keller, J. M. (2008). An integrative theory of motivation, volition, and performance. *Technology, Instruction, Cognition, and Learning, 6*, 79–104.

Keller, J. M. (2009). *Motivational design for learning and performance. The ARCS model approach*. Springer.

Khalil, M. K., Paas, F., Johnson, T. E., & Payer, A. F. (2005). Design of interactive and dynamic anatomical visualizations: The implication of cognitive load theory. *Anatomical Record. Part B, New Anatomist, 286B*, 15–20. doi:10.1002/ar.b.20078

Lee, M. J. (1990). *Effects of different loci of instructional control on students' meta cognition and cognition: Learner vs. program control*. Paper presented at the Annual Convention of the Association for Educational Communication and Technology, (ERIC Document Reproduction Service No. ED 323938).

Malone, T. W., & Lepper, M. R. (1987). Making learning fun. A taxonomy of intrinsic motivations for learning. In R. E. Snow & M. J. Farr (Eds.), *Aptitude, learning, and instruction, volume 3: Cognitive and affective process analyses* (pp. 223-253). Hillsdale, NJ: Lawrence Erlbaum.

Mayer, R., & Moreno, R. (2003). Nine ways to reduce cognitive load in multimedia learning. *Educational Psychologist, 38*, 43–52. doi:10.1207/S15326985EP3801_6

McMahon, M., & Luca, J. (2001). *Assessing students' self-regulatory skills*. Retrieved from http://www.ascilite.org.au/conferences/melbourne01/pdf/papers/mcmahonm.pdf

Nelson, B. C., & Erlandson, B. E. (2008). Managing cognitive load in educational multi-user virtual environments: reflection on design practice. *Educational Technology Research and Development, 56*, 619–641. doi:10.1007/s11423-007-9082-1

Newby, T. J., & Alter, P. A. (1989). Task motivation: Learner selection of intrinsic versus extrinsic orientations. *Educational Technology Research and Development, 37,* 77–89. doi:10.1007/BF02298292

Ormrod, J. E. (1999). *Human learning* (3rd ed.). Upper Saddle River, NJ: Merill Prentice Hall.

Paas, F., Tuovinen, J. E., Tabbers, H., & van Gerven, P. W. M. (2003). Cognitive load measurement as a means to advance cognitive load theory. *Educational Psychologist, 38,* 63–71. doi:10.1207/S15326985EP3801_8

Paas, F. G. W. C., & van Merrienboer, J. J. G. (1994). Instructional control of cognitive load in the training of complex cognitive tasks. *Educational Psychology Review, 6,* 351–371. doi:10.1007/BF02213420

Pannese, L., & Carlesi, M. (2007, May). Games and learning come together to maximise effectiveness: The challenge of bridging the gap. *British Journal of Educational Technology, 38*(3), 438–454. doi:10.1111/j.1467-8535.2007.00708.x

Papastergiou, M. (2009). Digital game-based learning in high school computer science education: Impact on educational effectiveness and student motivation. *Computers & Education, 52,* 1–12. doi:10.1016/j.compedu.2008.06.004

Pintrich, P. R. (1988). A process-oriented view on student motivation and cognition. In Stark, J. S., & Mets, L. A. (Eds.), *Improving teaching and learning through research: New directions for institutional research, no. 57.* San Francisco, CA: Josse-Bass. doi:10.1002/ir.37019885707

Prenksy, M. (2001). Digital natives, digital immigrants. *Horizon, 9*(5). Retrieved from http://www.marcprensky.com/writing/Prensky%20-%20Digital%20Natives,%20Digital%20Immigrants%20-%20Part1.pdf.

Reigeluth, C. M. (1999). The elaboration theory: guidance for scope and sequence decisions. In C. M. Reigeluth (Ed.), *Instructional-design theories and model, vol. 2: A new paradigm of instructional theory.* Mahwah, NJ: Lawrence Erlbaum Associates.

Rieber, L., & Noah, D. (2008). Games, simulations, and visual metaphors in education: Antagonism between enjoyment and learning. *Educational Media International, 45*(2), 77–92. doi:10.1080/09523980802107096

Ritterfeld, U., Shen, C., Wang, H., Nocera, L., & Wong, W. L. (2009). Multimodality and interactivity: Connecting properties of serious games with educational outcomes. *Cyberpsychology & Behavior, 12,* 691–697. doi:10.1089/cpb.2009.0099

Salen, K., & Zimmerman, E. (2004). *Rules of play game design fundamentals.* Cambridge, MA: The MIT Press.

Sankaran, S. R., & Bui, T. (2001). Impact of learning strategies and motivation on performance: A study in web-based instruction. *Journal of Instructional Psychology, 28,* 191–198.

Scheiter, K., & Gerjets, P. (2007). Learner control in hypermedia environments. *Educational Psychology Review, 19,* 285–307. doi:10.1007/s10648-007-9046-3

Schiefele, U. (1991). Interest, learning and motivation. *Educational Psychologist, 26,* 299–323. doi:10.1207/s15326985ep2603&4_5

Small, R. V., & Gluck, M. (1994). The relationship of motivational conditions to effective instructional attributes: A magnitude scaling approach. *Educational Technology, 34*(8), 33–40.

Song, S. H., & Keller, J. M. (2001). Effectiveness of motivationally adaptive computer-assisted instruction on the dynamic aspects of motivation. *Educational Technology Research and Development, 49,* 5–22. doi:10.1007/BF02504925

Suits, B. (1978). *The grasshopper: Games, life, and utopia*. Ontario, Canada: University of Toronto Press.

Sweller, van Merriënboer J. J. G., & Paas, F. G. W.C. (1998). Cognitive architecture and instructional design. *Educational Psychology Review, 10*(3), 251-96.

Thornbloom, S. A. (2009). *NSTC developing video computer training 'game'*. Retrieved from http://www.navy.mil/search/display.asp?story_id=42541

van Eck, R. (2006). Digital game-based learning: It's not just the digital natives who are restless. *EDUCASE Review, 41*(2), 16–30.

van Gerven, P. W. M., Paas, F., van Merriënboer, J. J. G., & Schmidt, H. G. (2006). Modality and variability as factors in training the elderly. *Applied Cognitive Psychology, 20*, 311–320. doi:10.1002/acp.1247

van Merriënboer, J. J. G., Clark, R. E., & De Croock, M. B. M. (2002). Blueprints for complex learning: The 4C/ID-model. *Educational Technology Research and Development, 50*, 39–64. doi:10.1007/BF02504993

van Merriënboer, J. J. G., & Sweller, J. (2005). Cognitive load theory and complex learning: Recent developments and future directions. *Educational Psychology Review, 17*(2), 147–177. doi:10.1007/s10648-005-3951-0

Vroom, V. (1964). *The motivation to work*. New York, NY: Wiley.

Weiner, B. (1985). Spontaneous' causal thinking. *Psychological Bulletin, 97*, 74–84. doi:10.1037/0033-2909.97.1.74

Westera, W., Nadolski, R. J., Hummel, H. G. K., & Wopereis, I. G. J. H. (2008). Serious games for higher education: A framework for reducing design complexity. *Journal of Computer Assisted Learning, 24*, 420–432. doi:10.1111/j.1365-2729.2008.00279.x

Zimmerman, B. J. (1989). Models for self-regulated learning and academic achievement. In Zimmerman, B. J., & Schunk, D. H. (Eds.), *Self-regulated learning and academic achievement: Theory, research, and practice* (pp. 1–25). New York, NY: Springer. doi:10.1007/978-1-4612-3618-4_1

KEY TERMS AND DEFINITIONS

Cognition Management (in Digital Game-Based Learning Systems/DGBLS): Managing cognitive learning in DGBLS is crucial for effective game-based learning. Learners need to mindfully plan and execute their actions in the DGBLS upon digesting the information retrieved from the DGBLS. Learners also need to manage their time well in DGBLS to guide the cognitive effort investment. Finally learners should always monitor their progresses in DGBLS pertaining to the intended learning objectives.

Cognitive Learning: Processes of information selection, information acquisition, knowledge construction, and knowledge integration. Cognitive learning also involves components of sensory registers, working memory, and long-term memory. Information needs to be located, encoded, stored, decoded, and retrieved between the aforementioned memory structures, to enable the completion of learning tasks.

Cognitive Load (by Cognitive Load Theory): A multidimensional construct that considers task-based mental load induced by learning tasks, learners' performance, and mental effort invested by students in their working memory to process information. Mental load represents the learning task's novelty and complexity in relation to learners' existing knowledge. Learners' performance refers to learners' achievement in terms of performance outcome and time spent on learning. Mental effort reflects the actual cognitive load, which indicates the cognitive load allocation by learners as the result of interacting with learning tasks.

Digital Game-Based Learning System (DG-BLS): A digital system that provides learning experiences through game playing. Computer-based games, video games, games on mobile devices, and online games can all be considered as digital gaming systems. The learning component of them, however, would require substantial instructional design efforts to integrate learning into playing.

Games: A game, regardless of its delivery mechanism, is a context in which individual players, teamed players, and the game system compete to attain game objectives by following sets of rules. The playing process intends to overcome challenges and winning (or defeating the opponents) is the ultimate goal of playing games.

Learning Motivation: Motivation is an internal state that drives our actions, directs our at-tention, and sustains our behaviors. Goal-directed behaviors are often stimulated and maintained by such state, which plays a critical role in learning. Its complexity involving self-regulatory skills, learner control and meta-cognitive activities, however, prevents it from being fully integrated into learning processes.

Motivation Management (in DGBLS): Learners should pay attention to efficient stimuli selections since DGBLSs are capable of delivering a plethora of cognitive, social, and affective stimuli to immerse the players. If learners take them all in, they might feel overwhelmed thus unable to fully experience the intended learning process. Therefore learners must focus on the needed stimuli and concentrate their efforts on the playing and learning processes. Any extraneous stimuli that can distract learners' attention should be avoided at all stages.

Chapter 11
Virtual Performance Assessment in Immersive Virtual Environments

Jillianne Code
University of Victoria, Canada

Jody Clarke-Midura
Harvard University, USA

Nick Zap
Simon Fraser University, Canada

Chris Dede
Harvard University, USA

ABSTRACT

Validating interactions in immersive virtual environments (IVE) used in educational settings is critical for ensuring their effectiveness for learning. The effectiveness of any educational technology depends upon teachers' and learners' perception of the functional utility of that medium for teaching, learning, and assessment. The purpose of this chapter is to offer a framework for the design and validation of interactions in IVEs as they are linked to learning outcomes. In order to illustrate this framework, we present a case study of the Virtual Performance Assessment (VPA) project at Harvard University (http:// vpa.gse.harvard.edu). Through our framework and case study, this chapter will provide educators, designers, and researchers with a model for how to effectively design immersive virtual and game-based learning environments for the purpose of assessing student inquiry learning.

DOI: 10.4018/978-1-61350-441-3.ch011

INTRODUCTION

The design and validation of learner interactions in virtual environments is critical for advancing assessment and interactive media in education. Although there has been much attention and speculation as to the effectiveness of the use of immersive virtual environments (IVE) in education, little research has been conducted that validates and provides concrete evidence that links the design of in-world interactions to learning outcomes. Starting with the learning objectives, a framework for evaluating and linking student in-world interactions to learning outcomes is essential. Validating those interactions throughout their development enables a clear connection to how and why students perform certain interactions in a given context. Selected interactions can then be captured in databases and scored for the purposes of establishing a cognitive model of the learner for a given domain.

Sophisticated interactive media, such as IVEs and serious games, enable the automated and invisible collection of rich and detailed event-logs on individual learners, in real-time, during the act of playing and learning (Clarke-Midura, 2009). Such event-logs provide time-stamped records and details of learners' interactions while they make choices and perform actions within the environment. Since the data captured is explicitly linked to learning outcomes and research questions, extraneous fuzzy data such as key strokes that do not provide information about the learning objectives become irrelevant. This data plays a key role in establishing the validity of in-world interactions for the purposes of assessing learning processes, such as science inquiry. Data can then be used to model students' thought processes and knowledge development providing a base for understanding the cognitive implications of those actions.

A cognitive model is required to make specific inferences about student learning. Cognitive models in educational measurement relative to serious games and IVEs are simplified descrip-

tions of problem solving on in-world tasks. These models help to characterize the knowledge and skills that students have acquired and facilitate the explanation and prediction of students' in-world performance. Since in-world interactions have been captured and stored, we propose that problem solving or inquiry in serious games can be described in terms of a cognitive model that can be used to characterize the knowledge, skills, and abilities of students at different stages in their development. As serious games and virtual worlds provide a medium in which to situate students to exercise inquiry practices, there are far reaching implications for serious games and virtual worlds as an assessment tool.

The purpose of this chapter is to offer a framework for the design and validation of interactions in IVEs as they are linked to learning outcomes. In order to illustrate this framework, we provide an overview of the Virtual Performance Assessment (VPA) project at Harvard University (IES# R305A080141). The VPA project is developing immersive technology-based performance assessments that measure middle school students' scientific inquiry knowledge, skills, and abilities (KSAs) aligned with national standards (College Board, 2009; National Research Council (NRC), 1996). In this chapter, we propose that validating interactions for the purposes of assessment is a multi-step process. First, to frame the discussion we provide a brief overview of the theoretical background of the Virtual Performance Assessment project. Next, we will discuss the process of designing and validating interactions back to the original learning objectives, using the VPA project as an example. Validating interactions back to the original learning objectives ensures the efficiency and content validity of the design. Third, we provide a case study of the VPA project and one empirical step in the process we are using to validate these interactions as outcomes of learning. Through our design framework and case study, this chapter will provide educators, designers, and researchers with a model for how to effectively design virtual and game-based learning environments for the purpose of assessing student problem solving and inquiry learning.

Background

Authentic assessment in science requires students to apply scientific knowledge and reasoning to situations similar to those they will encounter in the world outside the classroom, as well as to situations that approximate how scientists do their work (National Research Council (NRC), 1996). Thus, authentic assessment in science should examine students' understanding and appreciation of a scientific community of practice. The epistemic frame hypothesis (Clarke-Midura, Code, & Dede, 2011b) states that every community of practice has a culture whose basic value structure is composed of skills, knowledge, identity, values, and epistemology. Since existing assessment frameworks do not provide information on how inquiry processes develop, a cognitive model of inquiry is necessary to examine these processes *in situ*. This research uses the following model of inquiry (Figure 1) based on the work of White and colleagues (White, Collins, & Frederiksen, in press; White & Frederiksen, 1998).

Theorizing

Theorizing involves students' use and development of knowledge about the nature of scientific models and theories. Through this process, students develop an understanding of the similarities and differences in the types and purposes of scientific models, and how to create and connect models as a way of making sense of the world.

Identifying Questions and Hypothesizing

Identifying questions and hypothesizing involves students turning elements of theories into research questions requiring investigation. Through this process, students develop hypotheses as "different possible answers to a research question" (White, et al., in press) that help them understand the purpose and interrelated nature of research questions, and help them develop good research questions.

Accessing Data and Investigating

Accessing data and investigating involves students' developing an understanding of the different forms that scientific investigations can take and the goals of each type of investigation. Through this process, students follow steps to create an investigation, thereby developing an understanding of the cyclical, interrelated nature of investigations. As a result, students are able to discern limitations of studies.

Analyzing and Synthesizing

Analyzing and synthesizing involves students' ability to examine the information obtained during an investigation. Through this process, students develop an understanding of the purposes of qualitative and quantitative data analysis to support conclusions and guide theorizing. As a result, students develop the ability to carry out analyses and an understanding of how multiple analyses can be used to create a more complete view of phenomena.

The development and demonstration of higher-order cognitive skills involved in science inquiry are difficult to measure with open-response and multiple-choice tests (NRC, 2006; Quellmalz & Haertel, 2004; Resnick & Resnick, 1992). The focus of this chapter is not specifically about *what* inquiry is, but *how* inquiry can be measured through VPAs.

DESIGNING INTERACTIONS

Interactions in each VPA are designed with three aspects of assessment in mind (Pellegrino, Chu-

Figure 1. A model of the scientific inquiry process: Theorizing, identifying questions and hypothesizing, accessing data and investigating, and analyzing and synthesizing. © 2012, Jillianne Code, Jody Clarke-Midura, Nick Zap and Chris Dede. Used with permission.

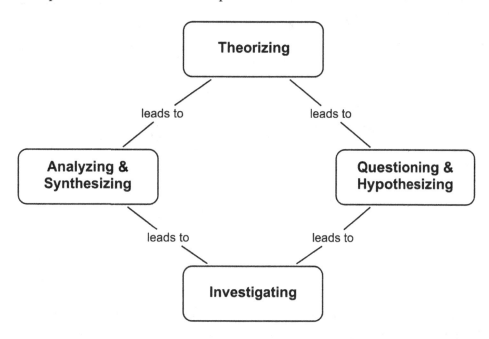

dowski, & Glaser, 2001): (1) the model of student cognition in the domain being assessed; (2) the set of beliefs about the kinds of observations that will provide evidence of students' competencies; and (3) the interpretation process for making sense of the evidence. Each of these aspects, cognition, observation, and interpretation, form the basis of the conceptual assessment triangle as proposed by Pellegrino and colleagues (Figure 2).

Validity is a central issue in test construction. "Validity is an integrated evaluative judgment of the degree to which empirical evidence and theoretical rationales support the adequacy and appropriateness of inferences and actions based on test scores or other modes of assessment…" (Messick, 1994, p. 1). In order to provide evidence that our assessment formatively diagnoses students' core concepts, we used the Evidence Centered Design framework (ECD; Mislevy & Haertel, 2006; Mislevy & Rahman, 2009) and conducted

a series of validity studies that provided evidence on construct validity.

Evidence Centered Design

Assessing complex interactions requires a comprehensive framework for making valid inferences about learning. One such framework is Evidence Centered Design (ECD; Mislevy, Steinberg, & Almond, 2003), which provides a formal, multi-layered approach to designing assessments as arguments (Mislevy & Haertel, 2006; Mislevy & Rahman, 2009; Mislevy, et al., 2003). The ECD framework helps to make explicit how high fidelity and rich assessment data in VPAs are established through iterative cycles of analysis, design, development, implementation, and evaluation instructional design decisions (Clarke-Midura, Code, Zap & Dede, in press). We have developed a modified version of the ECD framework by

Figure 2. The conceptual assessment triangle. Adapted from Pellegrino (2001). © 2012, Jillianne Code, Jody Clarke-Midura, Nick Zap and Chris Dede. Used with permission.

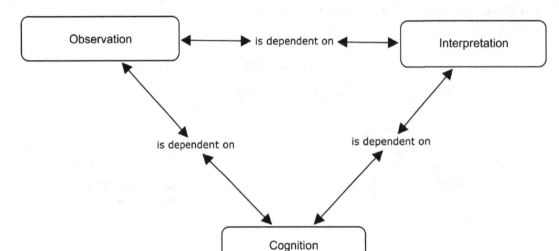

expanding the traditional approach to assessment design and applied ECD to designing complex interactions for virtual performance assessments. Using this approach, an evidentiary assessment interaction argument is formed that connects evidence and supporting rationales that essentially provide "a framework for developing [interactive] assessment tasks that elicit evidence that bears directly on the claims [we] want to make about what student[s] know and can do" (Mislevy, et al., 2003, p. 6). The ECD framework as developed by Mislevy and colleagues is a comprehensive framework that contains four stages of design: domain analysis, domain modeling, conceptual assessment framework and compilation, and four-phase delivery architecture.

The first two phases focus on the purposes of the virtual assessment interaction, the nature of knowing, and the structures required for observing and organizing knowledge. In Phase III, assessment interaction designers focus on the student model (what skills are being assessed), the evidence model (what in-world interactions elicit the knowledge and skills being assessed), and the task model (situations that elicit the behaviors/

evidence). These aspects of the design are inter-related. In Phase IV, the compilation phase, tasks are created. The purpose is to develop models for schema-based task authoring and developing protocols for fitting and estimation of psychometric models. Phase V focuses on the presentation and scoring of the task. The final phase, Phase VI, is an iterative and enables the refinement of the assessment as issues are encountered throughout the other phases. After piloting, the discrimination of individual items on each assessment is reviewed using point-biserial analysis to determine whether it requires modification.

As a part of our modification of the ECD framework, we have extended its application to include an examination of learning trajectories as opposed to individual test items. This was done so that ECD can be used with VPAs to measure student performance situated within an immersive narrative (e.g., students gathering data, identifying problems, making claims, and using data as evidence). To assist us with operationalizing this process, we used the Principled Assessment Designs for Inquiry system (PADI; Kennedy, 2005; Mislevy & Rahman, 2009). PADI is a design

Table 1. Extended ECD framework for VPA design and development

Modified ECD framework	Description
I. Domain Analysis	1. Establish the reason and purpose for assessing within the specified domain (science inquiry). 2. Compile research on the development of skills within the specified domain. 3. Develop a definition of competence within the specified domain. 4. Develop assessment objectives (competence of understanding). 5. Consult experts in the field about definitions of inquiry and assessment objectives.
II. Domain Modeling	1. Use information from the domain analysis to establish relationships among proficiencies, tasks, and evidence. 2. Explore different approaches and develop high-level sketches that are consistent with what they have learned about the domain so far. 3. Develop narrative descriptions of proficiencies of inquiry, ways of getting observations that evidence proficiency, and ways of arranging situations in which students provide evidence of targeted proficiencies. 4. Create graphic representations and schema to convey these complex relationships, and develop prototypes.
III. Conceptual Assessment Framework: • Cognitive Model • Student Model • Observation/Tasks Evidence • Interpretation	1. *Cognitive Model:* identify set of theory or beliefs about how students represent knowledge and develop competence in a subject. 2. *Student model:* What complex of knowledge, skills, or other abilities should be assessed. 3. *Observations/Tasks:* Identify kinds of tasks or situations (interactions) that will prompt students to say, do, or create something that demonstrates important knowledge, skills, and competencies. 4. *Evidence:* Identify behaviors and performances that reveal knowledge and skill identified in the student model. Identify and summarize evidence. 5. *Interpretation:* Develop a method for interpreting observations and evidence.
IV. Compilation: • Task creation • Statistical Assembly • Assessment Implementation	1. Develop tasks based on conceptual assessment triangle. 2. Develop models for evidence. 3. Develop statistical assembly and strategies and algorithms for test construction.
V. Four-Process Delivery Architecture: • Presentation • Response Scoring • Summary Scoring • Activity Selection	1. Develop data structures and processes for implementing assessments. 2. Develop back-end architecture that will capture and score student data. 3. Develop prototype. 4. Pilot prototype.
VI. Refinement	1. Refine assessment based on pilot data. 2. Repeat pilot test as necessary and refine assessment. This is an iterative cycle.

architecture for creating assessment templates for science inquiry within the ECD framework. See Clarke-Midura, Code, Zap & Dede (in press) for an example of what these PADI templates look like.

Within each of these PADI templates, we have detailed the KSAs we are measuring and then linked these KSAs to specific observable tasks within the VPAs that represent each of the science inquiry processes. Linking KSAs like this provides a measure of validity that research has found often lacking in performance assessments (e.g. Linn, et al., 1991). Using the ECD Framework,

we determined the constructs that were tapped by the assessment and selected interactions, or superobservables (Almond, 2009; Mislevy, et al., 2003), that were later used.

Some of the super observables were used in every assessment so that we are able to associate them with parallel forms of the assessments. After piloting, the discrimination of interactions in each assessment was reviewed using point-biserial analysis to determine whether modification was needed. Our research questions enable further validation of these VPA designs.

VALIDATING INTERACTIONS

Developing an effective performance assessment of complex tasks such as science inquiry requires the analysis of the cognitive processes and structures that contribute to task performance. This section describes the data collection procedures associated with a cognitive task analysis technique known as the Precursor, Action, Results, Interpretation technique (PARI; Hall, Gott, & Pokorny, 1995). The procedures derived from Hall et al. (1995) impose a structure on the performance tasks in the VPAs that captures the cognitive and behavioral components of science inquiry. This data provides critical validation evidence supporting the ECD design and alignment findings. Further, it enables additional refinement of tasks within the VPA before a larger scale implementation.

Cognitive Task Analysis and the PARI Process

As a skill analysis component of the technology, our adaptation of the PARI technique for middle school students allows a both broad and deep examination of science inquiry within the situated context of the VPA. This approach is a structured interview in which a research analyst uses standardized interview questions to systematically probe students during and after the VPA session. As they seek solutions, students are probed for reasons behind the actions they elected to take and for their interpretations of the results of their actions. In this way, the reasoning processes that are at the heart of inquiry are made apparent.

After the VPA experience, the students were asked to elaborate on solutions they just generated during a rehash session. They were explicitly asked to address the factors considered, or reasons for, the science inquiry decisions they made during the performance task. The question probes are a part of the structured interview designed to reveal knowledge and skill in the context of their use.

The PARI procedure thus yields fine-grained, but systematized, protocol data that capture both the inquiry steps and the supporting reasons for each decision made. From detailed protocol data, both precise targets for further in-depth instruction as well as broad skill commonalities were identified. We are currently in the process of triangulating this data with the trace data generated by the VPA system. We will use this data to form the basic framework for reporting student misconceptions in the inquiry process to teachers.

Standardization and Codification of PARI Procedures

Standardizing and codifying any task analysis methodology is important to its continued utility. The rationale is tied to our research goal to represent both depth and breadth of science inquiry proficiency. In order to investigate skill and knowledge commonalities and associated processes of transfer, a comparison of task analysis results across several VPAs was necessary. Comparisons of teacher identified novice and expert inquiry learners are also needed to examine the development of science inquiry skills. Comparative analyses require data having a standard form. Imposing a structure on the PARI inquiry sessions with the use of standardized probes ensures unified data structures across different task analyses, thereby facilitating these types of comparisons.

Task Sampling Variability

We also conducted an alignment study to test the alignment of our performance assessments to the cognitive model of inquiry we claim to be measuring (Quellmalz, et al., 2006). We used alignment procedures developed by Webb and colleagues (Webb, Schlackman, & Sugrue, 2000) that address: categorical concurrence, depth-of-knowledge consistency, range-of-knowledge correspondence, and balance of representation. Given the structure of the ECD framework, which requires us to articulate every aspect of our assessment design conceptually, our assessments align with the inquiry model. We will triangulate this data with results from the PARI Cognitive Task Analysis.

Assessment Utility

Integrating technology in the teaching and learning process goes beyond mere usability. Traditional usability relies heavily on an end-of-use judgment made by the user on the utility of the technology to satisfy the purpose for which it is used. Numerous reports and recommendations exist for evaluating the usability of technical content (i.e. Clarke-Midura, Code, Mayrath, & Dede, 2011a, 2011b; Code, Clarke-Midura, Zap, & Dede, in press) Less frequently studied is the evaluation of technology and its utility for teaching and learning (Nokelainen, 2006). For a technology to be useful in education, it must be both usable and hold some kind of utility for teaching and learning. Ultimately, the effectiveness of an educational technology depends upon teachers' and learners' choice, perception, and functional utility. We propose that both the teacher and the learner should judge the effectiveness of a technology to play a facilitative role in education along at least three dimensions: teaching, learning, and assessment. An important part of the iterative design of any teaching and learning environment involves users' process-use judgments between the beginning-of-use and end-of use cycle that reflect the ability of the virtual learning environment to perform its intended functions. The focus of the case study research presented below is to explore the learners' perspective and their judgment of the assessment utility (JOAu) of our virtual performance assessments.

CASE STUDY: VIRTUAL ASSESSMENT PROJECT

Research Goals

With funding from the Institute of Education Sciences (IES), the Virtual Performance Assessment project at Harvard University is developing and studying the feasibility of immersive virtual performance assessments to assess scientific inquiry of middle school students as a standardized component of an accountability program (see http://vpa.gse.harvard.edu). The goal is to provide states with reliable and valid technology-based performance assessments linked to state and national academic standards around science content and inquiry processes, extending capabilities to conduct rigorous studies that provide empirical data on student academic achievement in middle school science.

A constructivist, learner-centered approach to technology design requires a constructivist, learner-centered approach to the evaluation of that design (Mayrath, Clarke-Midura, Dede, & Code, 2011). Advances in information technology enable innovative ways for using performance-based assessments to measure learning (Pellegrino, et al., 2001). One such technology is IVEs. IVEs are three dimensional (3D) simulated contexts that provide rich, authentic contexts in which participants interact with digital objects and tools. The goal of our Virtual Performance Assessment (VPA) research project is to develop and study the feasibility of using IVEs as a platform for assessing middle school students' science inquiry skills in ways not possible with item-based tests. IVEs allow for performances and observations of these skills that are not possible via traditional testing formats (Clarke, 2009). The purpose of this particular study is to examine student perceptions of the assessment utility of IVEs for the evaluation of their science inquiry knowledge, skills, and abilities (KSAs). We present criteria for evaluating the assessment utility of virtual performance assessments and how this feedback is used to make experiential changes to the design and implementation of the IVE while keeping the same student assessment model.

Assessment 1: Save the Kelp!

To frame the discussion and illustrate the implementation of aspects of the design for Assessment 1, the following is a vignette of *Assessment 1: Save the Kelp!* highlighting the various design aspects of the learner experiences while establishing student understandings of the assessment outcomes (knowledge, skills and abilities; KSAs).

Thomas sits at his computer and logs into the student portal. He watches an introductory video telling him that they kelp in Glacier Bay are dying and he needs to help figure out why. He is given a brief description of Bull Kelp and why they are important to the ecosystem. Thomas opens the assessment and is immediately told how to navigate

the world. He also learnsthat he will be given quests to complete and he will know that there is a quest by a yellow "!" over a person's head. He is transported to Glacier Bay where Ranger Tina gives him his first quest.

Ranger Tina asks Thomas to travel under water by clicking on the scuba tank on the beach to see where the kelp live and learn more about kelp from a diver named Marc. Thomas sees the scuba tank on the beach, walks over to it, and clicks on the tank. He is then teleported to the kelp bed in the harbor.

While under the water, Thomas talks with Marc, where he learns more about kelp, and how he can use each of his tools in his toolbar. Thomas discovers that he has four tools he can use to take measurements around Glacier Bay. He tries to take a population sample of the Bull Kelp in the harbor by clicking on the tool and then clicking on one of the kelp in the bay. He finds out that

Figure 3. A character, Ranger Tina, in Assessment 1 that has a quest to give. © 2012, Jillianne Code, Jody Clarke-Midura, Nick Zap and Chris Dede. Used with permission.

Figure 4. Scuba Marc teaches about kelp and each of the data collection tools in the toolbar. © 2012, Jillianne Code, Jody Clarke-Midura, Nick Zap and Chris Dede. Used with permission.

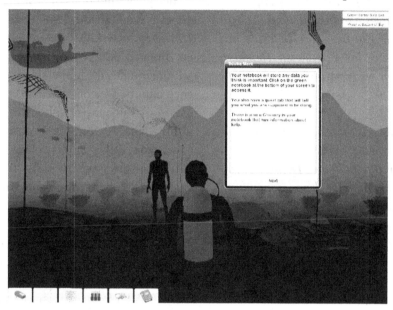

Figure 5. Two scientists on the beach have competing hypotheses and quests to give in Assessment 1. © 2012, Jillianne Code, Jody Clarke-Midura, Nick Zap and Chris Dede. Used with permission.

there are 20 Kelp in Glacier Bay. Thomas decides that this information is important and that he may need it later, so he saves it to his notebook. Marc tells Thomas to return to the shore and talk to Ranger Tina to receive his next quest. Thomas clicks on the tank on his back and is teleported back to the shore.

Ranger Tina tells Thomas there are two scientists on the shore have competing hypotheses about why the Kelp in Glacier Bay is dying. Thomas goes over to the scientists to talk to them about what they think is going on. Thomas talks to both of the scientists and they ask him to help them collect additional data to figure out if the Power Plant in Glacier Bay is causing the kelp to die. The scientists also tell Thomas to travel to a healthy bay, Green Cove, to collect comparison data.

The assessment utility of any IVE are guided by design assumptions of how the interactions in the IVE facilitate the demonstration of students' knowledge and skills. To examine our constructivist, situated design assumptions about how the VPA facilitates the immersive assessment of science inquiry, we conducted an empirical investigation of student perceptions of the assessment utility of the VPA for this purpose. Evaluating the assessment utility in this context focuses the research on the types of skills the VPA enables students to demonstrate, providing additional evidence that the VPA is a valid assessment of science inquiry. Building on the work of Noke-lainen (2006) on pedagogical usability we have developed the Meaningful Assessment of Learning Questionnaire for Virtual Environments (MALQ-VE). Items on this scale are loosely based on items from the Pedagogically Meaningful

Figure 6. Example of the Assessment 1 notebook containing measurements. © 2012, Jillianne Code, Jody Clarke-Midura, Nick Zap and Chris Dede. Used with permission.

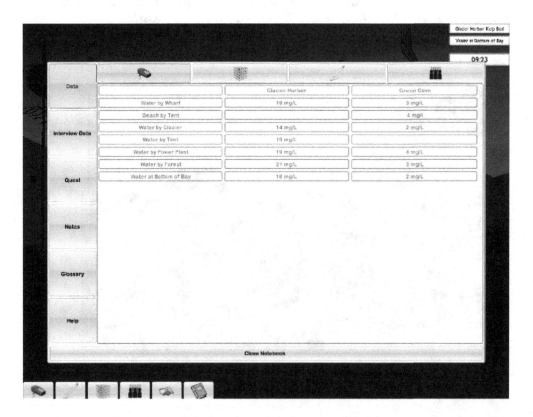

Learning Questionnaire (PMLQ; Nokelainen, 2006) and help to establish how well each of our VPAs enable learner control, engagement in activity, added value for learning, flexibility, feedback, and valuation of previous knowledge.

Methods and Data Sources

Using a sample of middle school science students ($N = 260$, 125 Female), we adapted 20 items from the Pedagogically Meaningful Learning Questionnaire (PMLQ; Nokelainen, 2006). This instrument included student perceptions of the following components of VPAs: learner control, learner activity, added value, flexibility, feedback,

and valuation of previous knowledge (for a copy of this instrument, please contact the first author). Following a 90 minute exposure to Assessment 1, students were asked to state their agreement with a series of items using a 5 point Likert scale from *1 = strongly disagree* to *5 = strongly agree*. A second study using Assessment 2 and validating the revised MALQ-VE is planned for Spring, 2011.

Results

Descriptive Statistics

A classical item analysis, including an exploratory factor analysis, was conducted to assess the uni-

Table 2. Classical item analysis of the MALQ-VE (N = 260, α = .80, CI$_{95}$ = .76, .83)

					Response Category[d]				
Item	M[a]	SD	CITC[b]	α[c]	1	2	3	4	5
1	3.06	1.09	**-0.13**	0.82	16	70	84	62	28
2	3.48	0.98	0.48	0.78	10	31	74	115	30
3	3.54	0.92	0.48	0.78	9	21	80	120	30
4	3.43	0.96	0.38	0.79	8	38	74	115	25
5	3.26	1.07	0.53	0.78	10	63	67	89	31
6	3.01	1.16	0.33	0.79	30	62	64	84	20
7	3.15	1.24	0.44	0.78	31	46	79	60	44
8	2.77	1.03	**0.20**	0.80	24	91	78	55	12
9	3.40	1.03	0.45	0.78	12	42	64	113	29
10	3.05	1.08	**0.15**	0.80	21	63	76	82	18
11	3.75	1.11	0.33	0.79	13	28	37	114	68
12	3.62	0.92	**0.20**	0.79	4	29	68	121	38
13	3.12	1.06	0.58	0.77	16	62	79	82	21
14	3.32	1.00	0.42	0.78	16	31	88	103	22
15	3.49	0.90	0.47	0.78	5	31	83	114	27
16	3.36	0.96	**0.19**	0.80	8	40	87	100	25
17	2.90	1.27	0.48	0.78	48	55	59	72	26
18	3.56	0.91	0.57	0.78	6	30	62	136	26
19	3.59	0.88	0.37	0.79	7	20	73	133	27
20	3.58	1.02	0.36	0.79	6	37	66	103	48

Note: CITC = Corrected Item Total Correlation; Bolded items have a *CITC* < .25 and are poorly discriminating; [a] Item mean is a classical test theory (CTT) indicator of difficulty. [b] Indicates item discrimination. [c] α if item is deleted; [d] 1 = *strongly agree*; 2 = *disagree*; 3 = *neutral*; 4 = *agree*; 5 = *strongly agree*.

dimensionality of this scale. A classical approach was chosen for this analysis because of the small relative sample size ($N = 260$). The results of a classical analysis for the MALQ-VE are presented in Table 2. The distribution of item correlations (CITC) was from -.13 to .58. Since the CITC for items 1, 8, 10, 12, and 16 are low (< .25) they are poorly discriminating. These items were removed from subsequent analyses.

Exploratory Factor Analysis

An exploratory factor analysis (EFA) was used to assess latent dimensionality of the MALQ-VE, since the original validation of the PMLQ was conducted with elementary students and was designed for evaluating Learning Management Systems. The factors were extracted using Varimax rotation with Kaiser Normalization. The EFA on this data set revealed a three-factor structure as reported in Table 3: learner flexibility and feedback (α = 0.77, CI_{95} = .72, .81), learner control (α = 0.69, CI_{95} = .62, .74), and learner activity (α = 0.59, CI_{95} = .50, .67). The calculated internal consistency of the entire scale is α = 0.83, CI_{95} = .80, .86, above the acceptable level of α_0 > .70 (Tabachnick & Fidell, 2006). However, learner control and learner activity scales could be improved. Items on each of these scales will be revised for the larger study.

Based on each newly defined factor, a summary analysis reveals (Table 4) that students strongly agreed or agreed that the IVE enabled increased learner flexibility and feedback (52.2%), control (46.5%) and activity (60.6%). However, these results reveal that there is still room for improvement of the overall student experience in each of these areas.

Table 3. Factor pattern and structure matrices for the MALQ-VE (α = 0.83, CI_{95} = .80, .86)

Item	Factor 1	Factor 2	Factor 3	h²
Learner Flexibility and Feedback (α = 0.77, CI_{95} = .72, .81)				
7	**0.62**	0.25		0.80
13	**0.60**	0.30	0.16	0.38
2	**0.58**	0.29		0.41
3	**0.56**	0.16	0.21	0.48
15	**0.52**		0.29	0.38
14	**0.42**	0.15	0.27	0.47
11	**0.37**	0.25	0.18	0.40
Learner Control (α = 0.69, CI_{95} = .62, .74)				
5	0.30	**0.62**		0.21
9	0.20	**0.56**	0.13	0.49
4		**0.49**	0.17	0.38
17	0.36	**0.45**		0.43
6	0.10	**0.44**	0.15	0.38
Learner Activity (α = 0.59, CI_{95} = .50, .67)				
20		0.24	**0.58**	0.27
18	0.28	0.35	**0.51**	0.39
19	0.23		**0.46**	0.36

Note: Items 1, 8, 10, 12, and 16 were removed as they were identified as poorly discriminating in the classical analysis; Items in bold indicate the highest factor loading.

Table 4. Summary of student responses by factor

	Response Category[a]				
	1	2	3	4	5
Learner Flexibility & Feedback	5.5%	13.7%	28.6%	38.9%	13.3%
Learner Control	8.3%	20.0%	25.2%	36.4%	10.1%
Learner Activity	2.4%	11.2%	25.8%	47.7%	12.9%

Note: [a] *1 = strongly agree; 2 = disagree; 3 = neutral; 4 = agree; 5 = strongly agree.*

Qualitative Analysis

In addition to the items in the MALQ-IVE, students were given a series of open-ended questions to provide them an opportunity for additional feedback on specific elements of the VPA. The following is a list of the top three elements that the students liked and disliked about Assessment 1.

Students liked:

- Taking samples
- Making their own decisions about the problem
- Moving around, choosing where to go and what to do, game-ness

Students didn't like:

- Time limits
- So many questions
- Didn't know if they were right at the end

Aside from specific elements of the VPA environment, the students had a lot to say about how they viewed this method of assessment. The following are some excerpts from student responses (note that these responses have been edited for grammar and spelling).

"I think instead of telling us if we were right or wrong, don't tell us at all because that makes it seem like a test and you get nervous so you tense up and forget what you are supposed to answer."

"This was very different and was a little bit more fun than pen and paper tests. It kept you thinking the whole time and it was fun playing a game at the same time as taking a test."

"Tests I take in school are stressful and more fact-based. This was more like learning."

Assessment 2: There's a New Frog in Town

To frame the discussion and illustrate the implementation of the design changes made from Assessment 1 to Assessment 2, the following is a vignette of *Assessment 2: There's A New Frog In Town* highlighting the changes in the user experience while maintaining the same assessment outcomes.

Arielle sits at her computer and logs into the student portal. She opens the assessment and is immediately allowed to choose what her avatar looks like. She selects an avatar and enters the world.

The ability for students to choose their own avatar (Figure 7) is a design decision that highlights for students that they have a sense of autonomy and control over their assessment experience. Further, an aerial overview of the farms helps provide situational awareness for students so that they are less likely to get confused and/or lost in the world.

Figure 7. An example of a VPA avatar selection screen. © 2012, Jillianne Code, Jody Clarke-Midura, Nick Zap and Chris Dede. Used with permission.

The camera slowly provides an aerial view of the world to orient Arielle to the problem space. Arielle sees that there is a village and what appear to be farms with ponds. The camera then focuses in on a multi-colored frog with 6 legs. Arielle wonders, "What could be causing this frog to have 6 legs?" The assessment begins. A scientist and farmers who have just discovered this mutated frog greet Arielle. The farmers all offer competing hypotheses for why the frog is mutated. The scientist turns to Arielle's avatar and tells her that she must conduct an investigation and come up with her own theory and back it up with evidence. He asks her if she thinks any of the hypotheses are plausible.

Having the characters present competing hypotheses sets up the context of the assessment (Figure 8). This question also allows us to identify in the assessment any misconceptions or prior knowledge that students may bring to the problem. Research has shown that this is an important part

of science inquiry that is often overlooked in assessments (Sadler, 1998).

The scientist shows Arielle a science lab and tells her to come find him when she is ready. Arielle inspects the 6-legged frog and puts in her backpack to investigate in the lab. She then walks around the village and sets out to explore the farms

At this point in the assessment, Arielle has a choice. She could have gone to the Internet kiosk and access information there such as research articles. However, she has chosen to explore. This choice is recorded on the back-end. We are recording students' choices and compiling them into patterns. These patterns are then built and compared to profiles of students' inquiry knowledge established during our cognitive task analyses. Because of this, the assessment has a built-in framework that enables us to examine students' intent and interpret their actions.

Figure 8. An example of characters presenting competing hypotheses in a VPA. © 2012, Jillianne Code, Jody Clarke-Midura, Nick Zap and Chris Dede. Used with permission.

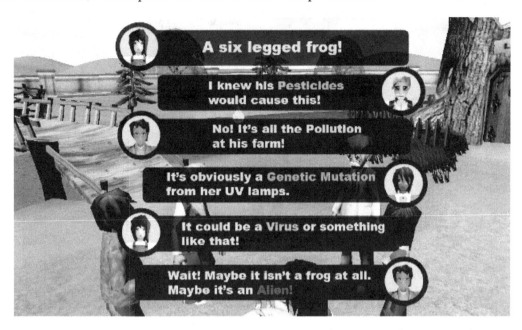

Before entering the first farm, Arielle is asked by the farmer what she is planning to do there. At the first farm, Arielle says she plans to collect a water sample. She enters the farm and collects a sample of the water. She also picks up a frog and a tadpole to bring back to the lab and run some tests. She finds a research article and starts reading it. It contains information on tadpoles and viruses so she puts it in her backpack and decides to visit another farm. At this point, Arielle has collected 5 pieces of data. Her backpack will only allow her to hold 8 pieces of data at a time.

Arielle will be forced to make a choice about what data she thinks is the most important or that she wants to investigate first. If students were allowed to pick up every piece of data in the world, then it would be difficult to make inferences about their knowledge of what data is important evidence in the investigation. If students were asked to evaluate a piece of data every time they collected it then the task would become boring. Thus, the

design is requiring students to make a choice through actions. She can go to the lab at any times to run tests on the data (e.g. water tests, blood test, genetic test). Any piece of discarded data from the backpack will go back into the world and can be picked back up at any time (given there is space in the backpack).

Arielle has collected 8 pieces of data from two farms. She does not want to discard any data and decides to go to the lab to run some tests. She arrives at the lab and examines the water samples. Her tests show that the lab water and water from one of the farms contains pesticides. However, one of the farms has clean water. She runs genetic tests on the 2 frogs she collects and sees that they are the same. She notes that both of the frogs have high counts of white blood cells. She decides that she needs more evidence and goes to collect water samples from the other two ponds. At this point, Arielle has spent her time collecting data and running tests.

Figure 9. The Internet kiosk for conducting literature searches. © 2012, Jillianne Code, Jody Clarke-Midura, Nick Zap and Chris Dede. Used with permission.

Figure 10. An example of the VPA backpack containing a limited number of items. © 2012, Jillianne Code, Jody Clarke-Midura, Nick Zap and Chris Dede. Used with permission.

Figure 11. An example of VPA lab results. © 2012, Jillianne Code, Jody Clarke-Midura, Nick Zap and Chris Dede. Used with permission.

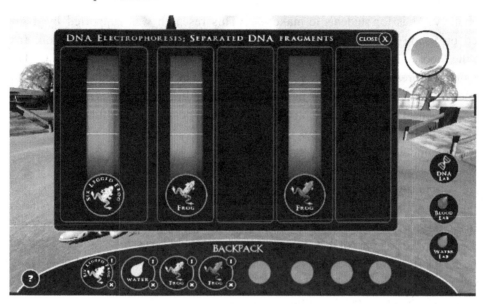

At the computer on her left, Maria has been tackling the assessment differently. As soon as Maria spoke with the scientist, she decides to go to the science lab. She examines the research that was available on frogs and tadpoles. She reads about viruses and genetic mutations in frogs and decides to go gather data to determine which is the cause. She goes to each of the four farms and collects a tadpole and a frog to run tests on. She gets back to lab and finds that all of the frogs have similar genetic make up. However, two of the tadpoles have small tails. She notes that a frog from the same farm also has a virus in its blood. She looks up the virus in the research documents and believes she has found evidence. She speaks to the scientist and builds a claim for why the frog is mutated, including evidence and then reasoning.

After class, Ms. Jones reviews the reporting tool to see the diagnoses the assessment provides about what each student knows and does not know about the various sub-skills involved in science inquiry. The tool presents data at both the individual and class level, and Ms. Jones finds that, while the majority of students are strong in providing evidence, they are weak in reasoning from evidence. Moreover, only a few of the students took Maria's approach and went to the research first to seek information on the problem. The rest of the class spent time exploring and gathering data and then analyzing it first. Some of the students did not even use the research. Some only collected one or two pieces of data before they attempted to make a claim.

FUTURE RESEARCH

In May and June 2011, we intend to implement Assessment 2 with middle school students. Currently we have a potential population of N = 7000. As a follow up to this analysis we intend on using Item Response Theory to provide additional validation evidence of the MALQ-IVE.

CONCLUSION

The goal of both VPAs is for students to make choices based on sound science inquiry skills that advance the theory that they are attempting to build. In both VPAs presented here, a student's measure of science inquiry performance is based on their in-world actions. Their actions and choices are given a range of scores and weightings that contribute to an ongoing student model of science inquiry temporally evaluated based on past, present, and future actions. In other words, a choice is evaluated in terms of the previous actions, the student's actual choice within the context of the available choices, and the outcome of that choice, which in turn sets the stage for the next set of actions. For example, if a character asks a student what they think the problem is and the student responds that they think the mutant frog is a result of pollution, the character will ask the student to provide evidence for their claim.

The evidence that a student gives will be weighted and evaluated based on their prior actions (data that they have previously collected) and by what they choose to present as evidence. Although both Assessment 1 and Assessment 2 evaluate the same learning outcomes and are tracked, measured, and scored in the same way, the user experience is qualitatively and markedly different which we hypothesize will provide a more valid, reliable, and accurate representation of the actual state of a students' science inquiry knowledge, skills, and abilities.

Validating interactions in IVEs used in educational settings is critical for ensuring their effectiveness for learning. Virtual performance assessment in IVEs involves designing in-world interactions that are linked directly to learning outcomes. Since sophisticated technologies enable the invisible and non-obtrusive capture of student in-world interactions, researchers and educators can use this information for diagnostic, formative, and summative assessment purposes.

ACKNOWLEDGMENT

This research was supported by a grant from the US Department of Education, Institute of Education Sciences awarded to Chris Dede (IES# R305A080141). Any opinions and conclusions are those of the investigators and do not represent an official position of the funding agency.

REFERENCES

Almond, R. G. (2009). Bayesian network models for local dependence among observable outcome variables. *Journal of Educational and Behavioral Statistics*, *34*(4), 491–521. doi:10.3102/1076998609332751

American Association for the Advancement of Science (AAAS). (1990). *Science for all Americans*. New York, NY: Oxford University Press.

American Association for the Advancement of Science (AAAS). (1993). *Benchmarks for science literacy: A Project 2061 report*. New York, NY: Oxford University Press.

Baxter, G. P. (1995). Using computer simulations to assess hands-on science learning. *Journal of Science Education and Technology*, *4*(1), 21–27. doi:10.1007/BF02211578

Baxter, G. P., Elder, A. D., & Glaser, R. (1996). Knowledge-based cognition and performance assessment in the science classroom. *Educational Psychologist*, *31*(2), 133–140. doi:10.1207/s15326985ep3102_5

Baxter, G. P., & Shavelson, R. J. (1994). Science performance assessments: Benchmarks and surrogates. *International Journal of Educational Research*, *21*(3), 279–298. doi:10.1016/S0883-0355(06)80020-0

Chooseco. (1977-2011). *Choose your own adventure*. Retrieved January 30, 2011, from http://www.cyoa.com/public/index.html

Clarke, J. (2009). *Exploring the compexity of inquiry learning in an open-ended problem space.* Unpublished Doctoral Dissertation, Harvard University, Cambridge, MA.

Clarke-Midura, J., Code, J., & Dede, C. (2011a). *Assessment 2.0: Rethinking how we assess science inquiry with technology-based assessments.* Paper presented at the National Science Teachers Association 2011 Annual Conference.

Clarke-Midura, J., Code, J., & Dede, C. (2011b). *Measuring students' scientific inquiry processes and skills with immersive performance assessments.* Paper presented at the National Association for Research on Science Teaching Annual Meeting.

Clarke-Midura, J., Code, J., Mayrath, M., & Dede, C. (2011a). *Exploring inquiry processes in immersive virtual environments.* Paper presented at the AERA 2011 Annual Meeting.

Clarke-Midura, J., Code, J., Mayrath, M., & Dede, C. (2011b). *Using evidence centered design to develop immersive virtual assessments.* Paper presented at the AERA 2011 Annual Meeting.

Clarke-Midura, J., Code, J., Zap, N., & Dede, C. (in press). Assessing science inquiry in the classroom: A case study of the virtual assessment project. In Lennex, L., & Nettleton, K. (Eds.), *Cases on Inquiry Through Instructional Technology in Math and Science: Systemic Approaches.* New York, NY: IGI Publishing.

Clarke-Midura, J., Dede, C., & Mayrath, M. (2010a). *Designing immersive virtual environments for assessing inquiry.* Paper presented at the Annual Meeting of the American Educational Research Association.

Clarke-Midura, J., Dede, C., & Mayrath, M. (2010b). *Ensuring the integrity of data in virtual immersive assessments.* Paper presented at the Annual Meeting of the American Educational Research Association.

Code, J., Clarke-Midura, J., Zap, N., & Dede, C. (in press). Virtual performance assessment in immersive virtual environments. In Wang, H. (Ed.), *Interactivity in e-learning: Cases and frameworks.* New York, NY: IGI Publishing.

College Board. (2009). *Science College Board standards for college success.* New York, NY: The College Board.

Cronbach, L. J., Linn, R. L., Brennan, R. L., & Haertel, E. H. (1997). Generalizability analysis for performance assessments of student achievement or school effectiveness. *Educational and Psychological Measurement, 57*(3), 373–399. doi:10.1177/0013164497057003001

Hall, E. P., Gott, S. P., & Pokorny, R. A. (1995). *A procedural guide to cognitive task analysis: The PARI methodology. Brooks Airforce Base.* TX: Air Force Human Resources Laboratory.

Kennedy, C. (2005). *Constructing PADI measurement models for the BEAR Scoring Engine (PADI Technical Report 7).* Menlo Park, CA: SRI International.

Kuhn, D., & Pease, M. (2008). What needs to develop in the development of inquiry skills? *Cognition and Instruction, 46*(4), 512–559. doi:10.1080/07370000802391745

Linn, R. L. (1994). Performance assessment: Policy promises and technical measurement standards. *Educational Researcher, 23*(9), 4–14.

Linn, R. L. (2000). Assessments and accountability. *Educational Researcher, 29*(2), 4–16.

Linn, R. L., Baker, E. L., & Dunbar, S. B. (1991). Complex performance-based assessment: Expectations and validation criteria. *Educational Researcher, 20*(8), 5–21.

Mayrath, M., Clarke-Midura, J., Dede, C., & Code, J. (2011). *A framework for designing assessment activities for virtual worlds.* Paper presented at the AERA 2011 Annual Meeting.

Messick, S. (1994). The interplay of evidence and consequences in the validation of performance assessments. *Educational Researcher, 23*(2), 13–23.

Mislevy, R., & Haertel, G. (2006). *Implications of evidence centered design for educational testing.* Menlo Park, CA: SRI Interantional.

Mislevy, R., & Rahman, T. (2009). *Design pattern for assessing cause and effect reasoning in reading comprehension.* Menlo Park, CA: SRI Interantional.

Mislevy, R., Steinberg, L. S., & Almond, R. G. (2003). On the structure of educational assessment. *Measurement: Interdisciplinary Research and Perspectives, 1*(1), 3–62. doi:10.1207/S15366359MEA0101_02

National Assessment Governing Board (NAGB). (2010). *Science framework for the 2011 national assessment of educational progress.* Washington, D.C.

National Research Council (NRC). (1996). *National science education standards.* Washington, DC: National Academies Press.

National Research Council (NRC). (2005). *How students learn: History, mathematics, and science in the classroom.* Washington, DC: The National Academies Press.

National Research Council (NRC). (2006). *Systems for state science assessment.* Washington, DC: The National Academies Press.

National Research Council (NRC). (2010). *A framework for science education: Preliminary public draft.* Retrieved December 12, 2010, from http://www7.nationalacademies.org/bose/Standards_Framework_Homepage.html

National Research Council (NRC). (2011). *Learning science through computer games and simulations.* Washington, DC: The National Academies Press.

Nokelainen, P. (2006). An empirical assessment of pedagogical usability criteria for digital learning material with elementary school students. *Journal of Educational Technology & Society, 9*(2), 179–197.

Organisation for Economic Co-operation and Development (OECD). (2007). *PISA 2006: Science competencies for tomorrow's world. Volume 1: Analysis.*

Pellegrino, J. W., Chudowski, N., & Glaser, R. (2001). *Knowing what students know: The science and design of educational assessment.* Washington, DC: National Academies Press.

Pine, J., Baxter, G. P., & Shavelson, R. J. (1993). Assessments for hands-on elementary science curricula. *MSTA Journal, 39*(2), 5–19.

Quellmalz, E. (1984). Successful large-scale writing assessment programs: Where are we now and where do we go from here? *Educational Measurement: Issues and Practice, 3*(1), 29–35. doi:10.1111/j.1745-3992.1984.tb00735.x

Quellmalz, E., & Haertel, G. (2004). *Technology supports for state science assessment systems.* Washington, DC: National Research Council.

Quellmalz, E., Kreikmeier, P., DeBarger, A. H., & Haertel, G. (2006). *A study of the alignment of the NAEP, TIMSS, and new standards science assessments with the inquiry abilities in the national science education standards.* Paper presented at the Annual Meeting of the American Educational Research Association.

Resnick, L. B., & Resnick, D. P. (1992). Assessing the thinking curriculum: New tools for educational reform. In Gifford, B., & O'Connor, M. (Eds.), *Changing assessments: Alternative views of aptitude, achievement, and instruction* (pp. 37–75). Norwell, MA: Kluwer Academic Publishers. doi:10.1007/978-94-011-2968-8_3

Rosenquist, A., Shavelson, R. J., & Ruiz-Primo, M. A. (2000). *On the "exchangeability" of hands-on and computer simulation science performance assessments.*

Sadler, P. M. (1998). Psychometric models of student conceptions in science: Reconciling qualitative studies and distracter-driven assessment instruments. *Journal of Research in Science Teaching, 35*(3), 265–296. doi:10.1002/(SICI)1098-2736(199803)35:3<265::AID-TEA3>3.0.CO;2-P

Shavelson, R. J., Baxter, G. P., & Gao, X. (1993). Sampling variability of performance assessments. *Journal of Educational Measurement, 30*(3), 215–232. doi:10.1111/j.1745-3984.1993.tb00424.x

Shavelson, R. J., Baxter, G. P., & Pine, J. (1991). Performance assessment in science. *Applied Measurement in Education, 4*(4), 347–362. doi:10.1207/s15324818ame0404_7

Stecher, B. M., & Klein, S. P. (1997). The cost of science performance assessments in large-scale testing programs. *Educational Evaluation and Policy Analysis, 19*(1), 1–14.

US Department of Education (USDE). (2010). *National Education Technology Plan 2010.* Washington, DC: US Department of Education.

Webb, N. M., Schlackman, J., & Sugrue, B. (2000). The dependability and interchangeability of assessment methods in science. *Applied Measurement in Education, 13*(3), 277–301. doi:10.1207/S15324818AME1303_4

White, B., Collins, A., & Frederiksen, J. (in press). The nature of scientific meta-knowledge. In Khine, M. S., & Saleh, I. (Eds.), *Dynamic modeling: Cognitive tool for scientific enquiry.* London, UK: Spinger.

White, B., & Frederiksen, J. (1998). Inquiry, modeling, and metacognition: Making science accessible to all students. *Cognition and Instruction, 16*(1), 3–118. doi:10.1207/s1532690xci1601_2

Wilson, M. (2009). Measuring progressions: Assessment structures underlying a learning progression. [10.1002/tea.20318]. *Journal of Research in Science Teaching, 46*(6), 716-730.

ADDITIONAL READING

Clarke-Midura, J. (2010). The Role of Technology in Science Assessments. *Better: Evidence-Based Education.*

Clarke-Midura, J., & Dede, C. (2010). Assessment, technology, and change. *Journal of Research on Technology in Education, 42*(3), 309–328.

Dede, C. (2009). Immersive interfaces for engagement and learning. *Science, 323*(5910), 66–69. doi:10.1126/science.1167311

Duschl, R., Schweingruber, H., & Shouse, A. (Eds.). (2007). *Taking science to school: Learning and teaching in grades k-8.* Wachington, DC: National Academies Press.

Mislevy, R., & Haertel, G. (2006). *Implications of evidence centered design for educational testing.* Menlo Park, CA: SRI Interantional.

National Research Council. (2011). *Learning Science Through Computer Games and Simulations.* Washington, D.C.: National Academy Press.

Pellegrino, J. W., Chudowski, N., & Glaser, R. (2001). *Knowing what students know: The science and design of educational assessment.* Washington, DC: National Academies Press.

Quellmalz, E. S., & Pellegrino, J. (2009). Technology and testing. *Science, 323*(5910), 75–79. doi:10.1126/science.1168046

Tucker, B. (February, 2009). Beyond the bubble: Technology and the future of student assessment (Education Sector Reports). Washington, DC: Education Sector.

U.S. Department of Education. (2010). *National Educational Technology Plan Washington DC*. Office of Educational Technology, U.S. Department of Education.

KEY TERMS AND DEFINITIONS

Avatar: Virtual representation of a person in a virtual world.

Evidence Centered Design (ECD): Design framework for assessments that focus on evidence of student learning.

Immersive Virtual Environment (IVE): 3-D computer-simulated environments where users interact with objects in the world and possibly avatars of other people. They can be single or multi-user. They have the look and feel of a videogame, but in the case of our research they are designed around educational experiences.

Performance Assessment: An assessment where students are asked to perform a task or create a product. Students are often rated on both the process and final product of their performance/action.

Science Inquiry: A cognitive process that entails theorizing, questioning and hypothesizing, investigating, analyzing, and synthesizing

Summative Assessment: An assessment of learning that samples from a domain of knowledge. Meant to measure cumulative growth or used as program evaluation.

Virtual Performance Assessment (VPA): Immersive technology-based performance assessments where students perform a task on the computer.

Section 3
Interpersonal Interactivity through Media

Chapter 12
A Case Study of Social Interaction on ANGEL and Student Authoring Skills

Ruth Xiaoqing Guo
Buffalo State College - State University of New York, USA

ABSTRACT

This case study examined a constructivist approach to creating an interactive learning environment on ANGEL for graduate students in a course: EDC 604—Authoring for Educators. The course curriculum was designed to help students construct knowledge to develop professional Websites. However, the class time was insufficient to meet the student learning needs and course objectives. The social interaction on ANGEL provided flexible time and space for participants to discuss the issues important to them. Findings revealed that practical action research combined with social interaction shed light on important issues of professional development through reflection on practice. The constructivist approach provided an interaction of two important sets of learning conditions: Internal and external levels for student cognitive development in authoring skills. Data were analyzed using a grounded theory approach. This study also identified issues for further research: The importance of curriculum design to meet students' needs, the effect of digital divide, and how student attitude impacts learning.

INTRODUCTION

This study examined the instructional practices of a constructivist approach to creating an online interactive learning environment on the students in a graduate course EDC 604—Authoring for Educators. Most students enrolled in this course were in-service teachers for K-12 public school learners.

The course curriculum was designed to help students construct knowledge to develop profes-

DOI: 10.4018/978-1-61350-441-3.ch012

sional Websites by a series of activities on HTML, Dreamweaver, Photoshop, Fireworks, and Flash. Most students entered the class without any background knowledge in these areas. This course has been based on face-to-face weekly classroom instructional mode. However, the class time for instructions and practice was insufficient to meet the student learning needs and course objectives.

I wish I could report that the course went off without a glitch, but that was not the case. To begin, the students experienced a great deal of anxiety over this fact: If the course was instructed on a regular meeting basis, would they be able to meet the course requirements and obtain the authoring skills? Additionally, most students did not have off-campus access to the programs such as Dreamweaver and Photoshop, which made content review after class difficult. The biggest hurdle for the instructor to overcome, however, was to understand what students had learned and what they did not yet know after each session of the instruction. While some students came to class with impressive knowledge of technology and they could acquire the new content at a faster pace, many others were helpless and panicked. Some of them asked the instructor questions by email, but the instructor could only respond to them individually at the cost of consuming a lot of time.

Effective interaction between and amongst instructor and class members became a key to the success of the course. Constructivist pedagogy would be helpful to enhance student learning. Student weekly learning journals would help me and the student themselves understand their learning process. In order to create an interactive learning environment, the instructor built a discussion forum on ANGEL, a Web-based application for curriculum, instruction and assessment, and required the students to post their learning journals online. The instructor read and responded to student questions and the other class members could access instructor's responses. This online activity allowed those who did have advanced skills to share them with their classmates; it afforded

them a safe space for acquiring and developing those skills; it afforded all the class members a friendly space for social and academic interaction. It is important to note that these students were overwhelmingly pleased with the idea. This study focused on the research question: How did social interaction on ANGEL enhance student learning and improve their authoring skills?

LITERATURE REVIEW

According to John Dewey (1933), education is a social process. Education is growth. Education is not a preparation for life; education is life itself. Therefore, building social interaction in class should be a contributory factor for enhancing learning. Dewey believed that learning was useful only in the context of social experience. Constructivism is a critical way of building knowledge through societal practices, including schooling, reflecting, and meaning making (Wonacott, 2001). Activity theory in general, and the zone of proximal development (ZPD) specifically, initiated by Vygotsky (1934, 1978), suggest that such zones exit when a less-skilful individual or student interacts with a more-advanced person or teacher, or is stimulated by an instrument, allowing the student to fulfill the task not possible when acting on his or her own. Activity theory encourages collaboration, social practice, and critical pedagogy. Russell (1995) defined activity theory in this way: "Activity analyzes human behavior and consciousness in terms of activity systems: Goal-directed, situated, cooperative human interactions, such as a child's attempt to reach an out-of-reach toy...a discipline, a profession, an institution, a political movement, and so on." (pp. 54-55). Utilizing an activity theory perspective, the participants of this study extend current understandings of societal practices to include not only how constructivist approach works but also why it is effective.

Alessi and Trollip (2001) stated that interactive multimedia must be built on sound human factors to be effective. This has a strong implication for this study because it underscores how learning practices with social interactions are deeply connected to both content and context. The participants in this study were required to design and create Websites, which included learning about the Website design and the pedagogies that the participants obtained from the course and then would apply to their classroom teaching in public schools. For most of the participants/students, it has been challenging to create Websites. Learning takes place within ZPD, an optimal challenge level that is neither too difficult nor too easy and meaningful to the learner. The ZPD is a range in which a learner can perform a task with help, including the development of languages, cognition, social practice, knowledge and skills. Vygotsky believed that learning is a dynamic process of social practice. Such development lies in two levels: internal and external levels. A person can make learning happen at certain internal levels, but he/she will do it better with external assistance, which includes the discursive environment such as tools being used and people providing support. The greatest advantage accrued from using ANGEL online communication is the flexibility and convenience this Web-based technology provides for a variety of learners with different needs. New technologies provide external stimuli for a student to interact with others. Some research has shown evidence of the use of Web-based technology as a catalyst empowering classroom teachers to play a role in shifting toward more constructivist pedagogy (Guo, 2009).

The explosive growth of the Web technology has been one of the biggest changes in the last two decades. Use of the Web-based technology has more impact on learning than all the developments in instructional technology of the past 30 years. Windschitl and Sahl (2002) documented their two-year study and examined how instructional technologies could be integrated into classroom teaching. This was mediated by their interrelated beliefs about learners in their school, about the concept of "good teaching" in the discourse of the institutional culture, and about the role of technologies in students' lives. Making a connection between the theoretical concept and practice helps learners construct knowledge in a meaningful way. A learner learns more effectively in any curriculum through a teacher's direct instruction, through practicing the skills, and through self-reflection, self-assessment, and receiving corrective feedback. John Dewey (1938) highly recommended the use of reflection: "To reflect is to look back over what has been done so as to extract the net meanings which are the capital stock for intelligent dealing with further experiences. It is the heart of the intellectual organization and of the disciplined mind" (p. 110). Dewey emphasized that "Keeping track is a matter of reflective review and summarizing, in which there is both discrimination and record of the significant features of a developing experience" (Dewey, 1938, p.110). Based on this guidance, reflection (e.g. weekly learning journal) and summary reflection (e.g. at the end of the semester) were parts of the course assignments. The instructor kept track and responded to the weekly reflections, and then analyzed the summary reflections at the end of the semester.

Journal writing has become a widely accepted approach to facilitating teacher candidates' reflection (Black, Sileo, & Prater, 2000; Lee, 2010). However, educators and researchers have argued that two critical aspects should not be overlooked in the process of reflection through journal writing.

First, reflection activities should be conducted within a specific context so that the students can understand how decisions on curriculum are influenced by contextual issues (Zeichner & Liston, 1996). Teaching students to connect context and content of reflection has been an important component in teacher education.

The second critical aspect is that the traditional journal writing is regarded as a personal process rather than an interactive communication (Lee, 2010; Putnam & Borko, 2000) and it causes a lack of potential to build a conversational community among class members. In order to overcome this limitation, Hatton and Smith (1995) recommended the use of social interaction. Dewey explained that "interaction" plays a main role for interpreting a learning experience in educational function—objective/external and internal conditions. A normal experience is "an interplay of these two sets of conditions", Dewey (1938, p. 39) claimed. Vygotsky (1934) strongly believed that cognitive development lies in two levels: internal and external levels. The traditional journal writing only provides internal condition. Combining both factors, the objective/external condition and the internal condition, social interaction can form an optimal learning situation. Using ANGEL to create social interaction provides both internal and external learning conditions.

Bandura (1977) suggested that environments that provide social interaction may develop greater reflection. Social interaction may enhance motivation and prolong engagement with the task. Social interaction would almost certainly bring forth more information and ideas that could be shared and would support student development of higher order thinking skills. This interaction might take place during the learning activity or it may occur later in formal or informal group discussions.

Students' lives are closely related to the ever growing speed of technology. With advancements in technology, online learning and computer-mediated communication among class members can be an effective tool for reflection activities (Harasim, 1990). There is a growing interest in exploring the possibility of using technology for students' reflection (Gomez, Sherin, Griesdorn, & Finn, 2008; Whipp, 2003). Gomez et al. (2008) stressed that "reflection has to be situated within a culture of practice that values reflection as part of ongoing work" (p.126). Participants in Lee's study (2010) reported that interactive online journaling facilitated their reflection in terms of (a) accessing each other's context, (b) obtaining a critical friend who asked in-depth questions, (c) offering additional ideas and suggestions, and (d)

providing confidence and social support. Online journal interaction can be a great opportunity to facilitate students' critical reflection by providing an opportunity to examine their beliefs and practices within a specific context.

Windschitl & Sahl (2002) argued that technology itself did not motivate teachers' movement toward constructivist pedagogy, rather, previous dissatisfaction with traditional teacher-centered practices made teachers take action to transform the classroom activities through collaborative student work and project-based learning environment. Coupled with online interaction for social construction, learning is enhanced in its broadest sense, sources of information are expanded, communication with others is improved and critical thinking is developed at an optimal level. Constructivist pedagogy provides a way to promote an effective model for cognition on the basis of interactions and discussions in an authentic online environment (Guo, 2005).

METHOD

The research site was in the Educational Technology graduate program at the Buffalo State College, State University of New York. Case studies were conducted with 28 students enrolled in the course: EDC604—Authoring for Educators in the fall 2009 and fall 2010 semesters. Fourteen students in fall 2009 and fourteen in fall 2010 semesters. Case study was employed because it takes into account the contextual nature of complex issues and explains how the process of these issues shift over time (Barton, Tan, Rivet, 2008; Donmoyer, 1990; Guo, 2009; Yin, 1994).

Case study was conducted to allow the instructor as a researcher to (a) explore and describe practical research action with a focus on the connection between online social interaction and student acquisition of authoring skills, and (b) document and describe how students applied those practices to engage themselves meaningfully in learning. To construct this case study, multiple sources of qualitative data were collected. The data collection included (1) surveys of students' information on technological skills administered at the beginning of the semesters, (2) student online learning journals and discussions, (3) students' projects, (4) students' summary reflections by the end of the semester, and (5) instructor observations during these two semesters. Observations were conducted during face-to-face class meetings, focusing on how online social interactions affected classroom meetings. To begin with the case study, the instructor created an E-Portfolio for each student enrolled in the course. Data collected from each stage of the practical action research were sorted into the E-Portfolios. There were totally 28 E-Portfolios developed during the semesters when the course was offered. The E-Portfolios included student pictures taken in the first week, survey information, activity assignments on HTML and CSS, proposal for final project, online learning journals, summary reflection, and final project.

Data were analyzed using a grounded theory approach. Data gathered from two semesters in this study were coded, classified, interpreted, and finally summarized to generate conclusions. Grounded theory is a qualitative research approach used to generate a theory that explains an action or interaction about a specific topic. A theory is grounded or rooted in the data. Ground theory approach was employed in this study because (a) grounded theory is an emergent research process with similarities to action research (Strauss, Corbin, 1998), (b) the grounded theory model of research is more flexible in structure and it recognizes the role of the researcher and the participants as a social interactive team (Charmaz, 2006; Guo, 2005). Charmaz called this approach the "constructivist" grounded theory model.

Students were guided to apply the method of practical action research to examine their progress in this course. Grounded in action research, practical action research focuses on the "how-to" approach on the processes of learning activities

(Mills, 2000). Schmuch (2006) described action research as "group dynamics," "collaborative, participatory, and reciprocal" (p. 30). Participants of action research carry out action research as partners. All the participants were students who enrolled in the course EDC604 Authoring for Educators. The students were informed that their participation in online communication was one of the assignments for the course work which would be used as a research purpose. Practical action research, "which takes a more applied and contextualized approach to action research" (Mills, 2000, p. 21), emphasizes the practicality of action research for teachers as they strive to enhance student learning. Allan and Miller (1990) pointed out that the emphasis of practical action research was on "real classrooms and real schools" (p. 196). Action research was implemented in the course EDC604 for students to create social interactions and then reflect on their practices.

Mills (2007) identified practical action research as follows: (a) the participants of practical action research are empowered to determine the nature of the investigation to be undertaken; (b) the participants are committed to continued professional growth and school/program/course improvement and that the participants systematically reflect on their practices; (c) participants choose their study of focus, design their data collection methods, analyze and interpret their data, and (d) develop action plans based on their findings. These characteristics of practical action research serve well for the purpose of this study.

Schmuck (2006) specified ten stages that help move from reflection to action research. The process of practical action research can be displayed in the following figure (see Figure 2). When the action reaches the last stage, the cycle has completed and a new cycle of action research begins.

There is a strong connection between reflection and action research. The ten stages of practical action research were implemented during the course of EDC604—Authoring for Educators. The course syllabus provided detailed instructions

Figure 1. Cycle in conducting action research

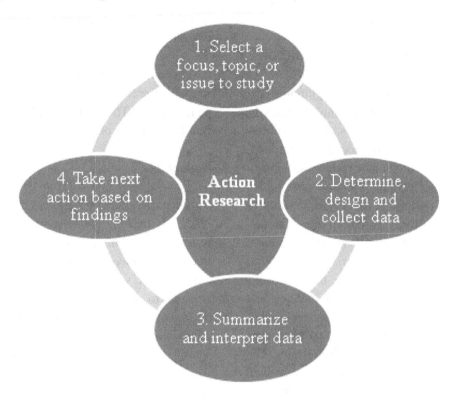

Figure 2. Process in conducting practical action research

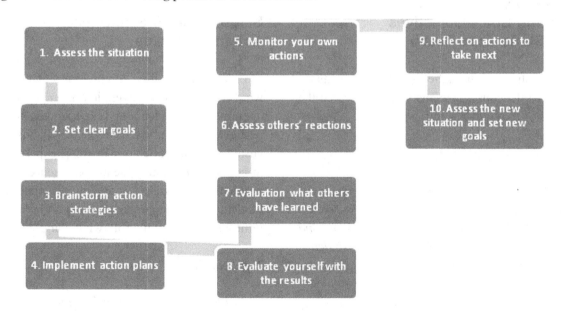

for students to participate in the cycle of reflection and action research as a group interaction.

Stage One: Assessing the Situation

A survey was administered at the beginning of the semester, assessing students' technological skills, students' attitudes, expectations, and capabilities of the authoring skills; and examining the situation and social actions that were enhancing or hindering student learning. Students were guided to apply action research to assess the possibilities of using ANGEL for constructing social interaction. To prepare for online social interaction, students were assigned into groups randomly to get to know each other as an ice break activity. They took individual and group pictures and posted them on ANGEL. They were required to edit the photos using Photoshop and to prepare their photos for future use in their Websites. The group members got to know each other pretty well within 20 minutes, and then got up in front of the class to introduce themselves as a group to the rest of the class. The practical action research started.

Stage Two: Setting Clear Goals: Setting Goals/Objectives for Students to Reach

After introductions at the first class, students reviewed the course syllabus which described the goals of the course as follows:

Goals of the Course

(a) To engage students in constructing knowledge of authoring tools for Web design; (b) To develop and integrate technology into instruction and learning in ways that support diverse students' attainment of high levels of learning; (c) To create learner-centered units using pedagogical approaches that support students' construction of their own knowledge; and (d) To create instruction that aligns with current state and national learning

standards, such as National Science Education Standards and the National Educational Technology Standards.

Particularly, approach to online learning journal interaction was applied to support student learning. The course syllabus provided this rationale for reflections as follows:

Rationale

By reflection, educators indicate both the learning processes and the learning outcomes. Through reflection, students construct knowledge by articulating connections among their expectations, learning, and self. Reflective activities introduce students to new kinds of self-assessment, often an outcomes-based self-assessment, which they carry into life outside of and beyond educational settings. In addition, through engaging in reflective activities, students develop the stance and practices of a reflective practitioner who can synthesize multiple sources of evidence and make contingent and ethical sense of them.

Stage Three: Brainstorming Action Strategies

In order to move from the present situation toward goals and objectives, it was important to use previous knowledge and experiences to make problem-solving plans. The course syllabus suggested students reflect on learning experiences in course work and presentations, and conduct problem-solving discussions with class members. Students were encouraged to focus on but not to limit themselves to the following components:

Key Learnings

List and describe your key learnings from the readings and/or the in-class presentations or activities. What new ideas/concepts stood out to you as being particularly important?

List and describe at least five ideas in a numbered list.

Pluses

What did you like most about what you learned? Were there any "A-Ha!" moments where confusing concept(s) were clarified?— Mention specific ideas, concepts, methods and/or tools.

Potentials

How might various ideas, concepts, activities, and/or skills that you learned be useful in the future? What are some possible applications in your own classroom or professional practice?

Concerns

What ideas did you find confusing or difficult to understand? What ideas might you disagree with? What ideas might require further clarification? List and describe at least three ideas in a numbered list.

Questions

What questions do you have about any topic or tool presented in the readings or in the in-class presentations or activities? List questions in a numbered list.

Stage Four: Implementing Action Plans

This stage carried out the action strategy created in Stage Three. The description was listed in the course syllabus:

Weekly Learning Journal and Summary Reflection

Description: You are required to post your leaning journal (the length of each journal is about 300 to 500 words) on ANGEL to discuss and to share the issues of Web design based on the lessons you have learned, such as what works for you and what doesn't. The class members and the instructor can be involved in your learning process and provide support in a timely manner. The last journal is a summary reflection of about 4 to 5 double-spaced pages, due in the last week. You can reflect on your learning process based on your biweekly journals posted on ANGEL. The total number of learning journals is 10 for the semester.

Submission: Each week, please upload your weekly entry in Discussion Forum on ANGEL. Name your entries by number in sequence.

FINDINGS AND DISCUSSIONS

Grounded theory is a complex process. The research began with a question "How did social interaction on ANGEL enhance student learning and improve their authoring skills?" which helped to guide this study. The actions from Stage Five to Stage Eight included: (5) Monitoring my own actions, (6) assessing others' reactions, (7) evaluating what others have learned, and (8) evaluating the results, are coped within this section to answer the research question. Data sources (learning journals coupled with assignments and instructor observations) were analyzed using grounded theory approach, accommodating with the stages of practical research action, on an ongoing schedule base. Learning journals were retrieved weekly from ANGEL. As the instructor began to gather data, core theoretical concept "online social interaction" was identified. In order to find if and how social interaction on ANGEL enhanced student learning and improved their authoring skills, tentative linkages were developed between the theoretical core concept and the data which emerged from each stage of practical action research: Social interaction and pedagogical decision-making in Stage Five; social interaction and positive support in Stage Six; social interaction and problem solving skills in Stage Seven; and social interaction and competent performance in Stage Eight. These four stages were basically the action-taking practices with a focus on a specific connection between the core concept and the data in each stage.

Stage Five: Monitoring my own Actions: Social Interaction and Pedagogical Decision-Making

Sarason (1990) suggested that educators, as they are still developing human beings, need to engage in personal and academic development as much as their students. Instructors cannot create and sustain the conditions for the productive development of students if those conditions do not exist for instructors. The social interaction-based practical action research is successful when participants work together with cooperation and equality. As an instructor and an equal member of the online social interaction, I took the role of leadership to create and provide supportive interaction which included understanding others' ideas, feelings, and concerns; encouraging others' inquiries and questions; acknowledging others' responses to questions; providing positive social support to enhance the ability of class members to perform competently.

From students' learning journals posted on ANGEL, the instructor could easily understand what students knew about the course content and what they did not know. As students assessed their levels of knowledge about Web design editors and graphics editing programs, the instructor could accommodate the teaching agenda accordingly. For example, the following message and

several other similar learning journals helped the instructor make a pedagogical decision: To start with the basic skills to teach in order to allow students to construct basic knowledge about the authoring tools.

Our first day of class was very interesting, especially because I have never used any of the mentioned programs throughout my education: Photoshop, Dreamweaver, or any sort of Website design tool.

Journal postings like the following one also provided some hints for the instructor to apply different pedagogies to reach teaching objectives:

I would have liked some more time with the different media we used throughout our first class, maybe a worksheet where everyone is doing the same activity with respect to the pictures we took so the pacing is better and people who are slower are not left in the dust.

To respond to a call like the one above, a constructivist approach was applied in classroom meetings and students were grouped to conduct hands-on activities. Within a group, the students with advanced technology skills could support those with beginning skills. As the semester proceeded, the journals revealed that students built more confidence in their skills. Creating a site was totally new to all students. Cascading Style Sheets (CSS) Styles and HyperText Markup Language (HTML) were challenging them, too. However, from reading the students' journals, the instructor understood that they got it and we could move on. The instructor noticed that the students enjoyed the challenge when they knew they could manage it. It was an encouraging finding! The following journal entries on ANGEL described the process of their learning experience with Dreamweaver after the second week's class:

"I learned the importance of creating a site and organizing the site in a way in which it is clean and easy for me to read. This skill will help me once I start to create my own personal site for the final project. One of the things that I really like about the lesson in Dreamweaver this week was learning how to enter in key words so that my site will be able to be searched for on a search engine. I think that learning the basics building blocks of creating a Web page are some of the most important skills that you need to be an effective site designer. These are the skills that you need to make the simplest page and also the most complex pages look beautiful and flow nicely."

"Once we had finished the basic formatting of a Web page we got into more advanced level of Dreamweaver. We started to look at how to change CSS styles and how to create new ones. This allows us to go in and change words and fonts for each line. We also worked on creating new style templates and changing preset headings. This allows you to quickly change formatting of the Web page in a quick manner and keep all the text the same."

"We also worked on editing the html code for our Web sites. It was neat to see how the code related to the text and how the text was related to the code. I like to see this because I have used code before to help me design my Web page when I was stuck. It was extremely helpful."

Learning Dreamweaver this time around is a lot more intense. I am enjoying the challenge and looking forward to applying what I have learned to my project."

From online journals, the instructor's attention was called to students' concerns. In the first few weeks of the fall 2009 semester, the instructor responded to individual questions on ANGEL so that other students could benefit from the responses by reading them. However, it was very time con-

suming to respond to individual questions. Once in a while, students approached the instructor and asked why the instructor had not responded to his or her last posting. In order to use the instruction time more efficiently and in an effort to answer these questions, the instructor collected all the questions from each of the journal entries and provided responses to the critical questions in the following class meeting. Particularly, the issues and the questions that were common to the class members were addressed in support of student engagement. In the fall 2010 semester, the class members were encouraged to respond to one another's questions. Interaction among students increased the scope of communication and the ability of students' problem-solving skills. This will be discussed in the following stages.

Stage Six: Assessing Others' Reactions: Social Interaction and Positive Support

Positive social interaction requires class members to communicate with esteem, respect, and share mutual responsibilities. Group social interaction and support enable the capability of group members to perform confidently and competently. For instance, group dancing performs more successfully when dancers communicate and cooperate with each other. Students learn more effectively when they feel accepted and respected by their class members. In the first week of the semester, the students formed groups to know one another by taking photos and then by introducing their group members to the class members. From the first week on, they built a positive learning community. In their first learning journal that they posted on ANGEL, they expressed that they enjoyed working with their community.

I enjoyed the time we spent at the beginning of class forming groups and learning about the path that others are taking to become better in their profession. The photographing exercise was a wonderful icebreaker that I hope to incorporate into my classroom someday.

Thanks for a nice first day of class everyone. Seems as though we have a great group of people and most are very knowledgeable in technology already. I enjoyed our "photo" session which was a good ice breaker for our groups. It was nice meeting Amanda and hearing where and what everyone teaches. We are all busy, so it's nice to hear that we're all in the same boat.

Since they remarked that they were in the same boat, they had a sense of belonging and feelings of inclusion which paved the path for development of social interaction trust. In such a situation, they were willing to support each other. They cooperated to solve problems to reach the goals important to all of the class members. For example, a student posted several questions in his learning journal, where other students responded with positive support and offered valuable suggestions.

Student's request for help: *I am a little confused how to place text labels on the slides in movie maker.*

Student's response: *Movie Maker certainly takes some practice. Be sure to sit near someone (if possible) with a little knowledge in these (and other) programs... (That's how I learned things last semester).*

Student's response: *Text labels..... (I think I know this one. Correct me if I'm wrong anyone.).... In Movie Maker, there are options for adding text on a screen, and also adding beginning and ending credits, etc. Example: Label your name on the screen if you appear in a 20 second video segment of your PPT/Movie Maker project, or over top of your photo.*

Instructor's response: *Thanks Mark for the good answer. To add text to the Movie frame, do the following: With the program Movie Maker open, click Edit Movie >click Make titles or credits>select "Add title at the beginning"> Type*

your title and then click Done to add the title to the movie. You can use the same method to add ending credits as Mark mentioned.

Student's question One: *What does it mean by slide transitions on Project #1?*

Student response: *The transitions are how the slides move from one to the next (ie. fade in, fade out, etc). You just have to click on the left of the screen where it says slide transitions and drag them in between the slides.*

Student's Question Two: *Do we need to write a lesson plan for our teachback activity?*

Student's response: *I say "no" to the lesson plan for the teach back.... Nothing in the syllabus mentions about one. This is a smaller project than the hypermedia (where you will do one).*

Students were inspired to respond to each other's postings, which became external stimuli for further reflections in meaningful ways in support of whom they were and what they wanted to do. They were satisfied that they could make contributions to the class community. Students were also highly encouraged to raise questions. Writing an APA style proposal for their final projects was challenging for most students. They had a lot of questions even though examples were provided on ANGEL. Questions like that could be answered by instructor and class members online anytime.

Students felt secure to ask questions. They knew they would be accepted no matter what kind of questions they raised, whether simple questions or high level thinking questions. When they met face-to-face in the classroom each week, they were still carrying on the discussions they posted on ANGEL. No one would feel embarrassed if he or she posted simple questions. A student had a question about the length of his first journal entry because his journal was beyond the length (300 to 500 words) required and described in the course syllabus.

Student's inquire: *"I want to know is this entirely too much writing for a journal entry? I would like to keep it shorter, so any suggestions for me would be happily accepted."*

Instructor's response: *"You have put invaluable insights into your journal. I really enjoyed reading it. You definitely built some depth in your understanding of the concepts and the class environment. Your concerns and questions are critical and they helped me understand your challenges and concerns. So in next session, I will be able to address your concerns, and together we will deal with the issues you mentioned in your journal. The length of this journal is fine with me. As long as it is rich in content, I enjoy reading it. But if you think it took you too much time, you can write it a little bit shorter and focus on the most important components (to address) in your journal."*

Positive social support and interaction provided an environment for class members that promoted esteem and respect. Students were acknowledged and felt proud to contribute important ideas and suggestions as they worked together. Without a strong foundation of positive social support and interaction, competent performance would not be achieved. Students commented on their learning conditions: "The professor provided a comfortable learning environment for students. If we encountered a problem, we were able to seek peers or the professor for help." Students felt that the most rewarding part of the experience was having the opportunity to work with "such a nice, helpful group of people." A student reflected on his learning journal: "Whenever I found myself stuck on a particular task there was always someone that was willing to take the time and help me find my way. I only wish I was more knowledgeable in certain areas so that I could return the favor."

Social interaction on ANGEL created an optimal learning situation. One student's learning journal was an inspiration for another posting. This constructivist approach provided an interaction of these two sets of learning conditions: Internal and external levels for student cognitive development in authoring skills.

Stage Seven: Evaluating what Others have Learned: Social Interaction and Problem Solving Skills

Stage Seven and Stage Eight focused on examining questions such as "Have my students developed the qualities that I was looking for when I set goals in Stage Two? Are the outcomes or results that I am getting desirable? Have there been any unexpected, undesirable outcomes?" Data sources were retrieved from student reflections on ANGEL, observations, and ANGEL postings. In this stage, however, focus was placed on the correlation between interaction and problem solving.

Online communication allowed the instructor to check students' postings anytime and give responses within a business day. It also allowed the class members to communicate efficiently. Students could get support from instructor and class members anytime. The following figure indicates the timely communication between students and instructor and among students. This timely communication helped solve the problems and allowed students to learn curricular matters week by week. So the instructor could be aware of and students could have a better control of the learning process. Even some students who were weak in technological skills at the beginning of the semester would not feel left behind when they participated in this social interaction environment.

Class members were willing to participate in the discussion and engaged in the process of others' projects. Each of them became an expert at least in one area and shared their knowledge and skills with others.

Student's inquiry: *I am not sure if I'm following the book correctly... I completed the first several pages in the book, and when I viewed it as a Webpage it looked exactly the same as my Word Doc. I went back and cannot find any errors... Help!*

Student's response: *It might just be how you saved it. When you save as, click the plain text or txt only first, then change the extension to html*

Figure 3. Timely interactions between instructor and students

[+] Post Title		Flag		Score	Author
⊟ Issue with Links	--		Tom	9/20/2010	1
RE: Issue with Links	--		Instructor	9/20/2010	0
Sources	--		Instructor	9/20/2010	0
Journal	--		Jackie	9/19/2010	0
⊟ Proposal Question	--		Tom	9/19/2010	2
RE: Proposal Question	--		Instructor	9/20/2010	0
⊞ RE: Proposal Question	--		Lucy	9/19/2010	2
⊟ Barbara learning journal	--		Barbara	9/16/2010	1
RE: Barbara learning journal	--		Instructor	9/16/2010	0
⊞ .css	--		Jim	9/13/2010	1
⊟ leftcurls.jpg	--		Ann	9/11/2010	1
⊞ RE: leftcurls.jpg	--		Lucy	9/11/2010	1
⊟ Quizzes	--		Nancy	9/11/2010	1
RE: Quizzes	--		Instructor	9/14/2010	0
⊟ KompoZer (helpful tips)	--		Jean	9/8/2010	1
RE: KompoZer (helpful tips)	--		Instructor	9/14/2010	0
⊟ Resume	--		Jean	9/8/2010	1
RE: Resume	--		Instructor	9/14/2010	0

afterward. If a box comes up with an encoding thing just click yes or save.

Student's inquiry: *I decided to use Word on my computer, but cannot open the Web page with a browser. The book keeps telling me to "Save files and then open the Web page with a browser." Any suggestions?*

Student's response: *Open the browser (internet explorer, etc). Click file->open. Then browse for your document (should be ceramics). It will open it for you in the browser, if you coded it as ceramics.html.*

It took a long time for one individual to solve a problem which might be a piece of cake to others. But it was eventually efficient in solving the problem within a supportive group as Vygotsky (1934, 1978) described in the zone of proximal development. One student reflected on his experience of facing a challenge in this way:

It's very helpful to have so many knowledgeable and helpful people around to offer suggestions or assistance. Within just a few minutes Mike managed to teach me how to generate a functional drop-down menu so that I could create multiple choice questions for my site. Without the help, I'm not sure I would have been able to learn using just the textbook.

The more things I learn with Dreamweaver the better I can improve my site. While is my site nowhere near perfect, I feel my most recent product offers more than my initial concept.

Students were looking forward to meeting together to complete their projects. The social support and interaction provided motivation and enthusiasm for the students to work together. In each stage of the practical action research, they reflected on the content area and fixed something to make improvement on their projects.

Stage Eight: Evaluating the Results: Social Interaction and Competent Performance

When the students first read the syllabus and saw that they would be working with Dreamweaver,

Photoshop, Fireworks, and Flash, they were nervous. Most students said they "have never really had an opportunity to work with any of the programs." Yet by the end of the semester, they had developed a good foundation of skills that they could build upon. Students pointed out: "From interactive activities, I learned authoring tools Dreamweaver, Fireworks and Flash." They took good control of their learning and implemented Adobe CS4 for their final projects—Web design. Based on their own positive learning experience from this course, students built interactive Websites for their students to enhance their learning outcomes. Teachers usually teach their students in the same way as they learned.

Analysis and evaluation of students' final projects showed that students had good knowledge and skills about the authoring tools—Adobe CS4 they learned during the semester. From the first day of the class when they started to collect data and worked on the skills of image editing using Photoshop and Fireworks to the final stage of publishing their Websites, they worked together as a group. The instructor created a discussion forum on ANGEL for students to post learning journals and to participate in discussions. The instructor also created an E-Portfolio Submission

Folder on ANGEL for students to submit their assignments and projects. Janet created a Website on writing for students between Grade Two through Grade Six. She combined the features of Flash, the Spry Accordion feature in Dreamweaver, audio, and videos to provide an interactive learning resource for young children to increase their interest and skills in writing. She was applying the constructivist model to create environments that provided both internal and external learning conditions.

Alice was teaching math at a middle school in Buffalo. She created an interesting Website for her school's math club. The math club was running the annual Pi Day celebration on March 14th for 3.14. Alice designed a Website to inform the parents of the students what would be going on. This was an engaging Website that would inspire students to find fun in mathematics, particularly the Pi Day activities.

All students' final projects were creative and geared toward their teaching. They were anxious to finish their final projects. With a practical action research perspective, they modified their projects to reach the best results. When they wrote a proposal for their final projects, they were not sure how much they could achieve. During the

Figure 4. Example of an interactive Web design project by student (source: http://bscstudent.buffalo-state.edu)

Figure 5. Example of website in math designed by student (source: http://bscstudent.buffalostate.edu)

process of the creating the Websites, they became more experienced and skillful. They adjusted the original design from time to time after they received feedback and self-assessed on their projects. One of the students reflected on the process of his Website design:

I'm looking forward to completing my final project in the weeks ahead. My site is starting to take shape and the overall goal has become clearer. I've strayed quite a bit from my original proposal, but I know it's for the best. When I first began I kept the design fairly simple because I wasn't sure what I'd be able to create.

Twenty-six out of twenty-eight students completed the course successfully with professional final projects that they would use as teaching resources. In the last day of the class, the students proudly presented their final projects. Two students failed the course. One failed because the student did not have the Internet at home to access ANGEL and he could not participate in online social interaction. Another student could not complete his course work because he did not take the previous course EDC601 Instructional Technology.

FUTURE RESEARCH DIRECTIONS

Stage Nine: Reflect on Actions to Take Next

Stage Nine—Reflecting on Action to Take Next and Stage Ten—Assessing the New Situation, Setting New Goals, and Starting a New Cycle of Action Research are dealt with in this section for future research directions. This stage virtually repeated Stage Three and Stage Four to examine the following processes: (a) If the brainstorm action strategies set up in Stage Three was appropriate; and (b) if the Action Plans in Stage Four were implemented properly or was it necessary to make modifications for actions to take next.

An assignment "Summary Reflection" was designed to require students to reflect on their actions and experiences. All students reflected that they had positive experiences. They developed a strong supporting community and hoped to carry on the social connection they made through this course. Students' summary reflections revealed the social interaction played a positive impact on their learning process and outcomes. Some students planned to expand the circle of the social community and decided to pass their knowledge on to others at their teaching schools and encourage them to use Dreamweaver, Flash, Fireworks, and many other programs in the Adobe Premium series; others hoped to continue the network with the class members they built through this course.

However, the course was filled with challenges. A few students admitted in their summary reflections that they were very intimidated when they found that they would be creating Websites from scratch at the beginning of the semester. But they enjoyed the learning experiences when the semester came to an end in a positive outcome with final products and content knowledge that students would take from this class and apply in their teaching career. It would not have been as successful had it not been for the social interaction on ANGEL.

A summary of actions to be taken for the next stage by students and by the instructor could be drawn from this study: (a) As technology is developing at an incredible speed, we all need social interaction and external support to inspire our internal desire to learn and to move on. No one can survive in this technology age in an isolated condition. (b) Action research process takes time. Ongoing analysis and reflection is a natural part of the action research procedure which allows the researcher and participants to use the data positively. Practical action research makes improvement possible but the improvement will not happen within one day. The researcher has to be patient enough to avoid the pitfalls of taking actions on premature analysis.

Stage Ten: Assessing the new Situation and Setting new Direction

As educators, we are supposed to be open to make continuous improvement in achieving effective teaching and learning outcomes. A lack of willingness to change is itself a serious weakness. Reaching this stage means the action comes to a full circle. It is time to summarize and to take a fresh look at the current situation, and to set new more doable goals. In addition to the findings

from previous stages, findings from this study also generated some unexpected outcomes:

First, some students had concerns that they would not be able to use the technological skills they obtained from the course due to the lack of access to the software in their working environments. They were looking for transferable and valuable information for their professional and academic growth. Accommodating students' needs should be one of the teaching objectives and curriculum has to be adjusted accordingly and the changes should be described in the course syllabus in the future. Particularly, these issues need to be addressed: (a) Software access and (b) basic knowledge of HTML and CSS. Most students reported on their survey that they did not have off-campus access to the programs such as Dreamweaver and Photoshop. Alterative solutions should be sought to solve this problem. For instance, free software KompoZer for Website design and free graphics editors GIMP can be introduced to students. Most students were weak in the area of writing HTML and CSS codes. More attention needs to be paid to strengthen and construct students' solid skills in this area.

Second, curriculum continuity is necessary within the graduate program. Curriculum disconnection created unnecessary anxiety for students. Students should be advised to take prerequisite course EDC601 Instructional Technology to avoid curriculum disconnection. Instructor needs to work cooperatively to guide students to the right direction.

Because I have not taken EDC 601 PREVIOUS to this course I am still working through things and trying to work out all the thinks on my site. I am however incredibly satisfied with my progress. My Web site layout is exactly how I wanted it and there are only a few minor things left to add or change. The rest will simply be adding in information and content.

The above journal entry and class observations showed that students who had a knowledge gap encountered frustrations and difficulties in this course. With a lot of help and support, the student struggled but completed the basic requirements of the course EDC604. However, the missing information from a previous course made him feel that he had been left behind from time to time. However, another student who had not taken the previous course EDC601 could not complete the course requirements of EDC604. That did not create a positive learning experience for that student. Some students realized that they missed the important information from EDC601. They turned back to take EDC601 after they had completed EDC604. They could have enjoyed more of the learning experience if they had done it the other way around.

Third, students who had no Internet access at home were excluded from the participation in social interaction on ANGEL and eventually failed. Interpretations can be made from this issue: (a) Conclusion can be made cautiously that social interaction on ANGEL played an important role in facilitating students' authoring skills in this course; (b) digital divide existed and it hindered learning opportunities; (c) however, student attitude toward learning and technology played a vital role in academic success.

One of the characteristics in grounded theory emphasizes theory generation by letting it emerge from the data rather than being caught up by scripted categories following a strict procedural guideline. Student attitude toward learning and technology was not the main focus of this study; however, the statement emerged from the data: The more active one participated in social interaction on ANGEL during the semester, the more competent and confident he or she was in authoring skills. The top students contributed more postings on ANGEL. One of the top students contributed 48 quality entries while one student who failed in the course posted five entries (the basic requirement was ten) for the whole semester. Even though the

Internet access was not available at home, there was 24 hour/seven day Internet access on campus. If one was willing to participate in online social interaction, he or she could come to use the Internet on campus anytime. In the future research, attention needs to be paid to examine if online social interaction helps change student attitude toward learning. When one feels a sense of belonging to a community, he or she will be motivated to make contributions to the community.

CONCLUSION

This case study revealed how social interaction on ANGEL has improved student authoring skills to help reach the course objectives. The constructivist approach provided an interaction of two important sets of learning conditions: Internal and external levels for student cognitive development in authoring skills. Online social interaction strongly supported learning. With a constructivist approach, social interaction on ANGEL brought the instructor and the class members together to serve the purposes of understanding student learning needs, decision-making on pedagogy, developing problem solving skills, accomplishing the academic achievements, and setting new goals for improvements.

From a practical perspective, social interaction on ANGEL solved the problem of time and space limit. It provided flexible time and space for participants to discuss the issues important to them. From a theoretical perspective, this is an idea from John Dewey: Reflection and inquiry create and inform meaningful learning. Practical action research with the process of ten stages emphasizes Dewey's belief in the important connection between teacher reflection and improvement of teacher practice. However, if the practical action research was conducted individually, some participants would be reluctant to admit "difficult truths" and challenges they encountered. Creating an online forum to share what everybody had learned and issues in which they had difficulties encouraged students to work out as a team. Students had a sense of belonging when they were involved in an interactive community.

Findings revealed that practical action research combined with social interaction shed light on important issues of professional development and curriculum change through reflection on practice, and reflection on connecting context and content. This study identified the following issues for further research and solutions: The importance of curriculum continuity to build solid knowledge foundation, curriculum design to meet students' needs, issues on digital divide and student attitude, the internal desire for learning and for mingling within the social learning community.

REFERENCES

Alessi, S. M., & Trollip, S. R. (2001). *Multimedia for learning: Methods and development*. Boston, MA: Allyn and Bacon.

Allan, K. K., & Miller, S. M. (1990). Teacher-research collaborative: Cooperative professional development. *Theory into Practice, 29*, 196–202. doi:10.1080/00405849009543454

Bandura, A. (1977). *Social learning theory*. Englewood Cliffs, NJ: Prentice-Hall.

Barton, A. C., Tan, E., & Rivet, A. (2008). Creating hybrid spaces for engaging school science among urban middle school girls. *American Educational Research Journal, 45*(1), 68–103. doi:10.3102/0002831207308641

Black, R., Sileo, T. W., & Prater, M. A. (2000). Learning journals, self-reflection, and university students' changing perceptions. *Action in Teacher Education, 21*(4), 71–89.

Charmaz, K. (2006). *Constructing grounded theory*. London, UK: Sage.

Clandinin, D., & Connolly, F. (Eds.). (1995). *Teacher's professional knowledge landscapes*. New York, NY: Teacher's College Press.

Dewey, J. (1933). *How we think*. Chicago, IL: Henry Regnery.

Dewey, J. (1938). *Experience and education*. New York, NY: Macmillan Publishing Company.

Gall, J. P., Gall, M. D., & Borg, W. R. (2005). *Applying educational research: A practical guide* (5th ed.). Boston, MA: Pearson Education.

Glaser, B. G. (1992). *Emergence vs forcing: Basics of grounded theory analysis*. Sage Publications, Inc.

Gomez, L. M., Sherin, M. G., Griesdorn, J., & Finn, L. (2008). Creating social relationships: The role of technology in preservice teacher preparation. *Journal of Teacher Education, 59*, 117–131. doi:10.1177/0022487107314001

Guo, R. X. (2005). Self-Assessment during online discussion: An action research perspective. In Mann, B. L. (Ed.), *Selected styles in Web-based educational research* (pp. 144–159). Hershey, PA: Idea Group Publishing. doi:10.4018/978-1-59140-732-4.ch010

Guo, R. X. (2009). *Information and communication technology (ICT) literacy in teacher education: A case study of the University of British Columbia*. Köln, Germany: Lap Lambert Academic Publishing AG & Co. KG.

Harasim, L. (Ed.). (1990). *Online education: Perspectives on a new environment*. New York, NY: Praeger.

Hatton, N., & Smith, D. (1995). Reflection in teacher education: Toward definition and implementation. *Teaching and Teacher Education, 11*(1), 33–49. doi:10.1016/0742-051X(94)00012-U

Lee, O. (2010). Facilitating preservice teachers' reflection through interactive online journal writing. *Physical Educator, 67*(3), 128–139.

Manfra, M. M. (2009). Action research: Exploring the theoretical divide between practical and critical approaches. [JoCI]. *Journal of Curriculum and Instruction, 3*(1), 32–46. Retrieved January 18, 2011.

Mills, G. E. (2007). *Action research: A guide for the teacher researcher*. New York, NY: Pearson Education, Inc.

Putnam, R. R., & Borko, H. (2000). What do new views of knowledge and thinking have to say about research on teacher learning? *Educational Researcher, 29*, 4–15.

Russell, D. (1995). Activity theory and writing instruction. In Petraglia, J. (Ed.), *Reconceiving writing, rethinking writing instruction* (pp. 51–77). Mahwah, NJ: Lawrence Erlbaum.

Sarason, S. (1990). *The predictable failure of educational reform*. San Francisco, CA: Jossey-Bass.

Schmuck, R. A. (2006). *Practical action research for change*. Thousand Oaks, CA: Corwin Press, a Sage Publications Company.

Strauss, A. (1987). *Qualitative research for social scientists*. Cambridge, UK: Cambridge University Press. doi:10.1017/CBO9780511557842

Strauss, A., & Corbin, J. (1998). *Basic of qualitative research: Technique and techniques and procedures for developing grounded theory* (2nd ed.). Thousand Oaks, CA: Sage.

Vygotsky, L. S. (1934, 1978). *Mind in society*. Cambridge, MA: Harvard University Press.

Whipp, J. L. (2003). Scaffolding critical reflection in online discussions: Helping prospective teachers think deeply about field experience in urban schools. *Journal of Teacher Education, 54*, 321–333. doi:10.1177/0022487103255010

Windschitl, M., & Sahl, K. (2002). Tracing teachers' use of technology in a laptop computer school: The interplay of teacher beliefs, social dynamics, and institutional culture. *American Educational Research Journal, 39*(1), 165–205. doi:10.3102/00028312039001165

Wonacott, M. E. (2001). *Technology literacy*. ERIC Digest. Columbus, OH: Clearinghouse on Adult Career and Vocational Education. Retrieved October 16, 2005, from http://www.ericdigests.org/2002-3/literacy.htm

Yin, R. (1994). *Case study research: Design and methods*. Thousand Oaks, CA: Sage.

Zeichner, K., & Liston, D. (1987). Teaching student teachers to reflect. *Harvard Educational Review, 57*, 23–48.

Zeichner, K., & Liston, D. (1996). *Reflective teaching: An introduction*. Mahwah, NJ: Lawrence Erlbaum Associates.

KEY TERMS AND DEFINITIONS

Action Research: Action research focuses on improvement and participation. Action research involves a cyclic process in which research, action, evaluation, and improvement are interwoven.

Activity Theory: Activity theory or the "zone of proximal development" (ZPD) specifically, was initiated by Vygotsky, Vygotsky believed a person could make learning happen at certain internal level, but he/she would do it better with external assistance, which included the discursive environment such as tools being used and people providing support. Activity theory suggests collaboration, social practice, and critical pedagogy.

ANGEL: ANGEL is a Web-based application for curriculum, instruction and assessment. Buffalo State College is using ANGEL for online teaching.

Constructivism: Constructivism is a critical way of building knowledge about self, school, daily life experience, and society practices through reflection and meaning making.

Grounded Theory: Grounded theory is a qualitative research approach used to generate a theory that explains an action or interaction about a specific topic. A theory is grounded in the data.

Practical Action Research: Practical action research focuses on the "how-to" approach to the processes of learning activities. It is a branch of action research.

Reflection: John Dewey's perspective of reflection as a meaning-making process and learning process; reflection as a systematic way of thinking grounded in scientific inquiry.

Social Interaction: Learning is a social practice. Learning happens when an individual interacts with others. Social interaction is an environment in which individuals engage with one another and cooperate to reach goals important to the community.

Chapter 13
Meaningful Connections:
"Going the Distance" in Distance Learning Through the Design and Generation of Community Building Online Learning Interactions

Terri Edwards Bubb
University of Houston – Clear Lake, USA

Denise McDonald
University of Houston – Clear Lake, USA

Caroline M. Crawford
University of Houston – Clear Lake, USA

ABSTRACT

This chapter explores the importance of collaborative and authentic learning in online distance learning environments. It focuses upon the interactive activities between the instructor, learners, online environment, and larger community, which are all engaged towards developing a community of learners in which meaningful connections enhance learner motivation (Ardichvili, Page & Wentling, 2003; Conrad & Donaldson, 2004) and acquisition of learning objectives. Built-in opportunities are integral to the process for socialization-type learning activities and instructor's awareness, and alignment of those activities to the readiness of individual learners and collective learning community (i.e., zone of proximal development) (Vygotsky, 1962, 1978). Practical instructional ideas and activities for building an online learning community are presented.

DOI: 10.4018/978-1-61350-441-3.ch013

INTRODUCTION

Imagine yourself as a first-time traveler on a train tour across a foreign country-side.

As a novice tourist, with limited knowledge of the native language, you make your way towards the train station and purchase your ticket. As you anxiously peer down the tracks for signs of the train that will transport you across an unfamiliar countryside to exciting new experiences, you study other passengers waiting on the train platform who are also gazing longingly for the train to pull into the station. At last, the train arrives and the conductor steps onto the platform preparing to check tickets and the tour guide greets you with maps and brochures. As each person boards, you notice other hopeful travelers with dreams of adventure on this shared journey. Although apprehensive about the journey about to begin, the excitement for the voyage, as well as the eagerness to meet these new passengers, you quickly quell any misgivings for making the trip.

As the researchers began collecting and organizing the data for this chapter, a metaphor of a journey began to develop. A journey of hopeful anticipation, adventure and the realization of new insights through experience of different landscapes and environments began to emerge. More explicitly, a train-based journey presented itself as a visible representation of the course experience and was integrated to support and enhance the reader's understanding related to developing communities of learning (Gannon Cook & Crawford, 2004; Palloff & Pratt, 2007; Swan, 2005) and communities of practice (Ardichvili et al., 2003; Wenger, McDermont, & Snyder, 2002) within the online learning environment. Online learning interactions, as well as other types of interactive activities (Bonk, Wisher, & Nigrelli, 2004; Haythornwaite, 2006) support and positively model the importance of meaningful connections within the learning environment. Although these types of community building activities may integrate into the face-to-face learning environment more easily,

it is of vital importance to not only design online learning interactions within the course framework, but also to model the importance of meaningful connections that engage the learner and support the development of higher order thinking skills (Bloom 1956, 1971; Anderson & Krathwohl, 2001). The researchers were inspired to integrate this metaphor as a conceptual underpinning to enhance and aid in the overall discussions related to how one might create a more interactive online environment for e-learners. The metaphor commences at the station while the passengers eagerly await the train's arrival on the station platform. Prior to the conductor emerging from the train ready to collect tickets, an initial inspection of the train's mechanical system, as well as a sweep of all cabins, has been performed, and a check of the train's destination including a report on possible track derailments was conducted. The train represents the virtual community of learning (online course environment and environmental usability, if you will), the train track that the train follows represents the course content, the train's conductor is the facilitative online instructor, and the passengers are the students, the eventual members of the community (all from different backgrounds, with varying experiences and different perceptions of ultimate destination). The journey that the passengers will undertake symbolizes the knowledge or learning that will take place within the distance learning course environment. To sum, the following designations have been offered:

- *First-time traveler, novice tourist = individual online learner*
- *Passengers = community of online learners*
- *Train = virtual community of learning within the course environment*
- *Station = virtual gathering place to "get on the train"*
- *Conductor and Tour Guide = facilitative online instructor*
- *Train engineer = instructional designer*
- *Journey = knowledge or learning to occur*

- *Tourist attraction stops, scenes & side trips = constructivist-based learning opportunities, that are learner initiated, generated or selected (exponential by nature)*
- *Bells and whistles = unique and aesthetically pleasing online attributes for communication and learning*
- *Separate traveler train cars = instructional tools implemented by the facilitative instructor and instructional designer*
  - *Engine car = course content*
  - *Fuel car = engagement and motivation content of course*
  - *Passenger car = assignments, interactions, and activities*
  - *Dining car = relational aspects of course*
  - *Observation car = constructivist learning*

This above illustration offers an opportunity towards a metaphoric representation of a similar situation that occurs within the distance learning environment; namely, the beginning of a semester. As the learners are waiting for their online course to begin, they are in a waiting period like one waiting for a train. The student learners (other train passengers) gather after logging into the online course for the first time. The learners are usually taken to the start page of the course which could be likened to the platform of a train station. Here, the student learner (A.K.A. first-time traveler, novice tourist) is "looking around" and trying to learn about everyone else within the course environment, as well as taking opportunities to try and make connections.

Additionally, the train conductor (facilitative instructor of the course) is seen on the platform beckoning the passengers (learners) "All aboard!" (as the invitation to begin learning together). Everyone enters the train (online course) carrying their luggage (learner tools and online perceptions) to begin their journey (knowledge acquisition). As we continue this conversation regarding online

learning and interactivity, this metaphor will be implemented throughout the chapter to support the discussion progression and to engage the metaphor to bridge theory with personal experiences and understanding regarding the importance of interaction and engagement within an online course environment.

BACKGROUND

As we progress through this chapter regarding interactivity and engagement in online course environments, it is appropriate to focus upon the shift from the online learning environment towards the online learning communities. Engaging the discussion more fully enhances the focus upon meaningful connections within the online learning environment and the design of community building within online learning interactions.

Online Learning Environments to Online Learning Communities

As a framework for this chapter, a look at the changing scope of online learning must be examined. Online education continues to grow as an instructional tool and researchers have begun to address the need of creating a sense of community within an online environment (Brown & Adler, 2008; Rovai, 2002a; Vesely, Bloom, & Sherlock, 2007). The definition of an online learning community is simply a common place on the Internet that addresses the learning needs of its members through proactive and collaborative partnerships (Palloff & Pratt, 2003). According to Crawford (2008):

Although the design, development and implementation of World Wide Web-based online learning environments has been an area of focus over the previous fifteen year period, it is only relatively recently that a growing number of researchers and developers who are focused upon online learning environments have been attentive towards making connections; this actively engaged creation of knowledge and practice communities that may also be referred to as learning communities. (C. Crawford, personal communication, June 20, 2008)

Today, research in creating successful online learning communities is needed to further promote social interactivity and student engagement between students while providing opportunities for students to develop a sense of group cohesiveness.

Definitions of Online Community of Learners

Definitions of community within an online environment include Rovai (2002b), who believes a community is a social group of learners who share values, goals, and knowledge within an online setting. Additionally, Renninger and Shumar (2002) classify a learning community as an online group that interacts with each other to provide knowledge and information while learning from others in the group. As previously defined, a learning community is a group in which its members socially interact purposefully and collectively to learn and give information (Renninger & Shumar, 2002). Therefore, online learning communities can be defined as groups of people who are separated physically yet engage collectively in the transaction or transformation of knowledge through technology (Browne, 2005). Rheingold (1993) further defines online communities as social groups who carry on discussions with sufficient human feeling to form personal relationships in cyberspace. Similarly, Rovai (2002a) explains that an online learning community encompasses several characteristics: (a) mutual interdependence among members, (b) a sense of belonging, (c) connectedness, (d) spirit, (e) trust, (f) interactivity, (g) common expectations, (h) shared values of goals, and (i) overlapping histories among members (p. 2).

These characteristics are not mutually exclusive, nor imperative for every learner to recognize within their own course experience; however, the aspects of association and community imperatives envelop not only the obscure but also the obvious necessities within the supportive, collegial relationship. The relational aspect of learning is heightened and can be capitalized upon in this social networking generational culture (Levy, 2008).

Learning Environment vs. a Community of Learning

A learning environment is different from a community of learning. Several researchers (Anderson, 2008; Bonk & Graham, 2006; Swan, 2005) concur that a *learning environment* is a forum for participants to learn together, where learning is gained horizontally. In comparison, a *learning community* is a relationship forged between the learner, instructor, and the subject matter (Ally, 2008; Vesely et al., 2007), and researchers are now advancing toward the definition of a community that learns, retains, and evolves knowledge (Conrad, 2007).

Student learners who participate in a community-type environment are exposed to more higher-order thinking opportunities that provide richer perspectives for learning experiences (Brown & Peterson, 2008). When learning behaviors and interactions occur electronically, the resulting environment is referred to as an *online learning community*. Through social networking and computer-mediated communication opportunities, the student learners work as a community to achieve a shared learning objective where learning objectives are proposed by an instructor or may arise out of discussions between participants that reflect personal interests (Bandura, 1986; Wenger et al., 2002). No longer is it acceptable for student learners only to obtain information in an online environment. Today, how learners gather and apply appropriate information to knowledge construction is fundamentally vital. This involves a shift from use of knowledge and comprehension, lower levels of Bloom's Taxonomy, to application, analysis, synthesis and creativity; higher levels of Bloom's Taxonomy (Bloom, 1956, 1984). Exploring the concept of community networks within an online learning environment has the potential to be a viable and groundbreaking instructional illumination, clarification, and revelation that effectively ensures learner success and provides opportunity for transformational learning.

Online Learning Community Enhancement Resources

In an online community, students communicate via synchronous or asynchronous textual discussion, audio, video, or other Internet-supported devices with the use of web logs (blogs), blending personal journaling with social networking to create environments with opportunities for reflection (McElrath & McDowell, 2008). Some types of online learning communities include electronic learning (e-learning) communities (groups intact and connected solely via technology) and blended learning communities (groups utilize face-to-face meetings as well as online meetings). Online learning communities may be categorized as knowledge-based, practice-based, or task-based and may focus on personal aspects, process, or technology (Riel & Pollin, 2004). These communities may use technology and tools in many categories: synchronous (such as instant messaging and video chats), asynchronous (such as message boards and email), content management systems such as Moodle, (http://moodle.org) and Lectureshare (http://www.lectureshare.com), collaborative Web 2.0 elements such as wikis, social networking such as Del.icio.us (http://delicious.com) and Flickr (http://flickr.com), learning object repositories, and blogs.

Online Community Characteristics: Facilitative Efforts

Bonk et al. (2004) advocate an online virtual community has many of the same characteristics as a real community. These elements offer support to its student learners so that they can feel safe to communicate openly, which in turn allows them to develop the shared vision that they need in order to learn together. Further, Palloff and Pratt (2003) posit that in online distance education, attention needs to be paid to developing a sense of community in the group of participants in order for the learning process to be successful. Wenger et al. (2002) describe online learning as focusing on *content*, in contrast with online learning communities, which focus on *interaction*. The challenge, for all facilitative instructors, is to combine these two ideas to integrate content and communication so that effective learning across all levels of the learning continuum takes place within a safe, open, and communicative learning environment.

Instructors in traditional face-to-face classroom learning environments act as academic experts and synchronously interact in the classroom to dispense the content, focus upon higher order thinking skills (Bloom, 1956) and carefully create appropriate face-to-face communities of learning. Palloff and Pratt (2007) point out that teaching in an online environment requires a move beyond traditional models of andragogy or pedagogy towards new practices that are more facilitative and constructivist in nature. Since online learning takes place through more asynchronous support and designed tasks, facilitative instructors and student learners can aid in their learning by managing the pace of conversations, asking questions, clarifying, summarizing, reflecting, making connections between topics while developing and maintaining a positive and supportive tone in the online space.

Moore (1989) affirms that interaction is the sole element that contributes to student success and learning in online courses. These interactions in online environments typically are displayed in the following ways:

1. **Student-to-Student:** Interactions designed to encourage students to interact with one another throughout the course.
2. **Student-to-Instructor:** Interactions between students and the instructor and can be instructional, supplementary, or evaluative in nature.
3. **Student-to-Material:** Interactions with the course content and the student. These interactions are typically independent as the student internalizes the material and makes meaningful connections. (Moore, 1989, pp. 2-4)

The relationships formed between the student learners, facilitative instructor, and the content may create a sense of community by building connections and making meaning so students feel part of the learning process. Research advocates students that are part of the learning process are more likely to succeed (Richardson & Swan, 2003). Further, several additional interactions have been recognized as occurring within the learning environment, specifically, *learner-interface* (Hillman, Willis, & Gunawardena, 1994), *learner-self* (Crawford, 2001), *learner-community* (Burnham & Walden, 1997), *instructor-community* (Crawford, 2001), *instructor-content* (Crawford, 2001), *instructor-interface* (Crawford, 2001), and, *instructor-self* (Crawford, 2001, 2003).

Although the interactions that occur between the student and other students, instructor and subject matter (Moore, 1989) are inherently integral to the success of the learning goals and objectives within the online learning environment, the additional types of interactions are also integral towards the success of the learning community towards engaging within higher order thinking skills (Anderson & Krathwohl, 2001; Bloom, 1984; Bloom & Krathwohl, 1956; Gronlund, 1970; Harrow, 1972; Krathwohl, Bloom, & Masia, 1964).

Enhancing the Metaphor: Separate Traveler Train Cars

As this chapter discusses the shift from the online learning environment towards the online learning community's enhancements, the student learner needs must be addressed. Specifically, what can the facilitative instructor and instructional designer of an online course do to promote interaction and engagement? To help answer this question, an in-depth look at our metaphoric representation is presented. As such, this metaphoric representation emphasizes the instructional tools implemented by the facilitative instructor.

Just as there are many cars in a train, there are many components in an online course. Each train car can be considered an instructional tool that the facilitative instructor and instructional designer use to promote interactivity and relationship-building within the online learning community. The following cars are presented along with a brief explanation of how the car is needed for an online learning community to take place.

Engine (Course Design and Content)

The first car in our metaphor is the engine. The train's engine burns the coal to make it move along the tracks, as well as houses the controls for movement. Similarly, the course instructional goals reside here to keep the course on-track and meet quality instructional goals and to ensure that passengers (learners) make their destination (gain knowledge). The engineer resides in this car maintaining fuel input and output, as well as keeping watch down the track for impending dangers that could destroy or stop the train, thereby preventing passenger arrival at their destination. The instructional designer's role is much the same. The design of the course is imperative to keep the course running smoothly as well as to help ward off concerns that could keep the course from meeting all of its instructional objectives. In many instances, the instructional designer and the facilitative instructor are the same, so it is important that as the course is planned, where attention to detail on such matters as types of assignments, setting clear expectations, communicating clear and understandable directions, and unambiguous explanation of how grades are computed are expressed to all members of the online learning community. Without these elements, the course will fail to meet the instructional objectives and learning could falter or stop altogether.

Of further importance is the consideration towards the subject matter expert. Although the facilitative instructor is normally the subject matter expert who works closely with the instructional designer, there is the occurrence that one person entertains all three rolls (i.e., subject matter expert, facilitative instructor, and instructional designer). The subject matter expert must be carefully entrenched, embedded, or otherwise engrained within the course content so as to ensure the appropriate and fully articulated information that is imperative towards the development of a decent learning environment experience. However, the facilitative instructor brings an understanding of the learning environment, and appropriate learner support and progression, into the instructional design process so as to offer a curricular and instructionally relevant progression of information and activities towards supporting the learners to accomplish or exceed the designated learning goals and learning objectives. The third necessary role is that of the instructional designer, who brings to the table the additional curricular understanding and instructional perspective but also the addition of the instructionally relevant tools and potential experiences that may also be inherently vital for the learner's understanding of the subject matter and meeting or exceeding the stated learning goals and learning objectives. As previously noted, the facilitative instructor and instructional designer may well be found within the same person; yet, the relevance of a subject matter expert, facilitative instructor and instructional designer comingled and fused into

one person is indeed a rare occurrence but may also be viewed as an extra enhancement wherein confusion through design and developmental communication would no longer be a concern. As such the engine, the course design and content, reflect the knowledge quality and vitality within the online course learning environment.

Fuel Car (Engagement and Motivational Construct of Course)

Directly behind the engine follows the fuel car. This car carries coal or the energy source for the train. The fuel or energy source symbolizes the motivational emphasis that must be constantly nurtured and supported throughout the course experience, so as to support the learner's constant and consistent progression through the course units of instruction and subsequent experiences within the course environment. To parallel the fuel car metaphor, the train's fuel car supports and nurtures the engine of the train, which is the primary opportunity through which to obtain fuel for the train; the course subject matter learning goals and objectives require constant support throughout the course experience, by the motivating factors such as through Keller's ARCS Model (Keller, 1979, 1983a, 1983b, 1984, 1987a, 1987b, 1987c) that emphasizes four specific progressive realms of focus, being: attention; relevance; confidence; and, satisfaction (Keller, 2010, para. 1). This motivational framework of thought suggests that the motivational fuel for the course learning journey is more important to implement at some times and less important to implement at other times, so as to support the learner's progression through the course learning and assessment opportunities, at other times.

It is the conductor's responsibility to keep an eye on the fuel supply like the instructor must monitor student engagement. This process can be done through several strategies; such as, student evaluations (i.e., formative, summative, etc.), conferences, surveys/questionnaires, and formal and informal chats.

Passenger Cars (Assignments, Interactions and Activities)

Each train carries a passenger car; several in fact. When entering, each car has its own personality with different passengers milling about, interacting with one another, discussing, and sharing ideas. Passengers, also by choice, traverse between cars for myriad reasons. Consider that each passenger car represents different assignments, interactions and activities within the course environment. In a robust online learning community, activities and assignments should vary from one another to keep student learners motivated and on-track. As passengers do not stay in one passenger car for the entire journey, learners move about freely in an online learning community interacting with various students while the course is in session. At times, the student learners will engage in conversations with a couple of other members trading seats and conversing about the journey ahead. Then, further down "the track" these student learners switch seats with other online community members.

Additionally, when designing assignments for the online learner, it is important to consider that assignments align with the students' career goals, offering real-life situations that are relevant to the course and workplace. Adult learners do not want to learn something for the sake of learning (Cross, 1981; Frey & Almann, 2003; Merriam & Caffarella, 1999). Their time is valuable, and usually when they are attending training/school, they are missing work, personal time, or both.

Dining Car (Relational Aspect of Course)

Most trains used for tours provide a dining car. Here passengers eat meals with other passengers while talking about their journey and sharing their experiences. Passengers have an option of entering this car at their own leisure for a bit of nourishment and sharing with others who are on the train. In an online learning community, nourishment is provided to all in the environment through the facilitative instructor, but also through peer informal interactions. Social bonding and community is developed more deeply through "shared meals"…as sustenance for the learning community through exchange and affirmation of newly gained knowledge. The instructor provides instructional reviews for those who need it on an as-needed basis. Additionally, the facilitative instructor may serve, or offer, "food for thought" to learners who need additional help engaging in the course readings or material.

One way to show a relational presence in an online course is through conferencing. Conferencing may occur via phone, video (such as Skype), chat or personal email. The objectives for the conference do not have to be formal. Initial conferences can include questions about the learners' personal experiences, interests, characteristics, hobbies, etc. This affords the instructor with key information for understanding learners' world views, dispositions, values, and perspectives. For example, one question that can solicit insightful information, "Would you rather be a big fish in a little pond or a little fish in a big pond? Please explain why." Subsequent conferences can include questions about the course, assignments, and degree plan. Through one-on-one conferences, these interactions potentially project a physical presence using conversational norms.

Observation Car (Constructivist Learning)

The last car on the train is the observation car. Adorned with windows and a platform at the end of the train, this carriage was designated as a place for passengers to view the surrounding landscape. Travelers could step out onto the platform for a bit of fresh air, or to wave to others travelers when pulling into a station. In the online environment, the observation car is a place for student learners to observe what others are doing in the course. One of the main concerns about online learning is that student learners can feel isolated at times and may have no sense of group connection or identity. One way to combat this concern is to allow student learners the chance to view other learners at work by sharing their course offerings and showing others in the community what they are doing, through some medium (e.g., student-created websites, wiki pages, blogs, rubric forms, peer evaluations, surveys, questionnaires, etc.). Here student learners have a chance to look at others' work without fear of critical feedback and this presents an Augmented Reality in which to interact and learn (See in this volume, Huang, 2011).

Additionally, the observation car is a place for the facilitative instructor to greet student learners and members of the community and set the tone of the course. For example, as the online facilitator, one can require students to evaluate peers' work with a created rubric. The students offer constructive feedback to each other's assignments to help improve the materials before final submission and instructor grading. Additionally, the students "see" other member's coursework to inspire and help them think outside of the box. Sometimes in an online course, the facilitative instructor is the only person that views the course offerings from student learners. Similarly, the facilitative instructor is the only feedback learners receive regarding assignments. The significance here is by allowing other members of the learning community to view and share course assignments, the facilitative instructor is allowing promoting a higher level of online interactions that optimize knowledge acquisition at the evaluative level of Bloom's Taxonomy (1956, 1984) and there is an opportunity for Distributed Cognition. Specific discussion of how these types of interactions and digital media can serve as Distributed Cognition

through archived course learning activities is discussed in this volume (Huang, 2011).

Bells and Whistles (Unique and Aesthetically Pleasing Online Attributes for Communication and Learning)

The last metaphor regarding creating vibrant online environments refers to the train's "bells and whistles" to inform passengers of stops and/ or emergency notifications. Online course designs can present a myriad of course "bells and whistles" that stimulate learner interest in course engagement. These additions are usually provided by the course management learning system that allows the course facilitator to provide enriching experiences that will aid the students and help them reach their destinations.

Some examples of course "bells and whistles" are adding video to the course. An example of this would be to ask students to create a video biography on the first day of the course. Students would produce a video that introduces themselves to their fellow classmates. Additionally, how the course is designed could be considered a "bell and whistle" of the course. Making sure the look of the course is aesthetically pleasing by incorporating color, graphics, and correct font styles and size may attribute to the overall perceptions of the online environment which may lead to students feeling comfortable enough to strive for academic success. Other suggestions include: providing self-help resources and materials to aid students in their studies in the course, slideshows to further exemplify course objectives, and tutorials in completing assignment tasks.

All of these cars combined make up the train; in this metaphor, the whole course learning community. However, these separate cars make up the different types of activities, interaction assignments, and instructional tools that are necessary towards meeting the learning goals and objectives. These student learners would be guided within each of these cars, or activities, by the facilitative instructor (conductor) so as to interact, collaborate and work together towards the required results. The facilitative instructor would guide the community building endeavors within the experiential journey through this framework.

Recommendations to Help Make the Online Environment an Online Community

Instructor Uses Combination of Constructivists and Cognitive Approaches

Ally (2008) points out that an online facilitative instructor should implement techniques that call for engaging and interactive activities to promote problem solving and reflective thought. Ingram and Hathorn (2005a) further assert that these techniques should be more constructive and cognitive in nature. When students are engaged in constructivist and cognitivist learning activities, the student learner is openly and actively immersed in the course environment to allow learning to take place (Jonassen, Cernusca, & Ionas, 2006). Additionally, when effective cognitive elements (such as open-ended questions) are combined with constructive elements (collaboration and reflective thought), the results engage student interactions that push the student learners' thinking above the knowledge and comprehension levels of Bloom's Taxonomy and into the higher order thinking levels of analysis, synthesis, and evaluation (Bloom, 1956, 1971). This is significant from an informational framework, so as to enhance the learners' understanding of the subject matter, but it is also imperative to consider the Anderson and Krathwohl (2001) revisions to the cognitive domain efforts so as to reframe the Bloom's higher order thinking skills (Bloom, 1956, 1971) towards the following: remembering, understanding, applying, analyzing, evaluating, and creating. This nurtures the 21st Century learner's efforts towards more fully working with the knowledge towards the

reframed higher order thinking skills of analyzing, evaluating and creating new ideas and products using the prior knowledge and rethinking about it in new and different, innovative ways. The cognitivist and constructivist approaches towards the understanding and usage of knowledge by the learners is of vital importance towards the success of the learner throughout the course instructional design while also expecting the learner to understand the subject matter in new and innovative ways. Galbraith (2004) states that adult learners and facilitators are involved in a continual process of activity, reflection upon activity, collaborative analysis of activity, new activity, further reflection, and collaborative analysis, and an example of this strategy would be to use a combination of discussion questions, reflective summaries, and evaluative assignments.

Facilitative Instructor as Co-Learner

Instructors, who truly value community and desire communities of learning to take place, must be willing to help students build their own community that is student-centered; not instructor driven (Palloff & Pratt, 2007). Instructors that take on the role as co-learner still provide facilitation necessary for keeping the student learners on-track, construct the course that prepares the students with needed information and resources, and provide instructional opportunities that call for members to take charge of their own learning. When members have an equal share in the learning process, the community flourishes with meaningful connections, collaborations, and interactions that keep the students engaged. This is significant because an engaging and effective instructor does not have to know everything in an online learning community environment or play the authority-figure dispensing information and content. In fact, when the instructor models the learner role, a level playing field is established where the focus on the act of learning is enjoyed and shared and allows all members to contribute with each other in knowledge-building and meaning making interactions. One way for online facilitators to take on the role of co-learner is to be a visible presence in discussion forums responding to students' posts with an open view of learning something new, posting responses and questions to students' comments by asking reflective questions, and affirming students for sharing their knowledge to the class.

Offer all Three Student Interactions in the Course

As previously discussed in the chapter, interactions in online learning community environments typically are displayed in the following ways:

1. **Student-to-Student:** Interactions designed to encourage students to interact with one another throughout the course.
2. **Student-to-Instructor:** Interactions between students and the instructor and can be instructional, supplementary, or evaluative in nature.
3. **Student-to-Material:** Interactions with the course content and the student. These interactions are typically independent as the student internalizes the material and makes meaningful connections. (Moore, 1989, pp. 2-4)

Suler (2004) and Stacey (1999) report that students felt interactions were a crucial part of their learning experience. Learner interactions may take a variety of forms, such as offering assistance, providing information, offering affirmations, or presenting feedback (McKeachie, 2002), and supports the development of critical interpersonal skills, such as cooperation and compromise, which are invaluable traits that easily transfer to workplace settings. This is significant because in order to foster a sense of community with an online learning environment, basic and functional student interactions are still needed to ensure student learner academic success, which is the priority goal in developing an effective and engaging learning community.

Modeling and Setting Expectations from Facilitative Instructor

Researchers posit the importance of modeling and setting expectations in the classroom (Swan, 2001; Thompson, 2004), and in the online genre it is imperative. The modeling behaviors of the facilitative instructor leads learners towards engaging in similar validating and affirming behaviors within the developing online learning community. The significance here is that when the facilitative instructor models community building behaviors, student learners are more inclined to model positive traits that build relationships with others in their online world. Modeling behaviors include posting discussion questions within the posting forum that ask students to defend or oppose course readings. An online facilitator needs to ensure use of a tone that encourages open dialogue and discourse free from bias in all coursework. Additionally, by correctly citing sources from course readings and ancillary materials, the instructor models professional accountability and the process of Distributed Cognition to be replicated by learners in the course (See Huang, 2011, in this volume).

Encourage Student Learners to Become the Facilitative Instructor

A learning community is an interactive and social environment that addresses the learning needs of its members through proactive and collaborative partnerships (Brown, 2001; Garrison, Anderson, & Archer, 2001; McElrath & McDowell, 2008; Rovai & Wighting, 2005). How learners actively gather and apply appropriate information for knowledge construction is more critical than simply obtaining information. In order for students to achieve, they need to be able to find other students in their online world with whom they feel comfortable engaging to collaborate and share. Students need to be able to join forces with other students in their virtual world to feel connected and supported. Encouraging student learners to take over the reins of an online course, allows them to take a more active role in their learning. This vested interest may lead to more in-depth research and knowledge acquisition for all members of the group. A simple way to allow students to become the facilitative instructor is to let them regulate a discussion question within the discussion environment. Students would write their questions and monitor the forum during the week, responding to other students' comments and questions.

SUMMARY

This section of the chapter focuses upon the background and research on the concepts of constructing a community of learners within an online learning environment. The word *community* was defined followed by characteristics of a learning community and research regarding online communities of learning. Facilitative instructors must carefully consider social communities and the interactivities that will help support the cognitive development of the learners in an online learning community. Furthermore, the facilitative instructor should purposely create communications and activities that are naturally occurring but also strategically designed into the course environment. Dependent upon the type of online learning community, such as a primarily text-based environment or a three-dimensional virtual world environment, the communicative support has the potential to catapult the student learners in successfully meeting stated learning objectives.

The social aspects that support the creation of autonomous, dynamic learning communities are enhanced not only by learner engagement regarding the development of bonds of understanding, but also thoughtful and professional collaboration by the facilitative instructor and instructional designer. Additionally, considerations towards student engagement and social interaction theory (Bandura, 1977, 1986; Jonassen, 2000; Vygotsky, 1962, 1978) help an online learning environment become a community of learner reality.

Returning to the train metaphor, the passengers (community of online learners) on the train (the course and learning community) are fully engaged with one another while traveling on their lengthy journeys (knowledge acquisition) through the countryside. The passengers are constantly switching seats, engaging in conversations with different passengers (making learning connections), and meeting others in their environment (learning community). These exchanges involve trading information to construct new knowledge which, in turn, opens new worlds and perpetuates the feeling that the journey (knowledge acquisition) never ends.

EFFECTIVE INSTRUCTIONAL TECHNIQUES FOR ONLINE LEARNERS

How online student learners learn is not a new concept. Just as there is not one instructional theory suitable for all learners, there is no one instructional technique that fits all characteristics of the online learner (Brookfield, 2006; Cross, 1981; Palloff & Pratt, 2007). Identifying effective teaching techniques that work well with online student learners is important for instructors when designing courses. Emphasis in online education should focus on techniques that afford rich and meaningful experiences. In the following section, relevant instructional techniques are presented and discussed.

Problem-Based Learning Activities

Problem-based learning is an instructional strategy that promotes active learning, critical thinking, and problem-solving (Duffy & Cunningham, 1996), where student learners work cooperatively in groups to seek solutions to real world problems. With this technique, problems are ill-defined and participants strive to find solutions to prepare students to think critically and analytically and to find and use appropriate learning resources (Gijselaers, 1996). Kovalchick and Dawson (2004b) outlined five steps in the problem-based learning process:

1. **Problem Formation:** Problem is presented and identified by the group. A hypothesis is then generated.
2. **Self-Directed Learning:** Students discuss what is known and work collaboratively to begin testing hypothesis.
3. **Problem Reexamination:** Students discuss results.
4. **Abstraction:** Students compare and contrast the problem with other problems.
5. **Reflection:** Students share research findings with their peers. (pp. 480-481)

In problem-based learning, teachers take on a minimal role when presenting problem-based learning scenarios and use open-ended questions to foster student metacognitive growth and guide students toward a goal. The instructor's role is that of a facilitator to stimulate, guide, integrate, and summarize discussions. Strategies to use with this technique include games, simulations, and role play (Kovalchick & Dawson, 2004b) as well as cooperative groups. In comparison to face-to-face settings when implementing problem-based learning, e-learning environments require accountability processes for individual contributions. For example, instructors could employ learning logs that document how each step was addressed and completed.

The ability to guide problem-based learning activities and embrace the team group case study offers the active engagement of the learners within the realm of problem-based learning that may be enhanced within the online learning environment. An interesting emphasis within the problem-based learning environment was offered by Hmelo-Silver, Duncan, and Chinn (2007),

There are two major flaws with Kirschner et al's argument. The first is a pedagogical one. Kirschner and colleagues have indiscriminately lumped together several distinct pedagogical approaches—constructivist, discovery, problem-based, experiential, and inquiry-based—under the category of minimally guided instruction. We argue here that at least some of these approaches, in particular, problem-based learning (PBL) and inquiry learning (IL), are not minimally guided instructional approaches but rather provide extensive scaffolding and guidance to facilitate student learning. (p. 1)

The " Kirschner et al" designation beginning this quotation is actually the Kirschner, Sweller and Clark (2006) journal article to which the Hmelo-Silver, Duncan and Chinn (2007) article responds. The interesting statement quoted refers to the importance of guidance and "extensive scaffolding" that must occur within problem-based activities so as to embrace and facilitate the learner's understanding of the information and experiential efforts. Within an online learning environment, this facilitative effort is even more imperative due to the distance in time and space usually associated with the online learning environment. As such, the constant, consistent and persistent facilitative efforts of the instructor are of utmost importance. Not only as regards the facilitative efforts of the instructor, but also towards ensuring that the learners maintain a progressive understanding of the subject matter without concerns related to cognitive load issues, as well as the need for self-regulation efforts modeled by the facilitator and embraced by the learner so as to steadfastly progress towards a successful end.

As an instructor recognizes, it is difficult to maintain this necessary level of response time and quality of communication within a face-to-face learning environment. Within an online learning environment, one may suggest that it has the potential to be impossible. Yet, the strengths of the digital realm come to the aide of the facilitative instructors and online learner colleagues. The ability to integrate regulatory aides into the learning environment is imperative to recognize, not only to ensure that any potential questions or concerns are directly addressed by the facilitative instructor within a perceived interactive and timely manner, but also so as to ensure that the learners have the immediate support and guidance desired. There are numerous ways through which to integrate regulatory support and information into the learning environment, no matter whether it be textual, auditory or through graphic representations. However, an interesting concept towards supporting the guidance and facilitative efforts necessary to support the learners, as well as a "fun" and different way through which to emphasize the desired support for the learner within the problem-based learning activity may be through an avatar product. Through the product Voki (Oddcast Inc., 2011), which offers the opportunity to create one's own avatar with personalized avatar characteristics and one's own integrated voice message, the ability to swiftly integrate clearly designated avatar support for the learner colleagues in a non-threatening manner. The facilitative instructor support efforts that embrace the self-regulatory efforts of the learner, while at the same time implementing support efforts through which cognitive load issues on the part of the learner may be lessened. Problem-based learning activities are inherently important within the team group and are instructionally relevant in the online learning environment because case studies and real world problems mandate the facilitative instructor to engage within the learning environment and each learner colleague to ensure the continuous support towards meeting the stated learning goals and learning objectives.

Discussion Activities

Discussion, collaborating verbally or in text, encourages student learners to discover solutions and develop critical thinking abilities (Arbaugh, 2008; Brookfield, 2006). Facilitative instructors using discussion as an instructional technique: (a) pose a problem; (b) monitor participant discussion; and, (c) summarize all participants' completed input (Bonk et al., 2004). Research finds discussion methods more effective compared to lectures when used with online student learners and allows for: (a) information retention; (b) transfer of knowledge to new situations; (c) problem solving and higher order learning; and, (d) motivation for further learning (Brookfield, 2006; Conrad & Donaldson, 2004). Discussion provides opportunity for an organic learning process to occur where learners, through their sharing, self-affirm their knowledge acquisition. Additionally, different from face-to-face discussions, online discussions (whether chat or discussion board) remain visible to student learners in an online environment and serve as a valuable resource or reference regarding their learning (See specific discussion of Distributed Cognition through archived course learning activities discussed in this volume, Huang, 2011).

To ensure in-depth and meaningful discussions are taking place in the online environment, facilitators can employ the Socratic questioning method in the discussion forums. Basically, the Socratic Method, named after the famous philosopher Socrates (Areeda, 1996), is based on asking open-ended and provocative questions to encourage critical thinking. Online facilitators use this method to stimulate disequilibrium in learners' thinking, thereby presenting opportunity for them to reevaluate their thought processes and expand their world views (Baxter Magolda, 1996). Ultimately, student dialogic exchanges are dynamic, where they begin to perceive their own answers as tentative, ephemeral and evolving. Ideally, dialogue lead to other learner questions about the course topics and content; thereby, providing depth and meaningfulness to discussions and anchoring content knowledge acquisition.

An interesting discussion should occur within the discussion perspective; specifically, whether the designed discussion activities are synchronous or asynchronous in nature. The instructional relevancy of the discussion activities must support and enhance the desired learning objectives, but must also consider the global time schedule and viability of synchronous activities for the instructor and learners. Within a synchronous activity, one must also consider the incorporation of archiving the synchronous events so that other learners, unable to attend the event, will have the ability to review the archived event. After all, it is of utmost importance to ensure that all learners are treated equally and have the ability to at least review the potential synchronous events so that one does not miss important knowledge acquisition nor perceived community building events. Therefore, within this discussion activity framework as well as all other forms of synchronous events, the archiving of potentially "lost" experiences and information must occur for future learner review.

After stating this emphasis upon archiving synchronous events, the ability to offer synchronous efforts related to discussion activities is rather exciting in scope. Dependent upon the subject matter and experiential efforts involved within a discussion activity it may be an interesting endeavor to integrate a mobile classroom response system, such as Poll Everywhere (n.d.) which may be described as "the world's first completely software based audience response system that connects presenters with their audience via mobile phones, twitter, and the web" (Condense, n.d., para. 1). As well, the opportunity to integrate Wiffiti (LocaModa Inc., 2009) into an online course wherein all the learners could synchronously post real-time messages to public displays has the potential to be

of significant interest, dependent upon the subject matter. How exciting, for the learners to publicly display their ideas and information within one public forum. For example, what if the learners were embracing a WebQuest (Dodge, 2007) effort or another form of scavenger hunt, with the Wiffiti display offering opportunities for the learners to share information that they've located so as to help and support other learner colleagues within a different type of discussion activity; although not a traditional discussion environment, Wiffiti does offer the opportunity to share information in a synchronous manner and offer short message responses that must be succinct, focused and embracing the energy of the discussion activity.

On the other hand, what of an asynchronous discussion activity consideration? The concept of podcast products, for example through the use of a mobile podcasting opportunity such as the use of iPadio (ipadio, n.d.) wherein one's mobile device can act as a broadcast device that allows a phone call to be reframed as a live web-based broadcast. How exciting, if group discussions were to be posted as audio products within the course environment, or perhaps small group discussions that were previously synchronous chat could then embrace the concept of true synchronous thought process and discussion activity without concerns related to word processing ability of the learners. Along these lines, one might consider Yodio (Audio Publishing Enterprises, Inc., 2008) as a storytelling device, but actually as a mobile digital storytelling environment wherein the storytelling activity can occur as more of a mobile endeavor and then make the storytelling product available within the larger learning environment so as to embrace a more holistic storytelling endeavor that may more fully support and reflect the learner's understanding and engagement with the subject matter information. These types of discussion activities, whether synchronous or asynchronous in nature, may also embrace the cooperative and collaborative learning activities.

Cooperative and Collaborative Learning Activities

Another effective online instructional technique involves cooperative learning. Cooperative learning is an instructional technique that places heterogeneous groups together to work on specific tasks (Stacey, 1999). Cooperative learners must share equal responsibility within the group; therefore, everyone must contribute and interact with one another in order to be successful. In cooperative learning, each group resembles a small community-type environment where decisions from assigning tasks, to offering constructive feedback must be handled by group exchanges (McKeachie, 2002). Student learners, working in groups, interact to share thoughts, opinions, and solve problems. Cooperative learning can be a successful instructional technique for the online student learner, because it promotes cognitive thinking for learners to manage their own learning, as well as constructivist elements such as discussion and dialogue to support rationales and elaborate basic content (Hannafin, 1989). An online instructor can establish cooperative learning opportunities through discussion board groups. These discussion board groups inherently present an organized structure to tasks and simplify communicative efforts amongst members. In discussion board groups, learners would operate cooperatively on different assignments or tasks.

Collaborative learning is a model of instruction that encourages student-to-community communication and interactions and is founded on assumptions associated with adult styles of learning that require independent, although interdependent, and interested participants (Knowles, 1973; Zimmerman, 2002). Collaborative learning is defined as "an activity that is undertaken by equal partners who work jointly on the same problem rather than on different components of the problem" (Brandon & Hollingshead, 1999, p. 111). Collaborative learning may appear comparable to cooperative learning, but collaborative learning has a less direct governance system, and is more student-centered paying attention to the individual abilities and contributions (McKeachie, 2002). When student learners are involved in collaborative processes, the facilitative instructor becomes less of an authority figure and is used more as a resource (Ingram & Hathorn, 2005b). The elements for collaboration are: (a) attributes of social construction of knowledge, (b) discussion of ideas and providing support via group communication, (c) sharing diverse perspectives and obtaining feedback from other group members, (d) group sharing of resources, and (e) seeking group solutions for problems and tasks (Stacey, 1999). Collaboration is an effective instructional technique for the online community environment for it allows student learners to interact with one another which increases communication with one another and decreases feelings of isolation (Palloff & Pratt, 2007). Collaborative learning projects need to be assignments that involve several components such as research gathering, evaluation of a technology product, a proposal to a company to improve workplace efficiency, designing or creating a new objective-based plan, or writing a formative or summative report. Members take on specific tasks to complete the entire project, and may work with partners to complete a specific objective or independently to contribute an individual component that adds to the whole presentation or product. When designing a collaborative project, the online facilitator should include a charter or contract that outlines how the team will complete the project. Students may add to the charter/contract or come up with their own that states how the group will work together, may include all group members' contact information, and outline procedures on how to handle conflict if the situation arises. Additionally the project should include a team (peer and self) evaluation by all members.

Exciting resources are currently available within the realm of cooperative and collaborative learning activities. One potentially robust activity embraces the communal realm of learning and understanding; a socially contextual embrace of knowledge that leads towards a stronger conceptual framework of understanding (Vygotsky, 1962, 1978) regarding the distinct shift from knowledge towards information that can be creatively embraced. This social emphasis upon understanding knowledge more fully, as well as the concept of double-checking the learner's understanding of the knowledge through others' understandings, helps to make connections in understanding and cognitively fit new information into previously framed understandings.

The first suggestion for implementation is a wiki environment, wherein a web site with a social construct is embraced. A course-specific or subject-specific wiki embraces the communal acquisition and socialization of the learners in the community while learning the information, wherein the emphasis is upon the ability of anyone within the community to add to, change, or delete any of the developing knowledge and more fully framing of information within the environment. The shift from a more passive understanding of the knowledge towards a wiki-embracing active engagement with the developing understanding of the knowledge is powerful, especially within an online environment wherein the ability to shift from an active learner into a more passive learner may rather easily transpire.

A second consideration is the concept of a course-based or communal blog. A blog is an interesting framework through which to consider cooperative and collaborative activities within an online learning environment because a blog, a web-based log or diary of events and experiences, offers the ability to post not only textual displays of information and hyperlinks to outside information but also offers the ability to integrate graphic images, digital videos, and audio products so as to enhance the occurring discussion. There are several free blog options available around the Web, such as Blogger (Google, 2011), WordPress (WordPress.com, 2011), Edublogs (Edublogs,

2011), and innumerable other blog options (Mashable, Inc., 2011). The ability to support the singular framing of acquired information through a public blog environment, or more fully within the social blog environment wherein learner colleagues can question, correct and reframe information within a supportive environment, is indeed a an impressive cooperative, collaborative activity within an online learning environment.

Finally, the communal environment offered by Facebook (2011) offers the ability to easily connect and share ideas, experiences and information with colleagues who are accepted as "friends" and colleagues. Within a learning environment, the socialization and ease of active engagement within an online environment merely urges the ease of cooperative and collaborative activities. One might consider the interest of Facebook "friends" within the FarmVille (Zynga.com, 2011) game application that is based within the Facebook environment. Consider this type of gaming environment within an instructionally relevant experience, and the potential impact this type of gaming application may have within a social environment, like Facebook, that offers the ease of usability that is preferential when one considers the potential for cognitive load issues involved in the learning process. As one may recognize, cognitive load relates to the overwhelming events that may occur as a learner delves into the subject matter and has difficulty conceptually framing the information within prior knowledge, so as to understand the subject matter; instead, the learner becomes overwhelmed with the knowledge and cognitively "shuts down" in confusion. The ease of use within a learning environment, especially when one considers the importance of the online learning environment, emphasizes the ability to support the learner's efforts through as little interface issue concerns as may be possible.

To further the consideration related to security concerns and control of the environment that may be desired by educational entities, the open source option towards a social networking engine application is worthy of discussion. Elgg (Curvender Limited, 2011) is a robust open source social networking engine, with the instrumental components necessary towards developing a cooperative and collaborative learning environment that may easily parallel the Facebook environment. Not only does Elgg offer the security desired so as to ensure a "safe" learning environment for learner colleagues, but the environment also offers the ability to design, develop and implement gaming applications with instructional learning goals and learning objectives.

These techniques and environmental application opportunities emphasize the socialization and social discourse necessary so as to support the conceptual framework of understanding as one works with knowledge and real-world applications with associated feedback and reflections.

Contextual Learning Activities

Contextual learning activities or situations are appropriate within the learning environment, no matter whether within a face-to-face environment or within an online distance learning environment. Contextual learning, also referred to as authentic learning, can be described as being structured or scaffolded around "real world" or "real life" situations and circumstances, such as offered by Adult Learning (n.d.):

In this approach, material is taught in the context in which it would be used in 'real life.' The underlying assumption is that the context provides meaningfulness to abstract information, making it more concrete and therefore, easier to learn. Related terms/concepts include: theme-based learning, authentic learning, experiential learning. (para. 10)

As such, the concept surrounding authentic learning is focused upon constructivist (Swan, 2005) and connectivist (Siemens, 2005) theories of learning; wherein, the learner-centered, learner-

focused approach towards learning is achieved within a community framework of understanding. To further emphasize the approach towards authentic learning,

Authentic learning builds on this concept of 'learning by doing' to create learning environments that move beyond merely allowing students to play a role. In the course of a project or problem, students engage in the type of multidisciplinary problem solving and critical thinking that researchers and experts use every day. Students learn how to investigate problems that require more than textbook formulas or rationales to solve. (Wyndham, 2007, p. 3)

Within the needs of the 21st century learner, the concept of authentic learning is of vital importance, so as to more fully support the student learners' understanding of the subject matter as well as ensure learners' ability to reuse the information or skills in new and different ways, as suggested by Lombardi (2007):

Student learners immersed in authentic learning activities cultivate the kinds of 'portable skills' that newcomers to any discipline have the most difficulty acquiring on their own:

- *The judgment to distinguish reliable from unreliable information*
- *The patience to follow longer arguments*
- *The synthetic ability to recognize relevant patterns in unfamiliar contexts*
- *The flexibility to work across disciplinary and cultural boundaries to generate innovative solutions. (Jenkins, Clinton, Purushotma, Robinson, & Weigel, 2006, as referenced by Lombardi, 2007, p. 3)*

The impact of authentic learning activities as an instructional design method within online distance learning environments may indeed enhance the instructional relativeness of the effort, as well as meet the needs of the learners, and ultimately, the larger global community.

Focusing upon Bloom's Taxonomy regarding higher order thinking skills (Bloom 1956, 1971, 1984; Anderson & Krathwohl, 2001), contextual learning activities are inherently important towards meeting the conception of higher order thinking skills. So as to embrace the realms delineated by Bloom (1956, 1971, 1984) as being analysis, synthesis, and evaluation, as well as Anderson and Krathwohl's (2001) revision of the higher order thinking skills designations as analyzing, evaluating and creating, one must embrace authentic learning opportunities as framed through contextual learning activities. Yet, how might one do this within an online learning environment? An initial thought is through virtual manipulatives that are focused upon the mathematics realm, such as the *National Library of Virtual Manipulatives* (Utah State University, 2010) which offers a lovely, simplistic way through which to explain basic mathematical concepts at the K-12 level although this is also worthy of consideration if one desires to explain basic constructs prior to building towards more advanced mathematical understandings. These web-based virtual manipulatives embrace the conceptual structure of the mathematical endeavor, which can be the first step towards embarking upon a more authentic learning opportunity.

Another consideration is a contextual learning activity framed through instructional gaming products. Gee (2005) states that, "A good instructional game, like many good commercial games, should be built around what I call 'authentic professionalism.' In such games, skills, knowledge, and values are distributed between the virtual characters and the real-world player in a way that allows the player to experience first-hand how members of that profession think, behave, and solve problems." (p. 1).

Within this thoughtful and potentially engaging environment, there are innumerable levels of learning occurring, whether knowledge-base, communal socialization, progressive cognitive problem-solving efforts, or innumerable perceived and real authentic activities. The socialization factor as embraced by Vygotsky (1962, 1978) and Wittgenstein (1922/2010, 1953) is enhanced by Gee (2005) through his instructional gaming discussion related to authentic professionalism:

Even young children learn best when they pick up "islands of expertise" (Crowley and Jacobs 2003). Whether those "islands" are model trains, toy dinosaurs, or Pokémon, they constitute centers of expertise that introduce learners to complex languages and the ways in which such languages are married to specific experiences, like gravity to a tossed coin. These experiences are then used to solve problems and answer questions. With authentic professionalism, "knowing" is not merely the mastery of facts; rather knowing involves participation in the complex relationships between facts, skills, and values in the service of performing a specific identity. Here, word and deed are united and the knower is a knower of specific kind—a type of active professional, not just a generic recipient of knowledge. (p. 4)

To delve further into the instructional gaming realm, one may desire to review *The Education Arcade* (n.d.) or the Serious Games Initiative (The Serious Games Initiative, n.d.).

Of further consideration is a more authentic view of team group case studies. Colorado State University (2011) offers the following description:

Case study refers to the collection and presentation of detailed information about a particular participant or small group, frequently including the accounts of subjects themselves. A form of qualitative descriptive research, the case study looks intensely at an individual or small participant pool, drawing conclusions only about that participant or group and only in that specific context. Researchers do not focus on the discov-

ery of a universal, generalizable truth, nor do they typically look for cause-effect relationships; instead, emphasis is placed on exploration and description. (para. 1)

The ability to analyze different case studies and then to delve into more authentic learning opportunities through more real-world cases to develop within the team's realm, is a potentially interesting effort.

The contextual learning activities, derived from authentic learning opportunities, embrace opportunities towards embracing higher order thinking skills (Bloom, 1956, 1971; Anderson & Krathwohl, 2001) within a social discourse environment (Wittgenstein, 1922/2010, 1953) so as to aide a learner's developing conceptual framework of understanding (Vygotsky, 1962, 1978).

Bloom's Taxonomy of Higher Order Skills Activities

Bloom (1956, 1971) developed a classification system to categorize student learning. These skills are arranged into six hierarchical levels, beginning from the simple, and building to the most complex. Bloom's Taxonomy of Educational Objectives (Bloom, 1956, 1971) levels include:

1. **Knowledge:** Students retain and recall information from memory;
2. **Comprehension:** Students explain information in their own words;
3. **Application:** Students apply learned information to different situations in their personal lives;
4. **Analysis:** Students uses prior information learned to solve problems by breaking it into smaller components;
5. **Synthesis:** Students are able to apply prior information learned in new situations; and
6. **Evaluation:** Students choose the best information and are able to support their choice

by making judgments. (Bloom, 1956, pp. 7-18)

Student learners that perform towards the lower level of the taxonomy (knowledge and comprehension) are demonstrating basic levels of cognitive thinking. Similarly, student learners that perform at the top of the hierarchy (analysis, synthesis, and evaluation) demonstrate higher or more sophisticated levels of thinking also known as critical thinking skills.

During the late 1990s, Anderson and Krathwohl (2001) updated Bloom's taxonomy to reflect the digital age. The revised levels may be represented as:

1. **Remembering:** Retrieving, recalling, or recognizing knowledge from memory to produce definitions, facts, lists, or retrieve material.
2. **Understanding:** Constructing meaning from different types of functions; written or graphic.
3. **Applying:** Applying related information and refers to situations where learned material is used through products like models, presentations, interviews or simulations.
4. **Analyzing:** Breaking material or concepts into parts, and determining how the parts relate or interrelate to one another or to an overall structure or purpose.
5. **Evaluating:** Making judgments based on criteria and standards through critiques.
6. **Creating:** Putting elements together to form a new pattern or structure. (Anderson & Krathwohl, 2001, pp. 67-68)

Bloom's Taxonomy (Bloom, 1956, 1971) and the revised Bloom's Taxonomy for the Digital Age (Anderson & Krathwohl, 2001) adhere well with effective techniques for the online learner, especially the higher levels of each hierarchy (Brookfield, 2006). Analysis, synthesis, evaluative, and creative skills encourage student interaction with other student learners and with the content, and align with Moore's (1989) student online interactions. Facilitative instructors, who desire student engagement with course content or other students, as well as utilization of problem-solving skills, find this taxonomy productive. De Wever, Schellens, Valke and Van Keer (2006) state that an advantage of online learning environments is the ability for students to have time to reflect on postings and access additional resources before contributing to the overall discussion which facilitates the development of higher order thinking. These critical thinking skills, such as analysis and synthesis learning, reflective thought, and evaluative thinking intensify the learning community experience. Additionally, higher order thinking skills help student learners recognize the close connection between social and intellectual development and offers new understanding that applies to students' own learning experiences. Opportunities for higher order thinking skills allow online members to form deeper bonds and create relationships that foster learning communities. The significance is that when higher order thinking assignments are incorporated into the course, the student learners' communications may be richer, more meaningful, and reflect critical thinking.

One example is to have students evaluate technology products, books, or other supplemental materials that relate to their major or degree. Students create their own evaluation rubric to speculate whether the item is beneficial to the student. This rubric can be used throughout the course to evaluate all products the students deem are necessary for their career. Specific discussion on how ability building impact e-learning is more fully discussed in this volume (See in this volume, Zheng, 2011).

Analysis and Synthesis Learning

Analysis and synthesis learning occur when students learn how to engage with new knowledge so that they can apply this knowledge into their world. In simplistic terms, the students focus upon their learning within the framework of higher order thinking skills; wherein, the students move across the continuum through the aspects of knowledge, comprehension, application, analysis, synthesis, and evaluation (Bloom, 1956, 1971), towards understanding the information and making connections within their conceptual framework of understanding (Vygotsky, 1962, 1978) and then apply their newly acquired knowledge within their professional worlds so as to emphasize the integration of newly acquired knowledge and skills while the student progresses through the higher order thinking skills of analysis, synthesis, and evaluation (Kovalchick & Dawson, 2004a). As such, the students appropriately progress through Bloom's Taxonomy of the Cognitive Domain (Bloom, 1971) by initial behaviors focused upon knowledge, comprehension, and application within the subject matter understanding and product development. Instructors' scaffolding skills and insight are crucial here (more fully discussed in this volume, Ge, Law & Huang, 2011).

For example, students help design assignment "templates" which can be generated to address mastery of content knowledge where students collect information on assigned topics and share with peers, either in an assigned discussion board group or with the whole class. The collective data are then individually selected and used to create a course "product" thereby demonstrating analysis and synthesis of knowledge acquired through course exchanges.

Reflective Thought and Evaluative Thinking

Reflection is the process of relating new knowledge in abstract and concrete ways to reconstruct ideas and strategies and turn them into new knowledge. Reflection helps students develop higher-order thinking skills by prompting them to relate new knowledge to prior knowledge, think in abstract and concrete terms, relate strategies to new tasks, and reconstruct their own thinking process (Schön, 1987; Zeichner & Liston, 1996). It supports development of a more sophisticated epistemology of the learner (Baxter Magolda, 1992, 1996).

Evaluative thinking is when students form and use criteria to judge the quality of an idea or task to make judgments on the worth of that idea or task. Evaluative thinking is a higher order level thought process that requires students to make judgments on ideas or tasks and assign value and meaning to determine the worth of the knowledge as it relates to their personal lives and existing belief systems.

Vygotsky (1962, 1978) suggests there is an interrelation between a learner's cognitive development and the nature of social interactions. Therefore, online learning communities' environments must carefully consider social communities and the interactivities that will help support the cognitive development of the learners through interactive activities and higher order thinking such as working collaboratively, and incorporating reflective or evaluative thinking. Online learning community environments mandate that communications be not only naturally occurring but also designed into the course environment to promote critical thinking skills. For example, online instructors have used individual blogs on Facebook pages, or teacher websites, as forums of reflective writing and expressive communication. These types of reflections must be developed within a community of trust for maximum effect; and must retain a level of decorum so that personal privacy is respected.

CONCLUSION

This section of the chapter concentrates on effective instructional strategies that should be used to enhance online student learners' academic success. Learning is about change; similarly, online learning is about change, often at an exponential level. Understanding effective online instructional strategies helps instructors to understand students and to design more meaningful learning experiences. There is not one online instructional technique that successfully applies to all online learning environments, but an understanding of the general principles will ensure student academic success (Brookfield, 2006; Frey & Alman, 2003; Merriam & Caffarella, 1999). In addition, a general understanding of online instructional techniques and strategies allows instructors to create experiences that will enhance the online learning environment (Arbaugh, 2008; Ardichvili et al., 2003; Bonk et al., 2004.)

Continuing with the metaphor of journeying on a train, an empty train (virtual community of learning within the course environment) is not beneficial to the owner of the railroad (university, workforce, or society). The train requires passengers (student learners and community members) to make the destination of their journey (acquisition of knowledge) along the countryside (subject matter and developing conceptual framework of understanding) justifiable. Additionally, the train (community) needs the conductor (the facilitative instructor) and engineer (instructional designer) to keep the vehicle on course, to plot the journey and not derail. All of these components work together, interacting with one another to support the train environment metaphor. If these interactions are absent, the train could simply stop or go off-track. An online community that does not participate in engaging interactions will practice futility, as these exchanges are vital in keeping the community alive and healthy, working towards ensuring student satisfaction and academic success. Additionally, as the train (virtual community of learning within the course environment) travels down the track while passengers (community of online learners) engage in interactions that are deeper, richer, and more comfortable allowing for insightful awareness about the journey (knowledge acquisition) to occur.

CHAPTER SUMMARY

This chapter discussed the findings as related to the current research in the construction and creation of successful interactions in an online course. As previously stated, a learning community is an interactive and social environment that addresses the learning needs of its members through proactive and collaborative partnerships (Brown, 2001; Garrison et al., 2001; McElrath & McDowell, 2008; Rovai & Wighting, 2005). If distance education is to succeed, interactive and engaging online learning communities are imperative for students to develop a sense of achievement and feel successfully engaged within the learning environment. In an online educational setting learning is increased when learners are actively engaged with others and the subject matter. Lee, Carter-Wells, Glaeser, Ivers and Street (2006) assert that forming social interactions through communication is best produced through instruction that is rich in student collaboration, social engagement, and student engagement, and when they are implemented into online courses, may create relationships for online learners, and as such, the union of technology, learning theories, and social presence for the adult learner may impact the landscape of distance education programs.

Representing the overarching metaphoric representation once again, the integral aspects related to the train journal have been put forward:

- *Passengers = community of online learners*
- *Train = virtual community of learning within the course environment*
- *Conductor and Tour Guide = facilitative online instructor*
- *Train engineer = instructional designer*
- *Journey = knowledge or learning to occur*
- *Separate traveler train cars = instructional tools implemented by the facilitative instructor and instructional designer*

These basic yet integral aspects within an online learning environment must be successfully executed, employed or realized in order to further engage the learners within the learning environment, towards meeting the course learning objectives.

This chapter suggests that student engagement and social interactions are possible in online learning environments through the use of simple instructional techniques incorporated into the online instructor's repertoire. As online learning continues to evolve, the chasm between online and face-to-face learning will widen. The days of taking a traditional course and modifying it for an online medium no longer works. Facilitators must begin with the instructional design for an e-learning genre incorporating the above strategies and techniques that are conducive to a vibrant and engaging environment where a physical presence is replaced by a virtual presence (See in this volume, Huang, 2011).

These activities are essential in developing relationships. The social aspects that support the creation of autonomous, dynamic learning communities are enhanced not only by learner engagement regarding the development of bonds of understanding, but also through thoughtful and professional collaboration. In order for student learners to achieve, they need to be able to find other students in their online world with whom they can collaborate and share. Learners need to be able to join forces with other students in their virtual world to feel connected, affirmed and supported.

Returning to the theme metaphor, as the sun sets, the train (community of learning) continues on its journey (knowledge acquisition), the passengers (community of online learners) are engaged in different activities on all train cars (instructional tools). Some are playing games with one another; some passengers are sharing photos of their trip with each other, while others are sitting together in intimate groups regaling others about certain facts in time (student learners' luggage of learning needs). All these interactions are engaging and meaningful, helping the passengers construct new meanings about their journey with other passengers. As the train travels down the track (course content or curriculum), towards its final destination a mysterious phenomenon occurs. The train seems to be growing in size becoming larger and larger in order to accommodate the passenger's growing collection of souvenirs, trinkets, and bags (ideas, thoughts, and opinions) they have collected on their journey. In real world terms, as the students interactions and collaborations increase in frequency, the knowledge gained from the interactions allow for student personal and professional growth.

REFERENCES

Ally, M. (2008). Foundations of educational theory for online learning. In Anderson, T., & Sanders, G. (Eds.), *Theory and practice of online learning* (pp. 1–31). Athabasca, Canada: Athabasca University.

American Psychological Association. (2010). *Publication manual of the American Psychological Association* (6th ed.). Washington, DC: Author.

Anderson, L. W., & Krathwohl, D. R. (Eds.). (2001). *A taxonomy for learning, teaching, and assessing: A revision of bloom's taxonomy of educational objectives.* New York, NY: Longman.

Anderson, T. (2008). Toward a theory of online learning. In Anderson, T., & Sanders, G. (Eds.), *Theory and practice of online learning* (pp. 45–74). Athabasca, Canada: Athabasca University.

Arbaugh, J. B. (2008). Does the community of inquiry framework predict outcomes in online MBA courses? *International Review of Research in Open and Distance Learning, 9*(2). Retrieved from http://www.irrodl.org/index.php/irrodl/article/view/490/1048.

Ardichvili, A., Page, V., & Wentling, T. (2003). Motivation and barriers to participation in online knowledge-sharing communities of practice. *Journal of Knowledge Management, 7*(1), 64–77. doi:10.1108/13673270310463626

Areeda, P. E. (1996). The Socratic method. *Harvard Law Review, 109*(5), 911–912.

Audio Publishing Enterprises, Inc. (2008). *Yodio: Audio for fun, fame and fortune!* Retrieved from http://www.yodio.com/

Bandura, A. (1977). *Social learning theory.* New York, NY: General Learning Press.

Bandura, A. (1986). *Social foundations of thought and action: A social cognitive theory.* Englewood Cliffs, NJ: Prentice Hall.

Baxter Magolda, M. B. (1992). Students' epistemologies and academic experiences: implications for pedagogy. *Review of Higher Education, 15*(3), 265–287.

Baxter Magolda, M. B. (1996). Epistemological development in graduate and professional education. *Review of Higher Education, 19*(3), 283–304.

Bloom, B. S. (1956). *Taxonomy of educational objectives, handbook I: The cognitive domain.* New York, NY: David McKay.

Bloom, B. S. (1971). Mastery learning. In Block, J. H. (Ed.), *Mastery learning: Theory and practice.* New York, NY: Holt, Rinehart & Winston.

Bloom, B. S. (1984). *Taxonomy of educational objectives.* Boston, MA: Allyn and Bacon.

Bloom, B. S., & Krathwohl, D. R. (1956). *Taxonomy of educational objectives: The classification of educational goals, by a committee of college and university examiners. Handbook I: Cognitive domain.* New York, NY: Longman, Green.

Bonk, C. J., & Graham, C. R. (2006). *The handbook of blended learning: Global perspectives, local designs.* San Francisco, CA: Pfeiffer.

Bonk, C. J., Wisher, R. A., & Nigrelli, M. L. (2004). Learning communities, communities of practice: Principles, technologies and examples. In Littleton, K., Miell, D., & Faulkner, D. (Eds.), *Learning to collaborate, collaborating to learn* (pp. 199–219). New York, NY: Nova Science.

Brandon, D., & Hollingshead, A. (1999). Collaborative learning and computer-supported groups. *Communication Education, 48*, 109–126. doi:10.1080/03634529909379159

Brookfield, S. (2006). *The skillful teacher* (2nd ed.). San Francisco, CA: Jossey-Bass.

Brown, J. S., & Adler, R. (2008). Minds on fire: Open education, the long tail, and learning 2.0. *EDUCAUSE Review*, (Jan/Feb): 16–32.

Brown, R. (2001). The process of community building in distance learning classes. *Journal of Asynchronous Learning Networks, 5*(2), 18–35.

Browne, E. (2005). Structural and pedagogic change in further and higher education: A case study approach. *Journal of Further and Higher Education, 29*(1), 49–59. doi:10.1080/03098770500037754

Burnham, B., & Walden, B. (1997). Interactions in distance education: A report from the other side. In *Proceedings of the Adult Education Research Conference* (pp. 49-54).

Colorado State University. (2011). *Case study: Introduction and definition*. Retrieved from http://writing.colostate.edu/guides/research/casestudy/pop2a.cfm

Condense. (n.d.). *Condense*. Retrieved from http://conden.se/

Conrad, D. (2007). Recognizing prior learning: Exploring the diversity of learners' experiential learning through PLAR. In Evans, T., Murphy, D., & Haughey, M. (Eds.), *World handbook of distance education*. Oxford, UK: Elsevier.

Conrad, R. M., & Donaldson, A. (2004). *Engaging the online learner: Activities and resources for creative instruction*. San Francisco, CA: Jossey-Bass.

Crawford, C. M. (2001). Developing webs of significance through communications: Appropriate interactive activities for distributed learning environments. [CWIS]. *Campus-Wide Information Systems Journal, 18*(2), 68–72. doi:10.1108/10650740110386675

Crawford, C. M. (2003). Emerging learning environments: Enhancing the online community. *Academic Exchange Quarterly, 7*(4), 131–135.

Cross, P. (1981). *Adults as learners*. San Francisco, CA: Jossey-Bass.

Curvender Limited. (2011). *Elgg: Introducing a powerful open source social networking engine*. Retrieved from http://www.elgg.org/

De Wever, B., Schellens, T., Valcke, M., & Van Keer, H. (2006). Content analysis schemes to analyze transcripts online asynchronous discussion groups: A review. *Computers & Education, 46*(1), 6–28. doi:10.1016/j.compedu.2005.04.005

Dodge, B. (2007). *WebQuest.org*. Retrieved from http://webquest.org/index.php

Duffy, T., & Cunningham, D. (1996). Constructivism: Implications for the design and delivery of Instruction. In Jonassen, D. (Ed.), *Handbook of research on educational communications and technology*. New York, NY: Simon & Schuster.

Edublogs. (2011). *Edublogs - Education blogs for teachers, students and institutions*. Retrieved from http://edublogs.org/

Everywhere, P. (n.d.). *Instant audience feedback*. Retrieved from http://www.polleverywhere.com/

Facebook. (2011). *Facebook helps you connect and share with the people in your life*. Retrieved from http://www.facebook.com/

Frey, B. A., & Alman, S. W. (2003). Applying adult learning theory to the online classroom. *New Horizons in Adult Education, 17*(1), 4–12.

Galbraith, M. W. (2004). *Adult learning methods: A guide for effective instruction.* Malabar, FL: Krieger Publishing.

Gannon Cook, R., & Crawford, C. M. (2004). From silos to communities: Addressing electronic isolation through interactivities. In R. Ferdig, C. Crawford, R. Carlsen, N. Davis, J. Price, R. Weber, & D. A. Willis (Eds.), *Society for Information Technology & Teacher Education International Conference Annual* (pp. 445-452). Norfolk, VA: Association for the Advancement of Computing in Education (AACE).

Garrison, D. R., Anderson, T., & Archer, W. (2001). Critical thinking, cognitive presence, and computer conferencing in distance education. *American Journal of Distance Education, 15*(1), 17–23. doi:10.1080/08923640109527071

Gee, J. P. (2005). What would a state of the art instructional video game look like? *Innovate 1*(6). Retrieved from http://innovateonline.info/pdf/vol1_issue6/What_Would_a_State_of_the_Art_Instructional_Video_Game_Look_Like_.pdf

Gijselaers, W. H. (1996). Connecting problem-based practices with educational theory. *New Directions for Teaching and Learning, 68,* 9–13.

Google. (2011). *Blogger: Create your free blog.* Retrieved from http://www.blogger.com/

Gronlund, N. E. (1970). *Stating behavioral objectives for classroom instruction.* New York, NY: Macmillan.

Hannafin, M. (1989). Interaction strategies and emerging instructional technologies: Psychological perspectives. *Canadian Journal of Learning and Technology, 18*(3), 167–179.

Harrow, A. (1972). *A taxonomy of the psychomotor domain. A guide for developing behavioral objectives.* New York, NY: McKay.

Haythornwaite, C. (2006). Facilitating collaboration in online learning. *Journal of Asynchronous Learning Networks, 10*(1), 7–24.

Hillman, D., Willis, D. J., & Gunawardena, C. (1994). Learner-interface interaction in distance education: An extension of contemporary models and strategies for practitioners. *American Journal of Distance Education, 8*(2), 30–42. doi:10.1080/08923649409526853

Hmelo-Silver, C. E., Duncan, R. G., & Chinn, C. A. (2007). Scaffolding and achievement in problem-based and inquiry learning: A Response to Kirschner, Sweller, and Clark (2006). *Educational Psychologist, 42*(2), 99–107. Retrieved from http://www.cogtech.usc.edu/publications/hmelo_ep07.pdf. doi:10.1080/00461520701263368

Ingram, A. L., & Hathorn, L. G. (2005a). Analyzing collaboration in online communications. In Howard, C., Boettcher, J., Justice, L., Schenk, K. D., Rogers, P. L., & Berg, G. A. (Eds.), *Encyclopedia of distance learning* (Vol. 1, pp. 83–89). Hershey, PA: Idea Group, Inc.doi:10.4018/978-1-59140-555-9.ch013

Ingram, A. L., & Hathorn, L. G. (2005b). Collaboration in online communications. In Howard, C., Boettcher, J., Justice, L., Schenk, K. D., Rogers, P. L., & Berg, G. A. (Eds.), *Encyclopedia of distance learning* (Vol. 1, pp. 264–268). Hershey, PA: Idea Group, Inc.doi:10.4018/978-1-59140-555-9.ch038

ipadio. (n.d.). *ipadio: Broadcast live to the web from a phone call.* Retrieved from http://ipadio.com/

& J. C. Moore (Ed.), *Elements of quality online education: Engaging communities* (Vol. 4, pp. 13–30). Needham, MA: Sloan-C.

Jenkins, H., Clinton, K., Purushotma, R., Robinson, A. J., & Weigel, M. (2006). *Confronting the challenges of participatory culture: Media education for the 21st century*. Chicago, IL: The MacArthur Foundation. Retrieved from http://www.digitallearning.macfound.org/site/c.enJLKQNlFiG/b.2108773/apps/nl/content2.asp?content_id=%7BCD911571-0240-4714-A93B-1D0C07C7B6C1%7D

Jonassen, D. H. (2000). Towards a meta-theory of problem solving. *Educational Technology Research and Development*, *48*(4), 63–85. doi:10.1007/BF02300500

Jonassen, D. H., Cernusca, D., & Ionas, I. G. (2006). Constructivism and instructional design: The emergence of the learning sciences and design research. In Reiser, R., & Dempsey, J. (Eds.), *Trends and issues in instructional design and technology*. Columbus, OH: Merrill.

Keller, J. M. (1979). Motivation and instructional design: A theoretical perspective. *Journal of Instructional Development*, *2*(4), 26–34. doi:10.1007/BF02904345

Keller, J. M. (1983a). Motivational design of instruction. In Reigeluth, C. M. (Ed.), *Instructional design theories and models* (pp. 383–433). New York, NY: Lawrence Erlbaum Associates.

Keller, J. M. (1983b). *Development and use of the ARCS model of motivational design*. Enschede, The Netherlands: Toegepaste Onderwijskunde, Technische Hogeshool Twente.

Keller, J. M. (1984). The use of the ARCS model of motivation in teacher training. In Shaw, K., & Trott, A. J. (Eds.), *Aspects of educational technology* (*Vol. XVII*, pp. 140–145). London, UK: Kogan Page.

Keller, J. M. (1987a). Development and use of the ARCS model of instructional design. *Journal of Instructional Development*, *10*(3), 2–10. doi:10.1007/BF02905780

Keller, J. M. (1987b). Strategies for stimulating the motivation to learn. *Performance & Instruction*, *26*(8), 1–7. doi:10.1002/pfi.4160260802

Keller, J. M. (1987c). The systematic process of motivational design. *Performance & Instruction*, *26*(9-10), 1–8. doi:10.1002/pfi.4160260902

Kirschner, P. A., Sweller, J., & Clark, R. E. (2006). Why minimal guidance during instruction does not work: An analysis of the failure of constructivist, discovery, problem-based, experiential, and inquiry-based teaching. *Educational Psychologist*, *41*, 75–86. doi:10.1207/s15326985ep4102_1

Knowles, M. (1973). *The adult learner: A neglected species*. Houston, TX: Gulf Publishing Company.

Kovalchick, A., & Dawson, K. (Eds.). (2004a). *Education and technology: An encyclopedia* (*Vol. 1*). Santa Barbara, CA: ABC-CLIO.

Kovalchick, A., & Dawson, K. (Eds.). (2004b). *Education and technology: An encyclopedia* (*Vol. 2*). Santa Barbara, CA: ABC-CLIO.

Krathwohl, D. R., Bloom, B. S., & Masia, B. B. (1964). *Taxonomy of educational objectives: The classification of educational goals. Handbook II: Affective domain*. New York, NY: David McKay Co., Inc.

Learning, A. (n.d.). Contextual Learning. *Adult Learning -. Theory into Practice*. Retrieved from http://www.nald.ca/adultlearningcourse/glossary.htm.

Lee, J., Carter-Wells, J., Glaeser, B., Ivers, K., & Street, C. (2006). Facilitating the development of a learning community in an online graduate program. *Quarterly Review of Distance Education*, *7*(1), 13–33.

Levy, Y. (2008). An empirical development of critical value factors (CVF) of online learning activities: An application of activity theory and cognitive value theory. *Computers & Education*, *51*(4), 1664–1675. doi:10.1016/j.compedu.2008.04.003

LocaModa Inc. (2009). *Wiffiti*. Retrieved from http://wiffiti.com/

Lombardi, M. M. (May 2007). Authentic learning for the 21st century: An overview. D. G. Oblinger (Ed.). *EDUCAUSE2007*. Retrieved from http://net.educause.edu/ir/library/pdf/ELI3009.pdf

Mashable, Inc. (2011). *40+ free blog hosts*. Retrieved from http://mashable.com/2007/08/06/free-blog-hosts/

McElrath, E., & McDowell, K. (2008). Pedagogical strategies for building community in graduate level in distance education courses. *Journal of Online Learning and Teaching, 4*(1), 117–127.

McKeachie, W. J. (2002). *McKeachie's teaching tips: Strategies, research, and theory for college and university teachers* (11th ed.). Boston, MA: Houghton-Mifflin.

Merriam, S. B., & Caffarella, R. S. (1999). *Learning in adulthood* (2nd ed.). San Francisco, CA: Jossey-Bass.

Moore, M. (1989). Three types of interaction. *American Journal of Distance Education, 3*(2), 1–7. doi:10.1080/08923648909526659

Oddcast Inc. (2011). *Voki*. Retrieved from http://www.voki.com/

Palloff, R. M., & Pratt, K. (2003). *Virtual student: A profile and guide to working with online learners*. San Francisco, CA: Jossey-Bass.

Palloff, R. M., & Pratt, K. (2007). *Building learning communities in cyberspace: Effective strategies for the online classroom* (2nd ed.). San Francisco, CA: Jossey-Bass.

Renninger, K. A., & Shumar, W. (Eds.). (2002). *Building virtual communities: Learning and change in cyberspace*. New York, NY: Cambridge University Press. doi:10.1017/CBO9780511606373

Rheingold, H. (1993). *The virtual community: Homesteading on the electronic frontier*. New York, NY: Harper Collins.

Richardson, J. C., & Swan, K. (2003). Examining social presence in online courses in relation to students' perceived learning and satisfaction. *Journal of Asynchronous Learning Networks, 7*(1), 68–88.

Riel, M., & Polin, L. (2004). Online learning communities: Common ground and critical differences in designing technical environments. In Barab, R., Kling, J., & Gray, H. (Eds.), *Designing for virtual communities in the service of learning* (pp. 16–50). Cambridge, UK: Cambridge University Press.

Rovai, A. (2002a). Building sense of community at a distance. *International Review of Research in Open and Distance Learning, 3*(1), 1–16. Retrieved from http://www.irrodl.org/index.php/irrodl/article/view/79/153.

Rovai, A. (2002b). Sense of community, perceived cognitive learning, and persistence in asynchronous learning networks. *The Internet and Higher Education, 5*, 319–332. doi:10.1016/S1096-7516(02)00130-6

Rovai, A. P., & Wighting, M. J. (2005). Feelings of alienation and community among higher education students in a virtual classroom. *The Internet and Higher Education, 8*, 97–110. doi:10.1016/j.iheduc.2005.03.001

Schön, D. (1987). *Educating the reflective practitioner*. New York, NY: Basic.

Siemens, G. (2005). Connectivism: A learning theory for the digital age. *International Journal of Instructional Technology and Distance Learning, 2*(1), 3–9.

Stacey, E. (1999). Collaborative learning in an online environment. *Journal of Distance Education, 14*(2), 14–33.

Stillwater, OK: Oklahoma State University. (ERIC Document Reproduction Service No. ED409460).

Stricker (Eds.), *Online counseling: A handbook for mental health professionals* (pp. 19-50). Amsterdam, The Netherlands: Elsevier.

Suler, J. (2004). The psychology of text relationships. In *R. Kraus*. J. S. Zach, & G.

Swan, K. (2001). Virtual interactivity: design factors affecting student satisfaction and perceived learning in asynchronous online courses. *Distance Education, 22*(2), 306–331. doi:10.1080/0158791010220208

Swan, K. (2005). *A constructivist model for thinking about learning online* (Bourne, J., Ed.).

The Education Arcade. (n.d.). *The Education Arcade*. Retrieved from http://www.education-arcade.org/

The Serious Games Initiative. (n.d.). *Serious games initiative*. Retrieved from http://www.seriousgames.org/

Thompson, S. C. (2004). Professional learning communities, leadership, and student learning. *Research in Middle Level Education Online, 27*(3), 35–55.

Utah State University. (2010). *National library of virtual manipulatives*. Retrieved from http://nlvm.usu.edu/en/nav/vlibrary.html

Vesely, P., Bloom, L., & Sherlock, J. (2007). Key elements of building online community: Comparing faculty and student perceptions. *Journal of Online Learning and Teaching, 3*(3), 234–246.

Vygotsky, L. (1962). *Thought and language*. Cambridge, MA: MIT Press. doi:10.1037/11193-000

Vygotsky, L. (1978). *Mind in society*. Cambridge, MA: Harvard University Press.

Wenger, E., McDermont, R., & Snyder, W. M. (2002). *Cultivating communities of practice*. Boston, MA: Harvard Business School Press.

Wittgenstein, L. (1922/2010). *Project Gutenberg's Tractatus Logico-Philosophicus* (Translated by C. K. Ogden). Retrieved from http://www.gutenberg.org/ebooks/5740

Wittgenstein, L. (1953). *Philosophical investigations*. (Translated by G.E.M. Anscombe).

WordPress.com. (2011). *WordPress.com – Get a free blog here*. Retrieved from http://wordpress.com/

Wyndham, C. (September 2007). Why today's students value authentic learning. D. G. Oblinger (Ed.). EDUCAUSE 2007. Retrieved from http://net.educause.edu/ir/library/pdf/ELI3017.pdf

Zeichner, K. M., & Liston, D. P. (1996). *Reflective teaching: An introduction*. Mahwah, NJ: Lawrence Erlbaum.

Zimmerman, B. J. (2002). Becomming a self-regulated learner: An overview. *Theory into Practice, 41*(2), 64–70. doi:10.1207/s15430421tip4102_2

Zynga.com. (2011). *FarmVille*. Retrieved from http://www.facebook.com/FarmVille

ADDITIONAL READING

Allen, I. E., & Seaman, J. (2008). *Staying the course: Online education in the United States, 2008*. The Sloan Consortium.

Brown, G., & Peterson, N. (2008). The LMS mirror: School as we know IT versus school as we need IT and the triumph of the custodial class. *Journal of Online Learning and Teaching, 4*(2), 190–197.

Cassell, J., & Tversky, D. (2005). The language of online intercultural community formation. *Journal of Computer-Mediated Communication, 10*(2), article 2. Retrieved from http://jcmc.indiana.edu/vol10/issue2/cassell.html

Chao, E., DeRocco, E. S., & Flynn, M. (2007, March). *Adult learners in higher education: Barriers to success and strategies to improve results.* Retrieved from http://wdr.doleta.gov/research/FullText_Documents/Adult%20Learners%20in%20Higher%20Education1.pdf

Duncan-Howell, J. (2010). Teachers making connections: Online communities as a source of professional learning. *British Journal of Educational Technology, 41*(2), 324–340. .doi:10.1111/j.1467-8535.2009.00953.x

Garrison, D. R., & Cleveland-Innes, M. (2005). Facilitating cognitive presence in online learning: Interaction is not enough. *The American Journal of Research on Distance Education, 19*(3), 133–148. doi:10.1207/s15389286ajde1903_2

http://delicious.com/

http://flickr.com/

http://moodle.org/

http://www.lectureshare.com/

Johnson, L., Smith, R., Willis, H., Levine, A., & Haywood, K. (2011). *The 2011 Horizon Report.* Austin, Texas: The New Media Consortium. Retrieved from http://wp.nmc.org/horizon2011/

Keller, J. M. (2010). *Motivation Design.* Retrieved from http://www.arcsmodel.com/home.htm

Kemp, L. (2010). Teaching and learning for international students in a 'Learning Community': Creating, sharing and building knowledge. *In-Sight: A Journal of Scholarly Teaching*, 563-74. Retrieved from EBSCO*host*.

Lave, J., & Wenger, E. (1998). *Communities of practice: Learning, meaning, and identity.* Cambridge University Press.

Lofstrom, E., & Nevgi, A. (2007). From strategic planning to meaningful learning: diverse perspectives on the development of web-based teaching and learning in higher education. *British Journal of Educational Technology, 38*(2), 312–324. doi:10.1111/j.1467-8535.2006.00625.x

Mackey, J., & Evans, T. (2011). Interconnecting networks of practice for professional learning. [Retrieved from EBSCO*host*.]. *International Review of Research in Open and Distance Learning, 12*(3), 1–17.

Oblinger, D., & Oblinger, J. (2005). Is it age or IT: First steps toward understanding the net generation. In D. Oblinger & J. Oblinger, (Eds.), *Educating the net generation* (pp. 2.1-2.20). Retrieved from http://net.educause.edu/ir/library/pdf/pub7101b.pdf

Oliver, K. M. (2007). Leveraging Web 2.0 in the redesign of a graduate level technology integration course. *TechTrends, 51*(5), 55–61. doi:10.1007/s11528-007-0071-3

Ouzts, K. (2006). Sense of community in online courses. *Quarterly Review of Distance Education, 7*(3), 285–296.

Russell, T. L. (1999). *The no significant difference phenomenon.* Raleigh: North Carolina State University.

Shea, P. (2006). A study of students' sense of learning community in online environments. *Journal of Asynchronous Learning Networks, 10*(1), 35–44.

Shea, P., Vickers, J., & Hayes, S. (2010). Online instructional effort measured through the lens of teaching presence in the community of inquiry framework: A re-examination of measures and approach. [Retrieved from EBSCO*host*.]. *International Review of Research in Open and Distance Learning, 11*(3), 127–154.

Smith, R. (2005). Working with differences in online collaborative groups. *Adult Education Quarterly, 55*(3), 182–199. doi:10.1177/0741713605274627

Vitale, A. (2010). Faculty development and mentorship using selected online asynchronous teaching strategies. *Journal of Continuing Education in Nursing, 41*(12), 549–556. .doi:10.3928/00220124-20100802-02

Weber, J. M., & Lennon, R. (2007). Multi-course comparison of traditional versus web based course delivery systems. *Journal of Educators Online, 4*(2). Retrieved from http://www.thejeo.com/Archives/Volume5Number1/LapsleyetalPaper.pdf.

Yu-Chu, Y. (2010). Analyzing online behaviors, roles, and learning communities via online discussions. [Retrieved from EBSCO*host*.]. *Journal of Educational Technology & Society, 13*(1), 140–151.

KEY TERMS AND DEFINITIONS

Andragogy: Andragogy is a term that refers to teaching adult learners.

Asynchronous: Asynchronous is a term in students in an online environment are separated from the instructor and other students through time.

Cognitive Learning Theory: A learning theory where memory plays a prominent role in instruction.

Collaborative Learning: Collaborative learning is a model of instruction that encourages student-to-student activities where students work together on an assignment or project.

Community for Learning: A community for learning describes a learning environment that is rich in vibrant discourse through student-to-student communications and assignment collaborations.

Constructivism Learning Theory: A theory of learning that explains how learners learn, and where the learner constructs his or her own knowledge to learn objectives.

Cooperative Learning: Cooperative learning is an instructional technique that places heterogeneous groups together to work on specific tasks including course assignments.

Online Learning Environment: An online learning environment is a distinct, pedagogically or andragogically meaningful, and comprehensive learning environment where learners and faculty can actively participate in the learning and instructional process through distance education.

Problem-Based Learning: Problem-based learning is an instructional strategy where student learners work cooperatively in groups to seek solutions to real world problems.

Socratic Method: The Socratic method, named after the famous philosopher Socrates is a discussion technique based on asking and answering questions to encourage critical thinking.

Synchronous: Synchronous, distance education term, refers to online instruction and means at the same time.

Chapter 14
Intentional Communities of Practice, the Challenge of Interactivity

Aaron Wiatt Powell
Virginia Tech University, USA

ABSTRACT

This chapter examines the support of social interaction in a cooperative, situated online learning environment, and the cultural barriers that hinder such intention and interactivity. The findings of a literature review suggest that the greatest challenge to intentional Community of Practice (CoP) is a sense of interdependence among CoP members, the authenticity of the practice or purpose, and a trajectory for the CoP's future. This case study attends to these issues with a cohort of practicing teachers. It explores an initiative to nurture CoP with cooperative projects and with the support of an online community portal. The case challenges CoP theory from an intentional or instructional standpoint, and informs design and technology in support of CoP.

INTRODUCTION

According to Jonassen, Peck, and Wilson (1999), human learning involves community and true life experiences lacking in the classroom:

In the real world, when people need to learn something, they usually do not remove themselves from their normal situations and force themselves into sterile rooms to listen to lectures on formal principles about what they are doing. Rather, they tend to form work groups (practice communities), assign roles, teach and support each other ... learning results naturally from becoming a participating member of a community of practice. (p. 177)

DOI: 10.4018/978-1-61350-441-3.ch014

Community of practice (CoP) is a "set of relations among persons, activity, and the world" (Lave & Wenger, 1991, p. 98) "created over time by the sustained pursuit of a shared enterprise" (Wenger, 1998, p. 45). Lave (1996) holds that learning is a social collective, rather than individual, psychological phenomenon. The extent to which this is the case may be the crux of the problem found in this study. The development and strength of a CoP hinges greatly on the degree of interactivity and interdependence of the CoP members, the extent to which knowledge is published to a broader audience and CoP members access and interact with this knowledge artifact and its author(s). Of course, such access is greatly facilitated by computer networks.

Teacher learning community is a main proposition of the NBPTS (National Board for Professional Teaching Standards, 2002). Teachers "cannot work and learn entirely alone or in separate training courses after school" (Hargreaves, 2003, p. 25). Rather, "It is vital that teachers engage in action, inquiry, and problem solving together in collegial teams or professional learning communities" (p. 25). There is a need for new teacher preparation and professional development strategies and for teachers to take more control of them through CoP (Stuckey, Hedberg, & Lockyer, 2001). Darling-Hammond (1996) found that teachers who have "access to teacher networks, enriched professional roles, and collegial work feel more efficacious in gaining the knowledge they need to meet the needs of their students" (p. 4). Similar arguments are made for other fields in general; the early literature and studies in this area were influenced by knowledge management in the corporate world, where there is a clear value in capturing the collective knowledge of a workforce (Hannum, 2001; Zahner, 2002).

Researchers (Moore & Barab, 2002; Schlager & Fusco, 2004) acknowledge that the current climate of teacher practice in the U.S. works against CoP. Indeed, teaching has been found to actually be a private practice (Riel & Becker, 2000; Schlager

& Fusco, 2004). This was confirmed by a pilot study (Powell & Evans, 2006) that examined the nature of community among a preservice teacher cohort during the last semester of their program, their practicum, at a large southern U.S. state university. It explored the degree of physical and online interaction between peers and with faculty and staff, and how knowledge artifacts were shared, or how accessible they were to others in the group. Outside of course work, there was very little communication between members of this cohort, let alone exchange of lesson plans and the like. When such cooperative work took place, it was random and one-to-one; it was private. And the preservice teachers, with one exception, observed a similar lack of cooperation between supervising teachers and their colleagues. The study found that activities provided little opportunity for cooperative work, academic competition individualized practice, paper-based artifacts limited accessibility and revisability, and a private portfolio process lacked consideration of a public audience.

The privatization of teacher practice likely starts with teacher preparation, which could lack the crucial interactivity required to support a thriving teacher CoP. If professional knowledge and practice are private when teachers enter the field, how can they become public later, per the NBPTS standards, and how do we ensure professional development in general? The study detailed herein was initiated by the main purpose of exploring how teacher participation in CoP facilitated with technology might contribute to a more public and cooperative professional development for teachers.

THEORY

Researchers on school learning and instructional design and technology (IDT) continue to rely more on socio-cultural, situated learning theories, in a move away from the strictly cognitive and psychological (Palloff & Pratt, 1999; Scardamalia

& Bereiter, 1996). These learning theories are still in development, and there is a diverse collection of opinions and understandings of their processes (Driscoll, 2000). Vygotsky (1978) and cultural historical activity theory have been a great influence for situated learning theory (Driscoll, 2000; Hung & Nichani, 2002; Lave & Wenger, 1991). Vygotsky challenged the notion that mental development must precede learning, suggesting that what people "can do with the assistance of others might be in some sense even more indicative of their mental development than what they can do alone" (Vygotsky, 1978, p. 85). 'Good learning' then "is that which is in advance of development" (p. 89); it "presupposes a specific social nature" (p. 88); "it awakens a variety of internal processes" that operate only through "interacting with people" and "cooperation with peers" (p. 90). A key element is that learning requires authentic social and cultural contexts, authentic work and activities. Vygotsky observed that learners' actual needs are often disregarded, that learning should be "incorporated into a task that is necessary and relevant for life" (p. 118).

A framework among the situated learning paradigm that seemed to hold considerable promise is that of communities of practice, or CoP (Lave & Wenger, 1991; Wenger, 1998, 2003). CoP theory is based on Lave and Wenger's (1991) observations and analysis of apprenticeship cultures and their learning processes. The theory assumes that learning is fundamentally social, and knowledge is integrated in the doing, the relations and the knowledge and expertise of the community and its members (Trentin, 2001). The theory holds that knowledge is inseparable from practice.

From a synthesis of definitions in the literature, a CoP is a self-organized, interdependent, sustained, social network that shares authentic purpose, knowledge, resources, and activity. The literature seems to support Wenger's (1998) three dimensions or elements of CoP: *joint enterprise, mutual engagement, and repertoire.*

- **joint enterprise:** members are bound together by their collectively developed understanding of their community's purpose, to which they hold each other accountable
- **mutual engagement or mutuality:** members build their community through mutual engagement. They interact with one another, establishing norms and relationships of mutuality that reflect these interactions.
- **repertoire:** communities of practice produce a shared repertoire of communal resources-language, routines, sensibilities, artifact, tools, stories, and styles. (Wenger, 1998, p. 73)

These elements offer valuable clues for structuring learning environments to better support social and authentic learning processes. They are quite interdependent. As evident in the results section, it is often difficult to treat one without including another. *Joint enterprise*, a shared and social purpose, is a crucial ingredient of CoP, where members are truly engaged in authentic shared activity. Too narrow a purpose is characterized by task-based or goal oriented learning communities (Henri & Pudelko, 2003; Riel & Polin, 2004; Trentin, 2001). A CoP has a trajectory of global expensiveness, a focus on the shared and social, contribution to something bigger than individual or course limited perspectives. There should be some interdependence among members, or *mutual engagement*. As Scardamalia (Fishman, et al., 1997) puts it, "A hallmark of student engagement in educational networks [CoP] is the production of knowledge of value to others, not simply demonstrations of personal achievement" (p. 16). Finally, the element of *repertoire* entails the crucial factor of access to the CoP tools and knowledge of specific aspects of its practice. Interactivity is an important factor of all three elements, but more so with the element of mutual engagement.

Unfortunately, many studies seem to treat the term CoP as a catch phrase for professional kinship or shared interest (Barab, Kling, & Gray,

2004; Schlager & Fusco, 2004). Few capitalize on the actual principles of CoP theory established by Wenger (1998), or examine his elements in a systematic fashion, if they are formally acknowledged at all. One primary level of analysis is that CoP must have continuity (Henri & Pudelko, 2003; Lave, 1996; Wenger, 1998). Henri and Pudelko (2003) explain that a *learners' community* typically exists at the whim of education programs, lacking "continuous character of the activity which characterizes the community of practice" (p. 481). Yet this simple principle is overlooked by researchers who attempt CoP interventions within time delimited courses or institutional settings, without any trajectory for further participation or production of, and access to, knowledge artifact beyond this limitation (Wenger, 1998).

The term *intentional* is an important qualifier in the title of this chapter. Barab et al. (Barab, MaKinster, & Scheckler, 2004) point to the common, intentional CoP linked to a course or other instructional intervention, not sustained beyond an academic term, not focused on authentic, "real-world" practice, and not characterized by interdependence (Barab & Duffy, 2000; Riel & Polin, 2004; Wenger, 1998). Instructional design and technology in support of CoP is a subject of this inquiry, which obviously implies some intention. A purpose of this study was to examine how intentional learning communities of the temporary nature can be better supported in their contribution to a more global CoP that might encompass them, or even supported in their transition to becoming more sustained and cooperative, actual CoPs themselves.

DESIGN

CoP theory considers knowledge to be public, with a social accountability, yet the literature reveals social accountability to be one of the greatest challenges for intentional CoP. Principles of instructional design and technology (IDT) contribute to this challenge. According to its traditions in behavioral psychology, instructional designers are primarily interested in individual learners' behaviors based on constructions of functional relationships and the discrimination and generality processes of these relationships (Burton, Moore, & Magliaro, 1996), but it is communication that an individual has within the social-cultural environment, CoP, that allows negotiation of these relationships (Lave, 1996; Vygotsky, 1978).

Traditional approaches of IDT are in many ways incompatible with CoP (Goodyear, 2000; Koschmann, 1996). Yet there has been a paradigm shift in IDT, away from the behaviorist and psychological toward more social and cultural perspectives, from the transmission model to computer supported collaborative learning (CSCL): situated activity and a cooperative, rather than competitive, pursuit of knowledge (Koschmann, 1996). Goodyear (2000) argues for a holistic perspective of lifelong learning for education, a shift from the creation of "tasks-in-objects" to "environments-for-activities," in support of "real-world" learning, not idealized teacher directed learning activities (p.3). Dede (1999) stresses the need for a reconceptualizing of "information technology in knowledge mobilization" with a shift from the transfer and assimilation of information to the creation, sharing, and mastery of knowledge, through the process of knowledge networking in communities of practice.

A challenge to design for CoP is that its currency is "collegiality, reciprocity, expertise, contributions to the practice, and negotiating a learning agenda, not affiliation to an institution, assigned authority, or commitment to a predefined deliverable" (Wenger, 2003, p. 97). Therefore, particular attention should be paid to informal learning processes, the meaningfulness of membership and participation, and technology platforms for shared discourse and knowledge (Wenger, 2003). A literature review on intentional CoP revealed Wenger's (1998) element of mutual engagement to be the greatest challenge, establishing the necessary level of interactivity, interdependence, and social accountability. Two specific factors align with Wenger's (2003) design concerns: (1) the best approach appears to be for CoP members to publish their knowledge and ensure *accessibility* of this knowledge beyond academic boundaries; (2) members need *authentic* reasons to both publish and access this knowledge, a margin of control and ownership in the purpose, process, and product of the CoP. After all, people in the real world don't set out to have communities of practice (Wenger, 1998); they are driven by solving authentic problems (Jonassen, 2005).

Regarding access, Wenger (1998) stresses three important processes: coordination, transparency, and negotiability. Technology amplifies Wenger's processes (Trentin, 2001). In most cases, online elements are assumed in the CoP research, and they are assumed in applications of CoP theory (Wenger, 1998). The dynamics of a CoP have been described as "Ensuring access to information, fostering a culture of sharing, enabling exchange of information, support and resources through technology, and prioritizing exactly what knowledge is to be managed" (Marshall & Rossett, 2000, p. 22). Riel and Polin (2004) suggest the use of online knowledge management systems as a repository for knowledge artifact, with the ability to link objects together for personal use, a collaborative or shared workspace, and the ability to push information to others (p. 45). Unfortunately, few studies directly attend to purpose, authentic reasons for CoP members to participate in these dynamics.

Regarding authenticity, design for CoP should be flexible and allow for community to adapt the design and take ownership (Engestrom, Engestrom, & Suntio, 2002; Lieberman, 1996; Palloff & Pratt, 1999; Riel & Polin, 2004; Trentin, 2001). This is also a form of access, allowing opportunity for the participant to have ownership in the process and product and make connections to personal experience. Many suggest including learners in the IDT and CoP process through participant and

iterative design (Carroll, 2001; Schwen & Hara, 2004; Suchman, 1983), a promising strategy for CoP that few seem to employ. The ultimate goal is to lighten the control of structures, in the aim of moving learners from "hierarchical to collegial interaction patterns, structured to conversational discourse, and passive to active participation" (Schlager & Fusco, p. 139). We cannot design CoP; we can only design *for* CoP. What is important is the interaction of the designed and the emergent, the crisscrossing of the design boundary object (Wenger, 1998).

INQUIRY

This study addressed two main issues that emerged from the literature on intentional CoP: access to public knowledge, and allowing for emergent, authentic practices. It is attention to these factors that is required for establishing the necessary level of mutuality or interactivity to maintain the synergy of the CoP. A presumption of this investigation is that we can design *for* intentional CoP within an academic course, with the support of activities that provide for authenticity, and technologies that amplify access and cooperative knowledge development and learning.

This study differs from previous research on three major points. One, the technology employed was quite flexible, and participants were encouraged to determine what tools to use and how to use them to meet their needs. Participants were not required, for example, to write two posts to the discussion board every week. Two, the purposes for using the technology emerged from authentic needs in the completion of a cooperative course project. The project needs and activities for meeting them were left fairly open, to be negotiated by the participants. Finally, this study took initial steps to ensure a trajectory (Wenger, 1998) for the CoP. Hargreaves (2003) criticizes attempts at institutionalizing CoP, as the support is inevitably withdrawn and the CoP gradually atrophies. This, in essence, is Wenger's (1998) point: with no future, there is no CoP. In this case, the technology support was not withdrawn, and the moral support was largely put in the hands of the participants. From the beginning, the instructors stressed to participants that the technology is theirs and would be utilized for the remainder of their program, two years, and open to use beyond graduation. Further, the initiative followed "the design principles for fostering, sustaining, and scaling a CoP in which the value of sharing one's practice and engaging in the dialogue outweighs the 'costs' of participation" (Barab, MaKinster, et al., 2004, p. 56). "Costs" such as various requirements an instructor might typically impose on format and quantity of contributions were kept to a minimum; they actually did not really exist in this case. Use was to be truly need driven.

This study used a case-study approach to examine a particular CoP, a graduate, reading-specialist cohort of practicing teachers taking a *Literacies and Technology* course at a large U.S. university. The study applied community support technology to support the cohort in completing a collective project: the design and development of a local support website for the clients served by the teacher cohort. The study explored the following questions:

The Activities

1. What activities emerge for the use of technology?
2. How do they come about?
3. Which are more supportive of CoP? The least supportive? Why?

The Participants

4. What changes occur with individual's perceptions of their community participation?
5. What changes occur in observed individual community oriented behaviors?

The CoP

6. How do online activities contribute to overall changes in community practice?
7. What concerns do participants have about the future of their CoP? Why?

METHODS

Yin (1994) argues that "case studies are the preferred strategy when 'how' and 'why' questions are being posed, when the investigator has little control over events, and when the focus is on a contemporary phenomenon within some real-life context" (p. 1). These were all important factors within this context. An essential element of case study design is to test or develop theory (Yin, 1994), which was an important purpose of this study.

Participants were a cohort of ten reading-specialist graduate students, and the program advisor who was the instructor for the course of the study. The cohort makes up the entire master's program; it was a CoP in the making. The participants had taken the same classes together for a year and a half and would for another two and a half years. Also, as employed elementary educators in the local area, the participants were viewed as more likely to maintain professional ties beyond the program. All participants were women between the ages of 23 and 57.

The cohort had relied heavily on course meetings, taking one course a semester that met one time a week for three hours at an urban higher education center. Before this course and research initiative, there had been little utilization of communication technologies among the cohort, except for limited email communication to coordinate activities. Also, the program had experienced very little cooperative work. For this class, the group met in a computer lab for the first time in their program of study. They had previously used only a course management system, Blackboard, only minimally. This was to be the first term the course would be more fully supported by an online community environment.

The instructor was a primary participant in the study, with more than 30 years of experience in elementary education and the field of literacy. As the leader of the group, she was expected to have significant impact on the tasks and activities of the cohort. However, she suffered a number of health issues during the course which limited her presence and influence. She was mindful of CoP principles, though she previously would not have articulated them as such. It was her teaching style to be a co-participant and allow students a great deal of independence. She did not micromanage student work, but she was directive when necessary. Though she uses a networked computer a great deal, she admitted that her technology knowledge is quite limited. However, she did not seem to have much trouble when she took the time to perform necessary tasks.

I, the key investigator, functioned as a participant observer in the study, as co-instructor assisting with the technology part of the course. For a study of this type, it is important for the researcher to share his predispositions (Maxwell, 1996; Yin, 1994). To *not* do so could conceal potential researcher effect, which poses a liability with regard to the generalizability of this study (however, I later discuss how avoiding researcher affect arguably resulted in lack of leadership, thus undermining the intervention). First, with years of experience as a student, teacher, and instructional technologist, I have observed that people responsible for instruction seem to fall short in recognizing or addressing learner needs. I am therefore guided by constructivist and situated learning theories to better involve students in the learning process. Furthermore, throughout my ten year teaching career, I experienced teaching as a practice that mostly happened behind closed doors. There was little collegiality, while at the same time, some of my more successful lessons were adapted from those few ideas that were

shared by colleagues. At one school, I developed a curriculum file cabinet in which teachers could share lessons and activities they had developed. I thought this would be a valuable resource, but after about two years, almost all additions to the filing cabinet were my own. I thought CoP theory could address this problem. Based on my own experience and the pilot study detailed above, I perceived a need for greater cooperation in teacher and preservice teacher practice. In essence, this need is for that shared filing cabinet I tried years ago, only now it is conceived in a more global form, supported by networked computing.

Sakai (2011) functioned as the online community workspace. Sakai had fairly accessible, flexible tools that better supported interactivity and collaboration. Though there were a few limitations of the system, such as a lack of a notification option for the discussion tool, Sakai offered a crucial, user-friendly shared folder space to which all members could upload, author, and revise content for the class and specific projects. This was an important advantage over mainstream tools at the time such as Blackboard or WebCT, which had no such feature. Sakai had significant momentum at the university with technical support and potential for longevity, important for the trajectory of the CoP.

A reminder that based on the review of literature, the technology itself is not so much a factor in the success of online support for CoP, particularly with such a novice group. Rather, the nature of the CoP, its needs and use of technology support in general are of primary concern. Thus, a minimal selection of tools and structure were set up initially in the Sakai site. All participants had permission to submit content to any of the Sakai tools. As participants negotiated their activities and tool needs, I provided support in reconfiguring initial tools. An email list in the Sakai worksite was utilized for group communication, with a central record of all correspondence in the Sakai Email Archive tool. The Announcements and Resources tools have the option for participants to have an email sent to the listserv to notify peers of a new contribution.

Data collection included the primary sources of focus group interviews and individual interviews, as well as the Sakai record of activities that took place within Sakai: discussion forums, email, and all files and contributions. A secondary source was memos authored by me, the key investigator, and the instructor of the course. Three focus-group interviews were unstructured and heavily dependent on issues raised by the participants. The instructor was interviewed at the start of the semester for a description of the current level of community for the group, the nature of its activities and use of technology to date. All participants were interviewed individually at the end of the semester. These interviews were semi-structured with a few planned questions along the lines of the research questions provided above. Additional inquiries were more targeted toward themes and concerns that emerged over the term or within the interviews. Participants were asked to confirm and elaborate on the class responses to course activities as observed by the researchers in their memos, or in focus groups. The interviews gauged the overall impact of the course worksite and the course activities with regard to learning and community. After the last course meeting, a final one-hour focus group confirmed preliminary findings with the participants.

Since both the instructor and I were quite busy with our participant roles during course time, field notes would be limited or nonexistent. Therefore, we each prepared memos to document observations and insights. I recorded my observations of CoP behavior as it related specifically to Sakai, the nature of interactions and artifact exchanged online, including in-class processes by which the group determined and carried out its online activities. The instructor dealt more generally with community and purpose. As expected, my role in providing technical support provided numerous opportunities for participants to provide direct feedback to me on the Sakai tools themselves

and how they were used to support the course project and program community. The memos were instrumental in capturing this data and providing a progressive interpretation of events as they unfolded.

The course and study procedure started with a group book report assignment. Small groups were assigned particular books for which they would prepare reports to be presented to the class. The intention was to immediately get the students collaborating, and exploring and using the Sakai tools. Students were also provided general guidelines of the term project, namely that small groups or the class as a whole would cooperatively prepare a website that would support literacy in some way. Students were provided with a limited pre-configured collection of support technologies within Sakai. For an hour during each of the first three class sessions, students received some basic training on the Sakai tools. Participants were encouraged to use the tools to support the book-report, using the Resources tool, for example, to upload PowerPoint slides. They were asked to begin thinking about and negotiating how they will utilize Sakai tools to support their class project of developing the website. The course began with little structure because the intention was to provide greater opportunity for activities to emerge from authentic work. Participants were encouraged to join the researchers throughout the semester in the purpose of further developing the online resources and activities in support of their professional community. Lessons on Sakai tools and other technologies continued throughout the term as needed. Participants were also introduced to basic website development skills with an initial activity that had them prepare a simple biographical webpage that they then shared in a collective place on the Sakai portal.

All data from the memos and interview transcripts were coded per emerging themes, *or non-equivalent patterns* (Yin, 1994) and then matched with Wenger's (1998) three main CoP elements: *repertoire, mutual engagement, and joint enterprise*. All data were coded such that it could be tracked back to the original source, thus keeping the data contextualized and grounded (Maxwell, 1996).

The *explanation-building* strategy (Yin, 1994) is helpful in considering explanations of data that do not match the variables, or cross over them. Here the memos were very helpful. According to Maxwell (1996), researcher bias is the main threat to interpretation and validity of inferences. Maxwell (1996) points to theory validity as well, that researchers should always consider "alternative explanations and understandings of the phenomena" (p. 90). The primary instructor's perspective as an expert in the literacy and teacher education fields provided confirmation of observations and inferences as well as some helpful consideration of alternative explanations. Probably the strongest method of protecting interpretation validity is with the multiple sources of data which provided converging lines of inquiry (Yin, 1994), offering triangulation to protect the reliability of findings. Further, member checks (Yin, 1994) within the personal interviews and the final focus group provided the opportunity for targeted questions to confirm emergent themes or inform plausible alternative explanations for what was observed and inferred. Of great concern is external validity, or generalizability of results to other settings. Due to the study's small study group and its possible uniqueness, results may be called into question in relation to other settings. The main protection of external validity is good documentation of procedures so that they can be replicated and have a chance of obtaining similar results (Yin, 1994, p. 95). The memos provided for this documentation, along with the data coding itself, breadcrumbs from inference back to original source of data. The methodology of this study was inspired by previous research on CoP (Harris & Niven, 2002; Preece, 2001; Rogers, 2000) that utilized Wenger's (1998) matrix; results of these and more recent studies can be compared to those of this study for consistencies and inconsistencies.

Also, this methodology will likely be used in future cases, potentially reinforcing theory building that resulted from this study.

RESULTS

Here the research questions are addressed in a brief narrative summary, as informed by the emergent themes from the data and analysis and how they fit each of Wenger's (1998) CoP elements: *repertoire, mutual engagement, and joint enterprise.*

Repertoire

- What activities emerge for the use of technology?
- How do online activities contribute to overall changes in community practice?

There were isolated uses of the various Sakai tools, but no systematic practices emerged. It would be difficult to argue that it became part of the group's repertoire. Sakai was used to handle the course tasks, for which the participants developed rudimentary skills. Otherwise, for the most part it was a novelty to play with and then set aside. Participants stated optimism for its future use, but it was clear that the Sakai worksite's longevity was very much in question. However, skills with Sakai transfer to other technologies, and some participants did seem to become more amicable toward sharing their work electronically or online in general.

There were definitely some technical difficulties, to be expected when introducing a number of new technologies in a new setting to people with limited technical skills. Participants certainly experienced some frustration at times. It was surprising how steadfastly confused many of the participants remained when it came to differentiating between the project website and web development vs. the community worksite of Sakai. Often investigator questions regarding

Sakai were misinterpreted to be about the website. This is evidence of their strong task focus, but it also illustrates their weak grasp of Sakai's purpose. Both the instructor and I were shocked that even the utility of Sakai for supporting the website project work was not fully appreciated by the participants until much later in the term.

Most participants did successfully meet the challenges they faced in developing the necessary technical skills that were expected of them to manage the course projects. However, there was a pre-existing repertoire with which Sakai had difficulty competing, such as standard email, storage disks, phone, and mainly physical presence. It was suggested by several that ideally, Sakai would have been introduced a previous term. They clearly experienced some cognitive overload with the technologies, as their level of technical skills was too limited to take on so much in one term. There were a number of surprising *firsts* for many of the participants, such as minimizing a window and retrieving it again, instead of closing it altogether. Of course, there was the additional burden of grappling with the higher order technical skills of developing and publishing a website and all of its associated technologies and tasks.

Community and shared practice were the key focus of this study, and in these areas, participants fell rather short in applying the technologies. A notable observation is the participants never really engaged in a discussion on a general protocol of where to put certain things, even for some project work, let alone other knowledge artifact they could share more randomly. Without better protocols, the notification tool was even more important, yet it was utilized only a few times the entire term, even for the website project. Though there were repeated invitations for participants to take ownership, it was a responsibility participants avoided. There was no long term outlook for organization because there was no long term outlook for Sakai's existence beyond the term. This was too high an expectation on our part, given their limited experience. It is difficult to discern, however, whether

the participants were handicapped in this area by a lack of technical skills or by a lack of interest or engagement in the process in general – "just tell us what to do, you're the instructor" or "this just isn't our way." Based on the interviews, it was likely a combination of both. Moreover, it is a point well taken that intentional CoP efforts would likely be even more difficult with other elementary teachers not engaged in a graduate program or the use of technology in general.

The participants had a legitimate case for some minor usability issues with Sakai's applications. The greatest complaint was with Sakai's discussion tool. However, participants generally had little experience of other technologies with which to compare their experience with Sakai tools, or other technologies employed for the study. For most, it was the first time they had really used an online discussion forum, so were the problems they associated with it really important usability issues, or was it simply a lack of practice or habit in using such a tool? Or were the usability issues simply an excuse?

The resources tool was more important because this was where files were shared. It worked pretty well, yet they had negative feedback on finding content there: it became too cluttered, disorganized. Yet there was also not enough content to draw them there. They consistently failed to recognize that the organization of the content was controlled by them. In my experience, these issues are generally not unlike the difficulty teachers have in finding files on their personal computers, due to poor file management skills or practices. Of course, the problem is compounded with a group of people managing one file space. Again, nobody stepped up to help establish protocols. This was where there was a lack of leadership in assigning roles perhaps, and maybe we should have provided more direction.

I was very surprised at the end of term to find in at least one interview that a student still didn't know how to use the email list. She didn't even seem aware of it, though it was mentioned repeatedly throughout the term. Others in the interviews still seemed to think that it was easier to simply email peers/coolleagues their traditional way. They had a tool they already knew how to use; it did not matter if another tool was easier and worked better.

In one way or another, all the participants commented on the technology barrier- the lack of skills and time to develop and use the skills. Therefore, when the technology *was* used, it was often frustrating and time consuming, and perceived as too much trouble. The physical method of hard copy and verbal conversation was therefore preferred. The participants verbally recognized benefits of Sakai and the other technologies, but they were apparently not important enough to warrant spending more time developing skills and habit in their use.

Another aspect of the *repertoire* element of CoP is community culture - other modes of communication and ways of sharing practice. There was much interactivity that occurred with the group outside of the course context and/or in the physical realm, all outside the purview of the study. Nonetheless, these activities certainly exist, as described by the participants in the interviews, and some of them are directly opposed to online support of CoP, such as a participant protecting a test as proprietary vs. sharing it with others who might have a use for it, or sharing a hard copy of it with *one* other teacher vs. making it available for all online. It is quite a challenge, the notion of taking individual teachers' repertoires, milk crates of professional knowledge artifact, and creating a collective database of that knowledge on which there is cooperative dialogue on how the knowledge base can be used and improved.

Mutual Engagement

- How do they [emergent activities] come about?
- Which are more supportive of CoP? The least supportive? Why?

- What changes occur with individual's perceptions of their community participation?
- What changes occur in observed individual community oriented behaviors?

In the span of one term, it was perhaps naïve to expect that any significant changes of the nature represented in these questions would occur, or at least to the extent they could be captured, particularly with a strong community to start. The activities that emerged for the use of Sakai were mostly the result of participants being asked to use the application in support of their group projects. Though a few interactions and postings occurred outside this boundary, they were certainly the exception and not the rule. The data were inconclusive on which activity or tool would be more supportive of CoP. Based on the interviews, it seemed the resources tool would be the most supportive, as a means to collect various documents of use to colleagues. The communications tools generally seemed to be less important because there were other means of communication already in place. It seems there was an increase in community oriented behaviors, but this was likely a function of the course related cooperative work, which of course came to an end. The use of Sakai had less of an impact in its support of the community than it did as a talking point on how to use the tools.

The group clearly had a strong social bond. They cared for each other and were social, and they had some amicable discussion on their professional knowledge. They were an established community. The study focused on how mutuality of the group would be affected by a general emphasis on the community and its longevity, and technology to support its activities. In the repertoire section we see how participants were not ready for such technology, particularly as it applies to the more abstract goal of supporting the community. It appears they were also not ready to take a closer look at their community, particularly in formalizing any of its activities in any way, online or otherwise. That sense of interdependent interactivity that is so crucial for CoP did not develop outside the tasks assigned within the course context. There was little exchange of knowledge artifact such as lesson plans, assessments, and the like, or anything outside the tasks of the course. Such exchange seemed to violate a sense of ownership. There did seem a chance, albeit a small one, that if the program were to continue using Sakai, there could be noticeable change in individual behaviors associated with mutuality and sharing. Alas, Sakai was not used for the next course as hoped.

There was certainly an impact on individual's perceptions of their community participation, but this was more a function of the cooperative, group activities, the tasks related to the course projects rather than community participation initiated by the participants. The group already worked well together, and from the beginning of the semester, they helped each other get a handle on the technologies. Some participants simply shared knowledge for the community's sake, but there was evidence that these same exceptions would have occurred regardless, by the more ephemeral channel of regular email or a brief encounter in the hall. In the end, perhaps a few participants were more open with the group, more likely to share something, and perhaps more likely to publish something online. There was certainly a strong feeling of potential from the interviews. But two years after the study, and after the group had graduated, there was no reason to believe that the community would even continue to exist, let alone make greater use of technology in facilitating its activities.

There was discussion in the third focus group on the "stinginess" of some teachers in not sharing their work, referred to by one teacher as "glory hogs." The exchange was remarkable in its unanimity on the existence of "glory hogs" and in its irony: that they all had documents of value to the group that they had *not* shared, and more importantly, that there is very little personal recognition

in their field, much less actual "glory." If their work remains private, not mutually engaging, who is aware of it to recognize it, let alone glorify it? Perhaps it is a fear that someday there might actually be a token of recognition, and someone else might actually get the credit? Or perhaps the individual work ethic and competitive nature of academics leading up to and including teacher education programs continues into their teaching careers, still an academic field?

A major theme in the individual interviews was the paradox of people appreciating the value in sharing, but not doing so. There appears to be an issue of ownership, particularly for things that took a good deal of investment of time and effort. There seemed to be a lack of trust in reciprocity; a couple participants directly indicated there would have to be a structured, balanced activity of exchange. A recurring theme was that notions of sharing and reciprocity are not part of teachers' culture, particularly online, that there is a lack of time for one thing, and that they prefer random acts of sharing in the physical realm, not in a public fashion online to all who might benefit.

The instructor and I attempted to make some motivational speeches on the importance of teachers sharing what they do. However, we may have been too soft in our approach, out of concern for authenticity and in an effort to prevent strong researcher influence. In hindsight, there was clearly a leadership vacuum, a clear dilemma of the students looking to us for leadership, as instructors of the course, and us providing the space and looking for some of them to emerge as leaders of their learning and professional community. A couple of them made tentative steps; it simply wasn't enough, and they did not necessarily have full appreciation in general of what we were trying to accomplish with online support for CoP.

Joint Enterprise

- What activities emerge for the use of technology?

- How do they come about?
- How do online activities contribute to overall changes in community practice?
- What concerns do participants have about the future of their CoP? Why?

As illustration of the degree of interdependence between the CoP elements, the joint enterprise reality of the group is to get a degree, and more topically, to successfully complete the course and related tasks, which means working on the cooperative projects successfully. However, from the perspective of this course and study, there was as much interest in the purpose of nurturing CoP beyond academic boundaries. In essence, the interactivity of *mutual engagement* was the *joint enterprise* from an intentional CoP perspective. Because we were concerned about authenticity, it was a secondary goal, not directly incorporated into the course tasks and activities, and this goal was, unfortunately, not really taken up by the participants. One could surmise that the truly authentic purpose for these participants, getting a degree and better job and pay, proved a significant handicap.

The participants voiced appreciation for the concept of online support for CoP, for greater mutual engagement and interaction, but their behavior spoke otherwise. When I pressed them on this contradiction, the participants responded with numerous reasons, the dominate one being community of practice was simply not *their* practice, at least in an online sense. Using Sakai did have an impact. If nothing else, it made the participants more aware and appreciative of the notion of sharing their knowledge, and the possibilities of doing it electronically, even if it is with their standby of more traditional channels. As one participant expressed it, "putting it into a computer is not our way." The general message among the participants in the interviews was that a great deal of time and effort would be needed to really get online supported CoP to happen. They were fairly explicit that CoP purpose would

need to be declared in the form of required tasks, and even then there was question as to what that would involve. The participants were distracted by the more concrete purpose of getting a good grade and graduating, for numerous reasons not relevant to CoP. Mutual engagement and greater interaction were not the assignments after all; it was the book reports and the website project.

Nonetheless, there were those "learning moments" as the participants called them, and according to the instructor in our final interview, the participants "knew how to do it at the end. They knew what it was for. They could see possibilities for the future." She felt this was a solid achievement for this group. That they challenged the use of Sakai and questioned its purpose is a normal part of the learning process, she said, and "it's part of virgins learning to use technology." She elaborates:

At the beginning I think they saw it [Sakai] as being useless, and they felt that we were sort of wasting their time. They didn't get it, they didn't see the value of it. It wasn't anything that we even should be spending class time on. Again, I think they weren't there. They weren't in the zone [of proximal development (Vygotsky, 1978)]. Ah, at the point when they started really asking questions about it, saying well why are we doing this? Well why aren't we just learning Front Page? What do we need this for? Ah, that's when they were getting in the zone. By the end of the semester they were there. I think almost everybody did see the value of it, they did appreciate it and at that point at the very end it was having a positive impact on the learning community.

As I was still in doubt, I questioned "how so?" Her response:

When we were getting all of the stuff up for (website project)...they were able to put all that stuff right up, go through it, put it on a projector, go through it as a group, they were so happy, so proud, so wow, look at this, look at what we have done, look at what we are gonna be able to do. Ah, I mean that was a moment and when I came into the classroom and after the two hours in the open house and I said okay show me what you have done, and they started, you know, putting it all up and showing me and telling me. I mean like that was a moment when I saw that they really got it and they were really there.

Perhaps they finally accepted the usefulness of the technology for their cooperative work in class, but whether they ever got the concept of using it to support their CoP beyond class is another question entirely. This would take reciprocity in sharing professional knowledge and artifact, voluntarily, outside course tasks. This concept never really took hold. Though they finally seemed to understand it, and perhaps appreciate it, there was never any ownership of this notion as their own purpose. As the data demonstrates, the teachers pointed to issues of technical skills, time issues, and the fact that this was "not the teacher way." Despite participants' positive statements for further growth of online support of the CoP over time, it did not happen. The access was there; the Sakai site was still live and active, but the participants stopped using Sakai and wanted little more to do with it, per the instructor's report from a year later. The trajectory was lacking, as the program did not continue with incorporating the use of Sakai in following courses; nor did it continue to emphasize CoP for that matter.

This exchange between the instructor and me took place about three weeks into the term, before I'd really collected any data. It sums up the study in many ways, when it had really just begun:

I: … one of the uses of the little bio page is that if we all get our pictures and a little bio and we can have something on the webpage that links to the creators of the webpage, and it has each of our names and can link to our bios

Me: This is something that maybe they should…you pretty much said up front, and I've been reinforcing this, that this is their project and I tried to reinforce this 3 or 4 times, that Sakai is their site and they can use it however they want, and the design, you know, their workflow.. however they like

I: Well but, I mean if we, you know, get right down and dirty and honest when we say "this is your site and you can do what you want to"

Me: They're clueless

I: But they, well, if they weren't in this class they wouldn't want to do anything, so... or I mean it's contrived for the class

Me: Yeah well this goes to that authenticity of the class. I think there're levels, you know, sure, the higher level course project is not authentic, but the activities they come up with to support that project, those would be authentic

I: Yeah, totally, totally

Me: They're establishing their needs and they're establishing how they're going to meet them

I: And I buy that

Me: Okay, that's the kinda argument I was trying to make about authenticity…

The difference between a CoP and a general learning community is that the CoP is continuously self-driven by authentic purpose. In an academic setting, establishing a sound authentic purpose is extremely problematic. What is authentic? In academics, one is essentially being asked to challenge the status quo of authenticity, to learn, to think or know differently, to participate in change. Instructional design and technology is about facilitating this intentional change. Such practice significantly challenges the notion of authenticity. Also, one must consider the purposes of the individuals in the academic program. Why are they taking the course or enrolled in the program? It is rarely for the sole reason to learn, if that is a reason at all, and it is certainly a rare individual whose primary purpose is to share knowledge with his or her peers. The dilemma of what is authentic in an academic setting is a resounding theme of this study's results. From my memos: "Though all the technology was used for *authentic* purpose, not simply utilized for technology's sake, it was *our* authentic purpose, the course's."

CONCLUSION

Though CoP is characterized in the literature "by warmth, cooperation, and mutual support," there is often a strong difference in the reality of what we observe empirically (Kling & Courtright, 2004, p. 98). Henri and Pudelko (2003) observe that researchers' disappointment with CoP "often comes from their implicit or explicit expectations" which may be "concerned by aspects of the activity of the community that it does not or cannot have" (p. 485). It is a question of authenticity. It was found in the literature that CoP initiatives have not allowed for the emergence of authentic community purpose, process, and product. We likely over-corrected for this shortcoming. We sacrificed structure for function, and the participants simply did not adopt the function of CoP. They were quite involved with decisions regarding course tasks to perform and complete; their engagement in cooperative work in this respect alone make the course a great success. Nonetheless, again, a CoP is a self-organized, interdependent, sustained, social network that shares authentic purpose, knowledge, resources, and activity. In this case, the level of authenticity was simply too low to truly develop a more self-organized (Trentin, 2001) and sustained (Barab, MaKinster, et al., 2004) online presence and interactivity.

For the joint enterprise of mutual engagement - interactivity or CoP itself as purpose, though a number of structures discussed in the literature were included in this initiative, they were perhaps too loose or informal. In hindsight, perhaps the instructor and I should have required certain activities such as sharing two lessons a week, or

sharing whatever was considered useful by the participants' for day-to-day practices with the children they teach. This would have developed more of a critical mass of content that could have activated more engagement and interactivity. More structured online places than we started with in this study would have to be provided in the CoP system for participants to post and organize their contributions. Perhaps a peer evaluation system could be set up that would both provide for assessment for the course, and valuation among the participants for their contributions. Leaders might emerge from such peer feedback, leaders who could begin taking more responsibility for the group's activities for when the term is over and the requirement is withdrawn. However, as previously expressed, the literature and experience suggests that when such artificial structures are withdrawn at the end of the term, the CoP is likely to collapse. The motivational factors one hoped would be authentic or internalized become permanently associated with a task, course, and term that are now completed – "We finished; we have our grade." There are a number of arguments for externalizing CoP initiatives outside an academic course, at the departmental or professional level.

Leadership was perhaps an issue that was understated in the data. Wenger (1998) stresses the importance of the community broker for bridging boundaries. Perhaps the instructor and I should have played a greater role as community brokers, modeling and evangelizing with even more emphasis the kind of CoP behaviors we had in mind. Or perhaps greater recognition of key members of the group would have further encouraged them to take on leadership roles, and the others to follow their lead. However, as the instructor noted, the age differences among the participants could inhibit younger, more active members (often the most technically proficient) from becoming leaders within the CoP. An area for future study would be a closer look at identities. Also, the intersection of contributor and audience could use some closer attention. What change agents would better motivate a potential contributor to contribute to the CoP and/or a participant to retrieve what has been contributed?

The proprietorship of knowledge or work is clearly an issue for teachers, and arguably students and faculty in general. For the younger, more active participants, it seems they might have benefited from greater focus on individual presence in the Sakai space, such as their sharing of work within a personal portfolio within Sakai. They did have their personal bio pages which they could have easily turned into more elaborate portfolios, which had been suggested as an option for the participants. They would not have had a thematic or typological index of resources as a whole, but then no such collection developed in this case anyway.

Wenger's (1998) trajectory contributes to mutuality by making knowledge processes and artifact accessible both within a particular group, local connectedness, and to a larger field, global expansiveness. Technology supports such access, with Wenger's (1998) boundary processes of coordination, transparency, and negotiability. Technology makes explicit and perennializes CoP process and product (Henri & Pudelko, 2003). Technology, such as Sakai, is an amplifier of CoP. However, establishing a more public audience and purpose is an area of importance largely ignored by many efforts in the literature, and in this study, the focus on this trajectory in correcting for this shortcoming fell largely on deaf ears. In an academic setting, it is questionable whether it would ever meet the test of authenticity, particularly at the course level. The participants lacked the necessary imagination, as witnessed by the instructor, and according to Wenger (1998), imagination is one of the three essential modes of belonging to CoP. The other two, alignment and engagement, were arguably satisfied in this study, though more in relation to the course and its tasks – too much alignment perhaps. This study group had a significant level of mutual engagement and interaction with each other, much more than a typical class one could argue, but it was apparently not strong enough

to support greater interdependence with online access to each other's resources, certainly not beyond the boundaries of the course.

In the end, there was an end. This study demonstrates that with the *more disciplined* definition of CoP used herein, CoP theory has little place in applications to instructional design and technology strictly at the course level, where there are other learning theories and methods that frame the social learning principles of CoP without the higher expectations. The trappings of academic courses simply offer too much interference; they are not self-organized or sustained, and motivating a commitment to CoP at the course level seems too great a challenge. The foundation of this study was preparing teachers to be better members of and contributors to professional community, not a temporary group of colleagues for a limited period of time. Still, though a thriving CoP did not result, centrally and online, the initiatives entailed here seemed to instill a greater appreciation of the importance of sharing knowledge and best practices and the efficiency of doing so with the support of online technology.

REFLECTION

Academic courses and programs are artificial entities for students, who are typically quite transient, posing a significant challenge to any intentional CoP initiative in academics. Still, an academic department is most definitely a CoP, with students typically at the periphery. However, in my experience with many academic departments at several colleges and universities, it has been troubling to witness how weak they can be as CoPs, the degree to which they can lack interactivity. Without exception, they have all have room for improvement simply with basic communications, often a great deal of room, and opportunities for performance improvement are endless. While a great deal of department knowledge might be available online, it is often published individually with many different methods, scattered to the winds. I've seen departments struggle to get even the most basic information about their programs and faculty available on a website. CoP theory still has significant relevance and potential benefit to an academic program or department as a whole, from the basic administrative work and practice level to the more advanced content and academic spheres. The presumptive advantage is that the program is already well established, self-organized and sustained. Courses, learners, and instructors would have a continuous presence to all members of the department via a departmental portal which contains course sites, individuals' portfolio sites, and sundry administrative resources, along with the necessary communication channels. Without these basic ingredients, access is considerably limited and, therefore, so is the CoP. With these basic ingredients, participants have significantly improved and sustained access to each other and valuable knowledge artifacts to support the future of the CoP. After years of experiencing such an active portal, authenticity could be better grounded, and alumni, who still have access, would be more likely to continue their contribution and/or branch off into other CoPs to globally benefit the profession. Of course, there are fiscal and other advantages to staying connected with alumni.

An academic department, however, could require some major cultural changes to be successful in strengthening its CoP, in making knowledge more accessible and increasing interactivity in general. Issues described here in the field of K-12 education are shared by higher education. A great deal of leadership and cooperation would be required. Also, a departmental CoP is small in scale; it is limited relative to larger professional organizations. Since this study was performed, there has been amazing growth in online communities for educators. There is now a number of open, knowledge sharing portals that have a wealth of content. Perhaps students should be guided toward becoming active with them.

Since this study was performed, there has also been incredible growth in the number and use of social networking and mobile technologies. These certainly have applications in the support of CoP. There is great advantage in the utilization of their metadata, or tagging, indexing, and search functions for example. One might create a network of individual student blogs with a comment/rating system, thereby addressing issues like identity, authorship and ownership. However, such systems do rely heavily on the appropriate input of the author (remember the protocols that did not take root in this study). I was challenged by some colleagues as to why I didn't use something like Ning (2011) for this endeavor. I must underline here that the difficulties faced by this initiative were not technical. Any technical challenges faced would have occurred with any technology. Moreover, it is generally a continuous, misguided notion that some other technology will be the solution to our instructional/learning problems. As always, technologies should be considered contextually, based on participant needs. I submit that a simple email list may be the best solution for some groups. Anecdotally, I have tried other technologies, including Ning, with no more success than with this study. I've used other course management systems to support professional development communities for faculty (there is something to be said for using a technology already well known to the community). The faculty did not jump at the opportunity to share knowledge in this way. In fact, professors can be even more concerned about intellectual property, in some cases for the most trivial of work. The problems are cultural and social, not technical. This is not to say that other technologies should not be examined. There is no question that these social networking and mobile technologies can be of great advantage in supporting CoP. I am also intrigued by the potential interactivity of e-texts. Take for example the popular highlights feature of the Amazon Kindle (2011). Indeed, consider the degree to which education centers on textbooks and the possibility that there could be a major paradigm shift developing as to the nature of a textbook. All the media-rich and social interactivity of today's dynamic websites will likely be built into textbooks of the future, and then there is the ability to customize one's own textbook and features.

Portfolios provide a good illustration of the social-cultural, technical phenomenon. In my teacher education program, we prepared our portfolios in 3-ring binders. A decade later, where I pursued my doctoral studies, students were preparing them as websites. I thought what a marvelous opportunity this could be to share them with a broader audience, yet with few exceptions, the websites were distributed on CDs! At the same time, various assessment and portfolio systems such as Livetext (2011) were the big thing at conferences. Again, I thought what a marvelous opportunity. After all, why should teachers have to become skilled with advanced level website development applications? Yet without exception, these systems were presented as tools for accreditation. Though these systems typically have features for packaging content in creative ways and sharing it with groups or as a public URL, nobody seemed even aware of these features, much less interested in having students use them to develop true professional portfolios that they could meaningfully share with peers and future colleagues. Today, years later, I have experience that this is still the case. How unfortunate that such collections of teacher knowledge are so private and then largely abandoned! Yet there does appear to be a new, more global portfolio movement in the works that could address these concerns, but it is unfortunately probably going to remain focused on the individual, when we should be envisioning online portfolios as identity representation in CoP. The CoP ingredients might already exist in many departments/programs, but they are trapped within traditional cultures of formal education. In closing, I encourage all to consider how they might apply CoP principles to improve communication and interactivity in their work and other com-

munity settings, how they might use the theory and strategies discussed here to develop a greater knowledge sharing culture. Consider sharing today something you have developed that could be useful to others.

REFERENCES

Amazon Kindle. (2011). *Most highlighted passages of all time*. Retrieved from https://kindle.amazon.com/most_popular

Barab, S. A. MaKinster, J. G., & Scheckler, R. (2004). Designing system dualities: Characterizing an online professional development. In S. A. Barab, R. Kling & J. H. Gray (Eds.), *Designing for virtual communities in the service of learning*. Cambridge, UK: Cambridge University Press.

Barab, S. A., & Duffy, T. M. (2000). From practice fields to communities of practice. In Jonassen, D. H., & Land, S. M. (Eds.), *Theoretical foundations of learning environments* (pp. 25–56). Mahwah, NJ: Lawrence Erlbaum Associates.

Barab, S. A., Kling, R., & Gray, J. H. (2004). Introduction: Designing for virtual communities in the service of learning. In Barab, S. A., Kling, R., & Gray, J. H. (Eds.), *Designing for virtual communities in the service of learning*. Cambridge, UK: Cambridge University Press. doi:10.1080/01972240309467

Bruner, J. (1996). *The culture of education*. Cambridge, MA: Harvard University Press.

Burton, J. K., Moore, D. M., & Magliaro, S. G. (1996). Behaviorism and instructional technology. In Jonassen, D. H. (Ed.), *Handbook of research for educational communications and technology* (pp. 46–73). New York, NY: Simon & Schuster Macmillan.

Carroll, J. M. (2001). Community computing as human-computer interaction. *Behaviour & Information Technology*, *20*(5), 307–314. doi:10.1080/01449290110078941

Darling-Hammond, L. (1996). The quiet revolution: rethinking teacher development. *Educational Leadership, 53*, 4–10.

Dede, C. (1999). *The role of emerging technologies for knowledge mobilization, dissemination, and use in education*. Retrieved from http://www.virtual.gmu.edu/EDIT895/knowlmob.html

Dewey, J. (1963). *Experience and education*. New York, NY: Collier Books.

Driscoll, M. P. (2000). *Psychology of learning for instruction* (2nd ed.). Boston, MA: Allyn and Bacon.

Engestrom, Y., Engestrom, R., & Suntio, A. (2002). Can a school community learn to master its own future? An activity-theoretical study of expansive learning among middle school teachers. In Wells, G., & Claxton, G. (Eds.), *Learning for life in the 20th century*. Oxford, UK: Blackwell Publishers. doi:10.1002/9780470753545.ch16

Fishman, L., Hoadley, C., Harasim, L., Hsi, S., Levin, J., Pea, R., et al. (1997, March 24-28). *Collaboration, communication, and computers: What do we think we know about networks and learning: Session overview and position statements*. Paper presented at the American Educational Research Association, Interactive symposium (learning environments), Chicago.

Goodyear, P. (2000). Environments for lifelong learning. In Spector, M. J., & Anderson, T. M. (Eds.), *Integrated and holistic perspectives on learning, instruction and technology: Understanding complexity* (pp. 1–18). Dordrecht, The Netherlands: Kluwer Academic Publishers.

Hannum, W. (2001). Knowledge management in education: helping teachers to work better. *Educational Technology*, (May-June): 47–49.

Hargreaves, A. (2003). *Teaching in the knowledge society: Education in the age of insecurity*. New York, NY: Teachers College Press.

Harris, R. A., & Niven, J. (2002). *Retrofitting theory to practice - A reflection on the development of an e-learning community*. Retrieved from http://www.scrolla.ac.uk/resources/Harris_Community_of_practice_Symp3.htm

Henri, F., & Pudelko, B. (2003). Understanding and analyzing activity and learning in virtual communities. *Journal of Computer Assisted Learning, 19*, 474–487. doi:10.1046/j.0266-4909.2003.00051.x

Hung, D., & Nichani, M. R. (2002). Bringing communities of practice into schools: Implications for instructional technologies from Vygotskian perspectives. *International Journal of Instructional Media, 29*(2).

Jonassen, D. H. (2005). *Let us learn to solve problems*. Retrieved September 30, 2005, from http://it.coe.uga.edu/itforum/paper83/paper83.html

Jonassen, D. H., Peck, K. L., & Wilson, B. G. (1999). *Learning to solve problems with technology: A constructivist perspective* (2nd ed.). Upper Saddle River, NJ: Merrill Prentice Hall.

Kling, R., & Courtright, C. (2004). Group behavior and learning in electronic forums: A sociotechnical approach. In Barab, S. A., Kling, R., & Gray, J. H. (Eds.), *Designing for virtual communities in the service of learning*. Cambridge, UK: Cambridge University Press.

Koschmann, T. (1996). Paradigm shifts and instructional technology: An introduction. In Koschmann, T. (Ed.), *CSCL: Theory and practice of an emerging paradigm* (pp. 1–23). New Jersey: Lawrence Erlbaum Associates.

Lave, J. (1996). Teaching, as learning, in practice. *Mind, Culture, and Activity, 3*(3), 149–164. doi:10.1207/s15327884mca0303_2

Lave, J., & Wenger, E. (1991). *Situated learning: Legitimate peripheral participation*. Cambridge, UK: Cambridge University Press.

Lieberman, A. (1996). Creating intentional learning communities. *Educational Leadership*, *54*(3), 51–55.

Livetext. (2011). *General overview*. Retrieved from https://www.livetext.com/overview/.

Marshall, J., & Rossett, A. (2000). Knowledge management for school-based educators. In Spector, M. J., & Anderson, T. M. (Eds.), *Integrated and holistic perspectives on learning, instruction and technology* (pp. 19–34). Dordrecht, The Netherlands: Kluwer Academic Publishers.

Maxwell, J. A. (1996). *Qualitative research design: An interactive approach* (*Vol. 41*). Thousand Oaks, CA: Sage Publications.

Moore, J., & Barab, S. A. (2002). The inquiry learning forum: A community of practice approach to online professional development. *TechTrends*, *46*(3), 44–49. doi:10.1007/BF02784841

National Board for Professional Teaching Standards. (2002). What teachers should know and be able to do. Retrieved from http://www.nbpts.org/UserFiles/File/what_teachers.pdf

Ning. (2011). *About Ning*. Retrieved from http://about.ning.com/

Palloff, R. M., & Pratt, K. (1999). *Building learning communities in cyberspace: Effective strategies for the online classroom*. San Francisco, CA: Josey-Bass Publishers.

Powell, A., & Evans, M. (2006). *Public vs. private interests: Design implications for teacher communities of practice*. Paper presented at the Annual Meeting of the American Educational Research Association.

Preece, J. (2001). Sociability and usability in online communities: Determining and measuring success. *Behavior and Information Technology Journal*, *20*(5), 347–356. doi:10.1080/01449290110084683

Riel, M., & Becker, H. (2000, April 6). *The beliefs, practices, and computer use of teacher leaders*. Paper presented at the American Educational Research Association, New Orleans.

Riel, M., & Polin, L. (2004). Online learning communities: Common ground and critical differences in designing technical environments. In Barab, S. A., Kling, R., & Gray, J. H. (Eds.), *Designing for virtual communities in the service of learning*. Cambridge, UK: Cambridge University Press.

Rogers, J. (2000). Communities of practice: A framework for fostering coherence in virtual learning communities. *Journal of Educational Technology & Society*, *3*(3), 384–392.

Sakai. (2011). *Sakai CLE*. Retrieved from http://sakaiproject.org/node/2260

Scardamalia, M., & Bereiter, C. (1996). Computer support for knowledge-building communities. In Koschmann, T. (Ed.), *CSCL: Theory and practice of an emerging paradigm* (pp. 249–268). New Jersey: Lawrence Erlbaum Associates.

Schlager, M., & Fusco, J. (2004). Teacher professional development, technology, and communities: Are we putting the cart before the horse? In Barbara, S., Kling, R., & Gray, J. (Eds.), *Designing virtual communities in the service of learning*. Cambridge, UK: Cambridge University Press. doi:10.1080/01972240309464

Schwen, T. M., & Hara, N. (2004). Community of practice: A metaphor for online design? In Barab, S. A., Kling, R., & Gray, J. H. (Eds.), *Designing for virtual communities in the service of learning*. Cambridge, UK: Cambridge University Press. doi:10.1080/01972240309462

Stuckey, B., Hedberg, J., & Lockyer, L. (2001, June 25-30). *Building on-line community for professional develolpment*. Paper presented at the Ed-Media 2001 World Conference on Educational Multimedia, Hypermedia, & Telecommunications, Tampere, Finland.

Suchman, L. (1983). Office procedure as practical action: Models of work and system design. *ACM Transactions on Office Information Systems*, *1*(4), 320–328. doi:10.1145/357442.357445

Trentin, G. (2001). From formal training to communities of practice via network-based learning. *Educational Technology*, (March-April): 5–14.

Vygotsky, L. S. (1978). *Mind in society: The development of higher psychological processes*. Cambridge, MA: Harvard University Press.

Wenger, E. (1998). *Communities of practice: learning, meaning, and identity*. Cambridge, UK: Cambridge University Press.

Wenger, E. (2003). Communities of practice and social learning systems. In Nicolini, D., Gherardi, S., & Yanow, D. (Eds.), *Knowing in organizations: A practice-based approach* (pp. 76–99). Armonk, NY: M.E. Sharpe. doi:10.1177/135050840072002

Yin, R. K. (1994). *Case study research: Design and methods* (2nd ed., *Vol. 5*). Thousand Oaks, CA: Sage Publications.

Zahner, J. (2002). Teachers explore knowledge management and e-learning as models for professional development. *TechTrends*, *46*(3), 11–16. doi:10.1007/BF02784836

Chapter 15
Embedded Librarians:
Delivering Synchronous Library Instruction and Research Assistance to Meet Needs of Distance Students and Faculty

Sheila Bonnand
Montana State University, USA

Mary Anne Hansen
Montana State University, USA

ABSTRACT

This chapter reports on one academic library's experiences with expanding instructional services by adding synchronous library instruction to better serve its online students and faculty located across the globe. Web conferencing software allows librarians to provide interactive, high-touch library instruction for online students equivalent to the experience of students in traditional face-to-face courses. While providing this real-time instruction on library resources and research skills, librarians are embedding themselves in online programs, becoming more readily accessible to online and distance students. By meeting the changing needs of academic library users wherever they are, librarians are reaffirming their integral role and relevance as partners in the educational endeavor.

INTRODUCTION

Librarians have long played an important role in the academic success of students and have traditionally provided on-campus students with face-to-face instruction on research and informa-

tion resources; librarians also play an integral role in facilitating lifelong learning. The Internet and online courses have changed the ways that libraries deliver research tools and resources in order to meet the needs students and faculty whatever their location. To remain relevant as instructors and to meet the information and research needs of

DOI: 10.4018/978-1-61350-441-3.ch015

distance and online students and faculty, librarians must go beyond providing web-based resources and static tutorials. It is not enough to be available within online courses for email and chat queries from students. For librarians to be truly embedded in the virtual academic enterprise, online library users should have the option to meet with librarians in real-time. The ability to provide live, synchronous library instruction allows librarians to offer interactive, high-touch research instruction, an experience similar to that of a face-to-face class. MSU librarians are using Adobe® Connect™ web conferencing software to deliver live library instruction sessions to students and faculty wherever they are located. This chapter discusses the successes, challenges, and surprises that librarians at Montana State University (MSU) have had in implementing synchronous library instruction to improve library services for distance and online students and faculty.

SERVING ONLINE STUDENTS

According to the Association of College and Research Libraries' (ACRL) *Standards for Distance Learning Library Services* (2008):

"Every student, faculty member, administrator, staff member, or any other member of an institution of higher education, is entitled to the library services and resources of that institution, including direct communication with the appropriate library personnel, regardless of where enrolled or where located in affiliation with the institution. Academic libraries must, therefore, meet the information and research needs of all these constituents, wherever they may be" (Executive summary, para. 1).

Fulfilling this mandate is becoming increasingly important as the number of distance and online courses continues to grow. Statistics from the 2006-2007 National Center for Educational Statistics (NCES) suggest that 66% of postsec-

ondary institutions were offering distance courses of some kind, whether online or hybrid (Parsad, Lewis, & Tice, 2008, p. 2). This number represents an increase of 10% from the 2000-2001 NCES survey (Waits, Lewis, & Green, 2003, p. 4). Though MSU has been involved with distance education for almost three decades, the number of courses has been relatively small and the institution has gathered few statistics. However, the statistics available suggest that MSU meets this trend of continued growth of distance education. As of spring semester 2010, 10% of MSU students were taking at least one class online while during the 2010 summer session 32% of students were enrolled in an online class.

The rapid expansion of online and distance instruction in higher education poses a number of challenges for academic libraries. Pival and Tuñón wrote in 2001 that "Bibliographic instruction (BI) is one of the major challenges facing libraries that support distance students" (2001, p. 347). To meet the library and information needs of students and faculty in this new environment, both on campus and at a distance, librarians must innovate. Cooke writing a few years later stated that, "Libraries cannot rest on their successes with traditional on-campus students; rather they must reinvent their support and services to accommodate distance learners" (2005, p. 55). To accomplish this, not only must ACRL distance education standards be applied, but libraries also have a responsibility to meet ACRL's information literacy standards which state that such standards are to be integrated "across curricula, in all programs and services" and that "competencies for distance learning students should be comparable to those for 'on campus' students" (Association of College and Research Libraries, 2000, para. 2). In standard 2.E of the new standards from MSU's regional accrediting agency, the Northwest Commission on Colleges and Universities (NWCCU), the importance of library support and information literacy instruction for students, faculty, and others involved in the institution's programs "...wherever offered and however delivered" is stressed (Northwest Commission on Colleges and Universities, 2E – Library and Information Resources section, 2010).

Who is this online learner? Generally, he or she is a student who "is constrained by distance, time, family or work responsibilities" (Caspers, Fritts, & Gover, 2000, p. 130). When online courses first started, participants were generally older (25 and up), working adults with some higher education experience already. That demographic soon changed and as early as 1999, NCES statistics suggested that enrollment represented a number of age groups as well as undergraduates and graduates. Many online courses are also attended by students not at a distance but on campus, for a variety of reasons (Palloff & Pratt, 2003, p. 3-4). MSU has followed these trends. Courses are designed for students truly at a distance but increasingly courses are being made available online or have an online component and are taken by both distance students and those on campus. According to Chakraborty and Victor, the main reasons students take online courses are "Convenience and flexibility...." (2004, p. 98). The rise in the number of online courses makes it even more important that librarians go where their users are located in order to meet their information needs.

SYNCHRONOUS LIBRARY INSTRUCTION

In order to provide equivalent services for online students and to meet professional standards, librarians at Montana State University have worked to meet the challenges and seek new opportunities in the world of virtual education. Recognizing that online courses and programs at MSU are only continuing to increase in number, MSU librarians explored ways that other distance librarians across the United States were reaching out to provide library services and resources to online students. One method for reaching online students that came to their attention was the use of web

conferencing software for delivering live library instruction. Web conferencing allows librarians to meet with the online learner in real-time to demonstrate relevant resources and strategies for searching them effectively.-

Web conferencing software emerged at the beginning of the 1990s, though the early commercial versions were generally expensive and had limited functionality and performance (Henning, p. 235). Libraries soon began experimenting with this software. However, in 2009, Lietzau and Mann reported "...a scarcity of research conducted within the past five years on the ... use of Web conferencing software packages to provide virtual synchronous, curriculum or course-related learning opportunities" (2009, p. 109). This observation remains true for libraries based on the literature reviewed for this chapter.

Pival and Tuñón reported that the Einstein Library of Nova Southeastern University in Florida experimented with Microsoft's NetMeeting in 1997 and "began delivering remote library instruction ... in April of 1998." In this case, students met at three or four remote sites. The training was well received by participants. A later software upgrade added the capability of including a video of the instructing librarian at the start of a class. Students reportedly "... liked seeing who was speaking to them" (2001, pp. 351-353), adding early support for the importance of a 'face' in the virtual environment.

In an effort to better support students at a distance, the library at the University of Northern British Columbia tried LearnLinc software. This was "a highly interactive synchronistic product" that met with "limited success" because of problems with the technology. The problems included a lack of compatibility with student computers and with some of the library's databases (Black, 2000, pp. 52-53).

Henning described the use of "desktop video conferencing" but this experiment again relied on designated computers at satellite sites which limited its flexibility. Henning observed that when working with technology, "glitches happen." She also reported that issues with peripheral devices, both audio and video, can "make or break" a web conferencing session (2001, pp. 243-244). Both issues were confirmed by MSU librarians during their web conferencing pilot project.

Two other studies purport the usefulness of web conferencing for reaching remote users. McCarthy's study comparing a library and information science course taught on-site to one using web conferencing to a remote site concluded "that interactive video technology is an effective pedagogical tool" (2004, p. 25). Additionally, Docherty described using webinars but for professional development rather than student engagement. However, her experiences led her to conclude that the technology could be employed "… to serve and instruct patrons and staff when and where they need it" (2004, p. 226).

Since these early experiments, interactive software has become more sophisticated, especially in its ability to allow users access from wherever they are. Students can log in from home, from work, from other libraries – anywhere there is a computer with a connection to the Internet. These web conferencing programs, like much software, have a high degree of functionality, but their basic features allow the instructor with average computer skills to get started easily.

MSU librarians made the decision to meet students virtually, but doing so required software that the Library at MSU did not have. Initial explorations of possible web conferencing software, and especially the cost of that web conferencing software, influenced MSU librarians to favor Adobe® Connect™ over other web conferencing software options. The decision to pursue this software for meeting students virtually was expedited by the opportunity on this campus to apply for funds through MSU's Teaching and Learning Committee, which yearly funds proposals of up to two thousand dollars through its Instructional Innovation Grants. Two MSU librarians successfully applied for a grant and used the funds to purchase

access to Adobe® Connect™ for two years. They were also able to buy webcams and headsets for the nine members of the library's reference team.

An additional reason for choosing this software arose through a partnership with another entity on campus, the Burns Telecommunication Center (BTC), which made it possible to get access much more cheaply through a shared subscription rather than the library subscribing alone. However, Adobe® Connect™ does include features that were important to MSU's pilot project, cementing the decision to opt into a group subscription with the BTC. Other than cost, ease of use was a priority. While Adobe® Connect™ has very sophisticated features, it can also be used easily 'right out of the box.' This web-based software is also easy for the end user, requiring only a quick plug-in on the first use. Because it is inevitable that not every student would or could attend a session, the ability to record sessions was also a priority; the fact that these recordings can be edited was an important criterion in the decision about which web conferencing software to purchase. Scales and Cummings summarized their review of an earlier version of this product by calling it "a very sophisticated tool that is flexible and powerful" (2009, p. 9), and it has been found to be so during MSU's web conferencing pilot project. Adobe® Connect's™ flexibility and ease of use allows students to participate wherever they are without requiring travel to satellite sites or designated computers.-

LIBRARY SUPPORT FOR ONLINE LEARNERS

The MSU Library has been serving online students since its campus started offering courses online and the librarians there are always working on initiatives to improve those services. Goodson's observation that "…distance education students are often the victims of benign neglect on the part of their institutions…" (2001, p. 3) does not apply to this institution. A member of the reference team has served as the library's distance education coordinator since the early 1990s, document delivery services are in place, and electronic resources are generally the preferred format for acquisitions. Patrons have the option to call, email, chat, text, or instant message reference questions. Reference librarians can take appointments for one-on-one consultations either in person or by telephone as part of the library's Research Assistance Program (RAP). The implementation of web pathfinders has made subject and course guides to specific library resources and services readily available online. A librarian role has been established in D2L, allowing instructors to add a librarian in a support capacity similar to that of a teaching assistant. However, except for telephone RAPs, none of these services is synchronous. Also missing is personalization, that direct contact with students that gives a face to the library.

Adding a live online instruction option embeds the idea that librarians and library resources are available to online and distance students in addition to on-campus students. For close to two years, MSU librarians have offered real-time, synchronous library instruction sessions for online students and faculty. After implementing web conferencing software, MSU librarians found that many of the distance students involved had not known that the MSU Library was an option for them until attending one of these sessions. Others have also reported that distance students, and often faculty members, do not realize the availability of their institution's library services and resources for online courses (Thomsett-Scott, 2009, p. 113). Reference librarians work to build relationships with students at the reference desk and in face-to-face classes so that students will be comfortable seeking help at a later date or for other courses. This practice holds true in the online environment where, according to Bower, a "…live interaction establishes a foundation between the librarian and remote students so that future interactions are more likely to follow in subsequent courses"

(2010, p. 479). The ability to meet synchronously with online students, to embed research instruction in online classes and programs, provides MSU librarians the ability to make connections with distance students especially, but also to on-campus students taking classes online. A recent library instruction session included students as far away as Dubai but also some from the local area. Graham stated it well: "… there is, in fact, no distinction between distant and local" (2009, p.46) in the current technological library world.

WEB CONFERENCING PILOT PROJECT

Over the nearly two years that MSU librarians have been providing synchronous library instruction via Adobe® Connect™ web conferencing software, they have delivered around 25 instruction sessions to approximately 300 students. A dozen or so different instructors teaching a spectrum of online courses have tapped the synchronous instruction services of MSU librarians since their pilot project started in 2009. These librarians have provided library instruction for both undergraduate courses and graduate courses; additionally, they have worked with some non-course-related groups needing to connect constituencies in real-time across the vast expanse of the state of Montana for various learning endeavors. The greatest success in repeat clientele using real-time instruction services has been with MSU's Master of Science in Science Education (MSSE) program, the largest fully online program at MSU. This online program offers K-12 science teachers the opportunity to complete a master's degree in science education from wherever they are without having to move to attend a face-to-face program. As such, it includes students from all across the United States, a few in Canada, plus a handful teaching in such far off places as Turkey and Thailand. Following the first semester of real-time instruction sessions, MSSE program directors and instructors praised this online library instruction and claimed it to be an essential component of the program, especially with the Foundations of Action Research course, thus establishing library instruction via web conferencing as an integral component of the course. The major reason for the MSSE program integrating real-time library instruction into their curriculum each semester was that instructors saw a dramatic increase in use of the MSU Library subscription resources by the MSSE students and a corresponding rise in the inclusion of quality resources cited in their assignments following the initial real-time library instruction sessions with their students.

At the beginning of each live instruction session, students are asked about their library usage: do they use the MSU Library, other libraries in the MSU system or their local libraries? It has been surprising to learn how many online MSU students have never used, or do not regularly use, the resources offered by the MSU Library, which provides far more databases and online journals than most online students would have access to through a local public library or small college library. Many online students have reported that they did not realize that MSU Library resources and services were available to them since they are not in face-to-face programs. In addition to connecting online students to library resources that are rightfully theirs to take full advantage of, live instruction sessions connect the students via webcam to friendly faces in the MSU Library that they can contact for questions about their research or access to resources. Prior to MSU librarians' use of web conferencing, the library's web page offered links to contact information about librarians, but this recently integrated, embedded role in online courses makes librarians far more accessible to online students. MSU librarians who teach via web conferencing are getting more research inquiries directly from online students, plus there has been an increase in overall reference statistics from online students since the debut of real-time library instruction. Like Lietzau and Mann, MSU

librarians have found that the faculty members and students involved in the pilot sessions "... consider web conferencing an enhancement to learning in the online environment, and they appreciate the interaction it provides" (2009, p. 116).

SERVING A WIDER CLIENTELE

When this pilot project began, it was anticipated that real-time library instruction would be provided solely to students and faculty in online courses. However, soon after beginning the web conferencing project, other campus units expressed interest in providing instruction to their staff and constituencies outside of MSU online courses. These groups included two federal grant-funded projects, one a National Institutes of Health (NIH) project and the other a National Library of Medicine (NLM) grant project. The NIH sponsors the MSU Center for Native Health Partnerships (CNHP), a community-based program to educate Native peoples on Montana's seven Indian reservations about health issues. Each reservation has a CNHP Community Organizer, a Native person employed to be the point person for the tribe on CNHP projects. MSU librarians were enlisted to provide library research training to these seven Community Organizers, who in turn are using their MSU Library research knowledge to help their local tribal constituencies research their own health-related topics.

The other grant-funded group interested in web conferencing was an NLM-sponsored Health Education for Rural Elderly (HERE) project that provided five real-time health information webinars over the course of several months to senior citizens in four rural communities in eastern Montana that are geographically isolated from major cities and all that cities have to offer regarding health facilities and health information providers. These rural seniors gathered in their local senior centers for each live webinar with MSU librarians, the HERE grant directors, and the various health information content presenters for each session. The use of web conferencing for both of these grant projects included the use of speaker phones in a conference room equipped with a computer and projector to make the sessions as fully interactive as possible. Participants could hear the presenters and they in turn could ask questions about the content being taught. While nontraditional teaching opportunities were a surprise, the chance to collaborate with these two grant projects on the MSU campus provided additional opportunities to use web conferencing software in new ways and to learn more about the meeting and teaching options available with it. Additionally, as the state's land grant university, it is within MSU's mission to provide outreach to not only immediate campus constituencies, but also to the citizens of the state. Both projects enabled collaboration with MSU constituencies and the clientele they serve in isolated pockets across Montana, further embedding the library within the academic community and the state as a whole.

Other non-course uses of web conferencing software have included sessions to explore professional development and training with several tribal college librarians from across the state; since all of Montana's tribal colleges are land grant institutions, it is within MSU's mission to provide them with outreach and training. Additionally, MSU librarians have used this web conferencing software for a number of other professional uses, including informal training on software products with librarians in other states. Adobe® Connect™ has also been used to conduct meetings among co-presenters in preparation for conference programs. Web conferencing has proven to be a valuable tool for service efforts as well, including meeting online in real-time with co-committee members on state and national library association committees, including the American Library Association and the Montana Library Association.

PILOT ASSESSMENT

Assessment has been an important component of this web conferencing pilot project. Just as it is important to assess face-to-face library instruction, it is equally important to assess instruction via web conferencing because student and instructor feedback will lead to improvements in format, content, and technical issues. Furthermore, gathering evaluative information about the impact of services on student learning is essential for multiple reasons, including tenure and promotion, ongoing and even improved financial support for the library, and accreditation.

An online evaluation form was used after each real-time instruction session to gather student input. The librarians emailed a link for the questionnaire to the course instructor, along with a link to the URL for the recorded library instruction session for him or her to post in the D2L course shell, allowing students who could not attend the instruction session synchronously to view it when convenient and also provide feedback on the recorded session. Additionally, students who were able to attend the real-time session could both provide feedback and watch the session again at their convenience.

Students were invited to provide feedback on each of the following points in the online survey form: name (optional); number of online courses currently enrolled in; how they viewed the course, i.e., synchronously or via recording; rate the quality of the technology; rate the quality of instruction; rate overall experience; name at least one thing they learned in the session; state one thing that should have been covered but was not; and any additional comments. The response rate for this optional feedback opportunity from the 300 students participating in the pilot has not been very high, with only about 25% completing a survey. This is not unlike the response rate for face-to-face classes at MSU. However, the feedback received still has yielded some valuable information for improving these online library instruction sessions.

Overall satisfaction with the sessions among participants was positive. For example, 70% of those responding indicated that the instructors were well versed in the content of the class with another 19% rating the instruction a four on a scale of one to five. When asked to rate the overall quality of the instruction session (technology plus instruction) on a scale from one (dull) to five (very engaging), 40% indicated that the session was "very engaging" and 38% rated it at a four. Coming from approximately 22% of respondents, lower ratings for the overall experience correlated with comments on difficulties with the technology.

Probably the most surprising information gathered from comments on the feedback forms was the number of distance students who did not realize that they could log in to MSU Library's subscription databases and journals from a distance. A few students even believed prior to their library session that MSU Library services and resources were not available to them. What follows is a sampling of some positive student comments gleaned from feedback forms:

"I have not used the MSU library for any of my previous courses simply because the web-site looks so daunting. Most of my fears have been laid to rest. Thanks!"

"The overview of library resources was excellent and I have already accessed some resources as a result of the session."

"I was very thankful for the session. I was really nervous about how I would be able to access information I need to complete my project. I feel much better now!"

"The library services for the virtual students was clearly confirmed. For example, I am now certain that the MSSE online students can easily obtain interlibrary loans and books from the MSU library.

Now I can better direct students to get resources from the MSU library."

"Dialogue was helpful—allowed students to get questions answered and made direct link to library personnel for future help. Thank you so much!"

"I was impressed with how helpful this service will be."

"I love being able to see the computer screen in the demonstration."

"Awesome vehicle for instruction!"

"I thought it was well done, and 45 minutes was about right in length."

Student feedback also yielded some helpful comments for improving web conferencing instruction, especially early on in the pilot project. One pedagogical issue revealed in the sessions was the need with some classes, especially lower division courses, to do some pre-instruction and perhaps post-instruction follow up. Unsurprisingly, the largest number of responses to the question of how to improve these sessions mentioned technical difficulties. Among the various technical issues gleaned through student feedback was screen size and this reinforced the importance of enabling the full-screen toggle for students so that they can enlarge their screens for clearer viewing of the instructor's desktop being pushed during database demonstrations. The other major technical challenge discovered was that the software is intended for reaching students individually in remote locations, not as a group in large classroom or computer lab where sound issues make it almost impossible for some students to hear the librarians. Here is a sample of comments from student regarding issues and challenges or suggestions for improvement:

"My screen was fuzzy. I didn't realize that I could enlarge it til almost the end."

"There were a lot of people on line in the room with speakers on so it was very hard to follow. I think this would be better on a personal level. I will try to access the library and now I know who to contact if I have trouble."

"I think a pre-session information sheet or agenda may have been helpful so that we could direct our thought process, but overall very good."

Instructors also provided valuable feedback, including the following comments:

"The sessions were great. I think there was a good balance of content and the presentation was dynamic. The sessions were rich in content and also helped to motivate students to use the MSU resources and to ask questions if they have problems. These sessions "opened the doors" of the MSU library to the virtual students. Thank you very much. I have few things to share: (1) For the people who had trouble hearing the audio, does Adobe® Connect™ Pro have a phone bridge option for those people. (I did not see this option on my page. Wimba has that option. People on dial ups might need a phone option for the audio). (2) It was difficult the read some of the Web pages displayed. If the areas of the page can be enlarged (zoomed in on) as they are used, it might help. Sometimes I was not able to read the text but I could see area of the page and listen to the description. I have a high speed DSL Internet connection and a rather fast computer and think that I might be able to see better. (3) It might be nice to have a possible follow up session while the students are actually using the resources for their conceptual framework. (This is just an idea for the future.) I think that many students will better understand that value of a library session or have questions once they are actually writing their conceptual framework section of their papers."

"Thank you so much for putting these sessions together. Initial feedback indicates that the sessions were of great value to our teachers. I'll pass on comments/thoughts from our instructors as I receive them. This is a great service to MSU's online students ... I suspect that we'll want to make them a regular part of our EDCI 505 courses each spring. "

"Just wanted to pass on a comment from one of our instructors regarding the MSSE Adobe® Connect™ session last night ... great job! These sessions will make such a difference in the comfort level for our distance students regarding library resources and access. This is a wonderful service ... thank you!"

BEST PRACTICES

These experiences with delivering library instruction via web conferencing software have provided some important lessons and the discovery of a few best practices. First, it was determined early on that the optimal length of time for a real-time instruction session, even with graduate students, is 45 to 50 minutes, a best practice confirmed by Docherty and Faiks (2005, p. 215). Any longer than that and participants have difficulty staying focused and interested in the lesson.

Additionally, online library instruction sessions are best delivered by two librarians working in tandem, with one delivering parts of the content on one computer, while the other monitors chat on a computer logged in to the participant view. This format allows the second librarian the ability to monitor that view for lag time in the transmission of database searches and library website navigation. Chat questions can also be fielded so that the librarian instructing can stay focused on the material being presented. While it is more labor-intensive to have two librarians teaching every online session, it provides for a more seamless and interesting experience for the online student.

MSU librarians have not experienced demand for real-time instruction to the point where the two-librarian instruction model is no longer sustainable. Kontos and Henkel reached a similar conclusion after their experiences using Wimba Live Classroom for online instruction, stating that such classes can be taught effectively by one instructor but that "… it is highly desirable to have two" (2008, pp. 5-6).

After a few initial web conferencing instruction sessions, it was also found desirable to ask participants to log in 10 to 15 minutes prior to the start of each session. This practice provides time to conduct sound checks and determine if anyone is experiencing technical difficulties without using up valuable instruction time. A bonus of building in the extra time is the opportunity to chat informally prior to the start of class with students as they log in, for example welcoming each participant individually, finding out where they are located, and answering their initial questions.

Another best practice for real-time library instruction is to include one or more polls for students to read and take as they are logging in prior to the start of the session. The use of polls serves to provide useful information about the students participating in the class, and it gets students interacting from the moment they log in to the live instruction session. Polls have been used, for example, to ask MSSE students, almost all of whom are educators out in the field, what grade levels they teach and what library or libraries they use, whether the MSU Library or another.

When MSU librarians first launched their Adobe® Connect™ pilot project, they anticipated that a best practice would be to initially greet each class over the webcam and then shut the camera off to avoid taking up too much bandwidth. However, experience has shown that the webcam can be left on the entire time, the bonus of which is to provide students with the enriched experience of both hearing and seeing their librarians during the instruction. Pival and Tuñón had the same result in their early experiments with web conferencing.

They found that students responded positively and "liked seeing who was speaking to them" (2001, p. 353) when a video image of a librarian was included in the instruction. Several MSU students have commented on library instruction evaluations that they really appreciate the human element included in the instruction sessions.

CHALLENGES WITH WEB CONFERENCING

Throughout the experience working with web conferencing for library instruction, technical difficulties were the most frequent problems encountered. A few students had issues with sound quality. The best fix for this issue is to have the student close out of Adobe® Connect™ and log back in again. When the sound quality just cannot be improved, a good practice is to send the student a chat message indicating that he or she might elect to wait for the URL to the recording of the session to be distributed and try viewing that for better sound reception. Another issue involves screen size. Students on small laptops or netbooks will find that there is a full screen toggle feature in Adobe® Connect™ that allows them to view a larger image of the desktop or files being shared by the instructor. Once students elect to use the full screen toggle, however, they lose the ability to monitor the chat questions from other students. In addition, they must toggle back and forth back to the smaller image in order to access the chat feature to pose any of their own questions. This issue of participants encountering technical problems is not unusual and has been a recurring theme since experiments with web conferencing began to be reported in the literature. Black, reporting on her library's trial of LearnLinc software wrote that those involved "didn't anticipate …the technical difficulties encountered …" (2000, p. 53). Lietzau and Mann surveyed students who participated in a class using Wimba web conferencing software and "… more than half mentioned technical or software/hardware problems as a drawback" (2009, p. 112). MSU librarians also discovered early on that this software cannot be used as broadcast medium. One of the first sessions conducted was with a group of MSSE students who had gathered in a classroom at a remote site. Audio feedback between the librarians and the remote instructor who was using a microphone made it difficult for the students to hear.

When working with students located across the country and beyond, finding a common meeting time can an issue because of the number of time zones involved. Bower and Mee mention the necessity of "compensating for time differences" (2010, p. 481) when instruction takes place via web conferencing. At MSU, librarians found that it was important to offer the option of several instruction sessions at different times and on different days. Instruction often takes place in the evening or on Saturdays. Providing the option of watching a recording was found to be another way to accommodate time zone variation.

Another challenge that MSU librarians have encountered in providing real-time library instruction via web conferencing is in the promotion and acceptance of it. Other than the MSSE program eagerly adopting this valuable service, there has not been widespread demand among other online courses or programs. It has become clear that that there is a need to continually market this service in order to get more online faculty to adopt its use and integrate it into their courses regularly. Part of the issue lies in the practice that many online courses across the curriculum rotate among departmental instructors semester by semester, so that someone who was an adopter of this service one semester might not be teaching an online course for another year. The other major issue encountered is the lack of familiarity and newness of web conferencing among faculty on this campus. Some faculty who are new to online instruction may feel overwhelmed in just developing and teaching one or more online courses; instructors faced with their own learning curve with online teaching may be

less motivated to explore online instruction with librarians because it is one more effort they will have to take for the course. Marketing efforts have emphasized that integrating real-time library instruction into an online course will not entail more work for faculty members other than posting the announcement in the course.

FUTURE PLANS

Once the pilot project grant funds for Adobe® Connect™ were exhausted, MSU librarians approached their administration about adding a subscription as a line item in the annual library budget, noting usage statistics and successes in meeting the needs of remote library users. Library administrators agreed that online library instruction with web conferencing should continue, and thus is a worthy expenditure of library funds. MSU librarians will continue providing synchronous instruction while also exploring ways to enhance the real-time instruction experience for students. One means for providing better interaction is the inclusion of the Adobe® Connect™ add-on feature of internal phone conferencing so that instructors do not have to rely on chat but can hear directly from students. The BTC, from whom the MSU Library subcontracts, has added this service to their base subscription, but there is an added per minute charge. MSU librarians will explore additional budgeting implications for utilizing this interactive audio feature of Adobe® Connect™.

Other plans for future uses of web conferencing for library instruction include experimenting with co-browsing with students so that they can take control and play more of a discovery role in trying database searches themselves with the librarians guiding them. This could be especially effective if demand grows for online RAP (one-on-one consultation) sessions. Additionally, MSU librarians will explore editing instruction session recordings. To date, the librarians have recorded every real-time instruction session in order to provide a means for those who could not fit live sessions into their schedules to view the recordings after the fact; recordings also provide a means for review for those who were able to attend the synchronous instruction session. However, they have not yet experimented much with editing the recordings, to delete, for example, unnecessary pauses and lag times to make a more professional copy.

MSU librarians will also continue efforts to promote this service to faculty members teaching courses online. The success with web conferencing to date has been the result of personal contact with faculty members in liaison areas and word of mouth. Plans are in place for librarians involved with the pilot project to make a presentation to faculty at an on-campus technology conference. Other plans include getting on the agenda of departmental faculty meetings at strategic times of the academic year and the creation of an informational brochure.

After working to gather statistics from the online evaluation tool, it was apparent that the categories in the rating scales were not precise enough, making it difficult to generate adequate granularity among responses. Improving the survey tool to gather more specific student feedback will help to further improve synchronous library instruction in the future.

CONCLUSION

To meet the changing needs of library users wherever they are located, MSU librarians have added another element to the multiple methods in place to reach and instruct students and faculty. With 10% to 30% of MSU students in an online class at any given time, it is clear that in order to provide equitable library services, librarians must be embedded in this virtual environment. By meeting students and faculty online, Montana State University librarians are not only fulfilling users' information needs, they are also maintain-

ing their relevance to those users. Though some technical difficulties were encountered during the web conferencing project, feedback from participants has been overwhelmingly positive. The implementation of synchronous instruction provides students a high-touch, personal library experience and reinforces the library's role in their academic success.

REFERENCES

Association of College and Research Libraries. (2000). *Information literacy competency standards for higher education.* Retrieved from http://www.ala.org/ala/mgrps/divs/acrl/standards/informationliteracycompetency.cfm

Association of College and Research Libraries. (2008). *Standards for distance learning library services.* Retrieved from http://www.ala.org/ala/mgrps/divs/acrl/standards/guidelinesdistance-learning.cfm

Black, N. E. (2000). Emerging technologies. *Journal of Library Administration, 31*(3), 45–59. doi:10.1300/J111v31n03_06

Bower, S. L., & Mee, S. A. (2010). Virtual delivery of electronic resources and services to off-campus users: A multifaceted approach. *Journal of Library Administration, 50*(5), 468-483. doi:10:1080/01930826.2010.488593

Caspers, J., Fritts, J., & Gover, H. (2000). Beyond the rhetoric: A study of the impact of the ACRL guidelines for distance library services on selected distance learning programs in higher education. *Journal of Library Administration, 31*(3), 127–148. doi:10.1300/J111v31n03_12

Chakraborty, M., & Victor, S. (2004). Do's and don'ts of simultaneous instruction to on-campus and distance students via videoconferencing. *Journal of Library Administration, 41*(1/2), 97–112. doi:10.1300/J111v41n01_09

Cooke, N. A. (2005). The role of libraries in web-based distance education. *Journal of Library & Information Services in Distance Learning, 1*(4), 47–57. doi:10.1300/J192v01n04_04

Docherty, K. J., & Faiks, A. H. (2004). *Science & Technology Libraries, 25*(1), 211–226. doi:10.1300/J122v25n01_13

Goodson, C. F. (2001). *Providing library services for distance education students: A how-to-do-it manual*. New York, NY: Neal-Schuman Publishers, Inc.

Graham, J. (2009). An uneven balancing act: One library administrator's view on providing library services for distance patrons. *Journal of Library & Information Services in Distance Learning, 3*(2), 43–46. doi:10.1080/15332900903057899

Henning, M. M. (2001). Closing the gap: Using conferencing software to connect distance education students and faculty. *Journal of Library Administration, 31*(1/2), 233–246. doi:10.1300/J111v32n01_02

Kontos, F., & Henkel, H. (2008). Live instruction for distance students: Development of synchronous online workshops. *Public Services Quarterly, 4*(1), 1–11. doi:10.1080/15228950802135657

Lietzau, J. A., & Mann, B. J. (2009). Breaking out of the asynchronous box: Using web conferencing in distance learning. *Journal of Library & Information Services in Distance Learning, 3*(3/4), 108–119. doi:10.1080/15332900903375291

McCarthy, C.A. (2004). Interactive video technology for distance learning: An assessment of interactive video technology as a tool. *Journal of Library & Information Services in Distance Learning, 1*(4), 5-31. doi:1300/J192v01n04_02

Northwest Commission on Colleges and Universities. (2010). *Standard two*. Retrieved from http://www.nwccu.org/Standards%20and%20Policies/Standard%202/Standard%20Two.htm

Palloff, R. M., & Pratt, K. (2003). *The virtual student: A profile and guide to working with online learners*. San Francisco, CA: Jossey-Bass.

Parsad, B., Lewis, L., & Tice, P. (2008). *Distance education at degree-granting postsecondary institutions: 2006–07*. Retrieved from http://nces.ed.gov/pubs2009/2009044.pdf

Pival, P. R., & Tuñón, J. (2001). Innovative methods for providing instruction to distance students using technology. *Journal of Library Administration, 2*(1/2), 347-360. doi:10:1300/J111v32no01_10

Scales, B. J., & Cummings, L. (2009). Web conferencing software. *Library Hi Tech News, 26*(9), 7–9. doi:10.1108/07419050911010732

Thomsett-Scott, B., & May, F. (2009). How may we help you? Online education faculty tell us what they need from libraries and librarians. *Journal of Library Administration, 49*(1/2), 111–135. doi:10.1080/01930820802312888

Waits, T., Lewis, L., & Greene, B. (2003). *Distance education at degree-granting postsecondary institutions: 2000–2001*. Retrieved from http://nces.ed.gov/pubs2003/2003017.pdf

KEY TERMS AND DEFINITIONS

Academic Libraries: Libraries located at post-secondary institutions, including colleges and universities.

Embedded Librarians: Librarians with an instructional role that have established collaborative working relationships with instructors and trainers and thus are integrated into programs, training efforts and courses. In the online realm, an embedded librarian is often an integral component of online courses and programs conducted via a learning management system. Embedded librarians are available to course and program participants for library instruction and research consultation throughout the duration of the course or program.

Information Literacy: The ability to understand the extent and scope of an information need, as well as the ability to locate, evaluate and apply or use the information once located.

Library Instruction: Also referred to as bibliographic instruction, library instruction is the teaching of library users by trained library personnel, usually degreed librarians, on the services and resources available through the library, including print and online subscription and proprietary information resources, as well as freely available information resources. In academic librarianship, library instruction is often highly tailored to a research assignment within a specific discipline and is a collaborative effort between librarian and course instructor.

Online Library Instruction: Library instruction conducted either synchronously or asynchronously via the web. Includes web conferencing and web tutorials.

Real-Time Library Instruction: Refers to library instruction conducted typically by web conferencing between librarian and library users, regardless of where they are located. Also referred to as synchronous library instruction.

Synchronous Library Instruction: Refers to library instruction conducted typically by web conferencing between librarian and library users, regardless of where they are located. Also referred to as real-time library instruction.

Web Conferencing: A method of synchronous, real-time communication using freely available or proprietary web software. Professional purposes for web conferencing include meetings among interested individuals for teaching, learning and training on any variety of topics. Web conferencing allows collaboration and co-browsing of websites, documents and resources, regardless of where participants are located. A web camera is often employed in web conferencing in order that participants may view an instructor or meeting leader, and at times each other, depending on situation and purpose.

Compilation of References

Adams, M. H., & Valiga, T. M. (2009). *Achieving excellence in nursing education*. New York, NY: National League for Nursing.

Adams, M. G. (2009, July). Engaging 21st-century adolescents: Video games in the reading classroom. *English Journal, 98*(6), 56–59.

Adams, W. K. (2009). Student engagement and learning with PhET interactive simulations. *Proceedings of Multimedia in Physics Teaching and Learning*.

Agostinho, S. (2006). Using characters in online simulate environments to guide authentic tasks. In Herrington, A., & Herrington, J. (Eds.), *Authentic learning environments in higher education*. Hershey, PA: Information Science Publishing. doi:10.4018/978-1-59140-594-8.ch007

Akilli, G. K. (2006). Games and simulations: A new approach in Education? In Gibson, D., Aldrich, C., & Prensky, M. (Eds.), *Games and simulations in online learning* (pp. 1–20). Hershey, PA: IGI Global. doi:10.4018/978-1-59904-304-3.ch001

Alchemy. (January 2010). *About the EVOKE game*. Retrieved from http://blog.urgentevoke.net/2010/01/27/about-the-evoke-game/

Alessi, S. M., & Trollip, S. R. (2001). *Multimedia for learning: Methods and development* (3rd ed.). Needham Heights, MA: Allyn and Bacon.

Allan, K. K., & Miller, S. M. (1990). Teacher-research collaborative: Cooperative professional development. *Theory into Practice, 29*, 196–202. doi:10.1080/00405849009543454

Ally, M. (2008). Foundations of educational theory for online learning. In Anderson, T., & Sanders, G. (Eds.), *Theory and practice of online learning* (pp. 1–31). Athabasca, Canada: Athabasca University.

Almond, R. G. (2009). Bayesian network models for local dependence among observable outcome variables. *Journal of Educational and Behavioral Statistics, 34*(4), 491–521. doi:10.3102/1076998609332751

Amazon Kindle. (2011). *Most highlighted passages of all time*. Retrieved from https://kindle.amazon.com/most_popular

American Association of Colleges of Nursing. (2008). *The essentials of baccalaureate nursing education*. Washington, DC: Author.

American Association for the Advancement of Science (AAAS). (1990). *Science for all Americans*. New York, NY: Oxford University Press.

American Association for the Advancement of Science (AAAS). (1993). *Benchmarks for science literacy: A Project 2061 report*. New York, NY: Oxford University Press.

American Psychological Association. (2010). *Publication manual of the American Psychological Association* (6th ed.). Washington, DC: Author.

Amory, A. (2007). Game object model version II: A theoretical framework for educational game development. *Educational Technology Research and Development, 55*, 55–77. doi:10.1007/s11423-006-9001-x

Anderson, J. R., Reder, L. M., & Simon, H. A. (1996). Situated learning and education. *Educational Researcher, 25*(4), 5–11.

Anderson, J. R. (2000). *Cognitive psychology and its implications* (5th ed.). New York, NY: Worth Publishers.

Anderson, L. W., & Krathwohl, D. R. (Eds.). (2001). *A taxonomy for learning, teaching, and assessing: A revision of bloom's taxonomy of educational objectives*. New York, NY: Longman.

Anderson, T. (2008). Toward a theory of online learning. In Anderson, T., & Sanders, G. (Eds.), *Theory and practice of online learning* (pp. 45–74). Athabasca, Canada: Athabasca University.

Ang, C. S., Zaphiris, P., & Mahmood, S. (2007). A model of cognitive loads in massively multiplayer online role playing games. *Interacting with Computers, 19*(2), 167–179. doi:10.1016/j.intcom.2006.08.006

Angeli, C., & Valanides, N. (2004). Examining the effects of text-only and text-and-visual instructional materials on the achievement of field-dependent and field-independent learners during problem solving with modeling software. *Educational Technology Research and Development, 52*, 23–36. doi:10.1007/BF02504715

Annetta, L. A. (2008). Video games in education: Why they should be used and how they are being used. *Theory into Practice, 47*, 229–239. doi:10.1080/00405840802153940

Apt, C. C. (1970). *Serious games: The art and science of games that simulate life in industry, government and education*. New York, NY: Viking.

Arbaugh, J. B. (2008). Does the community of inquiry framework predict outcomes in online MBA courses? *International Review of Research in Open and Distance Learning, 9*(2). Retrieved from http://www.irrodl.org/index.php/irrodl/article/view/490/1048.

Ardichvili, A., Page, V., & Wentling, T. (2003). Motivation and barriers to participation in online knowledge-sharing communities of practice. *Journal of Knowledge Management, 7*(1), 64–77. doi:10.1108/13673270310463626

Areeda, P. E. (1996). The Socratic method. *Harvard Law Review, 109*(5), 911–912.

Armstrong, A. M. (1989). Persistence and the causal perception of failure: Modifying cognitive attributions. *Journal of Educational Psychology, 70*, 154–166.

Arnold, K. E. (2010). Signals: Applying academic analytics. *EDUCASE Quarterly Magazine, 33*(1).

Association of College and Research Libraries. (2000). *Information literacy competency standards for higher education*. Retrieved from http://www.ala.org/ala/mgrps/divs/acrl/standards/informationliteracycompetency.cfm

Association of College and Research Libraries. (2008). *Standards for distance learning library services*. Retrieved from http://www.ala.org/ala/mgrps/divs/acrl/standards/guidelinesdistancelearning.cfm

Astleitner, H., & Wiesner, C. (2004). An integrated model of multimedia learning and motivation. *Journal of Educational Multimedia and Hypermedia, 13*, 3–21.

Audio Publishing Enterprises, Inc. (2008). *Yodio: Audio for fun, fame and fortune!* Retrieved from http://www.yodio.com/

Ausubel, D. (1968). *Educational psychology*. New York, NY: Holt, Rinehart & Winston.

Avedon, E., & Sutton-Smith, B. (1971). *The study of games*. New York, NY: Wiley.

Azevedo, R., Cromley, J. G., & Seibert, D. (2004). Does adaptive scaffolding facilitate students' ability to regulate their learning with hypermedia? *Contemporary Educational Psychology, 29*(3), 344–370. doi:10.1016/j.cedpsych.2003.09.002

Azevedo, R., Cromley, J. G., Winters, F. I., Moos, D. C., & Greene, J. A. (2005). Adaptive human scaffolding facilitates adolescents' self-regulated learning with hypermedia. *Instructional Science, 33*(5), 381–412. doi:10.1007/s11251-005-1273-8

Azevedo, R., & Jacobson, M. (2008). Advances in scaffolding learning with hypertext and hypermedia: A summary and critical analysis. *Educational Technology Research and Development, 56*(1), 93–100. doi:10.1007/s11423-007-9064-3

Baek, Y. K. (2008). What hinders teachers in using computer and video games in the classroom? Exploring factors inhibiting the uptake of computer and video games. *Cyberpsychology & Behavior, 11*(6), 665–671. doi:10.1089/cpb.2008.0127

Baker, M., Hansen, T., Joiner, R., & Traum, D. (1999). The role of grounding in collaborative learning tasks. In Dillenbourg, P. (Ed.), *Collaborative learning: Cognitive and computational approaches* (pp. 31–63). Amsterdam, The Netherlands: Pergamon.

Bandura, A. (1969). *Principles of behavior modification.* New York, NY: Holt, Rinehart and Winston.

Bandura, A. (1985). *Social foundations for thought and action: A social cognitive theory.* New York, NY: Prentice Hall.

Bandura, A. (1977). *Social learning theory.* Englewood Cliffs, NJ: Prentice-Hall.

Bandura, A. (1986). *Social foundations of thought and action: A social cognitive theory.* Englewood Cliffs, NJ: Prentice Hall.

Bandura, A. (1991). Self-efficacy mechanism in physiological activation and health-promoting behavior. In Madden, J. IV, (Ed.), *Neurobiology of learning, emotion and affect* (pp. 229–270). New York, NY: Raven.

Bandura, A. (1970). Modeling theory: Some traditions, trends, and disputes. In Sahakian, W. S. (Ed.), *Psychology of learning: Systems, models, and theories.* Chicago, IL: Markham.

Barab, S. A., Kling, R., & Gray, J. H. (2004). Introduction: Designing for virtual communities in the service of learning. In Barab, S. A., Kling, R., & Gray, J. H. (Eds.), *Designing for virtual communities in the service of learning.* Cambridge, UK: Cambridge University Press. doi:10.1080/01972240309467

Barab, S. A., & Duffy, T. M. (2000). From practice fields to communities of practice. In Jonassen, D. H., & Land, S. M. (Eds.), *Theoretical foundations of learning environments* (pp. 25–56). Mahwah, NJ: Lawrence Erlbaum Associates.

Barab, S. A. MaKinster, J. G., & Scheckler, R. (2004). Designing system dualities: Characterizing an online professional development. In S. A. Barab, R. Kling & J. H. Gray (Eds.), *Designing for virtual communities in the service of learning.* Cambridge, UK: Cambridge University Press.

Barton, A. C., Tan, E., & Rivet, A. (2008). Creating hybrid spaces for engaging school science among urban middle school girls. *American Educational Research Journal*, *45*(1), 68–103. doi:10.3102/0002831207308641

Baxter, G. P. (1995). Using computer simulations to assess hands-on science learning. *Journal of Science Education and Technology*, *4*(1), 21–27. doi:10.1007/BF02211578

Baxter, G. P., Elder, A. D., & Glaser, R. (1996). Knowledge-based cognition and performance assessment in the science classroom. *Educational Psychologist*, *31*(2), 133–140. doi:10.1207/s15326985ep3102_5

Baxter, G. P., & Shavelson, R. J. (1994). Science performance assessments: Benchmarks and surrogates. *International Journal of Educational Research*, *21*(3), 279–298. doi:10.1016/S0883-0355(06)80020-0

Baxter Magolda, M. B. (1992). Students' epistemologies and academic experiences: implications for pedagogy. *Review of Higher Education*, *15*(3), 265–287.

Baxter Magolda, M. B. (1996). Epistemological development in graduate and professional education. *Review of Higher Education*, *19*(3), 283–304.

Becker, K. (2007). Digital game-based learning once removed: Teaching teachers. *British Journal of Educational Technology*, *38*(3), 478–488. doi:10.1111/j.1467-8535.2007.00711.x

Becker, K. (2010). Chapter 2: Distinctions between games and learning: A review of current literature on games in education. In R. Van Eck (Ed.), *Gaming and cognition: Theories and practice from the learning sciences* (pp. 22-54). Hershey, PA: Information Science Reference, IGI Global.

Benner, P. (1984). *From novice to expert.* Menlo Park, CA: Addison-Wesley.

Benyon, D., Turner, P., & Turner, S. (2005). *Designing interactive systems.* Essex, England: Pearson Education.

Berge, Z. (1999). Interaction in post-secondary web-based learning. *Educational Technology*, *39*, 5–11.

Berliner, D. C., & Gage, N. L. (1998). *Educational Psychology.* Boston, MA: Houghton Mifflin Company.

Bernardi, R. (2003). Students performance in accounting: Differential effect of field dependence–independence as a learning style. *Psychological Reports, 93*, 135–142.

Berthold, K., Nuckles, M., & Renkl, A. (2007). Do learning protocols support learning strategies and outcomes? The role of cognitive and metacognitive prompts. *Learning and Instruction, 17*(5), 564–577. doi:10.1016/j.learninstruc.2007.09.007

Besnard, D., & Cacitti, L. (2005). Interface changes causing accidents. An empirical study of negative transfer. *International Journal of Human-Computer Studies, 62*, 105–125. doi:10.1016/j.ijhcs.2004.08.002

Betrancourt, M. (2005). The animation and interactivity principles in multimedia learning. In Mayer, R. E. (Ed.), *The Cambridge handbook of multimedia learning* (pp. 287–296). New York, NY: Cambridge University Press.

Black, R., Sileo, T. W., & Prater, M. A. (2000). Learning journals, self-reflection, and university students' changing perceptions. *Action in Teacher Education, 21*(4), 71–89.

Black, N. E. (2000). Emerging technologies. *Journal of Library Administration, 31*(3), 45–59. .doi:10.1300/J111v31n03_06

Blanton, W., Moorman, G., Hayes, B., & Warner, M. (1997). Effects of participation in the 5th dimension on far transfer. *Journal of Educational Computing Research, 16*(4), 371–396. doi:10.2190/0YAW-FYAN-2T2B-0LP3

Blaton, W. E. (n.d.). *Teaching and the 5th dimension: Novice and expert.* Retrieved from http://129.171.53.1/blantonw/5dClhse/teaching/expert.html

Bliss, C. A., & Lawrence, B. (2009). From posts to patterns: A metric to characterize discussion board activity in online courses. *Journal of Asynchronous Learning Networks, 13*(2), 15–32.

Bloom, B. S., & Krathwohl, D. R. (1956). *Taxonomy of educational objectives: The classification of educational goals, by a committee of college and university examiners. Handbook I: Cognitive domain.* New York, NY: Longman, Green.

Bloom, B. S. (1971). Mastery learning. In Block, J. H. (Ed.), *Mastery learning: Theory and practice.* New York, NY: Holt, Rinehart & Winston.

Bodhi, B. (1999). *The noble eightfold path: The way to the end of suffering.* Retrieved from http://www.access-toinsight.org/lib/authors/bodhi/waytoend.html.

Bogost, I. (2008). The rhetoric of video games. In K. Salen (Ed.), *The ecology of games: Connecting youth, games, and learning* (pp. 117-139). The John D. and Catherine T. MacArthur Foundation Series on Digital Media and Learning. Cambridge, MA: The MIT Press.

Boller, J., & Jones, D. (2008). *Nursing education for California: White paper and redesign and strategic action plan recommendations.* Berkeley, CA: California Institute for Nursing and Health Care.

Bonk, C. (2009). *The world is open: How Web technology is revolutionizing education.* San Francisco, CA: Jossey-Bass.

Bonk, C. J., & Graham, C. R. (2006). *The handbook of blended learning: Global perspectives, local designs.* San Francisco, CA: Pfeiffer.

Bonk, C. J., Wisher, R. A., & Nigrelli, M. L. (2004). Learning communities, communities of practice: Principles, technologies and examples. In Littleton, K., Miell, D., & Faulkner, D. (Eds.), *Learning to collaborate, collaborating to learn* (pp. 199–219). New York, NY: Nova Science.

Borthwick, F., Bennett, S., LeFoe, G., & Huber, E. (2007). Applying authentic learning to social science: A learning design for an inter-disciplinary sociology subject. *Journal of Learning Design Designing for Effective Learning, 2*(1).

Bower, S. L., & Mee, S. A. (2010). Virtual delivery of electronic resources and services to off-campus users: A multifaceted approach. *Journal of Library Administration, 50*(5), 468-483. doi:10:1080/01930826.2010.488593

Bowers, J. (1996). Conducting developmental research in a technology-enhanced classroom (Doctoral dissertation, Vanderbilt University, 1996). *Dissertation Abstracts International, 57*, 3433A.

Brandon, D., & Hollingshead, A. (1999). Collaborative learning and computer-supported groups. *Communication Education, 48*, 109–126. doi:10.1080/03634529909379159

Brey, P. (2005). The epistemology and ontology of human-computer interaction. *Minds and Machines, 15*, 383–398. doi:10.1007/s11023-005-9003-1

Bristol, T. J. (2006). *Evidence-based e-learning for nursing educators*. Iowa City, IA: Center for Health Workforce Planning, Bureau of Health Care access, Iowa Department of Public Health.

Brock, S. A., Otto, R. G., & Hoffman, B. (2004). Media as lived environments: The ecological psychology of educational technology. In Jonassen, D. (Ed.), *Handbook of research on educational communications and technology* (pp. 215–241). Mahwah, NJ: Lawrence Erlbaum.

Brookfield, S. (2006). *The skillful teacher* (2nd ed.). San Francisco, CA: Jossey-Bass.

Brown, E., Cristea, A., Stewart, C., & Brailsford, T. (2005). Patterns in authoring of adaptive educational hypermedia: A taxonomy of learning styles. *Journal of Educational Technology & Society, 8*(3), 77–90.

Brown, J. S., Collins, A., & Duguid, P. (1989). Situated cognition and the culture of learning. *Educational Researcher, 18*(1), 32–42.

Brown, A. L. (1997). Transforming schools into communities of thinking and learning about serious matters. *The American Psychologist, 52*(4), 399–413. doi:10.1037/0003-066X.52.4.399

Brown, S. L., & Vaughan, C. (2009). *Play: How it shapes the brain, opens the imagination, and invigorates the soul*. New York, NY: Avery.

Brown, J. S., & Adler, R. (2008). Minds on fire: Open education, the long tail, and learning 2.0. *EDUCAUSE Review*, (Jan/Feb): 16–32.

Brown, R. (2001). The process of community building in distance learning classes. *Journal of Asynchronous Learning Networks, 5*(2), 18–35.

Browne, E. (2005). Structural and pedagogic change in further and higher education: A case study approach. *Journal of Further and Higher Education, 29*(1), 49–59. doi:10.1080/03098770500037754

Bruce, V., Green, P. R., & Georgeson, M. A. (1996). *Visual perception: Physiology, psychology, and ecology*. Hillsdale, NJ: Erlbaum.

Bruner, J. (1996). *The culture of education*. Cambridge, MA: Harvard University Press.

Bruner, J. (2005). Foreward. In Sternberg, R., & Preiss, D. D. (Eds.), *Intelligence and technology: The impact of tools on the nature and development of human abilities* (pp. ix–xi). Mahwah, NJ: Lawrence Erlbaum.

Brünken, R., Plass, J., & Leutner, D. (2003). Direct measurement of cognitive load in multimedia learning. *Educational Psychologist, 38*, 53–61. doi:10.1207/S15326985EP3801_7

Brusilovsky, P. (2001). Adaptive hypermedia. *User Modeling and User-Adapted Interaction, 11*, 87–110. doi:10.1023/A:1011143116306

Brusilovsky, P. (2000). Adaptive hypermedia: From intelligent tutoring systems to web-based education. In G. Gauthier, C., Frasson, & K. ValLehn (Eds.), *Intelligent tutoring systems. Lecture notes in computer science* (vol. 1839, pp. 1-7). Berlin, Germany: Springer Verlag.

Buckingham, D. (2004). New media, new childhoods? Children's changing cultural environment in the age of digital technology. In Kehily, M. J. (Ed.), *An introduction to childhood studies* (pp. 108–122). Maidenhead, UK: Open University Press.

Bucy, E. P. (2004a). Interactivity in society: Locating an elusive concept. *The Information Society, 20*, 373–383. doi:10.1080/01972240490508063

Bucy, E. P. (2004b). The interactivity paradox: Closer to the news but confused. In Bucy, E. P., & Newhagen, J. E. (Eds.), *Media access: Social and psychological dimensions of new technology use* (pp. 47–72). Mahwah, NJ: Lawrence Erlbaum Associates.

Bulu, S., & Pedersen, S. (2010). Scaffolding middle school students' content knowledge and ill-structured problem solving in a problem-based hypermedia learning environment. *Educational Technology Research and Development, 58*(5), 507–529. doi:10.1007/s11423-010-9150-9

Burgoon, J. K., Bonito, J. A., Ramirez, A., Dunbar, N. E., Kam, K., & Fischer, J. (2002). Testing the interactivity principle: Effects of mediation, propinquity, and verbal and nonverbal modalities in interpersonal interaction. *The Journal of Communication, 52*(3), 657–677. doi:10.1111/j.1460-2466.2002.tb02567.x

Burnham, B., & Walden, B. (1997). Interactions in distance education: A report from the other side. In *Proceedings of the Adult Education Research Conference* (pp. 49-54).

Burns, H., Parlett, J., & Redfield, C. L. (2009). *Intelligent tutoring systems: Evolution in design.* New York, NY: Psychology Press.

Burton, J. K., Moore, D. M., & Magliaro, S. G. (1996). Behaviorism and instructional technology. In Jonassen, D. H. (Ed.), *Handbook of research for educational communications and technology* (pp. 46–73). New York, NY: Simon & Schuster Macmillan.

Burton, R., & Brown, J. S. (1982). An investigation of computer coaching for informal learning activities. In Sleeman, D., & Brown, J. S. (Eds.), *Intelligent tutoring systems.* Orlando, FL: Academic Press. doi:10.1016/S0020-7373(79)80003-6

Campbell, G. (Interviewer) & Medina, J. (Interviewee). (n.d.). *Personal interview.* Retrieved from http://hw.libsyn.com/p/5/c/6/5c614405b3bd577f/37-brainscience-Medina.mp3?sid=6341d3776c2c99f93b0aa9d671dd523b&l_sid=18369&l_eid=&l_mid=1550378

Carpenter, E. (1960). The new languages. In Carpenter, E., & McLuhan, M. (Eds.), *Explorations in communication.* Boston, MA: Beacon Press.

Carrier, C., & Jonassen, D. (1988). Adapting courseware to accommodate individual differences. In Jonassen, D. (Ed.), *Instructional designs for microcomputer courseware* (pp. 61–96). Mahwah, NJ: Lawrence Erlbaum Associates.

Carroll, J. M. (2001). Community computing as human-computer interaction. *Behaviour & Information Technology, 20*(5), 307–314. doi:10.1080/01449290110078941

Carroll, J. M. (1991). The Kittie House Manifesto. In Carroll, J. M. (Ed.), *Designing interaction: Psychology of the human-computer interface* (pp. 1–16). Cambridge, UK: Cambridge University Press.

Carter, K., & Sabers, D., Cushing, Pinnegar, S., & Berliner, D. C. (1987). Processing and using information about students: A study of expert, novice, and postulant teachers. *Teaching and Teacher Education, 3*(2), 147–157. doi:10.1016/0742-051X(87)90015-1

Caspers, J., Fritts, J., & Gover, H. (2000). Beyond the rhetoric: A study of the impact of the ACRL guidelines for distance library services on selected distance learning programs in higher education. *Journal of Library Administration, 31*(3), 127–148. .doi:10.1300/J111v31n03_12

Cazden, C. B. (1988). *Classroom discourse: The language of teaching and learning.* Portsmouth, NH: Heinemann.

Chakraborty, M., & Victor, S. (2004). Do's and don'ts of simultaneous instruction to on-campus and distance students via videoconferencing. *Journal of Library Administration, 41*(1/2), 97–112. .doi:10.1300/J111v41n01_09

Chan, T. S., & Ahern, T. C. (1999). Targeting motivation: Adapting flow theory to instructional design. *Journal of Educational Computing Research, 21*(2), 152–163.

ChanLin, L. (2009). Applying motivational analysis in a Web-based course. *Innovations in Education and Training International, 46*(1), 91–103. doi:10.1080/14703290802646123

Chaplin, H. (June 28, 2010). Schools use video games to teach thinking skills. *National Public Radio.* [radio news station]. Retrieved from http://www.npr.org/templates/story/story.php?storyId=128081896.

Charmaz, K. (2006). *Constructing grounded theory.* London, UK: Sage.

Charsky, D., & Mims, C. (2008). Integrating commercial off-the-shelf video games into school curriculums. *TechTrends, 52*(5), 38–44. doi:10.1007/s11528-008-0195-0

Charsky, D. (2010). Chapter 9: Making a connection: Game genres, game characteristics, and teaching structures. In R. Van Eck (Ed.), *Gaming and cognition: Theories and practice from the learning sciences* (pp. 189-212) Hershey, PA: Information Science Reference, IGI Global.

Chase, W. G., & Simon, H. A. (1973). The mind's eye in chess. In Chase, W. G. (Ed.), *Visual information processing* (pp. 215–281). New York, NY: Academic Press.

Chen, J. (2007). Flow in games (and everything else). *Communications of the ACM, 50*(4), 31–34. doi:10.1145/1232743.1232769

Chi, M. T. H., Feltovich, P. J., & Glaser, R. (1980). Categorization and representation of physics problems by experts and novices. *Cognitive Science, 5*, 121–152. doi:10.1207/s15516709cog0502_2

Ching, C. C., & Kafai, Y. B. (2008). Peer pedagogy: Student collaboration and reflection in a learning-through-design project. *Teachers College Record, 110*(12), 2601–2632.

Chinien, C. A., & Boutin, F. (1992). Cognitive style FD/I: An important learning characteristic for educational technologies. *Journal of Educational Technology Systems, 21*(4), 303–311.

Cho, K.-L., & Jonassen, D. (2002). The effects of argumentation scaffolds on argumentation and problem solving. *Educational Technology Research and Development, 50*(3), 5–22. doi:10.1007/BF02505022

Choi, J., & Hannafin, M. J. (1995). Situated cognition and learning environments: Roles, structures, and implications for design. *Educational Technology Research and Development, 43*(2), 53–69. doi:10.1007/BF02300472

Choi, I., & Lee, K. (2009). Designing and implementing a case-based learning environment for enhancing ill-structured problem solving: Classroom management problems for prospective teachers. *Educational Technology Research and Development, 57*(1), 99–129. doi:10.1007/s11423-008-9089-2

Chooseco. (1977-2011). *Choose your own adventure*. Retrieved January 30, 2011, from http://www.cyoa.com/public/index.html

Christensen, M. (1995). *Critical issues: Providing hands-on, minds-on, and authentic learning experience in science*. Retrieved September 27, 2010, from http://www.ncrel.org/sdrs/areas/issues/content/cntareas/science/sc500.htm

Clandinin, D., & Connolly, F. (Eds.). (1995). *Teacher's professional knowledge landscapes*. New York, NY: Teacher's College Press.

Clark, R., & Salomon, G. (1986). Media in teaching. In Wittrock, M. C. (Ed.), *Handbook of research on teaching* (3rd ed., pp. 464–478). New York, NY: Macmillan Publishing Company.

Clarke, J. (2009). *Exploring the compexity of inquiry learning in an open-ended problem space*. Unpublished Doctoral Dissertation, Harvard University, Cambridge, MA.

Clarke-Midura, J., Code, J., Zap, N., & Dede, C. (in press). Assessing science inquiry in the classroom: A case study of the virtual assessment project. In Lennex, L., & Nettleton, K. (Eds.), *Cases on Inquiry Through Instructional Technology in Math and Science: Systemic Approaches*. New York, NY: IGI Publishing.

Clarke-Midura, J., Code, J., & Dede, C. (2011a). *Assessment 2.0: Rethinking how we assess science inquiry with technology-based assessments*. Paper presented at the National Science Teachers Association 2011 Annual Conference.

Clarke-Midura, J., Code, J., & Dede, C. (2011b). *Measuring students' scientific inquiry processes and skills with immersive performance assessments*. Paper presented at the National Association for Research on Science Teaching Annual Meeting.

Clarke-Midura, J., Code, J., Mayrath, M., & Dede, C. (2011a). *Exploring inquiry processes in immersive virtual environments*. Paper presented at the AERA 2011 Annual Meeting.

Clarke-Midura, J., Code, J., Mayrath, M., & Dede, C. (2011b). *Using evidence centered design to develop immersive virtual assessments*. Paper presented at the AERA 2011 Annual Meeting.

Clarke-Midura, J., Dede, C., & Mayrath, M. (2010a). *Designing immersive virtual environments for assessing inquiry*. Paper presented at the Annual Meeting of the American Educational Research Association.

Clarke-Midura, J., Dede, C., & Mayrath, M. (2010b). *Ensuring the integrity of data in virtual immersive assessments*. Paper presented at the Annual Meeting of the American Educational Research Association.

Cobb, P., & Bowers, J. (1999). Cognitive and situated learning perspectives in theory and practice. *Educational Researcher, 28*(2), 4–15.

Code, J., Clarke-Midura, J., Zap, N., & Dede, C. (in press). Virtual performance assessment in immersive virtual environments. In Wang, H. (Ed.), *Interactivity in e-learning: Cases and frameworks*. New York, NY: IGI Publishing.

Code, J. R., Clarke-Midura, J., Zap, N., & Dede, C. (in press). *Virtual performance assessment in serious games and immersive virtual reality environments*.

Cole, M., & Derry, J. (2005). We have met technology and it is us. In Sternberg, R., & Preiss, D. (Eds.), *Intelligence and technology: The impact of tools on the nature and development of human abilities* (pp. 210–227). Mahwah, NJ: Lawrence Erlbaum.

College Board. (2009). *Science College Board standards for college success*. New York, NY: The College Board.

Collins, A., Brown, J. S., & Newman, S. E. (1989). Cognitive apprenticeship: Teaching the crafts of reading, writing, and mathematics. In Resnick, L. B. (Ed.), *Knowing, learning, and instruction: Essays in honor of Robert Glaser* (pp. 453–494). Hillsdale, NJ: Lawrence Erlbaum Associates.

Colorado State University. (2011). *Case study: Introduction and definition*. Retrieved from http://writing.colostate.edu/guides/research/casestudy/pop2a.cfm

Condense. (n.d.). *Condense*. Retrieved from http://conden.se/

Conrad, R. M., & Donaldson, A. (2004). *Engaging the online learner: Activities and resources for creative instruction*. San Francisco, CA: Jossey-Bass.

Conrad, D. (2007). Recognizing prior learning: Exploring the diversity of learners' experiential learning through PLAR. In Evans, T., Murphy, D., & Haughey, M. (Eds.), *World handbook of distance education*. Oxford, UK: Elsevier.

Cooke, N. A. (2005). The role of libraries in web-based distance education. *Journal of Library & Information Services in Distance Learning*, *1*(4), 47–57. .doi:10.1300/J192v01n04_04

Cooper, S., Khatib, F., Treuille, A., Barbero, J., Lee, J., & Beenen, M. … Foldit players. (2010) Predicting protein structures with a multiplayer online game. *Nature, 466*, 756-760. Retrieved from http://www.nature.com/nature/journal/v466/n7307/full/nature09304.html.

Cormode, G., & Krishnamurthy, B. (2008). Key differences between Web 1.0 and Web 2.0. *First Monday*, *13*(6). Retrieved from http://www.uic.edu/htbin/cgiwrap/bin/ojs/index.php/fm/article/view/2125/1972.

Cornelius-White, J. H., & Harbaugh, A. P. (2010). *Learner-centered instruction: Building relationships for student success*. Thousand Oaks, CA: SAGE Publications, Inc.

Corno, L., & Snow, R. (1986). Adapting teaching to individual differences among learners. In Wittrock, M. C. (Ed.), *Handbook of research on teaching* (*Vol. 3*, pp. 605–629). New York, NY: MacMillan.

Correia, A., Yusop, F. D., Wilson, J. R., & Schwier, R. A. (2010). *A comparative case study of approaches authentic learning in instructional design at two universities*. Paper presented at the American Educational Research Association 2010 Annual Meeting, Denver, CO, April 30-May 4, 2010.

Council on Education for Public Health (CePH). (n.d.). *Accreditation criteria*. Council on Education for Public Health. Retrieved March 14, 2011, from http://www.ceph.org/pg_accreditation_criteria.htm

Cowan, T. (2004). *Creative destruction: How globalization is changing the world's cultures*. Princeton, NJ: Princeton University Press.

Cox, J. (2004). E-books: Challenges and opportunities. *D-Lib Magazine, 10*(10). Retrieved April 26, 2011, from http://www.dlib.org/dlib/october04/cox/10cox.html

Crawford, C. (2005). *Chris Crawford on interactive storytelling*. Berkeley, CA: New Riders.

Crawford, C. M. (2001). Developing webs of significance through communications: Appropriate interactive activities for distributed learning environments. [CWIS]. *Campus-Wide Information Systems Journal*, *18*(2), 68–72. doi:10.1108/10650740110386675

Crawford, C. M. (2003). Emerging learning environments: Enhancing the online community. *Academic Exchange Quarterly*, *7*(4), 131–135.

Crawford, C. (1982). *The art of computer game design*. Retrieved from http://www.vancouver.wsu.edu/fac/peabody/game-book/Coverpage.html

Cristea, A. (2003). Adaptive patterns in authoring of educational adaptive hypermedia. *Journal of Educational Technology & Society, 6*(4), 1–5.

Cronbach, L., & Snow, R. (1977). *Aptitudes and instructional methods: A handbook for research on interactions.* New York, NY: Irvington.

Cronbach, L. J., Linn, R. L., Brennan, R. L., & Haertel, E. H. (1997). Generalizability analysis for performance assessments of student achievement or school effectiveness. *Educational and Psychological Measurement, 57*(3), 373–399. doi:10.1177/0013164497057003001

Cross, P. (1981). *Adults as learners.* San Francisco, CA: Jossey-Bass.

Crown, S. W. (1999). Web-based learning: Enhancing the teaching of engineering graphics. *Interactive Multimedia Electronic Journal of Computer Enhanced Learning, 1*(2). Retrieved on November 17, 2010, from http://imej.wfu.edu/articles/1999/2/02/index.asp

Csikszentmihalyi, M., & Csikszentmihalyi, I. S. (Eds.). (1988). *Optimal experience: Psychological studies of flow in consciousness.* Cambridge, UK: Cambridge University Press.

Csikszentmihalyi, M. (1975). *Beyond boredom and anxiety.* San Francisco, CA: Jossey-Bass.

Csikszentmihalyi, M. (1990). *FLOW: The psychology of optimal experience.* New York, NY: Harper and Row.

Curvender Limited. (2011). *Elgg: Introducing a powerful open source social networking engine.* Retrieved from http://www.elgg.org/

Danili, E., & Reid, N. (2004). Some strategies to improve performance in school chemistry, based on two cognitive factors. *Research in Science & Technological Education, 22*(2), 203–226. doi:10.1080/0263514042000290903

Darling-Hammond, L., Ancess, J., & Falk, B. (1995). *Authentic assessment in action.* New York, NY: Teachers College Press, Teachers College, Columbia University.

Darling-Hammond, L. (1996). The quiet revolution: rethinking teacher development. *Educational Leadership, 53*, 4–10.

Dascal, M., & Dror, I. E. (2005). The impact of cognitive technologies: Towards a pragmatic approach. *Pragmatics & Cognition, 13*(3), 451–457. doi:10.1075/pc.13.3.03das

Davis, B. G. (2009). *Tools for teaching* (2nd ed.). San Francisco, CA: Jossey-Bass.

Davis, F. D., Bagozzi, R. P., & Warshaw, P. R. (1989). User acceptance of computer technology: A comparison of two theoretical models. *Management Science, 35*(8), 983–1003. doi:10.1287/mnsc.35.8.982

Davis, F. D., Bagozzi, R. P., & Warshaw, P. R. (1992). Extrinsic and intrinsic motivation to use computers in the workplace. *Journal of Applied Social Psychology, 22*(14), 1111–1132. doi:10.1111/j.1559-1816.1992.tb00945.x

Dawson, S. (2010). Seeing the learning community: An exploration of the development of a resource for monitoring online student networking. *British Journal of Educational Technology, 41*(5), 736–752. doi:10.1111/j.1467-8535.2009.00970.x

De Bra, P. (2000). Pros and cons of adaptive hypermedia in web-based education. *Journal of CyberPsychology and Behavior, 3*(1), 71–77. doi:10.1089/109493100316247

De Bra, P., Brusilovsky, P., & Houben, G. (1999). Adaptive hypermedia: From systems to framework. *ACM Computing Surveys, 31*(4). Retrieved April 26, 2011, from http://www.cs.brown.edu/memex/ACM_HypertextTestbed/papers/25.html

de Crook, M. B. M., van Merriënboer, J. J. G., & Paas, F. G. W. C. (1998). High versus low contextual interference in simulation-based training of troubleshooting skills: Effects on transfer performance and invested mental effort. *Computers in Human Behavior, 14*, 249–267. doi:10.1016/S0747-5632(98)00005-3

de Wever, B., van Keer, H., Schellens, T., & Valcke, M. (2009). Structuring asynchronous discussion groups: The impact of role assignment and self-assessment on students' levels of knowledge construction through social negotiation. *Journal of Computer Assisted Learning, 25*(2), 177–188. doi:10.1111/j.1365-2729.2008.00292.x

De Wever, B., Schellens, T., Valcke, M., & Van Keer, H. (2006). Content analysis schemes to analyze transcripts online asynchronous discussion groups: A review. *Computers & Education, 46*(1), 6–28. doi:10.1016/j.compedu.2005.04.005

DeCharms, R. (1968). *Personal causation: The internal affective determinants of behavior.* New York, NY: Academic Press.

Deci, E. L. (1975). *Intrinsic motivation.* New York, NY: Plenum.

Dede, C. (1996). Emerging technologies and distributed learning. *American Journal of Distance Education, 10*(2), 4–36. doi:10.1080/08923649609526919

Dede, C. (1999). *The role of emerging technologies for knowledge mobilization, dissemination, and use in education.* Retrieved from http://www.virtual.gmu.edu/EDIT895/knowlmob.html

Dee-Lucas, D., & Larkin, J. H. (1992). *Text representation with traditional text and hypertext.* Pittsburgh, PA: Carnegie Mellon University.

DeNeve, K. M., & Heppner, M. J. (1997). Role play simulations: The assessment of an active learning technique and comparisons to traditional lectures. *Innovative Higher Education, 21*(3), 231–246. doi:10.1007/BF01243718

Derry, S., & Lajoie, S. (1993). A middle camp for (un) intelligent instructional computing: An introduction. In Lajoie, S., & Derry, S. (Eds.), *Computers as cognitive tools* (pp. 1–11). Hillsdale, NJ: Lawrence Erlbaum Associates.

DeSchryver, M., & Spiro, R. (2008). New forms of deep learning on the Web: Meeting the challenge of cognitive load in conditions of unfettered exploration in online multimedia environments. In R. Zheng (Ed.), *Cognitive effects of multimedia learning* (pp. 134-152). Hershey, PA: IGI Global Publishing.

Dewey, J. (1916). *Democracy and education: An introduction to the philosophy of education.* New York, NY: MacMillan.

Dewey, J. (1933). *How we think.* Chicago, IL: Henry Regnery.

Dewey, J. (1963). *Experience and education.* New York, NY: Collier Books.

Dewey, J. (2008). My pedagogic creed. In Pestritto, R. J., & Atto, W. J. (Eds.), *American progressivism: A reader* (pp. 125–134). New York, NY: Lexington Books.

Dickey, M. D. (2007). Game design and learning: A conjectural analysis of how massively multiple online role-playing games (MMORPGs) foster intrinsic motivation. *Educational Technology Research and Development, 55*(3), 253–273. doi:10.1007/s11423-006-9004-7

Dix, A., & Ellis, G. (1998). *Starting simple – Adding value to static visualization through simple interaction.* Paper presented at the Working Conference on Advanced Visual Interfaces (AVI '98), L'Aquila, Italy.

Docherty, K. J., & Faiks, A. H. (2004). *Science & Technology Libraries, 25*(1), 211–226. .doi:10.1300/J122v25n01_13

Dodge, B. (2007). *WebQuest.org.* Retrieved from http://webquest.org/index.php

Domagk, S., Schwartz, R. N., & Plass, J. L. (2010). Interactivity in multimedia learning: An integrated model. *Computers in Human Behavior, 28*, 1024–1033. doi:10.1016/j.chb.2010.03.003

Donovan, M. S., Bransford, J. D., & Pellegrino, J. W. (1999). *How people learn: Bridging research and practice.* Washington, DC: National Academy Press.

Dreyfus, H., & Dreyfus, S. (1985). *Mind over machine: The power of human intuition and expertise in the era of the computer.* New York, NY: Free Press.

Driscoll, M. P. (2000). *Psychology of learning for instruction* (2nd ed.). Boston, MA: Allyn and Bacon.

Driscoll, M. P. (2000). Introduction to theories of learning and instruction. In Driscoll, M. P. (Ed.), *Psychology of learning for instruction* (2nd ed., pp. 3–28). Boston, MA: Allyn and Bacon.

Dror, I. E. (2007). Gold mines and land mines in cognitive technology. In Dror, I. E. (Ed.), *Cognitive technologies and the pragmatics of cognition* (pp. 1–8). Philadelphia, PA: John Benjamins.

Duckworth, E. R. (2006). *The having of wonderful ideas and other essays on teaching and learning* (3rd ed.). New York, NY: Teachers College Press.

Duffy, T., & Cunningham, D. (1996). Constructivism: Implications for the design and delivery of Instruction. In Jonassen, D. (Ed.), *Handbook of research on educational communications and technology*. New York, NY: Simon & Schuster.

Duncan, J. (2008). Learning and study strategies for online teaching. In Kidd, T., & Song, H. (Eds.), *Handbook of research on instructional systems and technology* (pp. 532–546). Hershey, PA: Information Science Reference/IGI Global Publishing. doi:10.4018/978-1-59904-865-9.ch037

Eck, R. V. (2006). Digital game-based learning: It's not just the digital natives who are restless.... *EDUCAUSE Review*, *41*(2), 16–30.

Edery, D., & Mollick, E. (2009). *Changing the game: How video games are transforming the future of business*. Upper Saddle River, NJ: FT Press.

Edublogs. (2011). *Edublogs - Education blogs for teachers, students and institutions*. Retrieved from http://edublogs.org/

Educause Learning initiative. (2006, June). *7 things you should know about virtual worlds*. Retrieved from http://connect.educause.edu/Library/ELI/7ThingsYouShouldKnowAbout/39392

Educause Learning initiative. (2008, June). *7 things you should know about Second Life*. Retrieved from http://connect.educause.edu/Library/ELI/7ThingsYouShouldKnowAbout/46892

Eklund, J., & Sinclair, K. (2000). An empirical appraisal of adaptive interfaces for instructional systems. *Educational Technology and Society Journal*, *3*(4), 165–177.

Endsley, M., Farley, T., Jones, W. M., Midkiff, A. H., & Hansman, R. J. (1998-09). *Situation awareness information requirements for commercial airline pilots*. International Center for Air Transportation. ICAT 98-0.1

Engestrom, Y., Engestrom, R., & Suntio, A. (2002). Can a school community learn to master its own future? An activity-theoretical study of expansive learning among middle school teachers. In Wells, G., & Claxton, G. (Eds.), *Learning for life in the 20th century*. Oxford, UK: Blackwell Publishers. doi:10.1002/9780470753545.ch16

Engle, R. A. (2006). Framing interactions to foster generative learning: A situative explanation of transfer in a community of learners classroom. *Journal of the Learning Sciences*, *15*(4), 451–498. doi:10.1207/s15327809jls1504_2

Entertainment Software Association. (2010). *Sales, demographics and usage data: Essential facts about the computer and video game industry*. Retrieved from http://www.theesa.com/facts/pdfs/ESA_Essential_Facts_2010.PDF

Eow, Y. L., Ali, W. Z. B. W., Mahmud, R., & Baki, R. (2009). Form one students' engagement with computer games and its effect on their academic achievement in a Malaysian secondary school. *Computers & Education*, *53*, 1082–1091. doi:10.1016/j.compedu.2009.05.013

Epistemic Games. (2011). *Website*. Retrieved February 20, 2011, from http://epistemicgames.org/eg/category/games/front/

Ericsson, K. A. (1996). The acquisition of expert performance: An introduction to some of the issues. In Ericsson, K. A. (Ed.), *The road to excellence: The acquisition of expert performance in the arts and sciences, sports, and games* (pp. 1–50). Mahwah, NJ: Erlbaum.

Ericsson, K. A. (2000). *Expert performance and deliberate practice: An updated excerpt Ericsson*. Retrieved from http://www.psy.fsu.edu/faculty/ericsson/ericsson.exp.perf.html

Ertmer, P. A., & Newby, T. J. (1993). Behaviorism, cognitivism, constructivism: Comparing critical features from an instructional design perspective. *Performance Improvement Quarterly*, *6*(4), 50–72. doi:10.1111/j.1937-8327.1993.tb00605.x

Ertmer, P. A., & Stepich, D. A. (1999). *Case-based instruction in post-secondary education: Developing students' problem-solving expertise*. Paper presented at the Annual Conference of the Midwestern Educational Research Association (MWERA).

Etzioni, A. (1975). *Comparative analysis of complex organizations*. New York, NY: MacMillan Publishing Co.

Everywhere, P. (n.d.). *Instant audience feedback*. Retrieved from http://www.polleverywhere.com/

Eysenck, M. W., & Keane, M. T. (1990). *Cognitive psychology* (2nd ed.). Hillsdale, NJ: Lawrence Erlbaum.

Facebook. (2011). *Facebook helps you connect and share with the people in your life.* Retrieved from http://www.facebook.com/

Federation of American Scientists. (2006). *Harnessing the power of video games for learning.* Summit on Educational Games. Washington, DC: Federation of American Scientists.

Ferguson, S., Beeman, L., Eichorn, M., Jaramillo, Y., & Wright, M. (2004). High-fidelity simulation across cultural settings and educational levels. In Loyd, G. E., Lakem, C. L., & Greenberg, R. B. (Eds.), *Practical health care simulations* (pp. 184–203). Philadelphia, PA: Elsevier.

Filippidis, S. K., & Tsoukalas, I. A. (2009). On the use of adaptive instructional images based on the sequential-global dimension of the Felder-Silverman learning style theory. *Interactive Learning Environments, 17*(2), 135–150. doi:10.1080/10494820701869524

Fischer, K. W., Zheng, Y., & Stewart, J. (2002). Adult cognitive development: Dynamics in the developmental web. In Valsiner, J., & Connolly, K. (Eds.), *Handbook of developmental psychology* (pp. 491–516). Thousand Oaks, CA: Sage.

Fishman, L., Hoadley, C., Harasim, L., Hsi, S., Levin, J., Pea, R., et al. (1997, March 24-28). *Collaboration, communication, and computers: What do we think we know about networks and learning: Session overview and position statements.* Paper presented at the American Educational Research Association, Interactive symposium (learning environments), Chicago.

Foa, E. B., Keane, T. M., Friedsman, M. J., & Cohen, J. A. (2009). *Effective treatments for PTSD, 2nd ed: Practice guidelines from the International Society for Traumatic Stress Studies.* New York, NY: Guilford Press.

Ford, N. (1995). Levels and types of mediation in instructional systems: An individual differences approach. *International Journal of Human-Computer Studies, 43*, 241–259. doi:10.1006/ijhc.1995.1043

Ford, N., & Chen, S. (2001). Matching/mismatching revisited: An empirical study of learning and teaching styles. *British Journal of Educational Technology, 32*(1), 5–22. doi:10.1111/1467-8535.00173

Frederick, P. (1981). The dreaded discussion: Ten ways to start. *Improving College and University Teaching, 29*(3), 109–114.

French, J., Blair-Stevens, C., McVey, D., & Merritt, R. (Eds.). (2010). *Social marketing and public health theory and practice.* Oxford, UK: Oxford University Press.

Frey, B. A., & Alman, S. W. (2003). Applying adult learning theory to the online classroom. *New Horizons in Adult Education, 17*(1), 4–12.

Galarneau, L., & Zibit, M. (2007). Online games for 21st century skills. In Gibson, D., Aldrich, C., & Prensky, M. (Eds.), *Games and simulations in online learning: Research and development frameworks* (pp. 59–88). Hershey, PA: Information Science Publishing, Idea Group, Inc.

Galbraith, M. W. (2004). *Adult learning methods: A guide for effective instruction.* Malabar, FL: Krieger Publishing.

Gall, J. P., Gall, M. D., & Borg, W. R. (2005). *Applying educational research: A practical guide* (5th ed.). Boston, MA: Pearson Education.

Gannon Cook, R., & Crawford, C. M. (2004). From silos to communities: Addressing electronic isolation through interactivities. In R. Ferdig, C. Crawford, R. Carlsen, N. Davis, J. Price, R. Weber, & D. A. Willis (Eds.), *Society for Information Technology & Teacher Education International Conference Annual* (pp. 445-452). Norfolk, VA: Association for the Advancement of Computing in Education (AACE).

Gardner, H. (1993). *Multiple intelligence.* New York, NY: Basic Books.

Gardner, H. (1999). *Intelligence reframed: Multiple intelligences for the 21st century.* New York, NY: Basic Books.

Garris, R., Ahlers, R., & Driskell, J. E. (2002). Games, motivation, and learning: A research and practice model. *Simulation & Gaming, 33*, 441–467. doi:10.1177/1046878102238607

Garrison, D. R., Anderson, T., & Archer, W. (2001). Critical thinking, cognitive presence, and computer conferencing in distance education. *American Journal of Distance Education, 15*(1), 17–23. doi:10.1080/08923640109527071

Ge, X., Chen, C.-H., & Davis, K. A. (2005). Scaffolding novice instructional designers' problem-solving processes using question prompts in a web-based learning environment. *Journal of Educational Computing Research, 33*(2), 219–248. doi:10.2190/5F6J-HHVF-2U2B-8T3G

Ge, X., & Er, N. (2005). An online support system to scaffold real-world problem solving. *Interactive Learning Environments, 13*(3), 139–157. doi:10.1080/10494820500382893

Ge, X., & Land, S. (2003). Scaffolding students' problem-solving processes in an ill-structured task using question prompts and peer interactions. *Educational Technology Research and Development, 51*(1), 21–38. doi:10.1007/BF02504515

Ge, X., & Land, S. M. (2004). A conceptual framework for scaffolding ill-structured problem-solving processes using question prompts and peer interactions. *Educational Technology Research and Development, 52*(2), 5–22. doi:10.1007/BF02504836

Ge, X., Planas, L., & Er, N. (2010). A cognitive support system to scaffold students' problem-based learning in a web-based learning environment. *Interdisciplinary Journal of Problem-Based Learning, 4*(1), 30–56.

Ge, Z., Law, V., & Haung, K. (in press). Diagnosis: Supporting and fading: A scaffolding design framework for adaptive el-learning systems. In Song, H. (Ed.), *Interactivity in e-learning: Cases and frameworks*. Hershey, PA: IGI Publishers.

Gee, J. P. (2007a). *Good video games + good learning: Collected essays on video games, learning and literacy*. New York, NY: Peter Lang.

Gee, J. P. (2004). *Situated language and learning: A critique of traditional schooling*. New York, NY: Routledge.

Gee, J. P. (2007). *What video games have to teach us about learning and literacy*. New York, NY: Palgrave Macmillan.

Gee, J. P., & Hayes, E. R. (2010). *Women and gaming: The Sims and 21st century learning*. New York, NY: Palgrave Macmillan.

Gee, J. P., & Shaffer, D. W. (2010). Looking where the light is bad: Video games and the future of assessment. *Edge, 6*(1), 1–19.

Gee, J. P. (2005). What would a state of the art instructional video game look like? *Innovate 1*(6). Retrieved from http://innovateonline.info/pdf/vol1_issue6/What_Would_a_State_of_the_Art_Instructional_Video_Game_Look_Like_.pdf

Gee, J. P. (June 17, 2011). *The invective-filled tirade I would like to give if I wasn't so nice: A chat*. Games+Learning+Society Conference. Madison, Wisconsin.

Gee, J. P. (May 26, 2010). *Games and assessment discussion*. Games for Change Conference. New York.

Gibson, D., Aldrich, C., & Prensky, M. (2006). *Games and simulations in online learning: Research and development frameworks*. Hershey, PA: IGI Global. doi:10.4018/978-1-59904-304-3

Gibson, J. J. (1977). The theory of affordances. In Shaw, R., & Bransford, J. (Eds.), *Perceiving, acting, and knowing: Toward an ecological psychology* (pp. 67–82). Hillsdale, NJ: Lawrence Erlbaum.

Gijselaers, W. H. (1996). Connecting problem-based practices with educational theory. *New Directions for Teaching and Learning, 68*, 9–13.

Gladwell, M. (2008). *Outliers: The story of success*. New York, NY: Little, Brown and Company.

Glaser, B. G. (1992). *Emergence vs forcing: Basics of grounded theory analysis*. Sage Publications, Inc.

Gleick, J. (2004). *Isaac Newton*. New York, NY: Vintage Books.

Gobbet, F., Lane, P. C. R., Croker, S., Cheng, P. C. H., Jones, G., Oliver, I., & Pine, J. M. (2001). Chunking mechanisms in human learning. *Trends in Cognitive Sciences, 5*, 236–243. doi:10.1016/S1364-6613(00)01662-4

Goldberg, N. (2005). *Writing down the bones: Freeing the writer within*. Boston, MA: Shambhala Press.

Golightly, D. (1996). Harnessing the interface for domain learning. In M. J. Tauber (Ed.), *Proceedings of the CHI '96 Conference Companion on Human Factors in Computing Systems: Common Ground* (pp. 37-38). Vancouver, BC.

Golledge, R. G. (1999). Human wayfinding and cognitive maps. In Golledge, R. G. (Ed.), *Wayfinding behavior: Cognitive mapping and other spatial processes* (pp. 5–45). Baltimore, MD: The Johns Hopkins University Press.

Gombrich, E. H. (1974). The visual image. In Olson, D. (Ed.), *Media and symbols: The forms of expression, communication and education*. Chicago, IL: University of Chicago Press.

Gomez, L. M., Sherin, M. G., Griesdorn, J., & Finn, L. (2008). Creating social relationships: The role of technology in preservice teacher preparation. *Journal of Teacher Education, 59,* 117–131. doi:10.1177/0022487107314001

Gonzalez, J. A., Jover, L., & Cobo, E. (2010). A web-based learning tool improves student performance in statistics: A randomized masked trial. *Computers & Education, 55*(2), 704–713. doi:10.1016/j.compedu.2010.03.003

Goodson, C. F. (2001). *Providing library services for distance education students: A how-to-do-it manual*. New York, NY: Neal-Schuman Publishers, Inc.

Goodyear, P. (2000). Environments for lifelong learning. In Spector, M. J., & Anderson, T. M. (Eds.), *Integrated and holistic perspectives on learning, instruction and technology: Understanding complexity* (pp. 1–18). Dordrecht, The Netherlands: Kluwer Academic Publishers.

Google. (2011). *Blogger: Create your free blog*. Retrieved from http://www.blogger.com/

Google. (2011). *Google Voice*. Retrieved from http://www.google.com/googlevoice/about.html.

Graham, J. (2009). An uneven balancing act: One library administrator's view on providing library services for distance patrons. *Journal of Library & Information Services in Distance Learning, 3*(2), 43–46. doi:10.1080/15332900903057899

Gredler, M. (1994). *Designing and evaluating games and simulations: A process approach*. Houston, TX: Gulf Publishing Company.

Greenfield, P., & Yan, Z. (2006). Children, adolescents, and the Internet: A new field of inquiry in developmental psychology. *Developmental Psychology, 42,* 391–394. doi:10.1037/0012-1649.42.3.391

Greenhow, C., Robelia, B., & Hughes, J. (2009). Learning, teaching, and scholarship in a digital age. *Educational Researcher, 38*(4), 246–259. doi:10.3102/0013189X09336671

Greeno, J. (1997). On claims that answer the wrong questions. *Educational Researcher, 26*(1), 5–17.

Gregorc, A. (1982). *An adult's guide to style*. Columbia, CT: Gregorc Associates.

Griffin, R., & Franklin, G. (1996). Can college academic performance be predicted using a measure of cognitive style? *Journal of Educational Technology Systems, 24*(4), 375–379.

Gronlund, N. E. (1970). *Stating behavioral objectives for classroom instruction*. New York, NY: Macmillan.

Gunter, G. A., Kenny, R. F., & Vick, E. H. (2008). Taking educational games seriously: Using the RETAIN model to design endogenous fantasy into standalone educational games. *Educational Technology Research and Development, 56,* 511–537. doi:10.1007/s11423-007-9073-2

Guo, R. X. (2009). *Information and communication technology (ICT) literacy in teacher education: A case study of the University of British Columbia*. Köln, Germany: Lap Lambert Academic Publishing AG & Co. KG.

Guo, R. X. (2005). Self-Assessment during online discussion: An action research perspective. In Mann, B. L. (Ed.), *Selected styles in Web-based educational research* (pp. 144–159). Hershey, PA: Idea Group Publishing. doi:10.4018/978-1-59140-732-4.ch010

Hadwin, A. F., Oshige, M., Gress, C. L. Z., & Winne, P. H. (2010). Innovative ways for using gStudy to orchestrate and research social aspects of self-regulated learning. *Computers in Human Behavior, 26*(5), 794–805. doi:10.1016/j.chb.2007.06.007

Hall, E. P., Gott, S. P., & Pokorny, R. A. (1995). *A procedural guide to cognitive task analysis: The PARI methodology. Brooks Airforce Base*. TX: Air Force Human Resources Laboratory.

Hancock, T., Smith, S., Timpte, C., & Wunder, J. (2010). PALs: Fostering student engagement and interactive learning. *Journal of Higher Education Outreach and Engagement, 14,* 4.

Hannafin, M. J. (1989). Interaction strategies and emerging instructional technologies: Psychological perspectives. *Canadian Journal of Educational Communication, 18*(3), 167–179.

Hannifin, M. J., Land, S. M., & Oliver, K. (1999). Open learning environments: Foundations, methods, and models. In Reigeluth, C. M. (Ed.), *Instructional-design theories and models: A new paradigm of instructional theory* (*Vol. II*, pp. 115–140). Mahwah, NJ: Lawrence Erlbaum Associates.

Hannum, W. (2001). Knowledge management in education: helping teachers to work better. *Educational Technology*, (May-June): 47–49.

Harasim, L. (2000). Shift happens: Online education as a new paradigm in learning. *The Internet and Higher Education, 3*(1-2), 41–61. doi:10.1016/S1096-7516(00)00032-4

Harasim, L. (Ed.). (1990). *Online education: Perspectives on a new environment*. New York, NY: Praeger.

Hargreaves, A. (2003). *Teaching in the knowledge society: Education in the age of insecurity*. New York, NY: Teachers College Press.

Harley, S. (1993). Situated learning and classroom instruction. *Educational Technology, 33*(3), 46–51.

Harris, R. (2009). Improving tacit knowledge transfer within SMEs through e-collaboration. *Journal of European Industrial Training, 33*(3), 215–231. doi:10.1108/03090590910950587

Harris, R. A., & Niven, J. (2002). *Retrofitting theory to practice - A reflection on the development of an e-learning community*. Retrieved from http://www.scrolla.ac.uk/resources/Harris_Community_of_practice_Symp3.htm

Harrow, A. (1972). *A taxonomy of the psychomotor domain. A guide for developing behavioral objectives*. New York, NY: McKay.

Hart, R. (1981). Language study and the PLATO IV System. *Studies in Language Learning, 3*, 1–24.

Hatton, N., & Smith, D. (1995). Reflection in teacher education: Toward definition and implementation. *Teaching and Teacher Education, 11*(1), 33–49. doi:10.1016/0742-051X(94)00012-U

Haythornwaite, C. (2006). Facilitating collaboration in online learning. *Journal of Asynchronous Learning Networks, 10*(1), 7–24.

Health Resources and Services Administration. (2002). *National advisory council on nurse education and practice: Second report to the Secretary of Health and Human Services and Congress*. Rockville, MD: Author.

Heinich, R., Molenda, M., Russell, J. D., & Smaldino, S. E. (1996). *Instructional media and technologies for learning, 5/E*. Englewood Cliffs, NJ: Prentice-Hall, Inc., Simon & Schuster Company.

Henning, M. M. (2001). Closing the gap: Using conferencing software to connect distance education students and faculty. *Journal of Library Administration, 31*(1/2), 233–246. doi:10.1300/J111v32n01_02

Henningsson, S. (2003). *Deep learning with e-learning?* Master's thesis. Department of Informatics. Lund University. Lund, Sweden.

Henri, F., & Pudelko, B. (2003). Understanding and analyzing activity and learning in virtual communities. *Journal of Computer Assisted Learning, 19*, 474–487. doi:10.1046/j.0266-4909.2003.00051.x

Herbst, P. G. (2006). Teaching geometry with problems: Negotiating instructional situations and mathematical tasks. *Journal for Research in Mathematics Education, 37*(4), 313–347.

Hernandez-Serrano, J., & Jonassen, D. H. (2003). The effects of case libraries on problem solving. *Journal of Computer Assisted Learning, 19*(1), 103–114. doi:10.1046/j.0266-4909.2002.00010.x

Herrington, A., & Herrington, J. (2006). What is an authentic learning environment? In Herrington, A., & Herrington, J. (Eds.), *Authentic learning environments in higher education*. Hershey, PA: Information Science Publishing. doi:10.4018/978-1-59140-594-8.ch001

Herrington, J., & Oliver, R. (2006). Professional development for the online teacher: An authentic approach. In Herrington, A., & Herrington, J. (Eds.), *Authentic learning environments in higher education*. Hershey, PA: Information Science Publishing. doi:10.4018/978-1-59140-594-8.ch020

Hertel, J. P., & Millis, B. J. (2002). *Using simulations to promote learning in higher education.* Sterling, VA: Stylus.

Herzberg, F. (1966). *Work and the nature of man.* Cleveland, OH: World.

Hicks, R. E., & Young, R. K. (1972). Part-whole list transfer in free recall: A reappraisal. *Journal of Experimental Psychology, 96*(2), 328–333. doi:10.1037/h0033643

Hillman, D., Willis, D. J., & Gunawardena, C. (1994). Learner-interface interaction in distance education: An extension of contemporary models and strategies for practitioners. *American Journal of Distance Education, 8*(2), 30–42. doi:10.1080/08923649409526853

Hirumi, A., Appelman, B., Rieber, L., & Van Eck, R. (2010). Preparing instructional designers for game-based learning: Part I. *TechTrends, 54*(3), 27–37. doi:10.1007/s11528-010-0400-9

Hirumi, A., Appelman, B., Reiber, L., & van Eck, R. (2010). Preparing instructional designers for game-based learning: Part 2. *TechTrends, 54,* 19–27. doi:10.1007/s11528-010-0416-1

Hmelo-Silver, C. E., Marathe, S., & Lui, L. (2007). Fish swim, rocks sit, and lungs breathe: Expert-novice understanding of complex systems. *Journal of the Learning Sciences, 16*(3), 307–331. doi:10.1080/10508400701413401

Hmelo-Silver, C. E., Duncan, R. G., & Chinn, C. A. (2007). Scaffolding and achievement in problem-based and inquiry learning: A Response to Kirschner, Sweller, and Clark (2006). *Educational Psychologist, 42*(2), 99–107. Retrieved from http://www.cogtech.usc.edu/publications/hmelo_ep07.pdf. doi:10.1080/00461520701263368

Hollan, J., Hutchins, E., & Kirsh, D. (2000). Distributed cognition: Toward a new foundation for human-computer interaction research. *ACM Transactions on Computer-Human Interaction, 7*(2), 174–196. doi:10.1145/353485.353487

Holt, R. D., & Oliver, M. (2002). Evaluating web-based modules during and MSc programme in dental public health: A case study. *British Dental Journal, 193*(5), 283–286. doi:10.1038/sj.bdj.4801546

Holyoak, K. J., & Thagard, P. (1989). Analogical mapping by constraint satisfaction. *Cognitive Science, 13,* 295–355. doi:10.1207/s15516709cog1303_1

Horn, R. E. (1999). *Visual language: Global communication for the 21st century.* Bainbridge Island, WA: MacroVU, Inc.

Huang, J. S., & Andrews, S. (2010). Situated development and use of language learner strategies: Voices from EFL students. *Language Learning Journal, 38*(1), 19–35. doi:10.1080/09571730902717430

Huang, W. H. (2011). Learners' motivational processing and mental effort investment in an online game-based learning environment: A preliminary analysis. *Computers in Human Behavior, 27,* 694–704. http://dx.doi.org/10.1016/j.chb.2010.07.021. doi:10.1016/j.chb.2010.07.021

Huang, W. H., Huang, W. Y., & Tschopp, J. A. (2010). Sustaining iterative game playing processes in DGBL: The relationship between motivational processing and outcome processing. *Computers & Education, 55*(2), 789–797. .doi:10.1016/j.compedu.2010.03.011

Huang, W., & Johnson, T. (2008). Instructional game design using cognitive load theory. In Ferdig, R. (Ed.), *Handbook of research on effective electronic gaming in education* (pp. 1143–1165). Hershey, PA: Information Science Reference. doi:10.4018/978-1-59904-808-6.ch066

Huang, W., & Aragon, S. (2009). An integrated evaluation approach for e-learning systems in career and technical education. In Wang, V. C. X. (Ed.), *Handbook of research on e-learning applications for career and technical education: Technologies for vocational training.* Hershey, PA: IGI Global. doi:10.4018/978-1-60566-739-3.ch031

Huang, K., Ge, X., & Bowers, B. (2006). *Virtual Clinic: Simulated ethical decision making in nursing education.* Paper presented at the Annual Meeting of the Association for Educational Communications and Technology.

Huang, W.-H. D., & Yang, D. (in press). *Empowering digital learners: A self-managing learning process framework for digital game-based learning systems (DGBLS).*

Hung, D., & Nichani, M. R. (2002). Bringing communities of practice into schools: Implications for instructional technologies from Vygotskian perspectives. *International Journal of Instructional Media, 29*(2).

Hunt, L. (2006). Authentic learning at work. In Herrington, A., & Herrington, J. (Eds.), *Authentic learning environments in higher education*. Hershey, PA: Information Science Publishing. doi:10.4018/978-1-59140-594-8.ch019

Hutchins, E. (1995). *Cognition in the wild*. Cambridge, MA: MIT Press.

Hutchins, E., Hollan, J. D., & Norman, D. A. (1986). Direct manipulation interfaces. In Norman, D. A., & Draper, S. W. (Eds.), *User centered system design: New perspectives in human-computer interaction*. Hillsdale, NJ: Lawrence Erlbaum.

Hutchins, E. (2000). *Distributed cognition*. Retrieved October 5, 2009, from http://eclectic.ss.uci.edu/~drwhite/Anthro179a/DistributedCognition.pdf

Huzinga, J. (1950). *Homo Ludens: A study of the play-element in culture*. Boston, MA: Beacon Press.

IBM. (2009). *"Serious game" provides training to tackle global business challenges*. Retrieved from http://www-03.ibm.com/press/us/en/pressrelease/26734.wss

Ikegulu, P. R., & Ikegulu, T. N. (1999). *The effectiveness of window presentation strategy and cognitive style of field dependence status on learning from mediated instructions*. Ruston, LA: Center for Statistical Consulting. (ERIC Document Reproduction Service No. ED428758)

Ingram, A. L., & Hathorn, L. G. (2005a). Analyzing collaboration in online communications. In Howard, C., Boettcher, J., Justice, L., Schenk, K. D., Rogers, P. L., & Berg, G. A. (Eds.), *Encyclopedia of distance learning* (Vol. 1, pp. 83–89). Hershey, PA: Idea Group, Inc. doi:10.4018/978-1-59140-555-9.ch013

Ingram, A. L., & Hathorn, L. G. (2005b). Collaboration in online communications. In Howard, C., Boettcher, J., Justice, L., Schenk, K. D., Rogers, P. L., & Berg, G. A. (Eds.), *Encyclopedia of distance learning* (Vol. 1, pp. 264–268). Hershey, PA: Idea Group, Inc. doi:10.4018/978-1-59140-555-9.ch038

ipadio. (n.d.). *ipadio: Broadcast live to the web from a phone call*. Retrieved from http://ipadio.com/

Jacoby, S., & Gonzales, P. (1991). The constitution of expert-novice in scientific discourse. *Issues in Applied Linguistics*, *2*(2), 149–181.

Jana, R. (2007). *Microsoft's games get serious*. Retrieved from http://www.businessweek.com/innovate/content/dec2007/id20071220_808794.htm

Jenkins, H. (2006). *Convergence culture: Where old and new media collide*. New York, NY: New York University Press.

Jenkins, H., Clinton, K., Purushotma, R., Robison, A. J., & Weigel, M. (2006) *Confronting the challenges of participatory culture: Media education for the 21st century* [white paper]. MacArthur Foundation.

Jensen, J. F. (1998). Interactivity: Tracking a new concept in media and communication studies. *Nordicom Review*, *1*, 185–205.

Jensen, J. F. (2008). The concept of interactivity – Revisited. *Proceeding of the 1st International Conference on Designing Interactive User Experiences for TV and Video*. Retrieved May 19, 2011, from http://portal.acm.org/citation.cfm?id=1453831

Johnson, G. J., Bruner, G. C., & Kumar, A. (2006). Interactivity and its facets revisited. *Journal of Advertising*, *35*(4), 35–52. doi:10.2753/JOA0091-3367350403

Johnson, L., Smith, R., Willis, H., Levine, A., & Haywood, K. (2011). *The 2011 horizon report*. Austin, TX: The New Media Consortium.

Johnson, T. E., & Huang, W. D. (2008). Complex skills development for today's workforce. In Ifenthaler, D., Spector, J. M., & Pirnay-Dummer, P. (Eds.), *Understanding models for learning and instruction: Essays in honor of Norbert M. Seel* (pp. 305–325). New York City, NY: Springer. doi:10.1007/978-0-387-76898-4_15

Johnson, D. (2009). *Analysis and deconstruction of the institution*. Gamasutra: The art and business of making games. Retrieved from http://www.gamasutra.com/view/news/23960/Analysis_Portal_and_the_Deconstruction_of_the_Institution.php

Johnson, L., Levine, A., Smith, R., & Stone, S. (2010). *The 2010 Horizon report*. Austin, TX: The New Media Consortium. Retrieved from http://wp.nmc.org/horizon-k12-2010/chapters/game-based-learning/#0

Jonassen, D. H. (1985). Interactive lesson designs: A taxonomy. *Educational Technology*, *25*(6), 7–17.

Jonassen, D. H. (2000). *Computers as mindtools for schools*. Upper Saddle River, NJ: Prentice-Hall.

Jonassen, D. H. (2003). *Learning to solve problems with technology: A constructivist perspective*. Upper Saddle River, NJ: Merrill/Prentice Hall.

Jonassen, D. H., Peck, K. L., & Wilson, B. G. (1998). *Learning with technology: A constructivist perspective.* Columbus, OH: Prentice-Hall.

Jonassen, D. H., & Grabowski, B. L. (1993). *Handbook of individual differences, learning, and instruction.* Hillsdale, NJ: Lawrence Erlbaum.

Jonassen, D., & Hernandez-Serrano, J. (2002). Case-based reasoning and instructional design: Using stories to support problem solving. *Educational Technology Research and Development, 50*(2), 65–77. doi:10.1007/BF02504994

Jonassen, D. H. (2000). Towards a meta-theory of problem solving. *Educational Technology Research and Development, 48*(4), 63–85. doi:10.1007/BF02300500

Jonassen, D. H. (1988). Integrating learning strategies into courseware to facilitate deeper processing. In Jonassen, D. H. (Ed.), *Instructional designs for microcomputer courseware* (pp. 151–181). Hillsdale, NJ: Lawrence Erlbaum.

Jonassen, D. H., & Reeves, T. C. (1996). Learning with technology: Using computers as cognitive tools. In Jonassen, D. H. (Ed.), *Handbook of research for educational communications and technology* (pp. 693–719). New York, NY: Macmillan.

Jonassen, D. H., Cernusca, D., & Ionas, I. G. (2006). Constructivism and instructional design: The emergence of the learning sciences and design research. In Reiser, R., & Dempsey, J. (Eds.), *Trends and issues in instructional design and technology*. Columbus, OH: Merrill.

Jonassen, D. H. (2005). *Let us learn to solve problems.* Retrieved September 30, 2005, from http://it.coe.uga.edu/itforum/paper83/paper83.html

Kagan, J. (1966). Reflection-impulsivity: The generality and dynamics of conceptual tempo. *Journal of Abnormal Psychology, 71*, 17–24. doi:10.1037/h0022886

Kagan, J. (2002). *Surprise, uncertainty and mental structures*. Cambridge, MA: Harvard University Press.

Kalyuga, S. (2007). Enhancing instructional efficiency of interactive e-learning environments: A cognitive load perspective. *Educational Psychology Review, 19*, 387–399. doi:10.1007/s10648-007-9051-6

Kalyuga, S. (2009). Instructional design for the development of transferable knowledge and skills: A cognitive load perspective. *Computers in Human Behavior, 25*, 332–338. doi:10.1016/j.chb.2008.12.019

Kanfer, R., & Ackerman, P. (1996). A self-regulatory skills perspective to reducing cognitive interference. In Sarason, I. G., Pierce, G. R., & Sarason, B. R. (Eds.), *Cognitive interference: Theories, methods, and findings* (pp. 153–171). Mahwah, NJ: Lawrence Erlbaum Associates.

Kantrowitz, M. (2010, February 4). *Higher education funding in President Obama's FY 2011 budget.* Council on Law in Higher Education. Retrieved March 14, 2011, from http://www.clhe.org/marketplaceofideas/financial-aid/higher-education-funding-in-president-obamas-fy-2011-budget/

Karasavvidis, I. (2002). Distributed cognition and educational practice. *Journal of Interactive Learning Research, 13*(1/2), 11–29.

Kauffman, D., Ge, X., Xie, K., & Chen, C.-H. (2008). Prompting in web-based environments: Supporting self-monitoring and problem solving skills in college students. *Journal of Educational Computing Research, 38*(2), 115–137. doi:10.2190/EC.38.2.a

Ke, F., & Grabowski, B. (2007). Gameplaying for maths learning: Cooperative or not? *British Journal of Educational Technology, 38*(2), 249–259. doi:10.1111/j.1467-8535.2006.00593.x

Kebrichi, M. (2010). Factors effecting teachers' adoption of educational computer games: A case study. *British Journal of Educational Technology, 41*(2), 256–270. doi:10.1111/j.1467-8535.2008.00921.x

Keefe, J., & Jenkins, J. (1996). *Instruction and the learning environment*. West Larchmont, NY: Eye on Education.

Keller, J. M. (1987b). The systematic process of motivational design. *Performance and Instruction, 26*(9/10), 1–8. doi:10.1002/pfi.4160260902

Keller, J. M. (2008). An integrative theory of motivation, volition, and performance. *Technology, Instruction, Cognition, and Learning, 6,* 79–104.

Keller, J. M. (2009). *Motivational design for learning and performance. The ARCS model approach.* Springer.

Keller, J. M. (1979). Motivation and instructional design: A theoretical perspective. *Journal of Instructional Development, 2*(4), 26–34. doi:10.1007/BF02904345

Keller, J. M. (1987a). Development and use of the ARCS model of instructional design. *Journal of Instructional Development, 10*(3), 2–10. doi:10.1007/BF02905780

Keller, J. M. (1987b). Strategies for stimulating the motivation to learn. *Performance & Instruction, 26*(8), 1–7. doi:10.1002/pfi.4160260802

Keller, J. M. (1983). Motivational design of instruction. In Reigeluth, C. M. (Ed.), *Instructional design theories and models: An overview of their current status* (pp. 386–434). Hillsdale, NJ: Lawrence Erlbaum Associates.

Keller, J. M. (1984). The use of the ARCS model of motivation in teacher training. In Shaw, K., & Trott, A. J. (Eds.), *Aspects of educational technology* (*Vol. XVII,* pp. 140–145). London, UK: Kogan Page.

Kennedy, G. E. (2004). Promoting cognition in multimedia interactivity research. *Journal of Interactive Learning Research, 15*(1), 43–61.

Kennedy, C. (2005). *Constructing PADI measurement models for the BEAR Scoring Engine (PADI Technical Report 7).* Menlo Park, CA: SRI International.

Kester, L., & Kirschner, A. (2009). Effects of fading support on hypertext navigation and performance in student-centered e-learning environments. *Interactive Learning Environments, 17*(2), 165–179. doi:10.1080/10494820802054992

Khalil, M. K., Paas, F., Johnson, T. E., & Payer, A. F. (2005). Design of interactive and dynamic anatomical visualizations: The implication of cognitive load theory. *Anatomical Record. Part B, New Anatomist, 286B,* 15–20. doi:10.1002/ar.b.20078

King, D. B., & Wertheimer, M. (2007). *Max Wertheimer and gestalt theory.* New York, NY: Transaction Publishing.

Kirby, P. (1979). *Cognitive style, learning style and transfer skill acquisition.* Columbus, OH: The National Center for Research in Vocational Education, The Ohio State University.

Kirschner, P. A., Sweller, J., & Clark, R. E. (2006). Why minimal guidance during instruction does not work: An analysis of the failure of constructivist, discovery, problem-based, experiential, and inquiry-based teaching. *Educational Psychologist, 41,* 75–86. doi:10.1207/s15326985ep4102_1

Klawe, M. M. (1999). *Computer games, education and interfaces: The E-GEMS project,* (pp. 36-39). Retrieved from http://www.informatik.uni-trier.de/~ley/db/conf/graphicsinterface/graphicsinterface1999.html

Kling, R., & Courtright, C. (2004). Group behavior and learning in electronic forums: A socio-technical approach. In Barab, S. A., Kling, R., & Gray, J. H. (Eds.), *Designing for virtual communities in the service of learning.* Cambridge, UK: Cambridge University Press.

Klopfer, E., Osterweil, S., Groff, J., & Haas, J. (2009a). *Using the technology of today, in the classroom of today: The instructional power of digital games, social networking, simulations and how teachers can leverage them* [white paper]. The Education Arcade, MIT.

Klopfer, E., Osterweil, S., & Salen, K. (2009b) *Moving learning games forward: Obstacles, opportunities, & openness* [white paper]. The Education Arcade, MIT.

Knowles, M. (1973). *The adult learner: A neglected species.* Houston, TX: Gulf Publishing Company.

Koc, M. (2005). Individual learner differences in web-based learning environments: From cognitive, affective and social-cultural perspectives. *Turkish Online Journal of Distance Education, 6*(4), 12–22.

Koenders, A. (2006). An authentic online learning environment in university introductory biology. In Herrington, A., & Herrington, J. (Eds.), *Authentic learning environments in higher education.* Hershey, PA: Information Science Publishing. doi:10.4018/978-1-59140-594-8.ch004

Koffka, K. (1935). *Principles of Gestalt psychology.* London, UK: Lund Humphries.

Kohler, W. (1992). *Gestalt psychology: The definitive statement of the gestalt theory.* New York, NY: Liveright Publishing. (Original work published 1947)

Kolodner, J. L., & Guzdial, M. (2000). Theory and practice of case-based learning aids. In Jonassen, D. H., & Land, S. M. (Eds.), *Theoretical foundations of learning environments* (pp. 215–242). Mahwah, NJ: Lawrence Erlbaum.

Kontos, F., & Henkel, H. (2008). Live instruction for distance students: Development of synchronous online workshops. *Public Services Quarterly, 4*(1), 1–11. doi:10.1080/15228950802135657

Koschmann, T. (1996). Paradigm shifts and instructional technology: An introduction. In Koschmann, T. (Ed.), *CSCL: Theory and practice of an emerging paradigm* (pp. 1–23). Mahwah, NJ: Lawrence Erlbaum.

Koster, R. (2005). *A theory of fun for game design.* Scottsdale, AZ: Paraglyph Press.

Kovalchick, A., & Dawson, K. (Eds.). (2004a). *Education and technology: An encyclopedia (Vol. 1).* Santa Barbara, CA: ABC-CLIO.

Kovalchick, A., & Dawson, K. (Eds.). (2004b). *Education and technology: An encyclopedia (Vol. 2).* Santa Barbara, CA: ABC-CLIO.

Krathwohl, D. R., Bloom, B. S., & Masia, B. B. (1964). *Taxonomy of educational objectives: The classification of educational goals. Handbook II: Affective domain.* New York, NY: David McKay Co., Inc.

Kuhn, T. (1996). *The structure of scientific revolutions* (3rd ed.). Chicago, IL: University of Chicago Press.

Kuhn, D., & Pease, M. (2008). What needs to develop in the development of inquiry skills? *Cognition and Instruction, 46*(4), 512–559. doi:10.1080/07370000802391745

Kulik, C.-L. C., & Kulik, J. A. (1991). Effectiveness of computer-based instruction: an updated analysis. *Computers in Human Behavior, 7*(1/2), 75–94. doi:10.1016/0747-5632(91)90030-5

Lai, M., & Law, N. (2006). Peer scaffolding of knowledge building through collaborative groups with differential learning experiences. *Journal of Educational Computing Research, 35*(2), 123–144. doi:10.2190/GW42-575W-Q301-1765

Laidlaw, S. (2009, October 3). *The top 10 most important concepts in middle-school math.* Retrieved from http://www.imagineeducation.org/matharticles/

Laidlaw, S. (2010, January 31). *History of imagine education and our story-based math.* Retrieved from http://www.imagineeducation.org/matharticles/

Lajoie, S. (2000a). *Computers as cognitive tools: No more walls (Vol. II).* Mahwah, NJ: Lawrence Erlbaum Associates.

Lajoie, S. (2005). Extending the scaffolding metaphor. *Instructional Science, 33*(5), 541–557. doi:10.1007/s11251-005-1279-2

Lajoie, S., & Derry, S. J. (1993). *Computer as cognitive tools.* Hillsdale, NJ: Lawerence Erlbaum Associates.

Lajoie, S. (2000b). Introduction: Breaking camp to find new summits. In Lajoie, S. (Ed.), *Computers as cognitive tools: No more walls.* Mahwah, NJ: Lawrence Erlbaum Associates.

Lajoie, S. P. (2005). Cognitive tools for the mind: The promises of technology—Cognitive amplifiers or bionic prosthetics? In Sternberg, R., & Preiss, D. (Eds.), *Intelligence and technology: The impact of tools on the nature and development of human abilities* (pp. 87–101). Mahwah, NJ: Lawrence Erlbaum.

Lakoff, G. (2008). *The political mind: Why you can't understand 21st-century American politics with an 18th-century brain.* New York, NY: Viking, Penguin Books.

Land, S., & Zembal-Saul, C. (2003). Scaffolding reflection and articulation of scientific explanations in a data-rich, project-based learning environment: An investigation of progress portfolio. *Educational Technology Research and Development, 51*(4), 65–84. doi:10.1007/BF02504544

Larkin, J., & Simon, H. (1987). Why a diagram is (sometimes) worth ten thousand words. *Cognitive Science, 11*, 65–99. doi:10.1111/j.1551-6708.1987.tb00863.x

Lauerman, J. (2011, February 14). Higher education funding cut by $89 billion over 10 years in Obama budget. *Bloomberg.* Retrieved March 14, 2011, from http://www.bloomberg.com/news/2011-02-14/higher-education-funding-cut-by-89-billion-over-10-years-in-obama-budget.html

Lave, J., & Wenger, E. (1991). *Situated learning: Legitimate peripheral participation.* Cambridge, UK: Cambridge University Press.

Lave, J. (1996). Teaching, as learning, in practice. *Mind, Culture, and Activity, 3*(3), 149–164. doi:10.1207/s15327884mca0303_2

Law, V., Ataman, I., & Ge, X. (2010). *Virtual Drug Lab - Pharmacokinetics in an open-ended learning environment.* Paper presented at the The Annual Conference of Association for Educational Communications and Technology.

Leahy, R. (2009). *Authentic educating.* Lanham, MD: University Press of America, Inc.

Learning, A. (n.d.). Contextual Learning. *Adult Learning -. Theory into Practice.* Retrieved from http://www.nald.ca/adultlearningcourse/glossary.htm.

Lee, O. (2010). Facilitating preservice teachers' reflection through interactive online journal writing. *Physical Educator, 67*(3), 128–139.

Lee, J., Carter-Wells, J., Glaeser, B., Ivers, K., & Street, C. (2006). Facilitating the development of a learning community in an online graduate program. *Quarterly Review of Distance Education, 7*(1), 13–33.

Lee, J., & Park, O.-C. (2007). Adaptive instructional systems. In Spector, J. M., Merrill, M. D., van Merriënboer, J., & Driscoll, M. P. (Eds.), *Handbook of research for educational communications and technology* (3rd ed., pp. 469–484). New York, NY: Routledge.

Lee, M. J. (1990). *Effects of different loci of instructional control on students' meta cognition and cognition: Learner vs. program control.* Paper presented at the Annual Convention of the Association for Educational Communication and Technology, (ERIC Document Reproduction Service No. ED 323938).

Leutner, D. (2004). Instructional-design principles for adaptivity in open learning environments. In Seel, N. M., & Dijkstra, S. (Eds.), *Curriculum, plans, and processes in instructional design: International perspectives* (pp. 289–308). Mahwah, NJ: Erlbaum.

Levitin, D. (2007). *This is your brain on music: The science of a human obsession.* New York, NY: Plume/Penguin.

Levy, Y. (2008). An empirical development of critical value factors (CVF) of online learning activities: An application of activity theory and cognitive value theory. *Computers & Education, 51*(4), 1664–1675. doi:10.1016/j.compedu.2008.04.003

Liang, H.-N., Parsons, P. C., Wu, H.-C., & Sedig, K. (2010). An exploratory study of interactivity in visualization tools: 'Flow' of interaction. *Journal of Interactive Learning Research, 21*(1), 5–45.

Liang, H.-N., & Sedig, K. (2010). Role of interaction in enhancing the epistemic utility of 3D mathematical visualizations. *International Journal of Computers for Mathematical Learning, 15*(3), 191–224. doi:10.1007/s10758-010-9165-7

Lieberman, A. (1996). Creating intentional learning communities. *Educational Leadership, 54*(3), 51–55.

Lietzau, J. A., & Mann, B. J. (2009). Breaking out of the asynchronous box: Using web conferencing in distance learning. *Journal of Library & Information Services in Distance Learning, 3*(3/4), 108–119. doi:10.1080/15332900903375291

Lin, X., Hmelo, C., Kinzer, C., & Secules, T. (1999). Designing technology to support reflection. *Educational Technology Research and Development, 47*(3), 43–62. doi:10.1007/BF02299633

Linn, M., Clark, D., & Slotta, J. (2003). WISE design for knowledge integration. *Science Education, 87*(4), 517–538. doi:10.1002/sce.10086

Linn, R. L. (1994). Performance assessment: Policy promises and technical measurement standards. *Educational Researcher, 23*(9), 4–14.

Linn, R. L. (2000). Assessments and accountability. *Educational Researcher, 29*(2), 4–16.

Linn, R. L., Baker, E. L., & Dunbar, S. B. (1991). Complex performance-based assessment: Expectations and validation criteria. *Educational Researcher, 20*(8), 5–21.

Liu, Y., & Shrum, L. J. (2002). What is interactivity and is it always such a good thing? Implications of definition, person, and situation for the influence of interactivity on advertising effectiveness. *Journal of Advertising, 31*(4), 53–64.

Liu, M., & Reed, W. M. (1994). The relationship between the learning strategies and learning styles in a hypermedia environment. *Computers in Human Behavior*, *10*(4), 419–434. doi:10.1016/0747-5632(94)90038-8

Liu, X. J., Magjuka, R. J., & Lee, S. H. (2008). The effects of cognitive thinking styles, trust, conflict management on online students' learning and virtual team performance. *British Journal of Educational Technology*, *39*(5), 829–846. doi:10.1111/j.1467-8535.2007.00775.x

Livetext. (2011). *General overview*. Retrieved from https://www.livetext.com/overview/.

Lloyd, B. T. (2002). A conceptual framework for examining adolescent identity, media influence, and social development. *Review of General Psychology*, *6*, 73–91. doi:10.1037/1089-2680.6.1.73

LocaModa Inc. (2009). *Wiffiti*. Retrieved from http://wiffiti.com/

Lombardi, M. M. (May 2007). Authentic learning for the 21st century: An overview. D. G. Oblinger (Ed.). *EDUCAUSE 2007*. Retrieved from http://net.educause.edu/ir/library/pdf/ELI3009.pdf

Long, R. E. (2005). Using simulation to teach resuscitation: An important patient safety tool. *Critical Care Nursing Clinics of North America*, *17*, 1–8. doi:10.1016/j.ccell.2004.09.001

Lunsford, A. (2006). *The Stanford study of writing*. Retrieved February 28, 2011, from http://ssw.stanford.edu/

Macfadyen, L. P., & Dawson, S. (2010). Mining LMS data to develop an "early warning system" for educators: A proof of concept. *Computers & Education*, *54*(2), 588–599. doi:10.1016/j.compedu.2009.09.008

MacKay, C. (2000). The trial of Napoleon, a case study for using mock trials. *Teaching History: A Journal of Methods, 25*(2).

MacNeil, R. (1980). The relationship of cognitive style and instructional style to the learning performance of undergraduate students. *The Journal of Educational Research*, *73*(6), 354–359.

Macpherson, R., & Stanovich, K. E. (2007). Cognitive ability, thinking dispositions, and instructional set as predictors of critical thinking. *Learning and Individual Differences*, *17*(2), 115–127. doi:10.1016/j.lindif.2007.05.003

Magerko, B. (2009). The future of digital game-based learning. In Ferdig, R. E. (Ed.), *Handbook of research on effective electronic gaming in education* (*Vol. III*, pp. 1274–1288). Hershey, PA: Information Science Reference.

Malone, T. W., & Lepper, M. R. (1987). Making learning fun. A taxonomy of intrinsic motivations for learning. In R. E. Snow & M. J. Farr (Eds.), *Aptitude, learning, and instruction, volume 3: Cognitive and affective process analyses* (pp. 223-253). Hillsdale, NJ: Lawrence Erlbaum.

Manfra, M. M. (2009). Action research: Exploring the theoretical divide between practical and critical approaches. [JoCI]. *Journal of Curriculum and Instruction*, *3*(1), 32–46. Retrieved January 18, 2011.

Manlove, S., Lazonder, A. W., & de Jong, T. (2006). Regulative support for collaborative scientific inquiry learning. *Journal of Computer Assisted Learning*, *22*(2), 87–98. doi:10.1111/j.1365-2729.2006.00162.x

Manlove, S., Lazonder, A. W., & de Jong, T. (2009). Trends and issues of regulative support use during inquiry learning: Patterns from three studies. *Computers in Human Behavior*, *25*(4), 795–803. doi:10.1016/j.chb.2008.07.010

Mariano, G. J., Doolittle, P., & Hicks, D. (2009). Fostering transfer in multimedia instructional materials. In Zheng, R. (Ed.), *Cognitive effects of multimedia learning* (pp. 237–258). Hershey, PA: Information Science Reference/IGI Global.

Marino, M. T., Basham, J. D., & Beecher, C. C. (2011). Using video games as an alternative science assessment for students with disabilities and at-risk learners. *Science Scope*, *34*(5), 36–41.

Marshall, J., & Rossett, A. (2000). Knowledge management for school-based educators. In Spector, M. J., & Anderson, T. M. (Eds.), *Integrated and holistic perspectives on learning, instruction and technology* (pp. 19–34). Dordrecht, The Netherlands: Kluwer Academic Publishers.

Martin, F. (2008). Effects of practice in a linear and non-linear web-based learning environment. *Journal of Educational Technology & Society, 11*(4), 81–93.

Mashable, Inc. (2011). *40+ free blog hosts.* Retrieved from http://mashable.com/2007/08/06/free-blog-hosts/

Massey, B. L., & Levy, M. R. (1999). Interactivity, online journalism, and English-language Web newspapers in Asia. *Journalism & Mass Communication Quarterly, 76*(1), 138–151.

Mathur, S., & Murray, T. (2006). Authentic assessment online: A practical and theoretical challenge in higher education. In Williams, D. D., Howell, S. L., & Hricko, M. (Eds.), *Online assessment, measurement, and evaluation: Emerging practices.* Hershey, PA: Information Science Publishing. doi:10.4018/978-1-59140-747-8.ch014

Maxwell, J. A. (1996). *Qualitative research design: An interactive approach (Vol. 41).* Thousand Oaks, CA: Sage Publications.

Mayer, R. E. (2001). *Multimedia learning.* New York, NY: Cambridge University Press.

Mayer, R. E. (2003). Elements of science of e-learning. *Journal of Educational Computing Research, 29,* 297–313. doi:10.2190/YJLG-09F9-XKAX-753D

Mayer, R. (1997). Learners as information processors: Legacies and limitations of educational psychology's second metaphor. *Educational Psychologist, 32*(3/4), 151–161.

Mayer, R., & Moreno, R. (2003). Nine ways to reduce cognitive load in multimedia learning. *Educational Psychologist, 38,* 43–52. doi:10.1207/S15326985EP3801_6

Mayrath, M., Clarke-Midura, J., Dede, C., & Code, J. (2011). *A framework for designing assessment activities for virtual worlds.* Paper presented at the AERA 2011 Annual Meeting.

McCall, J. (2011). *Gaming the past: Using video games to teach secondary history.* New York, NY: Routledge.

McCall, J. (October 4, 2010). *Gaming the past: Simulation games in history class.* Goldberg Center and Digital Union Game-based Learning Conference. Columbus, Ohio.

McCarthy, J. P., & Anderson, L. (2000). Active learning techniques versus traditional teaching styles: Two experiments from history and political science. *Innovative Higher Education, 24*(4).

McCarthy, J. (in press). Connected: Online mentoring in *Facebook* for final year digital media students. In Song, H. (Ed.), *Interactivity in e-learning: Cases and frameworks.* Hershey, PA: IGI Publishers.

McCarthy, C. A. (2004). Interactive video technology for distance learning: An assessment of interactive video technology as a tool. *Journal of Library & Information Services in Distance Learning, 1*(4), 5-31. doi:1300/J192v01n04_02

McElrath, E., & McDowell, K. (2008). Pedagogical strategies for building community in graduate level in distance education courses. *Journal of Online Learning and Teaching, 4*(1), 117–127.

McFarlane, A. (1997). Where are we and how did we get there? In McFarlane, A. (Ed.), *Information technology and authentic learning.* New York, NY: Routledge. doi:10.4324/9780203440674

McFarlane, A., Sparrowhawk, A., & Heald, Y. (2002). *Report on the educational use of games.* Retrieved from http://www.teem.org.uk/publications/teem_gamesined_full.pdf

McGonigal, J. (2011). *Reality is broken: What games make us better and how they can change the world.* New York, NY: The Penguin Press.

McGovern, G. Norton, R., & O'Dowd, C. (2001). *Web content style guide: The essential reference for online writers, editors, and managers.* Upper Saddle River, NJ: FT Press.

McKeachie, W. J., & Svinicki, M. (2006). *McKeachie's teaching tips: Strategies, research and theory for college and university teachers.* Boston, MA: Houghton Mifflin, Co.

McLellan, H. (1996). Being digital: Implications for education. *Educational Technology, 36*(6), 5–20.

McLuhan, M. (1967). *The medium is the massage.* Corte Madera, CA: Gingko Press.

McMahon, M., & Luca, J. (2001). *Assessing students' self-regulatory skills*. Retrieved from http://www.ascilite.org. au/conferences/melbourne01/pdf/papers/mcmahonm.pdf

McManus, R. (2005). Web 2.0 is not about version numbers or betas. *Read/WriteWeb*. Retrieved July 18, 2011, from http://www.readwriteweb.com/archives/web_20_is_not_a.php

McNeill, K. L., Lizotte, D. J., Krajcik, J., & Marx, R. W. (2006). Supporting students' construction of scientific explanations by fading scaffolds in instructional materials. *Journal of the Learning Sciences, 15*(2), 153–191. doi:10.1207/s15327809jls1502_1

McPherson, S. L. (2000). Expert-novice differences in planning strategies during collegiate singles tennis competition. *Journal of Sport & Exercise Psychology, 22*(1), 39–62.

Medina, J. (2008). *Brain rules: 12 principles for surviving and thriving at work, home, and school*. Seattle, WA: Pear Press.

Medina, J. (n.d.). *Interview by Ginger Campbell*. Retrieved from http://hw.libsyn.com/p/5/c/6/5c614405b3bd577f/37-brainscience-Medina.mp3?sid=6341d3776c2c99f93b0aa9d671dd523b&l_sid=18369&l_eid=&l_mid=1550378.

Meringoff, L. K. (1980). Influence of the medium of children's story apprehension. *Journal of Educational Psychology, 72*, 240–249. doi:10.1037/0022-0663.72.2.240

Merriam, S. B., & Caffarella, R. S. (1999). *Learning in adulthood* (2nd ed.). San Francisco, CA: Jossey-Bass.

Messick, S. (1984). The nature of cognitive styles: Problems and promise in educational practice. *Educational Psychologist, 19*, 59–74. doi:10.1080/00461528409529283

Messick, S. (1994). The interplay of evidence and consequences in the validation of performance assessments. *Educational Researcher, 23*(2), 13–23.

Meyer, H. (2004). Novice and expert teachers' conceptions of learners' prior knowledge. *Science Education, 88*, 970–983. doi:10.1002/sce.20006

Michael, D., & Chen, S. (2005). *Serious games: Games that educate, train, and inform*. Course Technology PTR.

Michael, D., & Chen, S. (2005). *Proof of learning: Assessment in serious games. Gamasutra: The art and business of making games*. Retrieved from http://www.gamasutra.com/view/feature/2433/proof_of_learning_assessment_in_.php

Microsoft. (2010). *Microsoft Interactive Classroom*. Retrieved May 20, 2011, from http://support.microsoft.com/kb/2395492.

Miller, G. A. (1956). The magical number seven, plus or minus two: Some limits on our capacity for processing information. *Psychological Review, 63*, 81–97. doi:10.1037/h0043158

Milliken, J. (2007). Scaffolding cognitive processes in a marketing curriculum. *Higher Education in Europe, 32*(2-3), 185–191. doi:10.1080/03797720701840740

Mills, G. E. (2007). *Action research: A guide for the teacher researcher*. New York, NY: Pearson Education, Inc.

Mishra, P., & Koehler, M. J. (2006). Technological pedagogical content knowledge: A framework for teacher knowledge. [New York, NY: Columbia University.]. *Teachers College Record, 108*(6), 1017–1054. doi:10.1111/j.1467-9620.2006.00684.x

Mislevy, R., & Haertel, G. (2006). *Implications of evidence centered design for educational testing*. Menlo Park, CA: SRI Interantional.

Mislevy, R., & Rahman, T. (2009). *Design pattern for assessing cause and effect reasoning in reading comprehension*. Menlo Park, CA: SRI Interantional.

Mislevy, R., Steinberg, L. S., & Almond, R. G. (2003). On the structure of educational assessment. *Measurement: Interdisciplinary Research and Perspectives, 1*(1), 3–62. doi:10.1207/S15366359MEA0101_02

Mizuko, I. (2008) Education vs. entertainment: A cultural history of children's software. In K. Salen (Ed.), *The ecology of games: Connecting youth, games, and learning* (pp. 89–116). The John D. and Catherine T. MacArthur Foundation Series on Digital Media and Learning. Cambridge, MA: The MIT Press.

Moallem, M. (2008). Accommodating individual differences in the design of online learning environments: A comparative study. *Journal of Research on Technology in Education, 40*(2), 217–245.

Molenaar, I., van Boxtel, C. A. M., & Sleegers, P. J. C. (2010). The effects of scaffolding metacognitive activities in small groups. *Computers in Human Behavior, 26*(6), 1727–1738. doi:10.1016/j.chb.2010.06.022

Montessori, M. (1949). *The absorbent mind.* Madras, India: The Theosophical House.

Montessori, M. (1994). *From childhood to adolescence* (pp. 7–16). Oxford, England: ABC-Clio.

Moore, J. L., Dickson-Deane, C., & Galyen, K. (2011). e-Learning, online learning, and distance learning environments: Are they the same? *The Internet and Higher Education, 14*(2), 129–135. doi:10.1016/j.iheduc.2010.10.001

Moore, M. (1989). Three types of interaction. *American Journal of Distance Education, 3*(2), 1–7. doi:10.1080/08923648909526659

Moore, J., & Barab, S. A. (2002). The inquiry learning forum: A community of practice approach to online professional development. *TechTrends, 46*(3), 44–49. doi:10.1007/BF02784841

Moore, M. G. (1993). Three types of interactive learners. In K. Harry M., John, & D. Keegan (Eds.), *Distance education: New perspectives* (pp. 19-24). London, UK: Routledge.

Moreno, R., & Mayer, R. E. (1999). Cognitive principles of multimedia learning: The role of modality and contiguity. *Journal of Educational Psychology, 91*, 358–368. doi:10.1037/0022-0663.91.2.358

Morey, J., & Sedig, K. (2004). Using indexed-sequential geometric glyphs to explore visual patterns. In. *Proceedings of Interactive Visualisation and Interaction Technologies, ICCS, 2004*, 996–1003.

Morkes, J., & Nielsen, J. (1997). *Concise, scannable, and objective: How to write for the Web.* Retrieved March 2, 2011, from http://www.useit.com/papers/webwriting/writing.html

Morrison, G. R., Lowther, D. L., & DeMeulle, L. (1999). *Integrating computer technology into the classroom.* Upper Saddle River, NJ: Prentice Hall.

Morrow, D., Miller, L. S., Ridolfo, H., Kokayeff, N., Chang, D., Fischer, U., & Stine-Morrow, E. (2004). Expertise and aging in a pilot decision-making task. *Human Factors and Ergonomics Society Annual Meeting Proceedings. Aging, 5*, 228–232.

Moyer, P., Bolyard, J., & Spikell, M. (2001). Virtual manipulatives in the K-12 classroom. In A. Rogerson (Ed.), *Proceedings of the International Conference on New Ideas in Mathematics Education* (pp. 184–187). Palm Cove, Australia: Autograph.

National Assessment Governing Board (NAGB). (2010). *Science framework for the 2011 national assessment of educational progress.* Washington, D.C.

National Board for Professional Teaching Standards. (2002). What teachers should know and be able to do. Retrieved from http://www.nbpts.org/UserFiles/File/what_teachers.pdf

National Center for Healthcare Leadership (NCHL). (2010-2011a). *Graduate health management education demonstration project.* National Center for Healthcare Leadership. Retrieved March 14, 2011, from http://nchl.org/static.asp?path=2851,3223

National Center for Healthcare Leadership (NCHL). (2010-2011b). *NCHL measures of success.* National Center for Healthcare Leadership. Retrieved March 14, 2011, from http://nchl.org/Documents/NavLink/NCHL_Board_Measures_of_Success_7.09_uid8202009959251.pdf

National Council of State Boards of Nursing (NCSBN). (2005). *Meeting the ongoing challenge of continued competence.* Chicago, IL: Author.

National Research Council. (2011). *Incentives and test-based accountability in public education. Committee on Incentives and Test-Based Accountability in Public Education.* Washington, DC: The National Academies Press.

National Research Council (NRC). (1996). *National science education standards.* Washington, DC: National Academies Press.

National Research Council (NRC). (2005). *How students learn: History, mathematics, and science in the classroom.* Washington, DC: The National Academies Press.

National Research Council (NRC). (2006). *Systems for state science assessment*. Washington, DC: The National Academies Press.

National Research Council (NRC). (2010). *A framework for science education: Preliminary public draft*. Retrieved December 12, 2010, from http://www7.nationalacademies.org/bose/Standards_Framework_Homepage.html

National Research Council (NRC). (2011). *Learning science through computer games and simulations*. Washington, DC: The National Academies Press.

Nature Video. (2010). *Foldit: Biology for gamers* [video].Retrieved from http://www.youtube.com/watch?v=axN0xdhznhY

Nehring, W. M., & Lashley, F. R. (2010). *High-fidelity patient simulation in nursing education*. Sudbury, MA: Jones and Bartlett Publishers.

Nehring, W. M. (2010). History of simulation in nursing. In Nehring, W. M., & Lashley, F. R. (Eds.), *High-fidelity patient simulation in nursing education*. Sudbury, MA: Jones and Bartlett Publishers.

Nelson, B. C., & Erlandson, B. E. (2008). Managing cognitive load in educational multi-user virtual environments: reflection on design practice. *Educational Technology Research and Development*, *56*, 619–641. doi:10.1007/s11423-007-9082-1

Neuman, W. R. (1991). *The future of the mass audience*. New York, NY: Cambridge University Press.

Newby, T. J., & Alter, P. A. (1989). Task motivation: Learner selection of intrinsic versus extrinsic orientations. *Educational Technology Research and Development*, *37*, 77–89. doi:10.1007/BF02298292

Newhagen, J. E. (2004). Interactivity, dynamic symbol processing, and the emergence of content in human communication. *The Information Society*, *20*, 395–400. doi:10.1080/01972240490508108

Newman, D., Griffin, P., & Cole, M. (1989). *The construction zone: Working for cognitive change in school*. New York, NY: Cambridge University Press.

Newman, F. (1996). *Authentic achievement: Restructuring schools for intellectual quality*. San Francisco, CA: Jossey-Bass Publisher.

Newman, F., Sccada, W., & Wehlage, G. (1995). *A guide to authentic instruction and assessment: Vision, standards and scoring*. Alexandria, VA: Association for Supervision and Curriculum Development.

Ng, F., Plass, L., & Zeng, H. (2009). Research on educational impact of games: A literature review [white paper]. Institute for Games for Learning.

Ning. (2011). *About Ning*. Retrieved from http://about.ning.com/

Noble, K. (2006). *Effect of the NePPHRO program on the learning of students of physiology who exhibit variation in cognitive style*. Unpublished PhD Thesis, Temple University, Pennsylvania, PA.

Nokelainen, P. (2006). An empirical assessment of pedagogical usability criteria for digital learning material with elementary school students. *Journal of Educational Technology & Society*, *9*(2), 179–197.

Nolan, J., & Francis, P. (1992). Changing perspectives in curriculum and instruction. In Glickman, C. (Ed.), *Supervision in transition*. Alexandria, VA: Association for Supervision and Curriculum Development.

Norman, D. A. (1993). *Things that make us smart: Defending human attributes in the age of the machine*. New York, NY: Addison-Wesley.

Norman, D. A. (1991). Cognitive artifacts. In Carroll, J. M. (Ed.), *Designing interaction: Psychology at the human- computer interface*. Cambridge, UK: Cambridge University Press.

Northwest Commission on Colleges and Universities. (2010). *Standard two*. Retrieved from http://www.nwccu.org/Standards%20and%20Policies/Standard%202/Standard%20Two.htm

Novak, J. D. (1990). The concept mapping: A useful tool for science education. *Journal of Research in Science Teaching*, *27*(10), 937–950. doi:10.1002/tea.3660271003

Nuance. (2011). *Dragon NaturallySpeaking*. http://www.nuance.com/dragon/index.htm.

Oblinger, D. G. (2006). Games and learning: Digital games have the potential to bring play to the learning experience. *EDUCAUSE Quarterly*, *29*(3), 5–7.

Oddcast Inc. (2011). *Voki*. Retrieved from http://www.voki.com/

Oh, S., & Jonassen, D. H. (2007). Scaffolding online argumentation during problem solving. *Journal of Computer Assisted Learning*, 23(2), 95–110. doi:10.1111/j.1365-2729.2006.00206.x

Oliver, R. (2006). Reusable resources and authentic learning environments. In Herrington, A., & Herrington, J. (Eds.), *Authentic learning environments in higher education*. Hershey, PA: Information Science Publishing. doi:10.4018/978-1-59140-594-8.ch018

Oliver, R., Herrrington, A., Stoney, S., & Millar, J. (2006). Authentic teaching and learning standards that assure quality higher education. In Herrington, A., & Herrington, J. (Eds.), *Authentic learning environments in higher education*. Hershey, PA: Information Science Publishing. doi:10.4018/978-1-59140-594-8.ch021

Olson, D., & Bruner, J. (1974). *Media and symbols: The forms of expression, communication and education* (Olson, D., Ed.). Chicago, IL: University of Chicago Press.

Oregon Nursing Leadership Council. (2005). *Oregon nursing leadership council strategic plan: Solutions to Oregon's nursing shortage, 2005-2008*. Portland, OR: Author.

Organisation for Economic Co-operation and Development (OECD). (2007). *PISA 2006: Science competencies for tomorrow's world. Volume 1: Analysis*.

Orlando, J. (2011). What games teach us about learning? *Faculty Focus*. April, 2011. Retrieved from http://www.facultyfocus.com/articles/teaching-with-technology-articles/what-games-teach-us-about-learning/

Ormrod, J. E. (1999). *Human learning* (3rd ed.). Upper Saddle River, NJ: Merill Prentice Hall.

Ortega, K. A. (1987). *Problem solving: Expert/novice differences*. IBM Technical Report. TR54.422.

Orts, E. W. (2011). *Tragedy of the tuna*. Retrieved from http://beacon.wharton.upenn.edu/learning/management/tragedy-of-the-tuna/

Paas, F., Tuovinen, J. E., Tabbers, H., & van Gerven, P. W. M. (2003). Cognitive load measurement as a means to advance cognitive load theory. *Educational Psychologist*, 38, 63–71. doi:10.1207/S15326985EP3801_8

Paas, F. G. W. C., & van Merrienboer, J. J. G. (1994). Instructional control of cognitive load in the training of complex cognitive tasks. *Educational Psychology Review*, 6, 351–371. doi:10.1007/BF02213420

Palincsar, A. S. (1986). The role of dialogue in providing scaffolded instruction. *Educational Psychologist*, 21(1 & 2), 73–98.

Palincsar, A. S., & Brown, A. L. (1984). Reciprocal teaching of comprehension-fostering and comprehension-monitoring activities. *Cognition and Instruction*, 1(2), 117–175. doi:10.1207/s1532690xci0102_1

Palloff, R. M., & Pratt, K. (2003). *Virtual student: A profile and guide to working with online learners*. San Francisco, CA: Jossey-Bass.

Palloff, R. M., & Pratt, K. (2007). *Building learning communities in cyberspace: Effective strategies for the online classroom* (2nd ed.). San Francisco, CA: Jossey-Bass.

Pannese, L., & Carlesi, M. (2007, May). Games and learning come together to maximise effectiveness: The challenge of bridging the gap. *British Journal of Educational Technology*, 38(3), 438–454. doi:10.1111/j.1467-8535.2007.00708.x

Papastergiou, M. (2009). Digital game-based learning in high school computer science education: Impact on educational effectiveness and student motivation. *Computers & Education*, 52(1), 1–12. doi:10.1016/j.compedu.2008.06.004

Park, O., & Lee, J. (2004). Adaptive instructional systems. In Jonassen, D. (Ed.), *Handbook of research on educational communications and technology* (pp. 651–684). Mahwah, NJ: Lawrence Erlbaum.

Parry, G., & Reynoldson, C. (2006). Creating an authentic learning environment in economics for MBA students. In Herrington, A., & Herrington, J. (Eds.), *Authentic learning environments in higher education*. Hershey, PA: Information Science Publishing. doi:10.4018/978-1-59140-594-8.ch006

Parsad, B., Lewis, L., & Tice, P. (2008). *Distance education at degree-granting postsecondary institutions: 2006–07*. Retrieved from http://nces.ed.gov/pubs2009/2009044.pdf

Paulus, T. (2009). Online, but off-topic: Negotiating common ground in small learning groups. *Instructional Science, 37*(3), 227–245. doi:10.1007/s11251-007-9042-5

Pea, R. D. (1985). Beyond amplification: Using the computer to reorganize mental functioning. *Educational Psychology, 20*(4), 167–182. doi:10.1207/s15326985ep2004_2

Pea, R. D. (1987). Socializing the knowledge transfer problem. *International Journal of Educational Research, 11*(6), 639–664. doi:10.1016/0883-0355(87)90007-3

Pea, R. (2004). The social and technological dimensions of scaffolding and related theoretical concepts for learning, education, and human activity. *Journal of the Learning Sciences, 13*(3), 423–451. doi:10.1207/s15327809jls1303_6

Pea, R. (1993). Practices of distributed intelligence and designs for education. In Salomon, G. (Ed.), *Distributed cognitions* (pp. 47–87). New York, NY: Cambridge University Press.

Pedersen, S., & Liu, M. (2002). The effects of modeling expert cognitive strategies during problem-based learning. *Journal of Educational Computing Research, 26*(4), 353–380. doi:10.1092/8946-J9N7-E79U-M7CR

Pellegrino, J. W., Chudowski, N., & Glaser, R. (2001). *Knowing what students know: The science and design of educational assessment*. Washington, DC: National Academies Press.

Pendleton-Jullian, A. (2010). *Four (+1) Studios.* CreateSpace. Self-published. Retrieved from http://4plus1studios.com/

Pendleton-Jullian, A. (February 26, 2010). *Higher education and game-based learning: A faculty panel.* Digital Union Game-Based Learning Group Conference. Columbus, Ohio.

Perkins, D. N., & Martin, F. (1986). Fragile knowledge and neglected strategies in novice programmers. In Soloway, E., & Iyengar, S. (Eds.), *Empirical studies of programmers*. Norwood, NJ: Ablex.

Peterson, D. (1996). *Forms of representation*. Exeter, UK: Intellect Books.

Pham, A., & Sarno, D. (2010, July 18). The future of reading: Electronic reading devices are transforming the concept of a book. *Los Angeles Times*.

Piaget, J. (1967). *The child's conception of space*. New York, NY: Norton & Company.

Pike, W. A., Stasko, J., Chang, R., & O'Connell, T. A. (2009). The science of interaction. *Journal of Information Visualization, 8*(4), 263–274. doi:10.1057/ivs.2009.22

Pine, J., Baxter, G. P., & Shavelson, R. J. (1993). Assessments for hands-on elementary science curricula. *MSTA Journal, 39*(2), 5–19.

Pintrich, P. R. (1988). A process-oriented view on student motivation and cognition. In Stark, J. S., & Mets, L. A. (Eds.), *Improving teaching and learning through research: New directions for institutional research, no. 57*. San Francisco, CA: Josse-Bass. doi:10.1002/ir.37019885707

Pirnay-Dummer, P., Ifenthaler, D., & Spector, J. M. (2010). Highly integrated model assessment technology and tools. *Educational Technology Research and Development, 58*(1), 3–18. doi:10.1007/s11423-009-9119-8

Pival, P. R., & Tuñón, J. (2001). Innovative methods for providing instruction to distance students using technology. *Journal of Library Administration, 2*(1/2), 347-360. doi:10:1300/J111v32no01_10

Plowman, L. (1996). Narrative, interactivity and the secret world of multimedia. *The English & Media Magazine, 35*, 44–48.

Powell, A., & Evans, M. (2006). *Public vs. private interests: Design implications for teacher communities of practice*. Paper presented at the Annual Meeting of the American Educational Research Association.

Preece, J. (2001). Sociability and usability in online communities: Determining and measuring success. *Behavior and Information Technology Journal, 20*(5), 347–356. doi:10.1080/01449290110084683

Prenksy, M. (2001). Digital natives, digital immigrants. *Horizon, 9*(5). Retrieved from http://www.marcprensky.com/writing/Prensky%20-%20Digital%20Natives,%20Digital%20Immigrants%20-%20Part1.pdf.

Prensky, M. (2007). *Digital game-based learning*. St. Paul, MN: Paragon House.

Prensky, M. (2006). *"Don't bother me Mom, I'm learning!"*: *How computer and video games are preparing your kids for twenty-first century success and how you can help!* St. Paul, MN: Paragon House.

Prensky, M. (2010). *Teaching digital natives: Partnering for real learning*. Thousand Oaks, CA: Sage.

Puntambekar, S., & Hubscher, R. (2005). Tools for scaffolding students in a complex learning environment: What have we gained and what have we missed? *Educational Psychologist, 40*(1), 1–12. doi:10.1207/s15326985ep4001_1

Putnam, R. R., & Borko, H. (2000). What do new views of knowledge and thinking have to say about research on teacher learning? *Educational Researcher, 29*, 4–15.

Quellmalz, E. (1984). Successful large-scale writing assessment programs: Where are we now and where do we go from here? *Educational Measurement: Issues and Practice, 3*(1), 29–35. doi:10.1111/j.1745-3992.1984.tb00735.x

Quellmalz, E., & Haertel, G. (2004). *Technology supports for state science assessment systems*. Washington, DC: National Research Council.

Quellmalz, E., Kreikmeier, P., DeBarger, A. H., & Haertel, G. (2006). *A study of the alignment of the NAEP, TIMSS, and new standards science assessments with the inquiry abilities in the national science education standards*. Paper presented at the Annual Meeting of the American Educational Research Association.

Quintana, C., Reiser, B. J., Davis, E. A., Krajcik, J., Fretz, E., & Duncan, R. G. (2004). A scaffolding design framework for software to support science inquiry. *Journal of the Learning Sciences, 13*(3), 337–386. doi:10.1207/s15327809jls1303_4

Quintana, C., Zhang, M., & Krajcik, J. (2005). A framework for supporting metacognitive aspects of online inquiry through software-based scaffolding. *Educational Psychologist, 40*(4), 235–244. doi:10.1207/s15326985ep4004_5

Rafaeli, S. (1988). Interactivity: From new media to communication. In Hawkins, R., Wiemann, J., & Pingree, S. (Eds.), *Advancing communication science: Merging mass and interpersonal processes* (pp. 110–134). Newbury Park, CA: Sage.

Rafaeli, S., & Ariel, Y. (2007). Assessing interactivity in computer-mediated research. In Joinson, A. N., McKenna, K. Y. A., Postmes, T., & Rieps, U. D. (Eds.), *The Oxford handbook of internet psychology* (pp. 71–88). Oxford University Press.

Rafaeli, S., & Sudweeks, F. (1998). Interactivity on the Nets. In Sudweeks, F., McLaughlin, M., & Rafaeli, S. (Eds.), *Network and netplay: Virtual groups on the Internet* (pp. 173–189). Menlo Park, CA: AAAI Press/MIS Press.

Ragoonaden, K., & Bordeleau, P. (2000). Collaborative learning via the Internet. *Educational Technology & Society, 3*(3). Retrieved April 26, 2011, from http://www.ifets.info/journals/3_3/d11.html.

Reigeluth, C. M. (1999). The elaboration theory: guidance for scope and sequence decisions. In C. M. Reigeluth (Ed.), *Instructional-design theories and model, vol. 2: A new paradigm of instructional theory*. Mahwah, NJ: Lawrence Erlbaum Associates.

Renninger, K. A., & Shumar, W. (Eds.). (2002). *Building virtual communities: Learning and change in cyberspace*. New York, NY: Cambridge University Press. doi:10.1017/CBO9780511606373

Report, H. (2011). *The New Media Consortium and Educause*. Retrieved from http://net.educause.edu/ir/library/pdf/HR2011.pdf

Resnick, L. B., & Resnick, D. P. (1992). Assessing the thinking curriculum: New tools for educational reform. In Gifford, B., & O'Connor, M. (Eds.), *Changing assessments: Alternative views of aptitude, achievement, and instruction* (pp. 37–75). Norwell, MA: Kluwer Academic Publishers. doi:10.1007/978-94-011-2968-8_3

Reuber, A. R., & Fischer, E. M. (1992). Does entrepreneurship experience matter? *Journal of Small Business and Entrepreneurship, 9*(4), 50–62.

Rheingold, H. (1993). *The virtual community: Homesteading on the electronic frontier*. New York, NY: Harper Collins.

Rice, J. (2007). New media resistance: Barriers to implementation of computer video games in the classroom. *Journal of Educational Multimedia and Hypermedia, 16*(3), 249–261.

Rich, Y., & Almozlino, M. (1999). Educational goal preferences among novice and veteran teachers of science and humanities. *Teaching and Teacher Education, 15,* 613–629. doi:10.1016/S0742-051X(99)00010-4

Richards, J. P., Fajen, B. R., Sullivan, J. F., & Gillespie, G. (1997). Signaling, notetaking, and field independence-dependence in text comprehension and recall. *Journal of Educational Psychology, 89*(3), 508–517. doi:10.1037/0022-0663.89.3.508

Richardson, J. C., & Swan, K. (2003). Examining social presence in online courses in relation to students' perceived learning and satisfaction. *Journal of Asynchronous Learning Networks, 7*(1), 68–88.

Riding, R. (2000). *Cognitive style analysis – Research administration.* Birmingham, UK: Learning and Training Technology.

Rieber, L., & Noah, D. (2008). Games, simulations, and visual metaphors in education: Antagonism between enjoyment and learning. *Educational Media International, 45*(2), 77–92. doi:10.1080/09523980802107096

Riel, M., & Polin, L. (2004). Online learning communities: Common ground and critical differences in designing technical environments. In Barab, R., Kling, J., & Gray, H. (Eds.), *Designing for virtual communities in the service of learning* (pp. 16–50). Cambridge, UK: Cambridge University Press.

Riel, M., & Becker, H. (2000, April 6). *The beliefs, practices, and computer use of teacher leaders.* Paper presented at the American Educational Research Association, New Orleans.

Ritterfeld, U., Shen, C., Wang, H., Nocera, L., & Wong, W. L. (2009). Multimodality and interactivity: Connecting properties of serious games with educational outcomes. *Cyberpsychology & Behavior, 12,* 691–697. doi:10.1089/cpb.2009.0099

Rittschof, K. A. (2010). Field dependence–independence as visuospatial and executive functioning in working memory: Implications for instructional systems design and research. *Educational Technology Research and Development, 58,* 99–114. doi:10.1007/s11423-008-9093-6

Robinson, K. (2006). *Out of our minds: Learning to be creative.* New York, NY: Wiley, John & Sons.

Rogers, J. (2000). Communities of practice: A framework for fostering coherence in virtual learning communities. *Journal of Educational Technology & Society, 3*(3), 384–392.

Rogers, Y., & Scaife, M. (1998). How can interactive multimedia facilitate learning? In Lee, J. (Ed.), *Intelligence and multimodality in multimedia interfaces: Research and applications.* Menlo Park, CA: AAAI. Press.

Rosas, R., Nussbaum, M., Cumsille, P., Marianov, V., Correa, M., & Flores, P. (2003). Beyond Nintendo: Design and assessment of educational video games for first and second grade students. *Computers & Education, 40*(1), 71–94. doi:10.1016/S0360-1315(02)00099-4

Rosenquist, A., Shavelson, R. J., & Ruiz-Primo, M. A. (2000). *On the "exchangeability" of hands-on and computer simulation science performance assessments.*

Rovai, A. (2002a). Building sense of community at a distance. *International Review of Research in Open and Distance Learning, 3*(1), 1–16. Retrieved from http://www.irrodl.org/index.php/irrodl/article/view/79/153.

Rovai, A. (2002b). Sense of community, perceived cognitive learning, and persistence in asynchronous learning networks. *The Internet and Higher Education, 5,* 319–332. doi:10.1016/S1096-7516(02)00130-6

Rovai, A. P., & Wighting, M. J. (2005). Feelings of alienation and community among higher education students in a virtual classroom. *The Internet and Higher Education, 8,* 97–110. doi:10.1016/j.iheduc.2005.03.001

Russell, D. (1995). Activity theory and writing instruction. In Petraglia, J. (Ed.), *Reconceiving writing, rethinking writing instruction* (pp. 51–77). Mahwah, NJ: Lawrence Erlbaum.

Rymaszewski, M., Au, W. J., & Wallace, M. Winters, C., Ondrejka, C., Batstone-Cunningham, B., & Rosedale, P. (2006). *Second Life: The official guide*. Indianapolis, IN: Wiley.

Sadler, P. M. (1998). Psychometric models of student conceptions in science: Reconciling qualitative studies and distracter-driven assessment instruments. *Journal of Research in Science Teaching*, 35(3), 265–296. doi:10.1002/(SICI)1098-2736(199803)35:3<265::AID-TEA3>3.0.CO;2-P

Sakai. (2011). *Sakai CLE*. Retrieved from http://sakaiproject.org/node/2260

Salen, K. (Ed.). (2008). *The ecology of games: Connecting youth, games, and learning. The John D. and Catherine T. MacArthur Foundation Series on Digital Media and Learning*. Cambridge, MA: MIT Press.

Salen, K., & Zimmerman, E. (2004). *Rules of play game design fundamentals*. Cambridge, MA: The MIT Press.

Salen, K. (June 16, 2011). *Keynote: "What is the work of play?"* Games+Learning+Society Conference. Madison, Wisconsin.

Salen, K. (May 25, 2010). *Future of digital media talks*. Games for Change Conference. New York.

Salomon, G. (1979). *Interaction of media, cognition and learning*. San Francisco, CA: Jossey-Bass.

Salomon, G., Globerson, T., & Guterman, E. (1989). The computer as a zone of proximal development: Internalizing reading-related metacognitions from a Reading Partner. *Journal of Educational Psychology*, 81, 620–627. doi:10.1037/0022-0663.81.4.620

Salomon, G. (1993b). On the nature of pedagogic computer tools: The case of the writing partner. In Lajoie, S. P., & Derry, S. J. (Eds.), *Computers as cognitive tools* (pp. 179–196). Hillsdale, NJ: Lawrence Erlbaum Associates.

Salomon, G. (1974). What is learned and how it is taught: The interaction between media, message, task and learner. In Olson, D. (Ed.), *Media and symbols: The forms of expression, communication and education*. Chicago, IL: University of Chicago Press.

Salomon, G. (1993a). No distribution without individuals' cognition: A dynamic interaction view. In Salomon, G. (Ed.), *Distributed cognitions: Psychological and educational considerations* (pp. 111–138). Cape Town, South Africa: Cambridge University Press.

Salomon, G., & Perkins, D. (2005). Do technologies make us smarter? Intellectual amplification with, of, and through technology. In Sternberg, R., & Preiss, D. D. (Eds.), *Intelligence and technology: The impact of tools on the nature and development of human abilities* (pp. 71–86). Mahwah, NJ: Lawrence Erlbaum.

Salomon, G. (Ed., 1993). *Distributed cognitions: Psychological and educational considerations*. Cambridge, UK: Cambridge University Press.

Samples, R. E. (1975). Are you teaching online one side of the brain? *Learning*, 3(6), 25–28.

Sankaran, S. R., & Bui, T. (2001). Impact of learning strategies and motivation on performance: A study in web-based instruction. *Journal of Instructional Psychology*, 28, 191–198.

Santo, S. A. (2006). Relationships between learning styles and online learning. *Performance Improvement Quarterly*, 19(3), 73–88. doi:10.1111/j.1937-8327.2006.tb00378.x

Sarason, S. (1990). *The predictable failure of educational reform*. San Francisco, CA: Jossey-Bass.

Saulnier, D. (2008, January 23). *Immersive education and virtual worlds: Croquet and MPK20/Wonderland/Darkstar*. Retrieved February 25, 2011, from http://saulnier.typepad.com/learning_technology/2008/01/immersive-educa.html

Scales, B. J., & Cummings, L. (2009). Web conferencing software. *Library Hi Tech News*, 26(9), 7–9. .doi:10.1108/07419050911010732

Scardamalia, M., & Bereiter, C. (1994). Computer support for knowledge-building communities. *Journal of the Learning Sciences*, 3(3), 265–283. doi:10.1207/s15327809jls0303_3

Scardamalia, M., Bereiter, C., McLean, R., Swallow, J., & Woodruff, E. (1989). Computer-supported intentional learning environments. *Journal of Educational Computing Research*, 5(1), 51–68.

Scardamalia, M., Bereiter, C., & Steinbach, R. (1984). Teachability of reflective processes in written composition. *Cognitive Science*, *8*(2), 173–190. doi:10.1207/s15516709cog0802_4

Scardamalia, M., & Bereiter, C. (1985). Development of dialectical processes in composition. In Olson, D. R., Torrance, N., & Hildyard, A. (Eds.), *Literacy, language, and learning: The nature and consequences of reading and writing* (pp. 307–329). Cambridge, UK: Cambridge University Press.

Scardamalia, M., & Bereiter, C. (2006). Knowledge building: Theory, pedagogy, and technology. In Sawyer, K. (Ed.), *Cambridge handbook of the learning sciences* (pp. 97–118). New York, NY: Cambridge University Press.

Scheiter, K., & Gerjets, P. (2007). Learner control in hypermedia environments. *Educational Psychology Review*, *19*, 285–307. doi:10.1007/s10648-007-9046-3

Schiefele, U. (1991). Interest, learning and motivation. *Educational Psychologist*, *26*, 299–323. doi:10.1207/s15326985ep2603&4_5

Schlager, M., & Fusco, J. (2004). Teacher professional development, technology, and communities: Are we putting the cart before the horse? In Barbara, S., Kling, R., & Gray, J. (Eds.), *Designing virtual communities in the service of learning*. Cambridge, UK: Cambridge University Press. doi:10.1080/01972240309464

Schmuck, R. A. (2006). *Practical action research for change*. Thousand Oaks, CA: Corwin Press, a Sage Publications Company.

Schoenfield, A. H., & Hermann, D. J. (1982). Problem perception and knowledge structure in expert and novice mathematical problem solvers. *Journal of Experimental Psychology. Learning, Memory, and Cognition*, *8*(5), 484–494. doi:10.1037/0278-7393.8.5.484

Schön, D. (1987). *Educating the reflective practitioner*. New York, NY: Basic.

Schroeder, A. (2008). *Snowball: Warren Buffet and the business of life*. New York, NY: Bantam Dell Publishers.

Schwen, T. M., & Hara, N. (2004). Community of practice: A metaphor for online design? In Barab, S. A., Kling, R., & Gray, J. H. (Eds.), *Designing for virtual communities in the service of learning*. Cambridge, UK: Cambridge University Press. doi:10.1080/01972240309462

Sedig, K. (2004). Need for a prescriptive taxonomy of interaction for mathematical cognitive tools. In. *Proceedings of Interactive Visualisation and Interaction Technologies, ICCS, 2004*, 1030–1037.

Sedig, K., Klawe, M., & Westrom, M. (2001). Role of interface manipulation style and scaffolding on cognition and concept learning in learnware. *ACM Transactions on Computer-Human Interaction*, *1*(8), 34–59. doi:10.1145/371127.371159

Sedig, K., & Liang, H.-N. (2006). Interactivity of visual mathematical representations: Factors affecting learning and cognitive processes. *Journal of Interactive Learning Research*, *17*(2), 179–212.

Sedig, K., & Liang, H.-N. (2008). Learner-information interaction: A macro-level framework characterizing visual cognitive tools. *Journal of Interactive Learning Research*, *19*(1), 147–173.

Sedig, K., Rowhani, S., & Liang, H.-N. (2005). Designing interfaces that support formation of cognitive maps of transitional processes: An empirical study. *Interacting with Computers: The Interdisciplinary Journal of Human-Computer Interaction*, *17*(4), 419–452.

Sedig, K., Rowhani, S., Morey, J., & Liang, H. (2003). Application of information visualization techniques to the design of a mathematical mindtool: A usability study. *Journal Information Visualization*, *2*(3), 142–160. doi:10.1057/palgrave.ivs.9500047

Sedig, K., & Sumner, M. (2006). Characterizing interaction with visual mathematical representations. *International Journal of Computers for Mathematical Learning*, *11*(1), 1–55. doi:10.1007/s10758-006-0001-z

Sedig, K. (2011). Interactivity of information representation in e-learning environments. In Wang, H. (Ed.), *Interactivity in e-learning: Case studies and frameworks*. Hershey, PA: Information Science Reference/IGI Global Publishing.

Sedig, K. (2009). Interactive mathematical visualizations: Frameworks, tools, and studies. In Zudilova-Seinstra, E., Adriaansen, T., & van Liere, R. (Eds.), *Trends in interactive visualization: State-of-the-art survey* (pp. 343–363). London, UK: Springer-Verlag. doi:10.1007/978-1-84800-269-2_16

Shaffer, D. W., Squire, K. R., Halverson, R., & Gee, J. P. (2005, October). Video games and the future of learning. *Phi Delta Kappan*, 104–111. Retrieved from http://ddis.wceruw.org/docs/08%20ShafferSquireHalversonGee%20PDK.pdf.

Shaffer, D. W. (2006). *How computer games help children learn*. New York, NY: Palgrave Macmillan. doi:10.1057/9780230601994

Shafto, P., & Coley, J. D. (2003). Development of categorization and reasoning in the natural world: Novices to experts, naïve similarity to ecological knowledge. *Journal of Experimental Psychology. Learning, Memory, and Cognition*, *29*(4), 641–649. doi:10.1037/0278-7393.29.4.641

Shany, N., & Nachmias, R. (2000). *The relationship between performances in a virtual course and thinking styles, gender, and ICT experience*. Retrieved November 15, 2010, from http://muse.tau.ac.il/publications/64.pdf

Sharma, P., & Hannafin, M. (2004). Scaffolding critical thinking in an online course: An exploratory study. *Journal of Educational Computing Research*, *31*(2), 181–208. doi:10.2190/TMC3-RXPE-75MY-31YG

Shavelson, R. J., Baxter, G. P., & Gao, X. (1993). Sampling variability of performance assessments. *Journal of Educational Measurement*, *30*(3), 215–232. doi:10.1111/j.1745-3984.1993.tb00424.x

Shavelson, R. J., Baxter, G. P., & Pine, J. (1991). Performance assessment in science. *Applied Measurement in Education*, *4*(4), 347–362. doi:10.1207/s15324818ame0404_7

Shaw, J. P., & Chen, J. (in press). Transactional distance and teaching presence in e-learning environments. *International Journal for Innovation and Learning*.

Shaw, J. P., & Chacon, F. (2010). Structure and change in elearning: An ecological perspective. In Song, H. (Ed.), *Distance learning technology, current instruction, and the future of education: Applications of today, practices of tomorrow* (pp. 316–338). Hershey, PA: IGI Global Publishers.

Shaw, J. P. (2002). *A model for reflective processing using narrative symbols: Time and space coordinates in adult reflection.* Unpublished doctoral dissertation, Harvard Graduate School of Education. Cambridge, Massachusetts.

Shaw, J. P. (2005). Building meaning: Experts and novices in on-line learning. In *Proceedings for EdMedia International Conference,* Montreal, Canada.

Sherman, W. R., & Craig, A. B. (2003). *Understanding virtual reality: Interface, application, and design.* San Francisco, CA: Morgan Kaufmann.

Shernoff, D. J., Csikszentmihalyi, M., Schneider, B., & Shernoff, E. S. (2003). Student engagement in high school classrooms from the perspective of flow theory. *School Psychology Quarterly*, *18*(2), 158–176. doi:10.1521/scpq.18.2.158.21860

Shneiderman, B. (1983). Direct manipulation: a step beyond programming languages. *IEEE Computer*, *16*(8), 57–69.

Shute, V. J., & Zapata-Rivera, D. (2008). Adaptive technologies. In Spector, J. M., Merrill, M. D., van Merriënboer, J., & Driscoll, M. P. (Eds.), *Handbook of research for educational communications and technology* (pp. 277–294). New York, NY: Routledge.

Siemens, G. (2005). Connectivism: A learning theory for the digital age. *International Journal of Instructional Technology and Distance Learning*, *2*(1), 3–9.

Sims, R. (1997). Interactivity: A forgotten art? *Computers in Human Behavior*, *13*(2), 157–180. doi:10.1016/S0747-5632(97)00004-6

Skinner, B. F. (1974). The technology of teaching. In Bart, W. M., & Wong, M. R. (Eds.), *Psychology of school learning: Views of the learner* (*Vol. 2*, pp. 38–54). New York, NY: MSS Information Corporation.

Skylar, A. (2009). A comparison of asynchronous online text-based lectures and synchronous interactive web conferencing lectures. *Issues in Teacher Education*, *18*(2), 69–84.

Sloutsky, V. M., & Yarlas, A. S. (2000). Problem representation in experts and novices: Part 2. Underlying processing mechanisms. In L. R. Gleitman & A. K. Joshi (Eds.), *Proceedings of the 22nd Annual Conference of the Cognitive Science Society* (pp. 475-480). Mahwah, NJ: Erlbaum.

Small, R. V., & Gluck, M. (1994). The relationship of motivational conditions to effective instructional attributes: A magnitude scaling approach. *Educational Technology, 34*(8), 33–40.

Smartbean. (November, 2009). *What are 21ˢᵗ century skills?* Retrieved June 10, 2011, from http://www.thesmartbean.com/magazine/21st-century-skills-magazine/what-are-21st-century-skills/

Snelbecker, G., Miller, S., & Zheng, R. (2008). Functional relevance and online instructional design. In Zheng, R., & Ferris, S. P. (Eds.), *Understanding online instructional modeling: Theories and practices* (pp. 1–17). Hershey, PA: Information Science Reference/IGI Global Publishing.

Song, S. H., & Keller, J. M. (2001). Effectiveness of motivationally adaptive computer-assisted instruction on the dynamic aspects of motivation. *Educational Technology Research and Development, 49*, 5–22. doi:10.1007/BF02504925

Spence, R. (1999). A framework for navigation. *International Journal of Human-Computer Studies, 51*(5), 919–945. doi:10.1006/ijhc.1999.0265

Spence, R. (2007). *Information visualization: Design for interaction* (2nd ed.). Essex, UK: Pearson.

Spiro, R., Feltovich, P., Jacobson, M., & Coulson, R. (1991). Cognitive flexibility, constructivism, and hypertext: Random access instruction for advanced knowledge acquisition in ill-structured domains. *Educational Technology*, (May): 24–33.

Springer, S., & Deutch, G. (1985). *Right brain, left brain*. San Francisco, CA: W. H. Freeman.

Squire, K. D. (2011). *Video games and learning: Teaching and participatory culture in the digital age*. New York, NY: Teachers College Press.

Squire, K. D. (May 27, 2010). *Toward a theory of game-based assessment*. Games for Change Conference. New York.

Stacey, E. (1999). Collaborative learning in an online environment. *Journal of Distance Education, 14*(2), 14–33.

Stecher, B. M., & Klein, S. P. (1997). The cost of science performance assessments in large-scale testing programs. *Educational Evaluation and Policy Analysis, 19*(1), 1–14.

Steinkuehler, C. (June 15, 2011). *Keynote: National Research Council report: Learning science through computer games and simulations*. Games+Learning+Society Conference. Madison, Wisconsin.

Steinkuehler, C. (March 25, 2010). *Keynote: Massively multiplayer online games, learning and the new pop cosmopolitanism*. New Media Consortium Conference. Retrieved from, http://www.nmc.org/2010-nml-symposium/steinkuehler-keynote

Steuer, J. (1995). Defining virtual reality: Dimensions determining telepresence. In Biocca, F., & Levy, M. R. (Eds.), *Communication in the age of virtual reality* (pp. 33–56). Hillsdale, NJ: Lawrence Erlbaum Associates.

Stillwater, OK: Oklahoma State University. (ERIC Document Reproduction Service No. ED409460).

Strauss, A. (1987). *Qualitative research for social scientists*. Cambridge, UK: Cambridge University Press. doi:10.1017/CBO9780511557842

Strauss, A., & Corbin, J. (1998). *Basic of qualitative research: Technique and techniques and procedures for developing grounded theory* (2nd ed.). Thousand Oaks, CA: Sage.

Stricker (Eds.), *Online counseling: A handbook for mental health professionals* (pp. 19-50). Amsterdam, The Netherlands: Elsevier.

Stuckey, B., Hedberg, J., & Lockyer, L. (2001, June 25-30). *Building on-line community for professional develolpment*. Paper presented at the Ed-Media 2001 World Conference on Educational Multimedia, Hypermedia, & Telecommunications, Tampere, Finland.

Suchman, L. (1983). Office procedure as practical action: Models of work and system design. *ACM Transactions on Office Information Systems, 1*(4), 320–328. doi:10.1145/357442.357445

Suits, B. (1978). *The grasshopper: Games, life, and utopia*. Ontario, Canada: University of Toronto Press.

Suler, J. (2004). The psychology of text relationships. In *R. Kraus. J. S. Zach, & G.

Sundar, S. S. (2004). Theorizing interactivity's effects. *The Information Society, 20*, 385–389. doi:10.1080/01972240490508072

Suthers, D. (1998). *Representations for scaffolding collaborative inquiry on ill-structured problems.* Paper presented at the AERA Annual Meeting.

Svendsen, G. B. (1991). The influence of interface style on problem solving. *International Journal of Man-Machine Studies, 35*(3), 379–397. doi:10.1016/S0020-7373(05)80134-8

Swan, K. (2001). Virtual interactivity: design factors affecting student satisfaction and perceived learning in asynchronous online courses. *Distance Education, 22*(2), 306–331. doi:10.1080/0158791010220208

Swan, K. (2005). *A constructivist model for thinking about learning online* (Bourne, J., Ed.).

Sweller, van Merriënboer J. J. G., & Paas, F. G. W.C. (1998). Cognitive architecture and instructional design. *Educational Psychology Review, 10*(3), 251-96.

TechTarget. (2005, April 5). *Rich media.* Retrieved February 25, 2011, from http://whatis.techtarget.com/definition/0,sid9_gci212901,00.html

Thagard, P. (1996). *Mind. Introduction to cognitive science.* Cambridge, MA: MIT Press.

Thai, A. M., Lowenstein, D., Ching, D., & Rejeski, D. (2009). *Game changer: Investing in digital play to advance children's learning and health* [policy brief]. The Joan Ganz Cooney Center at Sesame Workshop. Retrieved from http://www.joanganzcooneycenter.org/Reports-abc.html

The Education Arcade. (n.d.). *The Education Arcade.* Retrieved from http://www.educationarcade.org/

The Serious Games Initiative. (n.d.). *Serious games initiative.* Retrieved from http://www.seriousgames.org/

Thomas, J. J., & Cook, K. A. (2005). *Illuminating the path: The research and development agenda for visual analytics. National Visualization and Analytics Center.* Richland, WA: IEEE Press.

Thompson, S. C. (2004). Professional learning communities, leadership, and student learning. *Research in Middle Level Education Online, 27*(3), 35–55.

Thomsett-Scott, B., & May, F. (2009). How may we help you? Online education faculty tell us what they need from libraries and librarians. *Journal of Library Administration, 49*(1/2), 111–135. .doi:10.1080/01930820802312888

Thornbloom, S. A. (2009). *NSTC developing video computer training 'game'.* Retrieved from http://www.navy.mil/search/display.asp?story_id=42541

Tileston, D. W. (2005). *10 best teaching practices* (2nd ed.). Thousand Oaks, CA: Corwin Press, a SAGE Publications company.

Trentin, G. (2001). From formal training to communities of practice via network-based learning. *Educational Technology,* (March-April): 5–14.

Trudel, C., & Payne, S. J. (1995). Reflection and goal management in exploratory learning. *International Journal of Human-Computer Studies, 42,* 307–339. doi:10.1006/ijhc.1995.1015

Tufte, E. R. (1997). *Visual explanations: Images and quantities, evidence and narrative.* Cheshire, CT: Graphics Press.

Tung, F.-W., & Deng, Y.-S. (2006). Designing social presence in e-learning environments: Testing the effect of interactivity on children. *Interactive Learning Environments, 14*(3), 251–264. doi:10.1080/10494820600924750

US Department of Education (USDE). (2010). *National Education Technology Plan 2010.* Washington, DC: US Department of Education.

Utah State University. (2010). *National library of virtual manipulatives.* Retrieved from http://nlvm.usu.edu/en/nav/vlibrary.html

Valli, L., Croninger, R. G., Chambliss, M. J., Graeber, A. O., & Buese, D. (2008). *Test driven: High-stakes accountability in elementary schools.* New York, NY: Teachers College Press.

van Eck, R. (2006). Digital game-based learning: It's not just the digital natives who are restless. *EDUCASE Review, 41*(2), 16–30.

van Gerven, P. W. M., Paas, F., van Merriënboer, J. J. G., & Schmidt, H. G. (2006). Modality and variability as factors in training the elderly. *Applied Cognitive Psychology, 20,* 311–320. doi:10.1002/acp.1247

van Joolingen, W. R., de Jong, T., Lazonder, A. W., Savelsbergh, E. R., & Manlove, S. (2005). Co-Lab: Research and development of an online learning environment for collaborative scientific discovery learning. *Computers in Human Behavior, 21*(4), 671–688. doi:10.1016/j.chb.2004.10.039

van Merriënboer, J. J. G., Clark, R., & de Croock, M. (2002). Blueprints for complex learning: The 4C/ID-model. *Educational Technology Research and Development*, *50*(2), 39–61. doi:10.1007/BF02504993

van Merriënboer, J. J. G., & Sweller, J. (2005). Cognitive load theory and complex learning: Recent developments and future directions. *Educational Psychology Review*, *17*(2), 147–177. doi:10.1007/s10648-005-3951-0

Vesely, P., Bloom, L., & Sherlock, J. (2007). Key elements of building online community: Comparing faculty and student perceptions. *Journal of Online Learning and Teaching*, *3*(3), 234–246.

Vincent-Morin, M., & Lafont, L. (2005). Learning-method choices and personal characteristics in solving a physical education problem. *Journal of Teaching in Physical Education*, *24*, 226–242.

Vroom, V. (1964). *The motivation to work*. New York, NY: Wiley.

Vygotsky, L. S. (1978). *Mind in society: The development of higher psychological processes*. Cambridge, MA: Harvard University Press.

Vygotsky, L. (1962). *Thought and language*. Cambridge, MA: MIT Press. doi:10.1037/11193-000

Waits, T., Lewis, L., & Greene, B. (2003). *Distance education at degree-granting postsecondary institutions: 2000–2001*. Retrieved from http://nces.ed.gov/pubs2003/2003017.pdf

Waldner, M. H., & Olson, J. K. (2007). Taking the patient to the classroom: Applying theoretical frameworks to simulation in nursing education. *International Journal of Nursing Education Scholarship*, *4*(1), 18. doi:10.2202/1548-923X.1317

Waneka, R. (2008). *California Board of Registered Nursing 2006-2007 annual school report: Pre-licensure nursing programs data summary*. San Francisco, CA: Center for Health Professions.

Wang, H. (2001). Effective use of WebBoard for distance learning. In T. Okamoto, R. Hartley, Kinshuk, & J. P. Klus (Eds.). *IEEE International Conference on Advanced Learning Technologies*. Las Alamitos, CA: IEEE Computer Society.

Webb, N. M., Schlackman, J., & Sugrue, B. (2000). The dependability and interchangeability of assessment methods in science. *Applied Measurement in Education*, *13*(3), 277–301. doi:10.1207/S15324818AME1303_4

Weigel, V. B. (2002). *Deep learning for a digital age: Technology's untapped potential to enrich higher education*. San Francisco, CA: Jossey-Bass Publisher.

Weiner, B. (1985). Spontaneous' causal thinking. *Psychological Bulletin*, *97*, 74–84. doi:10.1037/0033-2909.97.1.74

Wellings, J., & Levine, M. H. (2009). *The digital promise: Transforming learning with innovative uses of technology. A white paper on literacy and learning in a new media age* [white paper]. The Joan Ganz Cooney Center at Sesame Workshop. Retrieved from http://www.joanganzcooney-center.org/Reports-abc.html

Wenger, E., McDermont, R., & Snyder, W. M. (2002). *Cultivating communities of practice*. Boston, MA: Harvard Business School Press.

Wenger, E. (1998). *Communities of practice: learning, meaning, and identity*. Cambridge, UK: Cambridge University Press.

Wenger, E. (2003). Communities of practice and social learning systems. In Nicolini, D., Gherardi, S., & Yanow, D. (Eds.), *Knowing in organizations: A practice-based approach* (pp. 76–99). Armonk, NY: M.E. Sharpe. doi:10.1177/135050840072002

Werner, H., & Kaplan, P. (1960/1984). *Symbol formation*. New York, NY: Psychology Press. (reprint).

Westera, W., Nadolski, R. J., Hummel, H. G. K., & Wopereis, I. G. J. H. (2008). Serious games for higher education: A framework for reducing design complexity. *Journal of Computer Assisted Learning*, *24*, 420–432. doi:10.1111/j.1365-2729.2008.00279.x

Whipp, J. L. (2003). Scaffolding critical reflection in online discussions: Helping prospective teachers think deeply about field experience in urban schools. *Journal of Teacher Education*, *54*, 321–333. doi:10.1177/0022487103255010

White, B., & Frederiksen, J. (1998). Inquiry, modeling, and metacognition: Making science accessible to all students. *Cognition and Instruction*, *16*(1), 3–118. doi:10.1207/s1532690xci1601_2

White, B., Collins, A., & Frederiksen, J. (in press). The nature of scientific meta-knowledge. In Khine, M. S., & Saleh, I. (Eds.), *Dynamic modeling: Cognitive tool for scientific enquiry*. London, UK: Spinger.

Whitebread, D. (1997). Developing children's problem-solving: the educational uses of adventure games. In McFarlane, A. (Ed.), *Information technology and authentic learning*. New York, NY: Routledge.

Wiedenbeck, S. (1985). Novice/expert differences in programming skills. *International Journal of Man-Machine Studies*, *23*, 383–390. doi:10.1016/S0020-7373(85)80041-9

Wikipedia. (n.d.). *Serious games.* Retrieved from http://en.wikipedia.org/wiki/Serious_game

Williams, B. (2005). Case based learning – A review of the literature: Is there scope for this educational paradigm in prehospital education? *Emergency Medicine Journal*, *22*(8), 577–581. doi:10.1136/emj.2004.022707

Wilson, M. (2009). Measuring progressions: Assessment structures underlying a learning progression. [10.1002/tea.20318]. *Journal of Research in Science Teaching*, *46*(6), 716-730.

Windschitl, M., & Sahl, K. (2002). Tracing teachers' use of technology in a laptop computer school: The interplay of teacher beliefs, social dynamics, and institutional culture. *American Educational Research Journal*, *39*(1), 165–205. doi:10.3102/00028312039001165

Winner, E. (2010). *Cognitive and brain consequences of learning in the arts*. Association for Psychological Science 22nd Annual Convention, Boston, Massachusetts.

Witkin, H. A., & Goodenough, D. R. (1977). Field dependence and interpersonal behavior. *Psychological Bulletin*, *84*, 661–689. doi:10.1037/0033-2909.84.4.661

Witkin, H. A., Moore, C. A., Goodenough, D. R., & Cox, P. W. (1977). Field dependent and field independent cognitive styles and their educational implications. *Review of Educational Research*, *47*(1), 1–64.

Witkin, H. A., Oltman, P. K., Raskin, E., & Karp, S. A. (1971). *Group embedded figures test manual*. Menlo Park, CA: Mind Garden.

Wittgenstein, L. (1922/2010). *Project Gutenberg's Tractatus Logico-Philosophicus* (Translated by C. K. Ogden). Retrieved from http://www.gutenberg.org/ebooks/5740

Wittgenstein, L. (1953). *Philosophical investigations*. (Translated by G.E.M. Anscombe).

Wolf, M. J. P. (Ed.). (2008). *The video game explosion: A history from Pong to Playstation and beyond*. Westport, CT: Greenwood Press.

Wonacott, M. E. (2001). *Technology literacy*. ERIC Digest. Columbus, OH: Clearinghouse on Adult Career and Vocational Education. Retrieved October 16, 2005, from http://www.ericdigests.org/2002-3/literacy.htm

Wood, D., Bruner, J. S., & Ross, G. (1976). The role of tutoring in problem solving. *Journal of Child Psychology and Psychiatry, and Allied Disciplines*, *17*(2), 89–100. doi:10.1111/j.1469-7610.1976.tb00381.x

WordPress.com. (2011). *WordPress.com – Get a free blog here*. Retrieved from http://wordpress.com/

Wright, W. (April 2006). Dream machines. *Wired*. Retrieved from http://www.wired.com/wired/archive/14.04/wright.html

Wyndham, C. (September 2007). Why today's students value authentic learning. D. G. Oblinger (Ed.). EDUCAUSE 2007. Retrieved from http://net.educause.edu/ir/library/pdf/ELI3017.pdf

Yang, C. S., & Moore, D. M. (1996). Designing hypermedia systems for instruction. *Educational Technology Systems*, *24*, 3–30.

Yarlas, A. S., & Sloutsky, V. M. (2000). Problem representation in experts and novices. Part 1. Differences in the content of representation. *Proceedings of the 22nd Annual Conference of the Cognitive Science Society*.

Yi, J. S., Kang, Y. A., Stasko, J., & Jacko, J. (2007). Toward a deeper understanding of the role of interaction in information visualization. *IEEE Transactions on Visualization and Computer Graphics*, *13*, 1224–1231. doi:10.1109/TVCG.2007.70515

Yin, R. K. (1994). *Case study research: Design and methods* (2nd ed., *Vol. 5*). Thousand Oaks, CA: Sage Publications.

Zahner, J. (2002). Teachers explore knowledge management and e-learning as models for professional development. *TechTrends*, *46*(3), 11–16. doi:10.1007/BF02784836

Zeichner, K., & Liston, D. (1987). Teaching student teachers to reflect. *Harvard Educational Review*, *57*, 23–48.

Zeichner, K., & Liston, D. (1996). *Reflective teaching: An introduction*. Mahwah, NJ: Lawrence Erlbaum Associates.

Zellermayer, M., Salomon, G., Globerson, T., & Givon, H. (1991). Enhancing writing-related metacognitions through a computerized writing partner. *American Educational Research Journal*, *28*(2), 373–391.

Zhang, J. (1997). The nature of external representations in problem solving. *Cognitive Science*, *21*(2), 179–217. doi:10.1207/s15516709cog2102_3

Zhang, J., & Norman, D. (1994). Representations in distributed cognitive tasks. *Cognitive Science*, *18*, 87–122. doi:10.1207/s15516709cog1801_3

Zhang, J. (2000). External representations in complex information processing tasks. In Kent, A. (Ed.), *Encyclopedia of library and information science* (*Vol. 68*, pp. 164–180). New York, NY: Marcel Dekker.

Zheng, R. (2010). Effects of situated learning on students' knowledge acquisition: An individual differences perspective. *Journal of Educational Computing Research*, *43*(4), 463–483. doi:10.2190/EC.43.4.c

Zheng, R., Flygare, J., & Dahl, L. (2009a). Style matching or ability building? An empirical study on FDI learners' learning in well-structured and ill-structured asynchronous online learning environments. *Journal of Educational Computing Research*, *41*(2), 195–226. doi:10.2190/EC.41.2.d

Zheng, R., Yang, W., Garcia, D., & McCadden, B. P. (2008). Effects of multimedia on schema induced analogical reasoning in science learning. *Journal of Computer Assisted Learning*, *24*, 474–482. doi:10.1111/j.1365-2729.2008.00282.x

Zheng, R., Flygare, J., Dahl, L., & Hoffman, R. (2009b). The impact of individual differences on social communication pattern in online learning. In Mourlas, C., Tsianos, N., & Germanakos, P. (Eds.), *Cognitive and emotional processes in web-based education: Integrating human factors and personalization* (pp. 321–342). Hershey, PA: Information Science Reference/IGI Global Publishing. doi:10.4018/978-1-60566-392-0.ch015

Zheng, R. Z. (in press). The influence of cognitive styles on learner's performance in e-learning. In Song, H. (Ed.), *Interactivity in e-learning: Cases and frameworks*. Hershey, PA: IGI Publishers.

Zimmerman, B. J. (2002). Becomming a self-regulated learner: An overview. *Theory into Practice*, *41*(2), 64–70. doi:10.1207/s15430421tip4102_2

Zimmerman, B. J. (1989). Models for self-regulated learning and academic achievement. In Zimmerman, B. J., & Schunk, D. H. (Eds.), *Self-regulated learning and academic achievement: Theory, research, and practice* (pp. 1–25). New York, NY: Springer. doi:10.1007/978-1-4612-3618-4_1

Zimmerman, E. (June 15, 2011). *Keynote: Games are not good for you: a designer's perspective on learning and game*. Games+Learning+Society Conference. Madison, Wisconsin.

Zull, (2002). *The art of changing the brain – Enriching teaching by exploring the biology of learning*. Sterling, VA: Stylus Publishing.

Zynga.com. (2011). *FarmVille*. Retrieved from http://www.facebook.com/FarmVille

About the Contributors

Haomin Wang is an Associate Professor in the College of Education and Manager of Instructional Technology at Dakota State University. His research interests include media attributes, system affordances, interactivity in e-learning, instructional hypermedia, and database support for Web-based educational applications. He has co-authored *Designing and Developing Web-based Instruction* published by Pearson Education in 2006 and published a number of book chapters and journal articles. He has presented regularly at national and international conferences, and has conducted numerous seminars, panel discussions, and workshops on instructional technology and e-learning.

***

Michelle Aubrecht has been a Graduate Student at Ohio State University in the Art Education Department. She studied game-based learning, and game design. Her thesis work focused on how to support teachers in using games, specifically, Gamestar Mechanic, in an elementary art classroom. While a graduate student, she has been a Graduate Assistant at OSU's Digital Union, which supports faculty, staff, and students in using technology in the classroom. She has been the Digital Union's specialist in game-based learning for the past two years, where she has coordinated, grown, and facilitated a monthly brown bag group, taught workshops, and given and invited others to give presentations about game-based learning. She has written blog articles, taught workshops, and created a game-based learning wiki. Her current research is about how to support teachers in using video games in the classroom by making short, training videos for specific games.

Sheila Bonnand is currently a Reference Librarian/Assistant Professor at Montana State University in Bozeman, Montana. Her liaison responsibilities include the departments of computer sciences, earth sciences, mathematics, modern languages, and physics and overseeing the library's juvenile collection. She holds a Master's Degree in Library and Information Science from the University of Arizona and a Master's Degree in Education from the University of Montana as well as an undergraduate degree in Botany/Biology Teaching. Before moving in to academic librarianship, she worked as a community educator, a high school teacher and school librarian. Her research interests include information literacy, especially as it applies to distance and online education, and intellectual freedom issues. She has been involved in a project using web conferencing software for instruction for the past two years.

Terri Edwards Bubb, EdD, recently graduated from the University of Houston in Houston, Texas with a doctorate in Curriculum and Instruction with special emphasis in Instructional Technology. Dr.

Bubb is currently an Adjunct Professor with the University of Houston – Clear Lake facilitating Instructional Technology graduate students. Dr. Bubb's research interests focus in the area of creating engaging and stimulating learning environments within an online setting. Dr. Bubb may be contacted through her email address at tebubb@comcast.net.

Ann Leslie Claesson, PhD, BSN, a former health care executive and online faculty member for Capella University, has been in healthcare for over twenty years. Positions held include CEO of a consulting firm, Cardiovascular Service Line Director, Principal Investigator, Director of Clinical Education Department, Level I Trauma Program manager, and ICU staff nurse. Her experience includes 16 years of medical-surgical (14 years Cardiovascular, 5 years Oncology), 20 years management (13 years clinical, 8 years academic/training, 5 years surgical practice), 15 years research (13 years clinical, 8 year academic) and 5 years of pharmaceutical industry experience. Areas of expertise: development and analysis of healthcare delivery systems, clinical service optimization, organizational theory and management, public health and not-for-profit health systems management, staff mentoring/education, medical writing and clinical/outcomes research.

Jody Clarke-Midura is a Research Associate at the Harvard Graduate School of Education where she leads the Virtual Assessment Research Group. Her research bridges numerous areas: learning and assessment in virtual environments, issues of scale, and mixed methods research. She has participated in an access working group and research paper on technology enabled assessment and accessibility published in *The Journal of Technology, Learning and Assessment* (JTLA). Her most recent work on assessment is featured in the *Journal of Research on Technology in Education* and in volume she co-editing entitled, "Technology Based Assessment for 21st Century Skills: Theoretical and Practical Implications from Modern Research," published by Springer-Verlag. She holds a Master's in Technology in Education and a doctorate in Learning & Teaching from the Harvard Graduate School of Education.

Jillianne Code is an Assistant Professor of Educational Technology at the University of Victoria, BC, Canada and Co-Director of the Technology Integration and Evaluation (TIE) Research Lab. She recently completed a post-doctoral fellowship at the Harvard Graduate School of Education. Her research combines several areas including: the role of agency in learning, learning environments and social networks, and measurement methods in educational research. Jillianne has been recognized by the American Educational Research Association with a Graduate Student Research award based on her work using item response theory to validate psychological inventories. Her most recent work is being featured in the "Handbook of Research on Social Software and Developing Community Ontologies" and "Handbook of Research on Effective Electronic Gaming in Education."

Caroline M. Crawford, EdD, is an Associate Professor of Instructional Technology at the University of Houston-Clear Lake in Houston, Texas, United States of America. She earned her doctoral degree from the University of Houston in Houston, Texas, United States of America, in 1998, with specialization areas in Instructional Technology and Curriculum Theory, and began her tenure at the University of Houston-Clear Lake (UHCL) the same year. . At this point in Dr. Crawford's professional career, her main areas of interest focus upon communities of learning and the appropriate and successful integration of technologies into the learning environment; the learning environment may be envisioned as face-to-face, hybrid, and online (virtual or text-driven) environments. Dr. Crawford may be contacted through her e-mail address, crawford@uhcl.edu.

Chris Dede is the Timothy Wirth Professor of Educational Technology at the Harvard Graduate School of Education. His fundamental interest is the expanded human capabilities for knowledge creation, sharing, and mastery that emerging technologies enable. His teaching models the use of information technology to distribute and orchestrate learning across space, time, and multiple interactive media. His research spans emerging technologies for learning, infusing technology into large-scale educational improvement initiatives, policy formulation and analysis, and leadership in educational innovation. He is currently conducting funded studies to develop and assess learning environments based on modeling and visualization.

Xun Ge is an Associate Professor with the Program of Instructional Psychology and Technology (IPT), Department of Educational Psychology, at the University of Oklahoma. She earned her PhD in Instructional Systems from the Pennsylvania State University in 2001. Dr. Ge has been teaching graduate courses in instructional design and technology, including designing and developing instruction for multimedia learning. Her primary research interest involves designing and developing instructional scaffolds, learning technologies, and open learning environments to support students' ill-structured problem solving and self-regulated learning. Her other related research includes computer-supported collaborative learning and virtual learning communities. Dr. Ge has published over 30 refereed journal articles, 5 book chapters, and she has given over 80 conference presentations. Dr. Ge has been recognized for her two scholarly awards: "2003 Young Scholar" by Educational Technology and Research & Development, and "2004 Outstanding Journal Article" by Association for Educational Communications and Technology.

Deb Gearhart is the Director of eTROY at Troy University. eTROY provides twenty two of Troy University's degree programs online, with additional programs coming online Fall 2011. Dr. Gearhart has worked in the field of distance education for 25 years. Previously Deb served as the founding Director of E-Education Services at Dakota State University in Madison, South Dakota and was there for the 11 years. Before joining Dakota State she spent 10 years with the Department of Distance Education at Penn State, now Penn State World Campus. Deb was an Associate Professor for Educational Technology at Dakota State University teaching at both the undergraduate and graduate levels. She has co-authored at textbook entitled "Designing and Developing Web-Based Instruction" and edited another publication titled "Cases on Distance Delivery and Learning Outcomes: Emerging Trends and Programs," which was released in December 2009. Deb is a master reviewer and trainer for Quality Matters and has done consulting, training, and program review for distance education programs. Dr. Gearhart has earned a BA in Sociology from Indiana University of Pennsylvania. She earned a M.Ed. in Adult Education with a distance education emphasis and an M.P.A. in Public Administration, both from Penn State. Deb completed her Ph.D. program in Education, with a certificate in distance education, from Capella University.

Ruth Xiaoqing Guo is an Associate Professor in the Educational Technology graduate program of the Department of Computer Information Systems at Buffalo State College, State University of New York. Dr. Guo earned a PhD degree in Technology Studies and a Master's degree in Education from the University of British Columbia, in Vancouver, Canada. Her research interests include integrating technology into curriculum, digital divide, constructivist pedagogy, video ethnography, multiliteracies, information and communication technology (ICT) literacy, ICT assessment, and teacher education. Dr. Guo has taught courses in teacher education programs at the University of Ottawa (Ottawa, Canada), and at the University of British Columbia (Vancouver, Canada). She also has over 10 years of experience in teaching education courses at Chinese universities. In addition to teaching courses in educational technology to graduate students at Buffalo State College, State University of New York, Dr. Guo is also conducting research projects in this area.

Mary Anne Hansen is a Professor and Reference Librarian at Montana State University; she also serves as Distance Education Coordinator for the MSU Library. Her liaison responsibilities include Health and Human Development, Education, Psychology, College Writing, Student Athletics, Office for International Programs, and Residence Life. She also co-coordinates the MSU Library's annual Tribal College Librarians' Institute, a week-long professional development experience for librarians from across the globe who serve the research needs of indigenous college students. She holds a Master's Degree in Library and Information Science from the University of Arizona and a Master's Degree in Adult and Higher Education with a Counseling support area from the Montana State University as well as an undergraduate degree in Modern Languages Teaching. Her research interests include distance education, information literacy, and information services and issues for Indigenous populations.

David Huang currently holds a tenure-track faculty position at Department of Education Policy, Organization and Leadership at University of Illinois at Urbana-Champaign. His research interests mainly focus on cognitive as well as motivational issues in technology-enhanced learning and performance settings across organizations. In particular he investigates the empirical relationship between cognitive and motivational processing afforded by highly interactive learning environments such as digital game-based learning systems (DGBLS). His current projects also focus on the design differences between genders (and other social variables) in the context of game-enabled learning. Dr. Huang also carries out research projects in the context of online teaching and learning on a regular basis, to promote learner- and instructor-friendly online instructional practices.

Kun Huang is an Instructional Designer at the University of North Texas Health Science Center. She earned her PhD in Instructional Psychology and Technology from the University of Oklahoma and a MEd in Instructional Technology from the University of Virginia. Dr. Huang is an experienced instructional designer who has designed and developed numerous interactive online learning objects to scaffold students' critical thinking, metacognition, and problem solving. Her research focuses on the development of technology-supported learning environments and their effects on students' metacognition, knowledge transfer, and epistemological beliefs, particularly in the context of science education. Dr. Huang has published several empirical studies in refereed journals, and she has presented her research and instructional design works at various national and international conferences.

Victor Law is a PhD Candidate with the Department of Educational Psychology at the University of Oklahoma. He received a Bachelor of Science degree in Statistics from San Francisco State University and a Master of Applied Sciences degree from the University of Waterloo. In 1998 he received an MBA from the University of Illinois, Urbana-Champaign, with a concentration in MIS. Mr. Law's research interests include scaffolding, self-regulation, ill-structured problem-solving, computer-supported collaborative learning, and game-based learning. He has been conducting studies examining the effect of different scaffolding approaches, including massively multiplayer online games, computer-based simulation, and dynamic modeling, on students' complex problem-solving learning outcomes. He has presented his research results at prestigious national and international conferences, such as Annual Meeting of the American Educational Research Association, Association for Educational Communications and Technology, and International Conference of Learning Sciences. Recently, he has submitted several manuscripts to national and international journals.

Denise McDonald, EdD, is an Associate Professor of Curriculum and Instruction and Program Coordinator of Teacher Education at the University of Houston - Clear Lake. She has taught face-to-face, online, and web-enhanced undergraduate, Master's, and doctoral courses across a range of content areas including language arts, classroom management, curriculum planning, instructional strategies, critical inquiry, and qualitative research. She has also supervised undergraduate and graduate internships and currently chairs or serves as methodologist on multiple theses and dissertations. Her research interests include exemplary teaching practices, teacher identity formation, transformational learning, reflective pedagogy, and relational pedagogy, specifically explored through qualitative methodology such as ethnography and self study.

Betül Özkan-Czerkawski is an Assistant Professor of Educational Technology and program director at the University of Arizona. Prior to that, she served as the faculty coordinator of Instructional Technology at Long Island University (2006-2008) and was an Assistant Professor of Instructional Technology Research at the University of West Georgia (2003-2006). She has presented and published numerous papers on distance education, technology integration strategies, and emerging technology applications. Recently, she was the editor of the book "Free and Open Source Software in E-Learning: Issues, Successes and Challenges." Dr. Özkan-Czerkawski holds a PhD and a MA in Curriculum and Instruction from Hacettepe University, Ankara, Turkey, and a BA in Italian Philology from Ankara University, Ankara, Turkey. She completed her post-doctoral study at Iowa State University (2001-2003), where she also served as a project manager for a Fulbright Grant.

Paul Parsons is a PhD candidate in the Computer Science Department at the University of Western Ontario. His research is in the area of human-information interaction, a convergence of cognitive, information, computer, and learning sciences. His focus is on the design and analysis of interactive information interfaces that can be used to facilitate learning, problem solving, and other knowledge activities. His research has appeared in *Proceedings of the World Conference on Educational Multimedia, Hypermedia and Telecommunications*, the *Journal of Interactive Learning Research*, and other books and journals.

Felicity Pearson is a media course developer at Capella University. As one of the first writers assigned to the project, she helps to create the structure and storyline for the Riverbend City simulation. A varied career path which includes teaching writing at the University of Tennessee and serving as an environmental and occupational health technician in the United States Air Force, has contributed to Ms. Pearson's ability to bridge the subject matter expertise of faculty experts with the creative needs of the storyline.

Aaron Wiatt Powell, PhD, is an alumnus of the University of Georgia and Virginia Tech. He has been an educator for twenty years, ten as an English and writing teacher and ten as an instructional designer and technologist in higher education. He has taught courses on distance education and learning theories for instructional design, in addition to numerous professional development workshops. He is currently working on starting a design and development business with his wife.

Jesse Rosel, MS, is the manager of the course media team at Capella University. Jesse was involved from the very beginning as co-creator and producer of the Riverbend City simulation project. He manages a team of talented writers and designers, simultaneously cheerleading and challenging the team to keep pushing the project to new heights. A background in technology, business, and creative writing has allowed Jesse to manage the relationships between writers, designers, developers, business, and academic stakeholders.

Kamran Sedig is an Associate Professor in the Department of Computer Science and the Faculty of Information and Media Studies at the University of Western Ontario. He investigates how to design computer-based cognitive tools that support knowledge activities in which people work and think with information, such as learning, sensemaking, problem solving, and analytical reasoning. He is particularly interested in human-information interaction in the context of cognitive tools—that is, the design and evaluation of the information interface component of these tools where users interact with representations of information. Examples of the tools that he investigates include learning technologies, information visualization tools, mathematical visualizations, digital libraries as knowledge environments, and digital cognitive games. His research is published in a diverse set of journals, conference proceedings, and books, such as *ACM Transactions on Computer-Human Interaction, International Journal of Computers for Mathematical Learning, Computers in Human Behavior*, and *Interactive Learning Research.*

Julia Penn Shaw has integrated a systems view of e-learning through software development and process management at IBM; through her doctorate in developmental learning from the Harvard Graduate School of Education and an MS in system science/computer science; and as Associate Professor and Academic Coordinator at SUNY-Empire State College, Center for Distance Learning. In her current capacity, she has responsibility for curriculum design, course development, and academic delivery of the Human Development program. Her research, teaching, and publication interests include e-learning, the construction of meaning, adolescent/adult learning, and the development of personal wisdom.

Dazhi Yang, PhD is an Assistant Professor in the Department of Educational Technology at Boise State University, Boise, Idaho. Dr. Yang was a postdoctoral researcher and instructional designer in the School of Engineering Education at Purdue University prior to coming to Boise State. She earned both her PhD and Master's degrees in Educational Technology (now Learning Design and Technology) from Purdue University, West Lafayette, Indiana. Her research interests include computer-assisted learning and instruction, online and distance education, assessment, and evaluation. She also has research interests in STEM education, which consists of repairing and preventing student misconceptions of science and engineering concepts, and conceptual changes.

Nick Zap is an Instructional Designer with over 10 years experience in the design and development of educational games, 3D simulations, and online courseware. Nick is a past winner of the WebCT/Blackboard Exemplary Course Project whose goal is to identify and disseminate best practices for designing engaging online courses. His research includes problem solving, cognitive development and self-regulated learning in video game environments. Nick's most recent work is being featured in the "Handbook of Research on Social Software and Developing Community Ontologies" and "Handbook of Research on Effective Electronic Gaming in Education." Nick is currently a PhD candidate in Educational Psychology at Simon Fraser University with research focused on the development of a cognitive architecture for multimedia learning.

Robert Z. Zheng is an Associate Professor in the Department of Educational Psychology at the University of Utah. His research interests include online instructional design, cognition and multimedia learning, and human-computer interaction. He edited and co-edited several volumes including "Cognitive Effects on Multimedia Learning"; "Online Instructional Modeling: Theories and Practices"; and "Adolescent Online Social Communication and Behavior: Relationship Formation on the Internet." He has published numerous book chapters and research papers in the areas of multimedia, online learning, and cognition. He has presented extensively at national and international conferences.

Index